The I Hate to Cook Almanack

THE

I Hate to Cook Almanack

A BOOK OF
DAYS

Peg Bracken

HARCOURT BRACE JOVANOVICH

NEW YORK AND LONDON

Printed in the United States of America

Library of Congress Cataloging in Publication Data

Bracken, Peg.
The I hate to cook almanack.

1. Cookery.   I. Title.
TX740.B643   641   76–20512
ISBN 0–15–144050–6

First edition

B   C   D   E

ABOUT THE AUTHOR

For some time, Peg Bracken and cooking have been involved in an uneasy hate-love relationship. Though the course of it has never run smooth, still they can't quite leave each other alone.

When she wrote *The I Hate to Cook Book,* she wasn't aware that she was speaking for other people, too. But since the book's appearance several years ago, a great many other noncooks have come out of the kitchen closet, so to speak, fearlessly admitting that nearly anything is more rewarding than cooking is—an admission that unfortunately doesn't alter the fact that some cooking occasionally has to be done.

Hence these recipes, which are good, dependable, and mainly simple. Peg Bracken has no truck with glazes, sauces, boning things, or simmering them all day. She wants it known, too, that when she finally stands face to face with that Great Cook Up Yonder, she will be able to state unequivocally and unafraid that she never asked anyone to squeeze anything out of a pastry tube or told anyone to cover anything with a clean towel.

—The Publisher

FOR UNAUTHORIZED PERSONNEL ONLY

Before I quite finish typing it, I would like to explain some things about this book.

As I have found to my frequent distress, writing a book isn't easy, and writing even a cookbook isn't a piece of cake. It is more like a cross-country bus trip, with the writer driving. Sometimes there are more curves than straightaways, and some unexpected detours, so that driver and passengers alike may be a little uncertain of where they are going and whether they'll get there. And yet, with luck, it can be a good trip, too, sometimes brightened by new vistas and an occasional Rest Stop, and perhaps a few serendipitous dividends.

This is a Book of Days, or an Almanack, or a filled-up Calendar, or a Houseperson's Year, or quite possibly a Combination Plate. When I began it, I didn't know that so many things (besides recipes) and so many people would be trying to climb aboard. Many times I was firm and shut the door. But not always. Some kept coming back, and so I made room for them. After all, nearly anyone's Calendar, or Year, contains a fair amount of assorted this-and-that, as well as some new friends.

These people are all identified, either as they appear or else in the list at the back, except—I just noticed—for the occasional footnotes marked "Ed." This is Ed Scheidelman, who does the sidewalks and wastebaskets around the building where I was typing the manuscript. He took quite an interest, and I want to thank him. As for the words that are not attributed to anyone else, they are my own.

I thank *Family Circle* Magazine, too, for permission to use some material that originally appeared there. Some of these recipes were clipped out by its readers, who then misplaced them, and panicked, and wrote to me for help. I have recopied and sent them out more times than I care to think about, and I am glad I could include them here. Now they won't disappear so fast, for a book is harder to lose; and I won't have to copy things out any more.

Finally I want to salute all the reluctant cooks and the harried housepersons of this world who hang in there, doing as good a job as they can in the face of mountable odds. To them, with abiding respect and affection, I dedicate this book.

Peg Bracken

CONTENTS

Recipes

CONTENTS

CONTENTS

CONTENTS

CONTENTS

CONTENTS

CONTENTS

"All these things heer collected, are not mine,
But diverse grapes make but one sort of wine;
So I, from many learned authors took
The various matters printed in this book.
What's not mine own by me shall not be father'd,
The most part I in fifty years have gather'd,
Some things are very good, pick out the best,
Good wits compiled them, and I wrote the rest.
If thou dost buy it, it will quit thy cost,
Read it, and all thy labour is not lost."
—John Taylor

". . . The *Almanac* is a happy association of astronomy, prophecy, philosophy, and poetry . . . and a recipe for banana doughnuts. . . ."
—E. B. White

January

bringeth comforting Words about Cooking & other Things, too; it considereth Matters practical & impractical & introduceth new Friends; also featureth Receipts for

a most heartening New Year's Day Soup
Rain-or-Shine Moose
Aunt Henry's Eggless Raisinful War Cake
extraordinarily good Soya Short Ribs
a strange and easy pastry
the Engstead Cake

. . . and divers good Victuals too numerous for mention

Weariest of trees, The Christmas, now
(Once hung with jewels along the bough)
Irrelevant, just stands around,
Shedding its needles by the pound.

JANUARY 1   NOW ARRIVETH COLD JANUARY, the open Gate of the Year, and through it bloweth a keen Winde. Now sleepeth the Snaile warm under the dead Leaves & sleepeth the Houseperson late, an that be possible. But it proveth a fitful Sleepe with tossings & turnings, for this be the Start of the Year & All to do, Nothing done. Yet looking backwards & forwards achieveth mainly tennis-match Necke; and the wise do look hopefully to Janus, god of January & god of Beginnyngs. For all Beginnyngs are Adventures even though they do bear within them the sorrowful Seede of Completion, New Year's Day being but 364 days distant from Old Year's Night.

> *On this day in 1801,* Ireland became part of the United Kingdom of Great Britain and Ireland, to the considerable regret of them both ever after.

> *On this day in 1775,* the American colonies numbered 2,500,000 people.

> *On this day in 1976,* the United States numbered 218,-210,700 people and some of them weren't feeling very good.

In ancient Rome, Cato's preferred hangover cure was raw cabbage leaves. But since the invention of ice cream, a quart of vanilla has seemed therapeutic to many. Then some like a Canadian Red Eye: half beer, half tomato juice. Some like Moose Milk, a little whiskey in a lot of milk. Some swear by vitamin B_6 pills, four on retiring, four on arising; and some like pineapple juice in large amounts. Some take a Dramamine pill before going to bed, which seems to quiet the bed down. But the hollowest leg west of the Rockies, though it sloshed over last night, says the best remedy besides time is the hottest-available small red or green peppers eaten with soda crackers.

3

A HEARTENING NEW YEAR'S DAY SOUP
for 6 to 8

1 can tomato soup, undiluted
1 can beef or chicken bouillon
½ to ⅔ cup sherry

Stir it up, heat it, top it with sour cream, and sprinkle with chopped fresh dill or dried dill or parsley if any there be.

And on this day in 1907, President Theodore Roosevelt set the world's record for handshaking by shaking hands with 8,513 people, a remarkably friendly way to start a New Year.

JANUARY 2   Because of some problems yesterday, resolutions were postponed until today.

RESOLVED:

Not to open a new bottle of catsup till the old one is used up.

To read the newest news magazine instead of catching up with week-before-last's first, which is like always eating rotten apples.

To start a fresh rap sheet for certain people instead of adding to last year's.

To educate the kids out of the rollicking notion that just because something exists they have to have one of it.

To organize the kitchen tool drawer and keep it organized.

To hit the next person who says, "What are we having for dinner?"

". . . The man who does not at least *propose to himself* to be better *this* year than he was last, must be either very good or very bad indeed! . . . But, in fact, to propose to oneself to do well, is in some sort to *do* well, positively. . . ."

—*Mirror of the Months*

4

". . . Merely to have gotten as old as you are, and to move as far as you have in the tricky pageant of life, is reason for satisfaction—and thus respect. Just think of all the things you aren't, and are glad you aren't, and you have another solid ground for satisfaction, and respect of self."

—Charles McCabe

". . . It's not a small thing, you know, this learning to be less of an ass, to get in there and pitch; even to roll with the waves. And I do have limitations. . . . I'm forty years old, I must accept the small integrities of my life. You see that, don't you?"

—Anne Higgins

JANUARY 3   Now a fresh wind bringeth a fair day to ponder one's life-style and see if it has any.

"She's in a rut," someone said of a woman we both know. The lady in question spends every vacation in Colorado, reads only science fiction, and always wears navy-blue-and-something. But I considered the judgment hasty. How distinguish between a rut and a groove and a preferred pattern? It is the old adjective game, and we reserve the prettiest words for ourselves. (*I'm casual; you're messy; she's a slob.*)

I know a man who has eaten cream cheese on buttered whole-wheat toast every morning for breakfast for years. Though he has tried cereal, bacon-and-eggs, steak-and-eggs, bagels, and many other things, he has found that cream cheese on buttered whole-wheat toast suits him best. So it could be called a breakfast rut. But isn't it equally accurate to say that he has evolved his own preferred breakfast style?

MS. AESOP'S FABLES (No. 1)

A Dog was making the rounds of the neighborhood one morning and stopped to see his friend the Pig. The Pig was eating peanut butter with pickles, on crackers. "If that isn't just like a pig!" the Dog snorted, and walked on.

Next he came to the house of his friend the Ass. The Ass was eating peanut butter with pickles, on crackers. "What an ass he is!" the Dog exclaimed, and walked on.

Next he came to the house of his friend the Owl, who had sold several articles on high-class cuisine to high-class magazines. The Owl was eating peanut butter with pickles, on crackers. "H'm," the Dog thought, "must be pretty good stuff," and he went home and tried some and liked it very much.

Moral: It's also who's doing it.

JANUARY 4   Take a raincoat and a sweater;
              Weather to be cold and wetter
              (Unless the weatherman's a liar
              And it turneth warm and drier).

AN EXCELLENT RAIN-OR-SHINE MOOSE

    1 6-ounce package semisweet chocolate bits
    2 tablespoons sherry
    ¼ teaspoon salt
    4 eggs, separated

Find the double boiler, have water simmering in its bottom, and in the top part melt the chocolate bits. Take off the pan, turn off the burner, beat in the sherry, salt, and egg yolks. Now beat the egg whites till they're stiff and fold them in. Then, if you will pour it into eight little pudding dishes or demitasse cups and refrigerate them at least four hours, the world will be a better place.

JANUARY 5   How to Make Graham Crackers and Why

It was a raw, wintry day, a sharp wind pasting leaves to the windowpanes—a good day to stay home and do things that didn't need doing. Even the kitchen wasn't a bad place to be. So, having the ingredients as well as a mild curiosity as to whether this Graham Cracker recipe would really turn into graham crackers, I set about making some.

It wasn't long before I had a sizable supply of square, crisp, tan, faintly sweet objects you'd have recognized anywhere, which pleased me no end.

GRAHAM CRACKERS

½ cup shortening	1 cup enriched white flour
1 cup packed light brown sugar	1 teaspoon baking powder
½ cup granulated sugar	½ teaspoon baking soda
1 teaspoon vanilla	¼ teaspoon salt
2 cups whole-wheat flour	½ cup milk

First, cream the shortening with the sugars and vanilla. Then sift the dry things and add them alternately with the milk, mixing well each time. Chill about twenty minutes in the freezer.

Now the going gets mathematical: Divide it in 4 parts and roll each part ⅛ inch thick. Trim each into a long rectangle, 5 inches by 15 inches. Cut this into 6 smaller rectangles, 2½ inches by 5 inches. And there's your classic double graham cracker, lacking only a line down the middle. So make one with a table knife, indenting lightly, and add some dimples with a fork. This is important. No dimples, and they won't look official. Then, with a spatula, put them carefully on a couple of greased cooky sheets and bake in a 350° oven for ten to twelve minutes, till the edges are brown.

This makes forty-eight single graham crackers that keep well in a tin box in the refrigerator. They are also good to eat immediately, as I did for lunch, with a glass of milk and six chapters of a book I'd been wanting to get at for some time.

. . . As to why you would ever make graham crackers when you can buy perfectly good ones cheaper, I suppose the reason is that it's rather fun if you don't have to. Fun the way a walk in the mud can be, if you're dressed for it, or the way even cleaning a closet can be, once in a blue moon when the soul's own weather is right and your mind can roam free while your hands busy themselves with a not-too-demanding operation.

Sometimes I wonder if women who hate domesticity so vocally ever award themselves a day like this. I mean a day to roam around in and cultivate, whether it comes up flowers, weeds, or graham crackers. This kind of a day is a celebration, really, of those curious freedoms you can know, at home—even in this day and age, even in the much-maligned nuclear family. They are freedoms I'd certainly hate to be wholly liberated from.

". . . Don't get me wrong. I do not suggest that because the difficulties of housekeeping have been grossly exaggerated by writers of both TV commercials and feminist tracts—it is therefore lots of fun. Though many women (my wife included) find some aspects of home-making—cooking and preserving, for instance—reward-ing at least part of the time, much of it is incontestably dull. Though no duller, I would wager, than working in a typing pool or on an assembly line.

"Nor can I see it as 'degrading'—at least not until someone explains to me why it is degrading for a woman to sweep a floor but not for a man to sweep a street.

"Least of all am I suggesting that woman's place is in the home; her place is wherever her tastes, talents and luck can get her.

"I do say, however, that for those who approach the home with common sense, free from the manufactured obsessions of the housekeeping mystique, there are a lot worse places a woman could be. Or a man, for that mat-ter."

—Robert Claiborne

Now, it just so happened that the morning I read Mr. Claiborne's words was the same morning a letter came from my Aunt Henry Macadangdang.* She's worked at home and other places, and periodically she likes to sound off about it:

"Running a house is no rose garden. But it's no bramble patch either, and a lot of it's therapeutic, and you can't tell me a lot of women don't know it, whether they're holding down outside jobs or not. . . . I'll tell you something: the biggest problem people have is leisure. Anybody can handle a jampacked day. But filling an empty one with something that doesn't disgust you when you look at it tomorrow, *there's* your problem. That's why your retired men get heart attacks. They don't know how to design their own days. Women get more practice, earlier. . . ."

* Aunt Henry Macadangdang, nee Cafferty, is a staunch advocate of Marriage and the Home. Her fourth and present husband is Ramon Macadangdang, a handsome Filipino woodcarver she met on a package tour of the Far East in 1965. Sixty-two years old now, Aunt Henry is still a dynamo, ninety-three pounds and four-foot-ten from her shiny black topknot to the holes in her socks, though of course she doesn't wear any, there in Manila, where she has gone in heavily for stick-dancing and native crafts.

Here, by the way, are Aunt Henry's favorite

MANILA WAFERS

*(A great little cooky, she says—no rolling out and
stays crisp in a can with a good, tight lid)*

¼ pound butter	½ teaspoon baking powder
1⅛ cup sugar	1¼ cups flour
1 egg	1 teaspoon vanilla
¼ teaspoon salt	

She creams the butter with the sugar till they're well acquainted,
adds the unbeaten egg, then the sifted dry things and the vanilla.
Then she drops them by the teaspoonful onto a greased cooky sheet
and puts it on the middle rack in a 400° oven, to bake for seven or
eight minutes. And watches them. When they start to brown, she
says, they *brown*.

JANUARY 6   A day for some negative thinking, which is quite
              as good as the other kind, though most recipe
books don't think so. They love to tell you to do something (usually something you don't want to do), but they don't say what not
to do and why, which can be just as important.

9 KITCHEN NO-NO'S AND WHY
from Stella Trowbridge Hinky*

1

DON'T remove the blender's lid the minute you're done blending
something hot unless you are looking for an excuse to scrub the
ceiling.

---

* Stella Trowbridge Hinky was graduated *summa cum laude* from Jackson College,
in Hibited, N.D., in the field of Home Arts. Pompon girl, yearbook editor,
straight-A student, she was one of those girls you can't fault or stand either, for
very long at a time, and for a while they all called her Stinky, though she shaped
up later. Ms. Hinky majored in Cream Sauce and minored in Fly Spray, and whatever she says, you'd just better believe it. Now mother of three and wife of one,
she is active in Consumerism; recently mounted a nationwide campaign to outlaw
steri-seal plasticoat packaging of some 2,052 items including fingernail polish and
garden fertilizer; is active in the movement to get catsup packed in wide-mouthed
jars, so you can put some in a bowl on the table without the problem later of pok-
ing it back down that little skinny bottleneck. Author of several books, including
the ever-popular college text *The Houseperson's Houseperson*, The Garlick Press.

2

DON'T freeze a stew or anything else that has potatoes in it without first removing the potatoes, for they will end up revoltingly mushy. Only professional potato-freezers know how to freeze potatoes. Ditto carrots.

3

DON'T use a metal fork for fishing something out of a plugged-in electrical appliance like a toaster, or you can end up dead with a permanent wave.

4

DON'T whip an egg white when the egg is stone cold from the refrigerator if you can help it; you won't get the volume.

5

DON'T beat muffin batter till it's smooth or you'll have tough muffins.

6

DON'T measure anything right over the mixture you're adding it to unless you really want a half-cupful of pepper. Something or somebody's bound to jog your elbow.

7

DON'T add cream or salad dressing or nuts to a recipe without tasting them first, for these can all spoil when you're not looking and queer the whole thing.

8

DON'T store a once-opened bottle of green olives with the lid on, or green peppers with their seeds in, because they spoil faster that way.

9

DON'T think the oven is as good a place as any to store the breakfast biscuits that didn't get eaten (telling yourself that of course you'll remember to take them out before you heat the oven again, because you won't).

JANUARY 7   St. Distaff's Day.

". . . the Christmas holidays having ended, good housewives resume the distaff and other industrious employments."

—The Book of Days

A good day to attack the recipe collection and separate the Sheep from the Goats from the Dogs.

THE SHEEP are the good, docile recipes that always work. They go into the card file. THE GOATS are untried recipes from friends and untried recipes clipped in a moment of euphoria under the hair dryer. They go in a heap on the table. THE DOGS are (a) so-so but not worth doing again, or (b) so complicated you know you'll never actually try them. They go in the wastebasket, eventually to be recycled into magazines containing more recipes. But don't think about that.

Now assemble thirteen manila file folders. These are for stabling the Goats. Label them

BREAD & SO ON

CAKE, CANDY, COOKIES

CASSEROLES

CHICKEN & OTHER FOWL
   THINGS

DESSERTS (misc.)

DRINKS

FISH THINGS

MEAT THINGS

ODD THINGS

PASTRY, PIES

SALADS & SALAD DRESSINGS

VEGETABLES

and one more labeled ?????? for things even odder than Odd Things. Then file each untried Goat in its proper folder. Later, should one turn into a Sheep, it graduates to the card file.

> ". . . However jumbled his desk may be, there is some distant region of the spirit where his files are clearly labeled and his papers have been written in a neat hand on one side only and are stapled into bundles with their edges straight—the great plan encompassing every particular in every pigeonhole. There is something of this, too, in all of us."
>
> —John Radar Platt

JANUARY 8   The Battle of New Orleans ended on this day in 1815. This was the last battle in the War of 1812, when Andrew Jackson's army licked the British. As it turned out, they needn't have bothered to fight this particular battle, because the war had already been over for two weeks. It was harder to run a neat war then, back in the good old days before Alexander Graham Bell and the ten o'clock news.

However, during the course of the troubles, the citizens were undoubtedly eating War Cakes. A War Cake usually means an eggless cake, for reasons that escape the present scribe. Perhaps the hens get nervous and forget to lay, or maybe the chicken farmers get nervous and drop the eggs. No matter.

AUNT HENRY'S EGGLESS RAISINFUL WAR CAKE
(Fast, easy, and easy to double in the event of a larger war)

1 cup raisins	½ teaspoon salt
2 cups water	1 teaspoon soda
½ cup margarine	½ teaspoon cinnamon
1¾ cups flour	½ teaspoon nutmeg
1 cup sugar	

First she finds her big saucepan because it's the mixing bowl too, and she boils the raisins in the water for ten minutes. Then she adds the margarine and lets it cool. Then, without sifting, she adds everything else—some chopped nuts are good too but not essential—mixes it up, and bakes it in a greased ten-by-ten-inch pan for thirty-five minutes in a 350° oven. If you'd rather use a loaf pan, bake it fifty-five minutes to an hour, same temperature, and test it with a broom straw.

JANUARY 9   " '. . . You still don't understand nostalgia, do you?' he said with a sigh. 'Yesterday's kick in the head becomes today's treasured memory.' "
—Ralph Schoenstein

THE GOOD OLD DAYS
"In 1872 we used over 250,000 pounds of opium. . . . The habit of opium-eating seems to prevail chiefly among women. The fact may explain the great percentage of farmers' wives in lunatic asylums.

". . . The prevalence of the habit among women is probably explained by the unhappiness of most of them, the mental stagnation, the liability to nervous depression, and, in the country, the seclusion and grinding physical work. Moreover, women are excluded by public opinion from the beer-hall and the dram-shop, and stimulants must be secret. Opium, in its various forms of laudanum,

paregoric, and sulphate of morphia, can be taken readily in private and without interruption of duty. . . ."
—*Frank Leslie's Illustrated Almanac, 1875*

These people who want to get back to the womb! Maybe it wasn't so great in there. Maybe you're bored silly, and the food has a dreadful sameness, but there you are. It is just as well that we forget it, along with teething, which must have been a miserable business too, and diaper rash.

JANUARY 10   On this evening in 1976, Mrs. James (Muriel) ("Mumu") Harbottle, of 52 Oak Trees, Illinois, discovered at her buffet supper for ten that only three people ate the lettuce that was under their Waldorf salads. So, the next day, she telephoned Stella Trowbridge Hinky, long distance, to ask her if it would be okay if she didn't put lettuce under it any more—just stuck a sprig of watercress into it, or something, and Ms. Hinky said Yes, that would be okay.

JANUARY 11   New Words for a New Year!

ANTIPESTO	Italian roach powder.
BLANDWICH	Hamburger without any onions.
CANAPEW	A small, dank toast square smeared with curry mayonnaise or shrimp paste, served before dinner to spoil people's appetites.
CAVIAR EMPTOR	It's only some kind of fish eggs.
EATNIK	Health-food buff who won't touch it if it isn't enriched with granular kelp and blackstrap molasses.
HORSE D'OEUVRE	Steak Tartare made with finely ground horsemeat.
HUNTER-STYLE	Descriptive term for the dish you must hunt around for things to stretch it with. For example, Creamed Chicken Hunter-Style means padded with a cupful of sautéed chopped celery, several sliced hard-boiled eggs, and nine sliced stuffed olives.

NECHO (Etymologically related to the small boy who said he had three things for lunch that started with N—a Negg, a Norange, and a Napple.) A Necho is (1) a variation on a familiar theme, like last night's rice fried with onion and bits of leftover meat or (2) a simple rerun of last night's dinner: the roast, cold-sliced, and the rest of the mashed potatoes in potato cakes. "What are we having for dinner, Mommie?" "A Necho, dear, and shut up."

PIASCO What you're involved in when the pastry comes apart.

SCRUFFULOUS How the house looks when it's in good enough shape that you don't feel like doing anything about it but not good enough that you're dying to have anybody drop in.

STEWP Any mixture thinner than stew and thicker than soup.

SWALLUP The extra bonus of cake frosting left in the pan for somebody to lick.

JANUARY 12   A perfect day for celebrating Horatio Alger's birthday! Born in January in 1834, Horatio Alger wrote 120 books, after he grew up, all with invigorating titles like *Luck and Pluck, Work and Win, Strive and Succeed,* his thrust being that there is always a way. That is where he was wrong. He had probably never been inside a kitchen, where you can strive all you like but there is still no way to unburn the beans. There are only exceptions that prove the rule.

". . . Take Hollandaise sauce, for instance: nothing curdles more easily, and nothing is easier to fix with a tablespoon of boiling water and a bit of stirring."
—Mimi Sheraton

". . . Making a custard sauce, one memorable morning, I noticed to my considerable dismay that it had separated—indeed, looked rather like buttermilk. However, with that swiftness of reaction-*cum*-action that has long distinguished my every move in the kitchen, I tossed in a few marshmallows, stirred them a moment, and—Presto! Smooth as cream! . . . But even though the outcome isn't that happy, it must be remembered that every wife in the course of a wifetime has cooked things that had only one fault: they didn't taste good. It simply happens, occasionally, like hangnails and moles in the garden and other small unpleasantnesses which, taken in stride, are quickly forgotten."

—Stella Trowbridge Hinky

". . . In most recipes there are encouragingly few pitfalls. One mustn't go berserk with the thought, but a quarter cup of liquid, a tablespoon more or less of butter, five minutes or so of cooking time are all variable and the sooner the beginning cook learns it the better the food will be."

—Craig Claiborne

JANUARY 13   *A cold rotten day.*
        Now doth the harried houseperson put plastic sacks over the sick-looking house plants to humidify their individual atmospheres, for this doth often bring the invalid back to green-growing health but not always.

"We've got to accept the idea that plants just up and die for no apparent reason."

—Lynn and Joel Rapp

JANUARY 14   This is St. Hilary's Day, known to be the coldest of the year.

". . . a day to retreat and regroup as the sleet lashed the windows and the wind whistled. I went to bed with a stack of books and a bottle. But, presently, with a nod

15

toward the rugged life, I turned the electric blanket down to Medium. . . ."

—Albert Wooky*

As Mr. Wooky remarked recently on bringing some cookies to a hospitalized friend just back from skiing at Stowe, "It's cheaper and more fun to set fire to a few hundred-dollar bills, lock yourself in the freezer, and break both ankles with a tire iron."

THE WOOKY COOKY
(*Singularly crisp and buttery*)

1 cup butter
1 cup sugar
1½ cups flour
½ teaspoon baking soda
½ teaspoon baking powder

½ cup chopped nuts
½ cup Rice Krispies (not crushed)
1 teaspoon vanilla

Deftly he creams the first two ingredients together. Then without sifting anything, he adds all the rest and mixes it well. After cooling it in the refrigerator long enough to write a short review of a bum restaurant, he shapes it into balls, presses them firmly with a fork on a greased baking sheet, and bakes them at 325° for ten to fifteen minutes.

Aspects also favorable today for conceiving a female child if one be female. Aspects poor for cleaning the house, however, except for dusting. Science has now finished counting and reports that there are 250,000 dust particles in the average room. One room is sufficient.

---

* Bachelor, amateur chef, and essayist (author of *Regrets Only*), Albert Wooky was the first in Pittsburgh to know his Social Security number by heart and own a crêpe pan. He likes his lamb pink, his olives wrinkled, his mushrooms raw, and his telephone silent. He also believes in whole-grain cereals and General Utilities (Common Stock), of which he owns a small but tender fraction. A former newspaperman, Mr. Wooky still spends nine hours a day at his desk, covers the local bistro scene for the evening paper, hasn't had a cold or a headache or a hiccup in forty-eight years, and credits his excellent health to total avoidance of vigorous exercise. People over thirty who play tennis, he believes, should see a psychiatrist; and people who ski, once they have their second teeth, are certifiable.

JANUARY 15   STRANGE AND EASY PASTRY!

". . . This is the only recipe my mother ever saw fit to hand down to me. She kept a lovely home and set a good table, but she absolutely refused to teach the art of housecraft to her daughters, other than requiring us to keep our rooms picked up so we could find the beds.

"It's for piecrust. There are three ingredients: flour, shortening, water. There is one formula: use half as much shortening as flour, and half as much water as shortening. These proportions never vary.

"For a two-crust pie I generally start with a cup of flour. Then I have a little extra dough left to cut in strips, sprinkle with sugar and cinnamon and bake briefly till browned. My kids love them, and I feel like a Traditional American Mom.

"Okay. Dump 1 cup of flour in the bowl. Then add half as much shortening—hence, ½ cup. Cut in the shortening till it looks like a bowlful of small pebbles. Now add ½ as much water as shortening, so —¼ cup, cold, warm, or luke, as long as it's wet. Pour it all in at once and mix it with your hands. Apparently something about the heat of your bare hands has a magic effect on the dough, and it also provides the same sort of tensional release I'm told gardeners have when they dig in The Good Earth. Anyway, it's great therapy, and I can generally use some. . . ."

—Sarah Willett

Presently then, Mrs. Willett continues, when it is a sticky ball, you quit kneading, wash your hands, take half, and start rolling it out. "Use lots of flour," she says, "scattering it freely in all directions. Keep rolling from the middle, and don't go over the edge every time or the edge gets too thin. When it's the size you want, slap it into the pie pan and that's it. It's delicious every time, and it makes potpies and so forth very simple: even the scroungiest leftover is enhanced. . . ."

And so I tried it, adding a teaspoon of salt to that first cupful of flour, for luck, and found the piecrust to be just as good as Mrs. Willett said. She's right about using plenty of flour. I used another ¾ cup anyway, possibly more. But no-measuring is part of its charm. And the big virtue is handleability. No tearing and patching, and still it's a tender, flaky crust. I don't understand it at all.

JANUARY 16   Emmett Neitzelgrinder, M.D.,* was born sixty
                    years ago today. An exceptionally busy man,
his patients requiring as much counseling these days as they do
medicine, Dr. Neitzelgrinder still finds time to cook on weekends.
Here are four of his favorite recipes.

DR. N.'s
FRENCH-FRIED POTATO SKINS

> baking potatoes
> vegetable oil
> salt

He bakes some big Idaho potatoes as usual, then cuts them lengthwise in quarters and scoops out the pulp. (What he does with it
depends on how he feels; maybe throws it out, maybe saves it for
potato cakes sometime.)

Then he heats some vegetable oil to 365° and fries the skins till
they are golden-brown. About two minutes. Then he drains them on
brown paper sacks, salts them, and serves them forth.

Good plain, he says, or with sour cream or applesauce. They'll
stay crisp a good while, too, on a warm platter in a preheated 200°
oven.

"The test of a good cook is if you can't taste the vitamins."
—Dr. Neitzelgrinder

DR. N.'s GOOD SOYA SHORT RIBS

First he makes the sauce—mixes

1 8-ounce-can tomato sauce	2 tablespoons vinegar
¾ cup water	4 tablespoons soy sauce
2 teaspoons sugar	

Then he puts about three pounds of lean short ribs in a brown

---

* Dr. Neitzelgrinder, a graduate of Northwestern Med School, first practiced in a
small southern Illinois town—practiced very hard indeed, till he felt he was finally
good enough for a bigger place. After moving to Chicago, an interest in cooking
and nutrition led him to invent and patent several helps for housepersons. Among
them is a heavy-duty twin-bladed cleaver for people who have trouble cutting the
mustard; and for the cholesterol-minded, his ever-popular STIFFO, a special
butter that won't melt in your mouth. Author of the best-selling *The Truth about
Peanut Butter,* he is currently at work on another nutrition book, *Get Away from
Me with Those Soybean Cupcakes.*

paper sack with a little flour and gives them a good shake. Next he puts them in a heavy iron skillet with a tight-fitting lid. On top he puts plenty of sliced onions—two good-sized ones, anyway—pours the sauce on top, puts the lid on, and bakes for three hours at 300°.

When Dr. Neitzelgrinder goes fishing, he usually comes back with a couple of big ones. His wife perfected the following recipe for leftover fish, though he generally takes the credit for it; and that's all right with her, so long as he cooks it. Which he often does, even when there isn't any leftover fish, because it is remarkably good with canned salmon too.

DR. N.'s RICH FISH TURNOVERS

½ cup raw rice

3 eggs

enough pastry for a 1-crust pie

1 can browned-in-butter mushrooms

2 cups flaked cooked fish, any kind

½ teaspoon powdered dill

½ teaspoon powdered thyme

chopped parsley, fresh or dried

1 teaspoon salt

½ teaspoon pepper

another egg, beaten

First, the good doctor cooks the rice. It makes about a cup and a half, cooked. He also hard-cooks the eggs and eventually slices them.

Then he rolls out some pastry, generally from a ready-mix, into a dinner-plate-size circle about ⅜ inch thick, to put on a cooky sheet.

Next, he opens the can of mushrooms, drains them, and puts them where he won't forget them, because he did, once, and the thing wasn't as good.

Concentrating hard now, he seasons the cooked fish with all those seasonings, and then starts layering it all on ½ the circle: rice, mushrooms, egg slices dotted with butter, fish, and then he repeats it. Finally he folds the dough over, crimps the edges, brushes with the beaten egg, gashes the crust to let the steam out, and bakes at 450° for fifteen to twenty minutes.

In the meantime, Mrs. Neitzelgrinder is usually melting a cube of butter and adding some lemon juice to taste, plus some more chopped parsley, for a sauce. As she says, it's the least she can do, and that was her intention.

19

THE NEITZEL GRINDER*

(Tony Romagna, who owns a small bakery, paid off the doctor in bread for delivering his children. As the kids and the bread started to pile up, Dr. N. felt impelled to do something, at least about the bread. So he got into the habit of making a bunch of Grinders at one time, foil-wrapping and freezing them, so they're always on hand for a fast supper or a poker party.)

He takes small loaves of Italian (or French) bread, or cuts big loaves into ten-inch chunks. Cuts them in half the long way. Brushes both cut sides with garlicky olive oil; he keeps a cut garlic clove marinating in a bottle of olive oil for this very purpose.

What he puts on them depends on what is on hand. The last one is always different from the first one, because (as the good doctor has noticed) ingredients never run out simultaneously. Sometimes he arranges, sandwich-style, MOZZARELLA CHEESE, ANCHOVY FILLETS, SLICED BOLOGNA, or SALAMI. Or maybe it's JACK or SWISS CHEESE, stuffed OLIVES, PIMENTOS, HAM, or LIVERWURST, or SARDINES, or plain sliced COLD BEEF . . . whatever is there. The important thing is NO MAYONNAISE if he's going to freeze them, as he generally does.† Then he'll heat these, frozen and still foil-wrapped, in a 350° oven for about half an hour, and he generally inserts a few fresh tomato slices when people are ready to eat.

JANUARY 17   Mary, Mary, quite contrary,
              How goes the world in January?

                  Please, ma'am, it seems a desolate place,
                  Hardly snugger than Outer Space;
                  The weather hasn't improved a bit,
                  And every letter says "Please remit."
                  Now chill the dawns, and still the birds. . . .
                  Do you have, by chance, some heartening
                      words?

RIGHT HERE:

". . . Fortunately we don't need to know how bad the age is. There is something we can always be doing without reference to how good or bad the age is. There is at least so much good in the

---

* The Grinder is also known as the Submarine, the Hoagie, the Hero, the Po' Boy, the Torpedo, the Rocket, the Cuban, and the Bomber.
† He should look up the cooked salad dressing that freezes, on page 188. —Ed.

20

world that it admits of form and the making of form. . . . Fortunately, too, no forms are more engrossing, gratifying, comforting, staying than those lesser ones we throw off, like vortex rings of smoke, all our individual enterprise and needing nobody's cooperation; a basket, a letter, a garden, a room, an idea, a picture, a poem. For these we haven't to get a team together before we can play."

—Robert Frost

". . . The Buddha, the Godhead, resides quite as comfortably in the circuits of a digital computer or the gears of a cycle transmission as he does at the top of a mountain or in the petals of a flower. To think otherwise is to demean the Buddha—which is to demean oneself."

—Robert Pirsig

JANUARY 18   On this day in 1976, Albert Wooky somewhat reduced his postholiday tensions by writing a forthright note to the retarded computer that has billed him four times now for the alpaca sweater he paid for three months ago. He explained with anatomical precision what it could do with the bill, and, always a prudent man, he wrote it in invisible ink—a drop of salad oil in a teaspoon of household ammonia. It will be legible when it is dipped in water, but Mr. Wooky didn't believe the computer would think of that; and he hoped it developed a good pain in the circuitry.

JANUARY 19   On this day in 1976, and in considerable distress, Mumu Harbottle visited her friendly family physician.

"I just can't help worrying about what I'm feeding the family, Dr. Neitzelgrinder," she said, sitting on her hands because she had resumed her nail-biting after reading the latest news release from the Food & Drug Administration. "Like MSG. They say it causes brain damage in infant mice."

"Do you have some infant mice?" the good doctor asked, with interest. "With my kids it was mostly hamsters." (He is a big, comfortable man with a shiny pink bald head. Sometimes he paints a cheerful sun face on it for his younger patients.)

"No," said Mumu. "I'm raising children, not mice, but it makes me wonder."

Dr. Neitzelgrinder nodded. "Kwok's disease," he said.

"What?" said Mumu.

"Kwok's disease. The Chinese Restaurant Syndrome," the doctor said. "This Chinese doctor—a Dr. Robert Ho Man Kwok—found that certain people are allergic to MSG, and some Chinese cooks use it like there was no tomorrow. You use a whole lot of it, Mumu?"

"Well, no," she said. "I just sort of sprinkle it on eggs and things when I think of it. Only I'm scared of eggs now, all that cholesterol. But then—well, like cyclamates, remember *them?* In the diet soft drinks. They had me really worried. They said it gave rats cancer of the bladder."

Dr. Neitzelgrinder nodded sympathetically. "It's tough on the lab animals," he said. "Massive doses, you know, direct injection. It's a good question all right, mice or men? Does mankind have a right to—"

"Yes, it certainly is," Mumu said hastily. Let him get started and you'd be there all night. "But then they took cyclamates off the market and went back to saccharin and found that *it* wasn't so hot, and then they came up with something else—"

"Aspartame," supplied Dr. N., gently removing three fingers of Mumu's left hand from her mouth.

"That's right," she said, "and *it* wasn't so good either, and how are you supposed to know where you're *at?* —Organic things. What about that? I keep reading—"

"Hold it a minute," the doctor interrupted. "I'm going to give you a prescription." He reached for his pad and scribbled, then leaned back.

"All right, here's the thing, Mumu: there hasn't been a safe century for the world since the place opened. And we're all going to die of having lived, right? In the time and country we happened to land in, right? In some other century, in some other place, you'd have had your choice of childbed fever, ditchwater typhoid, mastoiditis, beriberi, the scurvy, the scrofula, the Black Plague, and the measles, not to mention spoiled pork and dirty milk. Listen, did you know they used to put red lead in cheese as a matter of course to give it a good rich color?" he said, really warming up. "And prussic acid in your port wine?" And Mumu thought, *O, my, there's no stopping him now.*

"Yes, but—" she began. He held up a finger.

"Use your head, Mumu, and you can eat better and live better than anybody ever did since the world began. You can also die of malnutrition from going macrobiotic or high-protein, or you can die of doctoring. Pills, pills, pills, a drug here and a shot there. *Moderation,* Mumu, that's the ticket. Listen: too many vitamins can kill you. Onions can give you anemia. Nutmeg can be poisonous. Spinach and rhubarb build kidney stones. Too many carrots and you get jaundice, too much cabbage can start a goiter. Yes, and before they're done they'll find that parsnips make your nose grow and mashed potatoes make your feet itch. But meanwhile, Mumu, moderation is the word. "Moderation," he repeated firmly. "Moderation in all things," he was saying, as Mumu backed out the door.

"Including moderation," he murmured, reaching into his middle desk drawer for his second Chocolate Wallop bar of the afternoon. It contained hydrogenated palm kernel oils, propylene glycol monostearate, hydroxylated lecithin, acetylated monoglycerides, and several other things, and it tasted darned good.

When Mumu finally deciphered the scrawl on the prescription blank, she found that it said, *Quit reading the paper.*

> ". . . This epitomizes the lack of sensitivity and intelligence of most plants; they don't even know the source of their food supply—whether they are fertilized by 'natural' (organic) or 'unnatural' (chemical—synthesized—made by man) materials. When the nutrients are broken down into their inorganic ions, *plants cannot tell their source of origin—whether they came from nature or factory.* And it really doesn't matter; an ion is an ion.
>
> "And the same thing applies to 'natural' versus 'synthetic' vitamins. The two are identical. The absorptive site in the small intestine simply could not care less about the pedigree of the vitamin. It recognizes that the vitamin is a vitamin. They are identical in every way—except for price."
>
> —Robert H. Moser, M.D.

"Drive far from us, O Most Bountiful, all creatures of air and darkness; cast out the demons that possess us; deliver us from the fear of calories and the bondage of nutrition; and set us free once more in our own land, where we shall serve thee as thou has blest us—with the dew of heaven, the fatness of the earth, and plenty of corn and wine. Amen."

—Robert Farrar Capon

JANUARY 20   Now beginneth the sign of dry AQUARIUS (controlling the Legs) which continueth through February 18, all this time being the time to
prune a cherry tree
shear a sheep
buy new boots
set herbs and teas in low oven for ten minutes to discourage mildew
reparaffin weeping jelly jars
wean a baby.
But the sociable Aquarian postponeth all these things and throweth a party.

JANUARY 21   Bringeth Interesting Medical Information!
"People consume too much carbonaceous food —as fats, oil, butter, lard, sugar, pork, fritters, doughnuts, greasy griddle-cakes, pies and pastry. Carbon dwarfs the soul."

—*Frank Leslie's Illustrated*
Family Almanac, 1872

JANUARY 22   ". . . The wise houseperson, cooking delicacies for the Christmas holidays, will set aside and hide a special hoard of them for personal enjoyment later in January; for it is seldom that she can enjoy the fruits of her labors during chaotic December, when the mere sight of a Christmas cooky is enough to turn her stomach. . . ."

—Stella Trowbridge Hinky

But if the houseperson didn't do this, today is a good day to make

ELEGANT SOUTHERN PRALINES

(Ms. Hinky points out that they are Elegant Northern Pralines
if they are made with walnuts instead of pecans.)

2 cups granulated sugar
1 cup buttermilk
1 teaspoon baking soda
a pinch of salt

2 tablespoons butter
2 cups nuts, halved or coarsely
  chopped
1 teaspoon vanilla

Pick a BIG saucepan, she advises. (The buttermilk and soda will foam with an exuberance that can shortly have you cleaning the whole stove.) In it, put everything except the butter, and nuts, and vanilla, and bring to a boil over medium-high heat. Keep right on stirring till the candy thermometer says 210°. (And don't be afraid you'll end up with white pralines. Somehow it all turns a beautiful dark gold.) Now add the butter and nuts, lower the heat a little, and keep cooking till the thermometer says 230°. If you haven't a thermometer, test it: the syrup should form at least a two-inch thread without breaking, when you tilt the spoon.

Take it off the heat, add the vanilla, and let it sit till it quiets down. Beat it till it loses its gloss, and drop it by spoonfuls on waxed paper. When they've cooled, wrap them individually in waxed paper squares and hide them in an unpleasant-looking used shortening can in the back of the refrigerator.

JANUARY 23   A Day for an Easy and Extraordinarily Good Cake.

My friend John mentioned a recipe for a chestnut cake he had acquired years ago from someone glamorous, I can't remember who. It was possibly, he said, the richest, most elegant, and best cake he had ever tasted.

In a rash moment, I volunteered to help him make one, and so, one sunny Saturday morning, we put it together with no trouble, hoping it would be only half as good as he remembered. Considering the ingredients, it would have to be at least adequate, I thought, despite Crumpacker's dependable 11th Law: *The quality of a dish decreases in inverse ratio to one's expectations.*

And so we baked it, frosted it, refrigerated it, and forgot it till desserttime, then brought it out. It looked handsome, cut superbly, and was by all means the richest, most elegant, best cake anyone there had ever tasted, including one man who was weaned on Sacher tortes as a little boy in Vienna.

I hardly knew what to think. Like discovering there really is a Tooth Fairy, a thing like this can reshape your world and restore your confidence. I always think of it as the day I had my faith lifted.

THE ENGSTEAD CAKE

¾ cup butter
1 cup sugar
4 eggs
1 tablespoon rum

2 cups chestnuts (shelled, cooked
  till tender, then ground fine)
¼ cup grated almonds
1 cup whipping cream

more almonds for decoration
plus ½ pound of bitter chocolate
and ½ cup of butter for frosting

Cream the butter, gradually beat in the sugar, then add the well-beaten egg yolks and the rum. Now add the ground chestnuts and grated almonds, beating thoroughly, and fold in the stiffly beaten egg whites. Pour it into two cake pans greased with Crisco and sprinkled lightly with graham-cracker crumbs. Bake them forty-five minutes at 350° and cool.

Put the two layers together with whipped cream: Whip a cup of whipping cream, add the merest minimum of sugar—say, a teaspoon or two—and spread it on one layer. Set the other layer neatly on top.

Now cover with chocolate frosting: Melt the ½ pound of Swiss bitter chocolate with ½ cup butter, in the top of a double boiler. Beat it till it's thick enough to spread. Then do so.

JANUARY 24   "Whatever Miss T. eats
               Turns into Miss T."
                           —Walter de la Mare

JANUARY 25   "The Guts uphold the Heart, and not the Heart
               the Guts."
                           —Thomas Fuller

JANUARY 26   A night to bundle up warmly, go outside, stand
               quietly, and see if it is possible to detect the
Chandler Wobble.

The Chandler Wobble (not to be confused with the Lindy Hop or
the Shrimp Wiggle) is the earth's wobble on its axis. It was invented
by the American astronomer Seth Carlo Chandler, who thought it
would be more interesting if the earth would wobble a little, not
just keep steadily turning in the same dull, dependable way. Now
that laser beams can be reflected off the moon, it may be possible
for Science to predict changes in the Wobble which, for reasons not
entirely clear to the present scribe, may be helpful in predicting
earthquakes.

JANUARY 27   A cold, forbidding day. Scudding clouds and
               charcoal skies and old snow like dirty laundry
filling the gutters. Wet. Raw. Chill Factor: —10. But a bright fire.
Stay indoors and curl up with a good friend. Or if that isn't convenient, a good book.

JANUARY 28   How the Houseperson can set little children to
               amusing themselves on a sleety weekend:

LET THEM MAKE AND BAKE THEIR OWN ZOO

Mix 1½ cups flour with 1½ cups salt, and enough water to make
it the consistency of a firm clay . . . start with ½ cup water and
add more by cautious spoonfuls. Divide it in several sections and
tint with food coloring.

Now the little children can mold some blue puppies and green
roosters and pink unicorns and bake them for an hour at 350°.
These are remarkably sturdy. In fact, you will have time to get good
and sick of seeing them around, because they last and last.

JANUARY 29   W. C. Fields was born Claude William Duken-
               field on this day in 1880. In his memory, take
all those cute little animals away from the kids and then insult the
dog.

JANUARY 30   Proper tides should neatly ebb and flow,
Like proper housewives, cleaning as they go.

But this one—see it now?—doth flow
and ebb,
And leaveth all its trash behind for
Feb.

JANUARY 31   And yet flowers come in stony places, as Masefield observed, and kind deeds are done by men with ugly faces. The elevator boy is getting over his sinus condition, and the couple in Apt. 24B made up again, and this morning's sunrise was a glorious full-color shout, audible and even visible, now that they've raised the emission standards over at the asbestos plant.

". . . At Sagamore Hill, Theodore Roosevelt and I used to play a little game together. After an evening of talk, we would go out on the lawn and search the skies until we found the faint spot of light-mist beyond the lower left-hand corner of the Great Square of Pegasus. Then one or the other of us would recite:

" 'That is the Spiral Galaxy in Andromeda. It is as large as our Milky Way.'

" 'It is one of a hundred million galaxies.'

" 'It consists of one hundred billion suns, each larger than our sun.'

"Then Roosevelt would grin and say: 'Now I think we are small enough! Let's go to bed.' "

—William Beebe

February

bringeth cold & storm & a garland of birthdays; considereth a rare Miscellanie of Topicks; also delivereth a purposeful Bevy of Delectable Breads: a Bread that

encourageth the novice
or filleth the lunch-bucket
or repaireth the health
or saveth the energy
or useth the milk gone sour
or scrimpeth on calories
or impresseth the neighbors
or gladdeneth the ego & the stomach

or even performeth these many tasks at once!

"... I went and did some baking, as it
all seemed beyond me and I felt frightened."
—Florida Scott-Maxwell
(age 82)

FEBRUARY 1   NOW IT IS BLEAK FEBRUARY, poor bobtailed February, robbed twice of a Day by arrogant Emperors; yet with what cool Revenge doth the shortest Month contrive to seem the longest! Now the pedestrian's Ankles congeal & the Chill Factor increaseth betwixt Apartment-dweller & Maintenance Engineer, while the Houseperson mendeth the frozen Pipe. In the north Countrie do small shivering Birds take cover from the piercing Ayre & the Snowmobiles; while in the south Countrie do Residents take cover & Traveler's Cheques from the Visiting Tourist. And yet there be small Stirrings below ground & Trees do a little begin to bud. And the reluctant Cook vieweth with Envie the early Robin feeding its Familie on raw Worms, while the harried Houseperson ignoreth with gallantry the Mudde upon the coat-closet Floor.

An Excellent Cure for Feminine Melancholie

"If any lady be sick of the sullens,* she knows not where, let her take a handful of simples, I know not what, and use them, I know not how, applying them to the place grieved, I know not which, and shee shall be cured, I know not when."

> —Sir Thomas Overbury, an
> English poet, imprisoned in the Tower
> in 1613 and slowly poisoned with blue
> vitriol by Lady Essex's agents, possibly
> for writing lines like these

But for a better cure, a kind of Shakespearean Lydia Pinkham's, let her try

HIPPOCRAS

"Take about three quarts of the best White-Wine, a pound and a half of Sugar, and an Ounce of Cinamon, two or three tops of Sweet Marjoram, and a little whole pepper; let these run through a Filtering Bag with a grain of Musk; add the juice of a large Limon,

---

* The sullens happen in months that do or do not have an *r* in them, and are generally preceded or followed by a case of the stupids.

and when it has taken a gentle heat over the Fire, and stood for the space of three or four days close covered, put it in Bottles, and keep it close stopt, as an Excellent and Generous Wine, as also a very Curious Cordial to refresh and enliven the Spirits. It easeth the Palpitations and Tremblings of the Heart and removes the Causes of Panick Fears, Frights, and Startings; it giveth Rest to weary Limbs and heats the cold Stomach."

—William Salmon, circa 1680

In This Month, in 1858, Galoshes Were Patented.

And it is remarkable that it took so long. February has always been a poor excuse for a month, so much so that some ancient Pollyanna turned its dependably foul weather into a pie-in-the-sky superstition, out of self-defense: the worse you've got it now, the better you'll have it later. And vice versa. Hence the old English proverb

"The Welshman would rather see his dam on her bier
Than see a fair Februeer."

Or, as the Scotsman put it,

"A' the months o' the yeer
Curse a fair Februeer."

(It took nearly as many years for the world to learn how to spell February as it did for it to learn how to keep its feet dry.)

However, galoshes eventually came along. And how merrily then they flopped and flapped when open! How snug they buckled against the elements, around the britches and the ankles! —Until the world regrettably regressed again to boots—boots that zipped or unzipped, if the zippers felt like it, or boots that fitted like skin and were just as painful to pull off.

In Bloomington, Indiana, this stormy day in 1974, a school-teacher was helping a small boy tug a pair of tight boots over his wet shoes. It was a traumatic time for them both, and, finally, as she tugged the last tug, he offered helpfully, "These aren't my boots."

"Not *yours!*" Grimly she pried them off, and reeling back, panting, the boots finally free in her hand, demanded, "Why didn't you *say* so?" And he explained, "They're my brother's, but I have to wear them; they don't fit him any more."

February can be like that.

FEBRUARY 2   MS. AESOP'S FABLES (No. 2)

One day early in February, an elderly ground-hog decided it was time to teach his son the family business from the ground up. So he said, "Elwell, get on up there and look around, and if you see your shadow, hurry home."

Elwell took off. But when he saw his shadow, he thought, *My, what a nice day to stay up here and play in the sunshine!* Which he did. Meanwhile, a bulldozer came along and bulldozed his old home into eternity right along with his parents, to make room for a parking lot.

> *Moral:* If you ever manage to get out of the hole, stay out.

FEBRUARY 3   A Dissertation on Homemade Bread

My trouble was that I captured, some years ago, the all-state amateur title for baking bread that wouldn't do what it was supposed to. Mainly, it wouldn't rise. And so, after some dazzling flops, I assumed that breadmaking required a special talent, like limbo dancing, and I abandoned the whole idea.

Or thought I had. But apparently I had only set it away in a warm place in my subconscious, where it finally rose, doubled in bulk, and surfaced one random morning when I found myself making a last gallant try, which worked. Either the yeast had improved in the long interim or I had. Possibly both. At any rate, I have been baking bread ever since when I'm not doing anything else, which is most of the time.

In my own mind, bread-baking and cooking have little in common. It isn't inconsistent to like one and hate the other. You *have* to cook, at least a little. But you don't have to bake bread, and electives are always more fun than requireds. Moreover, dinner doesn't keep, but bread does, for long, luxurious months in the freezer. I know jams and pickles last too, at least longer than dinner does. But they are trimmings, not fundamentals.

Perhaps it is this fundamental aspect of bread-baking that makes it therapeutic: comforting in worried times, like reading Wodehouse; and—if not stimulating—at least good for the morale in becalmed periods: at least there is something to show for the day. . . . There is no such thing, by the way, as a totally hopeless home-baked loaf. If it isn't even good toasted, it will still make

33

good crumbs (in the blender) for meat loaf; and if worst comes to absolute worst, it is an adequate doorstop. Shellac it.

. . . Now, it is a shame that all the experts have been busy recently making bread-baking so perfectly clear that it becomes unclear. Like sex, it has developed a mystique and an enormous literature all its own. The casual observer from another planet would conclude that both endeavors require a Ph.D., at the least, to get any pleasurable results. But of course this isn't true. Also, it isn't my intention to add to the literature. I only want to put down some points I wish I'd known sooner.

1. Any bread recipe in any standard cookbook will probably turn out fine. Just don't let them scare you with their nit-picking.

2. The world contains more bread recipes than the world needs. Still, they have their little differences. When you make an especially good one, write down the doubled proportions to one side (but don't quite double the salt). There is no point making less than two loaves of bread, and four is better, and there's nothing the matter with eight or ten. Some recipes, doubled, would nearly fill the bathtub, once the dough doubles in bulk, and maybe the bathtub is already occupied. So divide it and use two bowls, or even three, for the rising. Then borrow another oven to bake in.

3. Baking bread doesn't take much of your own working time. Mainly it is the yeast that works. (You'll notice that some recipes say, *Let the dough rest.* The dough, not you.) It generally takes fifteen to twenty minutes to mix up a batch for the first rising. Then it is only a matter of hanging around the place while it rises the second time and, finally, bakes.

The houseperson who thinks ahead will see to it that everyone else who is customarily or occasionally around the house—husband, wife, daughter, son, elevator boy —is familiar with the rising–punching–down–rising again–and–baking process, so the houseperson can mix it, knead it, and split.

4. Before you start a batch, put a medium-size cellophane sack by the telephone to slip your telephone hand into. At the start of the kneading process, there is usually a point where your hands look like the hoofs of some large, pathetic animal stuck in a clay bank; and if the telephone is going to ring once all day, this is the time.

34

5. Any kind of flour is all right except cake flour. Purists scream at the notion of using anything but unbleached. But purists will be purists.

6. Whatever amount of flour the recipe calls for, measure it all out first, in a separate bowl. That way you'll be sure to put in the right amount, regardless of absent-minded lapses.

7. Any homemade bread is even better for you if you add 1 tablespoon soy flour, 1 tablespoon powdered skim milk, and 1 teaspoon wheat germ, per cup of flour. This considerably increases the protein content in some mysterious fashion the nutritionists understand, and let's just take their word for it.

8. About kneading: most basic cookbooks tell how, and some have pictures. But just in case—

> *When the dough seems reasonably manageable, turn it out onto a floured board or kitchen counter, and sprinkle a little more flour on top. Now knead: press it down and away from you with the heels of your hands. Give it a quarter-turn, then pick up the opposite edge, bringing it toward you, then press it down and away from you again as you did before. Keep doing it. Set the timer if the recipe specifies a certain number of minutes—and add flour as necessary, till the dough is smooth and satiny. No pussyfooting, no delicate handling. Use muscle.*

This matter of adding more flour, by the way, doesn't come naturally to pastry cooks, who have been taught the more flour, the tougher the product. Not so, with bread, if it's thoroughly kneaded in. Moreover, in hot, humid weather, you'll often need as much as a cupful more than the recipe says. So add it, knead it hard, and don't worry about it.

9. If you're alone and have to leave it for an hour or so while you're kneading, it doesn't matter. If it's during the rising—first or second—punch it down before you go and let it rise again. When you get back, take a good look at it, if it's the second rising. You don't want it too high: it may use up the moxie it needs for the final surge as it bakes. Then your bread will be flatter: still good but not as handsome. So punch it back down and let it rise yet again, but not so high.

> *If you're suspicious of this day before it starts, and think you may be in and out like the tides, it's a good precaution to double the amount of yeast called for. Then, once*

the dough is shaped into loaves in the pans, refrigerate
them to bake that night or the next day. Take them out,
let them set ten minutes, and bake.

10. The one time you'd better stick close, or see that someone does, is while it bakes. Shift the pans around at least once during the baking time, so they will bake more evenly.

11. The handiest breadmaking tool for my dough costs less than a dollar in the kitchenware department. It is a rectangular metal scraper, about three inches by four inches, with a wooden handle down one side. At the sticky stage, it neatens things no end, besides doing a fast job of scraping the breadboard when you're done.

12. It's best to settle on one place for letting the dough rise, rather than schlep it around different places on different days. A dependable spot is the middle rack of a closed oven, with only the pilot light on (if it's a gas oven), or the oven light on if it's electric. Try that. If it takes longer to rise than the recipe predicts, next time use the pan-of-water system. Set a pan of it, hot and steaming from the faucet, on the oven floor, with the covered bread dough directly above it, and leave the oven door open a crack. Dough rises more slowly on humid days, and by using the pan of water, you're creating a humid day in your oven.

13. It is hard to hurt dough. If your mind wanders and you add things in the wrong sequence, it seldom matters. The bread may be a little different, that's all. Once I entirely forgot to add the last cup of flour to a batch of sour dough. It turned out odd-looking—rough-textured, dampish, and large-pored, like a real problem complexion. But toasted, it was crumpetlike—a chewy, muscular crust, and big holes that soaked up the butter. Very good, and I plan to do it again someday.

14. In fact, your bread may be different even if you make it exactly the way you did last time. That is one of its interesting features. Weather matters, and so does the flour, as well as—I strongly suspect—your state of mind. A recipe you've made a dozen times will, this time, be lighter, or firmer, or richer, or spongier. But nearly always good.

15. And you can make it different on purpose without undue risk. If the recipe says butter, you can almost always substitute lard, vegetable shortening, bacon fat, margarine, or cooking oil. Or change the liquid from water to bouillon to vegetable juice to

beer or wine, if you want to experiment. Or add chopped nuts or cheese or raisins or grated lemon peel. It will still be bread . . . maybe flatter, or yellower, or moister, or lighter, or holier . . . and possibly quite delicious. Also, many breads taste better and look prettier with sesame or poppy or caraway seeds or cracked wheat sprinkled on top before baking and after you've brushed them with egg white, melted butter, or water.

16. You can omit the salt from any bread recipe for people on salt-free diets. People who aren't can salt their toast or bread before they butter it. It won't be as good, but it won't be bad.

17. If bread calls for potato water, you don't have to boil potatoes to get it. Use three teaspoons of instant potatoes per ½ cup of water.

18. Any bread dough made with molasses or honey will be stickier, so add more flour if you have to. (Or substitute the same amount of brown or white sugar if you like, though you'd lose the distinctive taste of the molasses or honey, which may be what the recipe is all about.) Also, molasses gives bread a good color. Once when I substituted sugar for the molasses, the bread was the color of gray flannel underwear, though it tasted fine if you shut your eyes.

19. It is handy to have your own informal temperature gauge for the water the yeast goes into. A few degrees cooler than I like a hot bath works fine for me with dry yeast (the only kind I use, because it's least temperamental). Until you develop the feel of it, the deep-fat or candy thermometer should read 110° to 125°. (For cake yeast it's cooler—80° to 90°.) It's good to rinse the mixing bowl with hot water before you start. A cold bowl can chill the contents considerably.

20. To cover the rising dough, waxed paper is easiest. Don't use a dry cloth. The dough will eventually push against it, like a fat lady in slacks, and the sticky dough is a nuisance to wash out.

21. If it isn't brown enough once it's out of the oven, you can bake it another five or ten minutes till it is.

22. If it bulges fatly over the top when it is done, let it steam in the pan five minutes before putting it on the rack to cool. It will come out more neatly.

23. Any bread freezes and refreezes fine, sliced or unsliced. No need to bother with freezer tape, paper, and so on. Use aluminum foil or thick Pliofilm sacks. Just be sure the air is squeezed out.

24. As for keeping it, Bernard Clayton writes, in *The Complete Book of Breads:*

"In several studies by the flour companies, the most surprising finding was that bread stored in the refrigerator stales *faster* than bread at room temperature. Ideally, bread should be stored in a clean dry place at room temperature. There is nothing better than the traditional bread box or bread drawer. Bread in a plastic bag will be equally fresh but moist. Bread stored in the box (without wrapping) will better retain its crispness. Nevertheless, a loaf to be held for a long period should go into the refrigerator to prevent mold from forming."

FEBRUARY 4   "I really dug this bread thing because you don't have to sift the flour, you know? But I wasn't about to buy any bread pans till I found out if I could make the stuff. So I started out with the coffee-can kind. . . ."
    —Shirley Shimmelfenner,*
    My Kitchen & Welcome to It, vol. 8

SHIMMELFENNER'S
COFFEE-CAN BREAD

(Good-textured, and only rises once. Makes neat round slices that just fit the large-size baloney for a really well-tailored sandwich.)

First find some empty coffee cans that still have their plastic lids— one two-pound size or two one-pounders. Grease their interiors. Now assemble

1 tablespoon dry yeast	1 teaspoon salt
½ cup warm water	2 tablespoons salad oil
⅛ teaspoon ground ginger	4 or 4½ cups flour
3 tablespoons sugar	a little butter or margarine
1 can (13 ounces) evaporated milk	

* Details of Shirley Shimmelfenner's life would be redundant here, for she has revealed them all in her many books, starting with *I Was a Teen-Age Drudge* (1955) to *Shirley Shimmelfenner Rides Again* (1976), The Bar Nothing Press. Indeed, one wonders how, with her vast autobiographical output ("makes Anaïs Nin look tongue-tied," as one critic remarked), she finds time to do anything to write about. But find it she does, and at last reports was hard at work on a definitive study of the psychological aspects of deep-fat cookery, *Fear of Frying.*

In a big bowl dissolve the yeast in the water. Then add the ginger and one tablespoon of the sugar. Let it set about fifteen minutes while you do likewise. Have another cup of coffee. By then the yeast will be foaming like a stein of good beer and you'll know you're in business.

Now add the rest of the sugar, plus the milk, salt, and salad oil. Add the flour gradually till the dough is heavy, stiff, and reasonably unsticky. Knead it, five minutes by the timer, then put it into your greased can or cans and put their lids on.

Let them rise till the lids pop off—say one to 1½ hours. Put the lids somewhere safe for next time and bake the bread in a 350° oven—forty-five minutes for one-pound loaves, sixty minutes for a two-pounder. The crust will be quite brown. Brush it with butter if you remember to. They'll look like tall chefs' hats, and you'll feel pretty good about it.

Also on this fourth day of February in 1976, Mumu Harbottle made her first successful loaf of bread.

Mumu was positive that her bread wouldn't rise for her, the way it does for other people. Even though Jimbo kept urging her to try it, she kept putting it off. Finally, however, she gathered her nerve and made some. Sure enough, the dough didn't rise an inch.

When she told Dr. Neitzelgrinder about this, he suggested that she fish out of the kitchen wastebasket her used yeast envelope and check the expiration date. She did this, and learned to her considerable chagrin that she had dillydallied so long that the yeast was four months too old. And so she got some new yeast and double-checked the date and singlehandedly produced two beautiful loaves of

AMIABLE WHITE BREAD
(Fine-textured, good-flavored, and easy to handle)

3 packages active dry yeast
3 cups very warm water
¼ cup sugar or honey

8 to 9 cups white flour
5 teaspoons salt
5 tablespoons vegetable oil

In a good big bowl combine the yeast, water, and sugar (or honey). Stir it till the yeast dissolves. Add four cups of the flour, and the salt. Beat hard for a few minutes. Add the rest of the flour. When you have a fairly cohesive ball of dough, pour the oil over it and knead it in the bowl another two minutes. The dough will absorb

39

most of the oil. Now cover the bowl and let the dough rise till doubled—about forty-five minutes. Punch it down, knead it slightly, then shape into two large loaves in two one-pound loaf pans, greased. Cover and let it rise again, about thirty minutes. Bake at 400° for thirty to thirty-five minutes. Then take them out of the pans and let them cool on a wire rack.

A Little-known Fact!

You can deep-fry small balls of any basic bread dough— like this one—after the second rising, for good little DOUGHNUT-CRULLERS. When the hot-fat thermometer says 350° to 375°, drop them in it for a minute, drain them, and roll them in cinnamon and sugar. Or have them for breakfast with honey or jam.

FEBRUARY 5   "Tomato seedlings and window sills go to-
                    gether."   —Grace Firth
   This is an auspicious day to start some, in eggshell halves filled with sandy dirt.

FEBRUARY 6   Precisely on this day, winter is half over. To
                    help get you through the other half, make four
rousing good loaves of

WHOLE-WHEAT TIGER BREAD
*(One slice and you can move a piano. Two slices and
you can play it.)*

2 tablespoons dry yeast
½ cup warm water
3 cups hot water
⅔ cup brown sugar
4 teaspoons salt
6 tablespoons shortening

1 cup cracked wheat
2½ cups whole-wheat flour
½ cup wheat germ
6 cups white flour (and maybe
   a little more)

Soften the yeast in the ½ cup of warm water. In a big bowl, com- bine the three cups of hot water with the sugar, salt, and shorten- ing. Cool it to lukewarm. Then stir in the cracked wheat, the whole- wheat flour, the wheat germ, and about two cups of the white flour.

Beat it well, stir in the softened yeast, and add the rest of the white flour.

Knead it ten minutes by the timer, shape it into a ball, and put it in a big, greased bowl, turning it over once so the top surface is oiled too. Let it rise, covered, till doubled—about 1½ hours. Punch it down, divide it into four equal parts, let it rest ten minutes. Then shape it into round balls or loaf-shaped loaves, put it in greased pans, cover them, and let them rise again for an hour. Finally, bake at 375° about forty-five minutes. In half an hour, take a look, and if they're browning too fast, lay a piece of aluminum foil across the top.

FEBRUARY 7   ". . . Your proper Almanac deals in time: sidereal time, or clock-time, or sun-time. . . ."
                                               —Figgins

And if it also deals in bread, it should mention Meantime, which is one of the pleasantest kinds . . . time to do something else in too. There is ample Meantime in breadmaking: time to take a walk or a bath or a flute lesson or a sounding of the general situation. (But never trust a yeast-bread recipe that mentions jigtime. Even the no-knead kind takes rising time and oven time, and two hours is a long jig.)

FEBRUARY 8   Let us consecrate this day to James Payn, whose birthday it was, in 1830.

Later, Mr. Payn wrote voluminously and hard. He wrote *Carlyon's Year, Another's Burden, Lost Sir Massingberd,* and many another fat novel you never hear about or curl up with. All, all were swallowed without a trace by time's treacherous quicksand; so of his writing, only four short lines are alive and well:

> "I never had a piece of toast
> Particularly long and wide
> But fell upon the sanded floor
> And always on the buttered side."

And yet, a wistful quatrain is better than nothing. It is just as good as being remembered as the man who broke the bank or

41

threw the overalls, and it is considerably better than being remembered as the man who dropped the ball or dropped the bomb.

Apologia pro Sua Vita
"Little I said was very astute;
Little I wrote was deep or profound.
The gods gave me only a tiny flute
But some folks liked the sound."
—Morris Ryskind

FEBRUARY 9   *A Cheerful Day.*
It is possibly Shrove Tuesday, too, a day for forgiveness and pancakes. Or, at the very least, for good homemade bread, toasted.

A Capital Joke!
"Mama," said the little boy, drying a towel in front of the fire, "is it done when it's brown?"
The little stupe. But this is a good question with bread, and the answer is: Not always.

". . . So I finally learned, if the bread begins to smell great right after I put it in, to ask myself if it was supposed to smell that great that soon. Then I'd go turn off the broiler."
—Shirley Shimmelfenner (*Ibid.*)

If the oven was on BROIL, to heat faster, you get broiled bread dough. Precautions should be taken. Place an unlikely object like a tennis shoe on the stove top at the same time, to flag your attention as you put the bread in, and remind you to turn BROIL off and BAKE on.

FEBRUARY 10   Now the provident houseperson grates fine all the random ends of bread in the refrigerator and saves the crumbs in a refrigerated jar for some future need. The improvident houseperson doesn't do this, having learned from experience that when the future need arises, the i. h. forgets they're there and goes and buys some.

FEBRUARY 11   The Annual Pancake Race was held in Olney, England, on this day in 1975.

But it was never reported which pancake ran the fastest. More likely, they all just rolled, which must have been something to see, all right, though not much to eat. *A rolling pancake gathers no syrup.*

Biscuits roll better, and the following biscuits have other merits too. In 1974, they were voted most likely to get eaten before anything else was, at a school cafeteria in Decatur, Illinois, where they are served every Friday to take the curse off the creamed fish.

McGUFFEY BISCUITS

4 cups flour	½ teaspoon salt
¾ cup dry milk powder	1¼ stick butter
2 tablespoons baking powder	1¼ stick margarine
⅓ cup sugar	1¼ cup water

5 drops of yellow coloring;
makes them look lovely and rich

First mix the dry ingredients together, then cut in the shortening with a pastry cutter till it's all tiny lumps, like small peas. Put the yellow coloring into the water, then add it to the first mix, stirring just enough to moisten all the flour. Drop them by the tablespoonful (or the ice-cream scoopful) on a greased baking sheet and bake at 425° for twenty minutes.

This makes a lot of nice big biscuits that freeze well. Reheat them at 425° for ten to twelve minutes.

FEBRUARY 12   A good day for making Dr. Neitzelgrinder's

TENNIS-ELBOW BREAD

(No kneading. An honest man, the good doctor points out that it still must be beaten. So use your other elbow, he suggests, or hand it to the man who comes to read the meter. A good bread, with a hearty coarse texture and a staunch French-bread sort of crust.)

In a big bowl combine	In a little bowl stir together
1 tablespoon dry yeast	1¼ cups hot water
1 cup unsifted flour	1 tablespoon sugar
	½ teaspoon salt

until the sugar is dissolved. Add this to the flour and yeast you already put in the big bowl, and stir it up.

Beat it for three minutes and stir in *two more cups of flour*. Put the dough in a greased bowl, turning it over once, then cover and let it rise for an hour. Punch it down, cover, let it rest ten minutes, and grease a round casserole dish. (Or use a loaf pan, but the doctor says it tastes better round.) Sprinkle it generously with corn meal, put the dough in, sprinkle more corn meal on top, and let 'er rise forty-five minutes. Bake at 400° about forty minutes.

FEBRUARY 13   America's Oldest Public School Opened in Boston on This Day in 1635.

Almost immediately, then, the third-grade class went to work on America's first Valentine Box, the box they would need on the following day. It was a tasteful arrangement in red crepe paper and lopsided red construction-paper hearts. At the same time, some basic rules were formulated: everyone draws a name to give a paper Valentine to, and thus every child receives a Valentine.

Except that it never worked out that way, in 1635 or any year since, because some little blonde girl always gets seventeen plus a chocolate marshmallow heart. There will always be a little blonde girl.

FEBRUARY 14   With a truly deplorable lack of Aloha spirit, some hot, cross Hawaiian natives killed Captain Cook on this day in 1779. His widow, Elizabeth Cook, who was born Batts, survived him fifty-six years.

Also on this day, in 1842, Juliet Corson was born.

She opened the New York School of Cookery in 1876 and is generally considered to be the founding mother of Domestic Science. But just why she called it Science, no one has been able to figure out, inasmuch as its only underlying scientific principle is Heisenberg's Law of the Unexpected; and, always, the more scientific it gets, the less domestic it is.

> ". . . Of the home economists we have met in our lifetime, all had one trait in common: not one of them was at home."
> —E. B. White

FEBRUARY 15   A good day to bake bread in honor of Susan
                B. Anthony, who was born on this day in
1820 and headed the National Woman Suffrage Association from
1892 to 1900.

SUSAN'S LUNCH-BOX BREAD
(*The basic recipe makes five loaves, to slice and
freeze ahead for sandwiches. It's easy to double, too,
and that's a lot of bread, girls. Use a washtub.*)

5 tablespoons sugar
4 cups lukewarm water
2 packages dry yeast (or 2
   tablespoons)

18 cups flour
2 cups scalded milk
3 tablespoons melted shortening
4 teaspoons salt

Dissolve the sugar in the warm water. Next, stir in the yeast, add
six cups of the flour, beat it well, and put it aside for a little. (That's
a sponge you just made, and it's a good term to drop into bread-
baking conversations.) Meanwhile, scald the milk, add the shortening and salt, and let it cool. It will be lukewarm by the time the
sponge is ready. And when it is—when it's pretty puffy—add the
lukewarm milk to it and mix it, then enough of the flour to make
an easily handled dough. Knead it till it's smooth and elastic, then
grease some big bowls, the number depending on whether you
doubled it. If not, two are enough. Divide the dough in half, turn
it over once in the bowl, cover, let rise till doubled, about 1½
hours. Then shape it into five loaves, cover, let rise again about fifty
minutes. Bake at 425° for fifteen minutes, then at 350° for thirty.

FEBRUARY 16   Andrew ("One-Hoss") Shea* was born on
                this day in 1906.

A perennial bachelor, One-Hoss has always cooked for himself,
and he really knows his way around the kitchen except late some
Saturday nights, when he tends to bump into the refrigerator.

Most of One-Hoss's recipes involve some alcohol, one kind or
another, except for his granola (p. 99), and who knows what he
pours over it. A distinct fondness for spirits has run in the family,

* Author of *I Remember Mama, Daddy, Grammaw, Aunt Pert, and a Lot of
Other People* (© 1968, The Grape Press), first printing five hundred copies at a
cost to Mr. Shea of $2,000, and as soon as he sells the other 483 copies he'll break
even. Born in Boston, Mr. Shea eventually worked his way west to Surrey, Oklahoma, where he went to work in a buggy factory. The pay was minimal, and he'd
have quit sooner if it hadn't been for the fringe benefits.

ever since his great-granddaddy brought the first batch of fermented potato mash across the plains in a covered flagon.

One-Hoss also affirms that gin is the absodamlutely best eyeglass-polisher he ever ran into. Unless he's in too much of a hurry when he's pouring himself one, he puts a drop of gin on each lens, and for a while he sees a lot better. Also, in most bars, he reports, they give you paper napkins just the right size to polish them with.

ONE-HOSS BEER BREAD

(Fine texture, good taste. One-Hoss says people who don't like licorice can use dill or caraway seeds instead of fennel, but it would be a real shame.)

¼ cup warm water
2 tablespoons dry yeast
1¾ cups beer, which finishes a small bottle; One-Hoss
    points out that if you open a quart, you've got some
    to finish yourself

¼ cup melted shortening	1 tablespoon fennel seeds
¼ cup molasses	3½ cups rye flour
1 teaspoon salt	2 to 2½ cups white flour

First he puts the warm water in a cup and stirs in the yeast, then heats the beer and shortening together in a little saucepan till they're warm. He pours this into the big bowl with the red roses on it that used to be the washbowl in Grammaw's bedroom, then adds the molasses, salt, seeds, and the yeast mix.

After he's stirred it some, he starts in on the flour—adds all the rye, beats it good, adds enough white flour so he can handle it, and kneads it ten minutes. Good for the biceps and the bread too.

Next, he puts it in a warm, greased bowl, covers it, lets it rise an hour, punches it down, and lets it rise again for forty minutes. Then he shapes a round loaf to put in a greased casserole dish, and a long skinny loaf to put on a greased cooky sheet, and bakes them at 400°. The skinny one is done in about thirty-five minutes; the round loaf takes about an hour.

FEBRUARY 17   *A Great Day for Banana Bread*
                     in honor of Aunt Henry Macadangdang's husband, Ramon, whose natal day it is.

After Aunt Henry and Ramon got settled in Manila, we thought we'd never hear from her again. But she kept those cards and letters rolling in, especially at monsoon season. Her Banana Letter was especially memorable, and parts of it are included here.

". . . Anyway you won't believe what I learned today. At least I didn't till I tried it. You know how you grew up not putting bananas in the refrigerator. I mean, you just didn't *do* it any more than you'd cut the tag off a mattress. Well, any time you're over-bananaed, freeze them. That's right, wrap them separately in aluminum foil and they'll keep for weeks without the skins turning black, and, frozen, they taste exactly like banana ice cream."

Then she included her Fast Banana Bread recipe, and, for good measure, her Easy Banana Jam.

AUNT HENRY'S FAST BANANA BREAD
(*Rich and cakelike; fine toasted*)

1 egg, beaten
½ cup milk
3 cups biscuit mix

1 cup mashed ripe bananas
1 cup sugar
¾ cup chopped nuts

Beat the egg, add the milk, then add everything else. Mix it up, pour it into a good-sized greased loaf pan, and bake for an hour at 350°. Or use two smaller pans and bake for forty-five minutes.

How to Use Up Brown Splotchy Bananas, or

AUNT HENRY'S EASY BANANA JAM
(*Good on toast or ice cream, or in peanut butter sandwiches*)

6 very ripe bananas, mashed
juice of 6 lemons

Now add a cup of sugar to every cup of the banana-juice mixture and set it on low heat. Cook it about an hour, stirring frequently. If it starts turning pink, don't be upset; it depends on what kind of bananas they are. Maybe it will, maybe it won't. Anyway, skim off the froth as the jam cooks. Then refrigerate it if you're going to eat it pretty soon, as you probably will. Or pour it into sterilized jars and seal it with paraffin.

"Bread without jam ain't bread." —One-Hoss

"He who covers good bread with jam
would mix Grand Marnier with 7-Up."
—Albert Wooky

FEBRUARY 18   Ollie, a Guernsey cow, was the first cow to fly
🐄   in an airplane, on this day in 1930.

For reasons thus far unfathomed by your scribe, Ollie was milked
during the flight, the milk being then sealed in paper containers
and parachuted over St. Louis.

But flying never became really popular with cows, and understandably. When she got home again Ollie was probably able to hold
her enthusiasm down to a reasonable level. *Nothing to moo about,
girls. No scenery to speak of—couldn't see a thing, actually—but
you know the way it goes, business as usual, here comes old Icy
Fingers. Wonder it didn't curdle my milk.*

SOUR-MILK BREAD
*(Otherwise known as Irish soda bread. Good to know about if
you're out of yeast and the milk's gone west. This is a good, dependable loaf. If the milk isn't sour yet, add a good spoonful of
vinegar to sweet milk and use that. Or use a mixture of yoghurt
and sweet milk. You can also use all white flour, if you like, or
all whole-wheat, though a mixture of both is better.)*

1½ cups white all-purpose flour   1 teaspoon salt
1½ cups whole-wheat flour   3 tablespoons butter
1 teaspoon baking soda   1½ cups sour milk

Mix well till it's a soft and not-too-wet dough, then put it in a
greased loaf tin (making a little trough down the middle so it will
rise evenly) or put it in a round heap on a baking sheet. Bake at
375° to 400° for about an hour.

> ". . . As for my average Bookham day, there is not
> much to tell. Breakfast at 8:00, where I am glad to see
> good Irish soda bread on the table, begins the day. . . ."
> —C. S. Lewis

FEBRUARY 19   Now beginneth the moist, earthy sign of
🐟   PISCES (controlling the Feet) that continueth through March 20, each one of these days favorable for
     setting seeds in sunny window sills
     catching fish
     mending the porch
     writing a poem
     baking a good brown loaf

though the watery Piscean doth too often stopple both ears when Duty calleth, and sit, and cry.

FEBRUARY 20   On This Day of 1962, in the Spacecraft *Friendship 7*, John Herschel Glenn, Jr., Orbited the World Three Times.

FEBRUARY 21   *The New Yorker* Magazine was born on this day in 1925. Also on This Day in 1846, Sarah Bagley Became the First Woman Telegrapher.

History doesn't tell us what were the first words she telegraphed, and that is probably just as well. In all likelihood they were "Now is the time . . ." or "The quick brown fox. . . ." Unless a speaker gets a chance to sharpen up his historic first words before history gets hold of them, they usually don't amount to much. Like Thomas Stafford's remark when he learned that his Gemini 9 mission was finally, after great suspense, postponed. "Aw, shucks," he said, and unfortunately a man with a microphone was there to record it for posterity.

It is another matter, though, when you are warned in advance that some good First Words will be expected. The "one small step" remark on the moon had a nice professional polish to it. So did the alleged Hillary-Tenzing "because it's there" remark after they climbed Everest, although this one has a small but vocal group of detractors. Smart-ass, they say. "Why did you eat up all the cake, Junior?" "Because it was there." Whap. You'd belt him one. Hillary's actual first words when he finally made it to the top are better. "*Done* the old bitch!" he puffed. But this is an exception, so far as spontaneous First Words go.*

Come to that, one should be skeptical about famous Last Words too. It is surely a remarkable coincidence when a last remark is worth writing down. Even if you had a dandy all ready, the timing would probably be wrong. You'd come out with it just before heaving what you expected to be your final breath, but turns out it isn't. You live some more.

* It is also not 100 percent certain that these *were* his first words. Another equally reliable source says that when he staggered down from the summit, he announced to his waiting teammates, "Well, we knocked the bastard off!" Perhaps he said both. Perhaps he said neither. Perhaps we'll never really know.

Well, you can't say it again now; that would be like repeating the tag line of a joke. So you have to think of something else, and meanwhile you're saying a number of unmemorable things, like Ouch, or Please pass the Kleenex. The law of averages says that one of these will be your exit line.

Perhaps the best solution is to have a well-intentioned biographer at the bedside at the critical time—someone with a keen editorial ear and a pencil handy; someone who will select the best thing among several, and write it down.

Some Good Last Words:

JOHN LOCKE, the English philosopher: "Cease now." (He said this to Lady Marsham, who had been reading him the Psalms.)

ALBRECHT VON HALLER, the Swiss anatomist: "The artery ceases to beat."

GEORGE GORDON, LORD BYRON, the English poet: "I must sleep now."

MADAME DE POMPADOUR: *"Un moment, Monsieur le Curé, nous nous en irons ensemble."* (She said this to the curé, who had called to see her and was taking his leave.)

CHARLES II of England: "Don't let poor Nellie starve." (He meant his mistress, Nell Gwynne.)

TITUS OATES of the Scott Expedition (sick and unwilling to be a drag on his teammates) as he walked out into the blizzard to die: "I am just going outside and may be some time."

FEBRUARY 22   On this day in 1976, Mrs. Charles ("Edie") Grumwalt* finally divulged her easy Hot Roll recipe to a reporter for the local paper, and it was all over but the baking. Now she has to think up something else.

---

* "Chuck" and "Edie" Grumwalt are the acknowledged leaders of the Mervyn Meadows (Calif.) in-group. First on the block to have a bidet and a compost heap, first to join an encounter group and first to get out of it, they entertain frequently at their solar-heated beach cottage, formerly called "Laffalot" but rechristened "There" after they started meditating transcendentally.

EDIE'S EASY BUTTERY HOT ROLLS

(Mainly she likes to shape these like croissants. But sometimes she uses a little less sugar and shapes them into hamburger-size buns, or smaller round buns, which she makes into rare-beef or ham sandwiches, for hearty canapés.)

1 tablespoon yeast	4 tablespoons sugar
1 teaspoon salt	1 egg, beaten
1½ tablespoons shortening	3½ cups flour

Soften the yeast in two tablespoons warm water. Then, in a big bowl, put one cup of hot water and add the salt, shortening, and sugar. Cool it. Add the yeast and the egg, and beat in the flour, and add a trifle more if it seems really necessary. Let this rise till it's double in bulk. Then roll it out, as for piecrust. (It's easier to divide the dough in half first.) Cut in wedges, brush with melted butter, and roll up, for croissants. Let them rise, about thirty minutes, and bake ten minutes at 425°.

FEBRUARY 23   Samuel Pepys was born on this day in 1632, and John Keats died on this day in 1821.

There seemeth no logical connection between these facts and Dill Cottage Cheese Bread, but that is the way the ball sometimes bounceth.

DILL COTTAGE CHEESE BREAD

(A crusty savory loaf. Makes a big round one to serve with hearty soups and stews, or two smaller loaf-shaped loaves for sandwiches.)

1 cup (8 ounces) cream-style cottage cheese	1 tablespoon minced onion
	2 teaspoons dill seed
1 tablespoon dry yeast	1 teaspoon salt
¼ cup very warm water	¼ teaspoon baking soda
¼ cup butter or shortening	1 well-beaten egg
2 tablespoons sugar	2¼ to 2½ cups all-purpose flour

some melted butter and extra dill seed

In a little saucepan, heat the cottage cheese to lukewarm; and in a big bowl, soften the yeast in the water.

Now add the shortening, sugar, onion, dill seed, salt, and baking soda to the lukewarm cheese in the little pan. Add all this to the yeast-water mix, and beat in the egg. Add the flour a bit at a time, stirring to make a soft dough. Knead it for five minutes. Put in a greased bowl, cover it, let it rise till doubled—about an hour and twenty minutes. Punch it down, rest it ten minutes, then shape into two loaves for loaf pans or one big round loaf for a casserole dish, being sure to butter those pans first. Cover and let rise again about forty minutes, then bake at 350° for forty minutes.

FEBRUARY 24   There's Nothing Hard about Homemade FRENCH BREAD except the Crust.

Now, then. It's a good feeling, better than money in the bank, to have eight baguette-size loaves of French bread on hand. Money doesn't keep so well now; it shrinks in the bank. But this bread keeps fine in the freezer for at least a year, though chances are small that it will be allowed to, because the reluctant cook will start depending on it for so many meals, especially dinner. The knowledge of its comfortable thereness makes the thought of dinnertime more bearable: you can dispense with potatoes or pasta and have something much better besides. It also solves the problem of the small hostess gift, if you're plagued with small hostesses. A foil-wrapped baguette indeed solves many perplexities.

But first it's best to get some pans to bake it in. While heavy aluminum foil can be shaped into long narrow troughs (like gutters on a house) to use as baguette pans, it doesn't work as well as the ones Clyde Brooks developed after he left Paris. An air-force man, Mr. Brooks went to Paris in the early fifties

". . . when all the fresh food passed through Les Halles and the street markets, and bread came from your neighborhood boulangerie. Everyone walked to his local bakery twice a day, and in the afternoon—if you were early—you waited till your baker opened after his long lunch break. The bread came in several diameters and lengths, and each was named, but the one enjoyed by most Parisians [and Mr. Brooks] is the baguette. . . ."

He became, in a word, converted; and so he learned all he could from his own little *boulangerie* in Paris. Finally, back in the United States, he devised and is now making his PARIS X Baguette Pans, which make eight loaves, for $9.90, shipping costs included. His address is 5000 Independence Avenue, S.E., Washington, D.C. 20003.

Along with the pans, he includes a set of crystal-clear instructions for the tyro, as foolproof as anything can be in this imperfect world. Boiled down, the recipe is this:

> 5 cups warm water
> 2 tablespoons dry yeast
> 4 tablespoons sugar
> 2 tablespoons salt

1. Stir till dissolved.
2. Add fourteen cups white flour.
3. Knead ten minutes.
4. Raise till doubled.
5. Punch down, knead three or four times to remove air. Divide into eight equal pieces.
6. Shape into loaves, place in well-greased pans, and *slash*.
7. Brush with egg whites.
8. Raise.
9. Bake fifteen minutes in preheated oven at 450°, thirty minutes at 350°.
10. Remove from pans and cool.
11. Wrap in foil and freeze.
12. To serve, warm in foil twenty minutes at 350°, open, and cool.

"P.S. Try these: Cut ½-inch slices of bread, pan-fry in butter, and serve under a small broiled steak. You will be hard put to tell which is better—the bread or the meat—but the combination is unbeatable. ALSO: Split a half loaf of bread the long way, spread with butter and broil in the oven for the best toast you ever ate. And for a super breakfast treat spread with cream cheese and fruit jam."

—Clyde Brooks

FEBRUARY 25   This is my birthday, and a funny thing about your birthday is, no matter where you are on it or what you're doing, you feel somehow impelled to tell someone. Not how many birthdays you've had, necessarily, just the fact that it's your birthday. A number of other people were born on this day, too. I want to send them my greetings and earnest hopes that they have found it all, so far, worth the trouble.

FEBRUARY 26   Buffalo Bill was born on this day in 1846. And Dr. William Kitchiner died on this day, 1827, after a hearty supper and a most pleasant evening.
Dr. Kitchiner of London was a jolly M.D. and writer of cook-

books, as well as other books, with titles like *The Art of Invigorating and Prolonging Life* (though he died, himself, at the age of fifty) and *The Pleasures of Making a Will.*

Dr. K. was a popular host. Every Tuesday evening he gave a *conversazione,* at which he brought together people he considered interesting, for good talk and supper. On his mantelpiece, he kept a placard inscribed COME AT SEVEN, GO AT ELEVEN. On one occasion, a brash young guest found a chance to insert the word "it" between "go" and "at," which was considered by the guests to be a real knee-slapper, though it leaveth the present scribe unmoved.

The good doctor's menus were simple: a cold roast, a lobster salad, and ales and wine ready on the sideboard. He probably had bread or muffins there too, and he would undoubtedly have appreciated the many merits of

6-WEEK MUFFINS
Makes about 7 dozen
1. v. wholesome 2. v. good 3. makes a lot 4. batter keeps in the fridge for six weeks 5. sweet enough to serve as dessert when there isn't any

2 cups boiling water	5 cups flour
5 teaspoons baking soda	1 tablespoon salt
1 cup shortening	4 cups All-Bran
2 cups sugar	2 cups 40% Bran Flakes
4 eggs	2 cups chopped dates
1 quart buttermilk	1 cup chopped walnuts

Add the soda to the boiling water and cool it. In another pan, cream the shortening and sugar, then add the unbeaten eggs one at a time. Stir in the buttermilk, flour, and salt. Add the water and soda. In a *big* bowl now, mix the All-Bran, Bran Flakes, dates, and nuts together, then add the first mixture. Store it covered in the refrigerator. When you want to bake some, don't stir it—just spoon it into well-greased muffin tins, about ⅔ full. Bake them at 375° for twenty minutes.

FEBRUARY 27 On this day, Stephanie ("Fats") Stumflug went to consult Dr. Neitzelgrinder about her overweight problem.

"I've been baking bread till I doubled in bulk," she reported, "and now I've sworn off for keeps."

Dr. Neitzelgrinder explained to her, tactfully, that it wasn't the bread's fault. She was also (he pointed out) the sort of person who couldn't eat one chocolate, but must finish the box at a sitting. One slice of bread has only sixty-three calories, he continued, and if it's good enough bread, it needs nothing on it at all.

> ". . . Indeed, bread can be an important element in common-sense weight reduction and control, as demonstrated at the University of Nebraska where a group of students lost an average of 19.2 pounds in 8 weeks on a calorie-controlled diet containing large amounts of bread."
>
> —Bernard Clayton, Jr. (*Ibid.*)

And then Dr. Neitzelgrinder gave her his recipe for the flat, crisp Armenian bread called *lahvash*. Kept frozen, then briefly toasted and spread minimally with butter, a book-size piece of it has the dieter feeling loved—feeling that all is not lost but considerable may be, yet, and possibly even in the right places.

Lahvash must be made (the doctor explained) on a leisurely day with a mind at ease, or what passes for it, these troubled times. A fire to read by, or someone to play Scrabble with, is helpful, though not essential. The doctor admits that one June morning he delivered triplets, did a vasectomy, and played nine holes of golf before he came back to rolling it out. Much can be done in three hours.

LAHVASH

1½ teaspoons dry yeast
½ teaspoon white sugar
2 tablespoons warm water
¼ cup butter
2½ cups all-purpose white flour
1 cup whole-wheat flour

3 tablespoons sesame seeds, untoasted
1 cup very warm water
1½ teaspoons salt
another teaspoon sugar

1. In a small bowl put the yeast, ½ teaspoon sugar, and the 2 tablespoons warm water. Don't stir it.
2. Put the butter in a little pan over low heat to melt. Look out the window or go water the cactus. Come back and stir the yeast mix.

3. In a big bowl put both flours and the sesame seeds. Stir it a bit, then shape it into a pyramid and poke a deep well down the center. Into this, pour the yeast mixture, the cup of very warm water, the melted butter, the salt, and the teaspoon of sugar.

> (The Armenian rug peddler who gave this recipe to Dr. N. didn't explain the reason for this well routine, and Dr. N. freely admits he can't see the point of it. The minute the water goes in, it looks like the day the dam busted. But be that as it may.)

4. Stir it with a big spoon till everything is well blended, and then knead it, in the bowl or on a flat, floured surface. If necessary—it probably won't be—add a little more flour. Five minutes' kneading is enough.

5. Shape it into a ball, put it in a greased bowl, turn it over once, cover it with waxed paper, and let it rise. Now both of you get a three-hour recess, ample time for a walk and a little TM or the matinee at the Bijou.

6. After three hours, punch the dough down and take it out of the bowl.

7. Divide it into fourteen equal chunks. On a floured surface, roll each one out to its absolute paper-thin limit—an area of about ten by six inches.

> Dr. N. says the shape doesn't matter. Circles are fine if circles come natural, but inasmuch as the pieces are customarily broken into chunks before serving, it's up to you. He says his rolled-out pieces generally resemble undiscovered continents, though once he got such a good map of South America he could pinpoint Buenos Aires.

8. Put these on a lightly greased cooky sheet—one cooky sheet will hold two pieces. Prick with a fork.

9. Bake at 450° about six minutes, till partly gold and crisp.

They keep well, covered, in a dry place, and a year or more if they're antimoisture-wrapped, in the freezer. At breakfast-time, thirty seconds in a hot toaster is all they'll need. (This is good with a piece of cheese in the afternoon as a dieter's snack, too.) It is exceptionally good with soups, salads, and stews, on almost any occasion except possibly just after you've had a couple of teeth pulled, in which case, Dr. Neitzelgrinder says, dunk it.

FEBRUARY 28   As the day lengthens so the cold strengthens.

FEBRUARY 29   There may be one of these and then again there may not; but it is a shortsighted Almanack indeed that doesn't allow for it.

On the last day of the month say Bunny Bunny. Next morning, first thing, say Rabbit Rabbit. This makes for extraordinarily good luck the whole day long, according to a third-grader who knows all about these things.

March

*doth find us in that turbulent Body of Water called
Financial Straits & eating our Boot Tops in a high
Winde as the Rain descendeth, indicating that mayhap the Rainbowe's Ende discloseth no Pot of Gold
but a Pot of Beans; featureth*

> *7-Happiness Beef and Rice
> home-roasted soybeans
> cookies for when they're kicking sand
>   in your face
> Fancy Fishwiches
> some truly remarkable doughnuts*

and divers other good cheap things

lean month
mean month
branch all bare,
rag month
hag month
curlers in her hair

MARCH 1   NOW IT IS MARCH-MANY-WEATHERS &
            Spring engageth olde Winter in mortal Combat &
winneth always, yet always it seemeth touch-and-go, sun & cloud,
wet & winde, save us, Father, we have Sinned. The baby Lamb
bleateth & with good Reason; the Skunk Cabbage flowereth, yet
this lifteth not up the Heart. And in the Citie nerves do jangle, &
everywhere do the reluctant Cook & the harried Houseperson feel
hard-pressed, nay, Penniless, for always the long long month out-
lasteth the Money.

And it was in March that the charter was granted for the first
Savings Bank, in the City of New York, in 1816, though it didn't
open for business until July, for it takes time to chain all those desk
pens down.

But it is a good thing that the Savings Bank was finally invented.
Back in the good old bad old days, people used to keep their savings under the mattress, and this was the first place burglars looked.
Or else they taped it to the bottom of a dresser drawer, which was
the second. Or they buried it in the yard, where the dog dug it out
and ate it. Or they hid it in the oven, where it got burned up.

Then, with the advent of the freezer, certain shrewd folk started
keeping their extra cash in a frozen-vegetable carton tucked between
the Frozen Baby Onions in Cream Sauce and the Chopped Spinach,
which proved safe enough. But still these frozen assets gathered
only frost crystals, whereas in the Savings Bank they grew at least a
little, enough to pay for the shoe leather it took to get them down
there. And every little bit helps in March, the cold month, the broke
month, the worried old windy month, with wind from all quarters.

61

ONE MAN'S BEANS
6 servings

(This is Dr. Neitzelgrinder's recipe, given to him by a grateful patient. Some doctors get boats and digital wristwatches from grateful patients, but Dr. N.'s are never quite that grateful. He doesn't complain, though, because they've never sued him either.)

First he assembles, with ceremony, the ingredients:

    1½ pounds ground beef
    1 package dehydrated onion-soup mix
    several cans of beans: red kidney beans or pinto
        beans and some canned navy beans in tomato
        sauce, to total about 6 cupfuls
    1½ cups water
    ½ cup chili sauce

In a skillet he browns the crumbled beef. Then, parking his pipe with considerable care in a Limoges saucer, he opens the onion-soup package and all those bean cans, stirs them into the meat, adds the water and chili sauce, and lets it simmer half an hour (and longer won't hurt). If he thinks to do it, and sometimes he doesn't, he pours it all into a casserole dish and grates some cheese on top to melt under the broiler. Then he settles down and eats quite a lot of it.

> "Shake a Leicestershire yeoman by the collar
> And you shall hear the beans rattle in his belly."

> "Shake a Leicestershire woman by the petticoat
> And the beans will rattle in her throat."
>   —Old sayings from Leicestershire,
>   a great place for beans

MARCH 2   St. Chad Died on This March Day, A.D. 672

     It was St. Chad who introduced Christianity to the east Saxons. When he wasn't preaching, it was his habit to stand naked, praying, in a spring of cold water, probably praying that he wouldn't catch cold. And as it turned out, he didn't, though he did die, eventually, of the plague.

PARSLEY is nearly as good as prayer for preventing colds, because it is so full of vitamins A and C. This would be a good day for a

SPRING TONIC SALAD

Wash and dry a big bunch of parsley. Remove the coarser stems and chop the parsley somewhat. To it, add any likely spring vegetables, chopped or sliced: green onions, cucumber, celery, a little tomato and some black olives, sliced. For a dressing, mix olive oil and lemon juice together, 2 to 1. Pour it over the greenery, mix it well, and stop sneezing. *Gesundheit.*

MARCH 3   On this day in 1605, Edmund Waller was born.
When he grew up, he wrote a lovely poem to a rose, requesting that it go tell his shy lady to quit keeping her charms to herself, and requesting further that the rose then die, to show his lady "how small a part of time they share/That are so wondrous sweet and fair." In that day, swains seemed to be no less dogged in pursuit, but they were more lyrical about it.

On this day also, in 1847, Alexander Graham Bell was born.
To commemorate his birthday, make a nice cheap little cake, good enough and quick enough to call up Mother about, although if you do, there go your savings unless she lives in the same town. Better think twice and write home about it.

LETTER CAKE

> a package of golden-yellow cake mix,
>   enough for a one-layer cake
> 2 egg whites
> 1 cup brown sugar
> as many chopped nuts as you can spare

Put the cake together according to its directions, and pour the batter into a greased and floured eight-inch square pan. Now beat the egg whites till stiff, and gradually add the sugar. Spoon it onto the batter, sprinkle the nut meats on top, and bake at 350° for forty minutes.

MARCH 4   Mothering Sunday
was celebrated every March about this time, a couple of centuries ago in England. (The conscientious Almanack-

person has trouble pinning celebration dates down with any exact-
ness from year to year because they tend to slide around. But this is
approximately it.)

On Mothering Sunday, the great-great-grandmother of Mother's
Day, it was customary to visit the female parent on the mid-Sunday
of Lent and take her a game or a trinket. Whoever did this was said
to "go a-mothering." And then Mother, not to be outdone, would
prepare a special dainty called *frumenty,* a dish of wheat grains
boiled in sweet milk, sugared, and spiced, probably the great-great-
grandmother of Rice Pudding.

It is too bad that any of this happened, but we can't fight history.

MARCH 5   On this day in 1976, Mumu Harbottle thought-
              fully examined her hoard of 5¢-Off-Regular-Price
coupons for things like the Large Family Size Plastic Pudding, and
her BIG INTRODUCTORY OFFER coupons for items she didn't really
want to be introduced to. After asking Dr. Neitzelgrinder if it
would be okay, she then made a nice fire of them and sprinkled the
ashes around her rosebushes.

". . . When my children ask for a new food product they see on
TV, I always buy it once. I say, 'Let's see if this really tastes like on
TV. Look in the mirror as you eat. Does your face look as smiling
and as happy when you eat as the little girl in the TV?' They say,
'No, mommy,' and that's the end of that."

—Sita Byrne

". . . and I got to wondering who they think they're kidding,
whoever writes those articles about cutting your food bills. Have a
Gourmet Binge on a Budget! Throw a Pork Liver Party! They never
face facts. To cut your food bills
       "1. Go on a diet.
       "2. Don't have company.
       "3. When you're real hungry go visit somebody.
       "4. Send the kids to the neighbors on weekends.
       "5. Serve what nobody likes; it'll go farther.
       "6. Put the dog on a diet."
                —Shirley Shimmelfenner,
                  How Gray Were My Dishtowels, vol. 4

MARCH 6   Everyone should be allowed three things he won't eat, according to Aunt Henry Macadangdang.

But she admits that if there are five in the family and everyone chooses three different things not to eat, you've got trouble. Prima donnas (she amended hastily) must go.

MARCH 7   Luther Burbank was born on this day in 1849.

He was first to introduce a California dewberry to a Siberian raspberry and come up with a Primus Berry. Not one to rest on his laurels, he went on to mate a California dewberry with a Cuthbert raspberry to get a Phenomenal Berry, and a Japanese plum with an apricot for a Plumcot.

It is too bad he didn't think of introducing the sugar cane to the rhubarb, for a self-sweetening Subarb, or of applying his talents to certain vegetables that can't go anywhere but up. A fruitabaga would be nice, and so would a turnipeach.

> ". . . Looking back, of course I made a few mistakes. Giraffes. It was a good thought, but it really didn't work out. Avocados—on that I made the pit too big. Then there are things that worked out pretty good. Photosynthesis is a big favorite of mine. Spring is nice. Tomatoes are cute. Also raccoons."
> —God, as quoted by Avery Corman

MARCH 8   Frugal Day

> ". . . If there are bits of butter left on the plates, free from specks, let them be put away carefully for greasing tins. As butter is used with the knife only, and the knife never touches the lips, this piece of economy will shock no one."
> —Elisabeth S. Miller

Stella Trowbridge Hinky's Miserable Mean-spirited Penny Pinchers Which Are Nevertheless Very Sensible:

For a week, live off your hump; off the food that's already in the house. This will probably produce some picturesque menus, but it will save some cash, polish off some impulse buys, use up some items before they go west, and show the family you mean business.

See that everyone substitutes a cheaper eating habit for a frill: protein-enriched toast (p. 40) for fancy cereals; instant coffee, black, for percolated with cream; water instead of soda in the highball. Or, instead of chips and salted nuts,

HOME-ROASTED SOYBEANS
(Which aren't as good as salted peanuts, but then, few things are. At least the soybeans have less fat and more status.)

> soybeans
> butter
> salt

Soak a cup of dry soybeans in four cups of water in the refrigerator overnight. Next day, strain them, dry between paper towels, spread out on a baking sheet, and roast at about 200° for two hours, mussing them around once in a while. Then turn on the broiler and stir them frequently till the soybeans are a pretty shade of brown. Shake them up in a paper sack with a touch of salt and a little butter.

Set aside a refrigerator shelf for leftovers and print LOOK BEFORE YOU COOK on the door and then do it.

When a recipe calls for anything perishable that comes only in some quantity, figure ahead how you'll use it all before you get it.

Stay out of stores as much as possible.

When the butcher marks down the meat because it turned maroon, buy it. It was the fluorescent lights that changed the color, but they didn't hurt the meat any.

With meat, think for two nights instead of one, and steal some from the first night's before cooking it—*i.e.*, get a slightly larger steak and cut off strips for tomorrow's Stroganoff.

Praise the Lord and pass the peanut butter. Two and one-quarter tablespoons of dry milk powder mixed with six tablespoons of peanut butter and spread on enriched bread is a powerhouse protein combination. Use it for stuffing celery stalks.

As insurance against future bored or weary times when you'll want to eat out or send out for something, cook and freeze ahead in periods of energy and virtue.

Buy things together with a neighbor—turkey, ham, canned goods by the case, or flour by the big sackful—if they're cheaper that way.

Powdered milk is cheaper than bottled; frozen orange juice is cheaper than fresh or bottled; canned peas are cheaper than fresh or frozen. Buy brands you never heard of, if they cost less.

When you open a can of pimentos, put them separately in small plastic bags to freeze, so you eventually use them all instead of watching the rest grow whiskers. Or tomato paste. When a recipe calls for only a tablespoon, cover the top of the can with foil and freeze it. Next time, thaw it enough to take out what you want, then freeze it again.

Try hard not to burn things up. If you often pan-fry in butter, clarify a pound of it so it won't scorch so fast, and keep it cold in a labeled jar. *To clarify butter:* Put it in a deep saucepan and melt it over low heat so the foam disappears and there is a light-brown sediment in the bottom. The butter part should be clear and golden. Pour it off into a jar with a bit of nylon stocking stretched over its mouth to strain it.

Remember that the oven and the stove burners cost the most to cook with. When you can, use the electric skillet, the slow cooker, the pressure cooker, the toaster-oven, or the microwave oven—whichever you have.

Remember that it costs more to make things hot than to make things whiz around: seven times more to dry a load of clothes than wash them, a lot more to heat an oven than run a mixer, a lot more to dry the dishes in a dishwasher than wash them in it. Turn the machine OFF before it hits DRY, and open the dishwasher door.

Set the thermostat at 60° when you plan to be away for more than a day.

MARCH 9   But You Can Be Frugal for Only So Long

And if they don't stop kicking sand in your face, all your aggressions will come to the fore. That is the time to make

AGGRESSION COOKIES

(A fine cheap crisp cooky that makes quantities. This came via the Community Mental Health Center at St. Lawrence Hospital in Lansing, Michigan. They printed and mailed it out in the hope of channeling some energies away from throwing bricks. The more you knead, mash, and squeeze, the better you feel and the better the cookies. Makes fifteen dozen.)

3 cups firmly packed brown sugar
3 cups butter (or half butter-flavored margarine)
6 cups oatmeal, uncooked
1 tablespoon baking soda
3 cups all-purpose flour

Put all this in a big bowl and knead, mash, squeeze. Then form the dough into small balls and put them on ungreased baking sheets. Butter the bottom of a small glass, dip it in granulated sugar, then mash the balls flat. Bake at 350° for ten to twelve minutes. Let them cool a few minutes, then remove them with a spatula onto paper towels or brown grocery sacks. Put them in cans with good tight lids when the cookies are thoroughly cooled and crisp.

MARCH 10   March Hare Day

No one is quite sure what March hares are mad about, unless it is because we eat them and simultaneously make a big fuss over the twinkle-nosed Easter bunny, which does seem a little hypocritical.

The man who butchers the rabbits at the supermarket says he can taste the difference between a rabbit killed this morning and one killed this afternoon, but then he is a hare-splitter. Still, some people are supersensitive about chickens too, and they want a chicken that squawked its last squawk approximately six minutes before they buy it. This is getting harder to achieve. But sometimes these people bribe the butcher with a jug of his favorite tipple to tell them the Chicken Code. (In big markets, where packaged chicken is often coded as to which day of the week it came in, the butcher— the little dickens—is likely to spread out the stale chicken on top.)

MARCH 11   On this day in 1847, Johnny Appleseed died, after roaming for years about the Ohio River Valley, planting apple trees.

> A toast to Johnny now, a very
> Special kind of missionary
> Who roamed the hills and vernal glade
> By early Spring enchanted,
> Who did his praying with a spade
> And never preached, but planted.

And on the very next day, MARCH 12, in 1912, the U.S. Girl Scouts were founded, and the Girl Scout Cooky was invented the very same afternoon. In honor of them both, make

APPLE BROWNIES

First, cream together

    a stick of butter
    1 cup sugar

Add

    1 beaten egg
    2 medium-sized chopped
      apples
    ½ cup chopped nuts

Sift together and add

    1 cup flour
    ½ teaspoon each soda
      baking powder
      cinnamon

Pour it into a greased brownie-sized pan—eight by eight inches or seven by eleven inches—and bake at 350° about forty minutes. Cool it in the pan and cut in squares.

MARCH 13   A day of delicate sunshine and breeze nearly lyrical. Undoubtedly the weather is practicing up for an early springtime.

A Day for Flower Salad: Make it of nasturtium leaves, including some blossoms, plus the leaves of wild violets, "sweeter than the lids of Juno's eyes," as well as rich in vitamins A and C, a fact that Shakespeare probably didn't know or he would have mentioned it. Wild violets are usually found on sunny banks half-protected by hedges, or in woodsy vacant lots if you get there before the bulldozer does.

MARCH 14   On this day in 1879, Albert Einstein was born.

Many people are unaware that if he hadn't discovered the theory of photoelectric effect in 1905, we probably wouldn't have television yet. And if we didn't, the houseperson wouldn't be able to watch—among many other things—those exquisite feminine fingers whisk the charred sludge out of a skillet with touch of Magic *Voilà!*, which gives her hands a beauty treatment.

> Harken, friend and gentle neighbor,
> To a truth I know for sure:
> Manual—er—personual labor
> Never helped a personicure.

Baking soda is cheaper than *Voilà!* and two tablespoons of it in a cup of water, boiled for ten minutes or so in the burned skillet, will make the stuff easier to remove.

MARCH 15   Died, on this day in 1655, Theodore Turquet de Mayerne, a famous physician, doctor, and cook. In his cookbook, *Archimagirus Anglo-Gallicus,* a catchy title for those days, the chef-d'oeuvre is "A City of London Pie," which called for—among other things—eighteen sparrows, a peck of oysters, forty chestnuts, a pound of dates. . . . And this wasn't a particularly expensive recipe then, because both oysters and chestnuts were plentiful, and sparrows were free.

Times change. Today, ground beef is the stand-by, and the next three ground beef dishes will feed six or eight, cheaply.

7-HAPPINESS BEEF AND RICE

1. It is meat and starch combined.
2. Neither has to be cooked first.
3. Everything goes together at once.
4. Very young people and very old people like it, and the others don't mind it much.
5. The amount of meat depends on what's there.
6. Odds-and-ends of vegetables can go into it.
7. Though it looks like dog food when it goes into the oven, it doesn't when it comes out.

¼ cup salad oil
1 cup uncooked rice
½ to 1½ pounds ground beef
small bottle of stuffed olives, sliced

1 teaspoon salt, pepper, paprika
1 medium onion, chopped
2 cups V-8 or tomato juice
2 cups boiling water
grated cheese to spread on top

Crumble the raw beef in a big bowl. Add everything but the cheese and mix it up. Pour it into a nine-by-thirteen-inch baking pan and bake for an hour at 350°. Then reduce the heat and bake an hour longer. Half an hour before serving time, sprinkle the grated cheese on, and finish baking.

4-HAPPINESS SPAGHETTI

1. People with hearty, uncritical appetites like it and eat it—little kids, football players, and guests who had a third Martini.
2. It is quickly put together ahead of time.
3. It doesn't cost much.
4. It will sit in a 200° oven for an hour or longer without being noticeably affected.

2 pounds ground beef crumbled and browned in a little oil
2 large onions, chopped and sautéed till transparent
2 cans Franco-American or similar spaghetti
1 or 2 cans drained mushrooms, the more the merrier
8½-ounce can of petite peas, the petiter the better
½ pound sharp cheese
1 cup tomato juice (or enough that it comes about halfway up through the food)

Layer these things in this order: beef, onion, spaghetti, mushrooms, peas. Sprinkle it well with garlic salt and pepper, plus several squirts of Worcestershire sauce. Put the cheese on top and pour on the tomato juice. Freeze it if you like, or keep it in the refrigerator as long as thirty-six hours. (Either way, warm it to room temperature before you cook it.) Or bake it immediately, covered, in a 325° oven, at least an hour.

ITALIAN CHOP SUEY
(*or Chinese Macaroni*)

1½ pounds ground beef, lean 1 6-ounce tomato paste
2 medium onions ¼ cup soy sauce
2 green peppers 1 pound small shell macaroni
5 stalks of celery

Pan-fry the ground beef in a little oil till it loses its pinkness. Then add the sliced vegetables and let them simmer thoughtfully for ten minutes. Then add the tomato paste plus two or three cans of water (some like it wetter, some like it dryer) and the soy sauce. Simmer it, covered, forty-five minutes. Finally, cook the shell macaroni the way it says to on the package, drain it, add it, and serve.

MARCH 16 On this day last week, Mumu Harbottle started rubbing expensive French Turtle Butter into her face because her skin was rough enough to sand floors with. Now she says it would only sand smaller objects like footstools and bird-. houses.

". . . It makes little sense to skimp on groceries, only to spend the savings on cosmetics, when such splendid beauty aids are already in the pantry or the refrigerator. *Mayonnaise* is literally a cold cream that cleanses and protects—a real boon to sensitive skins. *Corn meal* sprinkled on a soapy cloth cleanses deep-down. *Egg white,* lightly beaten and allowed to dry on the face, is a mask that tones, stimulates, beautifies. . . ."
    —Stella Trowbridge Hinky (*Ibid.*)

A Powder to Make the Teeth Sweet!
  "Take the powder of Sage the Shavings of ivory put them amongft ye juice of lemons & every evening and morning rub your teeth therewith & it will make them both white & fweet."   —*Toilet of Flora*
        (15th century)

MARCH 17 Now the Length of the Day Exactly Equals the Length of the Night.
And St. Patrick was born on this day, A.D. 464.

"GOD KEEP US AND SAVE US!"
CRIED OLD MRS. DAVIS

"God love and presarve us!"
Cried old Mrs. Jarvis

"You're making me nervous,"
Said young Mrs. Purvis

Not everyone knows that St. Patrick rid the Emerald Isle of Druids as well as snakes, but nevertheless it is the absolute Irish truth. Pursuing the accepted modern policy of curing a country if it kills it, he cursed the fertile Irish lands so they became dreary bogs, cursed the rivers so they produced no fish, and cursed their very kettles so that no amount of fire and patience could make them boil. Finally—why didn't he think of it in the first place?—he cursed the Druids themselves, so that the earth opened up and swallowed them.

Indeed, St. Patrick had quite a way of doing bad while he was doing good, though presumably he didn't mean to. Once when the venerable saint had finally converted a stubborn Irish chief, he baptized him while leaning heavily on his crozier, unaware that the point of it was resting on the chief's big toe. It must have hurt like billy-be-damned, for the blood gushed forth. But the poor chief thought this was part of the act and never even said Ow. The place where this happened is called Struthfhuil (pronounced *Struill*).

GREEN PANCAKES
(pronounced *Frittaten*)

4 cups grated raw zucchini
1 cup flour
2 teaspoons baking powder

2 eggs, well beaten
salt and pepper
½ teaspoon thyme
butter for frying

Put the grated zucchini in a bowl. Sift the flour and baking powder together and beat the mixture into the vegetable. Then beat in the eggs, salt, pepper, and thyme. Blend it till it's a thick pancake batter, then drop by the spoonful into a skillet containing some good hot butter. What you're aiming for is pancakes about three inches wide. The British find them good accompaniment for the Sunday joint.*

* English families like to go out for Sunday-night supper, to some one special pub, which is called "the Sunday joint." —Ed.

73

MARCH 18   This was the day Noah and his wife entered the Ark. Legend has taken more liberties with Noah's wife than Noah probably ever did, because no one would dare take any with an old battle-ax like that. She not only sneered at Noah for being so gullible as to build the Ark in the first place, she refused to enter it when it was built. Then, when it really started to rain hard, she jumped into it and then jumped on *him,* beating him with her fists.

But we must look at her side of it. Perhaps Noah's track record wasn't so good. Perhaps he had tried and failed at many a darn-fool thing, and to Noah's wife this may have looked like just one more. Then too, as she watched all those animals filing in, she probably saw clearly who would get to play janitor, and it wasn't Noah; he'd be at the helm.

Worst of all must have been her swift realization after it started to rain that he was right, after all. She would never hear the end of his I-told-you-so's if she lived to be a thousand. It's no wonder she beat him up.

MARCH 19   This is the day when the swallows fly back to Capistrano, and if they don't always hit the date precisely, they come twittering in on some other day, sometimes after a journey of ten thousand miles, to the considerable relief of the Capistrano Chamber of Commerce.

This particular Capistrano swallow is the cliff swallow, *Petrochelidon pyrrohonta,* with a square tail and a light-brown patch on his rump. (A bird's tail is not synonymous with his rump; see any Bird Book.) The reason they fly back to Capistrano is that ten thousand miles is too far to walk. Swallows are noted for their strong wings and weak feet.

MARCH 20   Heigh-ho Spring-time,
✤ 〜   Pretty pretty ring-time!
                     Sun-time! Dance-time!
                     Aphids in the plants time!

". . . Chives will keep aphids away from roses; most of the aromatic herbs—such as borage, lavender, sage,

74

parsley, or dill—will repel great numbers of garden pests, while marigolds seem to protect almost any garden from almost anything!"

—*The Mother Earth News Almanac*

". . . Garden chores for March are numerous and unpleasant but, as Dostoevsky pointed out, happines is earned through suffering. . . ."

—Grace Firth

MARCH 21   Now beginneth the sign of ARIES (controlling ⚑ 🐏   the Head) that lasteth through April 19, all days mightily auspicious for

planting early peas
playing poker for large stakes
killing weeds in the gravel
conceiving children

and the enterprising energetic Arien doth hop to it with a right good will.

". . . When one's work gloves are temporarily mislaid, soapy lather is a fair substitute. Before gardening or garage work, I often soap my hands, working the lather well into and around the nails, then letting it dry. Grease and dirt will wash off easily then. I have always been rather proud of my hands. . . ."

—Albert Wooky (*Ibid.*)

MARCH 22   On this day in 1976 in Duluth, Minnesota, Dorothea Hoenig for the twenty-eighth time cremated a final cooky-sheetful of Nut Nuggets because she forgot to slip the timer into her pocket when she went into the other room to answer the phone. She estimated that it was a 42-cent mistake, not including the cost of the electricity.

MS. AESOP'S FABLES (No. 3)

A Stick and a Stone were of some small service to a Hindu holy man, and in gratitude he said he would transform them into any other Object they desired to be. The solid Stone said he would like

75

to become a Strongbox, to protect the holy man's Sacred Relics, but the vain Stick said it wanted to become a beautiful Hindu Robe.

Thus it came to pass: the Stone became a Strongbox and the Stick became a Robe. But on that night, a terrible fire ravaged the village, burning down the holy man's hut, burning up the Robe, but leaving the Strongbox untouched.

Moral: Better be Safe than Sari.

MARCH 23   On this day in 1769, William Smith was born. He is known as the Father of English Geology. And on this day in 1975, Mumu Harbottle visited her local Board of Environmental Control to try to get some things clear in her head.

"What can I do for you, Mrs. Harbottle?" said Firman Fuller, the head of the board.

"Well, I saw the cutest idea in a magazine," Mumu said.

"Yes?" said Mr. Fuller.

"About table settings," Mumu elaborated.

"Yes?" said Mr. Fuller, looking polite but restive.

"Well, and I wanted sort of an Environmental Impact Statement on it," said Mumu. "This article said to use little terry-cloth guest towels in napkin rings, instead of paper napkins. To save paper and, you know, like trees?"

"A sound idea," said Mr. Fuller. "And?"

"So I thought, fine," said Mumu. "And I bought some napkin rings, and then I got my little guest towels out of the drawer—you know how guests always sneak a corner of a big bath towel anyway; they don't want to mess up one of those little things—"

"Yes," said Mr. Fuller. "And?"

"And so I put them on the table, and that night my husband said, What's this? And I said it was his napkin. And he said, Are we having spareribs? And I said, No, it's your napkin, and you'll get a clean one next week."

Mr. Fuller nodded approvingly.

"So then the next night," Mumu continued, "Jimbo—my husband—said he'd rather have a clean paper napkin. And I said, But look at the trees we're saving!"

"That's right!" said Mr. Fuller. "It takes seventeen trees to make a ton of paper."

"Yes," Mumu said. "But Jimbo is an accountant, and he figured it out—so much detergent per wash-load, so much water, so much spray-and-wash for the bad stains, out of one of those aerosol cans. And then so much energy per dryer-load because I can't dry outside, it's so wet now. And actually the paper napkins are biodegradable, and . . ." She trailed off, unhappily.

"Well . . ." Mr. Fuller said judiciously, placing his fingertips neatly together, tent-fashion. "Your husband has an interesting point there, a ve-e-ry interesting point."

Fortunately his secretary came in then to tell him he had a long-distance call, and, taking the telephone, he waved Mumu away. She backed out, mouthing her earnest thanks.

> ". . . It's no wonder we spend so much of our daily
> life saving one another's faces. It's the least we can do."
> —Peter de Vries

MARCH 24   Conger T. Hatt Day
". . . We are bemused and befogged with trivia, so that we don't see the big issue. If most Americans—that is, the affluent among them—would say, once and for all, 'Okay: we'll settle for one car, one house, one bicycle, and we'll share appliances and quit keeping an eye on the Joneses . . .' maybe the Joneses would wither from insufficient attention. Then *all* Americans and a greater part of the world could live quite comfortably with less work, while honestly pursuing those goals to which, so far, they have given only lip-service."   —Conger T. Hatt

> "Who's first?"
> —Shirley Shimmelfenner,
> *Crack-Up!*, vol. 13

MARCH 25   Frogs haven't appeared yet in most places, which is just as well for them.

". . . As part of his fishing gear, my grandfather carried an empty beer bucket (a half-gallon container with a tight lid) in which he laid the cleaned frogs' legs for Grandma to fry like chicken when we got home.

"He liked to clean his meat or fish on the creek bank, because throwing the offal back into the water helped to sustain the balance of wildlife. 'I trade with the creek,' he declared. 'Other creatures' food for frogs' legs.' He believed that the earth was a gigantic balance, that when you used one resource you were obligated to trade back to the earth in another way. . . . 'You got to have something to trade, either with the earth or with other people,' he told me over and over."

—Grace Firth (*Ibid.*)

MARCH 26   On this very day a few decades ago, Adhesive Plaster was patented by Dr. Day and Dr. Shecut.

"Hooray for us!" cried Dr. S.
"Now bandages will stick!
For hospitals and such, I guess
The stuff will do the trick!"

"You're right, it's swell!" said Dr. D.,
"For First Aid—sea or land aid—
But dammit, think how rich we'd be
If it had been The Band-Aid!"

MARCH 27   And Now a Fine Cheap Way to Fill Up Chinks!
One-Hoss, who never feels too hard up if there's something around that he likes to munch on, occasionally makes himself a fast batch of

GOOD PHONY DOUGHNUTS

He buys a loaf of soft, spongy white store-bread, cuts the crusts off eight slices, and cuts them in quarters. Then, whistling gently through his teeth, he mixes up

1½ cups biscuit mix	1 beaten egg
1 tablespoon sugar	¾ cup milk
1 teaspoon baking powder	¼ teaspoon nutmeg

and some grated lemon peel if he can find the lemon. He also heats some oil in a saucepan—a few inches of it—till it's hot enough to brown a small cube of bread in about fifty seconds (or about 370° on a deep-fat thermometer, which he doesn't have). With a two-tined fork, he dips the bread quarters into the batter, drops them into the fat, and cooks them. Then he lets them drain on an old grocery sack before he rolls them in granulated sugar.

Somebody told him that if he'd make jam sandwiches* to quarter and dip the same way, he'd have some Jam Doughnuts. It sounded logical, and he's thinking seriously about it for next time.

Dear Aloise,
These experts that tell you to go buy some cheesecloth to strain your hot fat through make me laugh! Don't they know you can use old nylons? Or paper towels?
L. C.

Dear L.C.,
You're tops! I tried it and it works! What would we do without folks like you? I love you!
Aloise

MARCH 28   And Now a Good Reasonably Cheap Way to Fill Guests, if they can't be headed off

FANCY FISHWICHES

Thaw four frozen fillets of sole and cut each one in half. Spread four of the halves with this filling:

4 tablespoons mushrooms sautéed briefly in butter
2 tablespoons chopped onion
a little salt, pepper, tarragon

Top each one with the remaining fish halves and put the resultant Fishwiches in a buttered baking dish. Salt and pepper them lightly, and brush them with melted butter OR heavy cream. Finally, sprinkle them with fine cracker crumbs and bake at 500° about ten minutes —no need to turn them over. Garnish with plenty of parsley and quartered lemons.

MARCH 29   Vera Cruz Surrendered on This Day in 1847.
She was a pretty little thing, born of Mexican parents, and you know how strict they can be. But Pedro had been after her hammer and tongs for more than a year, and a girl's only

* Jam is better for this than jelly, which tends to run too much.

79

human, after all. However, he married her and everything worked out fine.

Vera turned out to be a good cook, of the economical sort, and Pedro really went for

VERA'S CLAM FRITTERS

She'd open two cans of minced clams and drain them.
Then she'd combine them with

> 2 well-beaten egg yolks
> 1 cup fine-toasted bread crumbs
> ½ teaspoon chopped chives and parsley
> 1 teaspoon salt
> ⅓ cup milk (approximately; she didn't want it too thin)

Then she'd whip the two egg whites till she was stiff and so were they, and she'd gently fold them into the first mix. Then she'd drop the batter by the tablespoon into clarified butter in the skillet, and presently they would turn into the prettiest little golden-brown clam fritters you ever saw.

MARCH 30   The Eiffel Tower Was Opened on This Day in 1889.

The French way of preserving eggs is to dissolve beeswax, mix a little olive oil with it, and use it to paint the eggs all over. If they are kept cool and unjostled, they will stay good for two years, which is probably true of most of us. Then the price of eggs will probably be cheaper than it was when you put them away, because that is how things usually work out. Still it is a good thing to know.

MARCH 31   is one of the Borrowed Days, borrowed by March from April. It is unlucky. John Donne died on this day in 1631. Beethoven died on this day in 1827. It is best to do nothing at all on this day besides wait for April.

April

bringeth Floods, Muds & Buds, with Puns & Riddles & suchlike Drolleries, yet introduceth the Houseperson's best Friend, plus eggstraordinary Receipts including

> a Shakel Egg Supper
> a Wagon-Wheel Cooky
> a Rootin-Tootin Sundae
> a Dazzleberry Pie

. . . and Easy Easter Buns, courtesy the Yeaster Bunny!

How to Remember Something:
If you will wear your left shoe
on your right foot and your right
shoe on your left foot, it will
remind you to switch them back
again pretty soon so they won't
feel so funny.

APRIL 1   NOW IT IS MERRIE APRIL that was named for
            Aphrilis, well rooted in the Greek name for Venus,
though Lovers in the Parke love it not as the vertical Dewe descendeth; and mayhap it was named for the Latin *aperio*, "I open,"
for so do the Heavens & the smalle winking Flowers & the Wallet
as the Tax Man cometh. Now the Bee goeth abroad for Honey
while the Physitian doth minister to a poor sniffling World, two
Aspiryns & bed-reste. Yet Hope punctually appeareth, in the shape
of an Egge; and appeareth too the merrie April Fool, who seeketh
the left-handed Monkey-wrench and dutifully returneth the telephone call to a certain Mr. Lion at the Zoo.

    Q. And why doth little Egbert cry so hard on Easter
       morning?

    A. He hates to see the Easter Egg dye.

    Q. And why is little Egglantine telephoning the
       Chinese restaurant?

    A. She wants to know what time the Egg Rolls.

On this day in 1974, U.S. Mailmen were first allowed to wear
shorts, and a good thing, too. It must have been awfully scratchy
without them, under those hot wool pants.

Now look to thy summer crop of scarecrows and plant thy scaraway
seeds!

Bet you didn't expert to meet a turkey on April 1!
But it is now ninety-nine days since you looked the Christmas turkey
in the cavity, and a good day to roast

THE BIRD UNSTUFFED

Get a big one. If it is frozen, thaw it in the refrigerator two or three
days for a twelve-to-twenty pounder. Or leave it in a pan at room

temperature for about half that long. Smear it lightly with mayonnaise, all over. Put it in a roasting pan. Tie the drumsticks together, and tie a string around the bird if you want to, to keep the wings flat. If you don't want to, the turkey will look unusually relaxed when it is done, but it will taste all right.

Now, then: turn him on his side for half the cooking time, and on the other side for the rest of it. When he is done, turn off the oven and turn him breast down for twenty minutes.

". . . Almost all cookbooks tell you to roast chickens, turkeys, pheasants and other birds breast up. This is quite wrong, for the following reasons. The breast and wings of a bird cook quicker than its other parts, and furthermore, the upper part of the oven is the hottest. Ergo, when a chicken is cooked breast up, the breast cooks more quickly and will be overcooked when the legs and other parts are done. And the juices produced by cooking will drain from the breast into the back, which is not eaten."

—Nika Hazelton

Before you start him to roasting, bend a piece of aluminum foil loosely over him. (Take it off half an hour before the turkey is done so the bird will brown.) And figure the cooking time twenty minutes per pound at 325° for sixteen pounds or less, and fifteen minutes per pound for a larger bird.

That's about it. Now you have pounds of turkey meat, to serve plain as long as they'll let you. ("Think of all the people in this world who'd just love to eat turkey every day!")

When this no longer works, freeze the rest, sliced, in bundles about the size of a box of kitchen matches. Re-present it pretty soon as turkey sandwiches, club sandwiches, or turkey salad: chopped turkey, celery, onion, lemon juice, and mayonnaise. You could add a touch of curry if you like. Or seedless white grapes. Or chopped nuts.

APRIL 2   "So we went to this fancy turkey dinner but the bird had been arrested!"
"How come?"
"He was a Peeping Tom!"

APRIL 3   Learn to Observe & Predict!

Spiders make larger webs as rain approaches.
Swallows fly low when rain is coming.
Insects bite harder when rain is near.
People scratch harder when insects are near.

APRIL 4   The Happy Book Cook!
Now take the wet, soggy book you left on the lawn swing, pop it into a microwave oven, and Presto—it's as dry as your old *Elementary Principles of Economics,* according to James M. Flink, assistant professor of food-processing at MIT, and no harm done.

The way to tear a telephone book in two and amaze your friends is to bake it first in a 350° oven for three hours.

APRIL 5   Some Almighty Olde-Tyme Jests!

A traveler, stopping for dinner at a roadside inn, found on the table nothing but a mackerel and a pot of mustard. When he inquired if that's all there was, the landlord said, "Why, there's enough mackerel there for six."
"But I don't like mackerel," the traveler said. And the landlord said, "Then help yourself to the mustard."

Mark Twain reports this one in *Overland Stagecoaching.* It was old in his great-granddaddy's day and in his great-granddaddy's day before that.
However, for the real vintage yuk, the fifteenth-century gut-buster, we look to a gentleman named Wynken de Worde, who shows us what they were laughing at in 1511, in his riddle book entitled *Demands Joyous:*

Demand   How many calves' tails would it take to reach from the earth to the sky?

Response No more than one, if it be long enough.

Dem.   What is the distance from the surface of the sea to the deepest part thereof?

Res.   Only a stone's throw.

Dem.   What is it that never was and never will be?

Res.   A mouse's nest in a cat's ear.

Dem.   Why doth a cow lie down?

Res.   Because it cannot sit.

Dem.   Who killed the fourth part of all the people in the world?

Res.   Cain when he killed Abel.

APRIL 6   Two Siamese kittens joined by a single caudal appendage were born on this day, 1944, to Mrs. Tabitha Katt (of the Cheshire Katts). See *Annals of Obstetrics & Gynecology, Felis domestica,* vol. 2, p. 366, "A Tail of Two Kitties."

APRIL 7   Hodag Day
        The hodag (*biggus mammalis hodaggus,* habitat North America) is a large, rough-skinned, bucktoothed, short-legged, and spiny-backed animal who mainly sits around and weeps copiously because he is so ugly.
Take a hodag to lunch today. They don't eat a great deal because of snuffling so much, and they're pretty nice once you get to know them. Presently you will find that some of your best friends are hodags.

APRIL 8   National Laugh Week ended today, and not a moment too soon.
"Its purpose: to promote a national sense of humor and a national sense of happiness."

—Chases' Calendar

"I'm glad my legs are broken—glad, glad, GLAD!"
—Pollyanna

"And so we went to this fancy Chinese dinner but the main course was in jail!"
"How come?"
"It was a Peking Duck!"

APRIL 9   And now in the village of East Whapping is held the merrie Dazzleberry Festival as men compete to grow the greatest Dazzleberry and little children do eat a bellyful and ladies do make

DAZZLEBERRY PIE

(If the dazzleberries aren't ripe yet, use canned cherry pie filling. Actually, canned cherry pie filling is much better in this particular pie, which is more of a cake or pudding anyway, and very good.)

Into a nine-inch pie pan pour a can of cherry pie filling (or apple or any other kind if the birds got all the canned cherries too). Sprinkle a one-layer box of golden-yellow cake mix over it, fairly evenly. Sprinkle a cup of coarsely chopped nutmeats over that. Now dot the whole thing with plenty of butter—a good third of a cupful—and bake it at 350° for forty-five minutes.

APRIL 10   On this important day in the annals of personkind and babykind did a certain Walter Hunt patent the safety pin in 1849.

> How promptly we commemorate
> With reverence each bloody date:
> Battles, wars and Lizzie Borden,
> Slaughter by the River Jordan!
> While the gun still belches hot
>   And ere the sound of carnage ceases,
> We raise the stone to honor not
>   The Man of Peace but man in pieces.
> So let us praise abundantly
>   A friend for every time and weather
> Whose gentle ingenuity
>   Has kept us—so far—pinned together.

APRIL 11   ". . . The uncertain glory of an April day."
                 —William Shakespeare

". . . Holsom as the Aprile showr fallyng on the herbes newe."
                 —John Lydgate

Why is it that *Bartlett* bulges with quotations by men? Why is it that they outnumber ten to one the quotations by women, when women (as men are the first to point out) do all the talking?

It is because whenever a man said anything, there was usually an admiring little woman around to exclaim, "I say! That's jolly good! *Awfully* good! I'll write it down!"

But now that men and women are done role-playing, the action changes.

SCENE:

A stormy night in Philadelphia. Benjamin and Ms. Franklin are at home, warming their toes at the Franklin stove, and reading. Ben sighs, then looks up from his copy of *The Saturday Evening Post*.

BEN: I don't like the way things are going, Deb. Not a bit.

MS. F: What things?

BEN: The country. I mean the colonies. I see but little evidence of that essential underlying unanimity of purpose that alone can make of all these disparate fibers a strong rope.

MS. F   (*absently, still reading*): Hmmmmmm . . .

BEN: I feel it strongly. We must indeed all hang together, or most assuredly we shall all hang separately.

MS. F   (*still reading*): Hmmmmm.

BEN: Say, Debby, that wasn't bad.

MS. F   (*looking up*): What wasn't?

BEN: What I just said. Or didn't you hear me? "We must indeed all hang together, or most assuredly we shall all hang separately." Might be good for the Almanac.

MS. F: I don't know, Ben. . . . I guess it's all right. (*Back to her book.*)

BEN: What do you mean, "all right"? It's damn good. Or maybe you don't get it. First I use "hang" in the sense of "stick"— *stick* together. Then I—

MS. F   (*impatiently*): Oh, I get it, all right. It's just—well, it strikes me as wordy. Long-winded. Needs sharpening. Actually, Ben—and I've been meaning to mention this—you've

88

been getting away with some pretty sloppy stuff lately. Last issue, wasn't it, you had something about "a penny saved is a penny got." Now *honestly!* What are you trying to say? If you save a penny, you'll have a penny? So what? And that one about patience—how did it go—"He that can have patience can have what he will." That's not a bit catchy, Ben, and, furthermore, it's a crock, and you know it. Sit in the same old office for fifty years and what do you get? Retired with a gold watch and a cheap dinner. Patience, my foot. What about the Pilgrims? Where'd we be if *they'd* been all that patient?

BEN: God defend me from a literal-minded woman.

MS. F: Yes, and another thing. You'd better knock off the sex stuff if you don't want to go down in history as the original male chauvinist pig.

BEN (*reddening a little*): You mean . . . uh . . .

MS. F: I mean advising that young man to take an old mistress "because they're so grateful." . . . Well, I have to admit it, a mature woman does find a young man a delightful change from wattles and potbellies and skinny shanks and toot-toot-puff-puff, the little old engine that couldn't. . . . Say, that's sort of cute, don't you think? Maybe I can use it somewhere. Will you pass me the quill pen, dear?

"Are women books? says Hodge, then would mine were
An Almanack, to change her every year."
—Poor Richard

"But not vice versa, dear," quoth Deb to Ben.
"At least, I know there *is* no changing men."
—Poor Peggie

APRIL 12   Shad running.

APRIL 13   Geese flying; things are picking up.

APRIL 14   Item from the Mervyn Meadows *Evening Clarion*
            Society Section, this day in 1976:

"At a pre-income-tax-day luncheon for the girls ('Come and eat cheap,' said the invitations, scrawled on brown paper!), Mrs. Charles ("Edie") Grumwalt got absolute raves on her delectable Tuna French Loaves, served with plenty of white *vin du pays,* which (she explained) was Safeway's cheapest. . . ."

TUNA LOAFWICH GRUMWALT
for 6

large loaf of French bread
butter
⅓ to ½ pound Swiss cheese
2 7-ounce cans flaked tuna
¼ cup sour cream

½ cup mayonnaise
¼ cup chopped parsley
½ teaspoon garlic salt
1 tablespoon lemon juice

Cut the bread in half lengthwise, butter both halves, and pave each half with thin slices of Swiss cheese. Then put them on a baking pan, mix up everything else and spread it on, with more cheese on top if some is left. Bake at 350° for about twenty-five minutes and cut in chunks.

APRIL 15   ". . . They did things better in old Egypt. Tax-
            delinquent citizens took a beating, and the longer they stood it, the less they had to pay. But we just take one while paying and we've stood it for years. . . ."

—Albert Wooky (*Ibid.*)

To sweeten the day, practice up on some

EASY EASTER-MORNING SWEET BUNS

Get an eight-ounce package of refrigerator Parkerhouse Rolls. Find enough muffin-tin pans to make twelve buns. Then, in a saucepan, mix

3 generous tablespoons brown sugar
⅓ cup light corn syrup
2 tablespoons butter
a dash of salt

Cook it over low heat and let it bubble placidly for a minute. Then add

 ½ cup coarsely chopped nuts

Cool it a little while. Then put a good spoonful into each muffin cup, put a roll in, and bake for fifteen minutes at 400°. Let them cool. Then turn them out onto a wire rack so they won't get soggy.

APRIL 16   How doth the hard-cooked Easter Egg
                   Improve the April scenery,
           A-gleam behind the table leg,
               A-twinkle 'midst the greenery,
       'Midst tender pansy-plant and pink,
          And gentle pussy-willow,
       But oh, that little chocolate fink
          Behind the sofa pillow!

". . . melted chocolate Easter Eggs (sludgies) are a real pain. You have to act fast. First, find out what jackass left one there and belt him one. Then scrape off the chocolate. Then read the label on the spray spot remover. If it claims to remove chocolate, give it a whirl. If it doesn't, and you've got a washable sofa, sponge it with cold water. Several times. Add some detergent the fourth time. If it's still a mess, and this is the day after the thing was dry-cleaned, as it usually is, put the pillow back where it was and wait till you have the job done again. People have no business prying behind the pillows on other people's sofas."
          —Shirley Shimmelfenner,
          Everything You Never Wanted to
          Know About Housekeeping, vol. 2

EGG-PLANT

Plant a hard-boiled egg in a claybank for a couple of months. Then dig it up and quarter it and eat it. This is how the modern Chinese achieve their allegedly 100-year-old eggs. Yours will be just as good as theirs and they couldn't possibly be any worse.

APRIL 17   Hard-cooked eggery:

1. Wash not thine egg before cooking-time.

2. Let not the water boil for it will toughen the egg therein.

3. A pinprick through the rounded end preventeth cracking.

4. The hard-to-peel egg spoileth the morning. But the egg started in cold water that simmered ten minutes and was peeled hot brighteneth the day.

5. A handy crayon to mark the Hard-cooked from the Raw preventeth profanity. Mark them T for 'Tis cooked, and T for 'Tain't cooked.

6. Water in which the egg hath cooked doth revitalize green-growing house planth.

Poached eggery:
   The tattered poached egg, how to avoid
   A. Walk around it.
   B. Let it sit ten minutes in very hot water in a cup before cracking it into a dish and slipping it gently into the simmering water.

APRIL 18   Ms. AESOP'S FABLES (No. 4)

The White Egg & the Brown Egg

A White Egg in the refrigerator told a Brown Egg, "I am better than you are," and the Brown Egg replied, "I am better than you are." Then a Scientist came along and, overhearing the argument, said, "Shut up, both of you, and I will find out who is right." So he took them both to his Laboratory, where he tested them, and finding no difference at all, scrambled them up for breakfast over his Bunsen burner.

Moral: You have no idea the silly talk that goes on inside the refrigerator once the light goes out.

As the hard-cooked eggs start piling up, have a

SHAKEL EGG SUPPER

Alternate layers of cooked broccoli with sliced hard-cooked eggs, pour cheese sauce over it, and bake at 350° for thirty minutes. (If you have no canned cream sauce, make your own: stir 2 tablespoons flour into 2 tablespoons melted butter in a saucepan, then add a cup of milk and ½ cup grated sharp cheese, and keep stirring till it's thick.)

APRIL 19   And as they keep rolling out, make a traditional

PETER ABBOTT SALAD
(To serve on a lettuce leaf or in sandwiches)

Slice about ten hard-cooked eggs. Then slice thinly, on the diagonal, about 1½ cups of celery. Drop it in boiling water for about a minute and drain. Cut half a green pepper in thin strips. Then mix together

> a green onion, chopped
> ½ cup mayonnaise
> 1 tablespoon Dijon mustard
> 1 tablespoon vinegar

and combine everything. Decorate it if you like with more green-pepper strips or pimento, chopped stuffed olives, sliced black olives . . . whatever is handiest.

APRIL 20   Now beginneth the sign of stubborn TAURUS (controlling the Necke) that continueth through May 20, this being a faire good time to

> plant potatoes
> paint the house
> shear a sheep
> slaughter a pig.

And the methodical Taurian doeth the first three (at his own slow pace) but leaveth the pig alive & well, for Taurus is tenderhearted.

APRIL 21   ". . . It is pleasant to see a great bed of tall dandelions on a windy April day shaking all their golden heads together; and common as it may appear, it is a beautiful compound flower. . . . How beautifully, too, the leaves are cut! and when bleached, who does not know that it is the most wholesome herb that ever gave flavor to a salad? . . ."

—R. Chambers

A SALAD BOTH PRETTIE & CHEAP
IF YOU GROW YOUR OWN DANDELIONS

They must be very young light-green dandelions—the plants, not the flowers. Wash them thoroughly and dry them thoroughly. Then sprinkle and toss them with salt, pepper, lemon juice (or vinegar if you have no lemon juice) and twice as much olive oil as lemon juice. Very good with crisp crumbled bacon and finely chopped cucumbers too.

> Q. Why did little Eggbert wear his asbestos suit to the produce market?
>
> A. He didn't want to get chard.
>
> Q. What hath a round face and ticks and strikes?
>
> A. A fat California lettuce-picker who got lost in a weed patch and never got his overtime.

APRIL 22   Prof. Arlo Crumpacker, Inventor (Ph.D., B.S.), was born forty-five years ago today.*

It is his collection of Household Laws that made him nationally famous. Crumpacker is to the daily household round as Newton was to the Fig, except that he formulated more laws.

Some of Crumpacker's Laws of Household Management:
1. It's in the other handbag.
2. No matter what the paint can says, the job will need another coat.
3. Whichever traverse-curtain cord you pull is the wrong one.
4. In making a three-egg meringue with the last three eggs in the house, it is the third egg yolk that oozes into the whites.
5. A level cupful of liquid cocoa becomes a quart of liquid

---

* Prof. Crumpacker's original field was Population Control, or Family Planning. However, he soon realized that he could do even more for the mental health of the home in other ways. Among his many popular inventions is a kitchen drawer that won't open, for keeping the vacuum cleaner's paint-spraying attachment in. Equally well received was the smartly tailored paper sack he designed for putting over a lady's head to cure her hiccups after reading what the magazines expect her to serve for an impromptu Springtime Brunch. At last reports, Prof. Crumpacker was hard at work on a ham that self-destructs on the morning of the fifth day.

94

cocoa when a child spills it on a white rug (Crumpacker's Law of Liquid Expansion).

6. If a fresh double-bed sheet is desired, it is a single-bed sheet that is unfolded.

7. Throwing the remaining mitten irretrievably out causes the missing mitten to reappear.

8. The missing red wool sock can always be located without difficulty in the wash load of white tennis clothes.

9. Any recipe calling itself foolproof isn't.

10. If you put on a pair of clean socks every morning, in a few days you won't be able to get your shoes on.

APRIL 23   ROOTIN-TOOTIN SUNDAE
À LA ONE-HOSS

First, make about a quart of Coffee Liqueur and let 'er mellow. A month should do it.

1 2-ounce jar of instant coffee
4 cups sugar
2 cups boiling water

1 pint brandy or vodka
a vanilla bean, cut in little pieces

Stir up the coffee and sugar in the boiling water till it is dissolved. Cool it. Add your brandy and vanilla bits, and pour it into some jars with tight lids. After a month in the icebox, it's ready to strain and pour over your ice cream—Mocha, Chocolate, Almond, Vanilla—and hot diggety.

APRIL 24   A good thing to have with it, or have anyway, is one of his

BIG WAGON-WHEEL COOKIES
*(Crisp, buttery, and, One-Hoss says,
the bigger the better)*

Sift
  ½ teaspoon baking soda
  4 cups flour
  1 teaspoon salt

Cream
1 cup butter
2 cups sugar

Beat
1 egg
½ cup milk

Add the dry stuff alternately with the wet stuff to the sugar-butter mix. Roll out, cut out, bake on a greased cooky sheet about fifteen minutes at 375°.

APRIL 25   ". . . Acronyms fill an increasingly important place in the superjet age. And naturally, for they save not only time but breath, energy, and paper."
—Conger T. Hatt

NATO, UNICEF, SNAFU, RADAR, SONAR. And SASE, Stamped And Self-addressed Envelope. And AKA, Also Known As. And ASAP, As Soon As Possible. Then there are abbreviations, like VIP and TGIF. And FYI, For Your Information, and FBI, for the government's information. Take an abbreviation to lunch today, say a PB&J or a BLT.

Apparently, the first real acronym to hit the top of the charts happened when an English police clerk booked a sailor for deflowering one of the village maidens. Scratching his head over how to record the change with suitable decorum, he finally settled on For Unlawful Carnal Knowledge,* which was later boiled down for convenience when the rest of the fleet hit port. And a good thing, too. Otherwise, literature would probably never have reached its present remarkable state of lucidity, and our armed forces personnel wouldn't be able to communicate at all.

After that, there was no stopping the acronym. Via the mails, on the backs of envelopes—MALAYA, My Anxious Lips Await Your Arrival, NELLY, No one Ever Loved Like You, POLAND, Please Open Lovingly And Never Destroy, SWAK, Sealed With A Kiss, BOLTOP, Better On Lips Than On Paper, HOLLAND, Hope Our Love Lives And Never Dies, and ITALY, I Trust And Love You.

And then the airlines—TWA, Try Walking Across. PIA, Please Inform Allah. ALITALIA, Always Late In Takeoff, Always Late In Arriving. BEA, Britain's Excuse for an Airline, undoubtedly full of the bellhop's GDT's, the Goddam Tourists.

Then there is the English teacher's handy NEASWAP, Never End A Sentence With A Preposition, an admonition we'd better not forget about. Nor can we afford to overlook the Organization Man's personnel approach—his WIGO, What Is Going On?, and his DFI,

* Sometimes confused with "Frigg" or "Frigga," the goddess of marriage in Norse mythology.

Damn Fool Idea, and his KITA, Kick In The Ass, all equally applicable in the domestic arena too.

When will the acronym hit the cookbooks? PIP, SLAM, POP. Put In Pan, Stir Like A Maniac, Pour Over Pie.

APRIL 26   ". . . If you've ever tried to scour a sink with Parmesan cheese, you know the wisdom of reading labels first. . . ."

—Dereck Williamson

This is especially vital with magical products named WHIFFO or JIFFO or CREAMO or DREAMO, which is a drain-cleaner if it isn't a spot-remover or a cake-frosting.

But as for the operating instructions that come with household appliances, reading them isn't necessary, because it wouldn't do any good. Mumu Harbottle didn't know this when she went to see Dr. Neitzelgrinder the other day with a sheaf of How to Operate manuals in her hand.

"I'm afraid something is the matter with my head, Doctor," she said. "Look. For my new vertical broiler. It says, 'Failure in adjustment of extruded Part A may support combustion. . . .' At first I thought they meant if I didn't tighten the knob, it would start a fire. But if they meant that, they'd have said it, wouldn't they?"

"No, Mumu," said the doctor sadly. "Not necessarily."

"And then it goes on," Mumu said, " ' . . . in which eventuality, suppression of conflagration may be effected by prompt application of sodium chloride.' "

Listening intently, Dr. Neitzelgrinder nodded. "Means if a fire starts, throw salt on it."

"Oh. Well, then, Doctor, this one, for the garbage grinder in the sink, it says, 'Do not introduce fibrous material to sink disposer unit.' Mrs. Sink Disposer Unit, may I present Mr. Fibrous Material? What are they talking about?"

"Artichoke leaves," said Neitzelgrinder. "Jerusalem artichokes. Celery. Stringy stringbeans. Stuff like that . . . By the way, Mumu, how old is your little girl now?"

"Two and a half," Mumu said.

"Just wait," said the doctor. "You think you've got trouble now, wait till you read the directions for putting your first Barbie Doll Dreamhouse together. You should see my waiting room the day after Christmas. This is the Acorn Academy."

Then he explained to Mumu that manufacturers spend so much money on TV time that they have to leave all instruction-writing to the President of the Board's nephew, who smiles a lot and collects tin foil and learned at Stupid School never to use a two-syllable word if a four-syllable word can be found.

Mumu gradually felt better as the doctor talked on, soothingly, about the millennium sure to come, some day, when expert instruction-writers will write instructions, and packagers will quit using triple-thick plastic where triple-thin tissue would do the job, and there won't be an aerosol can left in the world or a Barbie Doll either, and the lion will lie down with the lamb and have a pleasant conversation, clearly understood by both parties.

> We must learn to communicate with clarity, and if we can't, we must learn to shut up.

> "Mrs. Jones," said the doctor, frowning, "I don't like the way your husband looks."
> "I don't either," said Mrs. Jones, "but he's good to the kids."

Now let us stand for a reading of the Twenty-third Psalm.
". . . The Lord is my external-internal integrative mechanism. I shall not be deprived of gratification for my viscerogenic hungers or my need-dispositions. He motivates me to orient myself toward a non-social object with effective significance. . . ."

—*Time* Magazine, in an
article about jargon

APRIL 27   Mrs. Andreyev Taloff of Cleveland, Ohio, had an identity crisis today.

The Coffee Shop waitress asked her, poised with a plate held high, "Are you the lamb chop?" And when she gave the attendant her claim check at the parking lot, he said, "You the blue Volks?" And at the City Hall, where she works, the messenger boy said, "You Traffic Control?" And to her dentist she is the Twisted Lateral, and to her doctor she is the Post-nasal Drip, and to Macy's Alterations she is the Polyester Flares. And to her children she is Ma and to her husband she's Hon, and she says that sometimes she can't help feeling like considerably less than the sum of her parts.

APRIL 28   NOW!! More Jolly Breakfast Foolery from the Same Fun-filled Folks Who Brought You Chocolate Sugar-coated Krunchy-Nut Num-Nums!

This morning, in 1976, Stephanie ("Fats") Stumflug found she had granolaed herself right out of her caftan. Couldn't pry it on with a shoehorn.

The trouble—she explained to anyone who would listen—was that the side of the granola box said only 125 calories per ounce, but the pretty picture showed a generous bowlful . . . actually about five ounces, if she'd ever weighed a generous bowlful, but she never did.

"I might have known," she said bitterly. "You can't trust anything that tastes good."

". . . We've compiled information on more than 78 cold cereals of all types, and found that on a cup-for-cup basis most of the new 'naturals' contain four to seven times as many calories as other cereals—even the sugared 'kid stuff' cereals."

—Barbara Gibbons,
San Francisco *Chronicle*

But for those who can trust themselves with a measuring cup and for those who don't care, One-Hoss recommends his

GRANNY'S DATE GRANOLA
(You add the dates the last thing)

In a big bowl mix

4 cups quick-cooking oats	½ cup sesame seeds
1 cup finely chopped nuts	¾ teaspoons salt
½ cup shredded coconut	1 teaspoon cinnamon

Add

⅓ cup vegetable oil
½ cup honey
½ teaspoon vanilla

and mix it up good. Use your hands. Then spread it out on a couple of baking sheets and bake it at 325° for twenty-five minutes and stick around. Stir anyway every five. Then take it out, pour it into a big bowl, add

a cup of chopped dates

and let 'er cool. Then stir it around till it's crumbly and store it in jars.

APRIL 29   *A Capital Idea!*
". . . Dr. Strabismus (Whom God Preserve) of Utrecht has invented a small circular spoon, with a hole in the middle. Through this hole the cook can look at whatever she is about to stir.

"The spoon has no handle, so that when she is looking at, say, porridge, through the hole, the cook must hold the spoon by the rim of the circle. When the actual stirring is to begin, a handle can be fitted to the spoon, or else an ordinary spoon can be used."
—J. B. Morton

APRIL 30   And now be very wary.
This is Walpurgis Night, the Witches' Sabbath, and all hell busts loose in the Hartz Mountains.

Q. What is the difference between a deer that's trying to escape a hunter, and an undersized witch?

A. One is a hunted stag and I forget what the other one is.

May

openeth Buds, Windows & Bureau Drawers; pondereth the Order of Things (& lack of it); bringeth indispensable Receipts including a cowcumber Cure for Pimples & Pumples as well as

> a skinny fish dish for all seasons
> the fastest chocolate-chip cooky
> a most delicate noodle
> the handiest freeze-ahead casserole
> the easiest nonthinking dinner this
>   side of raw

and still other choice Viands!

O see the busy chickadee
    With agile cunning stop
The bugs that buzz the cherry tree
    From ruining the crop!

Then watch him, gloriously drunk
    On song and self and sun,
Devour the lot, the little shtunk,
    Before you've picked a one!

MAY 1   NOW IT IS MIRTHFUL MAY, with gossamer Aire
          in remote Places to delight the Senses and beckon to
city Folke who perforce increase its carbon monoxide content in
driving thither; and it is a Time for May baskets, May wine, May-
pole syrup!

Now behold the Moon in Taurus, all moist and earthy, as Countrie Mouse diggeth out his Wheelbarrow & Citie Mouse shifteth
the potted Begonia to catch the sweete Sunne. This month marketh
the Birthday of the great Linnaeus, who brought Order to a dis-
orderly World. And so doth the harried Houseperson desire to
neaten all Fuzz-and-Tousle made evident now by the clear & gentle
Light of the lengthened Daye.

> "I ponder with misgiving in
>   My rounds with broom and shovel
> That it doesn't take much living in
>   A house to make a hovel."
>   —Edwina Guest

MAY 2   A likely day to neaten things up. Shirley Shimmel-
          fenner once tried to.

". . . So I got this old two-drawer file and some file folders, and
labeled one drawer DULL and the other drawer INTERESTING. In
DULL I put tax stuff and appliance manuals and inoculation records
and so on. In INTERESTING I put plans for the guest room and like
that. But it didn't work. Nothing ever stayed Dull or Interesting. I
mean, the dog's rabies record got pretty interesting after he bit the
delivery boy in the pants. And the piece about growing bonsai trees
that I put in INTERESTING wasn't, very. Or I'd of done something
about it.

"So then I went alphabetical—Anchovy Dressing, Appliances,
Assessments. But I'd think 'salad,' not 'Anchovy dressing,' or I'd
think 'dishwasher,' not 'Appliance.' . . .

"Then I decided on special headings. CAR THINGS. TAX THINGS.
BANK BUSINESS. But everything belonged under two headings,

103

maybe three. Like the letter from the lawyer about my insurance policies, and the payments we made to the bank on the car.

"So then I put it all in a grocery carton on the closet floor. Now I use the top file drawer for sweaters and the bottom one for underwear. . . ." —Shirley Shimmelfenner, *A Day in the Life of* . . . , vol. 5

"There are boxes in the mind with labels on them: To study on a favorable occasion; never to be thought about; useless to go into further; Contents unexamined; Pointless business; Urgent; Dangerous; Delicate; Impossible; Abandon; Reserved; For others; My forte; etc." —Paul Valéry

MAY 3 On this day in 1975, Mumu Harbottle calculated that if she divided the number of ballpoint pens (in the desk drawer) that didn't work by the number of jar lids (in the pantry) that didn't fit anything, and multiplied that by the number of old lipsticks (in the dresser drawer) that she didn't like the color of and subtracted her Social Security number, she would still have quite a heap on her hands.

". . . Nobody should have to clean up anybody else's mess in this world. It is terribly bad for both parties, but probably worse for the one receiving the service." —Tennessee Williams

But this is not precisely so. The truth is, everyone should clean up someone else's detritus, because he isn't emotionally attached to it.

MS. AESOP'S FABLES (No. 5)

One day a Nanny-goat made her annual social call on her friend the Sow. As they settled down to a nice snack of slops and vegetable parings, the Nanny-goat noticed, leaning against the trough, the same old rusty hunk of radiator hood that had been there last year.

"I thought you were going to turn that into a planter," she said to the Sow. "Yes," the Sow said comfortably, "that'll make me a nice planter one of these days."

The following week, returning the call, the Sow was settling down with the Nanny-goat to a light lunch of mulberry branches and old gym socks when she noticed on the porch the same old corroded battery case that had been there last year.

"I thought you were going to have that wired for a lamp," she said. "Yes," said the Nanny-goat comfortably, "that'll make me a nice lamp one of these days."

Moral: It's a wise girl who knows her own garbage.

MAY 4   Pack Rats Anonymous was founded on this
            day, 1958.

Recently I attended an evening meeting of the group with my old friend Lester Chester. They met in a big bare room in an old house downtown . . . about twenty dedicated men and women from all walks of life.

Presently the Chairman called the meeting to order. "Attention, ladies and gentlemen. Before we get to the testimonials, will someone put the question?"

A short, balding man called from the back of the room, "Sure. Got some flotsam?"

At his words, the women dumped their open handbags onto the floor and the men emptied their pockets. Then they all picked various items out of the litter and carried them to the fast-growing heap in the fireplace. Crumpled Kleenex, empty film boxes, broken key chains, old grocery lists, sticky swizzle sticks . . . Finally the Chairman tossed in a match, and by the light of the cheerful blaze I could read, for the first time, the words on the two big placards on the wall. ANY WOMAN CAN. ANY MAN CAN TOO.

At a nod from the Chair, Lester stood up.

"My name is Les, and I'm a pack rat," he said quietly. Then, shoulders erect, voice steady, he gave a moving account of his past fifteen years, before he finally found PRA. Of the time he first began to realize that he couldn't pass up a reusable container. Or throw one out. Of how quickly he became unable to throw out a non-reusable container either. Of how he found himself retrieving it when anybody else threw one out, along with defunct flashlight batteries, torn shower caps, old third-class mail, and corks that didn't fit anything.

In harrowing detail he described the untold mental anguish of his wife and family as his condition deteriorated, till that final terrible Sunday afternoon, two years ago. Thinking to take a nap in his study, he couldn't find the couch under the pile of old tarps, magazines, paper sacks, gallon jugs, undershirts, car rags, empty Flit cans, check stubs dating back to 1949, a Hula Hoop, and nine unopened bottles of men's cologne, and had to sleep standing up.

The others listened with understanding. They had all been there. Indeed, some had been even farther, and when Lester finished, several told their stories too. One woman's was especially poignant. A guest had mistakenly opened the wrong dresser drawer and found a ruptured bicycle pump, 107 small aluminum-foil pans that formerly contained chicken pie, and an old girdle stuffed in a corn flakes box.

At meeting's end, heartened by sharing and comparing, they all stood up to repeat in unison the organization's motto: "Every day I'll throw something away, and I'll soon feel better and better." Then, after subdued good nights, they wended their separate ways home.

It was a memorable occasion. Never will I forget the courage and quiet resolve I had seen that evening, and I told Lester so as we stopped for a beer on the way home.

"I'm paying," he said, fishing in his pocket for change, which he finally dredged up along with some old dog-track tickets, a pair of dime-store sunglasses missing a lens, three Band-Aids that had lost their stickum, and a couple of outsize toggle bolts.

The bar was dark, though not so dark I couldn't see Lester flush as he put the objects back in his pocket. But he didn't mention them, and of course I didn't either.

> ". . . There are telltale signs of a really ordered life. Sooner or later every visitor walks into a cupboard in mistake for a room, and either is or isn't showered with fir-cones and old pingpong nets."
> —Katharine Whitehorn

". . . Twice a year, probably, things should come up for review, like prisoners. Some need a halfway house to stay in while you develop the mental starch necessary for getting them out of your life: clothes, books you outgrew or never grew up to, one-claw hammers, funny pictures from the bulletin board that aren't funny any more, the comical apron that never was. A big moving carton is a good halfway house. Then, after six months, don't look into it. Just move it."

—Stella Trowbridge Hinky (*Ibid.*)

MAY 5   An auspicious day for making fast, easy cookies.
         This is especially good for those times when the children threaten to turn into mean little misfits because of not enough home cooking.

SHUTTEMUP COOKIES
(The fastest chocolate-chip cooky)

Cream together

> 1 cup butter or oleo
> 1 cup brown sugar

Then add

> 2 cups flour
> 1 6-ounce package of chocolate chips
> 1 cup nuts, chopped

Mix it, press it into a thirteen-by-nine-inch jelly-roll pan, and bake twenty-five minutes at 350°. While it's still warm, cut it in bars. If you forget to, just break it up when it's cool.

Also on this day, in 1975, Mumu Harbottle took her inadequacies to the doctor, and in the very nick of time.

She explained that though she had tried and tried, her spice shelf never resembled the impeccable sparkling spice shelves in the magazine pictures. Dr. Neitzelgrinder then explained that only model kitchens to be photographed have spice shelves like that, because in real life, whatever spice you suddenly need isn't available in your pattern at the only store that's open then. It only comes in some tin box that won the Prix de Ugly at the Cans Festival. It also gets gummy, as time goes on.

He suggested, however, that Mumu separate the exotic things, like Fenugreek and Turmeric, from the everyday stand-bys, and put them in a shoe box with a legible list of contents pasted to the outside. If Mumu would keep this on the top shelf of a darkish, cool closet, he said, it would unclutter the spice shelf while increasing the longevity of the spices. It would also do something for Mumu's mental health, he added, because she wouldn't be perpetually reminded of all the fancy stuff she wasn't cooking.

MAY 6   Sigmund Freud was born on this day, in 1856, so that Mental Health Month could be celebrated in May. (Many people find it easier to be mentally healthy outdoors than in.)

Dr. Freud would have had an interesting time with my husband's Aunt Abilene, who lives, if you can call it that, in Toledo, Ohio, and is too busy cleaning everything to read anything. So it's perfectly safe to write about her.

Aunt Abilene doesn't approve of self-polishing floor wax or packaged Parmesan cheese or sex (she speaks darkly of someone's having relations, and you know she doesn't mean for Thanksgiving dinner) or Democrats or split infinitives or dirt. Most especially she disapproves of dirt.

She doesn't realize that dirt is only misplaced matter—matter that was perfectly okay and had its own place in the scheme of things, back at its original port of embarkation. Dirt is only foreign bodies—tiny tourists, so to speak. And constant cleaning only ages the skin prematurely and creates more dirt, one way or another, the way a bath leaves a ring around the tub, and all that detergent makes the algae grow in the lakes so the fish can't breathe and they die and start to smell.

> ". . . Keeping a place clean isn't all that hard if you can afford the soap, and it doesn't take any great brain. I guess that's why women give it a lower priority now. My former wife had just about enough sense to find her mouth with her fork, but she still kept the cleanest house in fifty states."   —Conger T. Hatt

Isabelline: A lovely soft pale gray, named for Isabella of Castile, who vowed she wouldn't change her underwear till Granada was retaken from the Moors, and it was a good long war.

MAY 7   "Still, you can't just bury your head in an ostrich. . . ."
           —Shirley Shimmelfenner (*Ibid.*)

"For scrubbing ze floor or shooting ze marbles,
safety-pin ze big sponges to ze pants-knees.
Très confortable, n'est-ce pas? . . ."
                                        —Brillo-Savarin*

MS. AESOP'S FABLES (No. 6)

Tiring of the nest, one bright spring day, a Mother Hen hired her teen-age Chick to housekeep it. "We 're low on soap," she said, "so get some," and then she flew the coop for a job in another part of the barnyard.

That night, when she came home, the place looked the same except for a shelf full of aerosol Grass-Cleaner, Hay-Brightener, Straw-Softener, Egg-Polisher, Roost-Freshener, and Trough-Wax, plus a bill that wasn't chicken feed. But no soap.

So the Mother Hen told her Chick she could either pay for it herself or take it back and get some soap. Which the Chick did, and they all lived just as clean ever after.

Moral: An old broom knows how to sweep clean cheaper.

MAY 8   And so, as the busy honey bee buzzeth outdoors,
          heavy-laden with golden dust, the houseperson raiseth
a little dust too.

When it comes to housework—and somehow it always seems to —I'd like to know how to maintain a respectable level of accomplishment, day in and day out, instead of being an overachiever one day and an inert mass the next.

Perhaps it averages out, and the sum total of what's done during a week is the same. Still, the stop-and-start approach certainly uses more gas—probably causes more wear and tear too. Like light bulbs. Turning a bulb on and off wears it out about as fast as letting it burn. . . . Wouldn't a glowworm last longer if it just kept on glowing? . . .

"When you're hot, you're hot; when you're not, you're not."
                                        —Shirley Shimmelfenner,
                                        and a lot of other people

* Brillo-Savarin was bucking for Chef at Le Tournedos in Marseilles till the day he burned the Béchamel. Since then he has been mainly in charge of cleaning things up.

"It is possible that Newton's law of action and inaction has something to do with the roller-coaster effect of many a housework pattern. And certainly the whirlwind-doldrum syndrome has its merits. Many a woman finds housework at least endurable if the place was so cluttered to begin with that she can see some results."
—Stella Trowbridge Hinky (*Ibid.*)

THE EASIEST NONTHINKING DINNER
THIS SIDE OF RAW
(*For whirlwind days*)

A good-sized eggplant, cut up any way, not peeled
A big can of tomatoes (or 3 or 4 fresh ones,
    unpeeled, just cut in chunks)
2 teaspoons rosemary, crushed between the palms
    or the oak trees; this doesn't matter

Put it all in an electric skillet and simmer it gently—lowest possible simmering temperature—about an hour and a half. Taste before adding any salt. (*Note:* No browning in oil—in fact, no oil. Yet it has a rich meaty taste and will do, in a pinch, as a main course.)

To Turn It into a Hearty Greek Stew: Add lamb, any kind, cut up any way. Brown it first in a little oil, then add the vegetables and cook the same way.

MAY 9   There Are Experts at Housekeeping . . .
            ". . . To assess her competence at cleaning, examine not the powder room, the sink, the living room. Regard, instead, the light-switch plate and the lamp shade; the telephone and its very cord; the underside of the lid of the step-on garbage can and the pedal that is daily stepped on; the steps of the household stepladder, and the medicine cabinet. . . . And, oh, examine most particularly the outsides of wastebaskets and cleaning-cupboard doors, as well as the shelf surfaces upon which the cleaning compounds and polishes have their being. All too often these are orphans. This is because, when they are in use, the mind is beamed purposefully elsewhere. One is emptying coffee grounds into the step-on can, not inspecting the can. One is urgently seeking the aspirin, not checking the sanitation level of the medicine cabinet. . . ."

—Stella Trowbridge Hinky

... and There Are Experts at Rationalizing, Another Handy Skill

Let's assume that two jobs need doing: (a) shoveling out The Child's room, which resembles a petrified storm, and (b) writing a steering-committee report.

Which one you do depends on which one seems the less repellent at the time. If the thought of the steering-committee business makes even The Child's room look inviting, tell yourself: *Though community involvement is important, one must know one's personal priorities; and with me, The Family comes first.*

However, if the thought of The Child's room makes your gorge rise and the report sound good, tell yourself: *The Child must develop organizational and cleaning skills. To do his work for him would be to deprive him of a Learning Experience.*

MAY 10   While intermittent probing sun
Proveth indoor work undone,
Intermittent gentle rain
Bringeth crab grass back again.

An auspicious day for straightening up outdoors, which is usually easier. When a tree or a bush drops something, you can safely assume it doesn't want it any more.

A fast dinner for an outdoor day:

4-ITEM MEXICAN CASSEROLE

(Taste the chili beans first, and if they lack authority, add a teaspoon of chili powder, or ½ teaspoon each of cumin and oregano. Also: If you forget to take the corn soufflé out of the freezer a couple of hours before dinner, it will thaw faster in a watertight bag immersed in tepid water.)

1 can chili beans with meat
1 cup taco-flavored corn chips, slightly crumbled;
    that should be enough to make an adequate layer
    on the bottom of a middle-size casserole dish
1 frozen corn soufflé, defrosted
1 cup shredded yellow cheese

Layer those things in that middle-size casserole dish—all the corn chips, all the chili—then spread it with the corn soufflé and sprinkle the cheese on. Bake it uncovered at 350° for about thirty minutes, till the soufflé is slightly puffed and the cheese melts.

MAY 11   On this day in 1976, the Hot Dog with Mustard on a Plain Soft Bun won the nationwide Pupularity Poll with schoolchildren between the ages of seven and eleven. From ages twelve through fifteen they wanted chopped sweet pickle too.

Facts like this are one of our country's greatest natural resources, and yet few people know where they come from. Actually, their source is an enormous silo about fifty miles north of Des Moines, Iowa, where they are kept to ferment for a while, before the silage is shipped to newspapers in all fifty states.

I happened to be walking past it once when the lid blew off, and a bunch of crisp facts blew out, frisking about like autumn leaves. Naturally, I grabbed a handful and ran.

> People with blue eyes and red hair are more apt to be nail-biters than people with brown eyes and brown hair.

> Only one out of thirty men over twenty-five can tell you (within 25 cents) how much change they have in their pockets; only one out of fifty women over thirty can tell you (within a dollar) how much change they have in their handbags.

> Families with three or more children eat pancakes three times a month.

> Twenty-two out of twenty-five people of Caucasian heritage put on their right shoe first.

MAY 12   For a Warm Day, a Cold Soup!

COLD WATERCRESS CREAM

Put together

    2 cans condensed cream of potato soup; delump it in
        the blender or a sieve
    1 soup can light cream
    1 cup chicken stock (made from chicken bouillon cubes
        or powder)
    1 bunch of watercress minus stems; should be about
        a cupful

Simmer it five minutes and chill it for the rest of the day—at least five hours. At serving time thin it with a little more light cream if it needs it.

MAY 13   Our Green-growing friends
          "Screaming and bickering households are not, as a rule, ideal surroundings for growing plants. I must define screaming and bickering as opposed to the yelling and hollering of children. Plants prefer a stable pattern of noise, rather than constant surprises like 'Boo!' and jumping through a doorway. Vicious and vindictive quarreling will turn almost all plants into neurotic introverts. . . ."
                                        —Jerry Baker

                    "Horse apples."
                                        —One-Hoss

MAY 14   Stella Trowbridge Hinky's Handy Dandy

                    LEMON PUD
          (*To make into pie or to eat as is*)

                    6 lemons
                    ½ cup butter
                    3 cups granulated sugar
                    6 eggs

Get the juice out of the lemons, some way, and grind up three rinds. Mix it. Now melt the butter in the top of a double boiler, stir in the lemon mix and the sugar. When it is all dissolved, stir in the beaten eggs and cook it all over simmering water—don't let the water boil. When it's as thick as thick molasses, cool it and pour it into jars to refrigerate.

This is handy to have on hand. You can eat it from little dishes, as pudding, or spoon it into any unbaked pie shell or crumb crust and bake it fifteen minutes at 375°. If you want to use up still more eggs, top it with a meringue and shove it for a minute or two under the broiler. If not, don't. Or use a squirt of whipped cream.

MAY 15   The St. Torquatus Olive Tree in Cádiz always blooms on this exact day every year, or is, at any rate, at least as accurate as the Capistrano swallows are.

And on this day in 1976, Winston Harbottle, age nine, of 52 Oak Trees, Illinois, concluded his fourth-grade science project on the Life Cycle of the Kidney Bean. He planted some in coffee cans, which he then set out on a tree stump, his experiment proving conclusively that raccoons certainly do like kidney beans.

MAY 16   Fulle sweete, the merrie month of May
              To lusty lads in raimente gay! . . .

But how sorry a thing it is (not only for the poet but for us all) to see honest old words so smogged over with new colorations that they can never again be scrubbed clean. When *gay* was liberated, the language was the loser.

And so it has always been, I suppose—the language changing daily, even hourly, being nibbled at, added to, and continually in the process of becoming, like the shore line of a continent. Not too long ago, a young woman could say, quite properly, "Yes, he made love to me but there was nothing improper about our intercourse." Not so very long before that, Spenser's "gentle Knight was pricking on the plaine." And now the innocent old query "How did you make out?" shows a rather unhealthy curiosity. . . .

Or consider the pimple. The not-very-attractive word *pimple* is well-calculated to produce an immediate image of the not-very-attractive thing itself. (There used to be a *pumple,* too—probably a larger or more mature pimple.) But after many generations of pimplehood, the eruption became—mysteriously—a *hickey,* which within present memory turned into a love bite, and now a pimple is a *zits.* No one seems to know where the zits comes from, except from too many potato chips, chili burgers, and surging adolescent hormones.

"The Cucumber or Cowcumber . . . chopped as herbs to the pot and boiled in a small pipkin with a piece of mutton, being made into potage with Ote-meale, even as herb potage are made, whereof a messe to breakfast, as much to dinner, and the like to supper; taken in this manner for the space of three weekes together without intermission, doth perfectly cure all manner of sauce flegme and copper faces, red and shining fierie noses (as red as red Roses) with pimples, pumples, rubies, and such like precious faces."
—John Gerard's *Herball* (circa 1575)

CHILLED DILLED CUCUMBERS

Slice a large cucumber thin enough to read through, but instead of doing that, beat together

⅓ cup salad oil
3 tablespoons vinegar
½ teaspoon dried dill weed (or 1½ teaspoons fresh)
¼ teaspoon each sugar and salt

and pour it over the cucumbers. Chill till dinnertime.

"Eat your green salad, it's good for your eyes," said Mrs. Ace to her little boy Goodman. "Did you ever see a cow wearing glasses?"

MAY 17   And now beginneth THIN EATING to prepare for the bikini season.

"You've got to get the lead out to get the lard off."
—Shirley Shimmelfenner,
The Valley of the Dishes, vol. 3

A HEALTHY SKINNY BREAKFAST
(240 calories)

½ cup orange or tomato juice
1½ cups high-protein nonsugar cereal
1 teaspoon sugar
½ cup skim milk
black coffee or tea

MAY 18   SKINNY FISH FOR ALL SEASONS

Dip fresh or thawed fish fillets—almost any kind—in well-salted milk. Roll them in fine crumbs mixed with paprika. Lay them out companionably side by side in a well-greased shallow baking pan. Drizzle just a little melted butter on top. Bake from eight to ten minutes in a 500° oven.

MAY 19   SKINNY MEAT LOAF

Mix together

2 pounds lean ground beef	1 cup skim milk
2 tablespoons melted whipped butter	2 tablespoons minced onion
	½ teaspoon white pepper
2 eggs, slightly beaten	2 teaspoons salt substitute

Pack this into a greased loaf pan and bake it about an hour at 350°
Or use a greased angel-food tin, which is more interesting, because
you can fill the hole in the middle with some skinny stringbeans
when you serve it.

MAY 20   bringeth something to hoot about!
On this day, 1975, One-Hoss trapped the big old
bird that had been eating his baby rabbits and really creamed him,
to make the first owleomargarine.

MAY 21   And now beginneth the sign of versatile GEMINI
(controlling the Nervous System), which extendeth
through June 20 and bodeth well for
        having the tonsils out
        setting hens
        consummating a business deal
        weeding the petunia patch.
But the restless mercurial Gemini decideth with difficulty which
to tackle first and so doeth a bit of each: one tonsil, one hen, one
phone call, one thistle. . . .

"Decisions were always terribly hard for me," said the Gemini
lady. "I would take the longest while to make up my mind. Tomato
juice or grapefruit juice? Green shirt or yellow shirt? Allan or
Henry? And suddenly one day, I thought, if it's that hard to decide,
there can't be a gram's worth of difference in how I feel about either
one. So I married Allan, and I guess I had to do that to find out
that it really should have been Henry, after all. . . ."

116

MAY 22   "Before scrubbing ze well-blackened pot bottom,
            place newspapers in ze seenk or you will be toot
sweet scrubbing ze seenk too."   —Brillo-Savarin

MAY 23   This day in 1967, in Liverpool, Humphrey the Dim-
            witted Computer who cost $125,000 was sold to a
British junk-dealer for $150.

Humphrey's only problem was that he couldn't think very well.
It took him a week to solve mathematical problems a college fresh-
man could do in half an hour.

But even if he'd been brighter, he would probably have created
about as many problems as he solved. That is the way computers
do. And according to latest reports, they are having trouble programming the computer that's supposed to replace the cook. They
can't seem to get the proper inflection into its "This isn't as good
as it usually is" when it sits down at the table.

". . . That night they had a big supper. . . . Mary Jane she
set at the head of the table, with Susan alongside of her, and said
how bad the biscuits was, and how mean the preserves was, and
how ornery and tough the fried chickens was and all that kind of
rot, the way women always do for to force out compliments; and
the people all knowed everything was tiptop, and said so—said
'How *do* you get biscuits to brown so nice?' and 'Where, for the
land's sake, *did* you get these amaz'n pickles?' and all that kind of
humbug talky-talk, just the way people do at a supper, you
know. . . ."   —Huck Finn

MAY 24   Now the weather groweth better and busier; a good
            day to cook and freeze ahead some Johnny Marzetti,
a virtually indispensable freeze-ahead casserole.

Cheryl ("Cherry") Pitts, of Pittsburgh, reports that before she
started making Johnny Marzetti, she and her husband, a dog-lover,
were seldom invited out to dinner, because her husband was such
a bore about his Bedlingtons ("That dog thinks he's *human*").
However, since she started making Johnny Marzetti, to freeze ahead

in individual portions, they're still not invited anywhere, but she doesn't mind. They probably wouldn't get fed anything they like as well, she says, and she can always read while she eats.

JOHNNY MARZETTI
10 to 14 servings

1 large onion
2 pounds hamburger
1 pound elbow macaroni
1½ pounds sharp yellow cheese, plus any odds and
      ends of Blue Cheese, et cetera, that you want
      to use up. If the yellow cheese isn't sharp
      enough, add a tablespoon of wet yellow
      mustard
1 can mushrooms—the more the better—plus the juice
1 large can (about 23 ounces) tomato sauce

Sauté the finely chopped onion till it's tender, add the hamburger, and cook till the meat stops blushing. Drain the grease. Boil the macaroni as long as the package says to, drain it, then add everything else. Pour this into casserole dishes to wrap and freeze. Or spoon it into tough pliofilm sacks, and freeze. (To cook these later, use the top of the double boiler; to heat the casserole dishes, use a 350° oven for about forty minutes.) Put a little more grated cheese on top during the reheating.

MAY 25   A Day to Think About Moving
      This was known as "Flitting Day" in bonnie old Scotland, where the Scots, for some reason, hated to stay put for more than a year. Usually the heather looked purpler on the other side of the moor, and May 25 was the day they moved.
    In early February, therefore, all landlords would ask their tenants, *Sit or flit?* Mostly they flat, and understandably, really. Sometimes moving is the only way to get a thoroughly fresh start, like with the floor under the refrigerator.

Big Moving Day!
    ". . . In maybe 50 years or longer, I think habitation of places beyond the Earth will become technologically feasible. There are

no planets in the solar system that could sustain human beings in an unprotected environment, so the best approach is to make a space city—perhaps many of them—closer to home.

"One interesting suggestion was made by Gerald O'Neill, a physics professor at Princeton. His concept is to use raw materials from the moon, fling them to places called the lunar Lagrangian points—places in space which are easy to get to and where things tend to hang around. It would be about as far from the Earth as from the moon. You would use the raw materials from the moon to build a space city. . . . Each might be self-supporting and have a living area about the size of the island of Bermuda. There would be artificial gravity so everybody could have his feet planted firmly on the ground. . . ."

—Carl Sagan

MAY 26   ". . . All the men there are in this world, and I had
          to pick the one that flunked birdhouses. . . ."
          —Shirley Shimmelfenner,
          *The 5 Little Shimmelfenners & How
          They Grew,* vol. 7

How to Make Closet-and-Shelf Room When You Can't Find the Hammer:
1. Remember that box room and shelf room are easier to come by than closet room, and many clothes are happier lying down than hanging up.
2. Get a flat-topped trunk to serve as an end table too, or paint and paper a moving crate. For a lid, have a thin piece of plywood cut to size and hinge it on.
3. Get some flat heavy-cardboard blanket-storage boxes to go under the bed. Most department stores have them.
4. Rest a thin, skinny board on two tall cans (or on two stacks of unreadable books) on a pantry shelf, to make a separate one for small objects like tuna cans.
5. Get a shoebag to tack inside the pantry door or the undersink door for polish, cleansers, and so on. Get another for coat-closet door for gloves, flashlights, rain hats, et cetera.
6. Or fill a sturdy shopping bag with the cleaning stuff and hang it from an inconspicuous doorknob.

7. Use a bookcase as a room divider instead of against the wall. If it has a back, pry it off, and put books in from both directions.

MAY 27   Now! Two Good Things to Go with Leftover Beef or a Ham That Won't Quit.

JET-SET NOODLES

Cook eight ounces of egg noodles the way the package says to. Meanwhile, combine

> 1 cup cream-style cottage cheese
> 1 cup commercial sour cream
> ½ teaspoon salt
> ⅛ teaspoon pepper
> ⅓ cup snipped chives or chopped green onion stems
> 1 tablespoon butter

Put it all together, mix it, and pour it into a good-sized casserole. Dot it with butter and bake forty minutes at 325°. If you'd like the noodles a little browner-looking, put it under the hot broiler a minute or so before you serve it.

RICE SHIMMELFENNER

> 3 tablespoons butter
> 2 medium onions
> 1 cup raw rice
> 1 can consommé, beef or chicken
> 1 teaspoon each rosemary and marjoram
> ½ teaspoon summer savory

Melt the butter in a skillet, sauté the chopped onions for five minutes, add the rice, and stir till it's a lovely beige. Then add the consommé plus enough water to total about three cups of liquid. Add the spices and simmer forty minutes more.

MAY 28   A Foolish Consistency Is the Hobgoblin . . .
        or, It all depends on how you're feeling at the time.

". . . I think I can understand that feeling about a housewife's work being like that of Sisyphus (who was the stone-rolling gentleman). But it is surely in reality the most important work in the world. What do ships, railways, mines, cars, government etc. exist for except that people may be fed, warmed, and safe in their own homes? As Dr. Johnson said, 'To be happy at home is the end of all human endeavor'. (1st to be happy to prepare for being happy in our own real home hereafter; 2nd in the meantime to be happy in our houses.) We wage war in order to have peace, we work in order to have leisure, we produce food in order to eat it. So your job is the one for which all others exist. . . ."

—C. S. Lewis

". . . Domestic drudgery is excellent as an alternative to idleness or to hateful thoughts . . . [but] as an alternative to work one is longing to do and able to do (*at this time* and Heaven knows when again) it is maddening."

—C. S. Lewis

MAY 29   A favorable day for perusing *Aunt Penny's Daily Thoughts,* linen-bound and hand-painted with violets.

> Clean when you are angry
> Shop when you are full
> Cook when you are hungry

But she neglected to add, And when the wind is right, skip all that and do what you were doing before you so rudely interrupted yourself.

"I don't do housework," Annie Dillard said flatly. "Life is too short, and I'm too much of a Puritan. If you want to take a year to write a book, you have to *take* that year, or the year will take you by the hair and pull you toward the grave. *Let* the grass die. I let almost all of my indoor plants die from neglect while I was writing the book. There are all kinds of ways to live. You can take your choice. You can keep a tidy house, and when St. Peter asks you what you did with your life, you can say, I kept a tidy house, I made my own cheese balls."

MAY 30   ". . . You owe it to us all to get on with what you're good at."

—W. H. Auden

MAY 31   "When Gary asked if I'd marry him, I said, 'I don't know, what are your views on takeout food?' He said he liked it, I said yes, and now it's nine years, one child, and lots of Chicken Delights later."

—Karen Geld, screenwriter

June

bringeth divers delights & dilemmas, including Marriage & Metrics & a 28-lb. Cat; giveth also the easy Rule for

> *a glorious Fruit Tart*
> *a swift spicy Chicken*
> *a most co-operative Main Dish*
> *a pioneer pone*

and other Good Things to know about

Butterflies taste with the soles of their feet!
    I read it myself in a butterfly book
And thought, what a pleasure, whenever they eat,
    For it's bound to be sole food, whatever they cook.

Just think, could we do it, how nice it would be!
    Imagine the difference such talent would make!
Shall we stroll through the meadow? Or hike to the sea?
    Ah no, let us go for a walk on the cake!

On desolate dawns when I sulk in the shower
    And my coffee is cold and my orange is sour,
I merely remember (and morning is sweet)
    Butterflies taste with the soles of their feet!

JUNE 1   NOW IT IS AMOROUS JUNE when the Turtledoves
                sit upon the lytle green Boughes in the sweet Ayre,
billing & cooing & billing yet again. And the Cat hath new Kittens &
the Nightingale tunes his Throate, though it availeth nought against
the Aire-conditioners keening the Night away in city Street &
countrie Lane. Yet young Lovers do make merrie, and middle-aged
Lovers too, whyle there be old Lovers who are not doing so badde
either. And it be in spite of everything a rare faire Month for Wed-
dyngs!

> "God saw thee most fit for me."
> —Popular inscription in old Irish
> wedding rings

> "Wedlock, as old men note, hath likened been
> Unto a public crowd or common route;
> Where those that are without would fain get in,
> And those that are within, would fain get out."
> —Poor Richard

Now, in the traditional wedding service today, the bride and
groom get out of their bed in the morning and change the baby before they all proceed to some body of running water—ocean, river,
park fountain, or open drain—to stand barefoot and read aloud to
each other from *Portnoy's Complaint* and *Jonathan Livingston Sea-
gull* as they pledge their continuing co-operative efforts at ecology-
oriented goal attainment, with background music by The Funky
Chicken.

But this is only one more variation of a ceremony that has
changed continually over the years, and not necessarily for the
worse.

Among the Anglo-Saxons in the Middle Ages, the bride was taken
"for fairer, for fouler, for better, for worse" and promised to be
"buxom and bonny" to her future husband, after which he hit her
over the head with a shoe. As a point of honor, too, he was officially
allowed the privilege of moderate castigation . . . three blows

with a broomstick being about right, according to old Welsh law, "on any part of the person except the head." However, the law thoughtfully provided that the stick be not longer than the husband's arm, nor thicker than his middle finger.

Sir Thomas More would have approved of today's wedding customs, with the possible exception of the music. In his *Utopia,* it was mandatory that young people behold each other naked before they were married; and in the case of his own two daughters, Sir Thomas didn't quibble. John Aubrey writes of the morning when Sir William Roper came to see Sir Thomas with a proposal to marry one of his daughters:

> ". . . My lord's daughters were then both together abed in a truckle-bed in their father's chamber asleep. He carries Sir William into the chamber and takes the Sheete by the corner and suddenly whippes it off. They lay on their Backs, and their Smocks up as high as their arme-pitts. This awakened them, and immediately they turned on their Bellies. Quoth Roper, I have seen both sides, and so gave a patt on her Buttock, he made choice of, sayeing, Thou are mine. Here was all the trouble of the wooing. . . ."

The observant reader will notice that the goose never got a gander at the old prospective bridegroom, who kept his clothes on; and there is no mention of Sir Thomas More's suggesting that he take them off. He is to be gently blamed for this. But it is written that no sensible man with two daughters is going to push his luck too far.

JUNE 2   And now Gemini ruleth the soil with the Moon in the sign of the Crab, surely as good a time as any to consider the Metric System.

It was about two thousand years ago, when Mayan priests were living where Guatemala is now, that one of them conceived the mathematical notion of zero.

> *1st Mayan Priest:* Maya ask what you invented today?
> *2nd Mayan Priest (scuffing a huarache in the dust):* Zero.
> *1st M.P.:* That's nothing.

And so no one bothered to get the word around to other civilizations, and the Hindus had to reinvent zero around A.D. 800. But the fact remains, if that Mayan priest hadn't invented nothing, they wouldn't have had nothing down there for so long. And, actually, the world has been in trouble ever since. If we didn't have a zero, we couldn't have a national debt, which consists mainly of zeros, and this is probably why nobody worries about it very much.

In fact, that Mayan priest has a great deal on his conscience. If it weren't for him, we wouldn't have to learn the grams and meters of the Metric System. But as our country moves ponderously to get in step with the rest of the world, the houseperson must move too. Otherwise the H.P. will end up getting gypped worse in the marketplace than she already is, and—in the kitchen—more confused. *31.103 grams of precaution is worth 0.4536 kilograms of cure.*

It is nice to have something to munch on while studying. Gold Nuggets are good with a book or a cold drink or both, and they freeze well.

GOLD NUGGETS

In a blender or mixer, combine
    1 pound Kraft Old English cheese cut in chunks
    1 cube butter
Add
    1 cup flour

Mix it, drop it in dollar-size bits on an ungreased cooky sheet, and stick a walnut half on each. Bake at 400° for six minutes.

JUNE 3   This is the birthday of Garrett Augustus Hobart, the twenty-fourth Vice President of the United States, who was born in 1844. Regretfully we bypass the celebration in order to continue with the Metric System.

It is hard to recapture, precisely, my mingled emotions on learning that our country is changing irrevocably over to the Metric System. Mainly, though, I was aflame with an intense desire not to learn anything about it, because it sounded like the dullest thing since tapioca.

However, when I really started to look into the subject, what was my surprise to find it even duller than I had expected, full of nitpicking ramifications you wouldn't believe. And yet, nevertheless, there are a few basic metric terms we must face up to, or be able to visualize. *There is the crux:* we must be able to visualize that metric quantity itself, without having to translate it into inches or quarts. This will be a small hedge against disaster, and it will also save an entire step in thinking.

JUNE 4   More Interesting Facts About the Metric System
Now, *milligrams,* or *mg.,* are only for pharmacists and doctors, and for the convenience of cigarette manufacturers, so they can count out the proper number of tar-and-nicotine bits to put into each cigarette. Otherwise, the *mg.* or *milligram* doesn't often concern the average houseperson.

Neither does the *tg.,* or *telegram,* which doesn't matter much any more, because the system has pretty much gone to hell and they hardly ever deliver them by hand the way they used to; they only telephone. Just remember that you still get only ten words, Day Rate, not counting your name; and it is important to choose them with care, as the sailor did, sending a telegram to his girl. "I love you, I love you, I love you [signed] Gunther," he wrote. When the clerk pointed out that he still had a word coming, he added, "Regards."

JUNE 5   And now the wild flowers wink in the feathery grasses
as the sun scatters warm gold, but here we are, still deep in our books.

Now, the *gram* is a different story. The gram is important to know about, even though it is hard to picture because it is so small. Only ¹⁄₂₈ of an ounce. (Actually, the gram is to the ounce as Connecticut is to California, if that makes it any clearer. You could put twenty-eight Connecticuts into one California.)

It was important to find something that weighed exactly one gram, and so I experimented with various objects on the postage scale. Aspirin tablets and kidney beans were too light, and anyway they kept rolling off. It was sheer good luck that led me to raisins, which were sticky enough to stay put, and seemed to be exactly the right weight too. . . . Twenty-eight middle-size raisins equal an ounce. Therefore,

a raisin = a gram

128

For practical purposes, I think of grams as being twenty-five to the ounce, because that's an easier figure to multiply or divide with. Those three grams aren't going to matter in any recipe I'll ever make, believe thee me, Bunky. And inasmuch as there are eight ounces to the cup, there are—roughly—two hundred grams, or raisins, in a cup. Knowing this may help you, someday, guess the correct number of beans in a jar and win a free trip to Las Vegas.

JUNE 6   This is the day of the International Sewage & Refuse Exhibition in Munich, Germany.
Celebrate it long distance with a bowl of

METRIC MUSH
(*A myghty picturesque old Receipt*)

Put fifty grams of rice (noninstant) and seventy-five grams of sugar in a casserole that has a lid. Add a liter* of whole milk and stir it up.† Add a little vanilla and cinnamon or nutmeg and bake it covered for 4½ to 5 hours, till desired consistency is reached, as the old book said, and this can be a stumper. How do you know what consistency is desired, and by whom? Actually, what you're after is sort of a gentle pablum. This was a popular dish for invalids some years ago, and it probably got them out of bed fast, knowing there was more where it came from.

JUNE 7   On this special day, the annual Mermaid Reunion is held in Weeki Wachee,‡ Florida.
On this special day also, Socrates was born, sometime in the fifth century, B.C. He was the Athenian philosopher who, being charged as an "evil doer and a curious person, searching into things under the earth and above the heavens, and making the worse appear the better cause, and teaching all this to others," refused to pay a fine for it, was sentenced to death, and drank the hemlock.

Know thyself. For a good beginning, measure thyself:
- wingspread, both arms stretched wide
- distance from tip of the third finger to the floor, arm

* Comes later. —Ed.
† This would translate to about two quarts of milk, four tablespoons raw rice, and ¾ cup sugar.
‡ Where the gents get Weeki from too much Wachee. —Ed.

straight at the side
· thumb-to-little-finger stretch
· length of stride

All these measurements are handy for furniture or rug-shopping when thou forgettest thy measuring tape.

And so back to Metrics, and the *kilogram,* which is 2.2 pounds and presents a special problem.

Examining it, one soon realizes that the *kilo* is basically an awkward conception—a product, perhaps, of the same keen minds that brought us the airplane seat and the morning horoscope, for it never quite fits. Nothing grows into a kilo as a rule, though the garden abounds in one-pound cantaloupes, and rutabagas and so on. Few manmade things turn out to weigh a kilo either.

A large cabbage is considerably more; a large cauliflower is invariably less. A No. 2 can of peaches comes close, but who can always remember offhand which size a No. 2 can is? And while five average bananas weigh almost exactly a kilo, it is no real help. Only a very few people are that familiar with the heft of five bananas.

Finally I settled for an extra-large coconut (without the husk), a real boomer, not the kind you commonly find in grocery stores or bopping tourists on the head in tropical places. This was the closest I could come except for a two-pound box of chocolates with an extra-heavy bow.

So the kilo is basically a personal thing. It is recommended that everyone find his own, to plant solidly in his own head.

JUNE 8   It was on this day in 1848 that Paul Gauguin was born.
It wasn't till he was forty-three years old that he dropped out and went to Tahiti. But then he made up for lost time, painting some of his finest pictures and enjoying the beautiful native girls and fruits. It is too bad they didn't have blenders then, for they could have made some chilled melon soup. But probably there weren't many refrigerators on the island then either, and from all accounts—certainly the ones I've read—Gauguin was busy enough as it was.

CHILLED MELON SOUP

a big ripe cantaloupe or two big ripe papayas
½ cup sherry
¼ cup sugar
1 tablespoon (more or less) lime juice or lemon juice

Cut the fruit in half, get rid of the seeds, and scoop out the meat. Put it in the blender, add everything else, and blend. Taste to see if you want more of anything. If so, add it. Serve it quite cold.

Also a favorable day for winding up the Metric System.

And so to the matter of length:

A *millimeter* (*mm.*) is the crack between the piano keys, big enough to spill things in but too small to clean them out of.

A *centimeter* (*cm.*) is a black piano key. And both of these are the tiny offspring of the *meter,* which is the root word as well as the main thing the houseperson must know about length. The *meter* (*m.*) is 1⅒ yards, which can be easily pictured as a skirt-length with enough left over for a ruffle.*

Then, for multiples of the meter, it is best that everyone nail down, as with the kilo, his own personal image. Five meters, to me, are about the width of my kitchen, or half as far as I can throw *The Joy of Cooking* overhand. A *kilometer* (*km.*) I think of as being a generous half a mile, or about the distance from our driveway to Ichiki's Grocery Store.

JUNE 9   Other Tables, Rules, and Misc. Information Important to the Houseperson.

Rule of thumb: Keep it out of the way when chopping vegetables with a Chinese cleaver.
Slide rule: Nine times out of ten a molded salad unmolded over the sink will slide down the drain.
Carpenter's rule: Time-and-a-half on weekends, double time on holidays.
Long rule: Victoria's, 1837–1901.
Fish scale: Easiest to remove while the fish is wet. Then scrape from tail to head, never vice versa, with a sharp knife.

* The same way a liter is 1⅒ quarts, or a couple of beers, with a dividend for the hostess.

Bathroom scale: Best avoided between Thanksgiving and New Year's.

Old walnut table: 1¼ pounds unshelled = 2 cups chopped.

Metric rule: Just when you think you're getting the hang of it, they bring out the hectares and kelvins and joules.

JUNE 10   It was on this day, 1974 (as recorded in vol. 12, *I Couldn't Stand the Heat So I Stayed Out of the Kitchen*), that Shirley Shimmelfenner spent five hours reducing the sauce in the French manner to pour over the whole chicken she had spent two hours boning in the French manner, which her well-sloshed guests polished off with no manners at all and in eleven minutes flat.

"Well then, says I, what's the use you learning to do right when it's troublesome to do right and aint no trouble to do wrong and the wages is just the same?"   —Huck Finn

JUNE 11   Now bloometh the wild poppy, in meadow and on the heath, and twinkleth too the bright strawberry, in market and strawberry barrel. Today, make a

STRAWBERRY FOOL

which is equal parts of crushed berries and whipped cream mixed together with a little honey. Or just as easy and good, make a

STRAWBERRY NINCOMPOOP

which is bowls of washed strawberries, their stems left on, with raw sugar (light brown will do) and sour cream to dunk them in.

JUNE 12   And still another remarkably effective way to treat a Strawberry!

A SHORTBREAD TART

The crust:
Mix 1 cup flour with 2 tablespoons confectioners' sugar, and with a pastry blender cut in ½ cup butter till it resembles corn

meal. Chill it half an hour, then press into a nine-inch pie pan or tart pan and bake ten minutes at 425°. Cool it.

The filling: Rinse and dry three cups ripe red strawberries, pinch off the stems, and arrange them points up in the pie-crust. Melt a ten-ounce jar of raspberry jelly over low heat and pour it carefully over, to glaze each berry. Chill it. Just before serving sprinkle a few nuts around—almonds, walnuts, pistachios.

JUNE 13   Now the daytime groweth longer and the wickets stickier.

". . . And something else that curdles my disposition is those recipes that don't say whether to cook it covered or not. Mostly you have to use your head, and I thought that was the cookbook writers' job. The way I finally figured it was, if you want it wet, you cover it. You want it drier with thicker sauce, you cook it *un*covered. If you can't make up your mind, split the difference—covered for a while, then take the lid off. On Mondays, Wednesdays, and Fridays I think it's harder to dry something that's too wet. On Tuesdays, Thursdays, and Saturdays I think it's harder to wet something that's too dry, especially since you're now out of sauce. . . ."
—Shirley Shimmelfenner (*Ibid.*)

JUNE 14   "What kind of cake recipe's that?" Joan Rivers said. "Three eggs, and it doesn't even tell you whether to to boil 'em or fry 'em."

". . . And that's only the start of it. Let's say you're rolling along with your Cheese-and-Chokeberry Surprise, till you trip over 'Cover and refrigerate up to twenty-four hours.' Is that the surprise? *Why* do you cover and refrigerate up to twenty-four hours? How long does it take a piece of cheese to buddy up to a chokeberry, for Pete's sake. This was supposed to be for tonight. All right then, wouldn't four hours be better than nothing? And what if you get busy and don't have it till day after tomorrow? What does it do after twenty-four hours, blow up? They never tell you these things."
—Shirley Shimmelfenner,
Crack-up!, vol. 13

JUNE 15   ". . . Regrettably, good cooks—like good painters
—can seldom tell you exactly how they did it. . . ."
—Albert Wooky

Take a piece of mutton and let boil a pretty while, goes an old recipe, which isn't too distant in spirit from "beat it till it *feels* right, then add a dollop of sour cream." It was with an eye to clarifying such culinary smog, as well as other kinds, that Prof. Arlo Crumpacker formulated his handy

TABLE OF EQUIVALENTS

Culinary Scale

Add a (whisper)
   2 whispers = a suggestion
   2 suggestions = a hint
   3 hints = a pinch
   2 pinches = a smidgen
   2½ smidgens = a dab
   3 dabs = a dollop
   2 dollops = a glob

Extent-of-Ignorance Scale

Doesn't know (beans)
   2 beans = from nothing
   2 from nothings = straight up
   2 straight ups = enough to
                roll over
   3 rolls = his arse from his
                elbow

Ease-of-Accomplishment Scale

Easy as (pie)
   2 pies = falling off a log
   2 falls = shooting fish in a tub
   3 shootings = one holler down
                a rain barrel

Worthlessness Scale

Not worth (a hoot)
   2 hoots = a tinker's damn
   2 damns = a plugged nickel
   3 nickels = the gunpowder to
                blow it up
   2 explosions = a fart in a
                windstorm

Certainty Scale

Sure as (shootin')
   2 shootin's = the vine grows round the stump
   3 vines = death & taxes
   2 d & t = fate
   2 fates = the Lord made little green apples

JUNE 16   On this day begins the week of National Old-time Fiddlers Contest & Festival in Weiser, Idaho.

And a good day almost everywhere for fiddling around. But sometimes the urge to do so happens on the way back from the grocery store with a sack containing some frozen things; and the mere thought of them glooming in their puddles can spoil your fun. Herewith, good news:

> ". . . After thawing, frozen foods are no more and probably not much less perishable than they would have been before they were frozen. . . . It is amazing how many women live under the dread illusion that they must rush home like mad from the market."
> —Poppy Cannon

"Contrary to popular belief, frozen foods that have thawed can be refrozen, according to the director of Rutgers University's food science department. Dr. Walter Maclinn states that thawed foods can be refrozen 'as long as they seem edible in appearance and odor.' He explains that manufacturers are against the practice not for health reasons but because they fear that products won't taste as good after refreezing—and sales may suffer as a result."
—*Moneysworth* Magazine, October 13, 1975

JUNE 17   A great many Chinese babies were born on this day in 1922, as well as on almost every day after that date and preceding it; clearly the Lord loves Chinese people as much as He loves poor people.

With all these mouths to feed Chinese home economists through the ages have understandably devoted considerable thought to quantity cookery.

> "She who double recipe without first writing down new proportions invite double trouble."
> —Hu Shih* (circa 550 B.C.)

---

* Hu Shih is sometimes confused with Hao Shih Minh, an earlier Chinese home economist whose recipes were terribly confusing.

JUNE 18   On this dark day for personkind in 1874, Susan B.
               Anthony was fined $100 for illegally voting in a
national election. Commemorate it with a good bowl of

BAIL-BOND BEANS

Cook more French-cut green beans than you can eat tonight till
they are just tender. In a little saucepan heat together

> 2 tablespoons lemon juice
> 2 tablespoons olive oil
> ½ cup sliced black olives
> some garlic salt and oregano

Pour it over the hot green beans and serve them.

JUNE 19   Add last night's leftover Bail-Bond Beans to a green
               salad for tonight. Very good.

JUNE 20   An exceptionally busy day all over. Tennessee cele-
ꙮ 🧍🧍   brates rhododendrons, Denmark celebrates Vikings,
and West Virginia celebrates the day it became the thirty-fifth
state. A good day for Dr. Neitzelgrinder's

5-MINUTE CHILI CHICKEN
*(He admits that the five-minute preparation time depends on how
fast you can cut up aluminum foil; and if someone stole the
kitchen scissors again, it's more like seven.)*

He lines up

> 8 to 10 chicken thighs or drumsticks
> 1 package of Chili Seasoning Mix
> ¼ cup cider vinegar
> some aluminum foil

and then he salts, peppers, and MSG's the chicken. Next, he mixes
the Chili Mix with the vinegar, paints each piece neatly with it, and
wraps each one snugly in a square of aluminum foil, so he won't
have to wash the baking dish later. Then he bakes them at 400° for
forty minutes.

JUNE 21   Now beginneth the sign of CANCER (controlling
🌹 ♋   the Breast and Stomach) that continueth through
July 22, this time being auspicious for
  cooking & freezing good things
  buying new clothes
  manicuring the lawn & the window box
  painting murals in the powder room.
And so the gentle, domestic Moon Child doeth these things, to have
all in readinesse for summer Guests. For summer beginneth now,
unless they changed it to yesterday, as they will sometimes do. The
longest day of the year, and plenty of time to make a bowl of
cheese potatoes that are good with cold meat.

SWISS POTATOES
4 to 6 servings
*(It's best to make more than you need because
they're good fried the next day.)*

1½ big baking potatoes, sliced thin as possible	2 beaten eggs
1 teaspoon salt	1½ cups milk, scalded
1 teaspoon minced dried onion	¼ pound Swiss or Gruyère cheese, grated

Mix it all together in a medium-sized baking dish, sprinkle more
cheese on top, and bake uncovered at 350° for an hour, or 300° for
an hour and fifteen minutes.

JUNE 22   No Problem Too Small! (Some problems too large.)

". . . One morning I found a raw scratch on the
fine old English desk my in-laws gave us for a wedding present. I
knew it was a fine old desk because it said Sheraton on the back, and
Waldo told me the trouble his dad had getting it out of the hotel.
Well, Grandma always said to rub scratches with a cut walnut
meat. So I got some walnuts and tried it. It seemed to work pretty
well, and that really surprised me, because most of those corny old
household hints aren't worth shucks. . . ."

—Shirley Shimmelfenner,
*I'll Tell You Who Threw the
Overalls,* vol. 6

JUNE 23   On this day in 1868, Chistopher Latham Sholes received a patent for the first practical typewriter.

And then writers quit writing those long novels, which seems illogical.

Consider Sir Walter Scott, who died thirty-six years before the typewriter was born. He started out writing naughty ballads like *The Lay of the Last Minstrel* but later mended his ways and started writing extremely long novels (which is why it is called "longhand") in pen-and-ink. Sir Walter would take six pages to say it was raining and another six to say how hard, and once he really got moving he could stretch one sentence from here to Glasgow with enough left over for a kilt.

However, many scholars believe there are sound reasons for the length (long-windedness) of novels before the invention of the typewriter, and for their comparative shortness thereafter. All handwriting being difficult to read, in quantity, authors were understandably reluctant to reread what they had written. Too, they were afraid they would find out how dull it was and feel they should rewrite it. So they would just take it to the publisher, who didn't want to read it either, and just handed it to the printer. Those were the days.

But after the typewriter appeared, writers could see how dull they were getting, and stop sooner.

Adhesive tape came along several years after the typewriter did, and it is a good thing it did, because it is such a help in cleaning striker keys. Press a piece on, then peel it off, and most of the impacted ink-and-lint will come with it. This improves even the fuzziest prose.

JUNE 24   A Foolish Paragraph!
". . . Pay attention to the cat of the house, for he can tell one not a little about the secrets of its larder. A good cook knows that her skill and the good name of the house are mirrored in the cat's coat and conduct, and that the absence of a cat is always interpreted in a sinister sense. A sleek cat, majestically slow in its movements, which languidly and voluptuously brushes your legs and occasionally, only very occasionally (for cats are naturally well-bred animals, if cynical individualists) stands up by your side to remind you with the velvety pressure of a paddy paw that grouse is

grouse, as much for *felidae* as for human beings, is a sure sign that your hostess has acquired a minor *cordon bleu,* or is quite capable of shaping one. . . ."

—P. Morton Shand

This illustrates a trouble with writers—how a pretty conceit will occur to them, something deft or whimsical or in some other way so appealing that they can't resist embroidering it, a lazy-daisy here and a French knot there. Presently they are so enamored of it that they don't care whether it's so or not. But there it remains for all time, or at least through its dusty life on the final mark-down table—a delightful ornament, a button that doesn't fasten anything.

The fact is, cats and cooks have no real connection, no more than adverbs and aardvarks, or mandolins and peanut butter. Indeed, it is tempting to argue the other way around: the fatter the cat, the worse the cook. I have generally found, myself, that card-carrying cat-lovers feed their cats the best tuna and kidney and chicken and the creamiest cream, with never a thought to what they feed themselves. If an ailurophile invites you to dinner, don't go.

Yet, here again is a generality constructed on the flimsiest of foundations. I know only three devout cat-lovers well enough to know what they cook and eat. The scientific method would demand intimate knowledge of three hundred to three hundred thousand, before any such theory could be formulated, which is a lot of cats and cooks. I am sure Mr. Shand hasn't known that many, any more than I have.

JUNE 25   It was on this very day in 1961 that a sow owned by Aksel Egedee of Denmark threw a litter of thirty-four piglets, though the record doesn't say how far.

On this day too, the mailman cometh with a letter from Rosemary of Yakima, who not only has a twenty-eight-pound cat with athlete's foot and a sinus condition, but also a semi-invalid purple finch and five children. Rosemary stands five foot, one inch tall, when she feels like standing. She used to be five foot nine but her kids picked on her a lot. She also has a neat husband.

". . . Here I am, Mrs. Casual," she writes, "married to Mr. Clean. Come summer he's out there weeding the flower bed with my eyebrow tweezers. Winters, he bleaches our snow. In his spare time he waxes the driveway. What am I doing? Putting the dinner plates down on the floor for the cats to lick. . . .

"Anyway this is a good casserole for times when people straggle in at all hours. You can shut it off and reheat it again till the cows come home or the family does."

ROSEMARY'S GREEN-PEPPER BEEF

1 pound ground beef
1 teaspoon salt
2 tablespoons mustard (plain or horseradish type)
1 medium onion, cut in rings

1 large green pepper, cut in rings
1 clove garlic, minced
1 can Mexican corn
½ cup chili sauce

Mix the first three things. In a large skillet sauté the onion and green pepper rings, not much, just enough to break their spirit. Add the ground beef mixture, mess it about a bit, and cook till browned. Add garlic and corn and simmer covered for fifteen minutes. Add chili sauce and mix lightly, re-cover, and simmer another ten.

JUNE 26   A fine fresh morning to *bake* some BACON.

For this is the Law of the Kitchen,
As old and as true as the sky:
Where bacon's concerned, you should bake it
(Though she who would break it may fry).

And the way of doing it is this: put the bacon on a rack in a shallow pan. Then put the pan in a 400° oven for ten to fifteen minutes.

PLUSES: It needn't be turned at all, or watched much. Also it will bake along with the biscuits and be a little less greasy.

MINUSES: Your oven uses 4,500 watts per hour and your small burner only 1,800, so your electric bill will be higher. When you come right down to it, it's a little like shooting rats with an elephant gun, and maybe frying is better, after all. Then you can skip the biscuits and make some

OLD-FASHIONED HARD-CORE PONE

1 cup white corn meal
½ teaspoon salt
boiling water

Add the salt to the corn meal, then enough boiling water to make a soft dough but not a batter. Use bacon fat to grease a medium skillet, have it hot, and apply the mixture, flattening it into one big thin cake with a spatula. When it is brown on the bottom side, turn it over and keep cooking till it's brown and crisp on the other.

JUNE 27   Now Cherries Are Ripe!
         ". . . A pleasantly sour wild red cherry that my grandfather called bird-cherry (*Prunus pensylvanica*) ripened in Missouri in June. I remember helping to pit them and Granddaddy saying that cherry pits contained a mild poison. There is a temptation to ferment cherries whole for wine, but unless you wish to slowly poison your drinking cohorts, cherries should be pitted before use, he said. I have seen hogs devour cherries by the bucketful and not show discomfort, but then, I can't tell a discomforted hog grunt from a comfortable grunt."
                              —Grace Firth (*Ibid.*)

JUNE 28   ". . . There lives the dearest freshness deep-down
                  things. . . ."
                              —Gerard Manley Hopkins

And appeareth now the frilled green lettuce.

> "Whoever thought up the idea that salad bowls should not be washed should be tossed summarily into a pot of rancid oil."
>   —Craig Claiborne

JUNE SALAD DRESSING

Blend together

1 cup sour cream or Imo	2 teaspoons celery seed
½ teaspoon garlic powder	½ teaspoon salt
2 tablespoons lemon juice	a dash of pepper
1 teaspoon dry mustard	

See that it's smooth, then chill it to serve later with fresh lettuce.

". . . Sometimes I'll pick nasturtium seeds or use the pretty blue flowers from chives for salads. Geranium leaves are excellent in blackberry jam."

—Emalee Chapman

JUNE 29   On this day in 1976, Edie Grumwalt secretly set over the buttons on all her husband's jackets so that they barely fastened, thus frightening him quite out of his burgeoning potbelly in time for their August vacation.

JUNE 30   ". . . What are you to do if your conscience is clear and your liver in order and the sun is shining?"

—"Elizabeth"

July

bringeth hot Weather & Hang-ups; considereth the Wayward Self as well as divers strange green-growing Objects; giveth also the easy Rules for

> *short rich Firecrackers*
> *the amazing Soccatumi Cake*
> *18 little-known Vegetables*
> *a most excellent Fruit Leather*

and still other memorable Delicacies!

I moved to the country
And grew a big tomato,
O, willy waly, willy waly.
I moved to the country
And grew a big tomato,
O, willy waly, wily waly O.

    I moved to the city
    and met a big tomato,
    O, willy waly, willy waly.
    I moved to the city
    And met a big tomato,
    O, willy waly, willy waly O!

JULY 1   NOW COMETH FIERCE JULY to breathe red upon
           the Back of the Necke & green upon the Vegetable
Patch. Now sweateth the Judge in his Gowne as the Laborer in his
Levi's & the Secretary at her Bus Stoppe, while the reluctant Cook
steameth like unto the fresh lytle garden Peas in her Pot.

Now the apartment Aspidistra drowneth through excess Zeal &
Water, as the high hot Sunne doth burn Grass & melt Macadam,
driving all to the Seashore for Picnicks & Fireworks; and little Children's Eyes do widen at these Wonders more wonderful than Telstar
or Moonwalk. Yet even at the Beach there be problems, as the harried Houseperson shoveleth away the Detritus of the Picnick before
him.

And there be Bugges.

JULY 2   A Time to Cover the Deviled Eggs and the Ankles!

Now, it is written that in the early 1500's, insects so
troubled Pope Clement VII that he commissioned Benvenuto Cel-
lini to make him a papal cursing bell, marvelously crafted of solid
silver, exquisitely chased with flies, gnats, mosquitoes, and other
sworn enemies of the drowsy season,

> So when they zeroed in, that hungry horde
> Of uninvited bugs to share his board
> (The microscopic fleas, the bees that sting,
> The tiny flies that bite like anything),
> Though hot and itchy grew the papal choler,
> Unseemly 'twas for popes to scratch and holler.

> And so he'd swing the trusty Cursing Bell
> To damn them each and all to bloody hell
> . . . A fairly futile gesture, probably,
> Though—grant it—godlier than DDT.

Certainly many bug preventatives have been tried, including
heavy black eye make-up in Cleopatra's time. They hoped it would
scare the bugs away, but it didn't, much to the surprise of the folk

who tried it, and this is probably the origin of the word "bug-eyed." Fringed hats have been hopefully worn too, but many bugs like to swing on the fringe.

What Is Known About Repelling Insects, Which Isn't Much:

1. Wear light colors. (Bugs prefer dark colors.)

2. Don't sweat, or else carry a fan to dry it off. (Bugs prefer moist surfaces to sit on.)

3. Don't use perfume. (Some bugs love it, and, in any case, it cancels the effect of any bug repellent you use.)

4. Ditto suntan lotions. (The chemical mix will probably add up to zero.)

5. If you use a chemical repellent, use it all over, not just in spots; any place uncovered will get bitten.

6. Be born a girl and stay that way. (Bugs find girl babies least inviting.)

"Don't water your lawn or flower beds for at least twenty-four hours before any outdoor party. An hour before the party starts, use a killer spray or light a bug-repellent smoke product in the area."

—Max Gunther

And there be Slugges. A pie tin full of beer will drown them, but it is a bad waste of good beer. And salt will melt them, but it is a sad thing to see. Better take a gallon of water, add a cup of sugar, mix in four 500-mg. vitamin-C tablets, pour it into pie tins, and leave it where the slugs were. They shortly become so healthy they can't stand it, and so they die, but presumably happily.

JULY 3   Now the sun pours tawny hot syrup on the sand, and a good thing, for otherwise everybody at the beach would catch cold.

"The ladies used to wear bathing suits down to the ankles and then they was wearing 'em down to the knees and now they ain't even wearing 'em down to the beach."

—One-Hoss

What to Do About Knock-Knees:

"A correspondent's advice and testimony are as follows: 'I commenced the practice of placing a small book between my knees, and tying a handkerchief tight around my ankles. This I did two or three times a day, increasing the substance at every fresh trial, until I could hold a brick with ease breadth ways. When I first commenced this practice I was as badly knock-kneed as possible; but now I am as straight as anyone. I likewise made it a practice of lying on my back in bed, with my legs crossed and my knees fixed tightly together. This, I believe, did me a great deal of good."
                                —From Mrs. Beeton's *All About Everything,* circa 1869

JULY 4   Today, also, the nation celebrates the birthday of Calvin Coolidge (in 1872), the thirtieth President of the United States. Commemorate it with a simple, shrewd, honest, and trouble-free picnic. Or, as they liked to put it then, Keep your cool with Coolidge.

CALVIN COOLIDGE PICNIC

Firecrackers
Baked Fried Chicken
Crumpacker's Cucumber Coleslaw   Whole Fruit
Potato Chips or French Bread
Soccatumi Cake
Beer or Iced Tea Punch

FIRECRACKERS

½ cup butter   several drops of Tabasco
¼ pound sharp Cheddar, grated   1 cup flour
¾ teaspoon salt   1¼ cups Rice Krispies
½ teaspoon red pepper

Cream the butter with the cheese, add the seasonings, then the flour and cereal. Shape into marble-size balls on a lightly greased sheet, flatten with a fork, and bake at 350° about twelve minutes. These are crisp, short, and hot. To cool them off, omit the Tabasco.

BETTY'S GOOD
BAKED FRIED CHICKEN

Sprinkle some chicken parts with garlic salt. Coat them with mayonnaise, roll them in Ritz-cracker crumbs, and spread them out on a baking sheet. Bake them at 300° for as long as it takes the New Ashmolean Marching Society followed by the Tri-County All-Girl Brass Band to get from Twenty-second & Main Street down to the Town Square, or, say, an hour and a half, though another half hour won't do a bit of harm.

CRUMPACKER'S CUCUMBER COLESLAW

(Coleslaw is to the vegetable compartment as meat loaf is to the whole refrigerator, according to Crumpacker's Coleslaw Equation, or 18th Law. Any raw vegetable sliced fine can go into it—radishes, turnips, zucchini, carrot. . . . This is a good basic rule.)

Shred a head of cabbage fine, then mix in two cups of chopped cucumbers and ¼ cup sliced green onions. Chill it while you mix the dressing:

2 eggs	1 tablespoon sugar
½ cup vinegar	2 teaspoons dry mustard
1 tablespoon salt	¼ teaspoon white pepper

Cook this till it's thick, and cool it. Then add 2 cups of SOUR CREAM, mix it, and keep it cold till you eventually put the coleslaw together. Add as much as you like to the shredded vegetables, then keep the rest handy for potato salad sometime later. Or for more coleslaw.

THE AMAZING SOCCATUMI CAKE

(Invariably rich, moist, and delicious. Actually, Soccatumi is the name of the Indian princess who often made it for the larger tribal functions. "Wow! Soccatumi!" the braves would yell as they waited for a piece, and a passing anthropologist thought it was the name of the cake.)

1 box yellow cake mix	4 eggs—add them one at a time,
½ cup sugar	unbeaten
¾ cup melted butter *or* Buttery- Flavored Wesson Oil	1 cup sour cream

Mix it all together with a big spoon, then beat it for five minutes with an electric beater. Pour it into a Bundt pan or angel-cake tube

148

pan. Bake it for an hour at 350°. Doesn't need frosting. Good all alone. Or with somebody else. Or with ice cream.

ICED TEA PUNCH

> 1 rounded tablespoon Instant Lemon Tea
> ½ cup concentrated Hawaiian Punch
> 2 cups cold water
> Plenty of ice

This serves 4 . . . multiply it as you like.

JULY 5   The Dog Days begin now, for dogs and everyone,
As Sirius, the Dog Star, rises with the Sun.
Now stare in mild paralysis at all the chores to do.
Plants wilt; ice melts; resolve does, too.

A Day to Ponder the Wayward Self.

"I am always saying to myself, *Look at you, and after a lifetime of trying.*"
—Florida Scott-Maxwell, at age 82

I am forever finding myself hung up on certain jobs—a particular letter that must be written, an especially miscellaneous cupboard to sort—all the things I know I ought to do and know I'd feel better if I did do. But don't do. Because I have a hang-up.

> HANG-UP: a cumulatively negative reaction to a particular stimulus, resulting in minimum achievement with subsequent significant risk to ego satisfaction and pattern maintenance domesticity-wise.

That would be the psychologist's definition, though it is only double talk for being caught on a barbed-wire fence by the seat of your mental britches so you can't move.

But I have learned at least one thing about managing my pig-headed Id when it gets hung up in this fashion. I have learned not to nag it—that is, not to let my Ego nag it. For then my Id will only dig in its heels. Apparently it hates to be nagged, and I am worse off than before.

149

And so, for me, it is better to assume philosophically that perhaps I am fated to live with the letter unwritten or the closet mussed up; better to give the thing only an occasional flick of the mind. Then I sometimes find, to my surprise, that my Id up and does the job when I least expect it, like a child who will sometimes, unbidden, scour the sink to surprise his mother.

Now that women have been more or less freed by the three c's—cars, can openers, and contraceptives—it seems too bad that the fourth one, Conscience, so often has to butt in.

A Report on Limbo:

Limbo is the suburb on Hell's outer fringes reserved for all those well-meaning but unfortunate souls either born too early or dead too soon to become Christians; people whose main error was timing.

Probably a corner of it is reserved for people whose flowers arrive at the hospital in time to greet the patient coming out, people whose soufflés rise high and ready before the salad greens are located and washed, people who are forever locking the stable door as the horse disappears down the road.

But apparently Limbo isn't a bad place; crowded, perhaps, but comfortable. According to C. S. Lewis, an authority on these matters, ". . . there are grand libraries in Limbo, endless discussions, and no colds. There will be a faint melancholy because you'll all know you missed the bus, but that will be a subject for poetry. The scenery is pleasant though tame. The climate endless autumn."

I think I'm going to like it there.

JULY 6 Thomas More is good and dead
     And hardly a man alive
     Remembers the day he lost his head
     In 1535.

The Hang-up (*continued*):

And then there is another kind of hang-up: the inaction that results from thinking something is harder than it actually is, despite all evidence to the contrary. There are small, stubborn cooking hang-ups.

Diced leftover chicken. Who has chicken left over? I don't, so I bypass recipes that call for it. Down where the truth lies, I know it isn't hard to simmer a couple of pieces of frozen chicken for half an hour with an onion and a celery stalk, then take the meat off the bones. But still . . .

Pastry tube. To me, that's like a GO BACK, YOU ARE GOING THE WRONG WAY sign on a freeway exit. When I come to a pastry tube in a recipe, I start over and make something else.

And just pastry. Some people bypass pastry on principle, even the prepared mixes. This is a good pie for them. It looks like a pie, tastes good, and uses only two apples.

NAKED APPLE PIE

Beat one egg in a middle-size bowl.
Then add

½ cup brown sugar
½ cup white sugar
1 teaspoon vanilla
pinch of salt
½ cup flour sifted with 1 teaspoon baking powder

½ cup chopped walnuts or pecans
2 medium-sized apples—peeled, then coarsely chopped or sliced

Spread it in a greased nine-inch pie plate and bake it half an hour at 350°.

And yet, when you come right down to it, what is so bad about a hang-up? Back in the comfortable old days, before quirks became problems that were supposed to be solved, a hang-up was a crotchet —just part of a person's engaging *is*-ness. I often think of Miss Jenkins, an elderly friend of the family when I was a little girl, whom we usually referred to as Miss Jenkins bless-her-heart.

Miss Jenkins bless-her-heart had a hang-up about keeping things covered. She felt that everything should be decently covered and stay that way. (She wouldn't have cared for Naked Apple Pie.) And, certainly, nearly everything in her house wore its own little sweater or jacket—her telephone, her teapot, her toaster, her terrier. . . .

You can imagine her dismay, then, when she developed a vitamin deficiency, and her doctor considered it advisable to administer the first of six vitamin shots, in the hip.

It was a traumatic moment for Miss Jenkins b-h-h. Weeks went by before she could bring herself to return to the doctor's office. It was a hang-up.

But she managed to live with it, most ingeniously. When she finally reappeared for the second shot, she had scissored a tiny slit in her underwear—approximately where the doctor had used the needle the last time—and neatly buttonhole-stitched it.

These were her going-to-the-doctor bloomers, and they worked just fine.

MISS JENKINS BLESS-HER-HEART'S PINK SALAD

She used to fix a three-ounce package of strawberry Jell-O the way the package said to, and chill it till it was half-thickened. Then she added a cup of unsweetened applesauce and let it chill till it set. She always brought this when she was invited to dinner, if the hostess mentioned turkey or chicken or pork or ham, and actually it was quite all right if you were ready for it.

JULY 7   On this brilliant blue-and-gold day in 1898, with the shiny palms waving like hula girls and the turquoise waves scalloping the shore, Hawaii was annexed to the United States.

Hawaii was first settled by Polynesians. Later, it was somewhat unsettled by Whalers and Sailors, as well as by a good many Missionaries. Many of them acquired pineapple fields and felt that Hawaiian pineapple should be pushed at all times. Indeed, this was the official missionary position.

Therefore, on Annexation Day, all U.S. restaurant owners swore a unanimous vow to call any dish containing pineapple Hawaiian-style, even if the pineapple came from Taiwan or Puerto Rico or Mexico, as it probably did. From that day to this, not one of them has broken his vow.

There are many ways to cook pineapple, but it is still best served fresh, as in a

FRESH PINEAPPLE SALAD (or dessert)
for 4

Quarter a pineapple but don't remove the leaves. With a sharp knife, remove the flesh and cube it—then put it back in the shell mixed with a few strawberries, banana slices, or whatever fruit you have. A squirt of lime juice never hurts, and it will keep the bananas, if any, from turning brown.

JULY 8   Quite probably muggy and unpleasant. A favorable day for a good book, a cool corner, and a cold drink. *SANGRÍA,* anyone?

First, find thyself a quart of ruby wine—
Not kitchen Burgundy, nor yet *too* fine.
A quart of sparkling soda cometh next,
Plus juice of lemons (2), an' be thou vex't
By tartness unrelieved, let sugar try
Its gentle blandishments to mollify
Thy sorely puckered palate—half a cup
Is adequate. So add and stir it up.

Next, oranges! Thou needest but a few—
One half a dozen fat ones will suffice.
Of juice itself, a gen'rous cup will do,
Forgetting not the roundly lucent slice
To charm the thirsty eye (for wise men know
'Tis eye that leads the trusting tongue). And so,
Well armed 'gainst summer *angst,* thou shalt not brood
But, beamish, lift thy ruby glass. *¡Salud!*

JULY 9   Elias Howe was born on this very day back in 1819. He is the one who invented the sewing machine, though he is often confused with Eli Whitney, who invented the cotton gin, which mustn't be confused with GIN-AND-GRAPEFRUIT JUICE, another good July drink. This one has the additional merit of coming with prose directions:

Mix the gin and juice in whatever proportions taste best, and dip the wetted rim of the glass in salt (before you fill it). Now it is called a SALTY DOG and it seems to taste best served in shorts or a bikini.

153

JULY 10   It was on this important day for the art world, in 1834, that Whistler's Mother produced Whistler.

If she could have foreseen that rocker bit coming, she probably would have dropped him on his head. Just think of the rich full life Mrs. Whistler must have enjoyed (for however it was, and even if she didn't enjoy it much, it must have been more interesting than simply sitting in a rocker in a bare room). Yet that is the only way posterity will ever know her. It is a real shame.

JULY 11   Still upset over Mrs. Whistler, let us name a good recipe for her:

MRS. WHISTLER'S ZUCCHINI BOATS

(The general principle here is the simple one of scooping out the innards to improve them, then piling it all back in to bake.)

1 cup chopped onion sautéed in butter till tender
6 medium zucchini
1 tablespoon additional butter
1 tablespoon flour
1 teaspoon instant chicken broth dissolved in ¼ cup hot water

¼ cup light cream
¼ cup bread crumbs
2 tablespoons grated Parmesan cheese
⅛ teaspoon pepper

While the chopped onion bubbles gently in the skillet, make boats out of zucchini: slice off the ends and cut a long vertical slice off each, a third of the way down. Simmer both tops and bottoms in salted water no more than ten minutes, scoop out the meat from both, and throw away the tops. Chop it, dry it a bit with a towel, and add it to the skillet.

Now make a white sauce: melt the one tablespoon butter in a small saucepan, stir in the flour, cook till bubbly, then add the chicken broth and cream. Stir till medium thick, then put in the skillet along with the bread crumbs, cheese, and pepper. Simmer five minutes, then pile it into the zucchini shells, put them in a greased pan, top with more Parmesan, and bake at 450° for fifteen minutes. Serve with a lemon wedge.

JULY 12   On this date, Dr. Emmett Neitzelgrinder throws his Annual Hand-wrestling & Pinochle Party, at which he invariably serves the doubled bean recipe of his that is on page 62.

"Men, cooking, are generally extremists. Stingy or lavish. Speedy or slow. Sloppy—you'd think the hurricane hit the gravy plant—or *neat* (some will even scrub the grout between the tiles just to shame you). As for their cooking, it's either good or terrible, with few in-betweens. The terrible men-cooks develop recipes like Fried Bologna & Rancid Mayonnaise on Charred English Muffin when their wives are away. The good ones do things like Quenelles and Filet en Croûte, but only when and if they feel like it."
—Stella Trowbridge Hinky (*Ibid.*)

"If you can't fry it or toast it, forget it."
—One-Hoss

JULY 13   Now Mars crosses the path of Saturn, and apologizes.
The nights are hot. Perhaps it would be well to freshen the bed, and it isn't hard to do, just as it was done back in the 1700's.

Then, a lady mixed water, wax, and flour together, then added powdered cloves and damask rose water. So do that, and brush it on the mattress ticking with a brush made of pig hair. You "fhall fmell your bed all over ye chamber," it being "both comfortable to ye head and ye ftomach and inoffencive to a woman in child bed."
—Book of Simples (mid-eighteenth century)

JULY 14   Avocados looking good now.

". . . That was the summer I went to visit Mother, and she threw me a (are you ready for this?) Tea Party. So I was lunging around for things to talk about and landed on Avocados, and you should of seen the fur fly. These dolls agreed there was only one way to do Avocados, but they all had a different one way, and I felt like the fellow and his restaurant soup, wished I'd never stirred it up."   —Shirley Shimmelfenner (*Ibid.*)

Dr. Neitzelgrinder prefers his avocado pitted, halved, and its middle filled with catsup. His wife likes a puddle of vinegar-and-oil dressing in hers. Albert Wooky likes a squirt of lime juice and a spatter of salt. One-Hoss fills his with rum, and Edie Grumwalt sets hers on lettuce, fills it with soy sauce, and surrounds it with mandarin oranges while tootling on her Chinese flute. She makes quite a thing of this recipe—even sent it to the newspaper. She named it Avocados Grumwalt.

". . . It is a blurry line between creation and accident, between adaptation and plagiarism, in food as it is in literature. Should Dracula turn transvestite, has the writer created a new horror, or only fouled up an old one? Similarly, with the cook who adds pineapple to a tuna–cashew nut casserole . . ."

—Albert Wooky

JULY 15   On this very day in 1869, margarine was patented by Hippolyte Mege-Mouries, of Paris. This first of the lower-priced spreads was compounded of suet, skim milk, pig's stomach, cow's udder, and bicarbonate of soda.

This is also St. Swithin's Day; and should it rain, it will rain for forty days more. That is because (legend saith) St. Swithin wanted to be buried outdoors, but his devoted followers brought him inside. At this, the spirit of the saint waxed wroth (became intensely annoyed) and made it rain till they moved him back out again.

It would seem to be a sort of reflex action on St. Swithin's part now. Whenever it sprinkles, he is reminded of that uncomfortable day when they were trucking him in and out like an old sofa, and he gets hot under the surplice all over again and makes it rain a lot.

However, I have noticed that on a couple of recent St. Swithin's Days there were showers, but it didn't keep on raining for forty days. It stopped almost immediately, as a matter of fact. Time heals most wounds, and apparently St. Swithin's spirit isn't so wroth any more.

JULY 16   "Now, you take a vegetable . . ."
said Aunt Henry Macadangdang. "If he grew *above* the ground, that's what he's used to—uncovered, warm in the sun. That's the way he likes it and that's the way he wants to be cooked:

uncovered." She examined, critically, the carrot she'd just peeled before she dropped it into the pot. "However; on the other hand," she continued, "if he grew under the ground, he likes his privacy. So cook him covered. That's what *he's* used to."

"He's probably used to worms, too," I said. "Should I throw some in?"

"None of your sass," said Aunt Henry. She doesn't like sass.

"Yes, but what if he's a frozen green bean?" I said. "He grew in the sunshine, but the directions always say 'Cook covered.'"

"Certainly," said Aunt Henry. "He's been living in that dark little box longer than he's been growing, and now he's accustomed to it. So cook him covered."

You've got to get up early in the morning to get ahead of Aunt Henry.

JULY 17   From Stella Trowbridge Hinky's
           Handy Garden Guide to Little-known Vegetables

"Some people would rather they stayed that way. But as more and more amateurs start vegetable gardens, more and more innocent bystanders are the puzzled recipients of the overflow, from kale to Chinese mustard. However, cooking and eating these things saves money; and some of them taste better than you would expect. Even the worst of them taste good to the person who grew them, the way a baby mud toad looks cute to its mother, and so it's really better to take the offensive and grow some yourself."

ANISE-FENNEL.   Sometimes called fennel, sometimes anise, but don't worry about it or cook it either if you don't like licorice. If you do, cook your fennel like celery. It also keeps fleas away from dogs. Plant fennel near kennel.

BEAN SPROUTS.   Fresh, glisteny, crisp. Chill in ice water, dry thoroughly between paper towels, and add to salads.

BLACK RADISHES.   Cook like turnips, if you ever do. Good in stews.

CACTUS LEAVES.   In Mexico they're called *nopales* till they're chopped and then they're *nopalitos*. It's a mean job taking the thorns out. Then after they've cooked ten minutes and been BSPed* they still only taste like green beans.

* Buttered-salted-and-peppered.

157

CARDOONS. A shirttail cousin of the artichoke; looks like a big thistle. Pare the prickles, destring it, treat it like celery.

CELERIAC. A.K.A. Celery Root. Very good with Hollandaise or melted butter. Peel it, chop it small, simmer in chicken bouillon till tender. Drain and add the sauce or butter, or drain and add to salad.

CHAYOTE. A confusing little affair that's also called Mango Squash, Vegetable Pear, or Mirliton. You want them dark if you want them at all, and hard. Wash, cut in quarters, steam till just tender, and BSP.

CHINA PEAS. Pretty, shiny, flat green pods that look like a case of arrested development with those little tiny bumps, but they're not; they're a different sort of pea. Wash, cook in boiling salted water two or three minutes only, and BSP. Good with sautéed mushrooms.

CHINESE BROCCOLI. Don't bother with it unless you're quite hungry. If so, wash it, steam it briefly, and pretend it's spinach.

CHINESE LONG BEANS. Really long: fifteen to eighteen inches. Trim the tips, treat like green beans.

CHINESE MUSTARD. One of Nature's graver blunders. Crumbled cooked bacon helps some.

CHINESE OKRA. Resembles enormous okra; not bad French-fried. Scrape off the brown ridges, wash, slice, steam five minutes, then drain. Dip in beaten egg plus a tablespoon of water, then in cracker crumbs. Pan-fry in butter or oil.

DAIKON. An overgrown Japanese radish. Good raw or thin-sliced in clear soup. Good in sandwiches: lightly salted sliced daikon and buttered homemade bread.

JERUSALEM ARTICHOKES. Scrub and simmer, unpeeled, in salted water about twenty minutes. Peel, cut in pieces, BSP. Or reheat in light cream. Also okay cubed in salads. Keep the peelings out of the garbage disposer or they'll tie it in knots.

LEEKS. Like an oversized green onion (shallot) but with its own taste. Wash, cut in edible-size pieces, simmer covered in a heavy skillet with a chunk of butter and some chicken bouillon. Good with cheese sauce.

SALSIFY. Shouldn't be creamed but often is. Good fried in butter if you like fried oysters. First, wash and simmer it fifteen minutes. Then put gloves on (it stains your fingers) and peel. Cut it in strips, put the fibrous inner cores in the garbage can. Dip strips in flour, pan-fry in butter, BSP.

WATER CHESTNUTS. Chestnutlike bulbs that stay crisp cooked. Wash, peel, slice (or not), and add to stews, salads, chow mein, whatever.

ZUCCHINI. Sauté a little chopped onion in butter. Add sliced zucchini, no water, simmer low for ten minutes. SP. Or alternate salted and peppered layers of it, coarsely grated, with layers of grated yellow cheese, ending with cheese, and bake uncovered, thirty minutes, at 350°. Or see Mrs. Whistler's Zucchini Boats, page 154.

JULY 18   An auspicious day for canceling any scheduled out-
            door camping trips in favor of a healthful vacation in
Akron, East St. Louis, or the General Motors parking lot.

"Fritz W. Went, a botanist at the University of Nevada, said that the fragrant pine, the pungent sage, and other related trees emit 1,000 per cent more pollutants than all man's fires, factories, and vehicles. . . .

"The botanist said that these trees send molecular substances known as terpenes and esters into the air, stimulating a chemical reaction similar to that caused by manmade pollutants. The reaction is 'summer haze' or 'blue haze,' the professor said.

"The terpene, from which turpentine gets its name, comes from pines and other trees, and is 'incredibly toxic,' he added."

—New York *Times*

JULY 19   On this day in 1695, the first matrimonial advertise-
            ment appeared in an English newspaper.
A middle-aged Englishman declared that he would like to "match Himself to some young Gentlewoman that has a fortune of 3000 pound-sterling or thereabouts."

It started something. Thereafter, it wasn't unusual for men to advertise their availability. However, it was unheard of for a lady to do so, and in 1727 when a lively spinster got into the act, advertising for a husband, the outraged citizens of Manchester demanded that an example be made. Forthwith, the Lord Mayor had her committed to a lunatic asylum for four weeks.

In Memoriam

Commemorate we now a gallant lass
  Unloved, unwed, and up till now unsung,
Most foully sentenced by some pompous ass
  To live four weeks the lunatics among.

Yet clear the moral shines, howe'er despotic
  The Mayor was, and loud the civic strife:
To want a husband's purely idiotic,
  But clearly sensible to want a wife.

On this day, too, in 1848, Elizabeth Smith Miller introduced the first pair of bloomers to the First Women's Rights Convention. History doesn't record what she called them. But it wouldn't sound right to put on your Millers, or your Smiths, or even your Lizzies, though that's better. It took Amelia Jenks Bloomer, a bit later, to put the item on the map—additional proof, if any were needed, that much depends on names.

JULY 20   The moon comes up, for thoughtful consideration. It was on this day in 1969 that we landed on it.

A good night to sit outdoors and stare at it . . . wondering if they took the poetry out of the moon by landing there, or whether in the last long analysis they put some in.

JULY 21   The sun also rises, and Ernest Hemingway was born on this day in 1898.

". . . Ernest was just as great an eater as he was a talker. He made a sandwich that I have always liked. Take a good piece of white bread, preferably French or Vienna. Butter the bread on one side quite heavily. Don't use margarine—the only good use for margarine is for children's suppositories. Spread a generous amount of peanut butter over the butter. I like the chunk style best myself. Then spread a heavy layer of chopped raw onions over the peanut butter. This sandwich leaves just nothing to apologize for to anyone. When you are saying your prayers say one for Ernest Hemingway."
                                        —George Leonard Herter

JULY 22   Aunt Henry Macadangdang says she doesn't know what anybody else is doing about the energy crisis, but she's taking lots of naps.

JULY 23   Now beginneth the sign of LEO (controlling the Heart) that extendeth through August 22 and bodeth well for
> restyling the hair
> picking blackberries
> finding new horizons
> getting married.

And strong prideful Leo doeth all these things, and well, though he roareth myghtily if crossed, like unto the finest Lion in the Jungle.

JULY 24   ". . . Fertilization of cucumber flowers by insects is also said to be affected by the moon. When the moon is a new sliver, the bugs rest at night and are vigorous by day. As the nights grow brighter with the waxing moon, fertilizing-type creatures romp all night and are too pooped to pollinate the cucumbers by day. . . ."
> —Grace Firth (*Ibid.*)

When your CUCUMBERS get ahead of you, slice them thin, salt, pepper, and flour them, and fry them in butter.

JULY 25   Tonight try to dream about carrots!
". . . These tasty roots in a dream prophesy an unexpected legacy or money windfall."
> —*The Dreamer's Dictionary*

JULY 26   "FRUIT LEATHER MAY BE MADE AT HOME!"
> (headline)

And then again, it may not; it all depends on whether you have enough fruit and sunshine. People who live under a peach tree in a warm climate can do this:

161

Peel and slice about ten big ripe peaches, or enough to make ten cupfuls. (Or the same quantity of apricots or strawberries.) Put it in a big saucepan with one cup of sugar. Bring it to a boil, stirring till the sugar is dissolved. Then pour it, in several batches, into the blender and purée it.

Now cover baking sheets tautly with plastic wrap. On each, pour some purée and spread it to the depth of about ¼ inch. Dry it all day under the bright, hot sun. (Obviously you'll have to do something to keep the bugs off, but you can't simply lay a piece of cheese-cloth on it, for it would stick. So stretch a piece of cheesecloth, or screening, tautly between two chunks of two-inch-by-four-inch boards placed far enough apart to straddle the cooky sheet.)

After its day in the great outdoors, bring it inside and finish the job in a 150° oven. It's done when the purée can be easily peeled off the plastic.

To store it, roll it up in the plastic, then wrap in more plastic and seal it tightly. At room temperature, it will keep for about a month; in the refrigerator, about 4 months; in the freezer, about a year.

JULY 27   Auspices good for making meat loaf.
            ". . . Meat loaf is one of the few purely creative endeavors left to the American cook. Not only is it creative, it is educational. As she serves it forth, she learns that (a) the family likes leftover poppy-seed noodles in their meat loaf, or (b) the family doesn't; while the family learns that (c) they'd better eat it anyway because (d) that's all they're going to get."
            —Stella Trowbridge Hinky (*Ibid.*)

JULY 28   Social Notes from Mervyn Meadows, Calif.
            "At the Friday Club's monthly Potluck, Mrs. Charles ('Edie') Grumwalt made a big 'hit' with her EASY-CHEESY MEAT LOAF, which 'Edie' confessed she just made up on the spur of the moment! What she did was make her regular meat loaf and then roll it into a rectangle, spread it plentifully with sharp cheese cubes, and roll it up like a jelly roll! Then she baked it in the regular meat-loaf pan at 350° for forty-five minutes. Your correspondent, who had a smidgen, agrees that it was a real 'breakthrough!' "

162

JULY 29   Dear Aloise,

I wonder if everybody knows about putting dry onion-soup mix in meat loaf. I use a package to about 2 pounds of ground meat. It gives a really great flavor and sure beats chopping up a bunch of onions!

I. K.

Dear I. K.,

You're a sweetheart! I tried it and you're right! It's people like you that make the world go 'round! I love you!

Aloise

JULY 30   From Our Science Correspondent:

"When you are wondering how hot it is, and only know it's too hot to go find out, listen for a cricket and count his chirps. If you add thirty-seven to the number of times he chirps in fifteen seconds, it will about equal the temperature. (The hotter it gets, the faster they chirp.)"

JULY 31   It was on this day in 1976, an extremely hot afternoon, that Mumu Harbottle managed to open a childproof container of aspirin tablets in the nick of time to stave off a severe headache. "I'd never in the world have been able to do it," she said later, "without the help of the children."

August

*descendeth like a sigh, to keep July & September from
sticking together; doth bring hammock Games & a
Consideration of the personal Letter & Receipts for
notable Edibles including*

> *Gigi's fish*
> *some remarkably good Toffee*
> *a salad to remember*
> *a swift & excellent ice cream*

and still other good Things

". . . Ideally, the body of a woman should feel like a
hot water bottle filled with Devonshire cream. You feel
like a paper bag crammed with curtain rods. Think of
your muscles one by one. Let them go slack. Relax.
Let the brain go blank. Relax . . ."
                              —Kurt Vonnegut, Jr.

AUGUST 1   NOW IT IS AUGUST, parched season of the Puffball & the Milkweed & the peeling Nose. And in the fayre Rivers (such as there be) swimming is a sweet Exercise, for the Sunne abateth not. Nor doth the Package Tourist slacken his Pace, all ardent to digest 22 Countries in 21 Days, nor even the Turtle, who striveth turtlefully in the International Turtle Creepstakes in Chicago (which is in Illinois). Yet can this be an amiable time for the reluctant Cook and the harassed Houseperson to fall back & regroup & read Novels of beautiful Folk & sinful Doings, or watch from some cool Shelter a Spyder go about her Homespynning, and think long Thoughts.

"The true business of people should be to . . . think about whatever it was they were thinking about before somebody came along and told them they had to earn a living."
—R. Buckminster Fuller

HAMMOCK comes from the Spanish *hamaca,* also from Sears, Roebuck.

AUGUST 2   A Good Day for Hammock Games
Games of 4's, 5's, and 6's

Four roads to skepticism:
    "Best of all, on this one you never feel the slightest bit hungry."

    "I know you folks don't feel like sitting around all night listening to speeches, so I'll make this short."

    "The decrease in administrative confusion will more than offset the slight increase in taxes."

    "Take the Lone Pine exit off 101 past the second red light beyond the Oak Creek turn-off this side of the next overpass and you'll be there in ten minutes."

Five ways to turn me off:

"Dear, I'm not trying to start something. But . . ."

"You're making a value judgment."

"But, Mother, you *said* . . ."

"If you'd read the book, you'd know what's the matter with the movie. Now, in the book . . ."

"May I be honest with you?"

Six ways to get my undivided attention:

"How nice you loo— Wait a minute. Turn around."

"Is that your red car parked across the street? Well . . ."

"Mom, I know you told me never to do it, but this afternoon . . ."

"Does your husband have a redheaded secretary, a real doll?"

"Now, I'm just going to tap that molar ve-e-ery gently with this little mallet, and you tell me if you feel anything."

"Due to changes in our billing procedure, some of our customers have been overcharged. We are pleased to advise . . ."

OR TAKE A MAGAZINE QUIZ TO DETERMINE THE EXTENT OF YOUR MALADJUSTMENT

Q. Do you think you smell as good as most people?

A. Yes.

Q. Are you now or have you ever been a member of an ethnic group?

A. Yes, want to make something of it?

Q. Do you often have feelings of inferiority?

A. Sure, if I compare myself to certain people, but if I compare myself to certain other people I feel pretty good. What a dumb question.

Q. Are you the same girl your husband married?

A. No, and I'll bet he's glad. My temper and my cooking have improved some, and I know how to take a vacuum cleaner apart and get it back together again.

Q. Do you daydream a lot?

A. Yes. Sometimes I daydream that dinner's all ready, and

sometimes I daydream I'm floating in a cool mountain lake at a posh resort, and sometimes I daydream I won the Nobel Prize, and sometimes for a real treat I daydream the kids are back in school.

AUGUST 3   It was on this day in 1893 that the Peary Expedition arrived in Greenland.

This shows how far some people will go to escape the heat. It is too bad that the Admiral didn't get the idea just one year sooner, so that Lizzie Borden could have joined the expedition, for it was precisely on

AUGUST 4,   1892 (Look-Out-Behind-You Day) that Lizzie Borden took an ax and gave her mother forty whacks, and when she saw what she had done, gave her father forty-one. Clearly it was a case of one of those extremely sticky August days when the temper runs short.

This is something to beware of, when the mercury climbs high and stays there. When people get mad, they're apt to say nasty things they mean, as Penelope Gilliatt has pointed out; and sometimes it helps to leave the room and come back with a couple of revitalizing cold drinks.

A TEMPER-SWEETENING MILKSHAKE

Keep small cans of baby-type mashed fruit in the refrigerator. Blend the contents of one with a scoop of ice cream and a little skim milk. A spatter of nutmeg will dress it up.

AUGUST 5   From *A Consideration of Womanual Labor,* by Stella Trowbridge Hinky:

". . . Periodically, then, ask yourself: Do I dust all floors daily and polish them weekly? Do I check all 'busy traffic' areas daily, to sort and put away, and do I give them a thorough cleaning every week? Do I . . ."

It is irresponsible talk like this that gives housekeeping a bad name. These words appear in Stella Hinky's master's thesis, which she wrote before she had a house and a family. But she smartened up fast. Now she dusts when it's dusty enough to make a difference, and she expects people to sort and put away their own things. If they don't, she throws them all into a big barrel at the bottom of the cellar stairs.

AUGUST 6   Now the corn crop is looking good, tassels as high as an elephant's. armpit, and Aunt Henry Maca-dangdang reminds us all that corn-on-the-cob is sweeter and tenderer if there is a little milk in the cooking water. She also admits there is nothing the matter with canned corn, especially in the following recipe, good to know when dinner is cold cuts again.

AUNT HENRY'S CORN-AND-CHEESE

Mix together

½ cup bread cubes
2 cups cream-style corn
3 teaspoons minced onion
¾ cup Cheddar cheese, grated

½ teaspoon salt
2 beaten eggs
½ cup hot milk

Pour it into a greased soufflé dish or baking pan, and put it in a pan of hot water. Bake at 350° for forty-five minutes to an hour or till it's firm.

AUGUST 7   JOHANNA'S DRESSING
but she paused long enough to write down her favorite way to treat salad greens. On humid days, she explained, with energy at one knot per hour gusting to two, dinner is generally cold meat—some kind—and salad. This makes plenty; lasts for weeks.

In a blender, blend

1 cup olive oil
4 tablespoons minced onion
2 tablespoons Parmesan cheese
3 teaspoons salt

1 teaspoon each
   Worcestershire sauce
   dry mustard
   basil
   oregano
   sugar
   pepper

Then add and blend for another thirty seconds

½ cup red wine vinegar
2 tablespoons lemon juice

Keep it cold and count on it.

According to University of Maryland researchers, the spurt speed of a snail is three inches per minute.

As for the previously mentioned cold cuts, they are apt to end up in a sandwich. Johanna finds it speeds up the sandwich-making (and improves the product) when she keeps a pot of her Better Butter ready in the refrigerator.

BETTER BUTTER FOR COLD MEAT SANDWICHES

One-half cup butter creamed with a teaspoon each of minced onion, prepared mustard, horseradish, and a dash of garlic powder. She keeps a pot of it cold.

AUGUST 8   On this warm August day in 1976, Charles ("Chuck") Grumwalt of Mervyn Meadows, California, cleaned from his swimming pool enough long brown hair to make a handsome doormat.

Hair is hard on swimming pools, which are equally hard on hair.

RECEIPT TO THICKEN THE HAIR
AND MAKE IT GROW AGAIN ON A BALD PART

"Take Roots of a Maiden Vine, Roots of Hemp, and Cores of soft Cabbages, of each two handfuls; dry and burn them; afterwards make a lye with the ashes. Before you wash your head with this lye, the part should be rubbed well with Honey, and this method persisted in for three days together." —*Toilet of Flora* (15th century)

AUGUST 9   On this historic day in 1841, the first U.S. train drawn by a steam locomotive chuffed and puffed its way from Albany to Schenectady.

And now returneth the Traveler from far exotic places, full of great food and conversation about it. Invite him to dinner before he has time to get his snapshops developed, and serve him a lovely French fish dish. This one serves four at 109 calories per serving, or possibly 110, depending on the amount of beurre.

GIGI'S FILLETS DE FISH

un lb. de fillets de fish blanc
demi-oignon dans les slices
un quartier lb. des mushrooms (aussi slicé)
un quartier coup de lait (skimmé)
la juice de demi-lemon
un demi tsp. de la sauce du Worcestershire

Maintenant! Puttez les fillets dans un pan greasé, et couvrez les avec les oignons et les mushrooms. Mixer les autres thingés tout ensemble et pourez les sur la fish. Appliez les dots de beurre, aussi du salt et poivre. Bakez le decouvert 15-20 minuits a 400°. Servez votre guest et dites-lui, Fermez la bouche.

AUGUST 10   Bad Smell Report
          ". . . The smell of a house is important always, but it is especially so in warm weather. Take careful note of any flowers in old putrid water, any vegetables rotting in cupboard or refrigerator. Remember that fresh air is a wonderful antidote for stale smells, ashes, smoke. . . ."
                    —Stella Trowbridge Hinkey (*Ibid.*)

"She who wax ash trays do slick cleaning job quicker."
                    —Wun Bum Lung
                    (Chinese sage, 1930–1951)

AUGUST 11   Good Smell Report.
          ". . . The most popular fragrance is the rose, closely followed by lilac and pine. Next in order are lily of the valley and violet, coffee, balsam, and cedar. Sixty-seven per cent of the group studied liked wintergreen, with the young group bringing up the vote for chocolate. Then in close succession come carnation, orange, and vanilla. Among popular resinous scents are

camphor, cedar, balsam, pine, witch hazel, menthol, and turpentine."   —Mary Davis Gillies

It is odd that no one mentioned clover, or bacon broiling, or hot
buttered popcorn. Or the smell of a new car or an old book or a
clean baby.

AUGUST 12   Now the end of the Dog Days brings a promise
              of coolness to come. A day to catch up on corre-
spondence and to consider some hurdles in the way.

    . . . It is discourteous to be too long in replying, and dangerous
too. I have noticed, myself, that I begin to dislike the poor innocent
friend to whom I owe a letter (for how *not* dislike a person who
makes you so uncomfortable?). And the longer I postpone the
writing, the heartier my resentment, to the point that it seems foolish to write a letter to anyone I dislike so much.

    Writing a good letter means summoning up the person you are
with that particular person. Sometimes this is impossible. Then
your letter doesn't sound like you. (It actually does, of course, but
it's a different aspect of your self from the one your friend may
know.)

    If you write someone twice a week, there is much to tell; twice a
year and there is hardly a thing.

    Any mimeo or carbon-copy letter of any kind from anyone at
any time is a bore.

    Finding the right complimentary close can be hard, if you
ponder nuances. *Sincerely* or *Faithfully* shouldn't be necessary,
though if they are, *Insincerely* and *Unfaithfully* should be correct
sometimes too; and to few people can you honestly promise that
you are theirs truly. *Love* is perhaps best, even for business letters.
There are many kinds of love, including a generalized bewildered
affection for one's fellow passengers on this wheeling planet. Moreover, the word might take some of the sting out of those letters
from banks and other large corporate structures that don't know
how to sound friendly even if they want to.

    A letter-writer's address should invariably be on the writing paper
itself as well as the envelope, because many people throw away the
envelope before they answer the letter.

Weather is as lame-brained a topic in a letter as it is in a conversation and it is just as handy.

It is usually more interesting for the letter-reader to hear what the letter-writer thinks or feels (unless the writer is an unusually poor thinker or always sick), but usually it is easier for the letter-writer to write what he did.

People should never apologize for typing letters; only, sometimes, for handwriting them.

It is a waste of good ink to apologize for not having written sooner, unless you were adrift on an Arctic ice floe or locked in a Turkish jail. Most other excuses ring phony as a lead dime. (If this were a love letter, you know you'd have somehow found the opportunity to write it if you'd had to pen it in blood or carve it in soap.) The truth is that until this very minute you didn't want to write the letter quite enough to make time for it. This has nothing to do with affection or even devotion; it is simply the way life is.

One of the big pleasures of rereading old letters is that they don't need answering.

> "You can always tell what you really think of some-
> body, anybody, by considering the first impression you get
> at the first sight of a letter from said party."
> —Lou Boyd

AUGUST 13   It is especially important on this thirteenth day of the month to get out of bed on the right side instead of the left, no matter how many people you have to crawl over. However, either side of the bed is the right side, depending on whether you're lying in it or looking at it, so don't worry about this.

AUGUST 14   *From Our Women's Page:*
Dear Aloise,
You may not believe this, but just for an experiment I planted an unpeeled garlic clove in a pot, and it grew just like chives. Handy!

M. S.

Dear M. S.,

In my book you're the tops! I tried it and it works! If everybody was like you the world would be a better place! I love you!

Aloise

AUGUST 15   On this historic day, the Social Security law was enacted, back in 1935.

And for quite a while now, Bessie Tyler Damm of Wichita Falls has been living on it. The following recipe for toffee is in honor of them both, because Mrs. Damm put herself through Writers' Correspondence School making and selling it. Not once did she ever get a rejection slip for her toffee, and so what with one thing and another, she decided to skip the short stories and stick to candy. She has kindly given permission to include her recipe here.

BESS DAMM TOFFEE

Butter a nine-inch square pan. Pour in, and spread evenly, a cup of chopped nuts—anything but peanuts. (Walnuts are Bessie's personal choice.) Now boil for seven minutes

> 1 cup firmly packed brown sugar
> ¾ cup butter

This should bring it to the hard-ball stage—from 250° to 266° on the candy thermometer. Anyway, that's what you're aiming for. So try it: drop a bit in cold water and see if it forms a hard ball that is still yielding. If so, pour the mixture over the nuts. Now sprinkle some semisweet chocolate bits—as many as you like—on top, and a few more chopped nuts on top of that. Press it all down firmly with a piece of aluminum foil, chill it, and break it in chunks.

AUGUST 16   ". . . My own house runs like clockwork. Sometimes it goes slow, sometimes it goes fast, often it stops altogether—just like clockwork."

—Katharine Whitehorn

AUGUST 17   A Sad Moment!

Waiting for take-off on the air strip, inside the big DC-10, the agile planes dipping and soaring in the distance, the three-year-old next to me was crying. He wanted to go on an airplane. He didn't know he was on one.

AUGUST 18　　A FAST, EASY STROGANOFF TO MAKE WITH CUBE STEAKS!

Start with 1½ pounds of cube steak, cut in one-inch strips. Then you'll need

> 1 medium onion, shredded
> 4 tablespoons butter
> ¼ pound sliced, cleaned mushrooms
> 1 cup beef broth
> 2 tablespoons lemon juice
> 1 cup sour cream

Sauté the onion a little while in 1 tablespoon of butter, till it's golden. Take it out, add another tablespoon and cook the mushrooms in it about five minutes. Flour the steak strips lightly and brown them in the rest of the butter. Put everything else back in the skillet, plus the broth and lemon juice. Simmer fifteen minutes, add the sour cream, heat it through *gently*. Serves six.

AUGUST 19　　Now the provident harvest mouse waits in readiness for the first plump wheat grains; and the provident Houseperson, in the cool of the early morning, rolls scoops of vanilla ice cream in coconut and puts them back in the freezer to serve later with fudge sauce.

AUGUST 20　　A Historic and Marital First!

Mr. and Mrs. A. D. Brandon ("Brandy" & "Ellie") of Los Altos, California, got lost on this day, in 1975, driving to a friend's new home for dinner, the reason being that Mr. Brandon had failed to get explicit directions. Promptly acknowledging his error, however, Mr. Brandon stopped at a public booth to telephone his friend for a verbal map, then later stopped again at a gas station to ascertain the correctness of his approach. The Brandons arrived approximately on time and in the best of spirits.

AUGUST 21　　Things to Do Today:
　　　　　　　Buy a roll of reflector tape to keep in the glove compartment, possibly to paste (some dark night) on the headlight glass. You can't predict when a headlight will burn out, these summer nights, on the long road back from the beach.

AUGUST 22　　It was on this very day in 1974 that Mrs. Ed-
🐾　　　　　　ward Ainsworth of Orinda (Calif.) cooked a salmon in her dishwasher. It was a seven-pounder. She placed it on a cupped sheet of heavy aluminum foil, poured on enough dry white wine to make it feel cherished, added an onion slice and an herb or two, wrapped it *snugly,* then put it through the dishwasher for two cycles. No detergent. She said it was beautifully poached, tender, and delicious . . . a good thing for anyone to know, she added, especially anyone who is faced simultaneously with a small salmon and a busted oven.

AUGUST 23　　Now beginneth the sign of **VIRGO** (controlling
🦁　　　　　　the Bowels) and a good thing too, as it extendeth through September 22, a fine fayre time for
　　　pulling teeth
　　　buying new overalls
　　　taking risks
　　　mowing lawns.
And the conscientious Virgoan doeth all these things, and nicely, though Perfectionism may hone itself to Nit-pickery as the Mercury climbeth.
　　A good time for fishing, and a good time to poach

SOME HANDSOME SALMON STEAKS

Combine in a large skillet

1 cup each water	2 teaspoons salt
white wine vinegar	1 teaspoon peppercorns
orange juice	¼ teaspoon ground allspice
lemon juice	1 teaspoon dried dill weed

Bring it to a boil and simmer ten minutes. In it, put

　　　4 salmon steaks (about ¾ inch thick)

and simmer ten more minutes or till the salmon flakes when tested with a fork. Don't overcook it. Take it off the heat and chill several hours (and it's all right to chill it for twenty-four). Finally, to serve it, take it out of the broth and garnish it with something pretty.

AUGUST 24   Another Cold Supper Day
It is commonly said that hot foods are cooling on a hot day. But this truth is inoperative, so far as the cook is concerned. The idea is to stay out of the kitchen entirely, if that is possible. If it isn't, then it is next best to have everything possible done in the early cool of the day. This Mexican-oriented salad is a hearty summer lunch or supper, with a loaf of good bread and a bottle of beer. It is also fast to fix.

SOUTH-OF-THE-BORDER SALAD
for 6

In the morning, mix and chill

½ cup mayonnaise	1 teaspoon Beau Monde
½ cup chili sauce	several drops Tabasco
1 teaspoon chili powder	1 teaspoon vinegar

Just before supper, put these things in a bowl:

> a medium head of iceberg lettuce, in edible-size pieces
> ½ cup sliced pitted black olives
> 1 cup grated Cheddar cheese
> 1 small purple onion, sliced thin
> seasoned salt and pepper
> a large chunked avocado
> 2 cups crumbled corn chips

Add the dressing, toss, and serve.

AUGUST 25   On this day in 1975, Mumu Harbottle went to see Dr. Neitzelgrinder.
"I want to quit smoking, Doctor," she said, lighting up.
"Then why don't you?" inquired the doctor, with interest.
"Well . . . because everything depends on something else," Mumu said uncomfortably. "I don't want to quit smoking till I've

lost fifteen pounds. And I don't want to start dieting till after my vacation, because it would be silly to diet on my vacation. And I can't take my vacation till my Department Manager takes hers. And she can't take hers till her in-laws go back to Tennessee. And her in-laws can't go back to Tennessee till the plumbers finish re-plumbing their kitchen. And—"

"I see," said Dr. Neitzelgrinder. "You can't quit smoking on account of some Tennessee plumbers you never even met."

"That's right," said Mumu. "I know it sounds silly to you but—"

"No, I understand how it is," said the doctor. "I want to start jogging again, to get rid of this potbelly, but I left my warm-up suit at my son's house in Colorado Springs. Only he's away trouble-shooting now, at the St. Louis plant, because the Chief Engineer is taking some cure in a Swiss clinic and maybe he'll stay another month if his eighteen-year-old daughter decides she wants to get some skiing in. So—"

"So you can't lose your—er—bay window on account of an eighteen-year-old ski buff you never met either," Mumu finished for him.

Dr. Neitzelgrinder nodded. "No man is an island," he said.

"No woman is either," said Mumu.

"All right, I'll tell you what, Mumu," the doctor said. "Why don't we start running our own ball game? I'll go buy another warm-up suit if you'll quit smoking."

"Just like that?" said Mumu.

"Just like that," said the doctor.

And so they did.

Beardsley Ruml had two maxims that he said were sufficient to live by. One was IT TAKES NO LONGER TO DO IT TODAY. The other was IN GOD'S GOOD TIME. These, he said, took care of most situations.

AUGUST 26   An Interesting Old Custom!

"Since Saxon days the people of Cheopham Bivney have brought in the snedge on August 26. Today at dawn the snedgebringers will assemble in the old tithe-barn. Then, led by the Master-Snedger, they will walk on stilts to the Gold Cross in the Market Place, singing the eighth-century huck-song, and wear-ing their gilt cardboard hats.

"The oldest woman in Cheopham Bivney, Mrs. Brass (104) will then read out the scrin-list, after which four young men will haul the snedge from Cow Down to the crossroads. It is a picturesque ceremony, and Professor Towell states in his East Mercian Folk Ceremonies that it probably goes back to the days of Eggfrith the Bald.

"PRODNOSE: But what is the snedge?

"MYSELF: That has never been disclosed."

—J. B. Morton

AUGUST 27   Confucius was born on this day in 551 B.C. And it wasn't long thereafter that Confucius say, *Hostess at pancake breakfast have most ups and downs.* Therefore, hostess who serve Very Slim Buttermilk Pancakes reduce two ways.

VERY SLIM BUTTERMILK PANCAKES

In 1 cup buttermilk, put

> 1 teaspoon each of baking powder
> > baking soda
> > salt

Beat 2 egg yolks and to them add

> 1 tablespoon sugar
> ½ cup flour
> the buttermilk mix you just mixed

Beat the egg whites till stiff, fold them in, and fry the pancakes on a lightly greased skillet.

AUGUST 28   A Little More about Confucius.

Confucius said a great many sound things in his time, and I've always felt that the reason he has lasted so well is that his advice was never exactly advice, but, rather, comments and observations from his undoubtedly vast store of experience. He stated what he considered to be a fact, and you drew your own conclusions. —None of those "If I were *you*" solutions that friends and other amateur sages are always so happy to contribute. (The sticker here is that I am not You, and You are not Me. Neither of us actually knows what weapons, if any, the other has in his arsenal.)

180

For instance. Recently, with only a few hours' warning, I was afflicted with two surprise guests for dinner, bed, and breakfast—a knowledgeable pair who had eaten widely and well in most of the world's gourmet meccas. Naturally concerned about what to stuff them with further, I was pondering the situation aloud with my neighbor, a skilled cook.

"If I were you," she said promptly, "I'd do a butterflied breast of lamb on the barbecue, and then I'd have that marvelous bulgar pilaf with the lemons and pecans—you remember, I gave you the recipe. . . ."

But my neighbor is not me. This is the sort of thing she does naturally. What *I* do, naturally and swiftly in a situation like this, is go to the telephone and make reservations for dinner at a local beanery. There we sit at ease, making snide remarks about the food, in which I join, Allah forgive me, for it is nearly always better than I would have been able to produce on short notice myself.

MS. AESOP'S FABLES (No. 7)

A certain Cat who had been roaming the countryside suddenly remembered an important Catfight he had been anticipating eagerly, back home. He turned around, and—traveling fast—soon came to a broad stream that must be crossed before he could continue his journey.

On the bank sat a friendly Dog, and so the Cat enquired, "When is the next ferry?" The Dog said, "There isn't one till tomorrow. If I were you, I'd just jump in. You can paddle across in no time."

The Cat jumped in, before he remembered he couldn't swim. "Oh, you dirty Dog," thought the Cat as he went down for the third time.

AUGUST 29   Ice Cream Facts

On this very day in 1974, Winston Harbottle, age nine, completed his third tour of all 31 Flavors and said Chocolate-Chip-Peppermint was still the hands-down winner.

Observers report that while the average grownup gets 170 licks from an ice cream cone, the average child gets 300. And yet the average child is right there, bright-eyed, sticky-chinned, and ready for another one while the grownup is still fumbling to pay the man.

EXCELLENT EASY BANANA ICE CREAM

2 cups mashed bananas   1 cup sugar
1½ cups buttermilk   1½ teaspoons vanilla
1 9-ounce container of frozen
     whipped topping

Blend it thoroughly in the blender, pack it in cartons, and freeze it.

"As for tasting other people's ice cream cones, never do it. If it tastes good, you'll wish you had ordered it; if it tastes bad, you'll have had a taste of something that tastes bad."

—L. Rust Hills

AUGUST 30   The best breakfast on a hot August morning is ¼ cup All-Bran sprinkled over a good scoop of vanilla ice cream.

AUGUST 31   August Andante

Regretfully the sun leaves, and dark comes late.
The soft shadows deepen now, along about eight;
And through an open window with the scent of warm clover
Comes the sound of Jane's piano, just a green yard over.

Listen . . . that's a scale now; she crosses hands here,
And now a little tune starts, halting, shy, clear. . . .
Rondo? Memories of Love? Elegy? Romance?
Or possibly a chorus of *The Primrose Dance?*

Summer isn't locusts, and shrill bright heat,
And the hot sun strumming with a harsh gold beat.
It's little cool piano notes, as falteringly sweet
As gentle petals falling
           through a dusky summer twilight
             down a quiet summer street.

September

*toucheth lightly upon Time & the Saving thereof &
the start of new Endeavors; landeth harder on some
lightning Receipts including*

> *Souper Chicken*
> *I Hate To Cookies*
> *4-way Meat Loaf*
> *the fastest fudge sauce*
> *the fastest lemon pie*

and other Swifties there isn't time to mention

". . . For the days grow short
when you reach September. . . ."

SEPTEMBER 1   NOW IT IS SEPTEMBER, Summer's fare-
                well, the brisk time, the gold time. Now
travelers do return to Offices throughout the Lande to tell great
Lyes of their Adventuryings & now the windes begin to knock the
Apples' heades together on the trees & the fallings are gathered for
Pyes. And Mothers do wave Children off to School, these little
ones now being a lump in the Throate that were so recently a pain
in the Necke. And yet this be the lively time, the yeasty time, the
Year in Geare, when all seemeth possible & is, to the reluctant
Cook & the harried Houseperson, given another Two Hours in the
Daye. And so to ferret these out be our worthy Endeavor.

SEPTEMBER 2   People so often talk about killing time but
                never about killing money. Perhaps we are
more reverent about money.

   The big difference between Time and Money is this: you can
save pennies in an old pickle bottle and watch them pile up. But
Time can't be saved that way; the snippets disappear. The capful
of detergent in the tub saves a ten-second swish later on. But where
do the ten seconds go? Out like a candle flame, melting into the
time-space continuum.
   Another example: the instant TV. No thirty seconds to warm up.
But what can you do with thirty seconds besides make instant
mashed potatoes? And this isn't the time for that, it's time to watch
the news.

   Why must we do everything fast? I'll bet it won't be long (I
thought) till they break the four-minute book the way they did the
old, slow, four-minute mile. Then we'll have the 3:58 book to aim
at, then the 3:56 book. . . .
   The idea bothered me, and so I decided to pay a call on our state
councilman in charge of Speedup.
   "Dr. Sonikboom," I said, for it was none other, "I'm sorry to

185

bother such a busy man on a busy Monday. But I'm confused about all this speed."

"Perfectly all right," he said, swallowing a cigar. (He swallows them instead of smoking them because it makes him feel just as bad, and it's faster.) "Nothing scheduled today anyhow, just a little project to provide free skate boards at the Art Museum. Do you realize that people have spent as much as a week in there and still haven't seen everything? On a skate board they can wrap it up in precisely—" he paused impressively—"one hour and forty-eight minutes, allowing a full five-second stop in front of the El Greco."

"Mercy me!" I said.

"Nothing to it," he said modestly. "Just a matter of taking the pleasure out and putting the speed in."

"But what about outdoor walking?" I said. "Some people still like to ramble around and look at the—"

"Clouds, trees, hills, all that stuff," he finished for me, nodding impatiently. "But we're fixing that. Stationary walkers. In the basement."

"Like mechanical bicycles?" I said.

"Right!" He beamed. "Strap yourself in, stand there, move your feet up and down and count the cobwebs! No fun at all! One hour is nine miles!"

"Heavens to Elizabeth!" I said. "But Dr. Sonikboom, people still spend a great deal of time listening to rock bands and opera and symphonies, don't they?"

He frowned. "It's a problem," he said. "The thing is, we still haven't figured out how you can listen faster than somebody plays. But we're programming it," he added confidently. "And we'll get there."

Still, there are two good reasons for doing something fast: because life is crowding in hard, and if the thing isn't done fast it won't be done at all, or because doing it isn't half so rewarding as doing something else.

Therefore: iron fast, or not at all, so you can paint slow. Shop fast, so you can sew slow. Cook fast, so you can study slow or read slow or write slow or take your time organizing an office or decorating a room. Or so you can spend some time with a child before it disappears into an adult.

SEPTEMBER 3   "You take some recipes, be my guest, they've got 14 ingredients before you come to the stuffing. This one has three, so you can remember it at the grocery store at quarter to five, and it tastes darn good."
—Shirley Shimmelfenner,
Breaking the 4-Minute Chicken, vol. 14

SOUPER CHICKEN

Mix
> 1 can undiluted mushroom soup
> 1 can undiluted onion soup
> 1 cup dry white wine

Pour it over two to three pounds of chicken parts, cover and bake at 300° for 2½ hours. Serve it. If you want gravy instead of sauce, thicken the juice with two tablespoons cornstarch or flour mixed in ⅓ cup cold water. And if you want stew, add some little onions and carrot chunks about thirty minutes before it's done. And if you just can't stop, put some refrigerator biscuits on top, about twenty minutes before it's done, and leave the lid off, for a nice Pot Pie.

Or make some

COCACHICKEN

Salt and pepper a flock of chicken parts—two or three pounds—or a whole chicken, cut up. In a skillet, warm ¾ cup catsup, add the chicken, and pour one cup of Coca-Cola over the whole thing. Cover it; cook half an hour. Then uncover it, cook another half hour, and it's done. And don't knock it till you've tried it. Then you can. But fair's fair.

Don't knock bottled barbecue sauce either. There are some good brands around—some smokier, some spicier. Get one you like, to keep handy for

BARBACHICKEN*

Simmer the chicken pieces in a little water for ten minutes, then drain them. Lay them out in a shallow pan, pour some sauce on top, and bake at 350° about forty minutes.

* That same barbecue sauce is good on any leftover roast meat if you've eaten it plain too long. Cut the meat in small chunks and heat them in it.

SEPTEMBER 4   An Auspicious Day for making sandwiches to
              freeze.

What not to put in them: mayonnaise, salad dressing, jam, jelly,
hard-cooked egg whites, lettuce, tomatoes, and carrots.

But to solve the mayonnaise problem you can make a freezable
cooked dressing. Then the sandwiches will be ready to eat when
they thaw.

FREEZABLE DRESSING

Over simmering water, mix well

> 2 tablespoons sugar
> 1 teaspoon salt
> 1 teaspoon prepared mustard
> 1½ tablespoons flour

Then beat an egg in ¾ cup of milk and blend it in. Now stir in
¼ cup of vinegar and keep right on stirring, over the hot water, till
it's thick—about twelve minutes. Blend in one tablespoon butter,
then cool it and refrigerate in a covered jar.

SEPTEMBER 5   Labor Day is a legal holiday on the first Mon-
              day in September, a day of rest and recrea-
tion, a day to bask in. . . .

Wash. Clean house. Cook. Locate everybody's back-to-school
gear. Explain to eight-year-old that the back-to-school dress from
Grandma isn't barfy. Explain that all her friends will be wearing
barfy dresses too. Explain that okay, she's going to wear it even
if it is barfy. Then explain that if she doesn't stop yowling you'll
give her something to yowl about. Then fish eight-year-old's patched
cut-offs out of wastebasket, barf, wash cut-offs, add additional vital
patch, and figure out something to tell Grandma.

SEPTEMBER 6   Look, Jane! Look, Jane, look!
              Look at the school bus! The school bus is
                coming!
              The school bus is coming to pick up the
                children.

See?
See, Jane? Did you see the school bus?
The school bus came and picked up the children!
Jump, Jane! Holler, Jane!
Jump high and holler!

SEPTEMBER 7   A good day to make

I HATE TO COOKIES*

(*Not a great cooky but a good cooky; a cheap cooky, a fast cooky, an easy cooky. No creaming, sifting, rolling out, cutting out, or pan-greasing.*)

Melt

    ½ cup butter (not margarine)

In it, stir

    1 cup brown sugar
    2 cups quick-cooking rolled oats
    ½ teaspoon baking powder
    1 teaspoon vanilla

Mix it, press it into a nine-by-fifteen-inch pan with a rim (a little bigger wouldn't hurt) and bake at 400° for ten to twelve minutes. It will still be bubbling when you take it out. When it's barely cool, cut in squares.

SEPTEMBER 8   The 4-way Meat Loaf, or
YOUR BASIC MEAT MIX
(from Hinky's book of the same name)

"Face it. The fastest food is raw food. Next comes the quick chop, steak, cutlet. Next, the Meat Mix, frozen in small balls to thaw fast and use half a dozen ways. In fact, the family can eat meat loaf most of the time and never know it."

Buy

    1 pound bulk sausage
    3 pounds hamburger

preferably on sale, but if it isn't, buy it anyway. (People who hate

* Registered.

to cook hate to shop, so bargains are a matter of luck.) Now add

½ cup milk
4 eggs
4 slices bread, crumbled
4 tablespoons parsley
2 tablespoons Worcestershire
sauce

1 cup minced onion
Salt, pepper, and garlic salt; or
dry mustard, celery salt, marjoram, thyme, or a bit of each

That's the MIX. Put ¼ of it in a meat-loaf pan and bake at 350° about fifty minutes. Make the rest into one-inch meatballs and divide them into three separate packages, about equal size, to freeze.

Second week: STUFFED PEPPERS. Remove tops and seeds from four green peppers, simmer them five minutes, then stuff them with the frozen meatballs right out of the freezer. Pour something wet over them—cheese sauce, tomato sauce, whathaveyou—and bake at 350° forty-five minutes.

Third week: JUST PLAIN MEATBALLS. Take out another package, flour the meatballs frozen, and brown them in a skillet. Put them in a casserole dish. Make gravy out of the pan drippings (or if you prefer a gravy mix, use that). Either way, add to it a half-cup of sour cream, pour it over the meatballs, and bake them covered at 350° for an hour.

Fourth week: STUFFED CABBAGE. Buy a small can of cream sauce or make a cupful, using 1½ tablespoons flour, 1½ tablespoons butter, and one cup milk. Now chop a small head of cabbage coarsely, cook it in boiling water five minutes, and drain it. Grease a big casserole dish. On the bottom put a chopped raw tomato. Next, half the drained cabbage. Next, a package of frozen meatballs. Now add the rest of the cabbage, dot with butter, cover and bake for an hour at 350°. *Before serving,* heat the cream sauce, add a pinch of nutmeg, and pour it over.

. . . Now, actually you needn't hold this down to four pounds of mix. If you have enough muscle and a big-enough bowl, make more. Those meatballs could show up with pastry wrapped around them, for a variation of Cornish Pasties. Or layered with pasta, mozzarella, and tomato sauce for free-style lasagna. . . .

SEPTEMBER 9   A day that augurs well for starting a project.

The civil war within: When I know beyond a doubt that I want to do a specific thing—will be happier, healthier, nicer, or richer for doing it—why then don't I do it? What absurd mental isometrics keep me immobilized? It is one-half the brain pitted against the other: the will and the won't. . . . A person divided against herself cannot stand, she sits.

SEPTEMBER 10   A Common Complaint!

My brain is not a satisfactory one. If I had a car like my brain, I would take it back and tell them they gave me a lemon. It is hard to budge out of neutral and it screams like an eagle when I shift gears into second, and the windows are usually stuck, only halfway open.

SEPTEMBER 11   A Comforting Reflection!

And yet, I suppose everyone knows more than he thinks he does. There are so many kinds of knowledge.

Think of all the things you know but don't believe! A table is only a mass of nervous electrons. Greenland is icy and Iceland is green. You are not as bright as you feel, after the second Martini.

And the things you believe but don't know. One kind of toothpaste is better than another kind. Cold showers are good for you. A male calico cat is worth a thousand dollars.

And the things you know but forget when possible. You probably look your age. If you try to get all your suntan in one weekend, you'll be as sorry as you were the last time.

And the things you take on consignment till they begin to look too foolish. The fattest people are the jolliest people. Everybody loves a good listener. You can trust anyone who looks you straight in the eye. The best things in life are free. . . .

SEPTEMBER 12   A Wise Observation!

" . . . Every act of conscious learning requires the willingness to suffer an injury to one's self-esteem. That is why young children, before they are aware of their own self-importance, learn so easily; and why older persons, especially if vain or important, cannot learn at all."

—Thomas Szasz

SEPTEMBER 13   A Valuable Word!

The *clochandichter,* in northeast Scotland, is the last rock that can be put on a heap of rocks before the whole lot collapses. —Not the rock that makes it collapse, mind you. (That would be the straw that broke the camel's back.) The clochandichter is the one just before it.

On a crisp September morning exactly a year ago, in Cleveland, Ohio, a certain Mrs. Andreyev (Frisia) Taloff woke to find the house unusually chilly. After investigating, Andreyev reported that they were out of oil. Frisia said she would telephone the fuel company as soon as their Customer Department opened.

Next, she washed a few dishes for the family's breakfast (the dishwasher was full of dirty ones because last night the dishwasher-detergent box had proved to be empty), then got Andreyev off to work and the children aimed for school, seven-year-old Boris having spilled his cocoa only once, to the considerable amusement of thirteen-year-old Natasha as she watched her mother clean it up.

From 9 to 9:30 at the telephone, Frisia got a busy signal from the fuel company. So she decided to stop and place the order, since their office was on the way to her own at the City Vocational Guidance Center, where she worked from 10 to 4.

Dressing, she discovered that Natasha had worn her mother's only pair of runless pantyhose to school, and so Frisia wore the pantsuit she had intended to drop at the dry cleaner's.

En route to the office, she had a flat tire that she replaced, herself, at the corner of Third and Taft, with her spare, which the garage told her, when she eventually limped in, was worse than the flat. So, $38.88 later, she arrived at the office, just in time to miss the department-head meeting during which she had been appointed Building Collector for the Heart Fund.

All afternoon it rained. At 4:30, returning to her car, she found she had left its windows open. At 5:15, arriving home after a stop at the supermarket, she found that Boris had a runny nose and that Natasha had thoughtfully run the dishwasher but used ordinary detergent, so the suds were now up to the kitchen sill.

By the time Frisia had wiped and dried the floor, the counters, and the dishes, Andreyev was home. She opened a can of corned beef hash.

Natasha wanted to know why they never got anything but corned beef hash around here. Frisia responded that sometimes they did, but not tonight.

Boris wanted to know if he had to eat a yucky poached egg on his. Frisia said, "Yes."

Then Andreyev said, over his shoulder as he twiddled the TV dial, "Say, it's still cold in here. Did you get the fuel company?"

Frisia said, "No."

Andreyev opened his mouth to say something else. But he happened to be looking at Frisia at the time. He closed his mouth again, promptly. He didn't say anything else. Fortunately, Andreyev recognized a clochandichter when he encountered one.

SEPTEMBER 14   "Woman's place is in the home, and that's where she should go just as soon as she gets done at the office."   —Anonymous

SEPTEMBER 15   On this day, 1847, the first ten-hour work-day law became effective in New Hampshire.

On this day, 1975, Artemus Thorncrotch, Economist, calculated that at his salary of $25,000 per year, one hour of his time was worth precisely $12.81.

Calculating in similar fashion for his wife, Alicia, who also holds a degree in Economics and pounds a typewriter down the hall for $10,000 per year, he informed her that one hour of hers was worth $5.12.

"Therefore," he said pleasantly, "when we spend an hour together, you should pay me the difference, precisely $7.69, or I'm wasting my time."

"You're wasting your time right now," she said, with equal cordiality. "Any decent call girl is $25 an hour—shall we say $3,600 a year? And the lousiest cook, which I am not, gets $600 per month —that's $7,200—plus minimum housework plus laundry, say $300 a month or another $3,600, plus weekend baby-sitter and chauffeur, that's another $6,000. So pay me my $20,400 annual back wages for fourteen years and maybe we can do business."

A smart girl, that Alicia. You can't say her degree in Economics went for nothing. Almost nothing, though.

SEPTEMBER 16   On this day in 1620, the *Mayflower* set sail from Southampton for Provincetown; and only twenty-eight years later the Pilgrims hanged their first witch, an occasion to commemorate with a

magic fast

RICH WITCH CAKE

(The magic is in the way the fruit cocktail disappears.
No one would ever guess.)

In a bowl, mix

1 cup white sugar	1 egg
1 cup all-purpose flour	1 small can (15-ounce) fruit
1 teaspoon soda	cocktail
½ teaspoon salt	

Pour it into a greased pan, about nine by eleven inches or there-abouts. Sprinkle the top with one cup brown sugar and ½ cup chopped nuts, mixed together, and bake at 350° for an hour. If you like, serve with ice cream or whipped cream. But think twice.

"To gild refined gold, to paint the lily,
To throw a perfume on the violet . . .
Is wasteful and ridiculous excess."
—Shakespeare

SEPTEMBER 17   A rare picturesque Phrase!
In the olden days, girls and boys, dolls were different. They didn't walk or talk or have bust measurements and ski outfits. What they had was wax heads and necks firmly attached to thoroughly stuffed stockinette bodies. And in Boston, some decades ago, certain well-reared children were taught to fold their little mitts over their breastbones, when offered another helping they didn't want, and say, "No, thank you. Dolly's wax!"

To dolly's wax a football team, make a

HEARTY BEEF GOULASH
to serve on noodles

(If it's the entire team plus the coach, add more beef, any handy vegetables, and cook more noodles. Or double or triple the whole thing.)

In a deep skillet with a lid, brown two pounds stewing beef in four tablespoons of oil. Remove the meat, and in the same oil sauté for about three minutes—

1 cup each onion, thinly sliced
celery, thinly sliced
green pepper strips
½ teaspoon garlic powder

Now stir in

3 teaspoons paprika
1½ teaspoons salt
½ teaspoon pepper
2 tablespoons tomato paste

1 can bouillon (undiluted)
1 cup thinly sliced carrots
a crumbled bay leaf

Bring the whole works to a boil, then simmer it, covered, about two hours, till the meat is quite tender. Do it hours ahead or the day before. Just before serving time, heat it through, keeping the heat low, and stir in

½ cup sour cream

Serve it on buttered noodles.

SEPTEMBER 18   Now beginneth a nation-wide week of mad revelry yclept *Pickle-Tickle Time,* sponsored by Peter Piper and his pixilated pickle-packing peers.

Beginneth also a

September Harvest of Extra-Simple Fast Recipes, each assembled before you can say *"precipitevolissimevolmente!"* and each one personally selected by Stella Trowbridge Hinky.

VEGETABLES & SALADS

SIMPLE SPINACH: Cook and drain a package of frozen chopped *spinach*. Press out the water. Add a one-ounce package of *cream cheese,* a dash of *garlic salt,* and stir over low heat till hot clear through.

CHEESE CABBAGE: Simmer quartered *cabbage* in a little water till tender. Heat and pour over it a can of undiluted *Campbell's Cheese Soup.*

SIMPLEST CORN CHOWDER: Pour a can of *cream-style corn* into a saucepan, add the same amount of *milk,* and heat, stirring occasionally. Pour into bowls, dot with *butter,* and serve.

CINNAMON YAMS: Open a No. 2½-size can of *yams.* Pour juice into the blender, add chunked yams, one *egg,* one teaspoon *cinnamon.* Blend, pour into a casserole dish, bake uncovered at 350° for forty minutes.

ONION RICE: In a saucepan put two cups of *water,* a tablespoon *oil,* a package of *Lipton Onion Soup Mix.* Bring to a boil, add one cup regular white *rice.* Turn to low, simmer twenty minutes, and don't peek while it cooks.

GOOD SALAD DRESSING: Equal parts *yoghurt* and *mayonnaise.*

GOOD SALAD DRESSING NO. 2: Thin *mayonnaise* with *catsup.*

SIMPLE FROZEN SALAD: Combine one can *whole-berry cranberry sauce* with one cup *sour cream* and one small can *crushed pineapple.* Freeze in oiled refrigerator tray, then cut in squares.

SEPTEMBER 19   Continueth the Hinky Collection, with two-and-three-ingredient recipes for

DESSERTS

FRESH FRUIT M*A*S*H: Leave one quart *vanilla ice cream* in refrigerator till slightly soft. Wash, cull, and/or peel one pint *fresh fruit.* Mash. Blend slightly with a big spoon. Chill in freezer before serving.

SWIFT FUDGE SAUCE: In the top of the double boiler, heat one can *Eagle Brand Condensed Milk,* three tablespoons *water,* three one-ounce squares *bitter chocolate.*

FASTEST LEMON-PIE FILLING: Mix a regular-size can of thawed *lemonade* with one can *Eagle Brand Condensed Milk* and one nine-ounce container of *whipped topping.* (Now it's ready to pour into a crust and chill.)

VANILLA SOUR-CREAM TOPPING: Prepare a small package of *Instant Vanilla Pudding* according to directions, add a cup of *sour cream,* mix, and refrigerate ten minutes. A good dip for fresh fruit.

SHORTBREAD: Mix ½ pound softened *butter* with ½ cup *sugar* and three cups of *flour.* Mix thoroughly, press into pan of proper size, so the mixture is ¼ inch thick and extends to the edges. Bake at 350° for fifteen minutes, 300° for thirty more.

> ". . . It was the Count de Laplace who discovered a very elegant way of eating strawberries, namely, of squeezing over them the juice of a sweet orange, or apple of the Hesperides."
>
> —Brillat-Savarin

AND ODDS-AND-ENDS

GOOD HEARTY SIDE DISH: Mix cooked *macaroni* with *cottage cheese, poppy seeds,* and *salt* and *pepper* to taste.

ICE CREAM MUFFINS: Mix two cups *self-rising flour* and one pint softened *vanilla ice cream.* Spoon it into greased muffin cups, bake at 425° for twenty to twenty-five minutes. (Add a tablespoon of sugar for a good shortcake base.)

CHEESE SAUCE: Add three ounces grated *sharp yellow cheese* and ½ teaspoon *dry mustard* to a small can of *evaporated milk.* Stir, heat.

TO GO WITH HAM OR TURKEY: Mix a good tablespoon of *Orange Tang* with a can of *applesauce.* Stir well and chill.

SEPTEMBER 20   On this day in 1974, Billie Jean King licked
the petticoats off Bobby Riggs in the Houston Astrodome. Celebrate with a

TRIFLE

". . . Lay mackroons over the bottom of your dish, and pour upon them a glafs of fack; then have ready a cuftard, made pretty ftiff, which lay over them. Make a froth of cream, fugar, wine, and juice of lemon, cover your cuftard over with it, and ftick citron in it."

—From *"The Complete Englifh Cook, or, The
Prudent Housewife,"* published 1746

SEPTEMBER 21   But if you can't decide where to ftick the
citron, make a

1976 TRIFLE

It takes

 1 strawberry jelly roll—about a pound
 2 small packages strawberry Jell-O
 1 cup sherry
 1 package cook-type vanilla pudding (not the kind
 you merely mix)
 whipped cream
 some maraschino cherries

and preferably a transparent bowl to put it in. Line the bottom with the jelly roll, cut in one-inch slices. Make the Jell-O according to directions EXCEPT use only half the water it calls for and make up the difference with sherry. (*Not* cooking sherry, which is salty.) Pour it on the jelly-roll slices and mush it together gently, then put it in the refrigerator to set while you cook the pudding. Pour it on top of the Jell-O and let it set. Before serving, decorate it with the whipped cream and the cherries.

SEPTEMBER 22   Have down-to-earth talk with potted house
plants that have been vacationing outside. Explain that life isn't all beer and skittles, and vacation is about

over, and the first frost is coming. Then move them closer to the house so you'll remember to bring them inside. Or get it over with and do it now.

SEPTEMBER 23   So beginneth the sign of magnetic LIBRA
♎   (controlling the Loins) that extendeth
through October 22 and augureth well for
>   painting a picture
>   writing a novel
>   composing a sonata
>   traveling to far places
>   buying rare fine new clothes.

And the born Libran charmeth all with his talents and warmth, yet keepeth his plans and projects ever to himself.

SEPTEMBER 24   Yet be not too careful at thy toilet.

"It is lucky to put on any article of dress, particularly stockings, inside out: but if you wish the omen to hold good, you must continue to wear the reversed portion of your attire in that condition, till the regular time comes for putting it off—that is, either bedtime or 'cleaning yourself.' If you set it right, you will change your luck."

                                    —R. Chambers

SEPTEMBER 25   And mark with precision the day of the week before cutting thy nails!

Cutting Fingernails:
"Cut 'em on Monday, you cut 'em for health;
Cut 'em on Tuesday, you cut 'em for wealth;
Cut 'em on Wednesday, you cut 'em for news;
Cut 'em on Thursday, a new pair of shoes;
Cut 'em on Friday, you cut 'em for sorrow;
Cut 'em on Saturday, you'll see your true love tomorrow;
Cut 'em on Sunday, and you'll have the devil with you all
    the week."
            —Forby's *Vocabulary of East Anglia*

SEPTEMBER 26 On this day, try Wun Long Chin's
CHOP SUEY
for People Who Don't Like Chinese Food

(Wun Long Chin, former chef at the Pewter Pavilion, was fired recently because his cooking was too Americanized. This isn't surprising, inasmuch as he's never been out of Peoria. However, his Chop Suey has a number of things going for it: kids like it, it freezes well, and it's handy for baby-sitter meals. Also you can make it with leftover turkey. Add some chopped ginger, some Chinese pea pods, some water chestnuts, and more soy sauce, to give it more thrust.)

Brown two cups finely diced fresh pork in three tablespoons salad oil. Add, and cook ten minutes

> 3 cups chopped celery
> 2 cups chopped onion
> 2 tablespoons soy sauce

Now dissolve two bouillon cubes in a cup of boiling water. Add it to the pork. Mix another tablespoon of soy sauce with three tablespoons cornstarch, one tablespoon molasses, and ½ cup water, and add this to the pork too. Finally, stir in a one-pound can of bean sprouts and a can of mushrooms, and stir till it's thick. Cook it another five minutes if it's to be served at once. If it's to be frozen, freeze it.

SEPTEMBER 27 Thirty days hath September,
Month of paler, cooler suns
(And if it didn't, who'd remember
The totals for the other ones?)

SEPTEMBER 28 "The old earth . . . is nearly half a degree
cooler than she was 30 years ago."
—*The Old Farmer's Almanac,* 1970

Helpful Healthful Facts!

COFFEE & TEA

". . . Coffee may be used with benefit by laboring men; but black tea is the best drink for sedentary persons. . . ."

SMOKING

"In consumption, catarrh, and nervous exaltation of the system, moderate smoking is always beneficial."
—*Frank Leslie's Illustrated*
Family Almanac, 1872

SEPTEMBER 29   This is the anniversary of the day Louise Riehl married Leo Todd, in Paducah, Kentucky, and it was a lovely wedding.

However, Louise, always active in the Women's Movement, wasn't about to give up her own name. Now Riehl-Todd, with four children, two in diapers, she hasn't yet found a way to lib herself from getting dinner. But she has found the following recipe to be of considerable help, because it is so easy, and the whole family likes it.

"This isn't the greatest-looking casserole in the world, why should I lie to you?" she writes. "But it *tastes* good—good and rich, for some reason. So cover the top with crumbs or cheese. It's really a dependable stand-by, sort of a foundation I can build on when I'm trying to figure out the week's meals."

LOUISE'S ALL-IN-ONE FOUNDATION

Brown 1½ pounds ground beef in a skillet with a little oil. Then mix into it

> 1 can Veg-All, drained
> 1 can chicken-with-rice soup, undiluted

Cover and bake at 325° for forty-five minutes, and if you decide to add the crumbs or cheese, bake it an additional ten minutes with the lid off. Serve it on Chinese noodles.

SEPTEMBER 30   Adam and Eve were banished from the Garden on this day, a long time ago.

And St. Jerome died on this day in A.D. 420. He was the one who removed a thorn from a lion's paw and wrote the Latin version of the Bible.

This is also Botswana Day, a national holiday for people who live in Botswana.

> Thirty days hath September,
> Thirty shining golden beads.
> Thirty days hath September.
> Actually, that's all it needs.

October

toucheth mainly upon Appearances; offereth ways to combat Obligations & presenteth divers Daynties to cook for Companie, including

> *Spinach and Love Apples*
> *a most delicious Carrot Cake*
> *the invariably successful Florentine*
>   *Casserole*
> *a worldly Hot Fruit Dish*

and many more Delicacies too

'Tis meet that we should dream the dream
And wish upon a gentle star
—Should do our earnest best to seem
A trifle couther than we are.

And so we sort the tousled house
Ere Guest descend, and rare the wife
Who hath not said to errant spouse,
Goddammit, use the butter knife.

OCTOBER 1   NOW IT IS RED-GOLD OCTOBER but the
Winde soon shaketh the Trees & wild Hogs grow
fat on harvest Nuts as doth the armchair Footballer. Now sparkleth
the new Season with theatre Openyngs & brave new Clothes all in
the winey Ayre; and kind Hearts & true Lovers lie close but do
ponder, on arising, their Sociall Obligations. For it is known to
both reluctant Cook & harried Houseperson that they who Entertain little will be but little Entertained; and the Holidays draw nigh,
which do take unaccustomed Forethought & Cooking & ardent Attention to Appearances.

> ". . . Everything that was of use, Mrs. Dancey hid
> away. Anything that was of no use to anybody, she
> proudly displayed. That was another reason Linnea knew
> she was a lady."
>   —Ardyth Kennelly

> ". . . At long last they had finished the painstaking,
> arduous, and expensive job of re-doing their house. All it
> lacked now was a discerning guest to appreciate how
> much more charmingly, luckily, and richly situated they
> were than he was."
>   —John Crispin

. . . The real reason for not dropping in at the dinner hour is
not (except in the wilderness) that people would feel constrained to
invite you to eat with them. It is because dinner is so personal a
thing, personal as undershirts, hair-curlers, and other comfortable
slovenries, and only distantly related to the way people eat when
you come as an invited guest. Many people hunker over the TV set
while eating, for nearly as many people watch TV and don't admit it
as eat TV dinners and don't admit it. And people read while they
eat, and eat in strange positions and make strange noises, and what
they eat is often strange, too.

205

OCTOBER 2   On this day in 1975, Mumu Harbottle forgot to buy her customary sour cream for the baked potatoes and served them plain with butter and salt. A guest telephoned the following day to say, among other things, that she had forgotten how delicious a comparatively unadorned baked potato can be, and she thanked Mumu for bringing the fact to her attention.

Style is sometimes a happy accident, while planned effects are not always effective. At one time, to hide a bad haircut, I was featuring a white turban—severe, yet not without a certain dash, or so I thought, until a doorman asked with real curiosity, "What happened to your haid?" Then, once I couldn't find any cuff links to wear with a French-cuffed shirt and wore the shirt anyway, open at the wrists. A friend told me later that she thought, *How chic!* and decided to wear her French-cuffed shirts that way too.

With me, other people's houses always get the benefit of the doubt. I see the odd off-color wall and think, *How carefully thought out, how interesting!* I look at my own and think, *Missed again.* . . .

". . . But a golden glow does seem to hang over the houses I visit; bald envy leaves me with a considerable re-entry problem into my own, and a depressing conviction that there's almost no place like home, dammit."   —Katharine Whitehorn

OCTOBER 3   A certain Mr. John S. Thurman did patent the motor-driven vacuum cleaner on this very day in 1899, a day that boded only good for universal personhood, that freed us (when we cleaned a room) from dusty bondage to the broom, from aches and pains and blistered mitts and periodic sneezing fits—that gave, from all of this, surcease, that we might henceforth sweep in peace. All hail!

From Aunt Henry Macadangdang's *Practical Entertaining Manual* that she has been making notes on for forty years:

Sometimes I sit at the dining table where guests will sit and look up (as they may do) at the undersides of things. I find considerable dust this way. Not that I necessarily do anything about it. But I find it.

Candle-lit rooms need less dusting than electric-lit rooms.

Flowers in the powder room get you more points than flowers on the table.

Raw vegetables are easier than hot canapés, and cheaper, because some are usually left over, for salad tomorrow.

When meat is expensive, serve salad as a first course, with plenty of breadsticks.

Always give people a chance to refuse dessert.

Always explain that it would be a crime to camouflage the vegetable's delicate spring taste, when you don't want the bother of making a sauce.

Don't ever admit the recipe came off the box. Say it is from a funny old cookbook that's been in the family forever.

It's really better to invite all the dull people one night and all the bright ones the next. The dull won't know it's dull, because it's always that way.

October is also Eat More Spinach Month. If the taste is sufficiently covered up, it isn't too bad, as is the case with Aunt Henry's two sound approaches to the problem:

1. MACADANGDANG SPINACH MEDLEY
(which provides a starch too)

2 tablespoons butter	4 eggs, slightly beaten
½ cup chopped onion	½ cup milk
1 pound spinach (fresh or frozen and thawed)	2 teaspoons salt
	¼ teaspoon pepper
1 teaspoon garlic powder	1 cup shredded mozzarella
3 cups cooked rice (1 cup raw)	cheese (about 4 ounces)
½ cup grated Parmesan cheese	

Melt the butter, add the chopped onion, and cook till it's tender. Add the spinach, garlic, rice, and Parmesan, and mix it well. Now combine the eggs, milk, and seasonings and stir this into the rice mixture. Turn it into a shallow rectangular baking dish, top it with the mozzarella, and bake at 350° for half an hour.

2. SPINACH AND LOVE APPLES

Get three or four big *tomatoes* and slice them into eight thick chunks. Lay them out in a flat buttered baking dish. Sprinkle with garlic salt. Now cook two packages of frozen spinach and drain it. With it, mix

¼ cup bread or cracker crumbs
⅓ cup chopped green onions
4 tablespoons melted butter
¼ teaspoon salt

⅓ cup grated Parmesan
½ teaspoon garlic powder
½ teaspoon thyme
2 beaten eggs

Spoon this on top of the tomato slices, shape into neat little humps, sprinkle more crumbs and Parmesan on top, and bake at 350° for fifteen minutes.

OCTOBER 4   A good day to celebrate Rutherford Birchard Hayes's birthday, because this is it. A good honest man, and a day for a good honest cake.

HONEST SHEEPWAGON CARROT CAKE
(Remember to start it the day before you want it.)

In a middle-size saucepan put

1⅓ cups sugar
1⅓ cups water
1 cup raisins (or chopped candied fruit if you like)
1 tablespoon butter

2 large carrots, finely grated
1 teaspoon each cinnamon
        cloves
        nutmeg

Simmer it all together for five minutes, then cover and rest it for twelve hours. Why it gets so tired is one of those little mysteries. But do it. Then add

1 cup chopped walnuts
2½ cups sifted flour
2 teaspoons baking powder

½ teaspoon salt
1 teaspoon baking soda

and mix it all up. Bake it in two oiled loaf pans or one tube pan at 275° for two hours. Cool, then wrap it in foil. A good-tasting, rich-looking, moist, sturdy pioneer cake this is, and good for every meal including breakfast.

OCTOBER 5   This is Opening Day of Unicorn-hunting Season.
Should you find one, treat him with utmost gentleness, for the unicorn is shy . . . a magic animal that only a maiden can catch. But you will recognize him instantly by his tail like a lion's and his hind legs like an antelope's. If you are persuasive (and only if he is looking for a place to sit down), he might consent to serve briefly as a center-*cum*-conversation piece, and a stunning one he would be, with his black-and-white-and-red horn growing out of his forehead—perfect for pretzels or doughnuts.

OCTOBER 6   An Unlucky Day. Sufficient unto it are the problems thereof.

". . . Cooking is a fickle and faltering art. Didn't Rembrandt ever ruin a picture? Then why shouldn't I have the right to ruin a dish? . . ."

—Raymond Oliver

". . . knights errant used not to complain of any wound, although their guts did issue out thereof."

—Don Quixote

. . . That night my salad was awfully good, but the sauerbraten tasted like fly spray. Thinking a simple admission of error was in order, I said philosophically, "Well, cooking is full of ups and downs," and my ten-year-old said, "It comes up right after it goes down." I didn't know whether to slit my wrists or hers, so I compromised and brought the dessert. *It* was good. . . .

Thinking about it later, I came to the conclusion that it was vanity, simple vanity, that troubled me. I didn't want my guests to think that this was my idea of something good to eat.

Vanity. Why don't I clean a room as thoroughly for myself as I do for a guest—any guest? You'd think I expected Queen Elizabeth, closely followed by Mrs. America and the Board of Health. Vanity again, vanity and hypocrisy overcoming my natural sloth. . . . And it is the same when I make something myself, say a pillow or a dress. I am torn between a desire to brag about the fact that I made it, and a desire to pass it off as the work of a professional. If I give

209

in to the first urge, as I generally do, then I invariably point to a flaw: "But the zipper puckers a little—see? Right here." Not modesty, but vanity. I am only trying to forestall their saying, "Who in the world laid that one on you?" Or thinking but not saying, *Doesn't she know a sloppy zipper when she sees one?*

"You are ungraceful [and you say] 'Excuse me, pray.' Without that excuse I would not have known there was anything amiss. . . . The only thing bad is the excuse." —Pascal

OCTOBER 7   Now doth the Noise of the Green Bay Belly-whoppers and the Back Bay Mastodons in valiant Battle joyned for fleeting Possession of the Pigskin make loud the Daytimes and yea the Eventides in darkened Livyngrooms throughout the Land.

A DOZEN THINGS A MAN CAN DO WHILE WATCHING FOOTBALL:

1. Isometrics: he can suck in his stomach hard and count to seven while trying strenuously, feet planted on the floor, to push them together without moving them.
2. Shell nuts.
3. String popcorn to freeze for the Christmas tree.
4. Give himself a manicure.
5. Give himself a pedicure.
6. Give you a pedicure.
7. Sort out your sewing box, getting the thread ends in the proper spool slots.
8. Roll newspapers into fireplace logs and fasten them with wire twists.
9. Polish silver.
10. Run in place.
11. Address Christmas cards.
12. Press flowers, just sitting there.

OCTOBER 8   A Heavy Trip!
On this day in 1906, the first permanent-wave machine was patented. It involved a dozen brass curlers weighing 1¾ pounds apiece, it took six hours, and it cost $1,000.

On that day, also, Great-Aunt Emily was probably thinking about her next party.

GREAT-AUNT EMILY'S FRIDAYS

My Great-Aunt Emily lived in a little Kansas town with red brick sidewalks where sage-green moss grew quietly between the bricks. This was a good while ago. I never knew her. But my mother has told me how she kept her social life in good repair.

On the first Friday of every month, dependable as the new moon, Aunt Emily had what she called her At Home, to which she asked perhaps a dozen people. Her habit was to prepare a large pot of beef stew, or Brunswick stew, or beans, or chicken-and-dumplings —with brown bread or biscuits, as the situation demanded, with raw carrot strips and celery her usual vegetables. She would bring out what pickles she had, and fruitcake, from her inexhaustible home-made supply, and that was it.

The big thing wasn't the menu. The big thing was that she always had something ahead to invite people to, a regular monthly occasion, which she could count on for keeping in touch with her old friends and repaying her social debts. The only entertaining she ever did, it was apparently enough. Great-Aunt Emily got around a good deal.

The theory is sound. Systematic entertaining is like a drawer to put things in—everything neat and in its place.

OCTOBER 9   A Reasonable Menu for a Punctual Friday Party

Parmesan-Wine Meatballs
on Noodles or Spaghetti
A Green Salad   Shivering Elizabeth
Breadsticks or Crisp Rolls
Rain-or-Shine Moose (p. 6)

PARMESAN-WINE MEATBALLS
for 10

Mix together

2 pounds ground beef
1 cup soft bread crumbs
1 cup milk
2 eggs, slightly beaten
1 cup grated Parmesan cheese

4 tablespoons dried minced
    onion
1½ teaspoons salt
1½ teaspoons pepper

Shape it into balls, pan-fry them briefly till brown, then take them out of the skillet and make the sauce: Add a little butter to the hot skillet, mix it with ⅓ cup flour, then gradually add

> 2 cups consommé (chicken or beef)
> 1 cup cream, sweet or sour
> juice from 8-ounce can mushrooms
> ½ cup dry white wine

Stir till it thickens but don't let it get too hot. Then put the meatballs back in, add salt and pepper to taste, and the mushrooms. Cover and simmer about twenty minutes.

SHIVERING ELIZABETH

> 1 package orange gelatin
> 2 small cans mandarin oranges
>   (drain but save the juice)
> 2 tablespoons lemon juice, plus enough of the mandarin juice
>   to make a cupful
> 1 pint orange sherbet

Heat the juice, then pour it over the gelatin and stir till the gelatin is dissolved. Take it off the heat, cool it, and watch it—or better yet, set the timer; it firms fast. Maybe ten minutes. When it starts to, add the sherbet and orange sections, stir it, pour it into a well-oiled six-to-eight-cup mold, and put it away in the refrigerator. (A good dressing: mix 1 cup sour cream with ½ cup chopped chutney and juice of half a lemon.)

OCTOBER 10   On this day in 1925, Art Buchwald first saw the light of this bewildering planet. A shrewd analyst and observer of the contemporary scene, founder and defender of the Ban the Peace Movement, he was first to point out that we could build ten hydrogen bombs with what it takes to build ten African universities. Send him a birthday cake. If you're too busy, a card will do nicely.

Also on this day, in 1639, the first U.S. apples were plucked from trees planted in Boston, Massachusetts. The record mentions "ten fair pippins."

212

OCTOBER 11   ". . . It was about this time I learned that
                when it comes to your own cooking, you can't
be a shrieking violet, you've got to *pass* things again.

"My hang-up was, I was bored with whatever I'd cooked by the
time I got it on the table, and anyway it's a pain when people push
things (they say, *Otherwise I'll just have to throw it out,* and you
want to say, *Go ahead*). But sometimes people are actually hungry.
Eating out one night, I never got a second chance at anything and
came home and made a sandwich and thought, *Even if you're not
the greatest cook in the world, there's no point getting a reputation
for being stingy too.*

"So you never know. But, probably, if you cooked it, you can't
judge it, so give it a chance. . . ."

—Shirley Shimmelfenner, *If I'd Known You Were
Coming I'd of Bought Some Cupcakes*
(*Shimmelfenner's Complete Works,* vol. 19)

FLORENTINE CASSEROLE
for 8 to 9
(*An exceptionally good recipe that your scribe hath copied out
for divers folk more times than she hath hairs on her head and
she be in no way bald.*)

6 ounces noodle bows or elbows—doesn't matter so long
    as they're noodles—cooked till barely tender, ac-
    cording to directions
2 to 3 cups spaghetti sauce made from a mix in one of
    those foil packets, using the tomato sauce it calls for
1 pound of ground beef, browned in a little fat, and
    crumbled into the sauce (get the habit of freezing
    ground beef in thin patties instead of a big chunk
    and it thaws fast)
1 package (10 ounces) frozen chopped spinach, thawed
    and well drained
1 cup sour cream
½ cup grated Parmesan cheese

After adding the beef to the sauce, mix it with the noodles. Cool it,
then layer it with the spinach, sour cream, and cheese (noodles,
spinach, sour cream, cheese; noodles, spinach, sour cream, cheese).
Bake thirty minutes at 375°. Freezes fine.

OCTOBER 12   Year older, wind colder, geese drumming, guests coming

". . . Finger bowls are dismal, but hot steamy scented guest towels are a great help after the entree as well as a great nuisance. *For those who care to bother:* have them steaming in the vegetable steamer over water to which you've added a drop of some man's after-shave lotion. Put on your oven mitts, roll the towels neatly, pass them on a tray. *For those who don't:* get some individual wash-and-dry towels, remove them midafternoon from their ugly commercial jackets, and repackage them in plain foil or any foil gift-wrap that suits the decor."

—Stella Trowbridge Hinky (*Ibid.*)

". . . Mrs. Guinea answered my letter and invited me to lunch at her home. That was when I saw my first fingerbowl. The water had a few cherry blossoms floating in it, and I thought it must be some clear sort of Japanese after-dinner soup and ate every bit of it, including the crisp little blossoms. Mrs. Guinea never said anything, and it was only much later, when I told a debutante I knew at college about the dinner, that I learned what I had done."

—Sylvia Plath

One wonders why Mrs. Guinea didn't give her a cue. What was she doing meanwhile with her own finger bowl? Had she dabbled her fingers in it, Sylvia would—presumably—have followed suit. Therefore, we can assume that Mrs. Guinea didn't. Why not? But apparently she didn't drink it either; and one would expect her restraint to have been a hint for Sylvia. After all, if your hostess simply sat and did nothing with *her* bowl of blossom-strewn water, wouldn't you suspect something? And quit drinking yours? Anecdotes like this leave quite a large number of tantalizing questions unanswered.

Once I, too, had a finger-bowl problem, at a dinner in a New York editor's apartment. The maid brought in the finger-bowls, a fact that didn't escape me. But I was talking so busily that when I finally dabbled my fingers, it was in the strawberry parfait, because she had already removed the finger bowls and had brought in the dessert.

OCTOBER 13   Simple Often Means Reassuring

". . . Unfortunately for Phyllis, she was too good a cook and a perfectionist as well. Her dinners were exquisite, talked about, marveled over, but never emulated. —Nor even, for that matter, was she invited back. Uneasy feelings pervaded the women of Fall River, followed by feelings of embarrassment and guilt. Presently they crossed the street when they saw her approaching, and she wondered what she had done wrong."

—John Crispin

"I think food should be uncomplicated and undisguised. A ham is beautiful to behold, but it has no business being decorated to look like a violin."   —Helen Corbitt

"My social instincts are primitive, centering around a fireplace and a pot of chili and beans."   —Adela Rogers St. John

OCTOBER 14   Of course there are ways to avoid cooking entirely.

". . . For a while there, living in town, I had it made. I'd just call up some people and say, 'I'm dying for Chinese food—if you'd come over I'd have a swell excuse to send out for some.' "
—Shirley Shimmelfenner (*Ibid.*)

OCTOBER 15   And there are uncomplicated entrees that frighten no one, including the cook.

YANKEE CASSOULET

(Beans with a French accent; good with caviar, fruit salad, Irish brown bread, and champagne)

2 cups small dried navy beans	2 (8-ounce) cans tomato sauce
2 cups water	1 cup dry white wine
1 teaspoon salt	1 pound bulk sausage
1 onion, chopped	2 cups cubed meat (chicken,
1 teaspoon garlic powder	beef, whatever you have)
½ teaspoon thyme	1 tomato, chopped
2 cups chicken broth	1 cup buttered bread crumbs

Bring the beans, water, and salt to a boil in an electric skillet or a Dutch oven and let them cook fifteen minutes, then stand for an hour. Add the onion, garlic, thyme, and the chicken broth. Cover, simmer for an hour, then add the tomato sauce and the wine. Re-cover it and simmer another hour.

Now brown the sausage and pour off the fat. Add it with the cubed meat and the chopped tomato to the beans. Pour it all into a bean pot or a casserole dish, sprinkle with crumbs and bake, un-covered, at 325° for an hour. If the top looks anemic, brown it under the broiler a minute or three before you bring it to the table.

OCTOBER 16   Ting Ling was born on this day, A.D. 450. A beautiful Chinese belle, she eventually married the Emperor and had to give large parties. It is an honor to present

TING LING'S CHINESE STEW
for 10 or more, and easy to double
(*When her kitchen staff asked her what to top it with, she told them to use their noodles.*)

Put two tablespoons of oil in a big skillet. In it, sauté for five minutes

1 cup chopped onions
1 cup sliced celery
and add
2 pounds crumbled ground beef

When it is brown, add

2 cans undiluted mushroom soup
1 cup uncooked rice
1 can bean sprouts with juice

1 flat can water chestnuts, drained and sliced
4 tablespoons soy sauce
salt and pepper

If you're making this in the morning, stop there and finish it later. If not, pour it into a big casserole dish and bake it covered for thirty minutes at 350°. Then add a package of frozen pea pods, thawed enough to separate, and stir them in. Then top it all with a can of chow mein noodles and bake for another thirty minutes, un-covered, same temperature. A green salad with some mandarin orange slices and cashew nuts added is good with this. Use a plain vinegar-and-oil dressing, three parts oil, one part vinegar. For des-sert, sherbet and cookies.

OCTOBER 17   There has always been a long, long Cocktail
               Hour.

Or reasonably always. Many years ago, when Antony and Cleopatra were living it up in Alexandria with a group of similarly blithe spirits known as "the Inimitable Livers," Cleopatra's cook invited a friend of Plutarch's grandpa to visit him, some night, and see the goings-on in the kitchen. When the friend did, he was goggle-eyed to see eight wild boars roasting whole.

" 'Surely,' he said, 'you have a great number of guests.' The cook laughed at his simplicity, and told him there were not above twelve to sup, but that every dish was to be served up just roasted to a turn, and if anything was but one minute ill-timed, it was spoiled.

" 'And,' said he, 'maybe Antony will sup just now, maybe not this hour, maybe he will call for wine, or begin to talk, and will put it off. So that it is not one but many suppers must be had in readiness, as it is impossible to guess at his hour.' "

—Plutarch's *Lives*

And thus it was that the long, long cocktail hour was allowed for. It was only a matter of time, then, till the cocktail was invented to go with it, and finally—an invention of lesser import to the gaiety of nations—the canapé, hors d'oeuvre, or appetizer, to go with the cocktail.

". . . Don't rush into complicated *hors d'oeuvre*. You have not the right, nor the time. In any case, they only attenuate the voluptuousness of your hunger for the principal dish, so use them with parsimony."

—Edouard de Pomiane

". . . Eventually one must take a stand. Pro-world, anti-nation. Pro-cat, anti-bird. Pro-people, anti-cockroach. Pro-dinner, anti-cocktail dip."

—Albert Wooky

OCTOBER 18   ". . . Well, the way it worked out, I was al-
               ways one thing behind. First it was fondue, a
big gummy lake of it, fondue from here to Whiddy Island. But the minute I got in step, it was quiche, everybody into quiche, and once I got a quiche pan, here came the crêpes. . . ."

—Shirley Shimmelfenner (*Ibid.*)

217

". . . Certainly there are fashions in food as in hem lines and wallpapers. Wise is the reluctant cook who disregards these seasonal breezes and makes only those dependable items that have earned her confidence. . . . However, she would be dim-witted indeed to disregard the obvious merits of the fondue served with cocktails when no dinner is to follow. Serving the ready-made fondue, either frozen or plain-packaged, is so easy it's worth the price of a fondue pot. Long fondue forks, chunked French bread, and that's it."

—Stella Trowbridge Hinky

A Good Canapé to Know About:

THE MINIQUICHE

Make a rich pastry of

> 1 cup butter
> 2 3-ounce packages cream cheese
> 2 cups sifted all-purpose flour

(Beat the butter with the cheese and gradually add the flour.) Chill it. Then form it into big-marble-size balls and press them into very small muffin tins or a tartlet pan. Put a teaspoon of deviled ham in each. Or crumbled bacon.

Mince a middle-sized onion and sauté it in two teaspoons of butter. Add ¼ cup grated cheese (American, Swiss, or Gruyère), mix it up, and spoon a bit of it on top of the ham in those little pastry cups.

Then make an uncooked custard; combine

> 1 large egg (or 2 medium)
> ⅓ cup milk
> ¼ cup *more* grated cheese
> a touch of nutmeg
> a dash of pepper

and spoon it evenly into the cups. Don't put in as much as you think you should; it will bubble up and run over. Now bake them at 450° for 10 minutes, then reduce the temperature and bake another fifteen minutes, till the custard sets and the quiches are golden brown.

Not so classy but easier: THE 4-WAY PIZZA

Get a frozen plain pizza. Score it lightly into four quarters. Put drained chopped clams on one, chopped ripe olives on the next, crumbled sausage on the next, anchovies or sautéed mushrooms on the last. Bake according to directions and serve in squares or slivers.

OCTOBER 19   On this day in 1975, Aunt Henry Macadang-dang found some more notes in the bottom of her embroidery basket.

Parkinson's Law applies to giving a dinner: it always takes as much time as you've got. So set some limits.

When you invite people, find out who doesn't like what. Say, "I want to do this great curried-oyster thing." If they say, "Do you?" think of something else.

Don't take any recipe on faith. There are some hostile recipes in this world.

If there's no time to do both an interesting vegetable and a special dessert, opt for the vegetable.

Big casseroles can fool you on reheating time. The deeper the dish, the longer it takes, so double-check the deep center.

Things go farther if you do the serving.

If you need help clearing the table, ask a man. He'll plunk the plates on the first clear surface and leave. Women hang around being helpful and hiding things.

> ". . . Few things are so annoying as unwanted help in the kitchen. When fools rush in, I tell them—as the great Samuel Johnson remarked on other provocation—'I do not say you should be hanged or drowned for this; but it is very uncivil.' "   —Albert Wooky

OCTOBER 20   Max Beerbohm Day
                An English critic, essayist, and caricaturist,
Max Beerbohm was given to frequent and rueful rumination about

The Host and The Guest. It was he who discovered that people are born basically one or the other, the natural-born guest being—in general—an inferior host, and vice versa.

Mr. B. himself tended toward guesthood, but he was often hard to catch:

". . . If anyone hereafter shall form a collection of the notes written by me in reply to invitations, I am afraid he will gradually suppose me to have been more in request than ever I really was, and to have been also a great invalid and a great traveler."

In spite of everything, it is still Host and Hostess. Why was it never Guest and Guestess? That would be convenient too.

OCTOBER 21   God bless the cook who doesn't ask me how I want my sandwich. (With or without mustard? Lemon-pepper? Mayonnaise?) She may simply bring it out. Unless she is thinking of something really bizarre like cherry marmalade on the sardines, I'll take my chances. One of the great pleasures in being a guest is not making decisions.

OCTOBER 22   ". . . And so we gather together to eat and to make what someone called those mutually reassuring noises known as polite conversation. . . . Strange that we customarily give so much more forethought to the first activity than to the second."   —Albert Wooky

OCTOBER 23   Now beginneth the sign of mysterious SCORPIO (controlling the Secret Parts) that extendeth through November 21, a time boding well for

betting the horses
mating the poodle
catching a mouse
heaping straw on strawberries.

And solitary Scorpio performeth these Duties but not to the Hurt of other Enjoyments, for he hath lusty Humors.

And on this day every year the Swallows leave Capistrano, but there is never much publicity about it.

OCTOBER 24   "Breakfast, an essentially unsociable meal, is
               an appropriate time to choose for disinheriting
one's natural heirs."   —P. Morton Shand

Once upon a time, two friendly couples who lived three hundred miles apart decided to visit each other. And so they both drove 150 miles the first day, to meet at a luxurious Motel Establishment where they had made advance reservations.

There, they talked, played tennis, swam, and talked some more, with no one responsible for host-and-hostessing except the motel management, which provided them with comfortable lodgings and an excellent dinner. (The ladies ordered the sweetbreads, which they never cooked at home because their husbands couldn't stand them, while the gentlemen enjoyed the prime rib.)

The following day, both couples swapped house keys and proceeded to each other's establishments, where they fed the rubber plant and watered the goldfish and enjoyed total privacy, new views, different places to go, as well as the glorious freedom from having to make small talk at unlikely hours.

At the beginning of the third day, they set forth once more, to meet again for lunch and the exchange of house keys, and then they drove back home.

Both couples agreed that it was the most satisfactory visit they had ever had. Each lady averred, as well, that there is nothing like knowing that your friend is going to have the run of your refrigerator for getting the damn thing really cleaned out and shiny.

OCTOBER 25   ". . . It was a chicken breast thing with an-
               chovies and apricots that taught me compli-
cated doesn't necessarily mean good. In fact, the more ingredients something's got, the bigger the chance it's going to be a lemon."
                        —Shirley Shimmelfenner,
                        Eat It Anyhow, vol. XI

"If there is one thing less appealing than another thing—and for the sake of discussion let us assume that there is—I cast my vote for the Steak-Lobster Combination Plate as featured in some of our drearier bistros. As Mencken remarked about vaudeville, some like it and some can stand it while they are drunk. With steak and lobster, I belong to neither category.

"But that is the way of it today. Silver screen, TV or bookshelf, pantry or restaurant, there is something for every warped taste."
—Albert Wooky

Let no man bring together what God hath set asunder.

A GOOD SIMPLE FISH DISH

2 tablespoons butter, melted
1 to 2 pounds sole fillets
salt, pepper
4 green onions, thin-sliced, including some of the green

3 tablespoons minced herbs—parsley, tarragon, chervil
1 cup fresh bread crumbs
⅓ cup dry vermouth

Melt the butter in a baking pan big enough to hold all the fish in a single layer. Then salt and pepper both sides of the fish. Dip them in the butter, both sides. Put the green onions and herbs in the pan, lay the fish out on it, and cover it neatly with the crumbs. Pour the vermouth over it all, dot with some more butter—three tablespoons should do it—and bake uncovered at 375° till the crumbs are brown and the fish cooked—about thirty minutes.

OCTOBER 26   ". . . Certainly it is no trick now to put a special meal together if there is a food market nearby and money in your wallet. Steaks, roasts, and lovely frozen arrangements that might as well be emeralds . . . But doing it out of the pantry is something else. The reluctant cook (who may well have spent the grocery money on something more interesting) will do well to keep handy the ingredients for a couple of easy out-of-the-pantry main dishes that still taste a little special. . . ."
—Stella Trowbridge Hinky

Mumu Harbottle is of the Minced Clam persuasion, *i.e.,* some grocer persuaded her to buy a case of canned clams on sale once (she'll never do *that* again), and she has been paddling her way out of a chowder sea ever since. But when she learned that clams can be nicely combined with pastry, she began to see lights on shore. Though her husband, Jimbo, is a real meat-and-potatoes man, he isn't so apt to ask, "Where's the rest of the dinner?" when he has finished a good wedge of Clam Pie.

JIMBO'S CLAM PIE

pastry for a 2-crust pie
2 eggs
2 7-ounce cans minced clams
¼ teaspoon pepper

½ cup coarse soda-cracker
crumbs
¾ teaspoon salt
¾ cup milk

She lines the pie pan with half the pastry. Then she beats two eggs and (if she remembers) sets aside a tablespoonful to brush the top crust with later. Next, she adds ¾ cup of the clam juice (throws the rest of it out) to the eggs. Then she adds everything else.

She pours it all into the pastry shell, dots it with butter, covers the pie with the rest of the pastry, gashes it, and brushes it with the tablespoonful of egg she saved, if she can find it now. It bakes for forty-five minutes altogether—fifteen minutes at 450° and another half-hour at 350°.

Another good thing to know about is

TUNA PIE
for 6

Roll out enough pastry for a one-crust pie and put it in a nine-inch pie pan. Next, pour two tablespoons oil into a big skillet, and in it put

> 1½ cups sliced carrots
> a large onion, chopped
> ½ teaspoon garlic powder
> ½ teaspoon anchovy paste

Cook it over medium heat about six minutes, and add

> ½ cup tomato-based chili sauce
> (not the Mexican pepper type, that is)
> 1 teaspoon oregano
> ¼ teaspoon pepper

Then drain a can of tomato slices, keep the juice, and into it stir two tablespoons flour. (If no canned tomato slices are around, small sliced fresh tomatoes are fine, but you'll need a half-cup of tomato juice from somewhere.) Anyway. Add the juice-flour mix to the onion-carrot business, cook, and stir till it's thick. Take it off the heat and add two 7-ounce cans of tuna, plus ⅓ cup sliced pimiento-stuffed olives (black will do if that's all you have) and ½ cup Parmesan cheese.

Pour it all into the pie shell, sprinkle with a lot more Parmesan, and bake at 375° about thirty-five minutes. Everything but the baking can be done several hours ahead.

OCTOBER 27   And sometimes the guest stayeth and stayeth and goeth not home.

". . . Whenever he [Steffansson] has visitors, he receives them seated behind a desk on a low platform in his small study. A visitor is placed facing him in an aged, overstuffed chair so saggy that the seat touches the floor. 'The arrangement gives me a feeling of great superiority,' he says. . . ."

—Robert Lewis Taylor

It was Ephraim Tutt who kept a special and subtly uncomfortable chair in his office for nonpaying clients (who always tended to stay too long). The front legs of the chair were an inch shorter than the back legs.

New At-Home Gown for Holiday Hostesses!
Send $10.98 plus $10.98 handling for a plain brown wrapper that fits all sizes, great for entertaining, stamped for embroidery, your choice of messages.

(1309A)   EAT IT & BEAT IT
(1310A)   CHEER UP OR PIPE DOWN
(1311A)   YES I'VE HEARD THAT ONE
(1312A)   GO HOME
(1313)   BED, ANYONE?

Shimmelfenner Products
33 Slippery Elm
Bugtussle, Oklahoma

OCTOBER 28   From the Mervyn Meadows *Sentinel:*
In an exclusive interview with the *Sentinel*'s "Chatterbox" editor, Mrs. Charles ("Edie") Grumwalt said that

she doesn't think it's right to pay back a dinner with a brunch because after all, as she put it, fair's fair, though she admitted she'd certainly done it.

"If you don't run out of booze, you can get by with murder at a brunch," she said. "That's why they're so great—I mean, to give, not to go to."

AN EASY BRUNCH PUNCH

Equal parts champagne and orange juice and plenty of ice.

OCTOBER 29   On this day in 1929, the stock market collapsed.
              On this day in 1740, James Boswell was born and thereafter grew up to report, with unflagging enthusiasm and no electric typewriter to help him, every audible word spoken by the late, great, and vocal Dr. Samuel Johnson, who did on one occasion declare himself as follows:

"Sir, when a man is invited to dinner, he is disappointed if he does not get something good. I advised Mrs. Thrale, who has no card parties at her house, to give sweetmeats, and such good things, in an evening, as are not commonly given, and she would find company enough come to her; for everybody loves to have things which please the palate put in their way, without trouble or preparation."

A most palate-pleasing dessert:

HOT WINTER FRUIT

1 orange and 1 lemon	8-ounce can sliced peaches
2 to 3 tablespoons brown sugar	8-ounce can pitted Bing cherries
8-ounce can apricots	(or plums)
8-ounce can pineapple slices	1 cup sour cream

Grate the orange and lemon rinds into the brown sugar. Cut the orange and lemon pulps into thin slices, removing as much of the white inner skin as you can, and the seeds. Mix these slices with the rest of the fruit and put a layer of it in a baking dish. Sprinkle it with part of the rind-and-sugar business and a spatter of nutmeg. Repeat the layers, then heat it in a 300° oven about half an hour. Top it with the cold sour cream.

OCTOBER 30   A smoky bitter-sweet time,
A ghost and trick-or-treat time,
And night falls soon
With a round orange moon.

". . . I myself am a pretty good operator with the forked twig. . . . Once I had a dowsing twig cut under a waxing moon from an apple-tree growing beside a graveyard. It was super-sensitive! Ignoring the nearby Charles River, it located a pint of bourbon in a friend's hip pocket."

—Harlow Shapley

Now drive thy broomstick in for a lube job and make some candied popcorn for tomorrow's gneighborhood gnomes.

BALDERDASH
(A descendant of old-fashioned crackajack and much improved. Also known as crackatooth if some shells get in by mistake.)

Pop ⅔ cup raw popcorn (or enough to make 2½ quarts). Mix with a cup of nuts—more if you like, any kind. Spread it out in a shallow pan with a rim and put it in a preheated 250° oven to bake slowly while you make the syrup:

> ½ cup butter
> 1 cup brown sugar
> ¼ cup light corn syrup
> ½ teaspoon salt

Combine those over medium heat and stir till the sugar dissolves. Then boil it without stirring till it reaches 248°—the firm-ball stage—on the candy thermometer. That will take about five minutes. Take it off the heat and stir in ½ teaspoon baking soda. Now pour it over the popcorn, stirring gently to coat everything, return it to the oven to bake for forty-five minutes. Stir it every fifteen. After it's cool, store in airtight cans.

OCTOBER 31   A Capital Rejoinder!
Old graveyards would be restful places if only the permanent residents would keep quiet. But, no, they must point their skeletal fingers, forever admonishing.

"Reader, stop and self behold,
Thou'rt made of ye same mould,
And shortly must dissolv'd be,
Make sure of blest eternity."

It was Charles Lamb who commented, "Every dead man must take it upon himself to be lecturing me with his odious truism, that 'Such as he now is I must shortly be.' Not so shortly, friend, perhaps as thou imaginest. In the meantime, I am alive. I move about. I am worth twenty of thee. Know thy betters."

"It is no problem to find someone who can make a good cobalt bomb but it is getting pretty hard to find someone who knows how to make a good jack-o-lantern."

—George and Berthe Herter (*Ibid.*)

November

freezeth the marrow & December's dinner; pondereth a Houseperson's Miscellanie, including the winter Colde & the unwieldy Leftover, & presenteth Receipts for

> some highly practical Chicken & Turkey
>   things
> jellied Moose Nose
> Salome's Molasses Crisps
> a painless ham casserole

and numerous other Daynties!

Although the choice is lavish now
    (They freeze whatever's salable)
I never thaw a Purple Cow;
    I don't think they're available.

NOVEMBER 1 NOW IT IS NOVEMBER with the Seas full roughe as the wild Goose leadeth a tattered Banner of Birdes through the chill Ayre, & the very Countrie doth rattle in a high Winde, for this be the Tyme of the political Oration. And in the Cities do Doormen & Apt. Supers show extra Courtesie from now till December 26, & in rural Places doth the long-tailed Fieldmouse curl up for his Nappe in the Weed patch behind the Shopping Centre. Now it is the nervous Tyme of late Meetings & Dinners postponed, of Bake Sales & Church Bazaars & all such divers Curves thrown the reluctant Cooke & the harried House-person, who do field them as best they can with what Weaponry lieth to hand.

And be it not forgot: that the peanut-butter-on-whole-wheat sandwich with an Orange & a Glass of Milke be an almost nutritionally perfect Meale.

NOVEMBER 2 This is the birthday of Marie (Let-'em-eat-cake) Antoinette, but she never really said that.

This is also Daniel Boone's birthday.

And on this day in 1976, Shirley Shimmelfenner came down off the mountain and delivered her Ten Freezer Commandments, en route to the airport and Kankakee, first stop on her preholiday lecture tour.

"Sure, it's easier to get up in the morning when your dinner's in the freezer, but you better be sure it's something you like and the family likes," said Ms. Shimmelfenner, looking great in her mackinaw and high-heeled Keds. "Otherwise, there you stand at quarter to six, freezer door open and your shins getting purple, wondering if you've got the nerve to unload that squid-and-gooseberry casserole on the family again. Remember, you thought you were so smart to double the recipe the first time you made it, so you'd have a frozen one in reserve? Ha."

231

SHIMMELFENNER'S TEN FREEZER COMMANDMENTS
for People Who Hate to Cook

1. Freeze a little of something new before you freeze a big dish of it. Don't trust anybody, even me.

2. Even if it tastes great, hot the first time, maybe it will freeze funny. Like, some flavors get stronger—cloves, garlic, black pepper, green pepper, pimento, celery. And some poop out—onion, salt, chili powder. And potatoes freeze mushy, and so do some beans. And if vegetables were cooked enough in the dish you ate hot, they'll be overcooked in the one you froze, by the time it's re-heated.

3. So better you cook two dishes to freeze, instead of one to eat now and one later. Do it some morning when you're eating out that night. That means three nights off. Better than money in the bank.

4. Don't give an all-frozen dinner party. You read these jolly articles, Be a Guest at Your Party!—Freeze it all ahead, lie around all day in your harem pants, then a couple of pirouettes and Presto, dinner's ready! Beautiful. But I'm here to say if it wasn't choreographed to a fare-thee-well, there'll be something limp and something over-garlicked and something stone-cold in the middle. Two prefrozen jobs is plenty.

5. You'd think frozen bacon and ham would stay good forever since they're smoked or pickled to start with, and would you ever be wrong. Two months for smoked ham in a 0° freezer, one month for bacon.

6. They make freezing sound so complicated it scares you. Special paper, tape, pencils, wraps, whatever. Nuts. Just so it's wrapped airtight and all the air squeezed out, you're okay—foil, solid paper, plastic wrap, nylon parachutes. Then borrow a freezer thermometer and make sure the freezer's at 0°.

7. Better arrange the food shelves in three sections: THIS WEEK OR ELSE . . . THIS MONTH . . . NO SWEAT. (That's for bread and ready-frozen things.)

8. Chances are good, whatever you're in the habit of making will freeze okay if it isn't full of mayonnaise and potatoes—check the freezer manual. Give your stand-bys a try.

9. If something looks dry when you take it out of the freezer—rice, noodles, and so on—add liquid, say ⅓ cup milk, broth, tomato juice, whatever's logical, before you reheat it.

10. Don't get suckered into too big a freezer. If you inherited one, use half for something else—wool sweaters, bathing suits, maybe popcorn chains for the Christmas tree. They freeze fine.

When there's a lot of it around, you never want it very much.
—Crumpacker's 22nd Law

NOVEMBER 3 ". . . I remember, after acquiring my first freezer, stopping short before an unexpected psychological hurdle. With a novice's enthusiasm I had prepared and frozen some nice items: a Coq au Vin, a Cassoulet, some lovely brioches. . . . Trying to choose from the attractive array one afternoon, I couldn't help thinking of old Franz Josef of Austria. One day he was reviewing his troops, splendid in their scarlet tunics and gold braid and shiny boots. And he simply stood there when it was over, the tears running down his face at the thought of sending such a beautiful little army off to war. That's the way I felt, looking at all those neat packages. That night I ate at a restaurant."
—Albert Wooky

NOVEMBER 4 A Day to Vote for Somebody

LIBERAL POTTAGE
(divers elements all stewing together)

Put a pound of lentils in a big kettle with three quarts of water. Bring it to a boil, turn off the heat, and let it stand two hours. Now fry

>   6 big chopped onions
>   2 garlic cloves
>   1 pound lamb meat (shoulder, neck, whathaveyou)

for fifteen minutes and put it in a big bean pot or deep casserole. Drain the lentils (but save the water) and add them, along with

>   a green pepper, seeded and chopped
>   a 15-ounce can stewed tomatoes
>   several stalks celery, chopped
>   4 chopped carrots

Stir it up and add some lentil liquor, just enough to cover everything. Salt and pepper to taste, then cover and bake in a slow, slow

233

oven, about 250°, for two hours. Longer won't hurt; just check once in a while for dryness and add more juice if it needs it.

NOVEMBER 5   The Carnegie Library was dedicated in Pittsburg on this day in 1895.

". . . Never have I lost my early faith that wisdom is to be found somewhere in a book—to be picked up as easily as a shell from the sand."

—Robert Lynd

"To make tough beef tender, soak it in vinegar and water (½ cup vinegar to 1 quart of water) for about twelve hours."

—Mrs. Crowen, *The American System
of Cookery,* 1870

"We derive a certain satisfaction from being sinned against. It is not only that a grievance adds content to our lives, but also that it makes less monstrous the flame of malice which like a vigil light flickers in the dimness of our souls."

—Eric Hoffer

"Take what you want," said God. "Take it, and pay for it."

—Spanish proverb

NOVEMBER 6   On this day in 1975, a certain Amaryllis Redd (of the Cincinnati Redds) calculated the cost of each individual almond and chicken chunk in the Frozen Chicken-Almond Casseroles she had been buying for the past year, and ever since then she has been inaccessible to her friends. Just sits in her bedroom staring straight ahead and keening softly.

". . . People who hate to cook and acquire a freezer generally start out by filling it with ready-frozen entrees, desserts, and fancy vegetable mixtures until they wake up broke, which generally doesn't take too long. Then if they have minimal sense, they settle for a few plain frozen vegetables by the sackful, plus a few simple guest-type entrees and vegetable casseroles they learn to make themselves. . . ."

—Stella Trowbridge Hinky

NOVEMBER 7   A DEPENDABLE BEEF BURGUNDY TO FREEZE

Cut two pounds of boneless beef chuck into two-inch chunks, brown it in a little oil, then pour on a cup of red wine. Stir it around. Then add

1½ teaspoons salt
¼ teaspoon pepper
1 teaspoon paprika
2 seeded and chopped green peppers, cut in rings

1 teaspoon marjoram
2 medium onions, sliced
½ pound fresh mushrooms, or the same amount canned

Cover and simmer it in the electric skillet (or in the Slow Cooker at medium or in the oven at 250°) for five hours. Then take the meat and vegetables out of the broth and keep them warm somewhere. Skim as much fat as possible off the broth. Better still, if you've time, semifreeze the broth so the solidified fat is easy to remove. Then boil it down to thicken it a bit, and if you want it thicker still, stir in a tablespoon of cornstarch or flour mixed to a smooth paste in cold water. Pour the whole works into a big casserole dish, or seven or eight little ones, wrap, and freeze. To serve it, eventually, reheat it in a 400° oven about forty minutes for the large, twenty-five for the small.

"Things that cooled fast in a bowl of ice water before they were frozen eventually taste better than things that didn't."
—Shakespeare
(Erwin Shakespeare, *sous-chef* at
Le Trianon, Kansas City)

"If a casserole calls for a crumb or cheese topping, do it before you reheat it, not before you freeze it. Otherwise it gets kind of a boardinghouse look."

—Napoleon Bonaparte

(Napoleon Bonaparte Mazzuti, head cook at the Elba Room, NYC. His great-uncle learned a lot about freezing, that winter in Russia)

Two Dependable Chicken Things to Freeze:

1. McCORMACK'S CHOICE

(The idea here is four items, layered and baked: broccoli, chicken-in-gravy, cottage cheese, and noodles.)

1 package frozen chopped broccoli
a 4-pound chicken, cut up
a celery stalk
an onion slice
½ cup butter

½ cup flour
½ teaspoon salt
½ teaspoon dried basil
8 ounces egg noodles
1 egg
16 ounces cottage cheese

Take the broccoli out of the freezer to thaw while you simmer the chicken in water to cover, with the celery and onion. Then get the meat off the bones and dice. Next, make some gravy: melt the butter, stir in the flour gradually, and add salt, basil, and three cups of the water you cooked the chicken in.

Cook the egg noodles eight minutes and drain them. Then beat the egg a little and mix it with the cottage cheese. Finally: layer these things like this, in a big casserole dish: chicken mix, noodles, cottage cheese, broccoli. Do it again, ending with chicken mix. Bake forty-five minutes at 350°, wrap it, and freeze. When you eventually reheat it, sprinkle Parmesan cheese on top and reheat it, frozen, for two hours at 350°.

2. McCLINTOCK'S BEST

(A good Mexican-type chicken arrangement that feeds 8 to 10 people and freezes well. Transfer it from freezer to refrigerator the night before you aim to serve it. On dinner day, heat it a good two hours at 300°.)

4 whole chicken breasts
  (or an equal amount of any
  chicken)
12 corn tortillas
1 can cream of mushroom soup,
  condensed
1 can cream of chicken soup,
  condensed

1 can chili without the beans
1 small onion, chopped
½ cup milk
1 cup green chili salsa
  (or taco sauce)
½ pound jack cheese, grated
½ pound sharp cheddar, grated

First, bake the chicken, wrapped in foil, for an hour at 350°. Then take the meat off its bones. Tear the tortillas into one-inch pieces. Now mix everything else except the cheese. That's your sauce. Layer chicken, tortillas, sauce, and cheese in a three-quart casserole, ending with the cheese, and bake at 350° for forty-five minutes.

And a Dependable Vegetable Dish to Freeze:

SPICY BAKED EGGPLANT

Get a good-sized eggplant and don't peel it, just cube it. Sauté it in ¾ cup olive oil for about 5 minutes. Then add

a 15-ounce can of tomatoes
small jar of pimentos drained
  and coarsely chopped
2 medium sliced onions

1 teaspoon garlic powder
2 tablespoons chopped parsley
1 teaspoon capers

Cook all this about fifteen minutes more, then pile it into a casserole dish, wrap it, and freeze it. Before you eventually reheat it to serve, put crumbs on top, heat half an hour at 350°, and double-check to be sure it's hot clear through.

NOVEMBER 8   This is National Dunce Day, named for Duns Scotus, a champion thirteenth-century nit-picker. Known as Dr. Subtilis, he was famous for his attention to tiny details that bored the whey out of everybody. To keep his memory green, do three dumb things, your choice, or

1. make gay matching plastic bloomers for all
   hanging house plants
2. wash and iron your floor rags
3. dust under the light-switch plates.

NOVEMBER 9   This day in 1974 was a very big day for
              Mumu Harbottle.

That year—it was the year she was an Avon lady and away from
home so much—Mumu had a traumatic time of it, thawing a frozen
roast for tomorrow. She found that if she transferred it from freezer
to refrigerator the night before, it wouldn't be thawed enough. On
the other hand, thawed at room temperature, it would eventually
be ankle-high in its own red juice, which meant considerably less
juice left in the meat.

Then, on this particular November 9 at 7:43 P.M., as she was
debating which dubious course to follow for tomorrow night's meat,
she noticed on the pantry shelf a small styrofoam cooler that had
cooled many a six-pack the previous summer. It occurred to her that
if she'd put the meat in it, its own chilly exhalations would cool the
small cubic area of the box enough so that it would be cooler than
room temperature but certainly warmer than the refrigerator. And
so she did and it was.

Greatly excited, then, Mumu wrote home to Mother about it, and
to her old college roommate, and she also placed a long-distance
call to Stella Trowbridge Hinky, a lady whose work she greatly
admired.

NOVEMBER 10   On this day in 1974, Stella Trowbridge
               Hinky returned Mumu Harbottle's telephone
call, Collect, and when Mumu delivered her big news, Ms. Hinky
said that was very interesting, but why did she bother to thaw it at
all? Why didn't she cook it frozen?

"I didn't know you could," Mumu said, crestfallen. (Her crest
falls easy.)

"Certainly," said Ms. Hinky. "Just figure twice the ordinary
roasting time for a roast that's frozen solid. Say, sixty-five minutes
per pound in a 325° oven, for medium to medium-rare. To make

sure, you can insert the meat thermometer after the meat has warmed a little."

Mumu said, "Oh."

"And," continued Hinky, "perhaps you'd be interested in knowing that the same thing is true for all kinds of steaks and chops. Cook them frozen—broiled or pan-fried at the same temperature you'd ordinarily use, but roughly twice the time. Actually, Ms. Harbottle, this preserves the juice and the flavor. Taste tests at Columbia University—"

"I'm sorry, I have to go," Mumu said, "my phone's ringing." After all, this was a long dime. That's the way with experts, she thought. Turn them on and you can't turn them off.

But that night in bed she had a sudden thought. When she was out all day and came home to a frozen three-pound roast, it would be three hours till dinner, Hinky's way, instead of an hour and a half the styrofoam-cooler way. Even if she put the frozen roast in the oven before she left in the morning, and set it on automatic, the meat would have thawed somewhat by the time the oven turned on. And she wouldn't be there to stick the meat thermometer in, and it would probably be well-done by the time she got home, and Jimbo would absolutely throttle her.

Why do things have to be so *fuzzy,* she thought, tossing fretfully, and presently she thought, The heck with it, and went to sleep.

NOVEMBER 11   On this day, observe a moment of respectful silence for Kurt Vonnegut, Jr.'s birthday.

NOVEMBER 12   Sky snoweth
                      kine loweth
                      cold groweth
                      nose bloweth

For the Common Winter (or Rotten Uncomfortable) Cold:

". . . Take half a pound of reafons of the Sun Stoned and 1 ounce of liquorifh and 1 ounce of Elicompane made into fine powder beat your reafons then pour in them till they come to a conferve adding thereto 2 or 3 fpoonfulls of Red rofe water if a thick

239

ruehm leffen your quantity of Elicompane & take of this morning noon and night. Probatum."*

—A Book of Simples, circa 1700

NOVEMBER 13   A Dissertation on Leftover Ham

From Shirley Shimmelfenner's *Hit It Again, Shirl!*, chapt. 27

". . . You read some great fiction in the food magazines. I mean, 'How Susie Thimblefinger Feeds Her Family of Four on $2.69 a Week,' all starting with this big ham she cooked on Sunday. Then it goes, MONDAY: Hot Clam Broth, Ham Timbales, Spinach and Mushrooms in Sour Cream, Herbed Carrots, Apple Crisp. TUESDAY: Ham-Asparagus Rolls with Macaroni, Broiled Green Tomatoes, Fresh Spinach Salad, Angel Fluff Pudding. And so on. — Out of sight! But anybody knows that in real life, Monday is Cold Sliced Ham with the rest of the scalloped potatoes, and maybe Tuesday is ham and eggs, and Wednesday is Cold Sliced Ham.

"After all, that's what you cooked it for, because it tastes all right cold, right? And why recook all the rest of the vitamin B out? I mean, quit messing with it till it gets right down to the tail end. It makes more sense to put your mind on something good to go with it. . . ."

NOVEMBER 14   Two good hearty dishes to go with a slice of Ham or any other cold meat:

1. JETTY SPAGHETTI

Into the blender put

2 cups parsley, stripped from the stems
1 teaspoon each basil
    oregano
    marjoram
    salt

½ teaspoon pepper
½ teaspoon garlic powder
½ cup olive oil

Blend it at high speed; occasionally you'll have to push it down the

* It is proven.

sides with a spatula. Ten minutes before dinnertime, cook and drain a pound of spaghetti (this will serve eight to ten, so cut it in half for four or five; no need to make less sauce, though, because it keeps) and mix it well with two tablespoons of butter. To it add ¼ cupful of chopped pecans or walnuts, and ½ cupful grated Parmesan cheese. Add the parsley sauce, see that it's all hot through, and serve.

2. WINE SPOON BREAD

3¼ cups milk
1 cup yellow corn meal
1½ teaspoons salt

2 tablespoons butter
4 eggs
¾ cup dry white wine

Scald the milk and stir in the corn meal and salt. Put an oven mitt on your hand, because the stuff sputters, while you stir it for three or four minutes. When it's a good thick mush, take it off the heat and add the butter. Beat the eggs, and to them add the wine. Stir the mixture slowly into the hot mush, then pour it into a well-buttered casserole dish. Put the oven rack just a notch below the center of the oven and bake the spoon bread at 375° about an hour. When its top is a pretty puffy light brown, it's done. Serve.

NOVEMBER 15   ". . . But comes a time [Shirley Shimmel-fenner continued] when the chips are down. Your ham looks like an ha'penny's worth of soap after a hard week's wash, and you'd love to give it to the dog. But with just two cups of chopped meat you can make a darned good

END-OF-THE-LINE HAM CASSEROLE

1 can cream of celery soup
½ cup milk
pepper

3 medium potatoes, peeled and sliced
1 medium onion, ditto
2 cupfuls chopped ham

Mix the soup and milk, add a good grind of pepper, then layer things like this, in a casserole dish: potatoes, meat, onion, celery-soup sauce. Cover and bake for an hour at 375°. Then take the lid off, which makes it easier to sprinkle some grated cheese on top, and bake it uncovered another twenty minutes.

Finally, if you can scrounge one more half-cupful of ham, you can make

AUNTIE SCROOGE'S BEAN SOUP

1 pound navy beans	½ teaspoon each celery salt and
3 quarts water	cardamom seeds
the chopped ham (and bone if	2 teaspoons salt
there was one)	2 drops Tabasco

Soak the beans in the water overnight. Next day, simmer them an hour, then add all the other things. Simmer for two more hours and it's done.

NOVEMBER 16   Tidy Tips for Thanksgiving Week

From Brillo-Savarin (as translated by S. T. Hinky)

1. Clean around doorknobs and damp-wipe the telephone before cleaning floors if there isn't time for both. Doorknob and telephone dirt is grime; floor dirt is just dirt.

2. With a rubber band, fasten an old sock to the end of a yard-stick to reach high cobwebs and dusty places.

3. After you polish your shoes with shoe polish, spit on the toes and buff them again. Nothing works like spit.

4. Everybody hates embroidered guest towels except the person who embroidered them.

NOVEMBER 17   A Story of Virtue Rewarded!

Once upon a time, a young bride invited her husband's boss and his wife to dinner. The employer, a kindly man, was also a gentleman chicken farmer; and on the snowy morning of the night they were to come, he sent over one of his nicest Wyandottes as a hostess gift.

The hen arrived crated, fully feathered, and clucking. Chicken and dumplings on the hoof. The bride telephoned her husband.

"Oh wow," he said. "We'll have to butcher it and pluck it," and he promised he'd be home early.

His bride didn't know anything about killing chickens and wouldn't have had the heart for it anyway. But she thought it would speed things up to start the plucking, which she did, twitching off a feather or two at a time.

By sundown, when her husband phoned to say the guests weren't coming after all because of the bad weather, the hen was looking pretty chilly. And when he finally got home, he found that his wife had made it a cozy kimono from an old flannel nightgown, and found some corn meal for its supper, and fixed it a cozy bed from shredded newspapers. The next morning, the little red hen laid a nice egg for their breakfast, and they all lived happily ever after.

A bird on the nest is worth two in the pot.

NOVEMBER 18   Now doth the Mighty Hunter don his red cap and fill his flask and his gun in the dark and go forth into the predawn cold to prove his Manhood in valiant tourney with the Wicked Moose!

". . . The king [James I], pleased, yet flushed and pale with excitement, his hunting-garb soiled with mire and bog-water from spur to bonnet-plume, reins up just in time to witness the finish, when the royal pack has fastened upon the quarry's throat. And when the deer has been broken up, and whilst the foresters, all unbonneted, wind the customary *mort* upon their bugles, our royal woodsman is plunging his unbooted limbs in the beast's warm, reeking entrails: an extraordinary panacea, recommended by the court physician, Sir Theodore Mayerne, as the 'sovereign'st thing on earth' for those gouty and rheumatic twinges, which too emphatically reminded the Stuart in the autumn of his days, how 'every inordinate cup is unblest and the ingredient thereof a devil,' though the warning produced no practical result. . . ."
—From a courtier's letter,
circa 1611

"HOW TO COOK A MOOSE NOSE: Moose nose is cooked by cutting off the upper jawbone just below the eyes. Drop this jawbone in a kettle of water and boil it for about 30 minutes. Remove, and cool, and skin it, taking the hairs and bristles and dark skin off. Now wash it well and place the skinned nose into a fresh kettle of water. . . . Cut the white and dark meat into thick slices and pack them into jars. Cover with the juice from the boiling. This will jell when chilled, and it can be sliced and eaten like sandwich meat. . . ."

—*How to Hunt a Moose,* by James E. Churchill

"After you've bagged your hunter, don't drape him over your automobile or mount him when you get home. Merely the cap or jacket will suffice."

—Cleveland Amory, founder
of the Hunt the Hunters Club

NOVEMBER 19 What Was So Great About Grandma?

". . . And so I finally learned that just because they call a recipe 'Grandma's Whatzis' doesn't necessarily mean it's any good. Plenty of grandmas can't cook worth shucks. In fact, a lot of girls today cook rings around their grandmothers, because their grandmothers grew up eating Grandma's Old-fashioned Store-bought Cookies by the boxful. It's their granddaughters and great-granddaughters that are cooking up a storm, cooking French, Korean, Italian, Basque, you name it. Pickling, preserving, baking . . . The only thing my grandma could really make was frozen Daiquiris.

"I got the following recipe from a belly-dancer named Salome, christened Mary Elizabeth, in a commune down the road. She makes them for her old man all the time. It's about the best, crispest, easiest cooky you'll ever make. Trust me on this."

—Shirley Shimmelfenner (*Ibid.*)

SALOME'S MOLASSES CRISPS

Cream ½ cup butter with ¾ cup sugar and beat in an egg. Then sift together

> 1½ cups flour
> ¾ teaspoon baking soda
> pinch of salt

and add it to the butter-sugar business alternately with

> ⅓ cup molasses

Finally, add ¾ cup of chopped nuts, more or less—whatever you have. Drop them by the teaspoonful on a greased cooky sheet and bake at 350° for twelve to fifteen minutes.

> "If they ain't molasses, they ain't cookies."
> —One-Hoss

NOVEMBER 20   Beware of Suppers!

SOME RULES FOR PRESERVING OF HEALTH BY DIET:
"Two meals a day is sufficient for all persons after fifty years of age, and all weak people; for the omitting of suppers does always conduce much to the health of the weak and aged; since if no suppers be eaten, the stomach will soon free itself from all rough, slimy humors, wherewith it is slabbered over on the inside, and thereby the appetite will be renewed and digestion made more strong and vigorous. Moreover, all that are troubled with sweating in the night or any ill taste in their mouths, belching, and troublesome dreams, must avoid suppers. . . ."

> —R. Saunders, 1770

NOVEMBER 21   Now on this day, or approximately, do all SANTA CLAUSES everywhere shake the mothballs and the moths out of their red plush pants.

And now is the wind sharp and the frost keen, and if one flower still standeth in the garden, it is with bowed head as though in mourning for its dead companions. And in such wise doth the reluctant Cook stand too, weighted down with sorry awareness of Thanksgiving dinner looming ever closer. And sometimes the Turkey doth even trouble her sleep.

"TURKEY: This bird has various meanings depending on the action in your dream. If you saw one strutting and/or heard it gobbling, it portends a period of confusion due to instability of your friends or associates. . . . However, if you ate it, you are likely to make a serious error of judgment, so be very careful regarding any important matters which may be pending."

> —*The Dreamer's Dictionary*

245

NOVEMBER 22   Now beginneth the sign of SAGITTARIUS
🏹   (controlling the Thighs) that extendeth
through December 21, all this time being mightily auspicious for
picking chives
exterminating the apartment
getting a haircut
going to Paris
falling in love
having teeth pulled.
And the born Sagittarian—restless, impetuous, impatient—doth
survey with unease the year's numerous unfinished projects all so
bravely begun, and even so (gallant optimist that he is) doth start
some more.

NOVEMBER 23   On this day, when Stephanie ("Fats") Stumflug found that she had gained another seven
pounds, she paid a call on her friendly neighborhood physician,
Emmett Neitzelgrinder, M.D.

"Well, now, I'll tell you, Fa— Stephanie," said the good doctor.
"Of course you eat too much. And one reason is that you eat too
fast. Now, I want you to observe something." He passed her a
doughnut from his file drawer labeled *D*.

"Take a bite," he said. "Taste it. Okay? Now try to taste it while
you're inhaling." Stephanie drew a deep breath as she chewed, and
her eyes went round with astonishment.

"You see?" said the doctor. "You can't do it. You can taste only
while you're exhaling or not breathing—*never* while you're breathing in. So just think of all the food you waste, taste-wise! If you will
take smaller portions and smaller bites and consciously *taste each
bite* when your lungs are comparatively empty, you'll get twice the
taste enjoyment for half the calories. Come see me after Christmas."

"Goodness gracious and Gloriosky!" Stephanie said to herself in
the elevator on her way down to the main-floor lobby; and when
she came to the newsstand she bought a chocolate bar so she could
practice her new technique on the way home.

"To acquire or maintain the perfect mean between fat
and thin is the life-study of every woman in the world."
—Brillat-Savarin

NOVEMBER 24   From *I'll Tell You Where to Stuff the Turkey* (Shirley Shimmelfenner, vol. 8, chap. 1)

". . . In the sink, because those bread crumbs really fly around, and otherwise you'll have the floor to sweep too. Somebody else's sink is best of all, because somebody else will probably be doing it then, not you.

"In fact, if you're any kind of a noncook, don't do Thanksgiving unless you potluck it. Doing the whole thing, you're out of your league—up against the pie purists, spud champs, and gravy artists, and every man there remembering the Thanksgiving dinner Mom used to put out. A wizard with a gizzard, Mom was, the way they tell it, even if she didn't know a giblet from her left foot. . . . And when you potluck it at someone else's place, put in for the relish and the dessert, and bring something Mom never heard of. You may not get Mom's reputation, but you'll get one for sure."

NOVEMBER 25   Make some

CRANBERRY CHUTNEY

In a big saucepan, combine

1 pound cranberries	1 tablespoon ground cinnamon
1 cup seedless raisins	1½ tablespoons ground ginger
1⅔ cups sugar	1 cup water

Simmer all this for about fifteen minutes, till the cranberries pop out of their skins and the mixture thickens. Then add

½ cup chopped onion
2 apples, pared and chopped
½ cup celery, sliced fine

Simmer it another fifteen minutes, then cool it and keep it cold.

NOVEMBER 26   On this day in 1789, the first nationwide Thanksgiving was celebrated.

George Washington chose the date as a day of national Thanksgiving, specifically for the adoption of the Constitution. But the purpose got lost in the general shuffle, and now we are mainly grateful for the long weekend and the chance to overeat and then to sleep it off.

A Good Thanksgiving Dessert:

KAHLUA CREAM
for 6

1 cup heavy cream
1 pint vanilla ice cream
¼ cup Kahlua

cupcake papers
⅓ cup finely chopped and toasted
   almonds

Beat the cream to the stiff-peak stage. Then put the ice cream in a bowl and beat it (with the same beaters) to soften it a bit. Then mix in the whipped cream and the Kahlua. Put the cupcake papers in muffin tins and fill them with the mixture. Sprinkle the almonds on top and freeze till firm.

NOVEMBER 27   A Reasonable Thing to Do with Leftover Turkey

". . . Nothing is easier than Sour Cream Turkey Curry, but since the family probably won't settle for nothing (that's my little joke!) a Turkey Curry is a good second choice, providing, as it does, a distinct change from the turkey taste."

—Stella Trowbridge Hinky

SOUR CREAM TURKEY CURRY

3 tablespoons butter
2 teaspoons curry powder
⅓ cup chopped onion
3 tablespoons flour

1 can chicken broth
3 cups cooked turkey meat,
   chopped
1 cup sour cream

Melt the butter over low heat, and add the curry powder and chopped onion. Cook about five minutes. Then stir in the flour and the chicken broth, stirring till it's a smooth sauce. Then add the turkey and the sour cream. Keep it hot in the double boiler (have the water barely simmering so the sour cream won't curdle) while you cook some rice to serve it on. Actually one should have done this first, but one doesn't always think to.

NOVEMBER 28   A good Italian treatment for Leftover Turkey.

ATSA MY TURKEY!

First, cook and drain half a pound of fettucini or plain egg noodles. Then simmer over low heat for five minutes

> 3 cups chopped cooked turkey
> ½ cup condensed chicken broth
> ½ cup dry white wine

Add the noodles to the turkey now, along with

¼ cup milk	2 tablespoons butter
6 tablespoons diced mozzarella or Monterey Jack cheese	1 teaspoon salt
6 tablespoons Parmesan cheese	¼ teaspoon pepper

Cook it over very low heat, stirring frequently, for ten minutes. (Or use the double boiler.) A fruit salad is good with it.

NOVEMBER 29   On this day in 1783, the American Revolutionary troops decided they'd won that war, and so they all demobilized.

Also on this day, in 1975, the Second Methodist Church of Piscataway, New Jersey, reported 100-percent co-operation from the female members of the congregation in making something for the Annual Home-Baked Goods Bazaar. Every one of them brought something.

"Actually, it was easy," explained Mrs. Patterson Wibblee, chairman and organizer. "We just had the minister announce that only the younger women were expected to contribute."

NOVEMBER 30   Mark Twain was born on this day in 1835, a very good day for the country.

> Low'ring sky,
> blizzard ny.
> Flick'ring sun,
> blizzard dun.

Augurs well for the end of the old month and the start of the festive new. Rest quietly now.

December

bringeth a consideration of sundry good things: the Gift & the Phlugerhaggen, the Card & the Comfit & the Sweetmeat; includeth

 a gentle jubilation of Cookies
 a remarkable Fried Fruit
 the world-famous Scripture Cake
 an almond-cranberry Delight

and other Delicacies befitting the Joyful Season!

Mary, Mary, quite contrary,
How does your Christmas garden grow?

Pine, poinsettias, holly berry . . .
The crocus sleeps now, under the snow.

DECEMBER 1   NOW IT IS DECEMBER and Frost lieth
               cold silver upon the Ground as the aging
Yeare creaketh to the Finish-line. Now the Apartment-dweller raileth
at the Super & the Homeowner complaineth to the Power Companie. And in 24 days shall the reluctant Cooke grapple with the
reluctant Turkie (or the sullen immortal Ham). And now doth the
harried Houseperson shut her Minde to the Cupboard that needeth
sorting & the Room that needeth repainting, wisely postponing
these Thyngs. For surely December bringeth problems enow & yet
bringeth Joys too, with good Thyngs to make & eat & think.

DECEMBER 2   What Do You Wear on Christmas Day?
               ". . . The trick about dressing for Christmas
is to get the dress *now*. Do it before the last of the money goes on
presents for forgotten relatives. . . . You probably need something
tough enough to cope with the kitchen, the children, serving the
turkey, getting drunk in, and general slouching about, yet pretty
enough to preside over your own family party or go out to someone else's. It should be loose enough to let you over-eat in comfort
without reminding you of the ruinous effect your gluttony is having
on your figure. . . ."
                              —*The Observer* (London)

"Don't eat too many almonds; they add weight to the breasts."
                      —Gigi (in *Gigi,* by Colette)

DECEMBER 3   Now lytle birds do search for seeds in the hard
               fields, and it is a time to replenish the Bird-
feeder and quarantine the Cat.

253

DECEMBER 4   Cooky Notes from Our Columnists
                  From "The Chatterbox," Mervyn Meadows
Sentinel:
   "Mrs. Charles ('Edie') Grumwalt's 'gang' is at it again! Last
Thursday, 'Edie's' charming kitchen was the scene of a pick-up
lunch and the Big Cooky Swap she instigated a month ago . . .
each of eight 'girls' going home with fourteen dozen cookies, seven
kinds! Only specification was that they had to freeze well. They all
looked just yummy. But would you believe they wouldn't give Your
Correspondent a single bite? 'No bringee, no eatee!' laughed 'Edie'
as she whipped up the Margaritas. So that's the way the cooky
crumbles with the 'Grumwalt gang'!"

From "One Man's Beat," Grand Rapids *Telegram:*
   ". . . On our block, swapping holiday baked goods is becoming
more complicated, now the Fimmisters have gone macrobiotic, the
Tuggleses low-carb, the Woodses high-protein, and the Wellmans
vegetarian-kosher. My wife wants to know how you make a
macrobiotic low-carb high-protein vegetarian-kosher Christmas
cooky. . . ."

   Dear Aloise,
      I just had to pass this great "tip" along! The next time
   you make any raisin-spice cookies, add some chopped
   dates too, and you'll find they stay moist and chewy
   and just delicious twice as long!
                                          Doreen

   Dear Doreen:
      You're a real live doll! I tried it and you're right!
   I love you!
                                          Aloise

DECEMBER 5   One year ago on this day, Stephanie ("Fats")
                  Stumflug read in the paper that basil is just as
good as mistletoe for getting kissed under. In Italy, it said, they
call it "Kiss-Me-Quick," and wearing a sprig is considered a cordial
invitation.
   Stephanie didn't have any fresh basil, so she just hung the
kitchen spice jar of it around her neck and it worked fine.

"Of course I had to tell everybody what it was for," she reported, "but what the heck."

Stephanie has always had a hard time keeping her mind on her cooking, especially vegetables, because she'd rather think about fruitcakes and fudge. The only holiday-type vegetable she can ever think to make is broccoli cooked as usual, seasoned with melted butter, salt and pepper, then jazzed up with pimento strips. She likes it because it matches the holly.

DECEMBER 6   Let us now celebrate the anniversary of Good St. Nicholas, who died on this day, A.D. 342, or else was born on this day, the book didn't make it quite clear.

Even as an infant, St. Nicholas was so good that he wouldn't suck on Wednesdays or Fridays, which were fast days then. Later, he became the patron saint of children, sailors, robbers, and virgins, most particularly virgins; and the way of it was this:

A nobleman in the town of Patera had three daughters and not much hope of marrying them off, for his fortunes had taken a terrible turn for the worse. Being something of a rotter, he had just about decided to sell them to a house of ill-repute, when word of his intention reached Archbishop Nicholas (he wasn't a saint yet) and perturbed him greatly.

Luckily, Nicholas had a great deal of money; and so, one moonlit night, he went by stealth to the nobleman's house and tossed a sack of gold through the open window, then vanished. This served as the eldest daughter's marriage portion, and the nobleman was thus able to unload her in holy matrimony.

Later, he did the same thing for the second daughter and later still for the third. (Doing it all at once would have been too hard on his pitching arm, because gold is heavy.)

But before he actually tossed the last sackful in, the nobleman—who had been dying of curiosity as to the identity of his unknown benefactor—caught him in the act.

"Oh, Nicholas! Servant of God!" he cried. "Why seek to hide thyself?" But Nicholas pledged him to secrecy, and understandably. There were probably many unmarried daughters in the town, and like the charity mailing list today, you get on one of them and you're on them all.

Anyway, that's why he is the patron saint of virgins.

DECEMBER 7   MS. AESOP'S FABLES (No. 8)

An Ass decided one autumn to do his Christmas shopping early. He got new trousers for the Pig and a cigarette lighter for the Dog and a rear assembly for the Worm (who had recently lost his in a lawn mower), and a nice big megaphone for the Owl, who was getting weak in the hoot.

A couple of weeks before Christmas, he saw his friends at a party. He found that the Pig had gained thirty pounds, and the Dog had quit smoking, and the Worm had meanwhile grown himself a new rear end, and the Owl was very excited about a new transistorized megaphone which he had made a down payment on that very day.

Moral: He who shops early shops twice.

**DECEMBER 8   From *Living Through Christmas*
by Stella Trowbridge Hinky:**

Christmas Shopping Rule No. 1: When you find a great little item that would suit several people on your list, *get* some, one for each, and all in the Fire Engine Red if that's the best color. No point getting them all different for variety's sake and then wondering who to stick with the purple one. Because you'll lose your nerve and end up with it yourself.

Christmas Shopping Rule No. 2: When you find something that looks about right, but you're not sure, get it anyway, instead of muttering, "Well, I'll think about it . . ." which gets you nowhere but tired. Even if you decide it's wrong, other gift times are coming around the bend. And other people.

Christmas Shopping Rule No. 3: Almost anyone can use another flashlight, flower pot, oven timer, timepiece, notebook, collapsible canvas traveling bag, pair of scissors, pencil sharpener, address book, dictionary, jar of caviar, dollar bill.

Just this one Christmas, One-Hoss wishes people would stop trying to spruce him up. He doesn't want an Aran Isle fisherman's cap or a Spanish beret or anything with leather on the elbows; he wants a new posthole digger.

DECEMBER 9   It is now sixteen days till Christmas and time to panic.

The fact is, so many objects are manufactured just to give to somebody else. Did anyone in her right mind ever buy herself a jeweled pancake turner? Or a set of crayfish forks? Or hurricane-lamp cozies? Or washcloths with sequins on them?

There is also the Phlugerhaggen. A Phlugerhaggen is a sort of non-thing, or thing-plus, which does or is whatever its builder wants it to do or be; and there is many a Phlugerhaggen around at Christmastime. (The winner in a recent Phlugerhaggen exhibit in Elmira, New York, was a wonderful creation that incorporated a bathtub, a 1915 gas engine, a steam whistle, a toilet, and a pair of walking shoes. It brushes the tub, plunges the toilet, blows the whistle, rings bells, and sweeps the ground in front of where its feet walk, while the water in the tub cools the gasoline engine.)

". . . My only enduring gift principle is the $5 cake of soap. Best of breed. Better the $20 coin purse than the $20 handbag. Better the $10 handkerchief than the $10 shirt. . . ."

—Albert Wooky

DECEMBER 10   From *Santa Claus Is Coming to Town & I'm Leaving,* by Shirley Shimmelfenner, chap. 22

". . . So there I was working my head off, Christmas coming, and suddenly I realized I was spending most of the time trying to make the house look like nobody lived in it and the kitchen look like nobody cooked in it. So I decided, Nuts to that, you expect to see some bodies around a battlefield. . . ."

BARLEY SHIMMELFENNER
(To bake along with a roast or serve with any cold meat)

2 tablespoons butter
1 cup barley, rinsed and drained
1 celery stalk, chopped
1½ teaspoons parsley, chopped

1½ teaspoons salt
¼ teaspoon pepper
2 cups chicken stock (made from bouillon cubes)

First she melts the butter in a skillet and sautés the barley briefly, not enough to brown it, then adds everything else and heats it to boiling. At that point she pours it into a casserole dish, starts to cover it, notices the dish doesn't have a lid, and mutters some basic English to herself while she hunts up the aluminum foil. When it eventually appears, she covers the casserole with that and bakes it for an hour at 350°. Serves six to eight and it's a nice change from spuds.

DECEMBER 11   A Personal Letter.
          ". . . You ask me [*my friend wrote*] why I don't send Christmas cards, and I suppose the answer is that I've gotten self-conscious about it—can't decide what sort of statement about myself I want to make. Because every card seems to make one. If it's all jolly ho-ho-ho, don't you look a trifle insensitive, these days? And foreign language cards always seem to say *Look who's been where,* don't they? And if it's a card sponsored by some terribly worthy cause, then it's *Oh, what a good girl am I. . . .* Only in that case it would be better to send a fat check straight to the Cause, wouldn't it, and skip the cards. I don't know. . . .

"Not that I haven't sent cards, some years. Once, I know my cards indicated that I was color-blind and broke, which wasn't so that year, but I'd bought them from an old Christmas-card peddler who was. And another time, all they said was that I was in a hurry when I picked them out, because I meant to check #184A, Snowbound English Village, and hit the #185, Andy Warhol Soup Cans, by mistake.

"And I do like to receive them, though under deep hypnosis I might reveal that any name-engraved Christmas card that comes without one personal note on it gives me the same warm good feeling as any piece of mail marked OCCUPANT. . . ."

DECEMBER 12   Make fome Rofewater for lytle giftf!
          ". . . The fcent of inflammable Spirit of Rofes is ravifhingly fweet; if only two drops of it are mixed with a glafs of Water, they impart to the Water fo high a perfume, that it exceeds the very beft Rofewater."
                    —From *Toilet of Flora* (15th century)

DECEMBER 13 And make fome feafoning falt alfo!

FEAFONING FALT

Altogether in the blender mix ½ teaspoon each of

dill seed	dried thyme
celery salt	marjoram
onion powder	garlic salt

and one teaspoon each of

dry mustard paprika

plus six tablespoons of plain table salt. Then make a green salad with a vinegar-and-oil dressing and some of your product and see how you like it. Perhaps you'll want a little oregano, or curry, or more garlic or paprika. Then you can quadruple the recipe, to pack in dime-store shakers. Tie one to a can of good olive oil for a nice lytle prefent!

DECEMBER 14 One-Hoss says things have sure changed. He can remember when he got 100 Christmas stickers and tags for 29 cents. Now it's four for a dollar. This year he's giving stickers and tags.

DECEMBER 15 Now begin the halcyon days. These be the seven days before and after the winter solstice—a time of such calm and tranquillity (or so said the ancients) that the halcyon, who was of the kingfisher family, would nest upon the sea.

But what has happened to the halcyon days? It was on this day, in 1975, that Mumu Harbottle went to see Dr. Neitzelgrinder about a persistent ringing in her ears.

"H'mmmm," said Dr. N. thoughtfully, after he'd looked her over. "It can't be the oven timer, way down here, and it's too early for sleigh bells. It's probably nerves. What's bugging you, Mumu?"

"Christmas, I guess," she said unhappily.

"Can't get your shopping done? Trying to take too much on?" asked the good doctor.

"Well, yes, but mainly it's— Oh, it's just the whole big commercial mess," Mumu said. "The canned carols—'Silent Night' in the

Ladies' Room at the dime store! And those awful Santa Clauses, two per block. What's the matter with little kids, are they feeble-minded that they can't figure it out by the time they're two years old? And buying overpriced stuff for people who don't need it. And sending a bunch of cards to people you hardly know when you ought to be writing a decent letter to somebody you *do* know. . . ."

"Then why don't you do that?" asked the doctor mildly.

"Because I'm so frantic at this point I couldn't write a decent note to the mailman," Mumu snapped. "Excuse me, Doctor. But that's something else. My temper. It's starting to go. And the kids. Gimme, gimme, gimme . . ."

The doctor nodded.

"And the whole mechanized Christmas-tipping routine," Mumu said bitterly. "We'd like to give the janitor someth—"

"Maintenance man," the doctor corrected.

"Okay, maintenance man. We'd like to give him something. And the garbagem—"

"Sanitation engineer," the doctor corrected.

"All *right*," Mumu said impatiently. "And the switchboard girl, whatever you call *her*. But what does the Super bring up last night? A list of what we're *supposed* to give everybody. Twenty dollars here. Ten dollars there. Twenty-five dollars there. About as spontaneous as a forced march."

"Have a cooky," said Dr. Neitzelgrinder, opening a shortening can beautiful with contact-paper daisies. "The scrub lady brought me s—"

"Maintenance woman," Mumu said.

"Right!" said the doctor. ". . . Darned good, aren't they? Really crisp."

They chewed awhile.

"Well, now, I'll tell you, Mumu," the doctor said. "You put too big a load on Christmas, it's not going to blow a fuse, *you* are. It's funny, everybody expects Christmas to change something. Going to make everything and everybody different. Well, it hasn't. Not in a couple of thousand years, it hasn't. Christmas is like old age. Just makes everybody more so. If you're miserable at Christmas, you're going to be more so, just because it *is* Christmas. If you're happy, you're going to be happier. What we've got is a big jolly commercial carnival with overtones."

"That's just what I said," said Mumu. "Commercial."

"But why is commercial a dirty word?" asked the good doctor. "This country of ours is commercial, among other things. If it weren't, we'd never have come up with mass production to spread things around so more of us can have decent comforts."

"Yes, but—" Mumu began. The doctor held up a finger.

"And the fact that certain people have such lavish ones that they're indecent doesn't change the fact. You listen to me, Mumu," he continued, and Mumu thought, *O, boy, here we go again.* "Decent comforts is what the whole world's been after since Og spread out a bearskin in the first cave, and the only thing wrong with decent comforts is that the whole world doesn't have 'em. And—shut up, Mumu—trying to see that they get 'em is the devout endeavor of some of the best brains we've got. Wouldn't you admit that that involves a good deal of what we call the Christmas spirit?"

"Well, yes," said Mumu. "But I—"

"And, meanwhile," said the doctor comfortably, settling back, "Christmas is still a time when you remind people that you love 'em or like 'em, isn't it? Or at least that you don't hate 'em. Or that you *thought* about 'em. Isn't it? And what in the heck is the matter with that?"

Mumu couldn't think of anything, and she noticed that the ringing in her ears had stopped, when she got up to go. "Thank you, Doctor," she said, as he handed her some more cookies to eat on the way home.

"Merry Crispness!" she said.

"Ho ho ho!" he said.

MERRY CRISPNESS COOKIES
(Very crisp with a smooth semishortbread texture)

1 cup butter	1 egg
1 cup sugar	2 teaspoons cream or canned
3 cups flour	milk
½ teaspoon salt	1 teaspoon vanilla
1½ teaspoons baking powder	

Cream the butter and sugar, and add the sifted dry ingredients. Then beat the egg, cream, and vanilla together and add them.

Maybe you'll need to chill it before you roll it. Then roll it thin, about ⅛ inch thick, put a walnut half on each if you like, sprinkle them with sugar, and bake on a greased cooky sheet about ten minutes, till they're gilt-edged. They'll stay crisp a good while in a closed can decorated with contact-paper daisies.

LITTLE CHRISTMAS THIMBLE CAKES

½ cup butter
⅓ cup confectioners' sugar,
    preferably sifted
1 egg, separated
½ teaspoon vanilla

1 cup unsifted flour
¼ teaspoon salt
¾ cup finely chopped pecans

jams, jellies, marmalade . . .

Cream the butter and sugar, add the egg yolk and vanilla, then the flour and salt. (Put the egg white in a little dish for dipping, later.) Mix it well. If it's hard to handle, chill it. Then shape it into ¾-inch balls, dip them in the egg white, and roll them in the chopped nuts.

Now we come to the thimble part: Put the balls on an ungreased baking sheet and, with a thimble, poke a little crater in each. Bake for five minutes at 350°. Then take them out and repoke them— the craters tend to level out—and bake about six minutes longer, till they're set. After they've cooled on racks, fill the centers with the jams and jellies. (If you're storing these, store them unfilled, or things will get pretty sticky.)

CURLED-UP CANDY COOKIES
(These give a lot of expression to a cooky plate.)

¾ cup unblanched almonds,
    grated or ground fine
½ cup butter
½ cup sugar
1 tablespoon each flour
             heavy cream
             milk

Put it all in a saucepan over low heat and stir it till the butter melts. Then whisk it a bit till it's smooth, and drop the batter by the tea-spoonful onto a well-oiled and floured cooky sheet—only three per sheet, because they spread like mad and, also, you have to roll each one while it's malleable, and they cool fast. Bake at 350° about eight minutes till the centers bubble a little and they're deep gold. Take them out, let them cool a few seconds, then quickly roll each one around a broom handle or a wooden spoon handle. Reoil and flour the cooky sheet each time or you may be sorry.

PEANUT-BUTTER POKIES

Liberate two egg whites from two eggs and slip them into a bowl.
Mix with 1½ cups of peanut butter and 1 cup of white sugar.
Drop by the teaspoonful onto a greased cooky sheet, press gently
with the tines of a fork, and bake eight to ten minutes at 350°.

DECEMBER 16   On this day in 1770, Beethoven was born.
               On this day in 1773, the Boston Tea Party
was held in Boston Harbor.
    And on this morning in 1975, a good brisk morning with a red
winter sunrise, Dr. Neitzelgrinder woke up hungry for pork chops.
—Hungry, specifically, for Mrs. Neitzelgrinder's pork chops. She
has always said he married her for her pork chops, an allegation he
denies but not very hard. And so she quit playing with holly sprigs
and styrofoam balls and the grandchildren's Christmas stockings
long enough to fix him a fine winter dinner, featuring her special
pork chops and her special cranberries with almonds.

MRS. NEITZELGRINDER'S PORK CHOPS
for 6

She gets six good-sized pork chops, at least an inch thick, and a
little thicker doesn't hurt. She also finds a brown paper grocery
sack and in it she puts

        ¼ cup flour
        ½ teaspoon garlic salt
        ½ teaspoon celery salt
        ½ teaspoon seasoned salt
        1 teaspoon paprika

    Now she drops the chops into it, bounces them around a bit, and
then browns them slowly in a couple of tablespoons of fat.
    While they brown, she's slicing a green pepper into six rings,
and three cored but unpeeled red apples into six thick chunks. On
each chop—when they're browned—she puts a pepper ring and an
apple slice.
    Now. In a cup, she mixes

        ½ cup water
        1 tablespoon brown sugar
        2 tablespoons Worcestershire sauce

263

and pours it over all the chops, then puts the lid on the skillet and simmers it for forty minutes.

(What he generally gets with this is scalloped potatoes out of a box. No point spoiling the man.)

As for the cranberry arrangement, she generally makes it in the morning, to give it time to get cold.

MRS. N.'S
CRANBERRIES WITH ALMONDS

½ cup almonds, blanched and 4 cups cranberries
   skinned* ⅓ cup orange marmalade
2 cups sugar juice of two lemons
1 cup water

She puts the sugar and water in a saucepan and lets them boil five minutes. Then she adds the cranberries and lets them cook for another five. When the skins burst, she takes the pan off the burner and adds the marmalade and the lemon juice. After it has cooled, she adds the cold almonds and then chills the whole thing.

DECEMBER 17   And on this splendid day in 1903, Orville Wright soared 120 feet high in the world's first power-driven heavier-than-air airplane! To commemorate it, make some

HIGH-RISE POPOVERS
(No one knows who started the unfounded rumor that popovers are risky or in any way a test of cooksmanship. These popovers can be easily made by anyone who is bright enough to blow her nose.)

Set the oven at 450°. Grease six custard cups with vegetable shortening (not oil), including the outside of the cup rims. Set them on a cooky sheet.

---

* If they're not already that way, she pours boiling water over them and lets them stand about five minutes. Then, with just a little pinch, the almonds squirt out, sometimes all over the kitchen. So she retrieves them, pours cold water on them, and lets them chill a couple of hours before she adds them to the cranberries. Finds they're crisper that way.

In a bowl, dump

> 1 cup unsifted flour
> ½ teaspoon salt
> 2 eggs (just break them over the bowl and
> drop them in so they're staring at
> you with their big yellow eyes)
> 1 cup milk

Beat this with an egg beater till it's just mixed—about fifteen seconds. Now fill the cups half full and set the cooky sheet in the 450° oven. Let them bake for twenty-five minutes. Then, without opening the oven, lower the temperature to 400° and bake another thirty—fifty-five in all. That's it. You will have six splendid popovers, so golden brown and exuberantly puffed up that it's almost embarrassing.

DECEMBER 18   A Good Christmas Punch.

is what One-Hoss says he'll give the next department-store clerk who directs him to the Suburban Swingers' Boutique when he asks the way to Women's Underwear.

He also has a recipe for a ripsnorter that he says don't take much doing, once the derned cloves are stuck in the oranges.

HOT POT PUNCH
Christmas spirits for 15 people

5 oranges	a fifth of apple brandy
plenty of whole cloves	½ gallon apple cider
cinnamon sticks, one per cup	

Stud the oranges with the cloves and roast them in a 350° oven half an hour, till they ooze a little and change color. Then put them in a metal pot, maybe the jam kettle. (One-Hoss used a glass punch bowl once, and he might as well have hit it with a pipe wrench.)

Heat the brandy—just put the bottle in hot water up to its neck over a low flame. Pour the apple cider into some big saucepan and heat it, too.

Then dim the lights, pour the hot brandy over the oranges, and light it. Whoosh! Put the fire out in a couple of minutes, after the flames have licked up the orange oils, and add the hot cider. Serve it by the big cupful, a cinnamon stick in each.

From Mrs. Beeton's *All About Everything*, 1869:

RUMFUSTIAN, a drink
greatly approved

Ingredients: 12 eggs, 1 quart strong beer, 1 pint gin,
1 bottle of sherry, 1 stick of cinnamon,
1 nutmeg, 12 lumps of sugar, peel of 1 lemon

Mode: Beat the eggs into a froth, and whisk them into
the beer; to this add the gin: meanwhile, boil a
bottle of sherry with the other ingredients, and
as soon as they boil, mix both together. Serve
quite hot.

One-Hoss says this'll grow hair on sidewalks.

DECEMBER 19   "Without the door let sorrow lie
And if for cold it hap to die,
We'll bury it in a Christmas-pie
And evermore be merry!"
—Old Christmas carol

". . . Old English cookery-books always style the
crust of a pie 'the coffin.' . . ."   —R. Chambers

A CHRISTMAS APRICOT PIE

2 cups dried apricots   ½ cup light brown sugar
1 cup orange juice   ¼ teaspoon salt
1 tablespoon cornstarch   butter
pastry for a 2-crust pie

Soak the apricots in the orange juice for two hours and line an
eight-inch pie pan with pastry at the same time, so it can chill while
the apricots soak. After two hours, drain the fruit but save ⅔ of
the juice. Put the liquid in the top of a double boiler, and blend in

1 tablespoon cornstarch
½ cup light brown sugar
¼ teaspoon salt

and let it cook till thick, stirring most of the time. Now spread the apricots around in the coffin, pour the syrup over them, and dot with butter. Cover it with a lattice top or a plain slit top—plenty of slits so the juice can bubble through—and bake for twelve minutes at 400°. Reduce the heat to 325° and bake another fifteen or twenty minutes, till the pastry looks pretty.

DECEMBER 20   On this bleak day in 1820, the sovereign State of Missouri leveled a Bachelor Tax. All unmarried men from the ages of twenty-one to fifty were liable for a special tax of one dollar per year.

Scholars of the period believe it was the husbands' lobby that got the bill through. They couldn't stand the thought of all those carefree unattached lads watching TV football the day before Christmas when they should have been messing with Christmas-tree lights.

DECEMBER 21   *A Dissertation on Camels.*
🍁 🍁   The Camel has not had an easy time of it, and it is no wonder he is bad-tempered. To begin with, he never liked his basic design and tried to get it changed. He wanted horns, according to Aesop—the kind of horns the buffalo had, or maybe a nice set of antlers, and so he took the matter up with Jupiter.

However, Jupiter not only refused to give him the horns he asked for, he cropped his ears short for being so impudent as to ask. The moral, Aesop says, is that *by asking too much we may lose the little that we had before.* Or, to put it another way, *Ask and ye shall receive, something else.*

It isn't true, by the way, that the Camel stores water in his hump. His hump isn't a reservoir, it is a pantry, for storing food. Mostly fat, the hump weighs about eighty pounds. When the Camel has little to eat, he lives off his hump which—naturally—shrinks. If things get tough enough, his hump can even slip off his back and hang to one side, so he loses his figure altogether—a development not calculated to sweeten the temper either. The moral here is *Keep your hump plump.* But of course the Camel is not always in a position to do so.

Carrying the Wise Men was really the high point for the Camel. Things have gone pretty much downhill ever since.

267

A good day to make a Scripture Cake.

THE FAMOUS OLD SCRIPTURE CAKE

(If you know your Bible well, this will pose no problems. If you don't know it quite that well, the translation is on pages 275–276.)

¾ cup Genesis 18:8
1½ cup Jeremiah 6:20
5 Isaiah 10:14 (separated)
3 cups sifted Leviticus 24:5
3 teaspoons 2 Kings 2:20
3 teaspoons Amos 4:5
1 teaspoon Exodus 3:23

¼ teaspoon each 2 Chronicles 9:9
½ cup Judges 4:19
¾ cup chopped Genesis 43:11
¾ cup finely cut Jeremiah 24:5
¾ cup 2 Samuel 16:1
whole Genesis 43:11

Cream Genesis 18 with Jeremiah 6. Beat in yolks of Isaiah 10, one at a time. Sift together Leviticus 24, 2 Kings 2, Amos 4, Exodus 30, and 2 Chronicles 9.

Blend into creamed mixture alternately with Judges 4. Beat whites of Isaiah 10 till stiff; fold in. Fold in chopped Genesis 43, Jeremiah 24, and 2 Samuel 16. Turn into ten-inch tube pan that has been greased and dusted with Leviticus 24.

Bake at 325° till it is golden brown or Gabriel blows his trumpet, whichever happens first. Usually it takes an hour and ten minutes. After fifteen minutes, remove it from the pan and have it completely cooled when you drizzle over it some Burnt Jeremiah Syrup.

BURNT JEREMIAH SYRUP

1½ cups Jeremiah 6:20
½ cup Genesis 24:45
¼ cup Genesis 18:8

Melt Jeremiah 6 in heavy skillet over low heat. Keep cooking it till it is a deep gold, then add the Genesis 24. Cook till smooth and remove from the heat. Add Genesis 18 and stir till it melts, then cool. After drizzling this on the cake, you can decorate it with whole Genesis.

DECEMBER 22   Now it is the first day of winter.
❦ ♑   And now beginneth the sign of persistent
CAPRICORNUS (controlling the Knees) that continueth through

January 19, a favorable time to
    pull teeth (if any be left now)
    bake a Christmas pudding
    execute the Christmas turkey
    start a romance
    continue one.
And Capricorn accomplisheth all duties, for in Capricorn the Desire
to be well thought of nearly equaleth the desire to follow the Heart.

DECEMBER 23   A day to give a passing thought to Christmas
                  Dinner.

". . . Since childhood, I have viewed with distinctly bridled
enthusiasm the general custom of cooking and serving a large
Christmas dinner. All I ever saw of my mother on that day was the
bow on her apron."

                        —Albert Wooky

A GOOD CHRISTMAS DINNER

Oyster Stew
or
Clam Chowder
or
Vegetable Soup
or
whatever soup the family likes best

A Platter of Cold Sliced Meat and Thin-sliced
Bread-and-Butter

Celery Stalks and Carrot Strips

A large tray of samplings from all edible gifts (and
freeze the rest), including Mrs. Finnery's Blue Ribbon
Cranberry Cake and the girl across the street's home-
salted Cashews, and some of those foil-wrapped Cheese
Wedges, compliments Dierdorff & Sons Insurance, and
some of Mrs. Diddlehopper's Dream Puffs

Champagne

DECEMBER 24   "Just for a few hours on Christmas Eve and
                 Christmas Day the stupid, harsh mechanism
of the world runs down, and we permit ourselves to live according
to untrammeled good sense, the unconquerable efficiency of good
will. We grant ourselves the complete and selfish pleasure of loving
others better than ourselves. How odd it seems, how unnaturally
happy we are! . . ."

                                   —Christopher Morley

Wrapping gifts on Christmas Eve, you will find that big brown
grocery sacks, cut up, make cheerful packages when tied with
bright yarn. As it grows later, small brown grocery sacks will prove
handy, as is. Drop the present in, and tie it with the yarn. Newspapers aren't bad either, and when you run out of yarn, there may
be some calico around, or an old printed shirt, to cut with pinking
shears into ribbon.

DECEMBER 25   Now riseth the hillock of crumpled Tissue
                 and emptie Boxes; now appeareth the bright
welter: the Gift Glorious & the Gift Poopy, the rich-packed Pudding
& the Toasts & the bright Sugar-plums. Yet through it all, the listening Ear heareth the sound of the Christmas Promise.

> "Then let us all rejoice amain,
>   On Christmas-day, on Christmas-day,
> Then let us all rejoice amain,
>   On Christmas-day in the morning!"
>   —Old English Christmas carol

DECEMBER 26   Aspects excellent for cooking the Christmas
                 ham (or turkey) that wasn't cooked yester-
day. A good thing to serve with it is

MAGGI COBB'S V. GOOD FRIED FRUIT

*(V. festive too, and it can be ready well in advance,
right up to adding the brandy)*

A 1-pound can each of
    peach halves
    pear halves
    pineapple rings
An 11-ounce can of
    mandarin oranges

1 cup seedless grapes, canned or
    fresh
1 6-ounce jar maraschino cherries
2 pared apples cut in wedges
3 sliced bananas

¼ pound butter
⅓ cup brown sugar
½ teaspoon cinnamon
½ lemon
⅓ cup brandy

Drain all the fruit and use the syrup for something else if you can think of something. Melt the butter in a skillet over low heat and add all the fruit. Sprinkle it with the brown sugar and cinnamon; squeeze the half-lemon over it. Cook till the apples are just tender. Before serving, turn up the heat and add the brandy. Stir till blended, and serve quite hot.

DECEMBER 27   Now drink a friendly toast to the memory of Dr. Crawford Williamson Long, who administered the first ether for childbirth, during the delivery of his second child, Fanny.

DECEMBER 28   One day can bring what the whole year hath not.
    —Old proverb

And perhaps this is the day for it: a letter or a new love or a check or an idea or a kick in the teeth or even a double rainbow.

DECEMBER 29   A True Account of a Curious Happening!
It was early in the seventeenth century that Kepler published his Laws of Planetary Motion. They were, of course, the wonder of the age, at least to the comparatively few people educated enough to understand them.

Lord Orrery, in the north of England, was one of these. In fact, he become so fascinated by Kepler's picture of the universe that he hired an ingenious jeweler to build for him a mechanical model of it in miniature, to place with all honor in his front hall.

There it stood, in its extraordinary shining complexity—a brass sun in the middle, the planets gravely revolving about it, four little moons revolving about Jupiter, one little moon revolving punctually around the earth, all exquisitely timed with a watchmaker's precision.

One morning, an atheist friend of Lord Orrery dropped by. Seeing it for the first time, he stood watching in awed fascination. Then he asked, "Who in the world made that for you?"

Lord Orrery said, "Nobody."

"Oh, come on, tell me," said his friend.

"That's right—nobody made it," Lord Orrery said. "It just happened. I came down one morning and there it was."

"Quit pulling my leg," his friend said with irritation.

And Lord Orrery said, "All right then, I'll make you a deal. If you will tell me who or what made the infinitely more intricate, mysterious, and beautiful universe we're living in, I'll tell you who made this one."

And for the first time, it is said, his atheist friend was without a ready answer.

GOD ISN'T DEAD, HE JUST DOESN'T LIKE BEING ON BUMPER STICKERS

DECEMBER 30   A good day to resolve to keep last January 2's Resolutions for the entire rest of the year.

DECEMBER 31   11:59 P.M. The neighbors went out for New Year's Eve. The kids went out. Even the tide went out, and it doesn't look like it wants to come back.

272

But your scribe goeth not out. (She did that once.) Your scribe sitteth in a new Christmas bathrobe by an old Christmas fire that will go out when the Old Year does. Listening to the wild bells ring out in Times Square and in the little church down the road, which were to ring out the thousand years of war and ring in the thousand years of peace but have not done so yet. Thinking the long thoughts that go with Old Year's Night. Viewing (as always) the Pandora's Box of a new year, unfailingly packed with Mischiefs of many kinds, yet also (like nuts in a cake) stuck therein with Pleasures & Goodnesses great & small; and also Hope therein, like a moth atremble, struggling to get her wings free.

And so your scribe now thinketh of the folk dear to her & of the folk who would be if she but knew them. Hopeth for them no troubles that cannot be in some good fashion coped with; wisheth them all (pray it be not too bold a wish) much joy in the year to come & the years thereafter. *Farewell.*

THE SCRIPTURE CAKE

GENESIS 18:8—"And he took *butter,* and milk, and the calf which he had dressed, and set it before them."

JEREMIAH 6:20—"To what purpose cometh there to me frankincense from Sheba, and the *sweet cane* from a far country?"

ISAIAH 10:14—"And my hand hath found as a nest the riches of the peoples; and as one gathereth *eggs* that are forsaken, have I gathered all the earth."

LEVITICUS 24:5—"And thou shalt take *fine flour,* and bake twelve cakes thereof."

2 KINGS 2:20—"And he said, Bring me a new cruse, and put *salt* therein."

AMOS 4:5—"And offer a sacrifice of thanksgiving of that which is *leavened,* and proclaim free will offerings and publish them."

EXODUS 30:23—"Take thou also, unto thee the chief spices: of flowering myrrh five hundred shekels, and of *sweet cinnamon* half so much."

2 CHRONICLES 9:9—"And she gave the king a hundred and twenty talents of gold, and *spices* in great abundance."

JUDGES 4:19—"And he said unto her, Give me, I pray thee, a little water to drink; for I am thirsty. And she opened a bottle of *milk* and gave him drink."

GENESIS 43:11—"Carry down the man a present, a little balm, and a little honey, spicery and myrrh, nuts and *almonds.*"

JEREMIAH 24:5—"Thus saith Jehovah, God of Israel: Like these good *figs,* so will I regard the captives of Judah, whom I have sent out of this place into the land of the Chaldeans, for good."

2 SAMUEL 16:1—"And when David was a little past the top of the ascent, behold, Ziba, the servant of Mephiboseth met him,

with a couple of asses saddled, and upon them two hundred loaves of bread, and a hundred clusters of *raisins*."

GENESIS 24:45—"And before I had done speaking in my heart, behold Rebekah came forth with her pitcher on her shoulder; and she went down to the *fountain,* and drew: and I said unto her, Let me drink, I pray thee."

MANY THANKS

All the people quoted in this book are real, though some are real only to me. That is, it was necessary to make some of them up, in order to be sure someone would say what I didn't feel quite comfortable saying myself. Accordingly, if they are not identified as they appear, or on this page or the following pages, that is probably the sort of people they are, and you are not likely to run into them anywhere again.

As for the others, I have identified them here if they seemed to need it, or if I could. (If I couldn't, it was because these writers were quoted in old old books, with no source given. Too bad.) If they seem to me familiar enough, I didn't bother to identify them. Identifying William Shakespeare, for instance, demands either innocence or effrontery, and at this point I haven't much of either.

But I want to thank everyone from whom I have quoted.

AMORY, CLEVELAND. Besides being the founder of the Hunt the Hunters Club, he is a social historian and writer, author of *Home Town, The Last Resorts, Man Kind?, The Proper Bostonians, Who Killed Society,* and *Vanity Fair.*

AUBREY, JOHN (1626–97). An English antiquary, folklorist, and gossip who delighted in the trivia of other people's lives, especially famous people, and preserved a lot of it in his *Miscellanies and Brief Lives.*

AUDEN, W. H. English-born and American-naturalized poet and playwright; author of *Poems, The Dance of Death, The Double Man,* and other books.

BAKER, JERRY. A popular garden writer, author of *Plants Are Like People,* which he seems to believe, and *Jerry Baker's Back to Nature Almanac.*

BEEBE, CHARLES WILLIAM (1877–1962). American explorer, naturalist, and writer of many books, including *The Arcturus Adventure, Half-Mile Down,* and *Book of Bays.*

BEETON, MRS. (nee Isabella Mary Mayson, 1836–65). English writer on cookery and housekeeping whose literary output was as voluminous as her life was short. Educated at Heidelberg, she became an accomplished pianist and gave it up in 1856 to marry the publisher Samuel Orchard Beeton. (Marrying a publisher is helpful to a writer, though not essential.) Her *Household Management,* published in several parts in 1859–60 and covering all branches of the domestic arts, made her name a household word. She died at age twenty-nine, after the birth of her fourth son.

BOYD, LOU. American syndicated columnist.

BRILLAT-SAVARIN, ANTHELME (1755–1826). French gastronome and writer. A minor politician, his passion was food—eating it, preparing it, thinking about it. He wrote his *Physiologie du Goût* in 1825, an elegant and witty compendium of the art of dining.

BYRNE, SITA. A Ceylonese woman who worked with the poor in Hong Kong, Korea, Japan, and Southeast Asia for the Lutheran World Federation.

CANNON, POPPY. Knowledgeable U.S. author of many cookbooks.

CAPON, ROBERT FARRAR. Episcopal minister as well as Professor of Dogmatic Theology and Instructor in Greek at The George Mercer Jr. Memorial School of Theology. Author of *Bed and Board, An Offering of Uncles,* and *The Supper of the Lamb.*

CATO, MARCUS PORCIUS. The Roman statesman who lived from 234 to 149 B.C. and didn't like the Carthaginians. His every speech ended with "As for the rest, I vote that Carthage should be destroyed," and he deserves most of the credit for bringing on the Third Punic War. We probably wouldn't know about his hangovers if it weren't for Plutarch and his *Parallel Lives.*

CHAMBERS, R. Scottish publisher and bookseller, born in 1802. He wrote voluminously on Scottish traditions, history, and biography. Singlehanded, he wrote *The Book of Days*—two immense volumes —working so hard on it that he lost his health and died in 1871.

CLAIBORNE, CRAIG. Food authority and author of several cookbooks. The lines quoted are from his *Kitchen Primer.*

CLAIBORNE, ROBERT. Free-lance writer for U.S. newspapers and magazines.

CLAYTON, BERNARD, JR. A former *Time-Life* war correspondent, now writer and editor attached to the School of Business at Indiana University, and author of a purely excellent and comprehensive bread book, *The Complete Book of Breads* (1973).

CORBITT, HELEN. Restaurant consultant to Neiman-Marcus and author of several books, including *Helen Corbitt's Cookbook, Helen Corbitt's Potluck, Helen Corbitt Cooks for Looks,* and *Helen Corbitt Cooks for Company.*

CORMAN, AVERY. U.S. advertising man; author of *Oh, God!*

DE LA MARE, WALTER JOHN (1873–1956). English poet and novelist who wrote many books, including *Songs of Childhood* and *Poems for Children.*

DE POMIANE, EDOUARD. French author of several charming cookbooks, among them one called *Cooking in Ten Minutes.*

DE VRIES, PETER. American author of *The Tents of Wickedness, Through the Fields of Clover, The Vale of Laughter,* and a number of other remarkable and remarkably funny books.

DILLARD, ANNIE. Poet (*Tickets for a Prayer Wheel*) and author of *Pilgrim at Tinker Creek;* also contributing editor to *Harper's.*

"ELIZABETH." Pen name of the Countess von Arnim, author of some delightful turn-of-the-century novels, including *Elizabeth and Her German Garden, Introduction to Sally,* and *The Father.* Born Mary Annette Beauchamp, she first married Count von Arnim and, next, a brother of Bertrand Russell.

FIRTH, GRACE. Missouri-born author of *A Natural Year,* a charming and fact-filled around-the-year book mainly concerned with how to live off the outdoors and like it (1972).

FROST, ROBERT. American poet. The quote is from a letter to *The Amherst Student,* published March 25, 1935.

FULLER, R. BUCKMINSTER. Designer and builder who developed, among other things, the geodesic dome, which is made of adjoining tetrahedrons, which are solids bounded by four plane triangular faces. He also wrote two good books: *Ideas and Integrities: A Spontaneous Autobiographical Disclosure* (1963) and *I Seem to Be a Verb* (1970).

279

FULLER, THOMAS (1608–1661). English clergyman, historian, and author of several books, including *History of the Holy Warre* and *History of the Worthies of England*. The remark about the guts and the heart quoted here is probably the shortest thing he ever said.

GILLIES, MARY DAVIS. Author of *The New How to Keep House* (1968).

GUNTHER, MAX. Free-lance writer, well versed in bugs.

HATT, CONGER T. I have been unable to track down his publisher, but I agree with a great deal that he says.

HAZELTON, NIKA. A good cook and writer on things culinary. The quote is from her *The Picnic Book* (1969).

HERTER, GEORGE LEONARD AND BERTHE. Authors of numerous books, all written, illustrated, and published by themselves in Waseca, Minnesota. Their works include *George the Housewife,* and three volumes of *Bull Cook and Authentic Historical Recipes and Practices*. They also run a thriving mail-order business in outdoor gear.

HIGGINS, ANNE. The quote is from her story "Maria at the Dentist," published in *Ms.,* April 1974.

HILLS, L. RUST. A man who writes and says quotable things. Author of several books, including *How To Be Good, or, The Somewhat Tricky Business of Attaining Moral Virtue in a Society That's Not Just Corrupt but Corrupting, Without Being Completely Out-of-it* (1976).

HOFFER, ERIC. The longshoreman-philosopher who wrote *The True Believer* and *The Passionate State of Mind*.

HOPKINS, GERARD MANLEY (1844–1899). Brilliant English Jesuit priest and poet, remembered for his God-haunted poems, not his sermons. Yet when he died, few of his obituaries mentioned that he was a poet.

KENNELLY, ARDYTH. Contemporary American novelist who knows and wrote about early Mormon days in Utah. Author of *The Peaceable Kingdom, The Spur, Good Morning, Young Lady, Up Home,* and *Marry Me, Carry Me*.

LAMB, CHARLES (1775–1834). English essayist who wrote, among other things, *Tales from Shakespeare* and *Essays of Elia*. These are fighting words from a very gentle man. But then, the people couldn't talk back.

LESLIE, FRANK. English journalist and artist whose real name was Henry Carter. In the mid-nineteenth century he came to the United States, changed his name for reasons of his own, and founded *Frank Leslie's Illustrated Newspaper,* a cozy and edifying sheet that contained something for everybody, as well as *Frank Leslie's Illustrated Family Almanacs.*

LEWIS, C. S. (1898–1963). English writer and Christian apologist; author of *Perelandra, Out of the Silent Planet, The Screwtape Letters,* and a number of other good books.

LYDGATE, JOHN. English monk and court poet who was born a couple of decades after Chaucer and wrote the same sort of thing Chaucer did but not so well.

LYND, ROBERT (1879–1949). Irish author of *It's a Fine World,* from which this quotation came.

MC CABE, CHARLES. New York–born newspaperman and professional Irishman, columnist for the San Francisco *Chronicle*.

MILLER, ELISABETH S. An early U.S. writer on the domestic arts. Author of *In the Kitchen* (1875).

MORE, SIR THOMAS. Well-known English writer and statesman who was beheaded at the age of fifty-seven because he wouldn't acknowledge Henry VIII as head of the English church.

MORLEY, CHRISTOPHER (1890–1957). Author of numerous novels, plays, poems, and casual pieces, who helped William Rose Benét found *Saturday Review of Literature* in 1924.

MORTON, J. B. Long-time columnist for the *Daily Express,* London.

MOSER, ROBERT. U.S. doctor and columnist, former editor of the A.M.A. *Journal.*

OLIVER, RAYMOND. Chef, writer, TV performer, and owner of Le Grand Vefours, a three-star Michelin restaurant in Paris.

PASCAL, BLAISE (1623–1662). An incredible and short-lived genius, mathematically, philosophically, and every which way. His *Pensées* were published after his death, and the quote is one of them.

PIRSIG, ROBERT. Author of the remarkable book *Zen and the Art of Motorcycle Maintenance* (William Morrow & Co., 1974). He studied chemistry, philosophy, and journalism at the University of Minnesota, and Oriental philosophy at Benares Hindu University in India.

PLATH, SYLVIA. American poet who wrote *The Colossus, Ariel, Uncollected Poems,* and *The Bell Jar.*

PLATT, JOHN RADER. American physicist and able writer. The quote is from *A Science Reader* (1962).

RAPP, LYNN AND JOEL. Authors of *Mother Earth's Hassle-Free Indoor Plant Book.*

RIVERS, JOAN. U.S. stand-up comedienne. It's always specified whether a comic stands up or sits down or lies down. Apparently it makes a difference in the quality of the work.

RUML, BEARDSLEY (1894–1960). Basically, a businessman but quite good at thinking. Chiefly remembered for inventing the pay-as-you-go Federal Income Tax plan.

RYSKIND, MORRIS. American playwright and collaborator of George Kaufman, George and Ira Gershwin, and Irving Berlin.

SAGAN, CARL. Director of the Laboratory for Planetary Studies and Professor of Astronomy and Space Sciences, Cornell University.

ST. JOHN, ADELA ROGERS. Contemporary California-born reporter and writer. The quote is from her most recent book, *Some Are Born Great.*

SCHOENSTEIN, RALPH. Columnist and free-lance writer. Author of *My Year in the White House Doghouse, I Hear America Mating,* and other funny books.

SCOTT-MAXWELL, FLORIDA. Writer and analytical psychologist. Author of several books, including *Towards Relationships, Many Women,* and *The Measure of My Days,* from the last of which the quoted lines were taken.

SHAND, P. MORTON. Self-termed gastrosopher; author of *A Book of Food.*

SHAPLEY, HARLOW. American astrophysicist, writer, and long-time director of Mt. Wilson Observatory. Among many other things, he figured out the size of our galaxy and the sun's position in it.

SHERATON, MIMI. A knowledgeable cook and writer. Author of *The Seducer's Cookbook.*

SZASZ, THOMAS STEPHEN. Contemporary Hungarian-born psychiatrist and author of several books, including *Pain and Pleasure, The Myth of Mental Illness,* and *The Second Sin,* from which the quoted lines were taken.

Helen Chen's

Chinese

Home

Cooking

Illustrated by Earl C. Davis

Hearst Books / New York

Library of Congress Cataloging-in-Publication Data

Chen, Helen.
    [Chinese home cooking]
    Helen Chen's Chinese home cooking.
        p.   cm.
    Includes index.
    ISBN 0-688-12756-8
    1. Cookery, Chinese.   I. Title.   II. Title: Chinese   home
    cooking.
TX724.5.C5C5374   1994
641.5951—dc20   93-49726
                                                          CIP

Printed in the United States of America

First Edition

2   3   4   5   6   7   8   9   10

Book design by Richard Oriolo

This book is lovingly dedicated to my mother,
Joyce Chen

My mother was diagnosed with multi-infarct dementia over ten years ago. All her symptoms and the progression of her illness lead her doctors to believe that she is also a victim of Alzheimer's disease. Today at seventy-six, my mother lives in a nursing home and cannot speak or care for herself.

Many years ago, before the illness manifested itself, my mother used to talk to me about her wish that one day we would write a mother-daughter cookbook. As the weeks became months and the months became years, our busy lives never brought us together in the kitchen to accomplish this collaboration. With the advance of my mother's illness and dementia I thought that dream was gone forever.

I was wrong. One morning I awoke with the realization that my book *was* the collaborative effort my mother wished for after all. Instead of having my mother beside me, I had her thoughts, her philosophy, her recipes, and her stories as my guide.

My mother's cookbook, which has been out of print for many years, contains many recipes from our family meals — those "hot and noisy" dinners with our Chinese friends, the simple family meals and get-together meals celebrating birthdays, festivals, and special events in our lives. I am happy to be able to bring some of those recipes, together with my own, for you to enjoy.

We can't recapture our past or change our destiny, but with my mother's recipes I truly feel that she has actually been with me, leading me through the maze of her recollections, stories, traditions, experiences, and food that she once prepared. Once in a while I'd be working on a recipe and think of her so much I would have to drive over to the nursing home to be with her.

In my mind I see her now as she used to be — smiling, talking, spatula in hand, apron on, warm fragrant aromas wafting from our little kitchen in Cambridge. That's how I remember my mother.

Acknowledgments

My mother used to say that we are all born the same. Everything we know comes from someone else. Although I cannot possibly thank all whose lives have influenced me, I wish to express my gratitude to those whose contributions made this book a reality:

First and foremost I wish to thank my mother, Joyce Chen, for teaching me everything I know about cooking. To my late father, Thomas Chen, for instilling in me the values of honesty, hard work, and perseverance.

I am grateful to my two brothers, Henry and Stephen, for answering questions, suggesting recipes, and helping me recall childhood stories and memories, of which there would be far fewer without them.

To my publicists, Lisa and Lou Ekus, for their friendship and guidance that led me to William Morrow and Company.

To Judith Weber, my agent, for her wise professional judgment and advice.

To Harriet Bell, my editor, for her encouragement, wisdom, and gentle guidance through the intricacies of writing a book.

To Skip Dye of William Morrow, who enthusiastically believed in me and my book from the start.

A special note of gratitude to Nancy Verde Barr for her insightful critique and editorial assistance.

And to the following people whose collective design and production talents made this book possible:

Bill Truslow, photographer; Jane Sutton, stylist; Susan Derecskey, copy editor; Richard Oriolo, designer; and Earl Davis, illustrator.

To my friends and neighbors who cheerfully tasted and honestly critiqued the recipes. In particular, a special thanks to close friend and fellow food enthusiast, Barry Lockard, who so generously offered his assistance in testing and tasting recipes.

To Mel Novatt, mentor, trusted adviser, and friend in business and in life.

To our family friend, Bob Bradford, who shared his expertise on wines.

To Wilson and Warren Wong of Sun Sun Company, Inc., who helped me with the glossary of ingredients.

To Shirley Fong-Torres and her husband, Bernie Carver, for their warm friendship and for introducing me to San Francisco's Chinatown.

To my cousins, Chen Zu-ying and Zhao Lung-hai, for their help with the *pinyin* spelling and Chinese characters. To my number one aunt, Wu Chen, and my sixth aunt, Chen Zai-chen, for being the link to my parents' China.

To Alice Chang and Lenny Li, for translation help; and to chefs Lee Yuen-gong and Li Xiao-xu, for their recipe ideas and suggestions.

To Betty Woodmansee for her computer expertise and Dorise Boujoulian for her ever-ready smile and administrative support.

To my sister-in-law, Barbara Chen, for information and advice on Chinese ingredients.

To my mother-in-law, Dorothy Ohmart, for her willing assistance with proofreading, and for being the best mother-in-law anyone could ask for.

To Gus Dallas, for his friendship, encouragement, and determination to have me taste every Chinese chicken salad in Los Angeles.

To longtime friends Deli Bloembergen and Anna Ku Lau, for recipe ideas, and to Valarie Hart Ross for inspiring me to create the only cookie recipe in the book.

To Gregory Lee for his assistance with the Chinese calligraphy.

To Nana, my loving cat, for her faithful companionship during the writing of this book.

And last but not least, to my devoted husband and partner-in-life, Keith, for his love, understanding, unwavering trust, and steadfast support in everything I do.

Acknowl-

edgments

Contents

Preface
前言
How It
All Began

My mother, Joyce Chen (Liao Jia-ai) 廖家艾, was born in Peking (Beijing), China, to the family of a prominent public official. She was the youngest in a family of nine, the seventh daughter. Being the youngest and only child of my grandfather's second marriage after the death of his first wife, she was the apple of her father's eye and often accompanied him on business trips. She was encouraged by both parents to be self-reliant and independent. Undoubtedly this early exposure and encouragement influenced her later interest and success in business. As a young girl, she also enjoyed spending time in the kitchen watching the family chef prepare meals. She would stir and mix and make miniature dumplings alongside the head chef's wife. Her parents frequently entertained friends at home, so her childhood memories were of parties, guests, and food.

My father, Thomas Chen (Chen Da-chong) 陳大中, was born in Hangchow (Hangzhou), China, to the principal of a high school. He was the youngest in a family of eleven (one died as a child) and was named Big Middle. It was his family's tradition that all the boys be named after the points on a compass and the girls after the seasons. By the time my father was born, all the compass points were taken, so he became Big Middle. My father's sixth sister was named Again Spring because she was the fifth daughter.

My older brother, Henry, and I were born in Shanghai, China — at home because in those days women were afraid their babies might be switched at the hospital. My brother Stephen, the youngest in the family, was born in Cambridge, Massachusetts. In the Chen tradition, all the children in the male line were given the same middle name. Only the last character of our name is our own. Thus all the Chen cousins have very similar names. Even if we never knew each other, we would realize our relationship because of our names. Henry's Chinese name is Chen Zu-ming 陳祖明, I am Chen Zu-hua 陳祖華 and Stephen is Chen Zu-chang 陳祖昌.

The foresight my mother's parents had in encouraging her interest in cooking so that she "wouldn't have to eat raw rice" was prophetic. In 1949, when my parents immigrated to the United States on the last boat to leave Shanghai before the closing of China, a new life was to start for them. In those early years in Cambridge, there were very few northern Chinese from Shanghai. Although many of us ate regularly in Chinatown where the food was southern — mainly Cantonese — there was nowhere to get our hometown specialties. My parents had become acquainted with a handful of northern Chinese students at nearby Harvard, M.I.T., and Boston University; they also were also homesick for their regional foods. My parents often played hosts to these students and my mother's reputation as a cook became established. She would cook wonderful meals for everyone, and they would talk and reminisce about China and sometimes play mah-jongg into the night. I remember having houseguests every weekend, and it is interesting that my childhood memories are of parties, guests, and food — just like my mother's.

My mother's reputation as an excellent cook grew and led to the opening in 1958 of the first of three Joyce Chen restaurants in Cambridge. She began teaching Chinese cooking at local schools and adult centers and in 1962 she published the *Joyce Chen Cook Book,* from which some recipes have been taken for this book. A year after her cookbook was published, she starred in her own public television series, "Joyce Chen Cooks." She was the first Asian to have her own television show. In 1972, also for public television, we made "Joyce Chen's China," a documentary recounting our trip to China and our reunion with our family. At that time my mother also founded Joyce Chen Products, a company that my husband, Keith, and I now operate. Joyce Chen Products designs, develops, and markets a line of quality Asian cooking utensils especially for the Western kitchen.

Although I have lived in America since childhood, I have a strong bond to China and to being Chinese. As a child I never knew any relatives outside of our immediate family. For a long time, I thought I had none. Since the opening of China in 1972, I have come to know some of my numerous relatives, who still reside all over China in such places as Hunan, Szechuan (Sichuan), Shanghai, Hangchow (Hangzhou), Peking (Beijing), and Nanking (Nanjing). I have assembled a family tree of Liaos (my mother's side) and Chens and discovered to my delight that we have over forty first cousins alone!

By writing this book, I hope to share with you, as my mother did, the rich cultural heritage of China, through my personal memories, traditions, and family recipes.

Introduction

For many people, Chinese cooking remains a mysterious and esoteric cuisine that requires exact and difficult cooking techniques with specialized cooking utensils and exotic ingredients. For others, it is a style of cooking that they occasionally do at home but find the taste is never on a par with the food at their favorite Chinese restaurant. Still others have unsuccessfully attempted Chinese cooking at home and given up in utter frustration. Do any of these sound like you?

What is it about Chinese cooking that people love — and why is it so elusive to most? In addition to the fact that it just tastes good, all of today's nutritional information points to Chinese food as "just what the doctor ordered." For the most part it is low in saturated fat and cholesterol, uses small amounts of meat, and incorporates an abundance of fresh vegetables cooked in a short amount of time to retain texture and nutrition. Unfortunately, there is so much misinformation as to cooking techniques and necessary ingredients that many people are confused as to what is actually right. High heat: What about the food burning in the pan? Small amounts of oil: What about the food sticking? When to cook vegetables and when to cook meat? Together? Separately? Pushed up the sides of the pan? Marinate the meat? Don't marinate meat? What's the answer?

As with most things, there is no one answer that will take care of everything. Cooking is a variable science and art. It all depends upon the kind of stove you have, the type and quality of the cookware you are using, the temperature, the size and type of ingredients, and so on. Understanding some simple techniques and controlling these variables will help you master the Chinese cooking experience.

Before you begin exploring on your own, you need to learn the basics in order to build a firm foundation for experiences yet to come. I will also try to tell you the "why" as well as the "how" of Chinese cooking. Once you understand why, rules become meaningful. Eventually you don't even have to try and remember them. They are yours.

Home-style Cooking

祿 Chinese cuisine holds a vast, largely untapped richness of family tradition, recipes that are passed down from generation to generation but are rarely written down. This is home-style or family-style cooking. It is a personal culinary expression. In spite of improved transportation and the institution of a national dialect, the Chinese still cling tenaciously to the provincial dishes of their home. People from Shanghai love Shanghai food and those from Peking (Beijing) prefer Peking food.

In preparation for this book, I spent a long time thinking about what I really wanted to do for you. I realized after a few false starts that what my mother said to me over thirty years ago, when she was writing her own cookbook, was still true today. Westerners love Chinese food for its quick cooking, economy, taste, nutrition, and variety. Isn't this exactly what the Chinese also love about their own cuisine?

Instead of concentrating on classic Chinese cuisine, this book focuses on the simpler, home-style cooking that I learned from my mother, and she from hers. It's a style of cooking that is simple to prepare. We stir-fry more than deep-fry; steam more than roast; use fresh, seasonal ingredients instead of exotic delicacies; and use less meat in favor of more fresh vegetables.

Besides a simpler approach to ingredients and cooking techniques, home-style cooking is also quick and economical. Although highly processed foods, frozen dinners, and fast-food restaurants are practically unknown in China, the Chinese have their own prepared foods. Understanding and learning to use some of these convenience foods provide a fast way to expand your Chinese cooking repertoire the way the Chinese do.

Although most of us love to get right down to the recipes in a cookbook, I encourage you to read each chapter to help build that foundation I talked about earlier. Once you have established a base of knowledge, you will be ready to put that knowledge to work in the kitchen.

A Word on Pinyin
Romanization

禧 After the founding of the People's Republic of China in 1949, the Mandarin dialect became the national language, thereby uniting all the provinces in a common tongue. This language is known in China as *putong hua,* or common speech. At the same time, China adopted a new system for romanizing Chinese words called *pinyin* or piece-together-sound. *Pinyin* is currently used by the Western world to replace the older Wade-Giles and Yale systems.

In most instances in this book, I have used the new *pinyin* words. However, some place names are more recognizable by their older romanized form and I have retained them for their familiarity to the reader.

Shopping in Chinatown

採購

Shopping at an Asian market can be daunting. The sights, sounds, and smells are all at once exotic, exciting, and intimidating. Although Chinese home cooking can be done without a single visit to a Chinese market, it adds to the culinary experience to browse through an Asian grocery store. And with the burgeoning Asian population in the United States, Asian markets are sprouting up in suburbs and shopping centers all over the country.

They are vibrant and active places, filled with live, fresh and frozen, canned and bottled, dried and pickled food. The shelves are usually stacked from the floor to the ceiling with every imaginable ingredient. Many will be new and unknown to even the veteran Chinatown shopper, for there are always new foods being imported from the Far East to tempt even the most jaded palate.

When I was a child, going to Chinatown was a family affair. Every Sunday we would all pile into the car and my father would drive from Cambridge to Boston's Chinatown. The first order of the day was to find a restaurant and eat. My mother was never one to just sit and wait, so while we waited for our food, she often ventured out to a nearby Chinese pastry shop to see what was fresh. She sometimes came back with some sweet dim sum for dessert. After our meal, the shopping would start in earnest at our favorite store on Hudson Street. It was a dusty dark place with wooden shelves that reached to the ceiling, wooden stools, and a hardwood table where the shopkeepers tallied and wrapped the purchases — and ate their meals. The store seemed to be an endless string of rooms since they had broken through the walls on either side to expand over the years. At the time, it was one of the largest markets in town and we used to spend hours there — or so it seemed to a five-year-old. Every week the owner would treat me to a piece of crystal-clear rock candy on a string that kept me occupied and quiet as my mother shopped. After the grocery store, there were stops at the noodle shop, pastry shop, roast-meat shop, and bean sprout factory.

Things have changed since those Sundays in the dark recesses of an old-fashioned Chinese market, but shopping and eating in Chinatown is a tradition that is carried on to this day. Just one look at the crowds and the bustle on weekends will confirm this. The grocery store we now frequent is a small but busy place. It is brightly lit, well stocked, and clean, with checkout counters just like Western supermarkets. It's only thirty-five hundred square feet, but it carries over three thousand different items!

Understanding and Using Chinese Ingredients

Thousands of different ingredients, from the common to the exotic, are used in Chinese cuisine. New food products from the Far East appear constantly, just as in American supermarkets. Since the opening of China in the 1970s and with the large influx of peoples from Vietnam, Laos, Thailand, and Cambodia, Chinese ingredients are imported from all over Asia and the Pacific Rim, making grocery stores truly pan-Asian. Although a Chinese grocery store may carry a huge variety of foods, not even the Chinese use all of them.

In this chapter, I will introduce you to the important special ingredients that are used in my recipes as well as to some standard ingredients that need some care in their use. I do not believe it's necessary to stock your pantry with many esoteric and expensive ingredients that you may use only once. Instead, I will show you how a few good-quality, well-chosen specialty ingredients will expand your Chinese cooking repertoire.

You will also be pleased to learn that most Chinese ingredients keep practically forever. Sauces, spices, preserved, dried, and pickled condiments seem to keep indefinitely. When I was young, I used to help my mother clean out the refrigerator and cupboards every once in a while. There would be jars and plastic bags containing, to my eye, indistinguishable matter in them. I would be ready to throw them out, having seen them there the last time we cleaned the cupboard. My mother would come rushing over to retrieve them from my hand saying, "Don't throw those away! They're still good." Now, I too have such jars and bags in my refrigerator and cupboard.

Ingredients are listed below in alphabetical order according to their English names. Below the English I have given the name in Mandarin romanization or *pinyin* (page 5). I have also given the Chinese calligraphy (all Chinese read the same characters) and for those ingredients that are sold most often by their Cantonese name, I have given that pronunciation. To be sure you are getting the right item, I suggest you bring your book with you or make a copy of the pages. If you are completely at a loss, you can show the shopkeeper the book and point to the ingredient you want. The shopkeeper, although perhaps reticent with English, often is happy to answer your questions.

Azuki Beans. See Dried Red Beans.

Bamboo Shoots

筍 *Mandarin:* sŭn

Recommended brands: Ma Ling (China) Winter Bamboo Shoots, Narcissus (China)

Bamboo is a grass, and it grows extremely fast. When the Chinese talk about things that grow quickly, they refer to them as "bamboo after a spring rain." My mother used to tell me that some people claimed they could hear the bamboo shoots pushing up through the ground in the spring!

Bamboo shoots are difficult to obtain fresh in the United States, so canned bamboo shoots are commonly used. As far as canned vegetables go, bamboo shoots and water chestnuts retain much of their original flavor and texture even when canned. Any slight metallic taste can be removed by blanching the shoots in boiling water, then immediately draining and refreshing them under cold water.

Canned bamboo shoots come in different sizes and cuts; sliced bamboo shoots are most common in American supermarkets. Chinese markets carry canned bamboo shoots that are whole, sliced, or in strips (shredded). They usually sell both the long, slender spring bamboo shoots and the thick, stubby winter bamboo shoots, which are favored by the Chinese. The winter shoots (*dong sun*) are more tender and flavorful. In general, higher quality bamboo shoots are canned whole.

Once opened, canned bamboo shoots may be stored for about one week, covered with cold water in a lidded container. Change the water daily. If the bamboo shoots smell sour or the water in which they are stored becomes viscous, the bamboo shoots are spoiling and should be discarded.

Bean Curd

豆腐 *Mandarin:* doù fú

Japanese: tofu

Bean curd, or tofu, is made from soy beans that are soaked, ground, and mixed with water to make a soy milk. The milk is heated, and when the curds separate, they are pressed into soft cakes. Bean curd is rather bland in flavor and takes on the taste of the sauce in which it is cooked. It is a healthy alternative to meat since it contains a high amount of protein and calcium without fat.

Chinese grocery stores sell individual three-inch square cakes of bean curd from water-filled tubs or pails. Fresh bean curd from a Chinese bean curd shop has a marvelous fragrance and an almost sweet taste, but it is very perishable and should be used as soon as possible for the best flavor.

Fresh bean curd is now readily available in supermarkets; it comes packed in sealed plastic containers. There are different kinds, but for the recipes in this book I use either the firm Chinese-style or the soft Japanese-style bean curd.

Store bean curd submerged in water in a covered container in the refrigerator. Change the water daily. Fresh bean curd will keep for five to six days, but if it smells sour, discard it. If I am unable to use the bean curd right away, or if I purchase extra cakes on sale, I put some in the freezer for longer storage. The water inside the bean curd freezes, and when it is thawed, the water flows away, leaving a spongy network behind. My mother used to cut frozen bean curd into bite-size cubes to add to a savory soup. They would soak up the tasty liquid in which they were cooked. Frozen bean curd is a traditional ingredient for the popular Peking (Beijing) winter dish called Fire Pot, in which raw ingredients are cooked in hot broth right at the table.

Besides the familiar fresh type, bean curd comes in many other forms — dried bean curd sticks and sheets made from the skin formed on the soy bean milk; little dark cakes of pressed and seasoned bean curd; light, airy puffs of fried bean curd; deep-fried bean curd; and bean curd noodles.

Fermented bean curd that is cured in salt and wine is known in Mandarin as *fú rǔ* 腐乳; it is also called wet bean curd. It is sold in small cakes packed in glass jars. The cakes are mashed and used for stir-frying vegetables such as watercress (page 272) and Chinese water spinach (page 29). It is also eaten right out of the jar as a breakfast condiment with rice gruel known as congee. Fu ru is available in a white (not spicy) or red (spicy) version. It keeps indefinitely in the refrigerator.

Chinese

Ingredients

Bean Paste or Bean Sauce

豆瓣醬

Mandarin: doù bàn jiàng

Japanese: miso

Recommended brands: Koon Chun (HK) Ground Bean Sauce (pureed or whole bean), Sze Chuan Food Products Co., Ltd. (Taiwan) Spicy Szechuan Sauce

Thick, salty, fermented soy bean paste is used as a base for sauces. It is available in whole-bean or pureed form; in this book I use only the puree. Both are sold canned and in thirteen-ounce glass jars. Choose the glass jars whenever possible.

Spicy Szechuan-style hot bean sauce is made with yellow soy beans, salt, flour, chili, sesame oil, sugar, and pepper and comes packed in cans or small jars. It is the base for such dishes as Szechuan Spicy Bean Curd (page 246).

The Japanese make a very good quality bean paste called miso (pronounced Mee-so) that is packed in sealed plastic bags or plastic tubs. There are many types of miso available, mainly white (*shiro*) and red (*aka*). My mother used to buy white and red miso and mixed them together half and half. I like to use the white miso for its lighter and slightly sweeter taste.

Store bean paste in the refrigerator after opening. If it came in a can, transfer it to a tightly lidded glass or plastic container. It will keep indefinitely.

Bean Sprouts

綠豆芽

Mandarin: lù doù ýa

Although at one time they could only be purchased in Asian markets, fresh mung bean sprouts are now popular and easily obtainable in most Western supermarkets. Be sure the sprouts that you buy are fresh and plump with no sign of wilting, browning, or sogginess.

I do not recommend canned bean sprouts. If bean sprouts are needed for flavoring such dishes as fried rice and are not available, substitute shredded pieces of the thick white part of iceberg lettuce. This does not work well in dishes where bean sprouts are the main ingredient.

The Chinese do not like to eat raw vegetables. Even for salads, they blanch the bean sprouts first to remove the raw taste. For special banquets they break off the hair root and head of each sprout by hand so the finished dish will look more beautiful.

Store bean sprouts in a plastic bag in the crisper in the refrigerator; they will keep fresh for about one week.

Chinese

Ingredients

粉絲 *Bean Thread*
Mandarin: fěn sī

Bean thread is also known as cellophane noodles, glass noodles, Chinese ver-micelli, and green bean thread. The first two names are a reference to the clear appearance the noodles have once they are cooked. Made from mung bean flour, the noodles are most often packed in tight two-ounce bundles and come eight bundles to a net bag. They are used in soups, stir-fried, or added to vegetarian fillings.

Bean thread will keep indefinitely in a cool, dark, dry place.

Black Mushrooms. See Dried Black Mushrooms.

白菜 *Cabbage*
Mandarin: bái cài
Cantonese: bok choy

Many different varieties of Chinese cabbage or bok choy (literally, white veg-etable) are available. Chinese cabbage has a milder flavor and softer texture than the common green cabbage. The first three varieties of Chinese cabbage listed below are the most versatile and widely available; they are the ones used most often in this book. The fourth, Shanghai bai cai, is currently available only in Chinese markets. The taste, texture, and appearance are so special, you should try to find it when you can.

山東白菜 *Napa cabbage.* Also known as Shandong Bai Cai, this is a barrel-shaped cabbage with tightly packed large crinkly leaves. The leaves are light yellow-green in color with white stems. Napa cabbage is a favorite of mine because it is extremely versatile, cooks up tender without a strong cabbage aroma, and stores well.

天津白菜 *Chinese celery cabbage.* Also known as Tianjin bai cai, this cabbage has long, slender leaves that form a compact, cylindrical head, hence the name celery. The pale green leaves are proportionally smaller than the more significant white stalk.

白菜 *Bok choy.* Called Bai Cai in Mandarin, this is a loose-leaf cabbage with thick white stems and dark green leaves. It is used most often in stir-fry dishes.

上海白菜 *Shanghai bai cai or bok choy.* Also called Shanghai bok choy, this diminutive (about six inches long) loose-leaf cabbage has a loose, green leaf structure similar to bok choy, but the leaf stems are green instead of white. The cabbage is usually split or quartered, if large, and stir-fried or parboiled.

Tight-leaf cabbages, like napa or Chinese celery cabbage, will keep a month or more, wrapped in plastic and stored in the vegetable drawer of the refrigerator. Loose-leaf cabbages, like bok choy or Shanghai bai cai, are more perishable and should be used within a week.

Cellophane Noodles. See Bean Thread.

Chili Oil
辣油 *Mandarin: là yóu*

Recommended brand: Joyce Chen (USA) Szechuan Stir Fry Oil

This bright red-orange chili oil is also known as hot oil. It may be purchased in Chinese grocery stores, or you can infuse your own (page 329). Chili oil is not meant for cooking but to be used as a garnish or seasoning for dips and stir-fry dishes.

The oil may be kept at room temperature in a cool, dark place for about six months or refrigerated for longer storage. If it begins to smell rancid, discard.

Chili Pepper
辣椒 *Mandarin: là jiāo*

Small (about 2 inches long) dried red chili peppers are useful to have on hand; they are a must-have if you like spicy-hot food. Most dried chili peppers come from Thailand and are packed in three- to four-ounce plastic bags.

To keep a finished dish looking attractive, I remove the pepper seeds before cooking. It's easy to do. Simply take a small pair of scissors, snip off the stem, and cut the chili open on one side. With one blade of the scissors scrape up and down the chili and the dry seeds will all fall out. Discard the seeds and use the pod only. Always add the dried peppers to cold oil and heat them up slowly to avoid burning.

You may substitute crushed red pepper for the whole chili. In general, if one teaspoon of flakes is added to a dish that serves four, it will be mild-hot; two teaspoons, hot; and three to four teaspoons, fiery!

Store dried chili peppers in a tightly lidded clean jar in your cupboard. They can get buggy over time.

芥藍 Chinese Broccoli or Chinese Kale
Mandarin: gài lán
Cantonese: gai lan

This vegetable is part of the cabbage family and resembles Chinese cabbage rather than broccoli. The flat leaves, which are the predominant part of the vegetable, grow from the stem, they are dark green with a blue haze. The narrow stalks often have small yellow or white flowers at the tips. Chinese broccoli is appreciated for its slightly bitter taste and the crunchy stems. As with regular broccoli, I peel the outer skin off the stalks if it is tough. Chinese broccoli may be substituted for regular broccoli.

韭菜 Chinese Chives or Garlic Chives
Mandarin: jǐu cài
Cantonese: gow choy

The long, grasslike leaves of Chinese chives are flat rather than round and have a stronger flavor and texture than regular chives. Chinese chives are green or if grown away from the light, yellow. If the white ends are tough, they should be snipped and the discolored or wilted leaves pulled off and discarded before use.

Chinese chives are easy to grow as a perennial herb. Seedlings or seeds are sold in garden shops as garlic chives (*Allium tuberosum*). You can use the greens in Chinese dishes and to garnish and flavor Western dishes much as you would use regular chives. The lovely swirl of white flowers that bloom in August are edible and make a nice garnish.

Store Chinese chives in a plastic bag in the vegetable drawer of the refrigerator. To prevent rotting from too much moisture, I like to lightly wrap the chives in a layer of paper towels before sealing in a plastic bag. They will keep fresh for about one week.

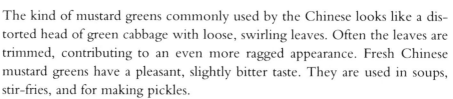

Chinese Mustard Greens

芥菜 *Mandarin: jīe cài*
Cantonese: gai choy

The kind of mustard greens commonly used by the Chinese looks like a distorted head of green cabbage with loose, swirling leaves. Often the leaves are trimmed, contributing to an even more ragged appearance. Fresh Chinese mustard greens have a pleasant, slightly bitter taste. They are used in soups, stir-fries, and for making pickles.

Mustard greens will keep about one week in a plastic bag stored in the vegetable drawer of the refrigerator.

Chinese Sausage

香腸 *Mandarin: xiāng cháng*
Cantonese: lop chong

Storebought Chinese sausages are very tasty, keep well, and are readily available in Chinese markets. The ones I use most often are the thin links about six to eight inches long, made with pork or with duck liver. The sausages are dried and shrink wrapped in plastic or, in some stores, hung from hooks in bunches. As with most sausages, they tend to be fatty, but they are versatile as a flavoring condiment or side dish. Since the taste is slightly sweet, they are sometimes referred to as sweet sausages. As a quick side dish, my mother used to fashion a tray out of aluminum foil, place the sausages, sliced into bite-size pieces, on it, and steam the sausage with the rice for the last ten to fifteen minutes of cooking.

Chinese sausage will keep for months in the refrigerator and indefinitely in the freezer.

Cilantro, Coriander, or Chinese Parsley

香菜 *Mandarin: xiāng cài*

The Chinese call cilantro "fragrant vegetable," and so it is. It resembles flat-leaf parsley but has a strong, distinctive aroma. Some people find the taste a bit too strong. I recently read that to many children, cilantro tastes like soap. I remembered that was the exact reaction I had when I first tasted it as a child. But now I love it and like to garnish cold meats, soups, and steamed seafood with sprigs of this herb.

Store cilantro in a plastic bag lined with a paper towel. Without the paper towel, the cilantro rots faster, especially if it was moist from the market. Be sure to rinse cilantro thoroughly before using as it can be gritty.

玉米粉 菱粉 Cornstarch

Mandarin: líng fěn (water chestnut starch)
Mandarin: yù mǐ fěn (cornstarch)

Cornstarch is used in Chinese cooking as a thickener, binder, and coating to hold in natural juices so that the food does not dry out. As a thickener, cornstarch is ideal. It mixes easily with water, cooks quickly, and makes a clear sauce. When used as a thickening agent, the cornstarch is always mixed first with water and stirred in quickly while the food is still cooking. It should never be added dry or it will form a lumpy, powdery mess. In Chinese restaurants a container of cornstarch mixed with water — a slurry — is always on hand, ready to use. The amount of slurry needed to thicken a dish depends upon how much liquid there is to thicken. If you like your sauces thicker, add a little more cornstarch slurry, judging the consistency as you stir. If the sauce is too thick, add some water or unsalted broth to thin it out.

As a binder, cornstarch is added to ground meat, as in Lion's Head (page 205). cornstarch locks in the juices and binds the soft meat together.

As a coating, cornstarch keeps the juices of meat and seafood sealed in during stir-frying and deep-frying. The drawback is that the cornstarch has a tendency to stick to the pan. If this happens, add some water — not oil — to the pan. The water will dissolve and lift the cornstarch, forming a gravy in the process.

When cornstarch is mixed with water to form a slurry or is used to coat meat or seafood, it has a tendency to separate and sink to the bottom of the bowl before it is added to the pan. Stir up anything that has cornstarch in it just before adding it to the pan. That way you'll be sure you haven't left most of the cornstarch behind.

If you are allergic to cornstarch, substitute Chinese water chestnut starch, available in Chinese grocery stores, or arrowroot.

You can store cornstarch indefinitely in a dark cupboard.

咖喱粉 Curry Powder or Paste

Mandarin: gā lí fěn

Curry is not a single spice but a combination of different spices; each curry has its own distinctive taste. I recommend purchasing Madras Indian curry in powder or, preferably, paste form in specialty ethnic markets since it has a

Chinese

Ingredients

good, strong flavor. Curry pastes with oil and chili have a more complex taste than curry powder.

I store curry paste or powder in the refrigerator. The paste will keep practically indefinitely. Curry powder should be replaced when it no longer has a rich aroma.

Daikon
蘿蔔 Mandarin: *luo bŏ*
Japanese: *daikon*

Known most commonly by its Japanese name, which means big root, this radish is also called icicle radish or Chinese white radish. It is long and white, inside and out. Good daikon is heavy, juicy, solid, and crisp, not fibrous and dry. It is used for soups, red-cooked foods, or for pickling (page 320). Mother and I also used to eat daikon raw if it was not too sharp. We would peel the radish, cut it into sticks, and dip them into peanut butter.

Store daikon in the refrigerator as you would carrots. It will keep for about one month.

Dried Black Mushrooms
冬菇 Mandarin: *dōng gū*
Japanese: *shiitake*

The Chinese call these winter mushrooms. The Japanese sometimes use these mushrooms fresh, but the Chinese always use them dried, in which case the smoky flavor is more concentrated. Black mushrooms come in a wide variety of size and thickness, which determine the quality and price. The most expensive ones have thick caps with white cracks. For everyday use, where the caps may be sliced for stir-frying, use the less expensive thinner ones. Reserve the more expensive, thick-capped ones for special occasions when the mushrooms will be served whole.

Dried mushrooms must be reconstituted before using. Soak them in hot water for fifteen minutes, squeeze out the water, and cut off the stems with scissors. Use whole or cut into pieces.

Dried black mushrooms should be stored in a tightly lidded container in a cool, dark place. They will keep almost indefinitely.

金針 Dried Golden Needles
Mandarin: jīn zhēn

These dried unopened blossoms of a certain kind of day lily are used in vegetarian and northern-style dishes such as Peking Hot and Sour Soup (page 72) and Moo Shi Pork (page 192). The dried flowers must be softened in hot water, the hard stem knob cut off, and excess water squeezed out. If the flowers are long, line them up, and cut them in half before using. Golden needles come packaged in cellophane or plastic bags.

Store in a tightly lidded container in a cool, dry, dark place. They keep almost indefinitely.

陳皮 Dried Orange or Tangerine Peel
Mandarin: chén pí

Dried orange peel is used to flavor braised and stir-fried dishes as well as desserts. The Cantonese favor their use more than the northern Chinese. I purchase a small box of dried orange peels in Hong Kong each year. They come in clear plastic boxes and look quite prehistoric! I also dry orange peels as my mother did. She preferred to use Honey Tangerines (Murcotts) because the skin is highly fragrant and the pith is very thin so you don't even have to scrape it off. Score the skin before peeling so you get nice, even quarters of skin. Air-dry for several days, and then store in a cool, dry, dark place. They will keep indefinitely.

Dried Red Beans
紅豆 *Mandarin: hóng dòu*

Japanese: azuki

Red beans may be purchased in Chinese grocery stores or in some health food stores. Unlike Western-style beans, these are generally used to make sweets. They are cooked whole as in Sweet Red Bean Soup (page 342) or sometimes pureed. The beans are also popular as the main ingredient in cold drinks during the summer. Store as you would any dried bean in a sealed plastic bag or lidded jar.

Already prepared sweet red bean paste (*hong dou sha*) is available in eighteen-ounce cans in Asian markets. Look for Companion brand. The paste is made from boiled and pureed red beans, sugar, and water and used as a filling for steamed buns and such desserts as Eight Treasure Pudding (page 344). My mother used to make her own the traditional way by pureeing the cooked beans and mixing the puree with sugar and lard into a rich paste. After opening, store the paste in a tightly lidded jar in the refrigerator. It will keep for several months.

蝦米 Dried Shrimp
Mandarin: xīa mī

These tiny shrimps are salted and dried. They have a strong fishy flavor and may not appeal to everyone. Chinese enjoy snacking on dried shrimp, and when we were children, my mother always kept a good supply on hand, enough for cooking and snacking! When they are used as a condiment in salads, soups, and stir-fried dishes, I soften and rinse them in water to rid them of excess salt. They are not a substitute for fresh shrimp.

Store dried shrimp in a covered jar in the refrigerator. They will keep for months. The color should be orange. Brown means that they are old.

木耳 Dried Wood Ears
Mandarin: mù ěr

Also known as Black Fungus, Cloud Ears, or Tree Ears, wood ears are a kind of black, gelatinous fungus that grows on trees. They are appreciated for their crisp texture and not for their flavor, of which there is little. Look for small, black flakes, about half an inch or smaller in size, not the large pieces with grayish color on one side.

Wood ears are always sold dried and must be reconstituted in hot water for fifteen to twenty minutes. When softened, they expand to five or six times the dried size. After soaking, trim off the sometimes hard stem end and rinse thoroughly to get rid of any grit. Cut or break the caps into smaller pieces for cooking. Do not cook them too long or they will lose their texture.

Store dried wood ears in a tightly sealed container or sealed plastic bag in a cool, dry, dark place. They will keep indefinitely.

Duck Sauce
Mandarin: none
Recommended brand: Joyce Chen (USA) Sweet and Tangy Duck Sauce

Duck sauce is a sweet and pungent sauce that resembles a fine chutney of apples, plums, and/or apricots, sugar, and vinegar. It has no duck in it, although it is delicious served with duck. I sometimes add duck sauce to fried rice at the table. Our sales director for Joyce Chen Products, John Eaton, adds a little bit to his stir-fry at the end of cooking for a tangy-sweet taste. Duck sauce is very popular with Americans and is often served with egg rolls, fried wontons, and barbecued spareribs. On the East Coast of the United States it is known as duck sauce, but on the West Coast they call it plum sauce. It is probably not authentically Chinese. Unfortunately, the duck sauce served at most Chinese restaurants is thin and runny. This is because many restaurants thin out the prepared duck sauce with applesauce and pineapple juice to extend it.

Egg-roll Skins or Wrappers

Egg-roll skins are sold in Chinese grocery stores and in almost any full-size supermarket. They are a standard six and a half inches square and are sold in one-pound packages. Wonton skins or wrappers are basically egg-roll skins, but cut into fours. I find that egg-roll or wonton skins from Chinese grocery stores or noodle shops tend to be thinner and more tender than the ones in Western supermarkets. The thinner skin gives better results. When you work with egg-roll skins, cover them with a lightly dampened towel to keep the edges from drying out and getting brittle.

If not using before the expiration date on the package, freeze the skins for later use.

Fermented Black Beans or Salted Black Beans

豆鼓 *Mandarin:* dòu chǐ

Recommended brand: Pearl River Bridge Co. (China) Yang Jiang Preserved Beans with Ginger

Not to be confused with dried black beans, these are soy beans that have been salted and aged with spices. They have a rich, salty taste and a tender texture. Some cooks like to rinse them before using, but I find that good-quality black beans are not loaded with salt and do not have to be rinsed. In general, however, if you add black beans to a dish that does not call for them, reduce the amount of salt. Black beans should be coarsely chopped before using to release the flavor. The quality of black beans varies from brand to brand. I highly recommend Pearl River Bridge beans, which are actually less salty than most. They are packed in a seventeen-ounce yellow, blue, and brown paper drum. Most fermented black beans are packed in eight- to sixteen-ounce plastic bags.

Black beans keep indefinitely in a tightly sealed container in a cool, dry, dark place.

Chinese

Ingredients

19

Five-spice Powder
五香珍 *Mandarin: wŭ xiāng fěn*

This prepared spice powder is made with about five (sometimes more) different ground spices, including cinnamon, star anise, licorice, fennel, cloves, ginger, anise seed, and pepper. In Chinese it is called five-fragrance powder. Five-spice powder is used by the southern Chinese to marinate meat and poultry as well as a seasoning for Oven-roasted Spiced Peanuts (page 321).

Store tightly covered in a cool, dry, dark place as you would other powdered spices.

Fu ru. See Bean Curd.

Gingerroot
薑 *Mandarin: jiāng*

Fresh gingerroot is an ubiquitous flavoring in Chinese cuisine. It is an irregular shaped fibrous rhizome with a strong, spicy taste and wonderful aroma. Ground ginger is not a substitute for fresh gingerroot.

Recipes call for gingerroot to be sliced, crushed, minced, shredded, or grated. Generally speaking, if the gingerroot will not be eaten, it does not need to be peeled. Minced and grated gingerroot that will be blended into a dish and consumed should be peeled first. Chinese chefs peel gingerroot with small, deft strokes of the Chinese knife. You may find it easier to scrape or peel the skin off with a small paring knife. Peel only as much as you will use at a time.

Slices of gingerroot called for in this book are one inch in diameter and an eighth of an inch thick, about the size of a fifty-cent piece. For grated ginger, the ginger should be peeled and the exposed end scraped over the raised teeth of a ginger grater. Use the grated ginger that accumulates at the end of the dish; the fiber caught in the porcelain teeth can be rinsed off and discarded. Crush gingerroot with the side of a Chinese knife.

Choose a piece of fresh gingerroot that feels hard with a skin that is light tan. If the skin is shriveled and darkened or the rhizome feels spongy, don't buy it.

I have short- and long-term storage methods for gingerroot that work very well.

Short storage: about three months. Wrap the fresh gingerroot in a plain white paper towel and place it in a plastic bag. Place in the vegetable drawer of your refrigerator. When the paper gets too wet, replace with a fresh paper towel. If any mold begins to grow on the gingerroot or a portion turns brown and becomes spongy, trim it off and use the portion that is still hard.

Long storage: one year or more. Rinse the gingerroot and slice one eighth of an inch thick. Place the slices in a clean glass jar with a good lid. Cover the gingerroot slices with pale dry sherry, seal the jar, and store in the refrigerator. When you need some gingerroot, remove the slices with a pair of chopsticks or a toothpick. Although sherry-packed gingerroot is easy to use, I prefer to use fresh gingerroot whenever possible.

Golden Needles. See Dried Golden Needles.

海鮮醬 *Hoisin Sauce*
Mandarin: hǎi xiān jiàng
Recommended brands: Koon Chun (HK) and Joyce Chen (USA)

This versatile soy bean sauce, which is flavored with spices and garlic and sweetened, is used in cooking and as a dipping sauce for dishes served with Mandarin Pancakes, such as Moo Shi Pork (page 192) and Peking Duck. Hoisin sauce is one of those commercial sauces that no one makes at home, like ketchup. It can be served as it comes from the bottle or garnished with a little sesame seed oil.

Refrigerate after opening. It will keep indefinitely.

辣豆瓣醬 *Hot Bean Paste. See Bean Paste.*

麵 *Noodles*

Many types of noodles are used in Chinese cooking. The most popular are made from wheat or rice flour.

Wheat Noodles

 *Mandarin: jī dàn miàn (egg noodles)*
miàn (water-and-flour noodles)

Wheat noodles may be egg or eggless, thin or thick. The thin kind is comparable to Italian thin spaghetti and the thick variety to fettuccine. Both varieties are available fresh or dried. Interestingly, it is easier to find fresh Chinese-style noodles in Western supermarkets than dried. This may be due to the fact that with the great popularity of Italian-style dried noodles, there's no room on the shelf for dried Chinese noodles.

Dried noodles are available in boxes or bags. I like to buy five-pound boxes of Chinese-style plain dried flat noodles about an eighth of an inch wide for general use. In the early years when Chinese-style noodles were only available in Chinese noodle shops, my mother often used Italian dried spaghetti from the supermarket as a substitute. I still use it and have never had a problem with the success of a dish. I use thin spaghetti, spaghettini, vermicelli, or when I want a wider noodle, linguine.

Dried wheat noodles keep almost indefinitely.

Fresh noodles are usually in the produce department of the supermarket and are packed in plastic bags. I have found that Azumaya brand noodles, thick or thin, are very good. You'll find many dried and fresh noodles in Chinese grocery stores. Fresh noodles, egg or plain, are packed in plastic bags.

Fresh noodles cook up very quickly, so be careful you don't overcook them.

Fresh noodles should be stored in the refrigerator until ready to use or frozen for longer storage.

米粉 *Rice Noodles*
Mandarin: mǐ fěn
Recommended brand: *Double Swallow Brand (China) Rice Stick*

Rice noodles are made from rice and water and come thick or thin, dried or fresh. The most common rice noodle used at home is the thin, dried variety called rice sticks.

Before using, soak the noodles in warm water for ten to fifteen minutes until soft. Do not boil. Drain and use in soup noodle recipes or with other ingredients in a stir-fry.

The thin rice noodles can also be deep-fried in hot (375°F.) oil while they are still dry. Break them into three-inch pieces and fry small portions at a time. Remove with a wire skimmer as soon as they puff up and drain on paper towels. Use them as a garnish for stir-fry dishes or in salads.

Dried rice noodles keep for a long time.

Fresh rice noodles, which are popular with the southern Chinese, are available in Chinatown. They are very perishable and must be stored in the refrigerator.

Chinese

Ingredients

22

油 *Oil*
Mandarin: yóu

There seems to be much confusion as to the *right* oil to use for Chinese cooking. There is no single right oil. Some are more right than others, however. Peanut oil has been touted by many, but my mother always used soybean oil because of its lighter flavor. Other oils that are fine to use are corn oil and so-called vegetable oil, such as Wesson or Crisco. I prefer canola oil, which is derived from the rapeseed, a plant of the brassica family. It is neutral in flavor and light in texture and does not interfere with the natural flavors of fresh or delicate ingredients. It is an excellent oil to use at high temperatures for stir-frying. Canola oil was used exclusively in the testing of all the recipes in this book.

If you would like to use a flavored cooking oil, the Joyce Chen cooking oils are all made with a base of canola oil.

Do not stir-fry with olive oil or sesame seed oil. These oils are not suitable for Chinese food because of their strong flavor and low smoking temperature.

蠔油 *Oyster Sauce*
Mandarin: háo yóu

Recommended brand: *Lee Kum Kee Premium (HK) Oyster Flavored Sauce*

This versatile and tasty Cantonese cooking sauce, also called oyster-flavored sauce, is made from oyster extract, salt, and spices. Contrary to its name, this thick brown sauce does not taste like oysters. Oyster sauce comes in glass bottles and is made by many manufacturers. If you are unsure of which brand to purchase, and the recommended brand is not available, choose a more expensive brand for better quality and taste. Refrigerate after opening. It will keep indefinitely.

Red Beans. See Dried Red Beans.

米 *Rice*
Mandarin: mǐ (raw rice)
飯 *fàn (cooked rice)*

Rice is the staple grain of Asia. There is long and short grain, brown and polished white rice, fragrant rices, like Basmati and Jasmine, popular in India and Thailand, respectively. The Chinese prefer long-grain white rice. This rice cooks up light and fluffy. The Japanese, on the other hand, prefer a short-grain white rice which is softer and stickier when cooked. For making congee, or rice gruel, we use short-grain rice for a smoother texture.

Originally, the northern Chinese ate many more wheat dishes like steamed breads and noodles because of the difficulty of growing rice in their cooler and drier climate. With better transportation rice is now served at every meal, although wheat remains a popular starch.

Rice is relatively inexpensive in the United States and easy to obtain in the supermarket or an Asian market. For convenience and savings, I buy a premium long-grain white rice by the twenty-five-pound bag. Precooked and instant rice are not recommended. They do not have the fresh flavor or soft texture of freshly cooked raw rice.

Glutinous rice, also known as sweet rice, is used in certain dishes as a filling or in desserts like the famous Eight Treasure Pudding (page 344).

Store raw rice covered in a cool, dry, dark place. It keeps indefinitely.

Glutinous rice is also ground into flour and used to make steamed sticky cakes, sweet rice balls like those in The Emperor's Nectar (page 340) and sweet soups like Almond tea (page 339). Sweet rice powder comes in one-pound boxes or bags from Japan, China, and Thailand.

Sweet rice wine is glutinous rice that has been yeast fermented. The rice is steamed, then mixed with a starter, covered and left in a cool, dark place until the rice is soft with a sweet, alcoholic liquid. Both the rice and its liquid are used in cooking such desserts as Emperor's Nectar. Although my mother always made her own sweet rice wine, I buy mine from the refrigerator section of an Asian market. It is sometimes called Sweet Rice Pudding.

麻油 Sesame Seed Oil
Mandarin: mā yóu

Recommended brand: Kadoya (Japan) or Joyce Chen (USA)

Oriental sesame seed oil is pressed from roasted sesame seeds. It is golden brown in color and highly fragrant. Since this oil has a low smoking temperature and is strongly flavored, it is not suitable for stir-frying. It is used as a garnishing oil or for making dressings and dips or added to fillings for flavor.

Store at room temperature in a dark, cool place. For longer storage keep in the refrigerator. Sesame seed oil tends to turn rancid in a few months. If it is used infrequently, buy a small bottle.

火腿 Smithfield Ham
Mandarin: hǔo tǔi
Recommended brand: Smithfield Packing Co. (USA)

The Chinese call ham "fire thigh," and the most famous in China is from Jinhua in Zhejiang Province south of Shanghai. The closest in flavor to the famous *Jinhua* ham is Smithfield ham from Virginia. My mother used to keep a Smithfield ham hanging in the basement; now I do the same! When we needed to use it my father would bring it up and with a hacksaw, saw off a piece. The ham would then be rewrapped and taken back down to the cellar. If you do not want to deal with a whole ham, you'll find many Chinese markets with a meat department that have pieces of Smithfield ham already cut and packed for sale. The ham is used to flavor soups (Ham and Winter Melon Soup), or it is minced for a garnish.

Whole Smithfield ham keeps well in a cool basement. If there is any mold, just scrape or slice it off. For longer storage you may freeze the ham. Slices of ham should be stored in the refrigerator.

雪菜 Snow Cabbage or Red-in-Snow
雪裏紅
Mandarin: xùe lǐ hóng or xùe caì
Recommended brand: Ma Ling (China) Pickled Cabbage

What a beautiful name for a pickled vegetable! The imagery comes from the fact that the roots are red and that this leafy vegetable, a member of the mustard family, often sprouts in early spring through the snow. The leaves are pickled in brine and have a distinctive salty, pungent taste and crisp texture. Pickled snow cabbage is used as a condiment and flavoring, in soups, in stir-fries with pork, and as a filling for dumplings. Snow cabbage is usually available in cans.

After opening, transfer to a clean, tightly lidded glass jar and store in the refrigerator. It will keep indefinitely.

雪豆 Snow Peas
Mandarin: xùe dòu

Unlike regular peas, the whole pod of the snow pea is edible. In fact, the important part is not the pea, but the pod. Only use fresh snow peas; frozen snow peas will ruin a fine dish. Also called pea pods, snow peas have bright green, unblemished pods; they should snap when bent in two. To use, snap the ends of the snow peas and pull down the strings. Other edible pods, such as sugar snap peas, may be substituted for snow peas.

Store snow peas in a plastic bag in the vegetable drawer of the refrigerator where they will keep about one week.

Chinese

Ingredients

25

Soy Sauce

醬油 *Mandarin: jiàng yóu*

Recommended brands: Dark — Pearl River Bridge (China) Soy Superior and Joyce Chen (USA), Light — Pearl River Bridge (China) Superior Soy, Thick — Koon Chun (HK)

A good Chinese soy sauce is critical to successful Chinese cooking. It is probably the most often used — and most misunderstood — Chinese ingredient. There are several different soy sauces, each with its own characteristic.

Supermarket soys are usually made from hydrolyzed vegetable protein, salt, caramel color, and preservatives. They lack both taste and texture. The popular Japanese soys are fine for Japanese food or for dressings and dips that call for their lighter, sweet flavor, but they are not suitable for Chinese stir-frying, which requires a more robust taste with a heavier, thicker texture.

The two most useful types of soy sauce to have on hand are dark and light. Dark soy sauce contains molasses and has a thicker texture (light refers to the thinner texture, not to the color or sodium content). You can tell the difference by shaking the bottle. Dark soy sauce will cling longer to the neck of the bottle. Light soy sauce, which is a little saltier than the dark, should be used for table dips and dressings or when a thinner coating is desired. Dark soy sauce should be used for cooking, where a richer taste and thicker coverage is desired.

The saltiness of different soy sauces varies a great deal. I suggest you omit or reduce the amount of salt called for when soy sauce is used. At the end of cooking, taste the dish and add salt as desired. This way, if the sauce you use is saltier than mine, you can adjust at the end of the cooking. This is especially true when using any Chinese prepared sauce, such as oyster sauce or bean sauce.

Many people ask me what restaurants use to give fried rice its dark color. It is not regular soy sauce, which would be too watery, but a thick, syrupy soy sauce called *thick soy sauce,* not to be confused with dark soy sauce. This has the consistency of honey and is made with molasses, salt, and soy bean extract. It is used primarily to give a deep, rich color to foods.

Store soy sauce in a cool, dark place. It is not necessary to refrigerate it. I like to buy large sizes of light and dark soy sauces and decant them into separate bottles with convenient pouring spouts.

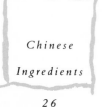

Chinese

Ingredients

八角 *Star Anise*
Mandarin: bā jiǎo

This lovely spice has five to eight cloves that form a star. The Chinese call them "Eight Corners" in reference to their star shape. They are most often used in Shanghai-style red-cooked dishes. Use star anise whole or break off cloves. Store in a tightly lidded glass jar in a cool, dark, dry place. Star anise keeps indefinitely.

Sweet Red Bean Paste. See Dried Red Beans.

花椒 *Szechuan (Sichuan) Peppercorns*
Mandarin: hūa jiāo

A dried spice, known as "flower pepper" in Chinese, Szechuan peppercorns are small reddish-brown husks that have partially opened to reveal tiny black seeds inside. They grow on bushes and are often packed with bits of twig that should be picked out before use. They are widely used in Szechuan cuisine for cooking, as well as for pickling and curing meats. They can be found in Chinese grocery stores, usually packed in four-ounce cellophane bags. Used in large quantities, they give a numbing sensation to the mouth. Transfer whole peppercorns to a covered glass jar and keep in a cool, dark, dry place. Use as long as they are fragrant.

Szechuan peppercorns are generally toasted and ground before use. Heat the peppercorns in an ungreased skillet over medium heat until the peppercorns are smoking and fragrant. Do not let them burn. How long it takes depends on the amount of peppercorns you are roasting. Let the peppercorns cool, then grind them in a mortar with a pestle or roll with a rolling pin between two pieces of paper. Sift through a strainer and discard the larger pieces that do not pass through. Store the powder in a clean, tightly lidded glass jar in a dark, dry place.

Szechuan peppercorns are also used to make a seasoned salt (page 332) that is used as a dip for fried foods. Stored in a tightly lidded container in a cool, dark, and dry place, the seasoned salt will keep indefinitely.

Chinese Ingredients

Szechuan Vegetable

榨菜 *Mandarin:* zhā cài

Recommended brand: Ma Ling (China) Zhejiang Preserved Vegetable

The knobby, fleshy stems of a particular kind of mustard green are preserved in salt and chili powder for this Szechuan specialty. Its salty, sour, spicy taste and crisp texture enrich soups and stir-fry dishes. Szechuan vegetable comes in cans and is available whole or shredded. I like to buy the shredded one because it is easier to use. I always keep a can or two on hand for that quick soup or soup noodle dish. I usually rinse off the coating of red chili powder before using to tone down the spiciness and salinity. After opening the can, transfer the vegetable to a clean tightly lidded jar. It will keep indefinitely in the refrigerator.

Tofu. See Bean Curd.

Vinegar

醋 *Mandarin:* cù

Recommended brand: Cider — Heinz (USA), Rice — Marukan (Japan and USA) Genuine Brewed Rice Vinegar (green label), Chinese black — Gold Plum (China) Chinkiang Vinegar

There are three types of vinegars used in this book — cider, rice, and Chinkiang or Chinese black vinegar.

Cider vinegar My mother always used Heinz vinegars. I also find the taste of Heinz to be preferable to other brands.

Rice vinegar Less acidic than cider, this clear or yellowish vinegar is made from rice.

Chinkiang or Chinese black vinegar This rich, flavorful vinegar is comparable in taste to balsamic vinegar. It is made from water, glutinous rice, and salt. It is known as Chinkiang vinegar, for the city in which it is brewed. Store in a cool place away from direct sunlight.

Chinese

Ingredients

馬蹄 *Water Chestnuts*
Mandarin: măˊti

Recommended brands: Ma Ling (China) or Companion (Taiwan)

Water chestnuts are available canned or fresh. Fresh water chestnuts are crunchy and sweet like apples, but it is difficult to find good-quality fresh ones. If the water chestnuts are spongy when pressed or are shriveled, don't buy them. Look for a hard fruit with a shiny mahogany-colored skin when rubbed. All fresh water chestnuts tend to be muddy. Wash, peel, and rinse thoroughly before eating. You may eat fresh water chestnuts raw or sliced and cook them in your favorite recipe. If the flesh is yellow or discolored, discard. Canned water chestnuts, available whole or sliced, are a fine substitute for the fresh. If your canned water chestnuts have a tinny taste or aroma, plunge them in boiling water for a few seconds, then immediately drain and rinse in cold water.

Store drained canned water chestnuts in a lidded container, covered with cold water. Change the water daily. If they begin to smell sour or the water becomes viscous, they are spoiled and should be discarded.

空心菜 *Water Spinach*
Mandarin: kōng xīn cài
Cantonese: ong choy

Water spinach is not related to spinach, but to the sweet potato. This trailing vegetable is available at Chinese markets. Stir-fried with fermented bean curd (page 9), it is a popular Cantonese country dish. The leaves become slightly slippery when cooked.

My introduction to the cultivation of water spinach was years ago when I lived in a two-family house in Somerville, Massachusetts, which I owned. My Chinese tenants downstairs asked permission one day to dig up a rather small and scraggly looking lawn for planting vegetables. I thought that neat rows of vegetables would look better than weeds, so I agreed. Little did I realize that they wanted to grow water spinach! True to its name it needs a very wet soil so instead of neat rows of tomatoes and peppers as I had imagined, the yard was transformed into wet, sunken beds filled with water spinach. When they moved out a few years later, it took quite a while to return the yard to lawn.

Water spinach will keep for about a week refrigerated in a plastic bag in the crisper.

Chinese

Ingredients

酒 *Wine*
Mandarin: jĭu

In Chinese cooking, rice wine is usually used as a seasoning to cover up certain unwanted flavors, like fishiness from seafood. In some recipes such as Drunken Chicken (page 180), it is the main seasoning. Shaoxing wine, from Zhejiang Province, is a famous high-quality rice wine used both for cooking and drinking. Chinese rice wines are available in Chinese grocery stores, but in order to sell them as cooking wines and not table wines, for which they would need a special license, the wines are salted. Do not confuse Chinese rice wines with the Japanese rice wine called sake or mirin. It is not necessary to use Chinese rice wine. My mother always used pale dry sherry both at home and at our restaurants. I also prefer dry sherry. It is easy to get, inexpensive, and provides an excellent taste.

冬瓜 *Winter Melon*
Mandarin: dōng gūa

A member of the gourd family, this melon is prized for its thick, white rind. It grows very large (like a pumpkin) and is cut into wedges and sold by the pound. The skin is green with a white fuzz that makes it look as if it's frosted with snow. Winter melon rind is used in soups. At fancy banquets, a whole winter melon may be carved with an intricate design and used as the container to hold the soup. The rind is also candied and served during the lunar New Year along with candied water chestnuts and coconut slivers to ensure a sweet year ahead. Slices of fresh winter melon should be wrapped in plastic film and stored in the refrigerator. The melon will keep for about one week.

Wood Ears. See Dried Wood Ears.

Note If you have difficulty obtaining any of the Chinese specialty ingredients or equipment used in this book, contact:
The Oriental Pantry
Mail Order Department
423 Great Road
Acton, Massachusetts 01720
Telephone: 1-800-828-0368
Fax: 617-275-4506

Tools in a
Chinese Kitchen

The traditional Chinese kitchen is a rather spartan place and it's hard to believe that a few simple hand tools and a single pan could produce such incredible delicacies. These tools seem to remain confusing and awkward to most Western cooks. I hope the following guide will dispel the mystery. Some items may not be available in local stores.

A Note on Quality

The cookware and cutlery of China are generally crudely made from inexpensive materials, such as cold rolled carbon steel and earthenware. This is not because the Chinese prefer them this way, but because China cannot afford better-made kitchenware. Just because a cooking tool comes from China or Taiwan doesn't necessarily mean that it is the best choice. The Western market is flooded with cheap Chinese equipment manufactured especially for export to be sold at low prices. It is ironic to me that so many home cooks insist on the "real" thing only to be disappointed with awkward-to-use, rusting cookware that ultimately ends up in the garage or trash can.

It was my mother's frustration with the lack of good or appropriate kitchenware that prompted her to create her own line of cookware, which continues to be distributed and marketed today under her name, Joyce Chen Products. Her original designs were the result of her knowledge of what a Chinese cook needs at home and what the Western kitchen can accommodate. I can recommend our products to you without reservation.

The Chinese Knife

福 The first piece of Chinese equipment people often think of is a wok, overlooking the most important tool — a good, sharp knife. Since the Chinese eat with chopsticks and not with knives and forks, almost all ingredients are cut up in the kitchen before cooking or serving. The most important cooking technique, stir-frying, is a fast sauté over high heat, and it is imperative that the ingredients be uniform in size so they cook quickly and evenly.

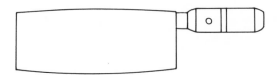

The traditional Chinese knife is a wide, rectangular carbon-steel blade with a wooden handle. It is sometimes referred to as a cleaver but I prefer to call it a knife, because the medium-weight style that is used most often is designed for cutting, slicing, and dicing, and not for chopping bones. Cleavers for chopping are heavier and made of a softer steel to avoid damage that may occur to a harder, more brittle blade.

A good knife should feel comfortable in your hand — well-balanced and solid. The blade and handle should be clean and properly packaged to prevent damage to the blade in transit. A poorly made knife will have a blade that is too thick and a handle that is awkward and fatiguing to hold.

The steel may be carbon or stainless. Some people feel that stainless blades are too difficult to sharpen because of their hardness, but I prefer a good stainless blade. It is much easier to maintain and won't rust, stain, or give a metallic taste to foods. The handle of a Chinese knife is traditionally made of wood, although there are some knives with metal, plastic, or rubber handles.

The top-of-the-line Chinese knife that we have designed for Joyce Chen Products is called the All-In-One Knife. It has a chrome molybdenum stainless steel blade and comes in two sizes, 85 mm (below left) and 63 mm wide (below right), with a full tang hardwood handle secured with three stainless steel rivets. The 85-mm knife is a full-size standard Chinese knife; the 63-mm is a slimmed-down version, made a little smaller and lighter for the smaller hand

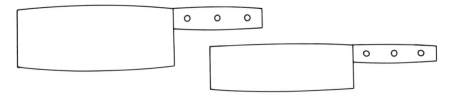

or for cutting vegetables. Our midline basic kitchen model is called The Chinese Kitchen Knife. It has a high carbon stainless steel blade with a traditional

round wooden handle. Which knife to use depends upon your personal preference.

A Chinese knife should be cared for like any other good knife. It should never be placed in the dishwasher. Store it carefully so the blade does not rub up against hard objects that will chip or dull its edge. Keep the edge honed by running it over a sharpening or honing steel each time it is used. If the edge needs sharpening use a whetstone or a good quality sharpening tool.

See pages 41–48 for instructions on holding and using a Chinese knife.

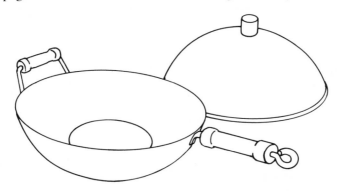

The Wok or Stir-fry Pan

禄 The next most important piece of Chinese equipment is the pan. Northerners who speak Mandarin call this pan a *guo,* or more familiarly *wok* in Cantonese. Manufacturers and distributors of Oriental-style cookware use the names stir-fry pan and wok interchangeably.

The original Chinese wok has a round bottom and metal ring handles on either side. It was designed to sit in an opening over a wood- or coal-burning brazier. This worked well for the Chinese for thousands of years, but on flat ranges in America, these round-bottom woks became inconvenient and even dangerous to use. To stabilize the wok, manufacturers devised a metal ring to be placed around a burner so the wok could sit on top. In the 1950s and 1960s this setup was all that was available to Western cooks wishing to stir-fry.

My mother never owned a round-bottom wok. She found it too difficult to use successfully on a Western stove. Before our cookware company was established, she used a pressure cooker or a deep heavy skillet from a professional kitchen supply house for stir-frying. It was the need for a proper pan that prompted her to develop the flat-bottom wok and stir-fry pan that became the hallmark of Joyce Chen Products.

When we introduced our first stir-fry pan, it was a revelation. My mother designed this new pan to be smaller and more compact than the fourteen-inch woks then available. The twelve-inch diameter fit better on a home stove top. She then eliminated the need for a ring stand by making the bottom of the pan flat. And instead of metal handles, she made one handle like a skillet

Tools

handle. The body of the pan was made of heavy-weight carbon steel; in later years we added a nonstick surface for lowfat cooking.

Which pan is right for you? Some people are traditionalists and swear by the round-bottom carbon-steel wok. If it works for you and you are happy, that's fine. But, I would not recommend it for anyone with an electric or porcelain top stove. There, a flat-bottom wok is essential. Flat-bottom woks are also much better for gas stoves.

Uncoated carbon steel or nonstick? Some people prefer the traditional carbon steel that is seasoned on a regular basis to prevent rusting and to create a black patina on the inside of the pan. I find, however, that most people do not use their woks enough to keep the seasoned patina in perfect shape. Chinese people use the wok many times every day, it is constantly being cooked in, cleaned, and reseasoned. The complaint about sticky, tacky, dusty and eventually rusting woks is often a result of underuse. With a carbon-steel wok, the more you use it the better it gets.

Nonstick woks and stir-fry pans, on the other hand, do not require seasoning. All nonstick pans, however, are not equal. In general, many nonstick coatings applied on carbon steel do not tolerate well the high heat demands of stir-frying and, interestingly, even less the abuse from boiling water when the wok is used for steaming. Nonstick aluminum is stronger and more tolerant of temperature changes because aluminum, unlike carbon steel, spreads heat across the whole pan rather than concentrating it in one place.

My personal preference is our top-of-the-line twelve-inch stir-fry pan called the Joyce Chen Peking Pan® Pro. It is made of heavy-gauge aluminum with a multicoat nonstick surface that helps you cut back on the amount of oil you use for cooking. Because the material is heavy-gauge aluminum you'll find that this pan takes a little longer to heat up than a carbon-steel pan. This is the pan I used to test all the recipes in this book.

If you choose a carbon-steel pan, make sure it is heavy for even heat conduction, but not so heavy as to be difficult to lift and move around. Handles should be securely attached to the pan with rivets or strong spot welds. Test the wok by holding the handles and pressing the sides together. A wok that is made of very thin gauge steel will be flexible, some can even be bent in half! Stay away from those. In addition to our Peking Pan Joyce Chen Products also offer a complete range of heavy gauge carbon-steel and nonstick woks.

Be wary of choosing wok sets by price alone. The difference between these sets may be more in the number of accessories than the quality of the pan.

Tools

I do not recommend electric woks. They generally do not provide enough heat for proper stir-frying, and they are difficult to control since the heating element is part of the pan itself.

How to Season a Carbon-Steel Wok

Carbon-steel woks are coated with a protective lacquer or oil to prevent rusting in transit. They must be cleaned and seasoned before use. Seasoning seals the carbon-steel cooking surface to prevent rusting. Successive uses of the wok will, over time, build up a black patina that will maintain the protective seasoning and provide a smooth, stick-resistant surface, much like a well-seasoned cast-iron skillet.

Thoroughly scrub the wok with hot soapy water to remove the factory-applied protective oil coating. Some woks come with a lacquer coating, this must be burned off before washing by placing the pan over medium-high heat until it smokes. Remove from the heat and cool. Wash and dry the pan thoroughly.

Pour about 2 tablespoons cooking oil into the wok and smear over the inside with a paper towel until the entire inside surface is coated with a film of oil. Place the pan over medium heat and allow it to heat up slowly for 10 to 15 minutes. With a paper towel, evenly distribute the oil over the entire cooking surface, tilting the wok over the burner so that the sides of the wok heat up as well as the bottom. The pan will be hot, so handle with care. The paper towel will blacken slightly as you do this. Repeat this oiling and heating process 3 or 4 times, letting the pan cool in between. Your wok is now seasoned and ready to use.

How to Maintain a Carbon-Steel Wok

After each use, rinse the wok with hot water and scrub away food particles with a dishwashing brush or nonmetallic scrubber. Use a dishwashing liquid only if necessary, as it may strip away the seasoning. Rinse the pan and dry thoroughly. To be sure all surface moisture is gone, place the wok over medium-high heat to finish drying. Allow the pan to cool. Before storing, wipe a thin film of cooking oil over the inside surface of the wok to prevent rusting and help maintain a seasoned surface. This last oiling may not be necessary every time if the pan is well seasoned and used often. If rust appears, simply scrub it away, rinse and dry the pan and season it again.

How to Maintain a Nonstick Wok

Wash a new nonstick wok with a mild dishwashing detergent and hot water. Dry thoroughly with a dish towel. After each use, clean with hot water and a mild detergent and dry by hand immediately. Never use scouring powder, abrasives, or metal scouring pads, which can damage the nonstick coating.

Never preheat nonstick woks without first adding cooking oil as called for in the recipe. The intense heat without something in the pan to help distribute it may damage the nonstick coating. Always use bamboo, wood, or plastic tools in your nonstick pan. Never use a metal spatula or sharp knives; these may scratch the nonstick coating.

To remove burned food, mix 3 tablespoons chlorine bleach with 1 tablespoon liquid dish detergent in 1 cup of water. Pour into the pan and soak for 20 minutes. Scrub gently with a soft nylon brush or sponge.

If you have a nonstick carbon-steel pan, apply a thin film of cooking oil to the entire surface of the pan after cleaning. This is to prevent rusting should the nonstick coating become scratched with use. It is not necessary to oil an aluminum nonstick pan.

Neither the carbon-steel or nonstick pans should ever be put into the dishwasher. Always wash by hand as soon as possible after cooking.

The Steamer

壽 After stir-frying, steaming is probably the most popular Chinese cooking method. Manufacturers now offer new electric steamers, but I prefer the Chinese stove-top steamers. They provide much more flexibility and control; flexibility in that larger steamers can hold whole fish or bowls of different sizes, control in that you can adjust the amount of heat as you wish.

The Chinese steamer is designed with numerous flat tiers — most commonly two tiers — and a lid. In the Far East, steamers can range in size from diminutive four-inch ones for dim sum to gargantuan tabletop steamers for commercial and restaurant use. For home use, the most common sizes are ten to twelve inches in diameter, these are available in bamboo, aluminum, and stainless steel.

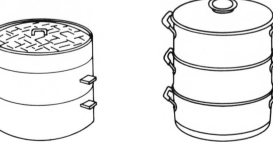

Bamboo steamers are handmade in Asia. Because bamboo can grow to over a hundred feet in height, very large as well as very small steamers can be made from this natural material. Some bamboo steamers in the American market are actually made of wood, with only the slats in bamboo. Some of the best bamboo steamers come from Sichuan (Szechuan) Province, where bamboo grows in profusion. The bamboo steamer is designed to sit over another pot, usually a wok, containing boiling water.

The benefit of a steamer made of bamboo is that as a natural material it absorbs condensation, keeping it from dripping back onto the food. When heated, it forms a hot container and can keep food warm for half an hour. A good bamboo steamer is also attractive enough to bring to the table and is generally reasonably priced.

Steamers made of aluminum and stainless steel come outfitted with a large base pot and tiers that fit snugly on top; there is no need to use a wok as the base. Metal steamers are the easiest to use if you plan do a lot of steaming. Most metal steamers have tiers that are high enough to accommodate a medium-size bowl for steaming soups. Ten-, twelve-, and fourteen-inch metal steamers are the most popular sizes for home use.

A drawback with metal steamers is that condensation forms inside the lid and drips onto the food, sometimes in a big stream when the lid is lifted. This is most troublesome when steaming breads and dumplings. To keep this from happening, the Chinese wrap the lid and the upper tier with a large piece of cotton cloth.

I use both metal and bamboo steamers at home. I prefer the bamboo steamers for steamed breads and dumplings because they don't allow condensation to form. I like the metal steamers because they accommodate bigger bowls and plates and can hold more water, so I don't have to replenish the boiling water as often. The larger steamers may be found in some Chinese markets or hardware stores in Chinatown.

The Rice Cooker

禄 Several kinds of rice cookers are available in the American market. Electric rice cookers are the most convenient to use. Once the rice and water are measured, all you have to do is to push a button and the rice cooker does the rest — cooks, turns itself off, and keeps the rice warm. Although an electric rice cooker can be expensive, it is a worthwhile investment if you like to eat rice.

Microwave rice cookers cook rice in twenty to thirty minutes. They are easy to use, although you need to cook the rice at two power levels and then let it sit to absorb moisture. Microwave rice cookers are inexpensive.

For saucepan-cooked rice a regular heavy-bottomed pot with a lid is fine. See page 88 for directions for cooking rice.

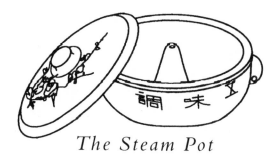

The Steam Pot

禧　The traditional Yunnan steam pot can also be used to cook rice. The steam pot is a special, hard-fired, unglazed clay pot that is handmade in China. It is designed with an interior chimney that rises from the floor of the casserole. It is through this tube that steam enters the casserole, condenses against the lid, and cooks the food in a moist, gentle heat. This pot comes from Yunnan Province. It is traditionally used to cook Yunnan Steam Pot Chicken, but can also be used to steam vegetables, rice, and fruit.

Accessories

福　The following are some useful accessories that make particular tasks easier. They are ones that I like to use.

Cutting Board. With all the cutting that is necessary for Chinese cooking, a good cutting board is essential. Traditionally, the Chinese used thick slices of hardwood tree trunks. They were often bulky and very heavy, about six inches thick and fifteen inches across. Many Chinese markets and restaurants use these, but they are not practical for home use. A fourteen-inch round or at least a twelve-inch rectangular board is sufficient. The material can be wood or plastic.

The item that started Joyce Chen Products was a solid polyethylene cutting board, which we called The Cutting Slab. It is nonporous so it won't absorb moisture or odors; it has the same density as wood, so it won't dull knives; it has a textured surface, so food won't slip and dough won't stick; and it is dishwasher-safe.

Spatula and Ladle. Because large restaurant woks are too heavy to lift, professional chefs use long-handled spatulas and ladles to stir and scoop food in and out. At home, a shorter spatula and shorter ladle are adequate for stirring and scooping sauces and soups.

I use a bamboo spatula that is well shaped and comfortable in the hand. Bamboo, unlike the softer beechwood popular in European wooden tools, is very strong and long-lasting and can go right into the dishwasher. Choose a twelve- to fifteen-inch spatula that is rounded to match the contour of a rounded pan. Be sure it is stiff and rigid, you cannot stir-fry properly with

a flexible spatula. I find that inexpensive plastic spatulas become soft when heated and are awkward to use. A metal spatula with a sturdy handle is fine for carbon-steel pans but can damage nonstick cookware.

Ladles are usually made of metal, because bamboo is not thick or wide enough to make into a ladle. Be careful not to scratch your nonstick pans. To be on the safe side, I use a plastic ladle on my nonstick cookware.

Wire Skimmer or Strainer. This utensil, with its long bamboo handle and wire mesh basket, is handy for lifting foods out of deep-fry oil and for blanching vegetables. A five- or six-inch wire basket is the most useful size for home use. Look for strainers that have strong, well-formed baskets made of either brass or copper wire.

Rolling Pin. The Chinese use a small rolling pin with no handles. It offers more control for rolling out scallion cakes, Mandarin Pancakes, or Peking Ravioli skins. A Chinese rolling pin is eleven to twelve inches long and one inch or slightly less in diameter. I purchased a beautiful professional pin in Hong Kong, but my mother used to make her own from wooden dowels available at almost any hardware store.

Kitchen Scissors. Every kitchen should have a pair of good scissors. I use scissors all the time, for such tasks as deveining shrimp, cutting off the stems from dried black mushrooms, trimming the fat from poultry, and cutting up a whole chicken or lobster. Joyce Chen Products distributes a unique, powerful pair of kitchen scissors called Joyce Chen Unlimited Scissors®. The handles are soft and flexible. And because the scissors have large loop handles, even hands slippery with chicken fat can't easily slip out. The scissors can be used right or left handed and are dishwasher-safe.

Ginger Grater. Ginger graters have raised teeth that separate the pulp from the root. They are made from a variety of materials from stainless steel to porcelain to bamboo. The best in my opinion are the porcelain ones.

Steamer Tongs. These look very much like canning jar lifters, but they open wider. They help you lift a plate from a tight steamer or place a plate or bowl into a hot steamer without burning your fingers.

Chopsticks. Bamboo cooking chopsticks are longer and thicker than chopsticks for table use. They are perfect for stirring green vegetables like spinach, for lifting noodles, and for plucking morsels out of hot oil. Bamboo is relatively inexpensive; when the tips get scorched, the chopsticks can be replaced.

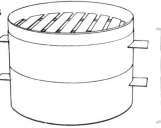

How to Use Chopsticks
筷 子

The Chinese call chopsticks "quick brothers" (*kwai zi*); they are the universal eating implement in China. They are very versatile, and you'll find them in the kitchen as well as on the dining table. Chopsticks are usually made of a nonconductive material such as bamboo, plastic, or wood but can also be made from silver, ivory, lacquer, enamel, or even jade and gold. I have two pairs of slim silver chopsticks intricately engraved and held together at the far end with silver chains. These were given to me by a Chinese friend as wedding chopsticks and are almost too beautiful to use. Chinese chopsticks have blunt ends; Japanese chopsticks are pointed. As a rule, the top end of the chopstick is square (so it won't roll off the table) and the eating end is round. Bamboo or wood chopsticks are inexpensive and good for beginners since they are not too slippery.

Adults should hold the chopsticks at the middle. It is easier for children to hold chopsticks lower down. Keep the ends of the chopsticks even and parallel; they must not cross. Every once in a while you can tap the eating ends on a plate if the chopsticks start to slip. This is not considered bad manners.

Some large foods or meat on the bone offer a special challenge to the uninitiated. The Chinese eat chicken and sparerib nuggets by holding the food with chopsticks and nibbling around the bone. After the meat is nibbled away, the bone is transferred by chopstick to a bone dish. To eat egg rolls, Peking Ravioli, or anything else that is not bite-size, you pick up the food with chopsticks and bite off pieces; return the rest to your bowl or plate or continue to hold it with the chopsticks.

Techniques
in a
Chinese Kitchen

Cutting Techniques

Since there are no forks and knives at the Chinese table, virtually all ingredients must be cut into bite-size pieces. Not only can they be eaten easily with chopsticks, they also cook evenly and look appealing. Although home cooking, unlike elaborate restaurant cuisine, does not utilize some of the fancier garnishing cuts, it does require many basic cutting techniques. Western cooks often seem afraid of preparing to cook a Chinese meal. There may be more cutting than you're used to, but with a good knife and a little instruction, you'll find it easier than you first thought.

First is the knife. Use either a sharp Chinese knife, the best choice, or an eight-inch chef's knife. Because of its shape and weight, a Chinese knife helps you cut quickly, evenly, and cleanly. It is surprisingly versatile. See pages 32–33 for a description of a Chinese knife and what to look for when buying one.

The rectangular shape of the Chinese knife may make it seem a bit front heavy and awkward at first, but it is held differently than a Western-style knife. Grip the Chinese knife at the bolster, firmly like a good handshake, with your bent forefinger resting on one side of the blade and thumb on the other. In this way, the center of balance is further forward, providing more control and less fatigue.

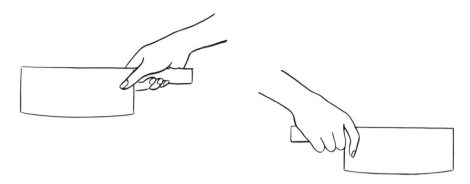

Your other hand should be relaxed with the fingers bent so that the fingertips are slightly behind the knuckles. In this way the knuckles guide the knife, while the fingertips hold down the food. Cut slowly and deliberately. Speed will come later as you develop strength, dexterity, and coordination. When cutting don't raise the knife above your knuckles, just lift the blade enough to move to the next clean cut. Since your fingertips are under and behind the knuckles, you can't cut yourself.

When you cut up ingredients for stir-frying, uniform shape and size is the rule. Tiny pieces of vegetables with large chunks of meat are not esthetically pleasing nor will the ingredients cook evenly. Sometimes you cannot change the shape and size of an ingredient. Bean sprouts, for example, are long, thin, and stringy. Since you can't make them larger, other ingredients should be made smaller — shredded instead of roll-cut or sliced.

How to Slice

The three slicing techniques that follow are the ones I use in this book. Although they are used for a variety of foods, I have focused on their use in my recipes.

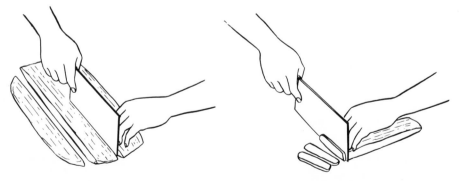

The Straight Slice. The straight slice is commonly used to cut meat and vegetables. This is the one to use when a recipe calls for sliced flank steak, for example. Meat cut this way cooks up very tender.

Trim the fat from the meat. With your knife vertical to the cutting board, cut *with* the grain along the full length of the meat. Cut it into long strips about 2 inches wide. Slice the long pieces *across* the grain into ⅛-inch-thick slices.

The Diagonal Slice. As with the straight slice, the blade is vertical to the cutting board, but at an angle. The more acute the angle, the longer the pieces. Cut each piece at the same angle for uniform size. This slice is most frequently used for cylindrical vegetables such as carrots, celery, cucumbers, and zucchini.

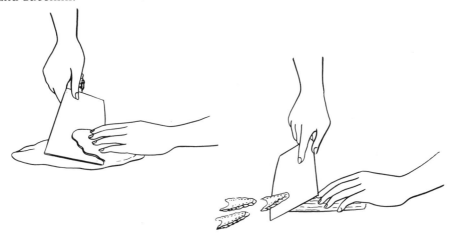

The Horizontal Slice. Horizontal slicing gives you thin wide pieces. In this book, I use this technique to slice chicken breasts and as the first step to shredding beef (page 44). To do this, it is easier to work with meat that has been partially frozen, and it is imperative to have a sharp knife. Wet the blade with water to help it glide smoothly.

Move the cutting board to the edge of the counter so your knuckles don't press on the counter as you work. Place your knife almost horizontal to, but angled down toward, the cutting board. Gently press down on the chicken. Slowly cut the chicken with a sawing motion into thin 2-inch-square pieces.

To cut vegetables, position your knife so you are cutting away from yourself.

Techniques

43

How to Shred

Chinese shredding is done by hand, and the results are quite different from what you get using a box grater. Shredding with a knife gives a matchstick shape about the size and shape of a bean sprout. It is easier to shred meat if it is partially frozen.

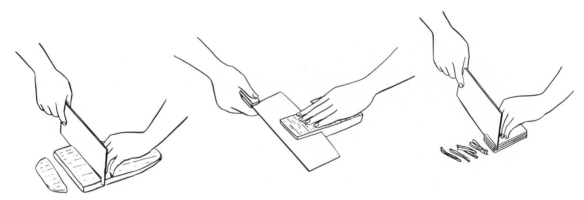

To Shred Flank Steak. Slice the flank steak *against* the grain into 2-inch-wide pieces. Using the horizontal slice, cut the meat into three or four pieces. Pile up the pieces and cut the meat into ⅛-inch shreds along the grain of the meat. Beef cut this way will be fairly chewy.

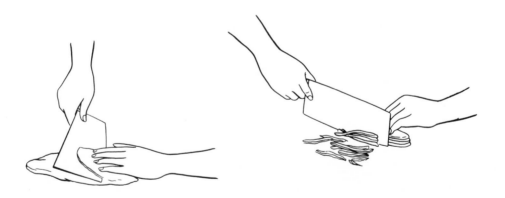

To Shred Pork and Chicken. For pork, I prefer to use thin-cut boneless chops. Thicker chops can be split and shred in the same manner as flank steak. Be sure to trim off the fat first.

For chicken breast, remove the bone and skin. With the blade angled down, slice the meat into wide thin pieces. Pile the pieces on top of each other and cut across into shreds.

To shred pork tenderloin, partially freeze the meat for easier cutting. Cut thin slices, then stack them up and cut across into shreds.

Techniques

44

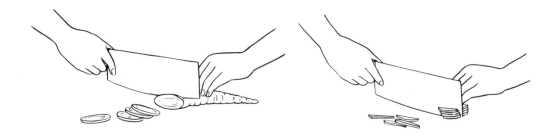

To Shred Vegetables. For carrots, daikons, and other root vegetables, use the diagonal slice to make thin flat pieces. Stack these pieces up and cut across with a straight slice into shreds.

When shredding large amounts of celery for fillings, where the appearance of the celery is not important, as for egg rolls, I save a lot of time by using the diagonal cut and slicing into very thin pieces.

For vegetables like cabbage and onions that are naturally layered, cut into thin pieces using the straight slice.

A convenient tool for shredding vegetables is a mandoline. You may be able to find a Japanese-style mandoline at a Japanese grocery store. You could also use a good-quality plastic slicer. The shred may be a little larger than you get with hand shredding, but you save an enormous amount of time. A mandoline works well with firm vegetables, like carrots and daikon, but does a poor job on celery and leaf cabbages.

To Shred Gingerroot. Peel and cut into thin slices. Stack the slices and cut across into fine shreds.

To Shred Snow Peas. Stack the snow peas and use the diagonal slice across the length of the snow peas to make long shreds.

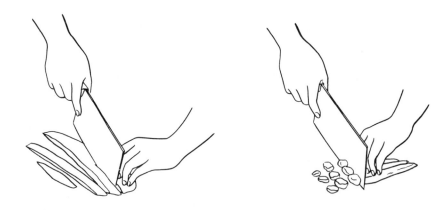

How to Dice or Cube

For dicing, split the item as thick as the size of the dice desired. Stack the slices, cut into like-size strips, and cut across into dice.

Cubing (¾- to 1-inch pieces) is used mainly for meats. Most of the stir-fried chicken breast in this book is cubed. Lay a trimmed chicken breast on the cutting board. Cut it lengthwise into ¾-inch-wide strips. Cut across the strips with a straight slice into ¾-inch cubes.

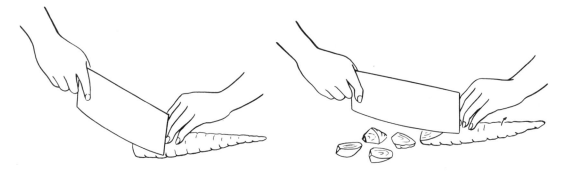

How to Roll-cut

The roll-cut is a useful and pretty cut for cylindrical vegetables such as carrots, zucchini, and parsnips. It is a way to get uniform pieces from vegetables that are not naturally uniform in shape. Roll-cut pieces have more surface area, move around the pan freely, cook evenly, and look attractive.

To roll-cut, place the vegetable horizontally on the cutting board. Starting at the thick end, slice off a section with a diagonal cut. The angle you use will determine the ultimate thickness and length of the piece. After the first cut, roll the vegetable toward you a quarter of a turn, then cut again at the same angle. Continue until you reach the end of the vegetable. If this is done correctly, you should not be able to distinguish the skinny-end pieces from fat-end pieces.

Techniques

46

How to Mince

For a regular mince, first slice the ingredients to a smaller size, then rock the knife from stem to stern while pivoting it from left to right (using the tip of the knife as the pivot point), pushing the pieces to the center every so often so that they are cut over and over again. This rocking mince cut is great for harder ingredients, like nuts, as it keeps them from flying this way and that. The number of times the knife is rocked across the ingredients determines how fine the mince is.

For a very fine mince (the Chinese do this when they need ground meat — since in general they do not have such modern conveniences as meat grinders, much less food processors), use two knives of equal size and weight. Hold the knife the way a Western knife is held, by the handle. With a knife in each hand, chop up and down across the pile, keeping the knives parallel with each other. Scrape the knives and scrape the ingredients toward the center occasionally so that every scrap is chopped until the proper consistency is achieved. This technique, by the way, results in a very different consistency from ground meat. Since the meat is actually cut into tiny pieces, the texture tends to be firmer. This fine mince technique is also useful for mincing cabbage for Peking Ravioli filling.

How to Crush

This is a neat way to peel garlic as well as to crush garlic cloves, knobs of ginger, or scallion bulbs to help release more aromatic flavor. If you want to peel a garlic clove, crush it first with the broad side of a Chinese knife, just enough to break the skin, then peel it away.

Knobs of ginger can be crushed with a more forceful blow. Be careful when you strike with the knife that the blade is perfectly flat and not angled. Otherwise you may damage your knife. And be sure to bring your cutting board to the edge of the counter so you don't bang your knuckles.

Peeled garlic and scallion bulbs are lightly crushed just to break the skin. You will have better control if you place the flat side of the knife against the ingredient and press down with your other hand.

How to Tenderize

Even the blunt edge of the Chinese knife is useful. My mother often used it to tenderize meat. Pound the meat first in one direction and then the opposite in a cross-hatch pattern. Do this on both sides. You can also use the crushing technique and slap the meat with the flat side of the blade to loosen and break up the meat fiber.

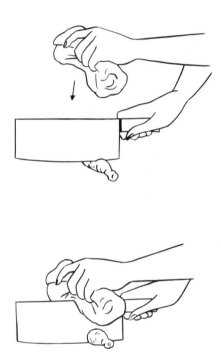

How to Chop

People always seem to want to chop big, heavy things with the Chinese knife, probably because of its relatively great size and weight. Chopping must be done properly, with care and with the proper knife (pages 32–33). More good Chinese knives are destroyed with this cut than any other.

Chop only light chicken or duck bones, not beef or pork. Use the back third of the blade, *never* the tip. Instead of using the knife as an axe, I prefer this safer, quieter, and more precise technique.

Place the knife in position on top of what is to be chopped. Wrap your other fist in a kitchen towel and use it like a hammer on the portion of the blade that is doing the chopping. The cloth will soften the blow to your hand. Do not twist the knife as it may damage or chip the blade. Instead of your fist, you can also use a rubber mallet.

Techniques

48

Cooking Techniques

壽　For the most part the Chinese home cook relies on five cooking techniques: stir-frying, deep-frying, steaming, boiling, and stewing. Smoking has a limited home application and roasting and baking are relegated to commercial establishments since the Chinese do not have ovens. Since ovens are commonplace in this country, however, I have included a few recipes for dishes that can be easily prepared in a home oven. Pickled and preserved foods are very popular in the Far East, but with the increasing availability of good commercial products, they are being done less and less at home.

The five basic techniques, which are the ones most often used in this book, are not difficult. It is the nuances within each that contribute to the subtle delicacy, incredible variety, and vast culinary panorama of Chinese cuisine.

How to Stir-fry

Stir-frying has become almost synonymous with Chinese cooking. It is believed that it began during the Han Dynasty over two thousand years ago in response to the lack of adequate fuel. Stir-frying requires quick, intense heat and short, rapid cooking. This not only conserved valuable fuel but also retained the natural nutrients and vitamins of the food.

In stir-frying, uniform, bite-size pieces of food are cooked in small amounts of oil over high heat. Sound easy? It is, but there are a few things to keep in mind, starting with a good-quality wok or stir-fry pan (pages 33–35). Put out of your mind any notion that stir-frying involves pushing food up the sides of the wok while cooking in the center. This is incorrect, and no Chinese I know cooks this way.

The Oil. You do not need a great deal of oil to stir-fry, especially if you are using a good quality nonstick pan. Generally I recommend using about three tablespoons of oil for a dish that serves four. A little oil does not, however, mean you can use a cooking-oil spray. That's not enough oil, not even in a nonstick pan.

To test the oil temperature for stir-frying I use this simple technique: Place the tip of a wooden or bamboo spatula in the oil; bubbles will form if the oil is hot enough. I sometimes dip the bamboo spatula in the moist ingredients; then the spatula not only bubbles but sizzles too. The intensity of the sizzle will indicate how hot the oil is. Most ingredients are added to hot oil, although delicate or dry ingredients may be added to warm oil.

I do not recommend that the pan be preheated before adding the oil as some cooks do. With nonstick cookware, heating up an empty pan may damage the coating. If you are using a carbon-steel wok, you may preheat the pan if you like, but it is not necessary.

Techniques

The Heat. Many people think Chinese cooking requires high, searing heat. This is true to a certain extent but with certain cautions and exceptions. High heat does not mean blasting away at the highest setting on your stove irrelevant of what is happening in the pan. Some recipes actually require lower heat to keep dry or delicate ingredients from burning. As with any cooking technique, control is the most important concept here.

Most of the stir-fry recipes in this book call for medium-high or high temperatures. The rule of thumb is to start at medium-high and adjust up or down accordingly. If the food appears to be cooking too rapidly or is beginning to stick, scorch, or burn, turn down the heat or remove the pan to a cool burner. I often add some water or broth, which brings down the temperature immediately.

If the food is cooking too fast on an electric stove, lift the pan right off the heat and replace it when more heat is needed. This up-and-down motion is easier and more efficient than constantly trying to adjust the heat. You may also move the pan to a cool burner, where you can continue stirring while the pan cools.

The Preparation. Have all the ingredients prepared and ready for cooking. Stir-frying goes very fast and demands a well-organized and efficient cook. As much as possible premix the sauces and organize cut ingredients in small dishes or bowls so that everything is within your reach. When I cook for a dinner party, I set out different trays or baking pans with the ingredients for each dish organized on its own tray in the order in which they will be used. This way, the cooking is choreographed and moves smoothly from one dish to the next.

The Cooking. Put food in the pan according to which ingredient takes longest to cook. Root vegetables and cabbage, for example, are put in first, while the more delicate fast cooking ingredients such as snow peas and bean sprouts are added in last. The first ingredients added to the hot oil should be as dry as possible to prevent spattering.

Do not overload your pan. A pan with too much food in it will cool down rapidly and never quite recover for proper stir-frying. A six- or eight-inch stir-fry pan is too small to cook a whole recipe; if that's what you have, you may have to cook in batches. Even with a fourteen-inch wok, you have to be careful when you double a recipe. The pan may be larger, but the heat source has not changed.

You will notice that in some recipes the salt is added to the oil before the ingredients. My mother told me that this helps keep spattering down, and the salt is evenly distributed throughout the dish. Because storebought ingredients, such as soy sauce, oyster sauce, hoisin sauce, and so on, vary in saltiness, I sometimes find it is more convenient to add the salt to taste at the end.

Techniques

The Serving. Most stir-fried foods should be removed from the pan and served immediately. The people should wait for the food, not the food for the people. When my mother prepared dinner, we had to be at the table when she brought the dishes out of the kitchen. That way, each one could be enjoyed at its peak. Nor should guests wait for the cook. The person cooking is always the last to come to the table.

How to Deep-fry

Deep-frying calls for ingredients to be submerged in a bath of hot fat. Traditionally the Chinese used lard, but because of concern about cholesterol in the diet, vegetable oil — soy, corn, peanut, or the more recently favored canola — is used. I don't deep-fry frequently at home because, in addition to the health issue, there is the inconvenience of handling large amounts of cooking oil. When this method is called for, however, keep the following in mind.

The Temperature. Oil that is either too hot or not hot enough will give you food that is burnt or, on the other hand, soggy and soaked with oil. Bring the oil to a temperature of 350°F. to 375°F. Test the oil by dropping in a small piece of bread, gingerroot, or wonton skin. The oil is ready if it foams actively along the edge. Use a deep-fat thermometer, especially if you are inexperienced.

Keep in mind that hot oil quickly drops in temperature once food is introduced. When deep-frying a second batch, be sure to allow the oil to return to temperature before adding food again. Be alert as well to oil that is too hot. If the food is scorching, turn down the heat. Regulate the temperature by turning the heat up and down as needed so that oil temperature remains as constant as possible.

The Cooking. Never crowd the pan when deep-frying. Crowding not only reduces the oil temperature rapidly and leads to greasy food but also makes the food cook unevenly. For even cooking, also be sure the oil is deep enough for the food to be submerged and to swim around freely.

Shallow-frying. For some dishes, such as Lemon Chicken, I use a home-style method of shallow-frying, which takes a smaller amount of oil, only one cup instead of the four or five needed for regular deep-frying.

Double-frying. Some recipes call for ingredients to be fried twice, Sweet and Sour Pork, Cantonese Style, for instance. The first frying is to cook the ingredient and the second to make the coating crisp. This method is often employed by restaurants. At home, you can plan such recipes ahead and deep-fry the first time, cool the ingredients, and refrigerate them until they are to be fried a second time and glazed with sauce.

Techniques

51

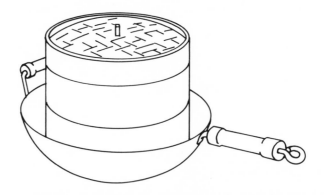

How to Steam in a Wok

Steaming is a common Chinese home-cooking technique. In most Chinese kitchens, the ubiquitous bamboo steamer is set in a wok or pan of boiling water to cook meats, seafood, and breads. In general the Chinese do not steam vegetables, which are parboiled or stir-fried. An exception is the recipe for Steamed Eggplant Salad. The steam that enters the covered steamer is trapped and cooks the food gently with moist heat. Although you can't burn food in a steamer, you can overcook it, so watch the timing. Here are some other points to keep in mind:

- Be sure the bamboo steamer fits into your wok. If your wok is fourteen inches in diameter, a ten- to 12-inch steamer will fit. The water should touch the bamboo steamer's bottom edge but still be at least one inch from the bottom tier. The food being steamed should never touch the boiling water.

- I'm often asked how to clean a bamboo steamer. I thought that a curious question until I realized that many people didn't understand that food is never placed directly on the steamer trays. Seafood and meat are steamed on dishes so the juices are not lost. Bread is steamed on small pieces of paper so they don't stick to the steamer.

- Have the water actively boiling before putting in the food. Keep the water at a constant boil over medium-high heat until the cooking is done. An exception to this is Steamed Egg Custard Soup which starts in a cold steamer so the eggs cook gently. Add more boiling water as necessary.

Constructing a Makeshift Steamer. If you don't have a Chinese steamer, you can create a makeshift steamer using a wok, stir-fry pan, or large stockpot. (Many wok sets come with steaming racks.) Be sure the pan is large enough to hold the dish used for steaming. It must have at least two inches of headroom and enough room around it so that it can be easily removed when hot. Remove the top and bottom of an empty tuna-fish can to make a stand

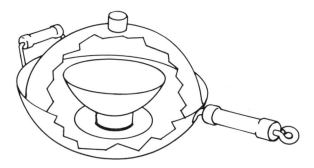

and place it in the bottom of your pan. Bring water to a boil. Put the plate or bowl containing the food on the stand, cover the wok with a lid, and steam.

If you plan to steam food often, you should buy a bamboo or metal steamer. Frequent steaming in a carbon-steel wok means you will have to reseason your wok often, and boiling water in a nonstick carbon-steel wok may shorten the life of the coating.

How to Boil

The Chinese employ boiling in specific ways. Sometimes they parboil vegetables to shorten the final cooking time, especially for multicourse banquets and at restaurants, where speed is essential. At home, this technique is useful when you cook for a dinner party.

To parboil vegetables, cut and wash them first, then stir them into enough boiling water for them to swim around freely. As soon as they are added to the water, the boiling will stop. Continue stirring for even cooking. If the vegetables are tender or you want them to remain very crisp, drain them after fifteen to thirty seconds, or just before the water looks as if it's going to return to a boil. Some harder vegetables such as carrots and green beans may require a little longer cooking; leave them in the water until it boils again. After draining, refresh the vegetables in cold water to stop the cooking and set the bright colors. If not using right away, store covered in the refrigerator.

Chinese cooks also use boiling water to sear meats and poultry, immersing them in a large pot of boiling water. Good examples are Shanghai Red-cooked Duck and Shanghai Red-cooked Ham. As soon as the water returns to a boil, the bird or meat is taken out and rinsed in cold water.

White-cooked meat is cooked only in hot water, without soy sauce or other flavorings. Simmering keeps the meat tender and seals in the natural flavor instead of washing it out into the water. The simmer must be slow and gentle with only one or two bubbles appearing at a time. Such meats are almost always served cold with a table dip for seasoning. This process is used frequently for larger pieces of meat such as a whole chicken (White-cooked Chicken), duck and ham (White-cooked Pork).

How to Stew

Stewing is slow cooking over low heat in a liquid, like braising. When stewing large pieces of meat, be sure your pot has a tight-fitting lid. After cooking, remove the lid and reduce the liquid over high heat while basting the meat constantly for even color and flavor. Many "red-cooked" dishes use this technique — Shanghai Red-cooked Duck and Shanghai Red-cooked Ham, for example.

Menu Planning
and Serving
Chinese Food

Menu planning plays a large and significant role in Chinese life, all the more since many foods are symbolic of good luck, prosperity, long life, and happiness. The arrangements and combinations of food fulfill a sense of harmony and completeness. Banquets celebrating marriages, births, birthdays, festivals, and the lunar New Year call for special foods and ingredients served in a particular manner.

The Chinese concept of menu planning is quite different from the American notion of a main dish accompanied by a side dish or two and followed by dessert. Chinese meals consist of a number of entrees with rice and a soup. Dessert is rarely served, except on special occasions. The number of entrees depends on how many people are eating. The more people there are at the table, the more variety there will be. It stands to reason that Chinese dinners are more fun with a crowd.

There are no rules about how many dishes to serve since much depends upon the number of people, individual appetites, and so on. Generally speaking, prepare two or three dishes plus a soup for four adults, four or five dishes plus soup for six. For only two people a single dish that combines meat and vegetables plus a soup, if desired, would be fine. White rice is served at all meals.

How to Pair Dishes

The Chinese seem to have an innate ability to choose dishes that provide a well-balanced and complementary meal that incorporates the ancient Chinese principles of yin and yang. It isn't that we are all versed in this concept, but experience has taught us what tastes and looks good together. Yin stands for cold, dark, and moist; yang stands for hot, bright, and dry. The balanced tension of these opposites creates a harmony that infiltrates all aspects of life.

When we plan our meals, we look for contrasts — hot and sour, warm and cold, crisp and soft, spicy and bland, etc. We would not serve a meal with two beef dishes or two spicy dishes. My mother was especially well versed in pairing, and whenever we went out, everyone turned to her to do the ordering. We were never disappointed.

For a multicourse meal, prepare a variety of dishes, choosing from meat, poultry, seafood, vegetables, and soup. For a Chinese family the soup is often the only beverage, so it is an important part of the meal. You may choose to leave it out when serving Westerners. Remember, what makes the meal interesting is not only the taste but the *contrast* and *balance* of taste, texture, temperature, and color of different dishes. Serve Chinese food the way it was meant to be served, with lots of steamed rice.

The number of servings indicated in each recipe in the book is the approximate number served Western style and Chinese style, that is, as part of a multicourse meal.

The sample menus on pages 60–61 will give you a good balance of taste, texture, color, and nutrition.

How to Serve Chinese Food

Family-style meals and banquets are served differently. For casual dinners at home all the dishes, including the soup and rice, are served at once at the center of the table. People use their own chopsticks to take food from the serving dish to their rice bowls. The dishes served at family meals are straightforward and simple. When we invite friends over to share a casual family meal, we humbly refer to it as *bian fan,* or simple rice.

At formal banquets, each dish is presented with its own serving spoon or serving chopsticks, and served alone so that the full enjoyment of its taste and appearance may be savored. Formal banquets offer as many as twelve different dishes. Sometimes in southern China strong tea is served in tiny cups as a palate cleanser. Rice is not served during the meal but at the end, and only as a polite gesture for those desiring it. It is considered a filler and is not served earlier so that guests will not fill up on rice and not be able to enjoy all the dishes to come. Dessert is often served in the form of fresh fruit, sweet soup, or steamed rice pudding, depending upon the season.

The Chinese like to use round tables, which make the serving dishes easily accessible to everyone and are conducive to conversation. Banquet tables usually seat eight, ten, or twelve — the Chinese prefer to set the table with an even number of places. The guest of honor is always seated facing the door and the host is seated across from the place of honor. There is traditionally much commotion before everyone is seated, with the guest of honor coyly refusing the place of honor and the host insisting. This is all part of Chinese ritual and good manners and is performed, and expected, at almost every social function.

To set the table Chinese style you will need a pair of chopsticks for each diner, a porcelain spoon and bowl for soup, a small dipping dish for bones, an eight-inch plate for holding food, and a rice bowl.

What to Drink with Chinese Food

禄 Many Westerners assume, incorrectly, that all Chinese drink tea at mealtimes. Only the southern Chinese, namely the Cantonese, drink tea at the dining table; everyone else has tea after meals. Most Chinese restaurants in America, however, do serve tea since the early groups of Chinese in the United States were from Canton (Quangzhou). Northern Chinese like to have soup, preferably a clear broth, as the beverage. Tea is then served after meals to cleanse the palate and to aid digestion.

There are hundreds, if not thousands, of types of tea drunk in China. They fall into three main categories — black (the Chinese call it red, since the color black is considered unlucky), green, and flower. One of the most famous green teas comes from my father's hometown of Hangchow (Hang-zhou) and is called *lung ching* or dragon well. Most Westerners are familiar with oolong tea, which is the one most often served at Chinese-American restaurants. Translated as black dragon, oolong is a semifermented black tea. At home after meals, our family always drank the green or flower-infused tea, such as jasmine, which are preferred by northern Chinese. These teas are not fermented and they brew up into a light amber or yellow color. Their delicate aroma and flavor should not be adulterated with sugar, milk, or cream.

Chinese tea should always be brewed with water that has boiled for only a few seconds. If you are using loose tea, sprinkle it into the pot and then pour the boiling water over the leaves. Cover and let steep for two to three minutes. Use about one teaspoon of tea leaves per cup of boiling water. The same tea may be used a second time for another pot of tea. We do the same thing if we are making it by the glass. Tea is best served in porcelain or glass cups; it is said that metal cups will spoil the flavor and color of tea. The Chinese don't mind the tea leaves, as good tea has whole tea leaves (not tea dust) that unfurl and sink to the bottom of the glass, out of the way. Many Chinese teas are

Pairing Wines with Chinese Food

Pairing Western wines with Chinese food presents a bit of a challenge. Since the typical Chinese meal may consist of meat, fish, and poultry, the wine choice should be based on the seasonings and not the main ingredients. My friend, Bob Bradford, a photojournalist and wine expert, shared his thoughts and suggestions on what wines best complement Chinese foods.

Bob suggests keeping a few basic principles in mind: How a wine's lively acidity, for example, can be like a squeeze of lemon, adding zest to food; or how white wines with big body and sweetness are often well suited to rich, spicy foods.

One of the most successful and versatile of assertive white wines for Asian dishes is a full-bodied Gewürztraminer, of which there are several good affordable selections from domestic producers. This perfumy, German-Alsatian grape has a pleasant spiciness that complements and enhances the intricate, sometimes exotic, flavors of Asia.

There are also many styles of Johannesburg Riesling that go well with Chinese food. Try a crisp, acidic dry version or one with a fresh, but full, sweeter big fruit character that can stand up to heavy seasonings and Szechuan specialties or a rich, honeylike late-harvest Riesling. Bob has been pleased with all three styles with Chinese food.

One of the most popular wines sold in Chinese restaurants is a full-style Chardonnay, and although Bob finds it agreeable, he doesn't find it the most interesting selection. He does find that full-bodied sparkling wines are excellent companions to most Asian dishes. Do not pair them with foods that are too heavy or sweet, however, since they can thin out and become a little bitter.

With delicate and lightly seasoned foods try a medium-bodied Chenin Blanc with its floral bouquet and crisp acid or a medium-style, fruity Semillon. Also worth trying are deep, black muscat wines or American berry wines such as raspberry and Bartlett pear.

Many assertive and robust young wines such as Chianti, Pinot Noir, the Cabernets, and Zinfandel also match up perfectly with many Chinese dishes.

Last, Bob suggests that you keep on tasting with an open mind and let your palate be the last word.

now also available in tea bags, but the finest teas are always purchased loose so that the quality and beauty of the leaves may be confirmed and enjoyed.

Beer and wine are also enjoyed by the Chinese, but usually only at a banquet setting. Chinese beers are beginning to appear in America. One of the earliest imports to America is the famous Tsingtao beer, named after the Shangdong port city of Tsingtao (Qingdao), occupied by the Germans in the late 1890s as a treaty port. It is said that Tsingtao beer is brewed according to an old German method. Many people enjoy beer with Chinese food. My husband enjoys fine beer and tells me that Tsingtao, as well as a number of Japanese beers, is excellent with Chinese food.

The Chinese have never developed a strong viticulture tradition. Instead of grapes, most Chinese wines are made from rice (*shiaoxing* is famous). Stronger spirits are distilled from grains such as millet (*mao tai*) and sorghum (*gaoliang*). The Chinese usually reserve alcoholic beverages only for celebratory meals.

Home-style meal for six

APPETIZER
Drunken Chicken (optional)

SOUP
Crab and Asparagus Soup

ENTREES
Mushrooms with Bean Curd
Sweet and Sour Shrimp
Spicy Beef with Carrots and Celery
Red-mouthed Green Parrot

RICE
White Rice

健康

Home-style meal for six

APPETIZER
Pickled Carrots and Daikon

SOUP
Mandarin Cucumber Soup

ENTREES
Chicken with Mushrooms
Kan Shao Green Beans
Coral and Jade
Stir-fried Asparagus

RICE
White Rice or Yangchow Fried Rice

Home-style meal for four

SOUP
Steamed Egg Custard Soup

ENTREES
Stir-fried Watercress with Fu Ru
Sweet and Sour Spareribs, Shanghai Style
Stir-fried Cauliflower and Broccoli

RICE
White Rice

禧

Home-style meal for four

SOUP
Watercress and Shredded Pork Soup

ENTREES
Stir-fried Green Beans
Steamed Salmon with Black Beans
Egg Foo Yung, Family Style

RICE
White Rice

Menu

Planning

and Serving

Eating the Chinese Way

吃

Chinese food is best when eaten the way the Chinese do, that is, with a bowl of rice as the mainstay of the meal. I find, however, that most Westerners are uncomfortable eating rice from a bowl the way the Chinese do. The problem seems to be in lifting the rice bowl to their lips; yet it is practically impossible to eat rice from a flat plate with chopsticks. Besides, when rice is put on a plate with other foods, it becomes an insignificant side dish instead of the substantial base of the meal, as it is intended to be.

Hold the rice bowl in one hand by the top and bottom edges. (The Chinese rice bowl has a foot on the bottom so you can hold it without burning your fingers on the heat from the rice.) Use your chopsticks to bring food from the serving dish to the bowl or, in some cases, directly to your mouth. The food is brought to the rice bowl so that it can rest lightly on the rice, allowing excess gravy or sauce to drip onto the rice.

To eat the rice, raise the bowl and push the rice gently into your mouth with the chopsticks. With practice, you'll soon be able to accomplish this movement with dexterity. In between courses or during conversation, place your chopsticks on chopstick rests or, as we do at home, across the top of the rice bowl.

Soup

A t Chinese family meals, soup is considered the beverage. Cold water, soft drinks, and mineral water are not served. In fact, it is an old wives' tale that you'll get a stomachache from drinking ice water with meals. As a child, I always liked a glass of water with my meals, but I was the only one at the table who had one.

In home-style eating, the soup and all the other main dishes are served at one time. This way the soup can be enjoyed throughout the meal to quench one's thirst. I like to add soup to my rice, although my mother always told me that this was a custom only for home eating and not appropriate for more formal occasions.

Since the soup is mainly a beverage and palate refresher, it is more common to serve clear soups made with a light broth base than thick soups. Most Chinese soups are based on chicken broth; sometimes pork bones are used to make broth, but never beef or lamb bones as the flavor would be too strong for Chinese tastes. Chinese Chicken Broth is much lighter than most chicken stocks and I always dilute canned chicken broth with water to approximate the chicken broth made at home.

Some more substantial soups, such as Wonton Soup, are served as snacks. Thick soups, such as Crab and Asparagus Soup and Chicken Velvet Corn Soup, are served on special occasions, when thinner, lighter soups would be considered too ordinary.

Chinese Chicken Broth

Makes about 10 cups

C hinese restaurants keep a large vat of chicken broth cooking at all times. It is used for soup and in stir-fry dishes instead of water for a richer flavor.

Instead of cooking a whole chicken for broth, I freeze chicken bones left over from other dishes. When I have enough bones saved up, I make my broth. I have to admit, though, that I do not always have homemade chicken broth on hand and sometimes substitute canned broth for convenience. Since the Chinese broth is made without salt and is quite light, I suggest you mix canned broth with water and not add salt to the recipe. Then you can adjust the salt later to your taste.

3 to 4 pounds chicken bones, such as backs, necks, wings, ribs, feet
2 tablespoons dry sherry
3 slices unpeeled gingerroot, 1 × ⅛ inch each
1 scallion

1. Bring a large amount of water to a boil in a stockpot large enough to hold all the bones and enough water to cover them. Blanch the bones by dropping them in the boiling water. When the water returns to a boil, about 3 to 5 minutes, drain the bones in a colander and rinse with cold water. This blanching ensures a clearer broth.

2. Rinse and scrub out any clinging scum from the stockpot. Put the chicken bones back into the pot with just enough cold water to cover them. Add the sherry, gingerroot, and scallion, bring the water to a boil over high heat, and immediately turn the heat down to maintain a simmer. Do not cover the pot.

3. Skim off any foam or impurities and discard. Simmer, uncovered, for 1½ to 2 hours, or until the chicken is tender and the bones fall apart easily. Remember, it's the slow simmering that makes a good broth, so don't rush this process.

4. Skim off the fat that is on the surface and remove any large bones. Strain the broth through a fine mesh strainer or through 2 layers of damp cheesecloth spread over a colander. Cool, uncovered, then refrigerate the broth in a sealed container until ready to use. (Remove any congealed fat before using.) Refrigerated, the stock will keep for about 5 days to 1 week. You may also freeze the broth in 1- or 2-cup containers for easier use. Serve the broth alone, salted to taste and garnished with chopped scallion, as a base for other soup recipes, or in stir-fry dishes in place of water.

Note   In China, where refrigeration is not available to everyone, people boil their stock each time before using it to kill any bacteria. It's still a good idea.

Variation   Pork bones may be added to the chicken bones to make a richer broth. To coax flavor out of the pork bone marrow, disjoint bones or crush them before cooking. Trim away all excess fat. The Chinese do not use beef or lamb bones, as the stronger flavor of these bones are not suitable for Chinese-style stock. For a clear stock, do not mix raw and cooked bones.

Wonton Soup

**Serves 2, or 4 to 6 as part of a
multicourse meal**

*I*n Chinese, the word wonton means "swallowing clouds." This fanciful name refers
not to the crispy, deep-fried wontons but to the wontons cooked in soup. They are
fluffy and float in the clear broth like clouds.

The Chinese eat Wonton Soup as a main course, not as the first course it has
become in Chinese-American restaurants. It is usually served in large noodle bowls as
a snack or lunch or at family get-togethers when all the family members help fold the
wontons.

4 cups Chinese Chicken Broth (page 64) plus 1 teaspoon salt or
    1 (13¾-ounce) can chicken broth and enough water to make 4 cups
1 slice unpeeled gingerroot, 1 × ⅛ inch
16 to 24 pork or turkey wontons, boiled and drained (pages 293–294)
Salt to taste
2 tablespoons thinly sliced scallions
4 tablespoons minced Szechuan vegetable (optional)
4 tablespoons finely shredded Egg Garnish (page 255) (optional)
1 teaspoon sesame seed oil

1.   Bring the chicken broth with the gingerroot to a boil and add additional salt to taste. Place 4 to 6 wontons in individual soup bowls. Sprinkle
the wontons in each bowl with some scallion and 1 tablespoon each Szechuan
vegetable and shredded egg, if desired.

2.   Pour the boiling soup over the wontons and drizzle with sesame
seed oil. Serve immediately.

Variation   Instead of the Chinese-style garnishes of Szechuan vegetable and shredded egg, add 4 ounces spinach leaves, which have been thoroughly washed, to the boiling broth just before serving. Cook the spinach
leaves only as long as it takes to wilt them.

Steamed Egg Custard Soup

Serves 3 to 4

*T*his smooth family-style soup requires the simplest of ingredients and very little attention. I like to prepare them when I'm in a hurry because once it's mixed and put in a steamer, it doesn't need to be watched. If you don't have a proper steamer, use a wok with a lid and place a low metal stand inside so the bowl doesn't touch the bottom of the wok. Fashion the stand from a tuna-fish can with both ends removed.

In China littleneck clams, still in their shells, are often added to this soup before steaming. The clams, a symbol of wealth, give it lots of flavor.

3 eggs
1 teaspoon dry sherry
3 cups cold Chinese Chicken Broth (page 64) plus 1 teaspoon salt or
   1 (13¾-ounce) can chicken broth and enough water to make 4 cups
2 teaspoons thinly sliced scallions or chives
½ teaspoon light soy sauce, for garnish

1.   Lightly beat the eggs with the sherry in a 1-quart heatproof bowl, using a fork or a pair of chopsticks. The eggs should be completely blended but not frothy or there will be bubbles in the soup.

2.   Stir the cold broth into the eggs. Mix thoroughly to get rid of lumps, which would cook up hard. Sprinkle the scallions over the mixture.

3.   Place the bowl in a steamer filled with 2 inches of water as described on page 52. Cover the pan and steam over medium-high heat for 20 minutes, or until the liquid becomes firm. (The soup will keep hot in the covered steamer off the heat for 15 to 20 minutes.) Drizzle soy sauce over the soup. Serve hot in the same bowl.

Soup

Egg Drop Soup

F or many people this soup with its delicate swirls of beaten eggs is the first soup they remember trying in a Chinese-American restaurant. This home-style version, not thickened with any starch, is lighter than its restaurant counterpart. The size of the egg swirls depends upon how fast you stir the eggs into the hot soup — the slower you stir, the bigger the pieces.

健康

4 cups Chinese Chicken Broth (page 64) plus 1 teaspoon salt or
    1 (13¾-ounce) can chicken broth and enough water to make 4 cups
2 slices unpeeled gingerroot, 1 × ⅛ inch each
2 eggs
½ teaspoon dry sherry
1 tablespoon thinly sliced scallions
Salt to taste

1. Combine the chicken broth and gingerroot in a medium saucepan and bring to a boil over medium-high heat.

2. While the broth is coming to a boil, beat the eggs with the sherry in a small bowl or measuring cup. When the broth is boiling, remove the gingerroot. Pour a thin, steady stream of egg into the liquid while stirring constantly. Remove the pan from the heat as soon as all the eggs are added. Salt to taste, and sprinkle the minced scallions over the top. Serve hot.

Meatballs with Crystal Noodle Soup

Serves 4, or 6 as part of a multicourse meal

*T*his easy soup makes a satisfying meal by itself, as well as a hearty soup course in a lighter multicourse meal of stir-fried vegetables and bean curd. Add the bean thread only when you're ready to serve. It overcooks easily and can become soft and gluey.

福

½ pound ground lean pork or beef (1 cup)
¼ teaspoon grated peeled gingerroot
1 tablespoon light soy sauce
½ teaspoon dry sherry
1½ teaspoons cornstarch
½ teaspoon salt, and additional to taste
2 ounces bean thread
5 cups Chinese Chicken Broth (page 64) plus 1 teaspoon salt or
    1 (13¾-ounce) can chicken broth and enough water to make 5 cups

1.   Mix the ground meat with the gingerroot, soy sauce, sherry, cornstarch, and ¼ teaspoon salt. Set aside.

2.   Soak the bean thread in warm water for a few minutes until soft. Drain carefully, keeping the strands together, and with scissors, cut into 6-inch lengths. Set aside.

3.   Bring the chicken broth and ¼ teaspoon of salt to a boil in a medium saucepan over medium heat. Scoop up one tablespoon of the meat mixture at a time and form about 16 to 18 smooth, small balls using your fingertips. Drop the meatballs into the boiling broth. Reduce the heat to low and simmer, covered, for 10 minutes. (You can cook the meatballs ahead and keep them warm or reheat them.) Just before serving, add the bean thread and stir a few times. Serve immediately.

Add additional salt to taste if desired.

Soup

Shredded Pork and Mustard Greens Soup

**Serves 4, or 6 as part of a
multicourse meal**

*C*hinese mustard greens are appreciated for their thick, green curved stems and distinctive, slightly bitter taste. They are available in Chinese markets and often have their leaves severely trimmed, leaving a rather ragged looking loose cabbage heart. Add mustard greens to soup only just before serving, or they will overcook and turn yellow.

⅓ cup shredded lean pork (3 ounces) (page 44)

2 teaspoons light soy sauce

1 teaspoon cornstarch

½ teaspoon dry sherry

¼ pound Chinese mustard greens

5 cups Chinese Chicken Broth (page 64) plus 1 teaspoon salt or

   1 (13¾-ounce) can chicken broth and enough water to make 5 cups

2 slices unpeeled gingerroot, 1 × ⅛ inch each

¼ teaspoon salt, or to taste

1.   Mix the pork, soy sauce, cornstarch, and sherry together. Set aside.

2.   Wash the mustard greens under running water and shake off the excess water. Cut the leaves and stems into 1-inch pieces. You should have about 1 cup.

3.   Bring the chicken broth and gingerroot to a boil in a 2-quart saucepan over medium-high heat. Stir in the pork and bring the broth back to a boil. Stir in the mustard greens and cook for 1 minute. Salt to taste. Serve hot.

Snow Cabbage with Shredded Pork Soup

Serves 4, or 6 as part of a
multicourse meal

*S*now cabbage (page 25), sold in cans in Asian markets, is a handy ingredient to keep in your pantry for flavoring otherwise simple dishes like soup noodles or stir-fry. A small dish of pickled snow cabbage is sometimes served as a condiment with breakfast rice gruel, known as congee. You can substitute shredded chicken for the pork in this recipe.

壽

½ cup shredded lean pork (4 ounces) (page 44)

1 teaspoon cornstarch

1 teaspoon light soy sauce

½ teaspoon dry sherry

4 cups Chinese Chicken Broth (page 64) plus ½ teaspoon salt or
    1 (13¾-ounce) can chicken broth and enough water to make 4 cups

2 slices unpeeled gingerroot, 1 × ⅛ inch each

¼ cup canned snow cabbage, coarsely chopped

¾ cup shredded firm tofu (bean curd) (optional)

Salt to taste

1.   Place the pork in a bowl, stir in the cornstarch, soy sauce, and sherry, and mix well. Set aside.

2.   Combine the chicken broth and gingerroot in a medium saucepan and bring to a boil over medium-high heat. Add the pork mixture and stir to cook the meat evenly and to keep the shreds separate.

3.   When the pork shreds change color and separate, add the snow cabbage and the bean curd, if using. Stir gently. Bring the soup back to a boil, then remove from the heat. Add additional salt to taste. Serve hot.

Soup

Peking Hot and Sour Soup

S e r v e s   4 ,   o r   6   a s   p a r t   o f   a   m u l t i c o u r s e   m e a l

This is one of mother's best-loved recipes, which she made famous in the 1950s at our first restaurant on Concord Avenue in Cambridge. What makes the soup sour is vinegar, what makes it hot is white pepper. If you like your soup extra hot, just add more pepper. In China, this soup is never served at banquets because the ingredients are considered too ordinary!

禧

¼ *cup shredded lean pork (2 ounces) (page 44)*

1 *teaspoon dry sherry*

3 *tablespoons cornstarch*

¼ *cup dried golden needles, soaked in 2 cups hot water for 15 minutes and drained*

¼ *cup dried wood ears, soaked in 2 cups hot water for 15 minutes and drained*

3½ *cups Chinese Chicken Broth (page 64) and 1 teaspoon salt or*
    1 *(13¾-ounce) can chicken broth and enough water to make 3½ cups*

1 *tablespoon light soy sauce*

½ *cup shredded firm tofu (bean curd)*

1 *medium egg, beaten*

2 *tablespoons cider vinegar*

¼ *teaspoon ground white pepper*

Salt to taste

1 *teaspoon sesame seed oil*

1 *tablespoon thinly sliced scallions*

1. Stir the pork, sherry, and 1 teaspoon of the cornstarch together in a bowl. Set aside. Dissolve the remaining cornstarch in ½ cup cold water. Set aside.

2. Cut off the tough stems from the golden needles and woody pieces from the wood ears, if any. Cut the golden needles in half and the wood ears into ½-inch pieces. Rinse, drain, and squeeze out excess liquid from both.

3. Put the vinegar and pepper in a large serving bowl.

4. Combine the chicken broth and soy sauce in a medium saucepan and bring to a boil. When the broth is boiling, stir in the pork. After 1 minute, stir in all the wood ears and golden needles. Bring back to a boil and boil for

Soup

1 minute. Add the bean curd. As soon as soup comes back to a boil again, mix the cornstarch mixture and stir it in. Stir until soup thickens.

5. Pour a stream of beaten egg into the hot soup while constantly stirring. Remove from the heat immediately and pour the soup into the serving bowl with the vinegar and pepper. Add salt to taste and garnish with sesame seed oil and scallions. Serve hot.

Watercress and Shredded Pork Soup

Serves 4, or 6 as part of a multicourse meal

W atercress is a popular green vegetable among the Cantonese. It is often served stir-fried or in soups.

健康

2 cups watercress sprigs (about 3 ounces)
⅓ cup shredded lean pork (about 3 ounces) (page 44)
½ teaspoon dry sherry
1 teaspoon cornstarch
4 cups Chinese Chicken Broth (page 64) plus 1 teaspoon salt or
    1 (13¾-ounce) can chicken broth and enough water to make 4 cups
2 slices unpeeled gingerroot, 1 × ⅛ inch each
Salt to taste

1. Wash the watercress and discard any wilted or yellowed leaves. Drain and cut the sprigs into 3-inch pieces. Set aside.

2. Place the pork in a bowl, add the sherry and cornstarch, and stir together well. Set aside.

3. Combine the chicken broth and gingerroot in a medium saucepan and place over medium-high heat. When the broth comes to a boil, mix up the pork again, stir it into the broth, and bring back to a boil. Add the watercress and stir for about 30 seconds, or just until the watercress is wilted. Remove from the heat and discard the gingerroot. Salt to taste. Serve immediately.

Frozen Bean Curd and Black Mushroom Soup

Serves 4, or 6 as part of a multicourse meal

*T*his is a light, subtly flavored soup. I like the texture of frozen tofu. It soaks up the broth like a sponge and has a tender, yet chewy consistency.

福

½ cup dried black mushrooms, soaked in hot water for 15 minutes
½ pound frozen tofu (bean curd), thawed and squeezed dry
4 cups Chinese Chicken Broth (page 64) plus 1 teaspoon salt or
*   1 (13¾-ounce) can chicken broth and enough water to make 4 cups*
1 slice unpeeled gingerroot, 1 × ⅛ inch
1 (8-ounce) can sliced bamboo shoots, drained (1 cup)
Salt to taste

1. Remove the mushrooms from the soaking liquid, rinse, and drain. Squeeze out excess liquid, discard woody stems, and cut into quarters. Set aside. Slice the bean curd into 1-inch squares, ½ inch thick.

2. Pour the chicken broth into a saucepan. Add the gingerroot and bring to a boil over medium heat.

3. Add the mushrooms, bean curd, and bamboo shoots. Return to a boil, reduce the heat, and simmer for about 10 minutes until the mushrooms impart their flavor to the soup and the ingredients are heated. Correct the seasoning. Serve hot.

Bean Curd and Daikon Soup

Serves 4

*T*ypical of clear soups served at family meals, this one combines two ordinary ingredients in a quick and easy way.

禄

1 daikon or Chinese icicle radish (about ½ pound)

4 cups Chinese Chicken Broth (page 64) plus 1 teaspoon salt or

   1 (13¾-ounce) can chicken broth and enough water to make 4 cups

2 slices unpeeled gingerroot, 1 × ⅛ inch each

½ pound firm tofu (bean curd), drained and cut into slivers

Salt to taste

1.   Trim away the ends of the daikon, pare, and shred through the large holes of a box grater. Squeeze the shreds in your hands to remove the excess water. You should have about 1 cup. Set aside.

2.   Combine the broth and gingerroot in a medium saucepan and place over medium–high heat. When the liquid comes to a boil, add the daikon and simmer for 15 minutes, or until it turns translucent.

3.   Add the tofu and stir gently until the broth returns to a boil. Taste for salt. Serve hot.

Mandarin Cucumber Soup

Serves 4, or 6 as part of a multicourse meal

My mother liked to prepare this soup because it reminded her of her childhood in Beijing. There was a small town nearby called Feng Tai 豐台 that once supplied the palace with both flowers and vegetables. The vendors at the Feng Tai train station sold tiny cucumbers, six inches long, from small woven trays. The cucumbers were too expensive to buy enough for a dish to feed a large family, so people bought just enough to make this special soup.

Both my mother and I use the young, thin cucumbers that are available during the summer at local produce stands. English seedless cucumbers that are wrapped in plastic and sold at most supermarkets can also be used. Since the skin of these cucumbers is tender and not coated with wax, you don't have to peel them. If you use regular cucumbers, peel them, leaving alternate strips of green skin behind.

壽

1 long seedless cucumber or 1 pound very young cucumbers
¼ cup thinly sliced lean pork (about 1 boneless pork chop)
½ teaspoon dry sherry
1 teaspoon cornstarch
4 cups Chinese Chicken Broth (page 64) and 1 teaspoon salt or
    1 (13¾-ounce can) chicken broth and enough water to make 4 cups
1 teaspoon sesame seed oil
Salt to taste

1. Cut the cucumbers in half lengthwise, remove seeds, if any, and slice on the diagonal ¼ inch thick. You should have 2 cups. Set aside.

2. Place the pork in a bowl, add the sherry and cornstarch, and stir together well. Set aside.

3. Bring the chicken broth to a boil in a medium saucepan. Add the pork and stir until the broth returns to a boil.

4. Just before serving, add the cucumber slices, stir 2 or 3 times, and remove from the heat. Drizzle with sesame seed oil. Salt to taste as desired. Serve immediately.

Soup

Note   The cucumbers cook very quickly and can overcook easily by just sitting in the hot broth.

Ham and Winter Melon Soup

Serves 4, or 6 as part of a multicourse meal

In China, the most famous ham comes from Jinhua. When we traveled by train in China on our first visit after the country became open to foreigners, we stopped briefly at Jinhua. Vendors were selling the hams at the station, and many people got on the train with whole hams tucked under their arms.

In this soup, a very acceptable substitute for Chinese ham is Smithfield ham. It is so heavily salted and well aged that even a little bit imparts a rich taste and fragrance to the soup. Be sure to cook the winter melon until tender and soft. It's almost impossible to overcook it.

禧

1 slice winter melon (1 pound)
¼ pound Smithfield ham
2 cups Chinese Chicken Broth (page 64) plus ½ teaspoon of salt or
    1 (13¾-ounce) can chicken broth and enough water to make 2 cups
2 slices unpeeled gingerroot, 1 × ⅛ inch each
Salt (optional)

1.   Cut the green skin off the winter melon and remove the seeds and soft, pulpy interior. Rinse, drain, and cut into ½ × 2-inch slices. Place the slices in 2 cups of water in a medium saucepan and bring to a boil over medium heat. Reduce the heat to low and simmer until the melon becomes translucent and tender, 15 to 20 minutes.

2.   Cut off and discard the dark skin and fat from the ham. Slice the meat into 2 × 1 × ⅛-inch pieces.

3.   Add the ham, broth, and gingerroot to the simmering melon and cook for 15 minutes over low heat. (The soup may be kept warm over very low heat or cooled and reheated until ready to serve.) Taste and add salt if desired. Serve hot.

Soup

Chicken Velvet Corn Soup

Serves 4 to 6, or 8 as part of a multicourse meal

*F*or this thick soup made with pureed chicken breast and creamed corn, I find that a good-quality canned cream-style corn — Del Monte is the brand I prefer — gives excellent results in a fraction of the time it would take to make it from scratch.

健康

½ pound skinless boneless chicken breast

½ cup water

1 teaspoon dry sherry

4¼ cups Chinese Chicken Broth (page 64) plus 1 teaspoon salt or
    1 (13¾-ounce) can chicken broth and enough water to make 4¼ cups

1 (16½-ounce) can cream-style corn

½ teaspoon salt, or to taste

Dash white pepper

2 slices unpeeled gingerroot, 1 × ⅛ inch each

2 tablespoons thinly sliced scallions

1 tablespoon cornstarch, dissolved in 2 tablespoons water

2 egg whites, lightly beaten but not frothy

1 teaspoon sesame seed oil

1.   Cut the chicken into 2-inch chunks and put into the workbowl of a food processor fitted with the metal blade. Add the water and sherry. Process for about 15 seconds, pulsing 2 or 3 times, until the meat is a smooth puree. Transfer to a small bowl. Set aside. (Or puree in a blender and discard any gristle that becomes lodged in the blades.)

2.   Place the chicken broth, salt, pepper, corn, and gingerroot in a 2-quart saucepan, stir together, and bring to a boil over medium heat.

3.   Add the chicken puree and stir so that the meat breaks up into small bits. The chicken will quickly turn white, indicating that it is cooked. Add the scallions, stir a few times, and taste. Add more salt as desired. Mix up the cornstarch solution again and pour it into the soup, stirring constantly until the soup thickens.

4.   Remove from the heat, discard the gingerroot, and pour the egg whites in a thin stream from about 6 inches above the saucepan. Stir gently a few times so that thin threads of egg white rise to the surface. Drizzle with sesame seed oil and give a few last stirs. Serve hot.

Crab and Asparagus Soup

Serves 4, or 6 as part of a
multicourse meal

*R*ather than hearty chowders, Chinese seafood soups are generally light, and the fresh taste of the seafood comes through. This soup is thickened with cornstarch to keep the bits of crabmeat suspended in the broth.

福

8 spears asparagus
1 (6-ounce) can crabmeat, drained (about ¾ cup)
1 teaspoon dry sherry
4 cups Chinese Chicken Broth (page 64) plus 1 teaspoon salt or
    1 (13¾-ounce) can chicken broth and enough water to make 4 cups
1 slice unpeeled gingerroot, 1 × ⅛ inch each
2 tablespoons cornstarch, dissolved in ½ cup water
1 egg, beaten
Dash white pepper
1 teaspoon sesame seed oil
Salt to taste

1.   Clean the asparagus, snap off the tough ends, and trim the leaves off the lower stalk. Cut on the diagonal into 1½-inch pieces. Set aside.

2.   Flake the crabmeat, removing any cartilage, and mix with the sherry. Set aside.

3.   Combine the chicken broth and gingerroot in a saucepan and bring to a boil over medium heat. Stir in the asparagus and crabmeat. As soon as the soup returns to a boil, add the cornstarch mixture and stir until the broth thickens and comes back to a boil. Stir in the egg and immediately remove from heat. Remove the gingerroot. Drizzle with sesame seed oil and adjust seasoning. Serve immediately.

Chinese Celery Cabbage and Dried Shrimp Soup

Serves 6 to 8

*T*his is comfort soup for me. It always reminds me of those childhood "hot and noisy" get-togethers — as the Chinese would call them — when my mother would cook all day. Traditionally this soup, served with Moo Shi Pork (page 192) and Mandarin Pancakes (page 118), made up a whole meal. Sometimes my mother used Smithfield ham in place of the dried shrimp. Don't use fresh shrimp, though; they are not suitable.

禄

¼ cup dried shrimp
1 teaspoon dry sherry
1 pound Chinese celery or napa cabbage
2 ounces bean thread
2 tablespoons canola, corn, or peanut oil
½ teaspoon salt
2 slices unpeeled gingerroot, 1 × ⅛ inch each
6 cups Chinese Chicken Broth (page 64) plus 1 teaspoon salt or
    1 (13¾-ounce) can chicken broth and enough water to make 6 cups

1. Place the shrimp in a small bowl or measuring cup and pour on the sherry and 3 tablespoons water. Set aside.

2. Discard the tough outer leaves of the cabbage and cut it into quarters lengthwise. Cut out the core and slice the cabbage quarters into 1½-inch chunks. Set aside.

3. Soak the bean thread in warm water for 3 to 5 minutes until soft. Drain carefully so that the strands stay together as much as possible. Cut into 6- to 8-inch lengths with scissors. Set aside.

4. Heat the oil in a stockpot. When the oil is hot but not smoking, add the salt, gingerroot, and cabbage chunks; the ingredients should sizzle. Stir and cook until the cabbage is wilted.

5. Pour in the chicken broth, add the dried shrimp with the soaking liquid, and bring to a boil. Cover and simmer until the cabbage is transparent and tender.

Soup

6. Just before serving, bring the soup to a boil, add the bean thread, and remove soup from the heat and check seasoning. Serve immediately.

Peking Fish Soup

Serves 6 to 8

his is a surprisingly quick soup to prepare and cook. The complex flavors and appearance with clouds of egg white belie its simplicity. The fish in this soup cooks very quickly. If you turn off the heat just before the fish looks completely done, it will continue to cook in the soup and be just perfect when you are ready to serve.

½ pound white fish fillets, such as cod or haddock
1½ teaspoons cornstarch
1 tablespoon dry sherry
1 egg white
5 cups Chinese Chicken Broth (page 64) plus 1 teaspoon salt or
      1 (13¾-ounce) can chicken broth and enough water to make 5 cups
½ teaspoon salt
½ teaspoon white pepper
3 tablespoons cider vinegar
1 tablespoon peeled, finely shredded gingerroot (page 45)
1 scallion, white and green parts, thinly sliced
2 sprigs cilantro, cut into 1-inch lengths

1. Slice the fish fillets into 1½-inch wide pieces. If necessary, cut the pieces crosswise so they are no longer than 2 inches. Mix the cornstarch, sherry, and egg white together until well blended. Add the fish and mix thoroughly. Set aside.

2. Bring the chicken broth to a boil in a 2-quart saucepan. Reduce the heat to medium and add the fish pieces. Stir gently for about 10 seconds.

3. Immediately stir the salt, pepper, vinegar, gingerroot, and scallion into the soup and simmer just until the fish turns white. Be careful not to overcook. Turn off the heat. Adjust salt to taste and add cilantro. Stir a few times and serve without delay.

Soup

Rice, Noodles, and Bread

Americans refer to wheat as the staff of life, but to Asians, the staff of life is rice. For the Chinese, there is nothing more comforting than the warm fragrance of rice cooking. It is as compelling as the aroma of fresh bread baking in the oven. The rice bowl is ubiquitous. Even in the wheat-growing North, rice is eaten at just about every meal, including breakfast. When Chinese greet each other they often say, "Have you eaten rice yet?" instead of "Hello."

My mother cooked long-grain rice for the dinner table and general eating but preferred short-grain rice to make congee, a thin rice gruel served at breakfast, for a late night snack, and to the elderly. At every lunar New Year, my mother made *nien gao,* a sticky cake made from glutinous rice, sweetened with sugar, and flavored with candied sweet olive blossoms from the *Osmanthus fragrans* tree. Following the Shanghai tradition, she often tinted the cake light green or pink. This special dessert symbolized the sticking together of the family and good luck for the new year in general.

In northern China, noodles, leavened and unleavened breads, and dumplings made predominately from wheat flour are the staple starch at meals. There are many varieties and types of noodles from thin, wispy noodles called dragon's beard to thick wide ribbons. Instead of birthday cakes we serve long noodles to symbolize long life.

My mother used to make birthday noodles by hand for each of us on our Chinese birthdays, which was based on the lunar calendar (our Western birthday was based on the Gregorian calendar). As a child I would brag to my amazed friends that I had *two* birthdays! We always had cake on our Western birthdays, but long-life noodles were traditional on our Chinese birthdays. The birthday person did not have to help, but everyone else was involved. Mother used to joke that she would make our birthday noodles so long that we would have to eat them from a ladder!

When I was growing up, Chinese noodles were available only at noodle shops in Chinatown. Fresh Chinese noodles are delicious, but noodle dishes can also be made successfully with packaged dried spaghetti or vermicelli. We often made noodle dishes with packaged spaghetti, and I still do. Noodles are served as a snack, lunch, or as a one-dish meal.

Other wheat dishes especially popular in the North are *man tou* (steamed bread) and *bing* (flatbread), such as scallion cakes (page 305) and Mandarin Pancakes. *Man tou,* the most common family-style steamed bread, is traditionally eaten with dishes cooked with a savory gravy. Various filled steamed breads are served mainly by street vendors or restaurants and not usually made at home.

Rice

福　The Chinese prefer plain white rice that has been cooked with water. The concept is that the rice serves as a blank canvas upon which the flavors and textures of the food play. Although not traditional, you may substitute chicken or beef broth for water if you like. Jade Rice, Onion and Garlic Rice, and Confetti Rice, all made with broth, are rice dishes that best accompany Western-style meals.

Fried rice is a way the Chinese use up leftover rice and pieces of cooked meat. Fresh rice would never be cooked just to make fried rice. Fresh rice is too soft and tender for stir-frying and gets mushy from the constant stirring. For the best fried rice, always use day-old rice, preferably day-old long-grain rice, which is firmer and will stand up to a second cooking better than short-grain rice. I store leftover rice in a plastic bag in the refrigerator and loosen the rice right in the bag. The two kinds of fried rice my mother made most often at home are Shanghai Golden Fried Rice and Choo Choo Train Fried Rice — both very easy and quick and neither of them brown. The brown color that is so popular in America comes from adding a little thick soy sauce to the rice.

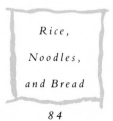

Proportions and Preparation

Two cups of raw rice will yield about five cups of fluffed cooked rice. This will serve three to four people with average appetites. The Chinese, in general, consume twice as much rice as Westerners. My theory about the complaint, "After eating Chinese food, you're hungry again an hour later," is that Westerners eat far too little rice. For the Chinese, rice is used not only as a palate cleanser and accompaniment to savory foods, but as a filler.

The Chinese wash and rinse the rice many times before cooking. This is a habit that just about every Chinese continues to practice, even though raw rice is cleaner than it used to be and sometimes enriched with vitamins that are washed away. I still wash and rinse the rice in cold water just as my mother did. I believe this not only rinses away any impurities but also helps to make the rice cook up whiter and fluffier and taste fresher. You can decide for yourself.

You will need 2¼ cups of water to cook two cups of washed and rinsed rice. If you like a harder, drier rice, reduce the water to 2 cups, an equal amount of water to rice. For short-grain rice, use two cups water. If you do not wash your rice, increase the water by four tablespoons.

Washing and Measuring Rice the Traditional Chinese Way The Chinese don't use calibrated measuring tools when they cook. It is a matter of feel and experience rather than strict proportions. This is especially the case when it comes to cooking rice. Since cooking perfect rice seems to elude many non-Asian cooks, it may come as a surprise that the Chinese approximate the correct amount of rice and water with only two fingers.

As you cook more and more rice, you'll get a sense of what a cup of rice looks like, so you'll eventually be able to pour rice directly into the cooking pot without measuring it. The Chinese usually use the same pot to cook rice, so after a while it really does become second nature. It's so simple even children can do it. Here's how to use this age-old method:

- Select a saucepan with straight sides. This works in automatic electric rice cookers, which usually have straight-sided inner pots.

- Add the raw rice to the pan, pouring in the approximate amount you think you'll need. If you are inexperienced, you may wish to measure the rice at first.

- Wash and rinse the rice three or four times right in the saucepan. After the last rinse, drain as much water out as you can by tipping the saucepan carefully without spilling the rice. You should proceed with the recipe immediately after washing since the rice will begin to absorb moisture. If allowed to sit in even a small amount of water for any length of time, the rice may cook up softer than desired.

- Smooth and level the surface of the rice with the back of your fingers. Then insert your index finger straight into the rice and touch the bottom of the pan lightly *(above left)*. Hold your index finger straight when measuring. Mark the depth of the rice by putting your thumb on the side of your index finger where the top of the rice touches it. Keep your thumb in place until all the water is measured.

- Pour warm or cold water into the pan just to the top of the rice. Then, with the tip of your index finger touching the top of the rice (not down into the rice), add water until it touches the tip of your thumb where it meets the index finger *(above right)*. If you like your rice harder or are using short-grain rice, use a little less water. If you like a softer, moister rice measure the water to slightly above the tip of your thumb.

Keeping Rice Warm The Chinese seem to know instinctively just when to start cooking the rice so that it will be ready when the meal is brought to the table. However, if you have to hold the rice for any reason, here are a few suggestions.

Saucepan rice will keep warm, as long as it is covered, for about thirty minutes, depending upon the temperature in the room, without extra attention. If you need to hold it for a longer time, turn off the heat and keep it covered. If necessary, you can give it some gentle heat later, sprinkling it first with a few tablespoons of water and turning the heat to very low. Cook for ten to fifteen minutes, being careful not to burn the rice.

Even the very basic electric rice cookers often have a "keep warm" feature. I find that it works well for about half an hour but if left on longer it sometimes browns the rice on the bottom of the pan. Even turned completely off, my basic, uninsulated rice cooker keeps the rice satisfactorily hot for up to an hour. Some deluxe models have a host of features that cook the rice as well as keep it warm for up to twelve hours. These cookers are bulky and expensive.

Rice that is cooked in a steam pot need only be left in the boiling water. The hot water surrounding the pot will keep the rice warm for up to forty minutes. If it needs reheating, simply turn the heat on and let the water boil again.

Reheating Leftover rice should always be wrapped and stored in the refrigerator to keep it from drying out. Cold rice reheats surprisingly well in the microwave oven. I generally transfer the amount of cold rice I want into a microwave-safe container and cover it with a lid or plastic wrap. Two cups of cold rice will reheat in about three minutes on high. There is no need to sprinkle any water on the rice as the moisture in the rice itself seems to be enough.

If you have an electric rice cooker, simply add three to four tablespoons of water to the cold rice in the cooker's inner pot and turn the machine on. It will turn itself off when the rice is ready.

You can also reheat cold rice successfully in a steamer. The steam keeps the rice from drying out. Place the cold rice in a heatproof bowl or dish, allowing for room on top of the rice to let the steam circulate freely. Steam for five to eight minutes, or until the rice is hot.

Serving

Freshly cooked rice is compact and should be fluffed with a pair of moistened chopsticks or a fork before serving. The Chinese eat their rice directly from a rice bowl. The family style is to serve everyone a bowl of rice. If people want seconds, they go to the rice pot and serve themselves another bowl.

If you are having a dinner party, you can transfer the cooked rice to a covered casserole of a contrasting color and let your guests serve themselves to a bowl or plate. The Japanese make heavy plastic rice servers that look like lacquerware with matching rice paddles. These handsome servers not only help keep the rice warm but are an attractive way to serve rice at the table.

Rice,

Noodles,

and Bread

Saucepan Rice

Makes about 5 cups cooked rice, enough to serve 3 to 4 people

*Y*ou *can make excellent rice in a regular kitchen saucepan. Be sure to read the notes on rice on pages 84–87. Watch the rice carefully so it does not boil over.*

健康

2 cups long-grain rice
2¼ cups water

1.　Pour the rice into a heavy-bottomed 2-quart saucepan. Cover the rice with plenty of cold water and gently rub the grains between your hands. Wash and drain the rice 3 or 4 times tipping the saucepan carefully to pour out as much water as possible without spilling the rice or drain in a strainer. Add the water and cover the pan.

2.　Bring to a boil over medium-high heat. Immediately reduce the heat to medium-low and stir the rice with a wooden spoon from the bottom up and around the sides of the pan. Scrape down the grains from the sides. Cover and cook until there is no visible liquid on top of the rice and there are holes on the surface of the rice, about 5 minutes. If the rice begins to boil over, place the cover askew until step 3.

3.　Immediately turn the heat down to very low, as low as you can, and cook for 20 to 30 minutes, or until the rice is tender and a grain no longer has a hard core when pressed between the fingers.

福

Note　If you inadvertently scorch the rice, use my mother's trick. Uncover the pan for a few minutes to release the steam, place a piece of bread over the rice, and put the lid back on. The bread absorbs much of the burnt flavor. Discard the bread before serving.

Electric Rice Cooker Rice

Makes about 5 cups cooked rice, enough to serve 3 to 4 people

*E*lectric rice cookers make such good rice and are so easy to use that the Chinese hardly cook rice in a saucepan anymore. I have been using a rice cooker for years, and it always makes perfect rice that does not have to be watched or monitored at all.

There are many models of electric rice cookers. The most convenient and popular size is the five-cup rice cooker. If you have a large family or need to cook lots of rice, though, you might want to consider the eight-cup size. In general, all rice cookers perform equally well; some newer models have special features that are nice but not imperative. My twenty-year-old Hitachi basic model is still used every day and has never missed a beat!

禄

2 cups long-grain rice
2¼ cups water

Wash the rice 3 or 4 times in plenty of cold water in a bowl or the inner cooking pot of the electric rice cooker. Tip the bowl or pot to drain as much water as possible without spilling the rice or drain in a strainer. Add the water, cover, and follow the manufacturer's directions. In my electric cooker, 2 cups of rice cook in about 20 minutes.

Steam Pot Steamed Rice

Makes about 5 cups cooked rice, enough to serve 3 to 4 people

*A*lthough the Yunnan steam pot is designed especially for cooking the famed Yunnan Steam Pot Chicken (page 177), I've found that it also makes perfect rice without any worry of burning or need to observe the different stages of cooking rice on the stove. What's more, the hard-fired clay retains heat and keeps the rice warm. The attractive and interesting design makes it a perfect serving dish as well.

2 cups long-grain rice
2¼ cups water

1. Place the rice in a bowl and cover with cold water. Rub the grains between your hands and then drain. Wash and drain 3 or 4 times. Drain by tipping the bowl carefully to pour out as much water as possible without spilling the grains or drain in a strainer.

2. Transfer the rice to a steam pot and pour in the water. Be sure all the grains are totally submerged and the surface of the rice is smooth and even. Cover the steam pot and place in a wok, stockpot, or roaster. Be sure there is enough room around the pot for you to lift it out when the rice is cooked. Add water so that the steam pot is sitting in water up to the bottom or middle of the handles. Do not overfill or the water will boil into the steam pot through the inner chimney or the lid. Cover the wok or pot and bring the water to a boil.

3. When the water reaches a boil, reduce the heat until the water maintains a slow boil. Cook for 30 to 40 minutes, or until a grain of rice is totally smooth when pressed between the finger tips. It is not necessary to stir the rice or check it during the cooking procedure. Just be sure that the water in the pot in which the steam pot is sitting does not boil away. Replenish with more boiling water as needed.

Onion and Garlic Rice

Serves 3 to 4 as a side dish

*R*ice is a wonderful accompaniment for Western-style beef or chicken stews. Instead of plain steamed rice, I often make flavored rice.

2 tablespoons canola, corn, or peanut oil

1 medium onion, chopped

2 garlic cloves, pureed or put through a garlic press

2 cups long-grain rice

2 cups Chinese Chicken Broth (page 64) plus 1 teaspoon salt or

    1 (13¾-ounce) can chicken broth and enough water to make 2 cups

3 tablespoons minced parsley

1. Heat the oil in a skillet over medium heat and brown the onion. Add the garlic and stir a few times. Remove the pan from the heat and transfer the onion and garlic to a 2-quart saucepan.

2. Add the rice and broth to the saucepan. Stir, cover the pan, and bring to a boil over medium heat. Reduce the heat to medium-low and cook until the surface of the rice is marked with holes and all the visible liquid has been absorbed, about 5 minutes.

3. Gently stir the rice, scraping down the sides. Immediately turn the heat down to very low. Cook, covered, for 20 to 30 minutes, or until the rice is cooked through and tender. Remove from the heat.

4. When ready to serve, transfer the rice to a covered serving dish and sprinkle with parsley. Serve immediately.

Rice Skin

鍋巴

Sometimes rice that has been cooked too long in a saucepan forms a brown crust on the bottom and sides. The Chinese call this "rice skin." My mother liked to cook it with lots of water to make a smoky rice porridge.

At the restaurant, the cooks dried the rice skin by placing the pan over very low heat. Once it had dried and shrunk, it could be removed easily from the pan. It was broken into smaller pieces and stored in a dry place. The chefs would deep-fry the rice skin in hot oil to make a crispy rice that crackled and sizzled when it was added to soups covered with sauce in the Peking fashion. The hot sizzling rice, called *guo ba,* has to be served as soon as possible after frying for the most explosive sizzle. When someone ordered a dish with sizzling rice, the waiters were instructed to stand by as the chef dropped the skin into the hot fat. As a child I loved sizzling rice with sugar sprinkled on top, so the chefs would often fry a little extra for me.

Jade Rice

Serves 3 to 4 as a side dish

My mother used to make this Shanghai steamed rice with chopped dark green bok choy leaves for the family. She would often pick through the trimmed bok choy leaves at our favorite Chinatown market to come up with a handful for her rice. She hated to see good food go to waste! I use pureed spinach leaves instead; they provide a uniform green color.

健康

¼ pound spinach leaves

2 cups Chinese Chicken Broth (page 64) plus 1 teaspoon salt or

 1 (13¾-ounce) can chicken broth and enough water to make 2 cups

2 cups long-grain rice

2 Chinese sausages, finely chopped

1. Wash the spinach thoroughly and parboil for 30 seconds. Rinse in cold water, drain, and squeeze out the water. Coarsely chop the leaves and combine with the broth in a blender or food processor. Blend or process until completely pureed.

2. Combine the rice, spinach puree, and sausage in a 2-quart saucepan. Stir together, scraping down the sides of the saucepan. Cover the pan and bring to a boil over medium heat. Cook until the liquid is almost absorbed and the top of the rice has small holes, about 5 minutes. Stir gently and scrape any grains from the side of the pan. Reduce the heat to very low and cook, covered, for 20 to 30 minutes, or until the rice has absorbed all the moisture and is cooked through. Serve hot.

Confetti Rice

Serves 4 to 5

*T*his dish gets its name from the riot of color created by the vegetables. It's a great alternative to fried rice since the chicken broth imparts a delicate flavor without any added oil. I have given directions for making the rice in a steam pot or saucepan. If you are using an electric rice cooker, follow the manufacturer's instructions and add the peas halfway through the cooking.

福

2 cups long-grain rice
2 cups Chinese Chicken Broth (page 64) plus 1 teaspoon salt or
    1 (13¾-ounce) can chicken broth and enough water to make 2 cups
½ cup diced fresh carrots or thawed frozen carrots
½ cup diced red bell pepper (about ½ pepper)
½ cup corn, fresh or frozen
⅓ cup thinly sliced scallions or diced red onion
½ cup fresh peas, parboiled, or thawed frozen peas
2 tablespoons minced parsley

1. Place the rice in a large bowl and cover it with cold water. Swish the rice around with your hands and then drain. Repeat 2 times and drain.

2. Place the rice in a 2-quart steam pot or in a 2-quart saucepan. Add the broth, 3 tablespoons water, carrots, red pepper, corn, and scallions. Mix well and smooth the surface flat so that every grain of rice is submerged in the broth. Put a lid on the steam pot or saucepan.

3. Place the steam pot in a bath of water in a wok, stir-fry pan, or other shallow pan wide enough to hold the pot comfortably. The water level should not come up any higher than 2 inches from the lid. Cover the pan holding the steam pot with a lid and bring the water to a boil. Reduce the heat to medium or medium-low and simmer for 20 minutes. Add more boiling water to the pan as necessary so it does not ever evaporate completely. (Or place the saucepan over medium heat. When the water boils, stir the rice, turn the heat to medium-low, and cook until there is no visible liquid over the rice and the surface of the rice forms holes, about 5 minutes.)

4. Uncover the steam pot or saucepan and stir in the peas. Re-cover the steam pot and the wok and cook for 20 minutes. (Or re-cover the saucepan, turn the heat as low as possible, and cook for 15 to 20 minutes.) The rice should be tender and no longer have a hard core.

5. Remove the steam pot from the water or the saucepan from the heat. Fluff up the rice with a pair of wet chopsticks or a bamboo rice paddle. If using the steam pot, sprinkle the parsley over the top and serve directly from the pot. Transfer the saucepan rice to a covered serving dish and sprinkle with parsley. Serve immediately.

健康

Shanghai Golden
Fried Rice

Serves 3 to 5

W hen we were children, my mother often made this simple fried rice for us at home. The light color might surprise you, but actually the Chinese are not used to the dark fried rice so familiar in Chinese-American restaurants. If you'd like a meatless version, simply omit the ham and, if desired, increase the salt slightly to adjust for the change.

4 cups cold cooked rice
2 large eggs
½ teaspoon dry sherry
3 to 5 tablespoons thinly sliced scallions, green and white parts, or minced onion
1 teaspoon salt, or to taste
4 tablespoons canola, corn, or peanut oil
½ cup chopped ham, bacon, or Chinese sausage (optional)

1. Place the cold rice in a large bowl and use your fingers to break up any lumps. Break the eggs directly onto the rice and add the sherry, scallions, and salt. Mix together thoroughly with your hands or with a wooden spoon.

2. Pour the oil into a wok or stir-fry pan and place the pan over medium-high heat. Heat until the oil is hot but not smoking. Test by dipping a spatula into the rice mixture and then into the oil; it should sizzle. If using the meat, add it to the hot oil and stir for about 30 seconds.

3. Turn the rice mixture into the pan, increase temperature to high, and stir constantly for 8 to 10 minutes, breaking up any lumps with the back of the spatula. The grains will be loose and fluffy and the rice heated through. Taste for seasoning. Serve hot.

Rice,

Noodles,

and Bread

Choo Choo Train
Fried Rice

Serves 3 to 5

Every Chinese person who travels a lot knows what train fried rice is — it's the type of fried rice usually served in dining cars in China. My mother coined this name when we were children because she thought we would find the dish more appealing. I guess she was right, because this was one of our favorite dishes.

4 cups cold cooked rice
2 large eggs
½ teaspoon dry sherry
4 tablespoons canola, corn, or peanut oil
2 tablespoons minced onion
1½ teaspoons salt
½ cup diced baked ham
½ cup fresh peas, parboiled, or thawed frozen peas

1.   Place the rice in a mixing bowl and use your fingers to separate the grains until they are loose. Set aside. Lightly beat the eggs and sherry together with a fork or chopsticks. Set aside.

2.   Heat the oil in a wok or stir-fry pan over high heat. When the oil is hot, stir in the onions and the eggs. Scramble until the eggs are dry and break into small pieces.

3.   Add the rice, salt, ham, and peas and stir constantly until the ingredients are well blended and heated, about 8 to 10 minutes. Serve hot.

Yangchow Fried Rice

Serves 3 to 5

From the Shanghai region, this attractive rice, flecked with yellow, green, orange, and pink is a popular snack since almost every kind of ingredient can be found in it.

健康

4 cups cold cooked rice

2 eggs

1 teaspoon sherry

4 tablespoons canola, corn, or peanut oil

½ cup diced cooked chicken

1 cup cooked small shrimp (6 ounces)

½ cup diced baked ham

1 cup diced carrots, parboiled, or thawed frozen carrots

1 cup fresh peas, parboiled, or thawed frozen peas

½ cup thinly sliced scallions

1 teaspoon salt, or to taste

Dash ground pepper, or to taste

1.   Place the rice in a bowl and use your hands to break up and separate the grains. Set aside. Lightly beat the eggs and sherry together with a fork or chopsticks. Set aside.

2.   Heat the oil in a wok or stir-fry pan over medium-high heat. When the oil is hot, add the eggs and scramble until they puff lightly but are still loose. Immediately stir in the rice and stir for about 2 minutes so that the rice heats up and the eggs are completely mixed in.

3.   Raise the heat to high and add the remaining ingredients and stir vigorously until they are well mixed into the rice and heated through. Correct seasoning as desired. Serve hot.

福

Note   This is a good recipe for leftover meat and shrimp. If you don't have all 3 kinds listed above, you can leave one out, but increase the other two so you have 1½ cups total. Fried rice heats up well in the microwave or in a stir-fry pan.

Fried Rice with Ham

Serves 3 to 5

*T*hick soy sauce gives this rice its brown color. If it's unavailable, you can omit it or use dark soy sauce, but the same amount will not color the rice. Add more gradually, taking care that the rice does not become too wet or salty.

禄

4 cups cold cooked rice

2 large eggs

1 teaspoon salt

½ teaspoon pepper

4 tablespoons canola, corn, or peanut oil

½ cup thinly sliced scallions or diced onion

1 teaspoon thick soy sauce (optional)

1 cup fresh peas, parboiled, or thawed frozen peas

1 cup diced carrots, parboiled, or thawed frozen carrots

½ cup diced cooked ham, chicken, turkey, or pork

1 cup fresh bean sprouts

1. Place the rice in a large bowl and use your fingers to break up any lumps. Set aside. Beat the eggs in a separate bowl with the salt and pepper. Set aside.

2. Pour the oil into a wok or stir-fry pan and place the pan over medium-high heat. When the oil is hot but not smoking, add the scallions; they should sizzle. Stir for about 15 seconds. Stir the beaten eggs into the pan with a spatula and scramble until the eggs are dry and separate.

3. Add the rice to the eggs and mix thoroughly. Pour the soy sauce evenly over the mixture. Add the peas, carrots, ham, and bean sprouts. Stir constantly until all the ingredients are well mixed and heated through. Serve immediately.

Oyster Sauce Fried Rice

Serves 6 to 8

My mother developed this fried rice to use as a stuffing in our Thanksgiving turkey. The giblets and oyster sauce give a wonderful savory flavor to the big bird. Even when we're having a traditional bread stuffing—at the request of my American husband—I like to make this rice as a side dish. It is tasty enough to stand alone and is even better the next day when the flavors have mellowed and blended. It warms up beautifully in the microwave. This dish may be prepared with or without the giblets and livers.

Giblets (liver, heart, and gizzard) from a turkey or ½ cup chicken giblets or
  livers (optional)
6 cups cold cooked rice
½ cup dried black mushrooms, softened in hot water for 15 minutes (optional)
4 tablespoons canola, corn, or peanut oil
1 onion, chopped (about ½ cup)
2 teaspoons minced garlic
1 cup chopped celery
¼ teaspoon black pepper
½ cup oyster sauce
Salt to taste
½ cup minced parsley

1. Chop the giblets or livers into small pieces. If you are using the gizzard, peel off and discard the thick membrane. Set aside. Put the rice in a mixing bowl and break up any lumps with your hands. Set aside.

2. Squeeze the water from the mushrooms, if using, and trim off the stems with a pair of scissors. Shred the caps and set aside.

3. Heat the oil in a wok or stir-fry pan over high heat until hot but not smoking. Test with a piece of onion; it should sizzle when added to the oil. Add the onions and stir-fry until lightly browned. Add the giblets, garlic, celery, and mushrooms. Stir constantly until the giblets change color and are separated.

Rice,

Noodles,

and Bread

4. Season with black pepper and oyster sauce and stir until well mixed. Add the rice. Stir constantly with a spatula until the rice is evenly mixed into the gravy and heated through. Taste and adjust seasoning as desired by adding more oyster sauce, 1 tablespoon at a time. Do not allow rice to become too wet; add salt if oyster sauce does not provide enough seasoning. Remove from the heat and stir in the parsley. If not ready to serve immediately, place in a covered casserole in a low oven. Serve hot.

Variation To use as stuffing for a turkey, rinse the turkey and dry inside and out with a paper towel. Stuff the cavity with the rice mixture only when you are ready to roast. Stuff lightly so the rice can expand during roasting. Any extras can be heated separately and served in a casserole. This recipe is enough for a 10- to 12-pound bird.

健康

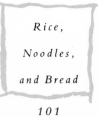

Shredded Pork with Stir-fried Noodles

Serves 3 to 4

Stir-fried noodles are a favorite snack food or lunch dish for the Chinese. We sometimes add vinegar or even ketchup to the individual servings. It may sound unconventional, but it's really quite good. Try it.

½ pound dried Chinese noodles, thin spaghetti, or linguine

1 teaspoon sesame seed oil

½ pound lean pork or beef, shredded (about 1 cup)

2 tablespoons light soy sauce

2 teaspoons cornstarch

1 teaspoon dry sherry

½ teaspoon sugar

1 cup dried black mushrooms, softened in hot water for 15 minutes

2 tablespoons canola, corn, or peanut oil

1 slice unpeeled gingerroot, 1 × ⅛ inch

2 cups shredded napa, Chinese celery cabbage, or bok choy

½ cup shredded carrots

½ cup thinly sliced scallions, white and green parts

1 teaspoon dark soy sauce

1.   Cook the noodles in a large amount of boiling water until a little more tender than al dente. Drain, rinse in cold water, and toss with the sesame seed oil to keep them from sticking together. Set aside.

2.   Place the pork in a bowl and add the light soy sauce, cornstarch, sherry, and sugar. Stir together well. Set aside.

3.   Drain the softened mushrooms, reserving 2 tablespoons of the soaking liquid. Strain the liquid through a fine sieve. Set aside. Snip off the stems of the mushrooms with scissors and discard. Cut the caps into thin shreds. Set aside.

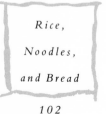

4.   Pour the oil into a wok or stir-fry pan and place it over high heat. Add the gingerroot and stir around the pan until the oil is hot but not smoking; the gingerroot will sizzle. Stir up the pork again and add it to the pan. Stir for about 2 minutes, or until there is no pink left in the meat. Add the cabbage, carrots, mushrooms, and scallions. Stir for about 2 to 3 minutes, or until the vegetables are tender-crisp.

5.   Add the reserved mushroom liquid and stir a few times to mix. Add the noodles and stir thoroughly until the noodles are heated through. Stir in the dark soy sauce until the noodles are evenly colored. Turn out onto a large serving platter. Serve immediately.

Note   See pages 44–45 for a description of how to shred meat and vegetables.

Both Sides Brown Noodles

Serves 6 to 8

Professional Chinese chefs brown these noodles at the same time as they are preparing the sauce. It is not always practical to do this at home, so I've suggested you brown the noodles first and keep them warm in a low oven while you make the sauce. Eat the noodles as soon as you can after browning while they are still hot and crisp.

禧

1 pound Chinese egg noodles, fresh or dried, or fettuccine or linguine

8 tablespoons canola, corn, or peanut oil

½ pound lean pork or beef, shredded (about 1 cup)

1 teaspoon dry sherry

7 teaspoons cornstarch

1½ cups Chinese Chicken Broth (page 64) or canned broth

1 slice unpeeled gingerroot, 1 × ⅛ inch

3 cups shredded green, napa, or bok choy cabbage (½ pound)

1 (8-ounce) can sliced bamboo shoots, drained (1 cup)

1 cup dried black mushrooms, softened in hot water for 15 minutes, drained, stems removed, and caps shredded or sliced fresh mushrooms

3 scallions, white and green parts, cut into 2-inch lengths

2 teaspoons salt

1. Stir the noodles into a large amount of boiling water and boil until a little more tender than al dente. Be sure not to overcook since the noodles will be cooked again. If the noodles are fresh they will cook in a very short time. Taste often as they cook. When tender, drain and rinse in cold water. Drain thoroughly and mix with 2 tablespoons of the oil to prevent them from sticking together. Set aside.

2. Mix the meat with the sherry and 2 teaspoons of the cornstarch in a bowl and stir together well. Set aside. Dissolve the remaining 5 teaspoons of cornstarch in ½ cup of the broth and set aside.

3. Heat 4 tablespoons of the oil in a large nonstick skillet or other flat-bottomed heavy pan over medium-high heat. Add the noodles and spread them out to the edges of the pan. Fry until the noodles are golden brown, 7 to 10 minutes on each side. Lift and peek every so often to see how they are browning. When the first side has browned, flip the noodles over and fry the other side. Remove from the pan and place on a serving platter in a warm oven. (If a large skillet is unavailable, cook the noodles in batches in a smaller pan.)

4.   To make the sauce, pour the remaining 2 tablespoons of oil into a wok or stir-fry pan and place the pan over high heat. Add the gingerroot and stir around the pan until it begins to sizzle. Mix up the meat again, pour it into the pan, and stir for about 2 minutes. Stir the cabbage, bamboo shoots, mushrooms, and scallions into the pan. Add the remaining 1 cup of broth and the salt. Reduce the heat to medium, cover the pan, and cook until the cabbage is tender, 3 to 5 minutes, stirring occasionally. Add the cornstarch slurry to the pan and cook until the sauce thickens.

5.   Remove the noodles from the oven and pour the sauce over them. Serve hot.

Note   See pages 44–45 for a description of how to shred meat and vegetables.

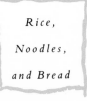

Noodles with
Peking Meat Sauce

Serves 6 to 8

My mother often used packaged spaghetti or vermicelli for this dish because in the early 1950s using Chinese egg noodles meant a special trip to Chinatown. When we had this dish in China, it was at a tiny restaurant that had a "noodle stretcher," a man who stretched noodles by hand. After he stretched the noodles, helpers immediately dropped them into a large vat of boiling water, then strained them right into a large noodle bowl. They scooped up a large ladle of sauce, poured it on, and added a crunchy vegetable garnish. People were lined up waiting to lunch on a plate of those Peking noodles! They were delicious, but I've always liked my mother's better.

禄

½ pound ground pork (about 1 cup)

1 teaspoon dry sherry

1 teaspoon cornstarch

½ cup bean paste, preferably Japanese miso

2 tablespoons hoisin sauce

1 tablespoon sugar

2 tablespoons dark soy sauce

1 tablespoon canola, corn, or peanut oil

1 teaspoon minced garlic

1 medium onion, minced

½ cup thinly sliced scallions, green and white parts

1 cup water

1 pound spaghetti, thin or regular

10 radishes, shredded, for garnish

1 medium cucumber, partially peeled, seeded, and shredded, for garnish

2 cups bean sprouts, parboiled for 15 to 20 seconds and drained well, for garnish

10 ounces fresh spinach, washed, parboiled for 15 to 20 seconds, squeezed dry, and minced, for garnish

5 garlic cloves, peeled and finely minced, for garnish (optional)

1.   Mix the pork with the sherry and cornstarch in a small bowl and set aside. Stir the bean paste, hoisin sauce, sugar, and soy sauce together in another small bowl. Set aside.

2.   Heat the oil in a wok or stir-fry pan over high heat. When the oil is hot, stir in the pork and cook for 2 minutes, or until the meat changes color and separates. Add the garlic and onion and stir for 1 minute. Add the scallions and stir constantly for 1 minute, or until the scallions are soft but not browned.

3.   Stir in the bean paste mixture and water and mix thoroughly with the meat. Turn the heat to low and simmer for 3 to 4 minutes, stirring occasionally. You will have a thin sauce.

4.   Bring 5 quarts of water to a boil in a large pot. Stir in the spaghetti and boil until a little more tender than al dente. Drain and rinse in hot water; immediately divide the noodles among 6 or 8 individual noodle bowls. Place the meat sauce in a serving bowl on the table. Set the vegetable garnishes out in individual bowls and let people sauce and garnish their own noodles.

Note   Shred the radishes and cucumber as described on page 45.

Variation   For a spicy version, substitute ½ cup Szechuan-style hot bean paste for the miso and add 1 tablespoon Chinkiang vinegar and 1 teaspoon toasted and ground Szechuan peppercorns.

Noodles with
Bean Curd Sauce

Serves 6

*P*reviously frozen bean curd with its open, spongy texture works very well in this sauce. It has a firmer texture than fresh bean curd, holds up to stirring and mixing, and soaks up the wonderful bean sauce flavor. Serve the dish with the same vegetable garnish as for Noodles with Peking Meat Sauce (page 106).

禧

1 pound firm bean curd, previously frozen
½ cup plus 2 tablespoons bean paste, preferably Japanese miso
2 tablespoons hoisin sauce
1 tablespoon sugar
2 tablespoons dark soy sauce
1 pound thin spaghetti
2 tablespoons canola, corn, or peanut oil
½ cup chopped onion
1½ teaspoons minced garlic
2 teaspoons minced peeled gingerroot
½ cup thinly sliced scallions, green and white parts
1½ cups water
1 tablespoon cornstarch, dissolved in 2 tablespoons water

1. Thaw the bean curd by placing it in a bowl of hot water. When it is completely thawed, gently squeeze out the excess water and cut the cake into ½-inch or smaller cubes. Set aside.

2. Blend together the bean paste, hoisin sauce, sugar, and soy sauce in a small bowl. Set aside.

3. Bring 5 quarts of water to a boil in a large pot. Stir the spaghetti into the boiling water and cook until tender.

4. While the spaghetti is cooking, heat the oil in a wok, stir-fry pan, or heavy saucepan over high heat until hot but not smoking. Test by dipping a piece of onion into the oil; it should sizzle. Add the onion to the hot oil and stir for about 1 minute. Add the garlic and gingerroot and stir for 30 seconds. Add the scallions and stir until they wilt. Stir in the bean curd and mix a few times. Add the bean paste mixture and the water. Blend well with the spatula. Reduce the heat to medium and simmer for about 1 minute. Pour in the cornstarch slurry and stir constantly until the sauce thickens.

5. Drain the spaghetti, rinse with hot water, and divide among 6 individual noodle bowls. Serve the bean sauce and vegetable garnish in separate bowls alongside the noodles and let people help themselves to sauce and garnish.

健康

Note   Bean paste, depending on the brand, can be very salty; a little bit goes a long way. In step 4, start by spooning on a small amount of sauce, mix and taste, and add more if desired.

福

Rice,

Noodles,

and Bread

Cold Noodles, Szechuan Style

Serves 6 to 8

The second time Keith, then my husband-to-be, met my mother it was her birthday. We had planned a family picnic, a sort of birthday potluck so my mother wouldn't have to cook. In honor of the special day Keith, who is not Chinese, decided to make cold Chinese noodles to symbolize long life. He was very brave—or very foolish—to try this, but everyone loved his noodles, including my mother.

Since these noodles are served at room temperature, they are ideal for picnics. Try them sometime instead of potato salad.

禄

1 pound thin spaghetti

4 tablespoons sesame seed oil

1 whole chicken breast (about 1 pound) or about 2 cups shredded, cooked chicken

¼ cup sesame seed paste (tahini)

2 teaspoons grated peeled gingerroot

3 teaspoons finely minced garlic

1 heaping teaspoon Szechuan peppercorns, toasted and ground

1 tablespoon rice vinegar

1 tablespoon chili oil

3 tablespoons light soy sauce

2 teaspoons sugar

½ cup thinly sliced scallions, green and white parts

3 tablespoons sesame seeds, toasted (optional)

Cilantro or parsley sprigs, for garnish (optional)

1. Bring 5 quarts of water to a boil and stir in the spaghetti. Boil until tender. Do not overcook or the noodles will be mushy. Drain and rinse under cold water. Drain thoroughly, transfer to a serving platter, not a bowl, and mix in 2 tablespoons of the sesame seed oil to the keep the noodles from sticking together. Set aside.

2. If using a whole chicken breast, put the chicken breast in a pot of boiling water. When the water returns to a boil, turn the heat down to a simmer. Simmer partly covered, for 20 to 25 minutes, or until the chicken is cooked through. Drain and set out on a plate to cool. When the chicken is cool enough to handle, remove and discard the skin and bones. Shred the meat by hand and spread over the noodles.

3.   Mix the sesame seed paste with the remaining 2 tablespoons of sesame seed oil and the gingerroot, garlic, Szechuan peppercorns, vinegar, chili oil, soy sauce, and sugar. Blend into a smooth thin paste. Pour the paste over the noodles. Reserve 2 tablespoons of scallions and 1 tablespoon of sesame seeds, if using, and sprinkle the remainder over the noodles. Toss together well. I find the best way to get the ingredients evenly mixed is to use my hands. Sprinkle the reserved scallions and sesame seeds, if using, over the top of the noodles and serve. (Or cover and refrigerate until ready to use. Bring back to room temperature and serve decorated with sprigs of parsley or cilantro.)

Dan Dan Noodles

Serve 6 to 8

D an Dan Noodles are Szechuan street food at its most traditional. Dan dan *refers to the thumping sound made by the pails of noodles and sauce at the ends of bamboo panniers as they are carried through the streets in a sort of traveling fast food restaurant.*

The noodles are served cold or tepid. Once assembled, the dish holds well, although the noodles absorb the sauce after an hour. If you like saucier noodles, dress them just before serving. I sometimes add blanched and shredded snow peas or blanched bean sprouts along with the scallions for texture.

禧

1 pound thin spaghetti
2 tablespoons sesame seed oil
¾ cup creamy peanut butter
¾ cup Chinese Chicken Broth (page 64) or canned chicken broth
2 tablespoons light soy sauce
2 teaspoons chili oil, or to taste
¼ teaspoon cayenne, or to taste
1 heaping teaspoon Szechuan peppercorns, toasted and ground
3 scallions, white and green parts, thinly sliced

1. Bring 4 to 5 quarts of water to a boil in a large pot. Add the noodles and cook uncovered, until a little more tender than al dente. Avoid overcooking, or the noodles will be mushy. Stir occasionally to keep the noodles from sticking together. When done, drain and rinse with cold water until thoroughly cool. Drain well, transfer to a large serving bowl, and gently toss with 1 tablespoon of the sesame seed oil (hands work best). Set aside.

2. While the noodles are cooking, blend the peanut butter and broth together in a bowl until smooth and creamy. Add the soy sauce, chili oil, the remaining 1 tablespoon of sesame seed oil, the cayenne, and Szechuan peppercorns and mix thoroughly. If you have the time, let the sauce sit for 30 minutes or more to allow the spices to develop.

3. Pour the peanut paste over the cooked noodles and add the scallions. I use my hands to toss the noodles because they mix the ingredients more evenly and the noodles don't break. Serve cool.

健康

Variation   For a vegetable garnish, blanch snow peas and bean sprouts in the boiling water that will be used to cook the noodles. For snow peas, snap off both ends and string ¼ pound of snow peas. Blanch for 10 to 15 seconds. Remove with a wire skimmer and rinse in cold water to refresh and drain. Cut on the diagonal into shreds. For bean sprouts, blanch 2 cups of bean sprouts in boiling water for 15 seconds. Remove with a wire skimmer and rinse in cold water. Drain well. Add the vegetables to the noodles with the scallions in step 3.

福

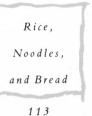

Rice,

Noodles,

and Bread

Chicken Soup with Noodles

Serves 3 to 4

Noodles are most popular in the wheat-growing north of China, but all Chinese enjoy a steaming bowl of noodles as a light meal or midnight snack. In Asia, noodle shops or noodle vendors with their carts are everywhere.

禄

½ pound Chinese dried noodles, thin spaghetti, or vermicelli
4 cups Chinese Chicken Broth (page 64) plus 1 teaspoon salt or
    1 (13¾-ounce) can chicken broth and enough water to make 4 cups
2 slices unpeeled gingerroot, 1 × ⅛ inch each
½ teaspoon salt, or to taste
⅛ teaspoon ground white pepper
1 pound skinless boneless chicken breast, shredded (page 44)
½ teaspoon cornstarch
1 teaspoon dry sherry
4 cups spinach, watercress, or napa cabbage, washed and cut into 2-inch pieces
Sesame seed oil, for garnish

1. Bring 3 quarts of water to a boil in a large pot. Add the noodles and cook until a little more tender than al dente but not mushy. Stir occasionally to keep the noodles from sticking together. When done, drain, rinse thoroughly with cold water, and drain well. Set aside.

2. While the noodles are cooking, mix the chicken broth, gingerroot, salt, and pepper together in a saucepan and heat to boiling.

3. Mix the chicken, cornstarch, and sherry together in a bowl. When the broth is boiling, add the chicken mixture, stirring constantly until the chicken shreds are separated and white, about 1 minute. Stir in the greens and cook just until they are wilted. If using napa cabbage, cook for about 2 minutes, or until the white parts are translucent.

4. When ready to serve, reheat the noodles by rinsing in hot water. Drain well and divide among 4 individual bowls. Spoon the hot soup over the noodles and top with pieces of chicken and vegetable. (Or put the noodles in the soup until they are hot, spoon them into the bowls with chicken and vegetables, and pour on the hot broth.) Drizzle ½ teaspoon sesame seed oil into each bowl. Serve hot.

Shredded Pork with Szechuan Vegetable and Noodles in Soup

Serves 3 to 4

I have found that people who are not adept with chopsticks find soup noodles difficult to eat. The noodles slip off a spoon and a fork won't pick up the soup! Chopsticks and a Chinese porcelain spoon are really the best and most efficient tools for eating soup noodles.

½ pound Chinese dried noodles or thin spaghetti

½ pound lean pork, shredded, about 1 cup (page 44)

2 teaspoons cornstarch

2 teaspoons dry sherry

2 teaspoons light soy sauce

2 tablespoons canola, corn, or peanut oil

2 slices unpeeled gingerroot, 1 × ⅛ inch each

½ cup shredded Szechuan vegetable, rinsed and drained

4½ cups Chinese Chicken Broth (page 64) plus 1¼ teaspoons salt or
    1 (13¾-ounce) can chicken broth and enough water to make 4½ cups

1 teaspoon sesame seed oil

1.   Cook the noodles in a large amount of boiling water until a little more tender than al dente. Stir a few times to prevent sticking. Be careful not to overcook. Drain in a colander and rinse thoroughly in cold water. Set aside.

2.   Place the pork in a small bowl. Add the cornstarch, sherry, and soy sauce and stir together until well mixed. Set aside.

3.   Pour the oil into a wok or stir-fry pan and place the pan over medium-high heat. Add the gingerroot and stir around the pan until the gingerroot begins to sizzle. Stir up the pork again, pour it into the pan, and cook for 1 minute, stirring constantly. Add the Szechuan vegetable and stir for 1 minute, or until the pork has changed color and is cooked through.

(continued)

4. Add the chicken broth. Bring to a boil and stir in the sesame seed oil. Discard the gingerroot. Taste and adjust the seasoning, adding more salt if desired.

5. When ready to serve, add the cooked noodles and let the soup return to a boil. Remove from the heat and divide noodles, soup, pork, and vegetable among individual bowls. Serve immediately.

Variation Add 2 cups shredded Chinese cabbage (celery cabbage, bok choy, or napa) when adding the Szechuan vegetable in step 3. Stir until cabbage is wilted. Add the chicken broth and proceed as directed.

Snow Cabbage and Shredded Chicken Soup with Noodles

Serves 3 to 4

*T*he leafy greens and stems of the snow cabbage (page 25) are chopped and pickled in brine for a handy ingredient. It is especially popular in the provinces of Zhejiang and Jiangsu. My father was from the former and my mother grew up in the latter, so it's no wonder that cans of snow cabbage were always kept in the pantry.

You may substitute shredded lean pork for the chicken as well as rice sticks for the wheat noodles.

健康

½ pound Chinese dried noodles, thin spaghetti, or vermicelli

¼ pound chicken breast, shredded (page 44)

1 teaspoon dry sherry

1 teaspoon cornstarch

1 tablespoon canola, corn, or peanut oil

1 slice unpeeled gingerroot, 1 × ⅛ inch

½ cup canned shredded bamboo shoots, drained

½ cup snow cabbage, drained

4½ cups Chinese Chicken Broth (page 64) plus 1¼ teaspoons salt or
    1 (13¾-ounce) can chicken broth and enough water to make 4½ cups

1. Bring 3 quarts of water to a boil in a large pot. Add the noodles and cook until a little more tender than al dente, but not soft. Stir occasionally to keep the noodles from sticking together. When done, drain, rinse thoroughly with cold water, and drain well. Set aside.

2. While the noodles are cooking, mix the chicken with the sherry and cornstarch in a small bowl. Set aside.

3. Pour the oil into a wok or stir-fry pan and place the pan over medium-high heat. Add the gingerroot and stir until it sizzles and becomes fragrant. Stir up the chicken mixture again. Add and cook for about 1 minute, or until the meat has turned white. Add the bamboo shoots and snow cabbage, stir about 30 seconds, and pour in the chicken broth. Bring the liquid to a boil. Taste and add salt if desired.

4. When ready to serve, add the noodles to the boiling soup and cook just until they are heated through. Divide the noodles evenly among individual soup bowls. Ladle the soup with pieces of meat and vegetable into each bowl. There should be enough soup to come up to the level of the noodles, but not submerge them. Serve hot.

福

Variation Substitute shredded lean pork for the chicken as well as thin dried rice noodles—also called rice sticks—for the wheat noodles. Soak the rice sticks in warm water until they are tender, then add them to the boiling broth in step 3 and heat through.

Rice,

Noodles,

and Bread

117

Mandarin Pancakes

Makes twelve 7-inch pancakes

Mandarin pancakes, called bao bing *in Chinese, one of the most popular foods in Peking, are the traditional accompaniment to Moo Shi Pork (page 192) and Peking Duck. It takes a fair amount of handwork to make Mandarin pancakes, but we used to make them by hand in our restaurant all the time. Once a week the entire kitchen crew—chefs, sous chefs, choppers, everyone—would congregate and roll out Mandarin pancakes on an assembly line. The dough was made in a huge commercial mixer, but the pancakes were formed one by one. It took all afternoon to make enough to last the week. The way to get them so thin is to roll two pancakes together. They come apart easily after being cooked because the sesame seed oil keeps them from fusing together. I would help separate the hot pancakes as they came off the griddle. The secret is to slap them between your hands, as if applauding, then find a loose spot and pull the pancakes apart with your fingers. After a while I had to exchange duties with the people rolling the pancakes because my fingers would get so hot!*

With the high cost of labor and advent of pancake-making machines, restaurants eventually turned to frozen machinemade pancakes from Chinatown. The packaged pancakes are very thin and quite excellent, but nothing will take the place of the memory of the sight, smell, and sound of everyone working together in the kitchen to make Mandarin pancakes.

1¾ cups unbleached all purpose flour
¾ cup boiling water
1 teaspoon sesame seed oil

1. Mix the flour and boiling water in a bowl with a wooden spoon or chopsticks. As soon as your hands can tolerate the heat, knead the hot dough together until smooth. Knead for 3 minutes, then cover the dough with a damp towel and set aside for at least 30 minutes. The Chinese say this "wakes" the dough.

Rice,

Noodles,

and Bread

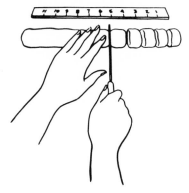

2. Roll the dough on a lightly floured board under the palms of your hands into a rope exactly 12 inches long. Using a ruler as a guide, cut the rope into 1-inch pieces.

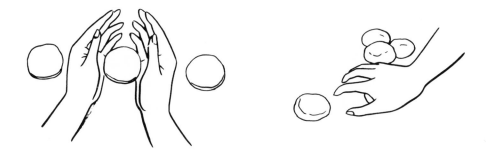

3. Turn a piece of dough on end and roll it between the palms of your hands into a cylinder. Flatten the cylinder with the palm of your hand into a circle. Continue until all are done.

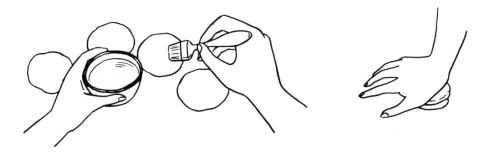

4. Brush 1 side of each cake lightly with the sesame seed oil. Place 1 cake on top of another, oiled sides together, and flatten the 2 cakes out with the heel of your hand, pressing evenly to keep the pancakes from sliding apart.

(continued)

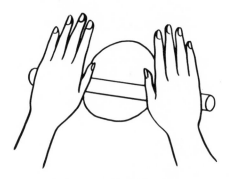

5.   With a rolling pin, roll the pairs of cakes to about 7 inches in diameter. Roll lightly and evenly to maintain a uniform thickness and even diameter of both pancakes. Rotate and turn over the pair of pancakes frequently, checking that the edges don't get too thick and the center doesn't get too thin. This will take some practice. Cover the pancakes with a dry cloth to keep them from drying out.

6.   Fry each pair of pancakes in an ungreased heavy-bottomed skillet or on a griddle over medium-low heat until light brown spots appear, less than 1 minute. Turn over to brown the other side for about 30 seconds. Check the heat frequently to be sure it doesn't get too high or too low. Be careful not to overcook the pancakes or they will become brittle and crack.

7.   Remove the pancakes and slap them a couple of times between your hands. This cools them a bit and forces any air bubbles out, creating an opening from which you can pull the pancakes apart. Pull them apart gently and slowly as soon as they are cooked. Once they cool, it's difficult to separate them without tearing. Pile the separated pancakes with the exposed side up. Keep them covered with a dry cloth to keep the edges from drying.

8.   Just before serving, reheat by steaming for 10 minutes, being careful that they don't touch the water. (Or reheat the Chinese home-style way: Place the pancakes on aluminum foil over simmering rice. The steam from the rice provides enough heat to warm the pancakes and the foil keeps them from sticking to the rice.) Serve the pancakes in a covered dish.

Note   For longer storage, stack the cooked pancakes in a plastic bag, seal securely, and refrigerate or freeze. When ready to reheat, thaw the pancakes and steam.

Variation   If you are planning to serve the pancakes with Peking Duck, make them smaller. Instead of one 12-inch rope, make two 12-inch ropes. You will have 2 dozen 5-inch pancakes.

Eating Mandarin Pancakes

People often seem to have trouble eating Mandarin Pancakes, but it's really very simple. Spread a pancake on a *clean* plate — it's very important that the outside remain dry. With a scallion brush, brush the pancake down the middle with a little Hoisin Sauce Dip (page 326), if desired. Put 2 to 3 tablespoons of Moo Shi Pork or 2 pieces of Peking Duck skin in the center. (The scallion brush is usually placed in the pancake with the meat.) Be careful not to overfill, or you won't be able to pick it up after rolling. Roll the pancake up, cigar style.

Place the roll in your left hand, supporting the ends with your thumb and little finger. Keep the little finger slightly raised and pressed against your ring finger to form a seal to prevent gravy or oil from dripping. Even so, it's best to eat over your plate since no matter how expert you are, gravy sometimes ends up dripping on your lap.

Chinese Steamed Bread
Man Tou

**Makes twelve 3-inch buns, serves 4 to 6
when not serving rice**

*T*here are many different types of bread in China, and because Chinese homes traditionally do not have ovens, the breads are steamed instead of baked. Some are plain, others are stuffed with sweet or savory fillings, but almost all use the same basic yeast dough. In the north of China, plain, unfilled bread, called man tou, is served in place of rice. My mother particularly liked to make plain steamed buns to serve with red-cooked dishes notably, Shanghai duck (page 187) and Shanghai Red-cooked Ham (page 217). The buns are great for soaking up the rich soy sauce gravy.

Because the bread is steamed, there is no crust and no browning; the bread is totally white. The Chinese in general prefer snowy white steamed breads and do not use whole wheat or any whole grain flour. In fact, when I was testing various types of flour for this recipe, my Chinese friends definitely preferred the whiter buns made from bleached flour even though the taste and texture of the unbleached flour buns were the same.

Man tou are easy to make at home, where they are formed in simple shapes. Because my mother was born in Beijing (Peking) and grew up in Shanghai, she made the buns round, which my Number One Aunt from Shanghai tells me is typical in that region. The Fujian chefs in our Cambridge restaurant like their steamed bread in a larger oblong loaf. You can do either, although I think the round shape is more delicate and attractive at the table.

2 tablespoons sugar

1 teaspoon active dry yeast

1 cup plus 3 tablespoons warm water (105°F. to 110°F.)

3½ cups all-purpose flour plus additional for kneading (1 pound)

1½ teaspoons canola, corn, or peanut oil

1 teaspoon baking powder

1.   Dissolve the sugar and yeast in the water in a measuring cup or small bowl. Place in a warm, draftfree place for about 10 minutes, or until it develops a head of foam.

2. To make the dough in a food processor, place the flour in the work-bowl fitted with the steel blade. With the machine running, pour in the yeast solution in a thin stream. Be sure to scrape in all the foam too. Process for about 15 seconds, or until a rough ball forms. If the dough appears very dry and does not form a ball, stop the machine and look. Sometimes the dough just needs a few more seconds. If you are sure the dough is too dry, add small amounts of warm water (¼ teaspoon or less at a time) until a rough ball forms. Transfer the dough to a lightly floured surface.

3. To make the dough by hand, place the flour in a large mixing bowl and add the yeast solution. Stir until it forms a coarse, lumpy dough. Use additional warm water, a little at a time, if the dough appears too dry. Turn the dough onto a lightly floured surface.

4. Knead for 5 to 7 minutes, or until the dough is smooth, firm, and elastic. After the first minute of kneading, the dough should not stick to either your hands or the work surface. If it is sticky, knead in more flour, a little at a time. Form the dough into a ball.

5. With a paper towel, spread ½ teaspoon of the oil in a bowl large enough to hold 3 times the bulk of the dough. Turn the dough around in the bowl a few times to cover it with a light film of oil. Cover the bowl tightly with plastic wrap and place in a warm, draft-free place to rise to double its volume. This will take from 1 to 2 hours.

6. While the dough is rising, cut out 12 pieces of wax paper or parchment, 3½ inches square for individual rolls. For loaves, cut out 8 pieces 5 × 3 inches. Pour the remaining 1 teaspoon of oil into a small dish. Set aside.

7. After the first rise, punch down the dough. Cover the dough and allow it to rise a second time to double its volume (30 minutes to 1 hour). Punch it down again. (The second rise is not necessary, but I have found that it seems to provide a smoother, finer texture.) If you are unable to proceed with the dough right away, you may refrigerate it at this point or after the first rise.

8. Sprinkle the baking powder over the work surface and knead the dough for 5 minutes, or until all the baking powder is well incorporated. Lightly flour the surface if necessary to keep the dough from sticking.

9. Roll the dough into a 12-inch-long rope. For Shanghai-style buns, cut the dough into 1-inch pieces, using a ruler as a guide. Pull each piece away as you cut it or the pieces will stick together. Roll each piece of dough into a ball. Using your fingertips, lightly oil one of the papers with oil and place a bun in the center. (For loaf-shaped buns, cut 1½-inch pieces of dough and place on the oiled paper without reshaping.)

Rice,

Noodles,

and Bread

(continued)

10. Place all the buns on a baking sheet or on the work surface and cover with a dry cloth. Allow the buns to rest in a draft-free place for 15 to 20 minutes, or until the dough slowly springs back when lightly pressed with a finger. The buns will not double in bulk but will be about 50 percent larger.

11. Prepare the steamer and have water boiling over high heat (page 52). Place the buns, with the paper liners, on each tier, leaving at least 1 inch between and above each bun to allow for expansion. (If you have only 1 tier or a small steamer, steam the buns in batches.) Stack the tiers over the boiling water, cover, and steam over high enough heat to maintain a steady stream of steam. If you are using a metal steamer, wrap the lid with a dish towel to prevent condensation from dripping on the buns and disfiguring them. Steam for 15 minutes, or until the buns are puffed up. Have boiling water in a kettle on hand to replenish the water in the steamer as necessary.

12. When the buns are ready, turn off the heat and allow them to sit in the covered steamer for a few seconds to avoid a sudden temperature change, which would wrinkle the surface. To serve, remove the buns to a plate or serve directly from the steamer. For casual family meals, leave the paper on the buns; for dinner parties, remove the paper before serving. To eat, bite or break off a section of the bun and eat it like rice between bites of braised or deep-fried meats or use it to soak up gravies, sauces, and soups.

健康

Note Don't bring all the steamed buns to the table at once, especially if it is a cold day or the air-conditioner is on. Keep them warm in the steamer. You can also refresh the buns or reheat ones that were made earlier in the day by steaming them for a few minutes before serving.

Extra buns may be cooled and packed in a plastic bag. Tightly sealed, they will keep well in the refrigerator for about 1 week to 10 days or in the freezer for a couple of months. Reheat for 10 minutes in a steamer just the way they were cooked. Frozen buns may be placed directly in the steamer without defrosting; they will need 15 minutes of steaming to heat through.

Leftover buns are also delicious as a breakfast bread or snack in a typical family-style way my mother often used. Slice a cold bun ⅝ inch thick and pan-fry in ½ inch of hot oil, turning so that both sides are browned and crisp while the inside remains soft and white. Sprinkle with light brown sugar. Or toast the slices and sprinkle lightly with a thin covering of brown sugar. I like these so much that I purposely make extra *man tou* so I'll definitely have some left over.

Seafood

Most Chinese meals have at least one seafood dish and no banquet is complete without a whole fish. The Chinese love of seafood and the special care and skill they give to its final presentation have made them experts at seafood preparation.

When it comes to fresh seafood, the Chinese are fanatics. If it's not alive, it's not fresh. In almost every restaurant in Hong Kong and Taiwan, there are aquariums with all kinds of fish and shrimp swimming around. Even land-locked areas of China have fish farms where freshwater fish are raised.

Once my husband, Keith, and I were in a Hong Kong seafood restaurant sitting next to an open tank holding live eels. Suddenly one large eel got out of the tank and squirmed under our table. We leapt up and watched with horror as this snakelike creature slithered around. No one else in the restaurant seemed the least bit upset. Then a cook appeared with a net, scooped up the eel, dropped it unceremoniously back into the tank, covered the tank with a screen, and walked back to the kitchen. We sat back down and ordered our meal as though nothing out of the ordinary had happened.

Goldfish or fancy colored carp, known as *koi* in Japan, are kept for decoration and good luck, not for eating. Many businesses have a large fish tank as part of the office decor for good luck. The Chinese word for fish is *yu,* which is a homonym for abundance. So whenever there is fish, on the dining table or in a tank, it symbolizes prosperity and having more than one needs. Certainly an important notion in a country where food was scarce and famine common.

Some larger Chinatown markets carry live freshwater fish in tanks. Other fish are usually displayed whole on a bed of ice, to be cleaned and filleted if you wish. To give you an idea of the variety of seafood the Chinese have at their disposal, I listed the number of different seafood I found on one day in a Boston Chinatown market. Eight varieties of live freshwater fish were swimming in tanks. Sitting on ice were butterfish, smelts, whiting, pomfret, grouper, squid, yellow croaker, hybrid striped bass, sea bass, bigmouth bass, scup (porgie), belt fish, gray sole, white perch, bighead carp, buffalo carp, grass carp, tilapia. Wiggling about in baskets were live blue crab and rock crab. Now that's quite a choice!

To get the best seafood, you should go to a market specializing in seafood if you can. The quality will be higher, and many fishmongers will order whole fish or a particular kind for you if you let them know in advance. The Chinese almost always buy a whole fish, unless of course the fish is so large that they have to buy portions of it. If you are buying a whole fish look for clear, smooth eyes, not sunken or cloudy; bright red gills; firm, smooth flesh without a trace of sliminess; and a fresh smell without a hint of fishiness. If you are buying fillets, use the last two tests.

Crustaceans and mollusks must be live. No Chinese will buy a dead lobster, crab, or clam. In the Far East all the shrimp are alive and swimming about seconds before they are cooked and brought to the table. A specialty in Hong Kong is freshly steamed shrimp with the heads still on. A dramatic dish in the Far East is something called Drunken Shrimp. Live jumbo shrimp are brought to the table in a clear heatproof bowl. The maitre d' pours in a vodkalike liquor, inebriating and flavoring the shrimp and flambés them, tossing them in the flames until they're cooked. The taste is incredible.

Dried seafood is commonly available in Chinese markets and sometimes, as in the case of dried scallops, they command a very high price. Since there is no refrigeration, salting, drying, and curing are ways to preserve seafood. Fish, shrimp, scallops, oysters, and squid are used in both the fresh and dried forms. Although the preference is always for fresh, the Chinese would rather use good dried seafood than seafood that is not fresh. Many recipes in this book use dried shrimp as a flavoring.

Steamed Whole Fish, Cantonese Style

Serves 2 to 3, or 4 to 6 as part of a multicourse meal

A *whole fish, with head, tail, and fins intact, is a symbol of prosperity and good luck. The Chinese word for fish is a homonym for the word abundance, and whole fish is always served on special occasions like the lunar New Year, birthdays, and weddings. The eyes and cheeks are particularly prized, and these are saved for the guest of honor or the eldest at the table.*

Since the fish is cooked with the skin on, I always scale the fish again even if it has been scaled at the market to make certain the skin is smooth and scaleless.

If you can't get flounder, substitute sea bass, striped bass, rock cod, trout, or red snapper.

健康

1 to 1½ pounds whole flounder, cleaned and scaled
½ teaspoon salt
1 teaspoon dry sherry
2 tablespoons light soy sauce
2 scallions, shredded
2 tablespoons finely shredded peeled gingerroot (page 45)
Dash white pepper
1½ tablespoons canola, corn, or peanut oil
1 teaspoon sesame seed oil
3 tablespoons coarsely chopped cilantro

1.   Rinse the fish, inside and out, and pat dry. It is not necessary to score flatfish like flounder, but if the fish you are using is thick, score both sides with long, parallel cuts almost to the bone. Scoring allows the flavors to penetrate and the fish to cook evenly. Place the fish dark skin up on a heatproof plate or platter and sprinkle with salt, sherry, and soy sauce. Scatter the scallions and gingerroot on top.

2.   Bring water in a steamer to a full boil and place the plate with the fish in the steamer. Cover and cook over medium-high heat for 10 to 15

(continued)

minutes, or until the flesh at the thickest part is white. Be careful not to overcook. Remove the fish from the steamer, being careful not to spill the juices from the platter. Sprinkle pepper over the fish.

3. Heat the cooking oil and sesame seed oil in a small saucepan until just smoking. Pour the hot oil over the fish and garnish with cilantro. Serve immediately.

Note Restaurants use huge steamers that hold a number of dishes all at once, including a whole fish on an oval platter. I use a 12-inch steamer and put the flounder on a 9-inch glass pie plate. The head and tail extend a bit over the edges, but most of the fish is in the dish. After steaming, I carefully slip the fish with all of its juices onto a 14-inch porcelain oval platter for presentation. This works with flounder because it is more round than long. If your fish is too long for your steamer, cut it in half and reassemble it on an oval platter before finishing it with the hot oil.

West Lake Fish

Serves 3 to 4, or 6 to 8 as part of a multicourse meal

My father was born in Hangzhou (Hangchow), a small town on the outskirts of Shanghai. It is a famous place, not only for the scenic beauty of its mountains and the West Lake but also for its food. The Chen family tomb is still in Hangzhou and is tended by my late fifth aunt's son. It is a Chinese tradition for children to say they are from the place where their father was born rather than where they were actually born. And so although I have never lived in Hangzhou, I feel a special bond to my father's home.

The first time we went to Hangzhou, in 1972, we traveled with my sixth aunt on my father's side and two first cousins. One of the first things my mother did was to take us to one of those big restaurants by West Lake to have West Lake Fish. She had often told us how a chef's helper would bring the fish to the table and slam it on the floor to kill it in front of you so you would know it was fresh. Fortunately, they no longer did this, but the fish was delicious and even more so with the view of West Lake in front of us.

After our fish lunch we spent the rest of the day walking on trails in the mountains, stopping at teahouses to drink Hangzhou's celebrated Dragon Well green tea brewed with mountain spring water from the famous Tiger Run spring. We had bowls of hot sweet soup made with the starch of lotus root gathered from West Lake and flavored with chestnut bits and flowers from the sweet olive tree (Osmanthus fragrans), which grows in abundance there.

My mother wrote this recipe in honor of my father's birthplace. Note that the fish is soaked in boiled — not boiling — water. That way it cooks gently and does not dry out. You need a fine-textured freshwater fish for this recipe. That was never a problem for us because my father loved to fish. He would bring the fish home live, and we would keep it in the extra bathtub until ready to cook it.

禄

1 freshwater bigmouth or smallmouth bass, cleaned and scaled (1½ to 2 pounds)
*   (If unavailable, use any firm, white-fleshed fish such as striped bass, cod, or*
*   red snapper.)*
1 tablespoon dry sherry
5 slices unpeeled gingerroot, 1 × ⅛ inch each
½ cup sugar
⅓ cup cider vinegar
1 tablespoon light soy sauce
1 garlic clove, crushed and peeled
2 tablespoons cornstarch

1. Rinse the fish in cold water and drain. Make 3 slashes, crosswise, on the meatiest part of each side of the fish for even cooking.

2. Bring water to a boil in a fish poacher or oval roaster large enough to submerge the whole fish. Slide the whole fish into the boiling water and add the sherry and 3 of the gingerroot slices. Cover the pan tightly and immediately remove from the heat. Let the fish soak in the hot water for 15 to 20 minutes, or until cooked through.

3. While the fish is soaking, chop up the remaining 2 slices of gingerroot and put it into a garlic press and squeeze to extract the juices. You should have about ¼ teaspoon. Mix the gingerroot juices with the sugar, vinegar, soy sauce, garlic, and cornstarch in a small saucepan. Heat the mixture over medium heat and stir constantly until it thickens. Discard the garlic.

4. Remove the fish from the roaster with a big spatula and flat plate held underneath. Drain off the water carefully. Place the fish on a large oval serving platter and pour the sauce over it. Serve immediately.

Seafood

Soy Sauce Fish, Shanghai Style

Serves 2 to 3, or 4 to 6 as part of a multicourse meal

've known Anna Ku Lau since kindergarten, longer than any other friend. Anna and her family are originally from Wu Xi, near Shanghai, where sweet soy-sauce dishes, known as "red-cooked," are popular. She told me that her favorite recipe from my mother's cookbook is this one.

In winter, especially around the lunar New Year, Soy Sauce Fish is cooked in large quantities and served cold as a side dish or with drinks. Sometimes instead of a whole fish, a large fish head is cooked; this is considered a real delicacy.

壽

1 whole fish, such as sea bass, perch, or scup, cleaned and scaled (1¼ to 1½ pounds)

¼ teaspoon salt

6 scallions, roots trimmed and cut in half

⅓ cup canned sliced bamboo shoots, drained

⅓ cup dried black mushrooms, softened in hot water for 15 minutes, stems removed and caps sliced

1 tablespoon dry sherry

¼ cup plus 1 tablespoon dark soy sauce

2 tablespoons light brown sugar

½ cup canola, corn, or peanut oil

2 slices unpeeled gingerroot, 1 × ⅛ inch each

1. Rinse the fish in cold water and dry both inside and out with paper towels. Make 3 equal diagonal cuts on each side for even cooking. If the fish is too large to fit into your pan, cut it in half. Sprinkle both sides with ¼ teaspoon of the salt. Let stand for 10 minutes.

2. Combine the scallions, bamboo shoots, and mushrooms in a bowl. Set aside. In another small bowl, mix together the sherry, soy sauce, sugar, and ¾ cup water. Set aside.

3. Pour the oil into a large wok over high heat. Add the gingerroot and stir around the pan until the oil is hot; the gingerroot will sizzle.

Seafood

130

4.   Slide the fish into the hot oil head first and fry over medium-high heat on 1 side for 3 or 4 minutes, or until golden brown. Cover the wok to keep the oil from spattering. When the first side is golden brown, remove the pan from the heat. Loosen the fish with a spatula and turn it over. Add the scallions, bamboo shoots, and mushrooms. Return the pan to the heat. Cook about 3 minutes or until the second side is lightly browned.

5.   When the fish is golden brown on both sides, remove from the heat. Pour off or ladle out the excess oil. Add the soy sauce mixture, cover, and bring to a boil. Boil slowly over low heat for 3 minutes, remove the lid, and raise the heat to medium-high. Baste the fish until a little more than ½ cup of the liquid remains. Transfer the fish and liquid to a platter. Serve hot or cold.

Note   If you have cut the fish in half, reassemble the pieces on the serving platter and use the vegetables to cover the division.

Steamed Fish Fillets

Serves 2 to 3, or 4 to 6 as part of a
multicourse meal

*T*he Chinese are experts with seafood, and steaming is a favorite way to cook fish. It is fast and retains the natural flavor of fresh fish. The natural juices are nutritious and very good over rice. My mother always steamed whole fish, but I often use fresh fillets for convenience.

1 pound whitefish fillets, such as haddock, flounder, or bass, skin removed

½ scant teaspoon salt, or less to taste

3 medium dried black mushrooms, softened in hot water for 15 minutes

1 teaspoon dry sherry

1 tablespoon light soy sauce

⅓ cup shredded bamboo shoots

2 ounces Smithfield ham, shredded

1 scallion, white and green parts cut into 2-inch pieces, and finely shredded

1 teaspoon finely shredded peeled gingerroot

1. Place the fish fillets on a heatproof platter with a rim or pie plate that will fit into your steamer. Sprinkle both sides with salt. Let stand for 10 minutes.

2. Drain the mushrooms, rinse and squeeze dry. Cut off and discard the stems and shred the caps. Set aside.

3. Sprinkle the sherry and soy sauce on the fish, then spread the mushrooms, bamboo shoots, ham, scallion, and gingerroot evenly over the fish.

4. Bring the water in the steamer to a fast boil. Place the plate with the fish in the steamer. Cover and steam over medium-high heat for 6 to 8 minutes for flounder and 10 to 12 minutes for thicker fish, or until the flesh is white all the way through. Do not overcook. Check the fish at the thickest part after the shorter cooking time. If the flesh is not white, then cook another 2 minutes. If the uncooked area is very small, turn off the heat and keep the steamer covered. The remaining steam in the steamer will finish cooking the fish by serving time.

Seafood

5. As soon as the fish is ready, it should be served without delay. Serve directly from the steaming dish, or transfer to a serving platter with the juices.

Variation In the traditional Chinese manner a whole fish may be cooked the same way; a 1½- to 2-pound sea bass, striped bass, flounder, red snapper, rock cod, or perch are good choices. Scale and clean the fish thoroughly. Rinse and score both sides of the fish, if thick on the diagonal, with long parallel cuts almost to the bone. This allows flavors to penetrate fish and cook more evenly. If the fish is too long for your steamer, you may have to cut it in half. Then follow the procedure above. Cook a whole fish for about 10 to 15 minutes.

Steamed Salmon
with Black Beans

Serves 2 to 3, or 4 to 5 as part of a
multicourse meal

*T*he deep ebony of black beans against the coral of the salmon makes this a very beautiful dish. The steaming time is very fast, so plan accordingly. The salmon should be served straight from the steamer to the table, at the peak of perfection. You can prepare bass or flounder fillets the same way.

1 pound salmon fillet or steaks

3 teaspoons dry sherry

1 teaspoon grated peeled gingerroot

¼ teaspoon salt

1 garlic clove, pureed

2 tablespoons thinly sliced scallions

1 tablespoon fermented black beans, coarsely chopped

1 teaspoon sesame seed oil

Cilantro or parsley sprigs, for garnish

1. Place the fish in a heatproof dish at least 1 inch deep, such as a glass pie plate. Stir together the sherry, gingerroot, salt, and garlic in a small bowl. Pour this mixture onto the fish and rub generously on both sides. Let stand for at least 15 minutes.

2. If you are using a fillet, turn it skin side down. Spread the scallions and black beans evenly on top. Drizzle with sesame seed oil.

3. Bring the water in the steamer to a vigorous boil. Place the pie plate on the steamer tray and cover. Steam for about 10 minutes, checking for doneness at about 8 minutes. The fish will look opaque and feel springy to the touch. It is better to slightly undercook than overcook since the heat in the fish itself will finish the cooking for you.

4. Serve directly from the steaming dish or transfer to a warm platter with the juices.

Kan Shao Scallops

**Serves 3 to 4, or 5 to 6 as part of a
multicourse meal**

*T*he Szechuan kan shao *or dry-cooked method intensifies the natural flavor of scallops.
You can use either bay scallops or sea scallops; if you use bay scallops, reduce the
cooking time.*

1 pound sea scallops

1 tablespoon minced peeled gingerroot

1 tablespoon dry sherry

⅓ cup fermented black beans, coarsely chopped

2 garlic cloves, minced

1 tablespoon crushed red pepper, or to taste

3 tablespoons canola, corn, or peanut oil

3 tablespoons dark soy sauce

1 teaspoon sugar

1. Rinse the scallops quickly and cut in half horizontally if they are
very large. Drain thoroughly and pull off the tough outer muscle. Place the
scallops in a bowl, add the gingerroot and sherry, and stir to mix. Set aside.

2. Combine the black beans, garlic, and red pepper in a small dish.
Pour the oil into a wok or stir-fry pan and place over medium-high heat. Add
the black bean mixture to the oil and stir until the oil is hot and the spices
fragrant; they will begin to sizzle. Don't let the garlic burn or it will become
bitter.

3. Add the scallops to the pan and stir-fry until they turn opaque, about
1 to 2 minutes. Add the soy sauce and sugar and stir for another 30 seconds
to 1 minute, or until thoroughly cooked. All the liquid will have evaporated.
Serve hot.

Seafood

135

Stir-fried Fish
with Vegetables

**Serves 4, or 6 as part of a
multicourse meal**

*U*se a firm whitefish for stir-frying and stir gently to avoid breaking up the pieces.

健康

1 cup dried black mushrooms, softened in hot water for 15 minutes

2 ounces snow peas (about 1 cup)

*1 pound firm whitefish fillets, such as cod, haddock, mahimahi, carp, hake, or
    pollack*

2 teaspoons dry sherry

1/4 teaspoon grated peeled gingerroot

1/2 to 1 teaspoon salt, or to taste

5 tablespoons canola, corn, or peanut oil

2 slices unpeeled gingerroot, 1 × 1/8 inch each

1 garlic clove, crushed and peeled

*1/2 pound napa or Chinese celery cabbage, quartered lengthwise, cored and cut
    into 1 1/2-inch chunks*

1/2 cup Chinese Chicken Broth (page 64) or canned chicken broth

1 (8-ounce) can sliced bamboo shoots, drained (1 cup)

2 teaspoons cornstarch, dissolved in 1 tablespoon water

1.   Drain the mushrooms, rinse, and squeeze dry. Cut off the stems with scissors and discard. Slice the caps in halves or quarters so the pieces are fairly uniform in size. Set aside.

2.   Rinse the snow peas and snap and string both ends. Cut the larger snow peas in half on the diagonal so the peas are of fairly uniform size. Set aside.

3.   Cut the fish into 2-inch square pieces and place in a bowl. Add the sherry, grated gingerroot, and 1/2 teaspoon of the salt. Mix together well.

4.   Pour 3 tablespoons of the oil into a wok or stir-fry pan and heat over high heat until the oil is hot but not smoking. Test by dipping the tip of a spatula into the fish mixture and then into the pan; it should sizzle. Stir up

the fish again and add to the hot oil. Stir gently for about 30 seconds, or until the fish is partially done. Remove to a platter.

5.   Add the remaining 2 tablespoons of oil to the same pan and add the gingerroot slices, garlic, and remaining ½ teaspoon of salt if using homemade broth. Stir around the pan until they sizzle. Add the cabbage and broth, stir, and cook, covered, for about 1 minute. Remove the lid and add the mushrooms, snow peas, and bamboo shoots. Stir-fry until the snow peas turn bright green.

6.   Return the fish to the pan and stir gently. Add the cornstarch slurry and stir until the sauce thickens. Taste and add salt, if needed. Discard the gingerroot and garlic, if desired. Serve immediately.

Sea Scallops *with Snow Peas*

Serves 3 to 4, or 5 to 6 as part of a multicourse meal

*F*ermented black beans give a rich yet not overpowering flavor to this delicate scallop dish, which is perfect for a dinner party. The snow peas lend a colorful and crunchy contrast.

福

1 pound sea scallops

1 teaspoon sherry

1 teaspoon cornstarch

½ pound snow peas

1 (8-ounce) can sliced water chestnuts, drained (1 cup)

4 tablespoons fermented black beans, coarsely chopped

2 teaspoons light soy sauce

1 teaspoons sugar

3 tablespoons canola, corn, or peanut oil

1 garlic clove, thinly sliced

2 slices unpeeled gingerroot, 1 × ⅛ inch each

2 to 3 tablespoons broth or water (optional)

(continued) *Seafood*

1.   Rinse and drain the scallops. Remove the crescent-shaped muscle and discard. Cut larger pieces in half horizontally so all the scallops are about the same size. Place the scallops in a bowl, stir in the sherry and cornstarch, and mix well. Set aside.

2.   Snap and string both ends of the snow peas. If desired, cut larger ones in half on the diagonal. Rinse and drain. Set aside. Place the black beans in a small bowl and add the soy sauce, sugar, and 2 tablespoons water. Set aside.

3.   Pour the oil into a wok or stir-fry pan and place over high heat. Add the garlic and gingerroot and stir around the pan until the oil is hot but not smoking; the garlic and gingerroot will sizzle. Add the scallops and stir briskly for 1 to 1½ minutes, or until the scallops just begin to turn opaque and are partially cooked. Be careful not to overcook at this stage, since the scallops will continue to cook after the vegetables are added.

4.   Add the black bean mixture and continue stirring for 15 seconds. Add the water chestnuts and snow peas. Add broth or water for more gravy, if desired. Stir constantly for another minute until the snow peas turn darker green. Discard the gingerroot, if desired, and transfer the scallops to a serving platter. Serve immediately.

Celery and Dried Shrimp Salad

Serves 4 to 5 as part of a multicourse meal

*D*ried shrimp have a long shelf life and are extremely versatile — my brother Henry especially enjoyed snacking on dried shrimp when he was a teenager. I always have them on hand to use in fried rice or soups or to stir-fry with vegetables. A little goes a long way.

4 cups shredded celery (about 8 stalks) (page 45)

1 cup shredded carrot (about 1 medium) (page 45)

¼ cup dried shrimp

1 tablespoon plus 1 teaspoon light soy sauce

2 tablespoons rice vinegar

1 tablespoon sugar

½ teaspoon grated peeled gingerroot

1 teaspoon sesame seed oil

1.   Blanch the celery and carrots in boiling water for 30 seconds. Drain and refresh under cold water until completely cool. Drain thoroughly and place in a covered bowl in the refrigerator until ready to use.

2.   Place the dried shrimp in a bowl and pour on 1 cup water to soften and to remove the excess salt. Soak for 15 minutes or more. Drain.

3.   When ready to serve, mix the soy sauce with the vinegar, sugar, and gingerroot. Combine the celery, carrots, and shrimp and toss with the soy sauce dressing. Garnish with sesame seed oil. Serve immediately.

Note   Although traditionally the Chinese do not eat raw vegetables, I have prepared this dish very successfully with unblanched carrots and celery.

Sweet and Sour Shrimp

**Serves 3 to 4, or 5 to 6 as part of a
multicourse meal**

M ost restaurant-style sweet and sour shrimp is coated in a thick batter, fried in lots of
oil, and served in a cloying sauce — completely unappealing and nothing like my
version. The shrimp here are lightly coated in a thin cornstarch paste, shallow-fried,
and served in a light tart sauce that does not overwhelm their delicate flavor.

禧

1 pound large shrimp, shelled

1 tablespoon dry sherry

3 tablespoons light soy sauce

5 tablespoons cornstarch

1/2 teaspoon salt

1 medium red bell pepper, cored, seeded, and cut into 1-inch cubes

1 medium green bell pepper, cored, seeded, and cut into 1-inch cubes

1 cup canned pineapple chunks, well drained, syrup reserved

1 garlic clove, crushed and peeled

1/3 cup cider vinegar

1/3 cup plus 1 tablespoon sugar

1/3 cup syrup from the canned pineapple

1/4 cup ketchup

1 cup plus 1 tablespoon canola, corn, or peanut oil

1. Cut a slit along the back of the shrimp and pull out and discard the
vein. Rinse in cold water and drain thoroughly. Combine the sherry, 1 tablespoon soy sauce, 3 tablespoons cornstarch, and salt in a bowl and stir until you
have a smooth paste. Add the shrimp and mix. Let stand for 20 minutes or
more.

2. In the meantime, add the peppers to a small saucepan of boiling
water. As soon as it comes to a boil, drain and rinse in cold water to stop
cooking. Add the pineapple to the peppers and set aside.

3. Combine the garlic, vinegar, sugar, syrup, ketchup, 2 tablespoons
soy sauce, and 2 tablespoons cornstarch dissolved in 1/3 cup water in a bowl.
Set aside.

4.   Heat 1 cup oil in a wok or stir-fry pan over medium-high heat. When the oil is hot (350°F. to 375°F.), drop half of the shrimp, one at a time, into the pan. Stir and turn the shrimp carefully and slowly with a slotted spoon or wire skimmer. Cook for 2 to 3 minutes, or until the shrimp turns opaque and pink and are lightly crisp along the edges. Transfer to a dish lined with paper towels. Continue with the rest of the shrimp until all are cooked. Keep in a warm oven while you make the sauce.

5.   Pour out the oil in the wok and wipe with paper towels. Pour the sauce mixture into the pan and heat over medium heat, stirring constantly, until the mixture comes to a boil. Stir in the cornstarch slurry and continue stirring until the sauce thickens and becomes translucent. Discard the garlic and stir in 1 tablespoon oil. Add the pineapple chunks, peppers, and shrimp. Give a few big turns with a spatula to coat the shrimp. Transfer to a platter and serve immediately.

Soy Sauce Shrimp in the Shell

Serves 3 to 4, or 5 to 6 as part of a multicourse meal

When the Chinese cook shrimp in the shell, they leave the shell on when they serve it because that's where the sauce is. Some people are quite adept at shelling the shrimp in their mouth. My mother was a real artist at this. The shrimp never touched her fingers as she gracefully lifted it to her mouth with chopsticks and after a few barely noticeable swishings, delicately spit the shell into the discard dish.

健康

1 teaspoon dry sherry
1 tablespoon dark soy sauce
1 tablespoon light soy sauce
3 teaspoons brown sugar
1 pound large shrimp in the shell, deveined
1 cup canola, corn, or peanut oil
1 garlic clove, crushed and peeled
1 slice unpeeled gingerroot, 1 × 1/8 inch
2 tablespoons thinly sliced scallions, white and green parts

1.   Stir the sherry, both soy sauces, brown sugar, and 2 tablespoons water together in a small bowl until the sugar is dissolved. Set aside.

2.   Devein the shrimp by cutting through the back of the shell with scissors. Do not remove the shell. Pull out and discard the vein. Rinse and drain thoroughly and pat dry with paper towels.

3.   Heat the oil in a wok or stir-fry pan over medium-high heat to 375°F. Dip an end of a shrimp into the oil; it should sizzle. Carefully, so not to make the fat spatter, add all the shrimp to the hot oil and fry for no more than 1 minute, stirring with a wire skimmer so each shrimp cooks evenly. When all the shrimp turn pink, remove them to a plate lined with paper towels. Reserve 2 tablespoons of the oil and discard the rest.

4.   Heat the reserved oil in the wok or stir-fry pan over medium-high heat. Add the garlic, gingerroot, and scallions to the pan and stir until fragrant,

about 30 seconds. Do not burn. Pour in the soy sauce mixture and return the fried shrimp to the pan. Stir briskly until all the shrimp are coated. Transfer to a platter. Serve immediately.

Crystal Shrimp

Serves 3 to 4, or 5 to 6 as part of a multicourse meal

*T*here is no soy sauce to darken the clear white sauce in this Shanghai dish. That's why the shrimp are described as crystal. The original recipe calls for deep-frying the shrimp, but I prefer this version.

1 pound medium shrimp, shelled

¼ teaspoon grated peeled gingerroot

1 teaspoon dry sherry

1 teaspoon cornstarch

1 scant teaspoon salt

1 scallion, green and white parts, cut into 2-inch pieces

4 tablespoons canola, corn, or peanut oil

1. Cut a slit along the back of the shrimp and pull out and discard the vein. Rinse the shrimp in cold water, drain and place in a bowl. Add the gingerroot, sherry, cornstarch, and salt. Stir until the shrimp is well coated, then mix in the scallions. Set aside.

2. Heat the oil in a wok or stir-fry pan over high heat until hot but not smoking. Test by dipping a spatula into the shrimp and then into the oil; it should sizzle. Stir up the shrimp mixture again and pour it all into the hot oil. Stir briskly until the shrimp turn opaque, about 1 to 2 minutes. Transfer the shrimp to a platter with a slotted spoon. Discard the scallion if desired. Serve immediately.

Seafood

Coral and Jade

Serves 3 to 4, or 5 to 6 as part of a multicourse meal

M y mother coined this name for a popular shrimp dish that we serve at our restaurant. The shrimp is stir-fried in a light tomato sauce, which accentuates the pink color of the cooked shrimp and makes it resemble coral. Snow peas when cooked take on the green color of imperial jade, so prized by the Chinese. What lovely imagery for a lovely dish!

禄

1 pound large or medium shrimp, shelled

1 teaspoon grated peeled gingerroot

1 teaspoon dry sherry

1 teaspoon cornstarch

½ to 1 teaspoon salt, or to taste

3 tablespoons canola, corn, or peanut oil

¼ pound snow peas, ends snapped off and strings removed, cut in half on the diagonal

2 tablespoons ketchup

1 (8-ounce) can sliced water chestnuts, drained (1 cup)

1. Cut a slit along the back of the shrimp and pull out and discard the intestinal vein. Rinse the shrimp in cold water, drain, and place in a bowl. Stir in the gingerroot, sherry, cornstarch, and ¼ teaspoon salt and mix well. Set aside.

2. Heat 1 tablespoon of the oil in a wok or stir-fry pan over medium heat until hot but not smoking. Dip an end of a snow pea into the pan; it should sizzle. Add the snow peas and stir just until they turn a darker green, about 30 seconds. Do not scorch the tender snow peas inadvertently by heating the oil too hot. Remove the snow peas and spread out on a plate. Set aside.

3. Pour the remaining 2 tablespoons of oil into the same pan and heat over high heat. Stir up the shrimp mixture again, pour into the pan and cook, stirring constantly, for 1 to 2 minutes, or until the shrimp just turn pink and opaque. Stir in the ketchup, water chestnuts, and remaining ¼ teaspoon salt and stir-fry for about 30 seconds. Return the snow peas to the pan and mix together for 30 seconds to 1 minute. Remove from the heat and taste, adding more salt if desired. Transfer to a serving dish. Serve immediately.

Seafood

Note   Use large or medium shrimp depending on the number of people you are serving; medium shrimp will serve more people.

Shrimp with Peas

**Serves 3 to 4, or 5 to 6 as part of a
multicourse meal**

 eas go nicely with shrimp, complimenting but not overpowering them, and their bright green color is pretty against the pink of cooked shrimp.

1 pound medium shrimp, shelled

¼ teaspoon grated peeled gingerroot

1 teaspoon dry sherry

1 teaspoon cornstarch

1 teaspoon salt

1 cup green peas, fresh or frozen and thawed

1 scallion, green and white parts, cut into 2-inch pieces

3 tablespoons canola, corn, or peanut oil

1.   Cut a slit along the back of the shrimp and pull out and discard the intestinal vein. Rinse the shrimp in cold water, drain, and place in a bowl. Add the gingerroot, sherry, cornstarch, and salt and stir to coat the shrimp. Set aside.

2.   If using fresh peas, drop them into boiling water and boil for 1 minute. Drain immediately and run under cold water to stop the cooking. Set aside.

3.   Heat the oil in a wok over medium-high heat. When the oil is hot, add the scallion pieces; they should sizzle. Stir a few times. Add the peas and stir for 1 minute. Stir up the shrimp mixture again and pour it all into the pan. Stir for another minute, or until the shrimp turn opaque and pink. Transfer the shrimp and peas to a platter. Discard the scallions if desired. Serve immediately.

Seafood

145

Shrimp in Tomato Sauce

Serves 3 to 4, or 5 to 6 as part of a multicourse meal

A lthough ketchup is a commonplace American staple, this sauce is anything but mundane. Many people don't realize that ketchup originated in Asia.

健康

1 tablespoon dry sherry

1 tablespoon cider vinegar

4 tablespoons ketchup

1 teaspoon light or dark soy sauce

½ teaspoon salt

2 teaspoons sugar

1 teaspoon grated peeled gingerroot

1 pound medium shrimp, shelled

2 teaspoons cornstarch

2 teaspoons dry sherry

3 tablespoons canola, corn, or peanut oil

2 garlic cloves, crushed and peeled

1 slice unpeeled gingerroot, 1 × ⅛ inch

3 tablespoons thinly sliced scallions, green and white parts

1.   Stir the sherry, vinegar, ketchup, soy sauce, salt, sugar, and gingerroot together in a bowl and set aside.

2.   Cut a slit along the back of the shrimp and pull out and discard the vein. Rinse the shrimp in cold water, drain, and place in a bowl. Add the cornstarch and sherry and stir to coat well. Set aside.

3.   Pour the oil into a wok and place the pan over high heat. Add the garlic and gingerroot and push them around the pan until the oil is hot; they will sizzle. Stir the shrimp up again and turn it all into the hot oil. Stir-fry for 1 minute, or until the shrimp are opaque and pink. Pour the sauce mixture into the pan and stir until the shrimp are evenly coated. Sprinkle the minced scallions over the shrimp, mix with a couple of big turns of a spatula, and transfer to a platter. Discard the gingerroot and garlic if desired and serve immediately.

Seafood

Shrimp with Black Beans

**Serves 3 to 4, or 5 to 6 as part of a
multicourse meal**

S eafood and fermented black beans are commonly combined in Cantonese-style dishes. It's amazing how everyday ingredients take on a whole new character with just a little of this extraordinary seasoning. This family-style dish is not usually served at banquets. It is not considered elegant enough because the dark sauce covers the coral shrimp. At home it is enjoyed with great relish.

1 pound large shrimp, shelled
1 teaspoon dry sherry
1 teaspoon cornstarch
3 tablespoons canola, corn, or peanut oil
1 tablespoon thinly sliced scallions
1 tablespoon minced peeled gingerroot
1 garlic clove, crushed and peeled
3 tablespoons fermented black beans, chopped
Salt to taste (optional)

1.   Cut a slit along the back of the shrimp and pull out and discard the intestinal vein. Rinse the shrimp in cold water, drain, and place in a bowl. Mix well with the sherry and cornstarch. Set aside.

2.   Heat the oil in a wok or stir-fry pan over high heat until hot but not smoking. Dip a spatula into the shrimp and then into the oil; it should sizzle. Add the scallions, gingerroot, garlic, and black beans and stir a few times. Mix up the shrimp again and add it to the pan. Stir constantly. Add 2 tablespoons of water and cook until the shrimp is opaque, about 2 minutes. Taste the sauce and add salt, if desired. Serve immediately.

Seafood

Shrimp in Lobster Sauce

**Serves 3 to 4, or 5 to 6 as part of a
multicourse meal**

*T*his has always been a popular American-Chinese dish, and it was a favorite in our
original restaurant in Cambridge, Massachusetts. There is no lobster in the dish at
all. Rather, the shrimp is cooked in the type of sauce the Cantonese use for lobster.
You can omit the pork if you wish.

禄

1 pound medium or large shrimp, shelled

2 teaspoons dry sherry

3 tablespoons cornstarch

1¼ cups water

¼ pound ground lean pork (about ½ cup)

2 tablespoons dark soy sauce

¼ teaspoon sugar

3 tablespoons canola, corn, or peanut oil

2 slices unpeeled gingerroot, 1 × ⅛ inch each

2 garlic cloves, crushed and peeled

2 tablespoons fermented black beans, minced

Salt

1 egg, beaten

1. Cut a slit along the back of the shrimp and pull out and discard the
vein. Rinse the shrimp in cold water, drain, and place in a bowl. Stir in 1
teaspoon of the sherry and 1 tablespoon of the cornstarch and mix well. Set
aside.

2. Mix the remaining 2 tablespoons of cornstarch with ¼ cup of the
water. Set aside. Mix the pork with the remaining teaspoon sherry, the soy
sauce, and sugar in a small bowl. Set aside.

3. Heat the oil in a wok or stir-fry pan over medium-high heat until hot but not smoking. Test by dipping the end of a shrimp into the oil;
it should sizzle. Stir up the shrimp mixture again, pour it into the pan, and
cook, stirring constantly, until the shrimp is just pink. Remove the shrimp
from the pan with a slotted spoon, leaving as much oil as you can in
the pan.

4. Add the gingerroot, garlic, and black beans to the same pan and stir a few times. Add the pork mixture. Stir about 30 seconds. Add 1 cup of water. Bring to a boil, cover the pan, and lower the heat. Simmer for 2 minutes and taste carefully for seasoning. Add a small amount salt, if needed.

5. Uncover the pan and return the shrimp to the pan. Discard the gingerroot and garlic, if desired. Add the cornstarch slurry and stir until thickened. Pour the beaten egg into the pan in a thin stream. Give 2 big stirs. Serve hot.

Lobster, Cantonese Style

**Serves 2, or 4 as part of a
multicourse meal**

The Chinese like to cook lobster — as well as crab and shrimp — in the shell because it holds the moisture in and because it makes a beautiful presentation. For the fullest enjoyment of this dish, dispense with table manners and use your fingers. Suck the sauce from the lobster pieces, then remove the meat from the shell.

My mother always insisted on getting an active live lobster; it had to be flapping vigorously when she picked it up. Some people are a bit squeamish when it comes to chopping up a live lobster. The first cut, which splits the lobster in two, kills it instantly, but if this bothers you, plunge the lobster in boiling water first. I do not recommend buying ready cooked lobster because the meat is usually dry and overcooked. Be sure to cook the lobster as soon as it is chopped.

1 live lobster (1½ to 2 pounds)

¼ pound ground pork (about ½ cup)

2 slices unpeeled gingerroot, 1 × ⅛ inch each

2 garlic cloves, crushed and peeled

1½ tablespoons fermented black beans, coarsely chopped

2 teaspoons dry sherry

½ teaspoon salt

1½ tablespoons dark soy sauce

¼ teaspoon sugar

3 tablespoons canola, corn, or peanut oil

1½ tablespoons cornstarch, dissolved in ¼ cup water

1 egg, beaten

1.   Rinse the lobster in cold water and dry with paper towels or plunge it into a pot of boiling water for a few seconds. Cut and chop the lobster through the shell into 14 pieces as shown. Make the first cut down the middle, splitting the lobster in two. Collect the tomalley, place it in a bowl, and break it into small pieces. Discard the legs, intestine, sacks in the tip of the head, and spongy gills.

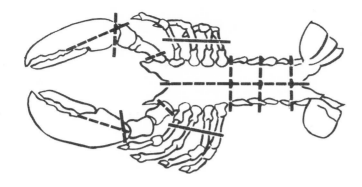

2.   Combine the pork, gingerroot, garlic, black beans, and sherry in a small dish. Set aside. Mix together salt, soy sauce, sugar, and ¾ cup water in another dish. Set aside.

3.   Heat the oil in a wok or stir-fry pan over medium-high heat. When the oil is hot but not smoking, add the pork mixture and the tomalley; they should sizzle. Stir for 2 to 3 minutes, or until the pork is no longer pink.

4.   Add the lobster pieces and give a couple of big turns with a spatula. Add the soy sauce mixture. Cover and bring to a boil. Reduce the heat to a simmer and cook for 3 to 4 minutes, or until the lobster shell turns bright coral and the meat turns white and pink.

5.   Uncover the pan and transfer the lobster pieces with a slotted spoon to a serving plate. Increase the heat to medium-high. When the liquid begins to boil, stir in the cornstarch slurry. When the liquid thickens, add the egg, stirring a few times to create ribbons. Return the lobster to the pan and give a couple of big turns with a spatula to mix well. Serve hot.

Stir-fried Squid
with Mixed Vegetables

**Serves 3 to 4, or 5 to 6 as part of a
multicourse meal**

*S*quid, naturally low in fat, is an excellent choice for stir-frying, but it becomes tough *and rubbery if overcooked. The squid body should be scored and blanched before stir-frying so it will cook quickly. Most markets now offer squid already cleaned. If you need to clean it yourself, see the directions below.*

The Chinese also use dried squid, which is golden in color; it must be softened and reconstituted in water before using. Sometimes a combination of fresh and dried squid is used. I prefer fresh squid because it's more tender than the dried kind.

健康

1 pound fresh squid, cleaned
3 tablespoons canola, corn, or peanut oil
2 garlic cloves, crushed and peeled
2 slices unpeeled gingerroot, 1 × 1/8 inch each
1 carrot, peeled and thinly sliced on the diagonal
1/2 green bell pepper, cut into 1-inch chunks
1 cup broccoli florets
2 cups bok choy chunks
1 small onion, quartered
1/2 cup Chinese Chicken Broth (page 64) or canned chicken broth
2 tablespoons fermented black beans, chopped
1 cup snow peas, ends snapped off and strings removed
1/2 teaspoon salt, or to taste
2 teaspoons cornstarch, dissolved in 2 tablespoons water

1. Rinse the squid thoroughly, inside and out, with cold water and drain. Cut down 1 side of the body tube and spread out flat with the inside facing up. Lightly score the flesh in a fine crisscross pattern and cut into pieces about 2 to 3 inches square. If the head with the tentacles is large, cut it in half. Bring water to a boil in a saucepan, remove from the heat, and plunge the squid in the water for 15 seconds. The squid will turn opaque and it will curl.

Immediately drain in a colander and rinse in cold water to stop further cooking. Shake out excess water and drain thoroughly. Set aside.

2.   Heat 1 tablespoon of the oil with the garlic and gingerroot in a wok or stir-fry pan over high heat, stirring until the oil is hot but not smoking; the garlic and gingerroot will sizzle and become fragrant. Add all the vegetables except the snow peas. Stir for about 30 seconds. Add the broth, reduce the heat to medium, and cover the pan. Cook, covered, for 1 to 2 minutes, or until the vegetables are tender.

3.   Return the heat to high and add the blanched squid, black beans, and snow peas. Stir for 30 seconds to 1 minute. Taste and add salt, if necessary. Add the cornstarch slurry. Stir until sauce is thickened. Serve immediately.

Note   To clean squid, peel off and discard the spotted skin from the body. Rinse the body and tentacles thoroughly. Pull off the head and tentacles together. The intestines will follow. Cut the tentacles from the head and reserve. Discard the remainder. Be sure to remove and discard the small hard beak at the center of the tentacles if it is still attached. Pull out the long, clear cartilagelike quill from the center of the body and discard. Rinse the cleaned body and tentacles in cold water and drain thoroughly.

Clams in Black Bean Sauce

Serves 2, or 4 as part of a multicourse meal

*T*he Chinese serve clams cooked in their shells on special occasions like the lunar New Year. They are considered symbolic of prosperity and wealth because when the clam shells open they resemble the shape of the silver ingots used in old China.

禄

12 littleneck or cherrystone clams (about 2 pounds)

2 garlic cloves, lightly crushed and peeled

2 slices unpeeled gingerroot, 1 × ⅛ inch each

1 scallion, green and white parts, cut into 1-inch lengths, bulb split

3 tablespoons fermented black beans, coarsely chopped

2 tablespoons dark soy sauce

1 tablespoon dry sherry

2 teaspoons sugar

2 tablespoons canola, corn, or peanut oil

2 teaspoons cornstarch, dissolved in 1 tablespoon water

Cilantro sprigs, for garnish

1. Cover the clams with fresh cold water and soak for about 30 minutes. Scrub the shells with a stiff brush and rinse thoroughly to remove all sand and grit. Remember shells and all will cook in the sauce and you don't want it to become gritty. Drain. Set aside. If not cooking right away, place in the refrigerator.

2. Combine the garlic, gingerroot, scallion, and black beans in a small dish. Set aside. Combine the soy sauce, sherry, sugar, and ½ cup water in another dish. Stir until the sugar is dissolved. Set aside.

3. Pour the oil into a wok or stir-fry pan and place over high heat. Add the black bean mixture to the pan and stir until fragrant. Add the clams and stir for about 30 seconds. Add the soy sauce mixture, stir to mix, and cover the pan. Cook over medium heat for about 5 minutes, or until the clams just open. Stir occasionally for even cooking.

4. Remove the lid and thicken the sauce with the cornstarch slurry. When the sauce has thickened, transfer the clams to a serving platter and garnish with cilantro. Serve immediately.

Seafood

154

Poultry

oultry, especially chicken, is almost as ubiquitous as pork in China. Chickens, like pigs, are simple to care for, mature quickly, and can be raised by almost anyone with a little plot of land.

As with seafood, the Chinese like their chicken freshly killed for the best flavor. A walk through the open markets in the Far East reveals stalls with live chickens in bamboo cages and shoppers walking home with a live chicken strung up by its feet.

It is very convenient that Western supermarkets have available an array of whole chickens and chicken parts all neatly packaged and ready to cook. In China, chickens are only available whole, so it is up to the cook to prepare it and decide which portions should be used in which dishes. In general, the drier breast meat is used for stir-frying or deep-frying; the dark meat (legs, wings, thighs) is used for braising and stewing.

Since Chinese dishes use a lot of chicken breast meat, you can save substantially on food costs by deboning the chicken breasts yourself instead of buying fillets. Not only will you have the satisfaction of learning a new skill, you'll also be able to make a tasty chicken broth with the bones. (Directions for deboning chicken breasts are on pages 168–169.) We always remove and discard the skin and fat before cooking chicken breasts. This reduces the fat content substantially since most of the fat in poultry lies right under the skin.

When it comes to serving whole chicken, the Chinese do not carve it Western style, but chop it up, bones and all, into bite-size pieces. These pieces are then reassembled on a platter.

The Chinese prefer the dark meat near the bone. We feel it is tastier. My mother liked to eat the bone marrow too and would break the larger bones open to suck it out. Traditionally, the Chinese like to have whole chicken cooked on the rare side with a little blood still apparent near the bones. This is especially true for such dishes as White Cooked Chicken, Drunken Chicken, and Soy Sauce Chicken. However, for health reasons it is not advisable to eat rare chicken.

Duck is popular with the Chinese as well. There are many regional duck specialties, of which Peking Duck is the most well known outside of China. There are restaurants in Peking that feature only Peking Duck and side dishes prepared with duck parts (tongues, feet, etc.). The Chinese rarely prepare Peking Duck at home since they do not have ovens. It was really a specialty left to the realm of a restaurant chef. The one duck recipe featured in this book, Shanghai Duck, is an easy, family-style whole duck that we regularly prepared at home; it's a real favorite for Shanghai people. At other times, we would buy Cantonese-style roasted ducks in Chinatown or have Peking Duck at our own restaurant.

Sliced Chicken with Broccoli

Serves 3 to 4, or 5 to 6 as part of a multicourse meal

*F*resh vegetables always give the best results. After one cooking class I taught, a student remarked how much crisper the broccoli was in my dish than in hers when she prepared the same recipe at home. It turned out she had used frozen broccoli. If you are rushed, you can get all kinds of cut-up raw vegetables at a supermarket salad bar. They may cost more than starting from scratch, but it's better than going to the freezer.

1 pound broccoli

1 pound skinless boneless chicken breasts, sliced (page 43)

2 teaspoons dry sherry

3 teaspoons cornstarch

1 teaspoon salt

3 tablespoons canola, corn, or peanut oil

¼ cup water

1 slice unpeeled gingerroot, 1 × ⅛ inch

1 garlic clove, crushed and peeled

1 (8-ounce) can sliced bamboo shoots, drained (about 1 cup)

1. Trim the broccoli stalks and peel them with a small paring knife. Slice the flower head off the stalks and cut it into bite-size florets. Roll-cut the peeled stalks into 1½-inch pieces as described on page 46. You should have about 4 cups. Set aside.

2. Place the chicken in a bowl, add the sherry, 1 teaspoon of the cornstarch, and ½ teaspoon of the salt, and stir. Set aside. Mix the remaining 2 teaspoons cornstarch and ½ teaspoon salt with ½ cup of cold water. Set aside.

3. Pour 1 tablespoon of the oil into a wok or stir-fry pan and place over high heat. When the oil is hot but not smoking add the broccoli and stir for about 30 seconds. Stir in the ¼ cup water, reduce heat to medium, and cover the pan. Continue cooking, stirring occasionally, for about 2 to 3 minutes, or until broccoli turns a darker green and is tender-crisp. Pour onto a shallow platter and set aside.

4. Heat the remaining 2 tablespoons of oil in the same pan over high heat until hot but not smoking and add the gingerroot and garlic, stirring until they are fragrant and release their flavor, about 30 seconds. With a spoon, stir up the chicken again and turn it all into the pan. Stir briskly for about 3 minutes, or until the chicken turns white. Add the bamboo shoots and return the broccoli to the pan, stirring constantly. Pour in the cornstarch mixture and continue stirring until the gravy is slightly thickened. Remove and discard the gingerroot and garlic, if desired. Serve hot.

Stir-fried Chicken with Cucumbers

**Serves 3 to 4, or 5 to 6 as part of a
multicourse meal**

*Y*ou've probably noticed how important cutting is to Chinese cooking. The ingredients
are usually cut in a uniform shape for a pleasant presentation. In this unusual, refreshing dish, the chicken is sliced to the same flat shape as the cucumbers. It takes a
little practice to get the technique just right. You can cut the chicken into cubes instead, but the slices make a lovelier dish.

1 long seedless cucumber or 1 pound regular cucumbers

1 pound skinless boneless chicken breasts, sliced (page 43)

3 teaspoons cornstarch

2 teaspoons dry sherry

1 teaspoon salt, or to taste

3 tablespoons canola, corn, or peanut oil

2 garlic cloves, crushed and peeled

1 tablespoon fermented black beans, coarsely chopped

1. Wash the cucumber. European cucumber can be left unpeeled. If
using regular cucumbers, partially peel by removing alternating ½-inch strips
of skin down the long side. Trim away ¾ inch from each end and split the
cucumbers lengthwise. Scrape and discard the seeds from regular cucumbers
with a teaspoon. Slice the cucumbers on the diagonal ½ inch thick. You should
have about 3½ to 4 cups. Set aside.

2. Place the chicken in a small bowl, stir in the cornstarch, sherry, and
salt, and mix well. Set aside.

3. Pour the oil into a wok or stir-fry pan and place the pan over high
heat. Add the garlic and stir around the pan until the oil is hot but not smoking;
the garlic will sizzle. Stir up the chicken again and add it all to the pan. Stir
briskly for 2 to 3 minutes, or until the chicken is opaque.

4. Add the cucumber slices and stir another 2 minutes. Toss in the
black beans and stir for another 30 seconds, or until the ingredients and flavors
are evenly mixed. Taste and add another ½ teaspoon of salt if you wish. Discard
the garlic, if desired. Serve hot.

Chicken with Mushrooms

Serves 3 to 4, or 5 to 6 as part of a
multicourse meal

*I*f *you want to make this recipe more exotic, use half fresh and half dried black mushrooms. Soften the dried mushrooms in hot water, trim the stems, and cut the caps into pieces similar to the fresh mushrooms. You may also wish to try other kinds of fresh mushrooms, such as porcini or shiitake.*

1 pound skinless boneless chicken breast, cut into ¾-inch cubes (about 2 cups)

1 teaspoon dry sherry

2 teaspoons cornstarch

1½ teaspoons salt

3 tablespoons canola, corn, or peanut oil

2 slices unpeeled gingerroot, 1 × ⅛ inch each

1 garlic clove, crushed and peeled

¾ pound fresh button mushrooms, cleaned and quartered (2 cups)

¾ pound fresh snow peas, ends snapped off and strings removed (2 cups)

1 (8-ounce) can sliced bamboo shoots, drained (1 cup)

1.   Place the chicken in a bowl. Add the sherry, 1 teaspoon of the cornstarch, and salt and stir together until the chicken is well coated. Set aside. Dissolve the remaining teaspoon of cornstarch in 1 tablespoon water. Set aside.

2.   Pour the oil into a wok or stir-fry pan and place over high heat. Add the gingerroot and garlic and stir around the pan until the oil is hot but not smoking; the gingerroot and garlic will begin to sizzle.

3.   Stir the chicken again and pour it into the pan. Stir constantly until the chicken turns white, about 2 minutes. Add the mushrooms, snow peas, and bamboo shoots. Continue stirring until the snow peas turn a darker green.

4.   Give the cornstarch mixture a quick stir to be sure it is completely dissolved and pour it into the pan. Continue stirring until the liquid thickens. Remove and discard the gingerroot and garlic. Serve immediately.

Chicken with Mixed Vegetables

Serves 3 to 4, or 5 to 6 as part of a
multicourse meal

*Y*ou can use many kinds of vegetables for this dish, but I like this particular mix because the colors are bright and the flavors combine well with the chicken. Since there is
no soy sauce in this dish, the colors of the vegetables and the chicken shine right
through.

1 pound skinless boneless chicken breast, cut into ¾-inch dice (about 2 cups)

1 tablespoon cornstarch

2 teaspoons dry sherry

3 tablespoons canola, corn, or peanut oil

1 carrot, peeled and roll-cut (page 46)

2 celery stalks, sliced on the diagonal ¼ inch thick

1 medium red bell pepper, seeded, cored, and cut into 1½-inch dice

2 cups bok choy, washed, drained, and cut into 2-inch pieces

½ cup Chinese Chicken Broth (page 64) or water

2 slices unpeeled gingerroot, 1 × ⅛ inch each

1 teaspoon salt, or to taste

1. Place the chicken in a bowl and add the cornstarch and sherry. Stir
until well mixed. Set aside.

2. Heat 1 tablespoon of the oil in a wok or stir-fry pan over high heat
until the oil is hot but not smoking. Test by dipping the end of one of the
vegetables in the oil; it should sizzle. Add the vegetables to the pan and stir
for about 2 minutes. Add the broth, stir, and cover. Reduce the heat to medium and steam for 2 minutes, or until the vegetables are tender-crisp. Transfer
the vegetables and their juices to a platter.

3. Add the remaining 2 tablespoons of oil to the same pan. Place over
high heat and stir in the gingerroot and salt. Stir for about 30 seconds or until
the gingerroot sizzles; do not let it burn. Stir up the chicken again and add it
to the pan. Stir for 2 to 3 minutes, or until the chicken is almost done.

4. Return the vegetables and any juice from the platter to the pan, mix thoroughly, and cook until vegetables are heated and chicken is done. Taste and add salt, if necessary. Remove and discard the gingerroot. Transfer the chicken and vegetables to a platter. Serve immediately.

Chicken Chop Suey

Serves 4

*C*hop Suey, *which loosely translates as "mixed up," is not authentically Chinese. Like Chow Mein, it was conceived in the United States and was extremely popular with Americans who thought it was a Chinese dish.*

When our restaurant opened in 1958, my mother did not want to serve either Chop Suey or Chow Mein, but she quickly found that customers were unhappy not to find them on the menu. She reluctantly added sections to the back of the menu for these two categories. As our customers came to appreciate real Chinese food, they stopped ordering Chow Mein and Chop Suey and did not miss them when they eventually disappeared from the menu.

Yet, old favorites die hard for some people. Our close friend and business associate, Mel Novatt, himself a world traveler and gourmet, surprised, even shocked, me one day when he admitted that one of his favorite Chinese dishes was Chicken Chop Suey and that he was disappointed that it had become almost impossible to get. In one Cantonese restaurant in Boston, he implored me to order it for him. The waiter was taken aback and asked two times if American Chop Suey was really what I wanted. Mel was a happy man that evening.

I am including a simple Chop Suey recipe here because although it is not authentic, it is nutritious and tasty when it is made well. Always use fresh vegetables and be sure not to overcook the bean sprouts. They are best when they are tender but still crisp. Serve the dish with steamed rice or crisp chow mein noodles.

(continued)

禧

3 tablespoons canola, corn, or peanut oil

2 slices unpeeled gingerroot, 1 × ⅛ inch each

½ pound skinless boneless chicken breast, cut into ¾-inch cubes (about 1 cup)

1 medium onion, shredded (about 1 cup)

2 celery stalks, shredded (1 cup)

1 (8-ounce) can bamboo shoots, drained and sliced or shredded (1 cup)

2 cups shredded napa cabbage (about ½ pound)

2 chicken bouillon cubes, dissolved in ½ cup hot water

3 cups bean sprouts (about 6 ounces)

1 tablespoon cornstarch, dissolved in 2 tablespoons water

1. Pour the oil into a wok or stir-fry pan and place over high heat. Add the gingerroot and stir around the pan for about 15 seconds or until the oil is hot but not smoking; the gingerroot will sizzle.

2. Add the chicken and stir constantly for about 1 minute. Stir in the onion, celery, bamboo shoots, cabbage, and chicken bouillon solution. Stir around a few times and cover the pan. Cook, covered, for about 3 minutes, stirring occasionally, until the vegetables lose their raw look. Add the bean sprouts and stir another minute, or until the sprouts are lightly wilted but still crisp.

3. Stir in the cornstarch slurry and cook, stirring constantly, until the sauce thickens. Serve hot.

健康

Note See directions for shredding vegetables on page 45.

Mandarin Orange Chicken

Serves 3 to 4, or 5 to 6 as part of a multicourse meal

My version of the classic Orange Chicken requires no deep-frying, so there's a saving of time, effort, and calories. I use frozen orange juice concentrate, which blends exceptionally well with the spicy hotness of chilies. If you don't like chilies, you can omit them.

Stir-frying the snow peas separately and using them to ring the chicken makes a very nice presentation for dinner parties. For a family meal, you can return the peas to the pan just after the oranges and mix them in.

福

1 pound skinless boneless chicken breasts, cut into ¾-inch dice (about 2 cups)

2 teaspoons dry sherry

3 teaspoons cornstarch

2 teaspoons sugar

1 tablespoon cider vinegar

3 tablespoons light soy sauce

3 tablespoons frozen orange juice concentrate

4 tablespoons canola, corn, or peanut oil

¼ pound snow peas, ends snapped off and strings removed, cut on the diagonal into ½-inch pieces

2 to 4 dried chilies, seeds removed (see page 12)

1 garlic clove, crushed and peeled

2 slices unpeeled gingerroot, 1 × ⅛ inch each

1 (11-ounce) can mandarin oranges, drained

1.   Place the chicken in a bowl, stir in the sherry and cornstarch and mix well. Set aside. In another bowl, combine the sugar, vinegar, soy sauce, and orange juice concentrate and mix well. Set aside.

2.   Heat 1 tablespoon of the oil in a wok or stir-fry pan over medium heat until hot but not smoking. Test by dipping the end of a piece of snow pea in the oil; it should sizzle. Add the snow peas and stir just until they turn a darker green, about 30 seconds. Transfer the snow peas to a large serving platter and spread them out. Do not pile up the snow peas, but spread them out so they will not overcook in their own heat.

3.   In the same pan, heat the remaining 3 tablespoons of oil with the chili peppers over medium heat. As the oil heats up, the peppers will turn dark brown and become very fragrant. Discard the chilies when they are almost black but not burned. Add the garlic and gingerroot and stir around the pan a few times until they begin to sizzle.

4.   Increase the heat to high, stir up the chicken again, and add it. Stir for about 1 minute, add the orange sauce, and continue stirring another minute or two. When the chicken is almost done, discard the garlic and gingerroot. Add the mandarin oranges and stir gently to heat the oranges and finish cooking the chicken — not more than 1 minute or the oranges will fall apart.

5.   Arrange the snow peas in a ring around the edge of the platter and spoon the chicken and oranges into the center. Serve hot.

Cutting up a Whole Cooked Chicken, Chinese Style

切

When the Chinese cook a whole chicken, they like to chop it all up into bite-size pieces for serving. The pieces are reassembled on a platter to look like a whole chicken with the wings and legs positioned properly. Here's how to do it.

Allow the chicken to cool for a few minutes to firm up the meat and reduce splattering. Be sure to wear a large apron.

- Cut off the wings and then cut them apart at the joints. Leave the wingtip whole but chop the other two pieces in half. Place the pieces on either side of an oval platter, reassembled to look whole.
- Cut off the legs at the hip joint, close to the body. To do this, pull the legs away from the body and bend at the hip to expose the joint for easier cutting. Cut the legs apart. With a Chinese knife, chop the thigh and drumstick into 3 pieces about 1 inch wide. Reassemble the pieces on either side of the platter below the wings.
- With the chicken breast side up, cut through the breast with a knife or a pair of scissors. Take your time and place the knife down into the bird and cut-chop firmly. Pull open the cavity to expose the backbone. Chop (or cut with scissors) along the side of the backbone, then along the other side, separating the neck and backbone from the carcass. If desired, chop the backbone crosswise into 1-inch pieces and reserve it to enrich and flavor soup noodles.
- Place a body half, skin side up, on the cutting board. Chop into 2 pieces lengthwise and then crosswise into 1 × 2 inch pieces, being careful to keep the pieces together so they can be easily reassembled on the serving platter. Repeat for the other half.
- Assemble the body pieces, skin side up, in the middle of the serving platter. Always have the most attractive and meaty breast pieces on top, over the bonier rib pieces, for a beautiful and rich presentation. Garnish the platter with sprigs of parsley or cilantro.

Note When you get Cantonese duck or chicken in Chinatown, they chop up the whole carcass without removing the backbone. The Chinese usually serve the neck and backbone along with the other meat, hidden under the breast pieces. I save those pieces to use in another meal.

Almond Chicken

*N**uts appear frequently in Chinese cooking in desserts, fillings, sweet soups, and stir-fry dishes. The almonds offer a crunchy contrast to the chicken and vegetables. In this dish, all the ingredients should be diced to about the size of whole almonds.*

1 pound skinless boneless chicken breast, cut into ½-inch dice (about 2 cups)

2 teaspoons cornstarch

1 teaspoon dry sherry

1 teaspoon salt, or to taste

3 tablespoons canola, corn, or peanut oil

1 slice unpeeled gingerroot, 1 × ⅛ inch

½ cup canned bamboo shoots, drained and diced

½ cup canned whole water chestnuts, drained and quartered

1 medium green bell pepper, seeded, cored, and diced

1 medium red bell pepper, seeded, cored, and diced

½ cup whole almonds, blanched or natural, toasted

1.   Place the chicken in a bowl. Add the cornstarch, sherry, and salt and stir to coat the chicken thoroughly. Set aside.

2.   Pour the oil into a wok or stir-fry pan and place over high heat. Add the gingerroot and stir it around until the oil is hot; the gingerroot will sizzle. Stir the chicken up again and pour into the pan. Stir constantly for 1 to 2 minutes, or until the chicken pieces are separated and almost cooked.

3.   Add the bamboo shoots, water chestnuts, and peppers. Stir well for 1 minute, or until the peppers are tender-crisp. Add the almonds and mix thoroughly. Remove and discard the gingerroot, if desired. Serve immediately.

Variation   To give the dish a slightly sweet taste, add 1 to 1½ tablespoons hoisin sauce when adding the vegetables and reduce the salt to ½ teaspoon.

Chicken with Cashew Nuts

**Serves 3 to 4, or 5 to 6 as part of a
multicourse meal**

This chicken recipe has been an outstanding favorite at our family's Cambridge restaurant for as long as I can remember. There, the cashews are deep-fried, but at home I prefer to toast the nuts instead. This reduces the amount of oil without reducing the flavor.

禧

1 pound skinless boneless chicken breast, cut into ¾-inch cubes (about 2 cups)

2 teaspoons cornstarch

2 teaspoons dry sherry

½ teaspoon grated peeled gingerroot

2 tablespoons dark soy sauce

2 tablespoons hoisin sauce

1 teaspoon sugar

4 tablespoons canola, corn, or peanut oil

1 garlic clove, crushed and peeled

1 cup whole blanched cashews, toasted

1 teaspoon sesame seed oil

1. Place the chicken in a bowl. Add the cornstarch, sherry, and gingerroot and stir together until well mixed. Set aside.

2. Combine the soy sauce, hoisin sauce, sugar, and 2 tablespoons water in a small bowl and stir until smooth. Set aside.

3. Pour the oil into a wok or stir-fry pan and place the pan over high heat. Add the garlic and stir it around the pan until the oil is hot and the garlic sizzles, about 30 seconds. Do not let it burn. Stir up the chicken mixture again and add it all to the hot oil. Continue stirring until the chicken is almost done, 1 to 2 minutes. Remove and discard the garlic.

4. Reduce the heat to medium and stir in the soy sauce mixture. Continue stirring until the ingredients are well blended. Add the cashew nuts and stir another 30 seconds. Drizzle with sesame seed oil and give a couple of big turns with a spatula. Serve immediately.

How to Debone a Whole Chicken Breast

Deboning a chicken breast is done easily with just a few strokes of a good sharp knife.

- Tear off and discard the skin and fat. Cut or tear away and discard any loose membrane or excess fat from the cavity. Rinse the breast in water and pat dry with paper towels.
- Lay the breast, bone side up, on a cutting board and with the tip of your knife or with kitchen scissors cut into and through the center bone, splitting the breast in two.

- Lay the breast half, bone side down, on the cutting board. Make a slash through the meat at its thinnest part over the rib cage. Do not cut through the rib bones.

- Insert your index finger into the slash and run it up to the center bone, keeping it close to the bone and loosening the flap of meat from the bones underneath.

- If necessary, use the tip of the knife to loosen the meat from the bones. Lift the meat from the bone and set it back down on the cutting board. Pull the tenderloin free from the larger fillet. (If it is still attached to the breast bone,

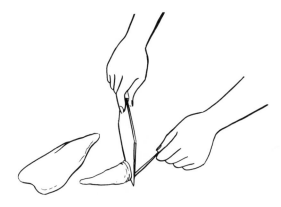

cut around the membrane that holds it in place.) Repeat with the other piece.
- You should now have four pieces of meat, two fillets and two tenderloin strips. Save the bones to make Chinese Chicken Broth (page 64) or place in a bag and freeze for later use.
- Cut and trim away any peripheral fat and membrane. I do this by using my hand to spread the membrane to the sides and then trimming it with the tip of my knife.
- Place the tenderloin on the cutting board and grasp between your fingers the end of the tendon that runs from one end of the meat, where it is clearly visible, into the meat. If it is slippery, use a piece of paper towel for a better grip. Using the edge of the knife blade, lightly scrape the tendon to expose enough for a good grip. Hold the knife down on the meat and pull the tendon out toward you. The knife will hold the meat in place while the tendon is neatly extracted.

Kung Pao Chicken

**Serves 3 to 4, or 5 to 6 as part of a
multicourse meal**

*T*his is a famous Szechuan dish known as Kung Pao Chi Ting. At the time of the
Qin (pronounced ch'in) dynasty, the person in charge of protecting the heir apparent
to the throne held the title of Kung Pao, Kung meaning castle and Pao, to protect.
During one period, the Kung Pao was a man from Szechuan Province whose favorite
dish was spicy diced chicken with peanuts. It came to be named after him.

福

1 pound skinless boneless chicken breasts, cut into ¾-inch cubes (about 2 cups)

3 tablespoons dark soy sauce

1 teaspoon salt

1 tablespoon cornstarch

1 teaspoon dry sherry

1 tablespoon sugar

1 tablespoon cider vinegar

1 teaspoon sesame seed oil

2 to 4 dried chilies, seeds removed

3 tablespoons canola, corn, or peanut oil

½ teaspoon Szechuan peppercorns, toasted and ground

1 garlic clove, peeled and sliced

1 scallion, green and white parts, cut into 1½-inch lengths, bulb split, plus
    2 tablespoons thinly sliced scallions

2 slices unpeeled gingerroot, 1 × ⅛ inch each

½ cup unsalted blanched peanuts, toasted, or unsalted dry-roasted peanuts

1.   Place the chicken in a bowl. Add 1 tablespoon of the soy sauce, salt,
and cornstarch and mix well. Set aside. Mix the remaining 2 tablespoons of
soy sauce together in a small bowl with the sherry, sugar, vinegar, and sesame
seed oil. Set aside.

2.   Pour the cooking oil into a cold wok or stir-fry pan and add the
chilies. Heat the pan over medium-high heat and stir the peppers until they
turn dark brown. Add the peppercorns, garlic, scallion pieces, and gingerroot
and stir a moment or two. Mix up the chicken again and pour it into the pan.
Stir briskly.

3. After stirring for about 1 minute, add the soy sauce mixture, the peanuts, and the thinly sliced scallions. Turn the heat up to high and stir for about 30 seconds until well mixed. Remove the chilies and gingerroot, if desired. Serve hot.

Note   You may substitute 1 to 3 teaspoons crushed red pepper for the dried chilies. Add with the peppercorns, garlic, and scallions.

壽

Chicken Livers and Snow Peas

Serves 3 to 4, or 5 to 6 as part of a multicourse meal

*T*he *Chinese appreciate organ meats, but I find that many Americans — even my own husband — do not. Those who do like liver (and I know there are many of you out there) will find stir-fried liver dishes different and easy to prepare.*

禧

½ pound chicken livers (about 1 ½ cups)
1 teaspoon dry sherry
3 tablespoons dark soy sauce
3 teaspoons cornstarch
3 tablespoons canola, corn, or peanut oil
¼ pound snow peas, ends snapped off and strings removed
1 slice unpeeled gingerroot, 1 × ⅛ inch
1 (8-ounce) can sliced bamboo shoots, drained (1 cup)
¼ teaspoon salt, or to taste

1. Peel the membrane off the chicken livers with your fingers. Cut into ½-inch pieces and place in a bowl. Stir in the sherry, 1 tablespoon of the soy sauce, and 1 teaspoon of the cornstarch and mix well. Set aside.

2. Dissolve the remaining cornstarch in the remaining soy sauce and ¼ cup cold water. Set aside.

3. Heat 1 tablespoon of the oil in a wok or stir-fry pan over medium-high heat until the oil is hot. Test by dipping an end of a snow pea into the oil; it should sizzle. Add the snow peas to the hot oil and stir for about 1 minute, or until the peas turn a darker green. Do not overcook. Remove and spread out on a platter.

4. Heat the remaining oil in the same pan over high heat. Add the gingerroot and stir around the pan until it is fragrant and sizzles. Stir up the chicken livers again and pour into the pan. Stir constantly for about 3 minutes or until blood no longer seeps out.

5. Add the bamboo shoots and stir for 30 seconds. Stir up the cornstarch mixture again and add it. Return the snow peas to the pan and continue stirring until the sauce thickens. Serve immediately.

Poultry

172

Curry Chicken

**Serves 3 to 4, or 5 to 6 as part of a
multicourse meal**

For this dish, I use Indian curry powder. My mother preferred curry paste, which is available in specialty stores or Asian markets. She would then omit the chili powder.

The traditional Chinese recipe calls for small pieces of chicken with the bones left in, but I have changed it to boneless chicken to make it easier to eat. Serve the dish with steamed white rice or brown Basmati rice, steamed vegetables, and Spicy Mango Chutney (page 330) on the side.

健康

2 tablespoons curry powder

1 tablespoon chili powder

2 cups chicken broth or water

2 tablespoons all-purpose flour

3 tablespoons canola, corn, or peanut oil

1 large onion, sliced (about 2 cups)

1 to 1¼ pounds skinless boneless chicken breast, cut into 1½-inch chunks

1 teaspoon salt

⅓ to 1 cup chopped cilantro leaves (optional)

1 to 2 cups Spicy Mango Chutney (page 330) (optional)

1. Stir the curry and chili powders together with ½ cup water or broth in a small bowl until thoroughly mixed. Set aside. Combine the flour and ½ cup water or broth in another small bowl. Stir until smooth, with no lumps. Set aside.

2. Heat the oil in a stir-fry pan or heavy pot over medium-high to high heat. When the oil is hot, add the onion and stir until translucent and just beginning to brown around the edges. This will take about 5 minutes.

3. Add the curry mixture and stir a few times. Add the chicken and stir for 2 to 3 minutes, or until all the chicken is coated with the curry. Pour in the remaining 1 cup water or broth and bring to a boil. Cover the pan and simmer over low heat for 10 to 15 minutes, or until the chicken is fully cooked.

4. Stir in the salt. Remove the chicken and onions with a slotted spoon to a serving dish. Quickly bring the curry sauce to a boil over medium-high

(continued)

heat and pour in the flour slurry, stirring constantly until the sauce thickens, about 3 minutes. Pour the gravy over the chicken. (The curry may be made ahead and reheated. Warm over low heat, stirring constantly.) Serve hot with small dishes of chopped cilantro and chutney for individual garnish, if desired.

Lemon Chicken

Serves 2 to 3, or 4 to 5 as part of a multicourse meal

*A*t our restaurant the chicken is dredged in water-chestnut starch, which is available in Chinese grocery stores, instead of cornstarch, for a crisper crust.

2 skinless boneless chicken breasts, with small fillet removed (about ¾ pound)
1 egg
½ teaspoon salt
Juice of 1 lemon, strained (about ¼ cup)
5 tablespoons (firmly packed) light brown sugar
1 slice unpeeled gingerroot, 1 × ⅛ inch
2 tablespoons cornstarch plus additional for dredging chicken
1 cup canola, corn, or peanut oil
1 teaspoon sesame seed oil
Lemon slices and parsley, for garnish

1. Place the chicken breasts on a cutting board and remove any visible fat. With the broad side of a Chinese knife or a heavy object such as a rolling pin, pound the chicken breasts to flatten slightly.

2. Lightly beat the egg and salt in a shallow bowl. Place the breasts in the egg mixture and turn a few times to coat evenly. Set aside for 10 minutes.

3. Combine the lemon juice, sugar, gingerroot, and 1 cup water in a small saucepan on an unlit burner. Remove a third of the mixture and combine with the 2 tablespoons of cornstarch, stirring until the cornstarch is dissolved.

4. Heat the oil over medium heat in a stir-fry pan or skillet large enough to hold the breasts. Place cornstarch in a pie pan. Remove the breasts from the egg and press into the cornstarch, coating both sides well and shaking off excess. When the oil is hot, fry the breasts for 8 to 10 minutes, turning until both sides are lightly browned and chicken is cooked through. Remove to a plate lined with paper towels to absorb the excess oil. Cut each chicken breast into ¾-inch-wide slices. Arrange on a shallow platter and keep warm as you cook the sauce.

5.   Heat the lemon mixture in the saucepan over medium heat. When it comes to a boil, stir up the cornstarch slurry and pour it in. Stir until the sauce is thickened. Taste for tartness and add more sugar if desired. Discard the gingerroot. Stir in the sesame seed oil. Pour the sauce over the chicken and garnish with lemon slices and parsley. Serve hot.

Note   Chicken breasts cook more evenly and remain flatter when the small fillet underneath is removed. You can leave it on, but you should at least remove the tendon. Once I've removed the tendon, I separate the fillets and freeze the smaller ones for stir-fry dishes.

Empress Chicken

*T*his is a lofty name for a convenient family dish when you don't have the time or
appetite for a whole chicken. Not only does this dish take under an hour to prepare
and cook, it holds very well in a warm oven. It can also be made a day ahead and
reheated without any loss of texture or flavor. Serve it with hot white rice.

4 chicken wings

4 whole chicken legs

1 cup dried black mushrooms, soaked in hot water for 15 minutes

1 scallion, folded to 3 inches and tied with a cotton string or thread

1½ cups canned whole bamboo shoots, drained and cut into chunks

½ cup dark soy sauce

2 cups Chinese Chicken Broth (page 64) or water

3 whole star anise

2 slices unpeeled gingerroot, 1 × ⅛ inch each

1 tablespoon dry sherry

1 teaspoon salt, or to taste

1. Cut the chicken wings into three through the joints. Discard the
wing tips or save them for making broth. Cut the chicken legs in two through
the joints. Chop the leg and thigh into 2 pieces each.

2. Bring water to a boil in a large pot and scald the chicken by dropping
the pieces into the boiling water. When the water returns to a boil, drain the
chicken in a colander, rinse with cold water, and drain again.

3. Squeeze out the water from the mushrooms and cut off the woody
stems with scissors and discard. Leave the caps whole.

4. Put the blanched chicken with the rest of the ingredients into a large
saucepan or Dutch oven. Cover and bring to a boil. Reduce the heat and
simmer, covered, for 30 minutes, or until the chicken is tender. Stir occasionally to prevent sticking and for even color.

5. Uncover, increase the heat to medium, and bring the liquid to a
boil. Baste the chicken for even color and flavor and continue cooking for 10
minutes, reducing the liquid. Remove the scallion and discard. Serve hot or
warm.

Yunnan Steam Pot Chicken

Serves 3 to 4, or 6 as part of a multicourse meal

ou will need a Chinese steam pot (page 38) with at least a two-quart capacity to prepare this dish in the traditional manner. The steam enters the closed container through an inner spout. The slow cooking results in a rich, flavorful broth.

禧

2 to 2¼ pounds chicken, cut through the bones into 2-inch pieces

3 slices unpeeled gingerroot, 1 × ⅛ inch each

2 scallions, green and white parts, cut into 2-inch lengths, bulb split in half

8 dried black mushrooms, soaked in hot water for 15 minutes, woody stems discarded and caps quartered

½ cup sliced bamboo shoots, drained

¼ pound Smithfield ham, fat removed, cut into 2-inch slices

2 cups Chinese Chicken Broth (page 64) plus ½ teaspoon salt or
      1 (13¾-ounce) can chicken broth and enough water to make 2 cups

1 tablespoon dry sherry

½ teaspoon salt

1. Arrange the chicken with the gingerroot, scallions, black mushrooms, bamboo shoots and ham in a steam pot. Combine the chicken broth and sherry and salt and pour over the chicken.

2. Cover the steam pot and place in a water bath in a large stockpot, wok, or covered roaster. The water should come up just to the handles of the steam pot. Cover the stockpot or wok and steam for about 1½ hours, or until the chicken is cooked through. Replenish the water in the outside pot as needed.

3. Remove steam pot from the pan, discard the gingerroot and scallions and skim off any surface fat. Serve the chicken and broth directly from the steam pot at the table.

Poultry

White-cooked Chicken

Serves 6 to 8 as part of a
multicourse meal

T his Chinese method of poaching chicken uses the passive heat of boiled water to cook. It is slow, but the result is well worth the wait.

The quality of the chicken is very important here. My mother always insisted on using fresh-killed chickens. When I was a child, every week we would make the trek to a shop in the back of Harvard University where my mother could pick out a live chicken. It would disappear through an open doorway to a back room to be butchered. The butchering took place in full view of the shop entrance. The butcher would leave on the head and feet and put all the innards back into the cleaned and dressed bird.

My mother always brought along a jar partially filled with a water-and-salt solution. She would give it to the butcher to collect the blood, which she made into a delicious blood pudding for soups. Nothing was wasted.

健康

1 whole chicken, freshly killed if possible (3 to 5 pounds)
1 tablespoon dry sherry
3 slices unpeeled gingerroot, 1 × 1/8 inch each
1 scallion
Soy Sauce Dip (page 324), for serving

1.   Carefully lower the chicken into a large pot of boiling water and let sit for 2 to 3 minutes to clean and sear. Drain and pull out any pinfeathers with tweezers. Set aside.

2.   Choose a large pot that will hold the whole chicken comfortably and fill it with enough water to submerge the chicken. (If you are unsure of how much water is enough, put the chicken in the pot, cover with water, and remove the bird.) Bring to a boil over high heat. Carefully slip the chicken into the water. Be sure it is totally submerged. Add the sherry, gingerroot, and scallion. When the water starts to boil again, turn off the heat, cover the pan tightly, and leave the chicken in the hot water for 1 hour.

3.   After 1 hour, remove the cover and turn the heat to high. Watch the pot carefully and as soon as the water returns to a boil, immediately turn off the heat, cover tightly, and let sit for another hour.

Poultry

4. Check for doneness by piercing the thigh with a chopstick or testing with an instant-read thermometer. The juices should be clear and the temperature 165°F. If the juices are bloody, repeat the boiling and soaking procedure a third time, letting the chicken stand in the water for 30 minutes before draining. Discard the liquid, it doesn't have much taste.

5. Let the bird cool. Serve at room temperature. (Or refrigerate the chicken, covered, overnight.) Serve the chicken chopped up, Chinese style (pages 164–165), or carved Western style with a soy sauce dip.

Drunken Chicken

*T*his traditional Shanghai-style cold appetizer is a great dish for a hot summer's day when served with a salad or steamed garden vegetables. The chicken is poached whole and then marinated in wine for at least twelve hours. The Chinese marinate it in different kinds of rice wine, but excellent results can be had with the more readily available pale dry sherry.

I have offered two poaching techniques. The first, which my mother taught me, takes longer but gives better texture and flavor. The second is faster, and I find it is still good. Marinating the bird in sherry brings back its moisture and flavor. This dish is best served as part of a multicourse meal.

1 whole chicken, freshly killed if possible (3 to 4 pounds)
4 slices unpeeled gingerroot, 1 × ⅛ inch each
1 tablespoon salt
3 cups dry sherry
Cilantro sprigs, for garnish

1.   Rinse the chicken and remove the neck and giblets. Discard excess fat from the cavity opening. If there are still pinfeathers, pluck them out with tweezers.

2.   Cook the chicken as described on page 178 or bring water to a boil in a pot large enough to hold the chicken and enough water to cover it. When the water boils, add the gingerroot and submerge the bird. When the water returns to a boil, turn the heat to low. Cook, covered, at a very slow simmer for 40 minutes. Turn off heat and let stand for 30 minutes. Test for doneness by piercing the thigh with a chopstick; the juices should be clear with no tinge of pink. Or, test the thickest part of the thigh with an instant-read thermometer; the temperature should be 165°F. If the bird is not done, turn heat back on to medium and bring just to a boil. Turn heat off and let stand for 15 minutes. Test for doneness again.

3.   When the chicken is done, drain thoroughly and let cool until you can handle it. Place it in a plastic bag large enough to hold the whole bird and still be tightly secured. Place the bag in a large bowl or baking pan to catch any drips or leaks. Mix the salt with the sherry and stir until all the salt has dissolved. Pour mixture into the plastic bag with the bird, squeeze out air from bag, and secure tightly. Refrigerate for at least 12 hours, turning occasionally for even marinating.

4. When ready to serve, chop the chicken up, Chinese style (pages 164–165), or place it on a platter and carve at the table. Garnish platter with sprigs of cilantro.

Drunken Chicken Breasts

Serves 4, or 6 to 8 as part of a
multicourse meal

This nontraditional version of Drunken Chicken (page 180) uses only the breast meat. The sliced chicken makes a lovely light summer lunch when served with freshly tossed mixed greens and crusty French bread. Or you can cut the pieces smaller and serve them as a cold appetizer.

2 whole chicken breasts (about 2 to 3 pounds)
4 slices unpeeled gingerroot, 1 × ⅛ inch each
1 tablespoon salt
3 cups dry sherry
Cilantro sprigs, for garnish

1. Bring water to a boil in a pot large enough to hold the chicken comfortably. Rinse the breasts and trim away excess fat. Add the chicken and the gingerroot to the water. When the water returns to a boil, reduce the heat to low. Cover and simmer for 15 to 20 minutes. Turn off the heat and let stand for 20 minutes. Test for doneness by piercing the thickest part of the breast with a chopstick. The juices should be clear without any tinge of pink.

2. Remove the chicken from the water, cool and place in a plastic bag. Dissolve the salt in the sherry and pour over the chicken in the bag. Squeeze the air from the bag and secure tightly. Set the bag in a roasting pan or dish to catch any drips or leaks and marinate in the refrigerator for at least 12 hours. Turn occasionally for even marinating.

3. Remove the meat from the breast bone and slice into ¾-inch-thick pieces. Arrange in an overlapping design on a platter, pour about ¼ cup of the marinating liquid over the chicken and garnish with cilantro sprigs.

Soy Sauce Chicken

Serves 3 to 4, or 6 to 8 as part of a multicourse meal

For the Chinese, Cantonese-style soy sauce chicken, duck, and pork are as poplar and versatile as cold cuts are to Americans. They aren't used in sandwiches but as appetizers, side dishes, or as part of a multicourse meal, usually served at room temperature. Leftover pieces, especially the bony backs, are saved to add to soup noodles to make the broth even tastier. You can see the prepared meats hanging in the windows of grocery stores in Chinatown. You can buy a whole or half chicken and have it chopped up — bones and all — into bite-size pieces. It's quite a show to watch the chefs chop. They often work behind a clear plexiglas wall, both for sanitary reasons and to keep the juices from splattering everywhere and making a mess.

You can prepare your own Soy Sauce Chicken with this recipe. I often drop a few shelled hard-boiled eggs into the cooking liquid at the point when the chicken is turned over. They should be basted and turned occasionally for even color. The giblets may also be cooked along with the chicken. Be sure to allow them to simmer for at least twenty-five minutes to ensure that they are cooked through. Serve the chicken with Chinese Steamed Bread (page 122) to dip in the delicious gravy.

1 chicken (3 to 4 pounds)
3 slices unpeeled gingerroot, 1 × ⅛ inch each
2 whole star anise
1 (3-inch) stick cinnamon
1 (3-inch) piece dried or fresh orange peel
½ cup dark soy sauce
3 tablespoons dry sherry
½ cup sugar
1 tablespoon sesame seed oil (optional)

1.   Rinse and drain the chicken. Remove any excess fat from the cavity and discard.

2.   Place the gingerroot, star anise, cinnamon, orange peel, soy sauce, sherry, sugar, and 1 cup water in a Dutch oven or roaster large enough to hold the whole chicken. Stir to dissolve the sugar and bring to a boil.

Poultry

3.   Add the chicken, breast side down, and with a large spoon or bulb baster, baste a few times. Turn the heat to low, cover, and simmer for 25 minutes. Baste frequently and check that the liquid remains at just the barest simmer.

4.   Turn the chicken over and continue to simmer, covered, for 20 to 25 minutes. Uncover the pan, bring the liquid to a boil over medium heat, and baste frequently for about 10 minutes, or until the skin is brown. Turn off the heat and let stand, covered, for 1 hour. Test for doneness by sticking a chopstick into the thigh; if the juices run clear the chicken is done. If not, turn the heat on to medium and bring to a boil again. Turn off the heat and let stand for 15 minutes. Check for doneness again and repeat if necessary.

5.   Carve the chicken, place on a platter, and sparingly pour some of the cooking juices over it. Mix sesame seed oil, if using, into the cooking liquid and serve the remaining juices on the side. (To serve Chinese style, see pages 164–165, cut up the chicken and reassemble all the pieces on the platter. Mix the sesame seed oil, if using, into the cooking liquid and lightly drizzle the juices over the chicken pieces.) Serve cold.

Chinese Chicken Salad

Serves 4 to 6

*I*t wasn't until I was an adult and visited Los Angeles that I ever tried a Chinese chicken salad. Our Los Angeles sales representative and friend, Gus Dallas, introduced me to it, and I came back to Boston determined to develop a chicken salad of my own. This one is much lighter and lower in fat than Western chicken salads. Serve it with Pan-fried Scallion Cakes (page 303) or Minute Scallion Pancakes (page 305) and fill a bowl with extra noodles to let guests add more if they like. Add the noodles to the salad just before serving or they will become soft and soggy.

健康

½ cup rice vinegar

1 tablespoon cider vinegar

4 teaspoons sugar

2 teaspoons sesame seed oil

½ teaspoon grated peeled gingerroot

1 pound skinless boneless chicken breast, poached, or about 2 cups shredded cooked chicken

4 cups shredded iceberg lettuce (½ medium head)

2 cups grated carrots (about 2 medium)

¼ cup chopped chives or scallions

1½ cups chow mein noodles

½ cup sliced almonds, toasted

1. Combine the vinegars, sugar, sesame seed oil, and gingerroot in a small bowl or lidded jar and stir or shake until the sugar is dissolved. Set aside.

2. Tear the chicken with your hands into tiny shredded pieces. Combine the pieces in a large salad bowl with the lettuce, carrots, and chives. Just before serving, pour the dressing over the salad and toss until thoroughly mixed. Sprinkle with chow mein noodles and almonds. Serve immediately.

Note　See page 45 for directions for shredding vegetables.

The Best Part of the Chicken Breast

The tender meat of the chicken tenderloin is considered the best part of the chicken. In Chinese families where the elderly are revered, this special part is often saved for the grandparents. But nothing is wasted in China — even the tendon that is removed from the tenderloin has its place. It is saved by placing it in an out-of-the-way place like the kitchen window to dry. Then it is deep-fried in hot oil until it puffs up, much like pork rind, and used to garnish dishes.

Cold Cucumber Salad
with Chicken Shreds

Serves 4 to 6 as part of a multicourse meal

*T*his dish was often served at our dinner table, especially during the summer, and it was one of my first potluck contributions when I was in school. If you have any leftover roast chicken or turkey, use it here.

祿

1 long seedless cucumber or 1 pound regular cucumbers
¼ cup smooth peanut butter
½ teaspoon salt, or to taste
1 tablespoon sesame seed oil
½ cup shredded cooked chicken or turkey

1. Wash the seedless cucumber, split in half lengthwise, and slice on the diagonal, ¼ inch thick. If using regular cucumbers, partially peel, leaving strips of green skin, split in half lengthwise, and with a teaspoon scoop out the seeds and discard. Slice on the diagonal, ¼ inch thick.

2. In a small bowl, gradually stir ¼ cup cold water into the peanut butter and mix with a rubber spatula to make a smooth paste. Add the salt and sesame seed oil. Set aside.

3. When ready to serve, mix the cucumber slices with the shredded chicken and peanut dressing.

Shanghai Red-cooked Duck

**Serves 4 to 5, or 6 to 8 as part of a
multicourse meal**

M y late father loved to have this dish in the traditional manner with Red-mouthed
Green Parrot (page 271) and Chinese Steamed Bread (page 122) to soak up the
delicious soy sauce gravy. When he moved to Hawaii for health reasons and would
return to Boston for visits, I often prepared this for him.

I also like to make this dish for dinner parties since it can be prepared in advance and kept warm or made a day ahead and warmed up. The Chinese do not use
knives at the table, even when a whole duckling is served; they pull off pieces with
chopsticks. For company, I cut pieces off the duck so everyone can pick up tasty morsels of duck without a struggle.

1 duckling, thawed if frozen (4 to 5 pounds)
½ cup sugar
1 tablespoon dry sherry
¾ cup dark soy sauce
8 scallions, green and white parts, cut into 3 pieces
2 slices unpeeled gingerroot, 1 × ⅛ inch each
3 whole star anise

1.   Remove and discard any large pieces of fat from the cavity. Carefully
lower the duckling and the giblets into a large pot of boiling water and let
soak 2 to 3 minutes until the skin shrinks and is covered with goose bumps.
This will clean the duck and open the pores. Drain and pull out any pinfeathers
with tweezers. Rinse and drain the bird thoroughly.

2.   Combine the sugar, sherry, soy sauce, and ½ cup water in a small
bowl. Stir to dissolve the sugar.

3.   Put the scallions, gingerroot, star anise, and giblets in the bottom of
a heavy oval pot or Dutch oven that will just hold the whole bird comfortably.
Place the duckling, breast side down, in the pot and pour the soy sauce mixture
over. Cover the pot and bring to a boil.

(continued)

4. Reduce the heat to low and simmer for 1½ to 2 hours, or until the duckling is tender. Halfway through cooking, turn the duckling over so the breast is facing up. If much of the liquid has evaporated, add another ½ cup of water. Test if the duckling is done by piercing the thigh with a chopstick. If it goes in easily, the bird is done.

5. When the duck is ready, remove the cover and skim off the fat with a spoon or bulb baster. Turn the heat to medium and baste the duck frequently for 15 minutes, or until the skin becomes dark brown and about ½ to 1 cup of liquid remains. Transfer the duckling and the liquid to a large oval platter with enough depth to hold the liquid. Or serve directly from the cooking pot. Remove and discard the gingerroot and star anise if desired. Serve hot.

禧

Pork

Pork is the national meat of China. When we say *rou,* which means meat, we mean pork; the words are synonymous. Other meats are described as beef meat or sheep meat, but pork is so universal it doesn't need a modifier.

The reason for pork's popularity is a practical one. Land in China is scarce and valuable but pigs are easy to raise on small plots. Every household can raise its own pigs in the backyard.

Pork works well in Chinese dishes. It has a mild taste that does not interfere with milder sauces and light soups. It also has a smooth texture that is not fibrous, so it is a good choice for quick cooking such as stir-frying.

My mother's name is a good example of how ubiquitous pork is to the Chinese. Her name in Chinese is *Liao Jia Ai* 廖家艾 . Chinese women retain their maiden name throughout their life, even after marriage. Married women may be called Mrs. So-and-So, but when they are called by their own name, it's always their maiden name. My mother's middle name, which is part of her given name, is the character *Jia* 家, which means house or home. If the character is taken apart and examined, the radical or top portion of the ideogram looks like the roof of a house with a chimney 宀 . The character that is under the roof is the literary term word for pig 豕. I find it significant that the word for home uses the ideogram of a pig under a roof. Doesn't "A pig in every home" sound a little like the Chinese version of "A chicken in every pot"?

I like to use boneless lean pork chops when I need a small amount of meat. I buy the chops and freeze them individually so they don't stick together.

This way I can take out only as much as I need. Pork tenderloin is another lean cut I like to use. It has very little fat and is easy to cut into slices, cubes, or medallions.

The Chinese like to eat pork fat. The thick fat under the skin in the pork shoulder, which is used for Shanghai Ham, has always been considered a delicacy. Much of that tradition comes from the need for extra calories in a land where famine was chronic. Of course, we know now that animal fat is very high in cholesterol and is not healthy to eat. For health reasons everyone, even in China, is now well aware that excess consumption of animal fat is not good for you. Choose lean meat and trim it well before cooking.

Pork Shreds *with Green Beans*

Serves 3 to 4, or 5 to 6 as part of a multicourse meal

*M*y husband and I are partial to green beans in season. In this dish, they are practically a meal-in-one.

健康

1 pound green beans

1 cup shredded lean pork (about ½ pound)

1 teaspoon dry sherry

2 teaspoons cornstarch

2 tablespoons dark soy sauce

3 tablespoons canola, corn, or peanut oil

1 cup thinly sliced onion

1 slice unpeeled gingerroot, 1 × ⅛ inch

½ cup water

Salt to taste

1.   Snap the ends from the green beans and break them into 2-inch pieces. Wash and drain thoroughly.

2.   Place the pork in a bowl, stir in the sherry, cornstarch, and soy sauce, and mix well. Set aside.

3.   Heat 2 tablespoons of the oil in a wok or stir-fry pan over high heat. Add the gingerroot and stir a few times until the oil is hot and the gingerroot sizzles. Add the onion to the pan and stir-fry for 1 minute. Stir up the pork again and pour it into the pan. Stir-fry for about 3 minutes, or until pork is cooked through. Transfer the meat and onions to a platter.

4.   Add the remaining tablespoon of oil to the same pan and stir in the green beans. Stir-fry for about 1 minute. Add the water, stir, bring to a boil, and cover. Reduce the heat to medium-low and cook, covered, for 9 to 12 minutes, depending upon how crisp you like your beans. Stir occasionally for even cooking.

5.   Return the meat to the pan and stir thoroughly until the pork and gravy are well mixed into the beans. Taste and add salt, if desired. Discard the gingerroot, if desired, and transfer to a serving platter. Serve hot.

Note   See page 44 for directions for shredding the pork.

Moo Shi Pork

Serves 4, or enough to fill about 12 pancakes

Moo Shi refers to the fragrant yellow flowers of the sweet olive tree (Osmanthus fragrans), which are used in China as a flavoring, because the scrambled eggs in this dish are believed to resemble the tiny flowers. In China, only wood ears and golden needles are used in the dish. Restaurants in this country add fresh mushrooms, bamboo shoots, cabbage, and sometimes bean thread. I have given my recipe, which is enriched with bean sprouts, cabbage, and mushrooms, because that's the one I prefer.

Moo Shi Pork is served with Mandarin Pancakes (page 118), sometimes called "doilies" because of their delicate composition. Hoisin sauce is spread on a pancake, 3 or 4 tablespoons of Moo Shi are placed in a strip down the middle, and the pancake is rolled up and eaten. Don't overfill the pancake or it will be impossible to eat neatly. The pork is on the dry side so it won't drip out of the pancake. If you don't have time to make your own pancakes, you can purchase them frozen in Asian markets. You can also eat Moo Shi Pork in an unconventional but equally good manner — over steamed rice. In that case, serve a small dish of hoisin sauce as a condiment.

3 tablespoons dried wood ears

¼ cup dried golden needles (about ½ ounce)

½ cup shredded lean pork (about ¼ pound)

1 teaspoon dry sherry

3 tablespoons light soy sauce

1 teaspoon cornstarch

4 tablespoons canola, corn, or peanut oil

2 eggs, beaten

2 slices unpeeled gingerroot, 1 × ⅛ inch each

1½ cups shredded green cabbage (about 5 ounces)

1 cup sliced mushrooms

2 cups bean sprouts (about 6 ounces)

2 scallions, green parts cut into 1-inch pieces, bulbs split in half

1½ teaspoons salt, or to taste

1.   Soak the wood ears and golden needles separately in hot water to cover for 15 minutes, or until soft. Squeeze out the water, clean, rinse, and drain. Remove any tough parts and chop the wood ears coarsely into pieces about ½ inch in size. Cut off the stems of the golden needles if they are tough, and cut in half. Set aside.

2.   Place the pork in a bowl, stir in the sherry, soy sauce, and cornstarch, and mix well. Set aside.

3.   Heat 2 tablespoons of the oil in a wok or stir-fry pan over medium-high heat. When oil is hot, pour in the eggs and scramble into fine pieces. Remove the eggs from the pan. Set aside.

4.   Pour the remaining 2 tablespoons of oil into the same pan and place over high heat. Add the gingerroot and stir a few times until the gingerroot begins to sizzle. Stir up the pork again and pour it into the pan. Add the cabbage and 2 tablespoons of water. Stir about 2 minutes, or until the pork turns color and the cabbage just begins to wilt. Add the mushrooms, bean sprouts, scallions, wood ears, and golden needles. Stir constantly for 1 minute, or until the fresh vegetables are tender and the pork is thoroughly cooked.

5.   Return the eggs to the pan and stir until well mixed. Taste for salt. Discard the gingerroot. Serve hot.

Note   See pages 44–45 for directions for shredding the pork and cabbage.

Bean Sprouts with Shredded Pork and Chinese Chives

Serves 4, or 8 as part of a multicourse meal

C hinese chives are also known as garlic chives because they have a deep garlic flavor. They are easy to grow, but be sure to plant plenty of them since you need to use a whole bunch at a time.

禧

1 cup shredded lean pork (about ½ pound)
2 teaspoons dry sherry
2 teaspoons cornstarch
½ teaspoon sugar
3 tablespoons light soy sauce
¼ pound Chinese chives or scallions
3 tablespoons canola, corn, or peanut oil
2 slices unpeeled gingerroot, 1 × ⅛ inch each
¾ pound bean sprouts (4 heaping cups)

1.   Place the pork in a bowl, stir in the sherry, cornstarch, sugar, and soy sauce, and mix well. Set aside.

2.   If using the chives, trim off and discard the white ends. Wash the leaves thoroughly and cut into 1-inch lengths. If using scallions, trim away root ends and wash the scallions well. Split the bulb and cut the whole scallion, white and green part, into 2-inch pieces.

3.   Pour the oil into a wok or stir-fry pan and place over high heat. Add the gingerroot and stir around the pan until the oil is hot; the gingerroot will sizzle. Stir up the pork again and pour into the pan. Stir constantly until the pork pieces are separated and lose their pink color, about 2 minutes.

4.   Add the chives or scallions and the bean sprouts and stir until the sprouts wilt, 2 to 3 minutes. Discard the gingerroot, if desired. Serve immediately.

健康

Note   See page 44 for directions for shredding the pork.

Pork

Pork Shreds with Bean Thread and Napa Cabbage

Serves 3 to 4, or 5 to 6 as part of a multicourse meal

*B*ean thread, made from mung beans, is also known as cellophane noodles because when it is cooked it becomes transparent. Bean thread has no flavor itself, but it soaks up the flavors of the gravy and other cooking ingredients. Be careful not to overcook the bean thread and be sure to serve the dish as soon as it is ready, or the noodles will become very soft and sticky.

禄

1 cup shredded lean pork (about ½ pound)

1 teaspoon cornstarch

3 tablespoons light soy sauce

1 teaspoon dry sherry

¼ pound bean thread (2 2-ounce packages)

½ pound napa cabbage, about 4 cups

3 tablespoons canola, corn, or peanut oil

1 slice unpeeled gingerroot, 1 × ⅛ inch

⅓ cup thinly sliced scallions

½ cup chicken broth or water

1. Place the pork with the cornstarch, soy sauce, and sherry in a bowl and stir together well. Set aside.

2. Soak the bean thread in hot (not boiling) water until soft. Drain carefully, keeping the strands together, and cut into 6-inch lengths with scissors. Set aside. Wash the cabbage leaves thoroughly, drain and cut into 1½-inch chunks. You should have about 4 cups. Set aside.

3. Pour the oil into a wok or stir-fry pan and place over high heat. Add the gingerroot and stir until the oil is hot; the gingerroot will begin to sizzle. Add the scallions and stir for about 15 seconds. Stir up the pork again and pour into the pan, stirring constantly for about 1 minute. Add the cabbage and stir again for 1 minute.

(continued)

Pork

195

4. Pour the broth into the pan, stir to mix, and cover. Let steam for about 4 minutes. Uncover, reduce the heat to medium, and stir in the softened bean thread. Stir for about 2 minutes, or until the bean thread becomes translucent. Serve immediately.

Note See page 44 for directions for shredding pork.

Shredded Pork with Bean Sprouts and Szechuan Vegetable

Serves 2 to 3, or 4 to 5 as part of a multicourse meal

W*hen Szechuan vegetable, also called Szechuan preserved vegetable, is added to a dish, it gives a distinctive pungent flavor to the other ingredients. It is a very versatile canned condiment with a long shelf life, even after opening. My mother and I keep some on hand at all times.*

1 cup shredded lean pork (about ½ pound)

1 teaspoon cornstarch

1 teaspoon dry sherry

½ cup shredded Szechuan vegetable (page 45)

3 tablespoons canola, corn, or peanut oil

2 slices unpeeled gingerroot, 1 × ⅛ inch each

¾ pound bean sprouts (4 heaping cups)

2 tablespoons light soy sauce, or to taste

1. Place the pork in a bowl, stir in the cornstarch and sherry, and mix well. Set aside.

2. Place the Szechuan vegetable in a strainer and rinse to remove excess salt and chili. Drain well. If not shredded, cut into thin slices, and shred. Set aside.

3. Pour the oil into a wok or stir-fry pan and place the pan over high heat. Add the gingerroot and stir until it begins to sizzle. Stir up the pork again, add to the pan, and cook for about 2 minutes, or until all the pink is gone from the meat. Break the meat up as you stir to keep shreds from sticking together.

4. Add the Szechuan vegetable and the bean sprouts. Stir thoroughly for 1 minute. Drizzle the soy sauce over the mixture and stir until it is well mixed and the bean sprouts are tender-crisp. Discard the gingerroot, if desired. Transfer to a platter. Serve immediately.

健康

Note I always rinse Szechuan vegetable before I use it. If you like a spicier and more savory dish, use it as it comes from the can. Adjust the amount of soy sauce accordingly.

See pages 44–45 for directions for shredding the pork and Szechuan vegetable.

Stir-fried Pork
with Asparagus

**Serves 3 to 4, or 5 to 6 as part of a
multicourse meal**

I keep a few boneless pork chops, individually wrapped, in the freezer for easy last-minute stir-fry dishes like this one. Hoisin sauce lends a delicate sweetness to the sauce, which enhances the natural goodness of fresh asparagus.

福

1 pound asparagus

½ pound lean pork or boneless loin chops

2 teaspoons cornstarch

1 teaspoon sherry

1 tablespoon dark soy sauce

2 tablespoons hoisin sauce

1 teaspoon sugar

3 tablespoons canola, corn, or peanut oil

¼ cup water

1 garlic clove, peeled and sliced

1. Break off or cut the tough ends from the asparagus, trim away the lower scales from the spears, and wash well. Cut on the diagonal into 1½- to 2-inch pieces.

2. Cut the pork into ¼-inch-thick strips the same length as the asparagus. Place in a bowl, stir in the cornstarch and sherry, and mix well. Set aside. Combine the soy sauce, hoisin sauce, and sugar in another bowl. Set aside.

3. Heat 1 tablespoon of the oil in a wok or stir-fry pan over high heat until hot but not smoking. Test by dipping an asparagus into the oil; it should sizzle. Add the asparagus and stir for about 30 seconds, or until they just turn a darker green. Add the water and cover the pan. Cook, covered, over medium heat until tender, 3 to 5 minutes, depending upon the thickness of the spears. Stir occasionally for even cooking. Remove the asparagus and any liquid to a platter.

4. Pour the remaining 2 tablespoons of oil into the same pan, add the garlic, and place over high heat. When the garlic sizzles, stir up the pork again and pour into the pan. Stir constantly until the meat is no longer pink, about 2 to 3 minutes. Add the soy sauce mixture and stir for about 20 seconds, return the asparagus to the pan, and stir another 30 seconds or so, until well mixed. Serve hot.

Chungking Pork

**Serves 3 to 4, or 5 to 6 as part of a
multicourse meal**

*T*his is a classic Szechuan dish named after Chongqing (Chungking), a major city in Szechuan Province. It is also known as Twice-cooked Pork, although the literal translation of the Chinese name is "return the meat to the pan," because the pork is first poached and then stir-fried. I have simplified the recipe, without sacrificing flavor, by eliminating the first cooking.

¾ pound pork tenderloin

2 teaspoons dry sherry

4 teaspoons cornstarch

2 tablespoons fermented black beans, coarsely chopped

1 teaspoon crushed red pepper, or to taste

3 tablespoons hoisin sauce

2 teaspoons dark soy sauce

4 tablespoons canola, corn, or peanut oil

½ pound green cabbage, cut in 1½-inch chunks (about 3 cups)

1 medium green or red bell pepper, seeded, cored, and cut into 1½-inch chunks

3 slices unpeeled gingerroot, 1 × ⅛ inch each

2 garlic cloves, crushed and peeled

(continued)

Pork

1. Slice the tenderloin crosswise ⅛ inch thick. If necessary, freeze briefly first. Place in a bowl, stir in the sherry and 2 teaspoons of the cornstarch, and mix well. Set aside. Dissolve the remaining cornstarch in ¼ cup of water. Set aside.

2. Stir the black beans and crushed red pepper together in a small bowl. Set aside. Combine the hoisin sauce and soy sauce in another small bowl. Set aside.

3. Heat 2 tablespoons of the oil in a wok or stir-fry pan over high heat. When the oil is hot but not smoking, add the cabbage; it should sizzle. Stir-fry for about 3 minutes. Add the peppers and cook for 2 minutes. The cabbage may slightly brown. Remove the vegetables to a plate.

4. Pour the remaining 2 tablespoons of oil into the same pan and place over high heat. Add the gingerroot and garlic and stir around the pan until they become fragrant and begin to sizzle. Do not brown. Stir the pork up again and add to the pan, stirring briskly, until the meat is no longer pink, about 2 to 3 minutes.

5. Stir in the black bean mixture, mix around a few times, add the sauce mixture, and stir a few times to mix. Return the vegetables to the pan, stir, then add the cornstarch slurry, and stir for 30 seconds. Discard the gingerroot and garlic, if desired. Serve hot.

Kan Shao Green Beans with Pork

Serves 4, or 6 as part of a multicourse meal

*K*an shao, which means "dry cook," is a Szechuan style of cooking in which the ingredients are stir-fried over high heat until the liquid has completely reduced. The result is a truly rich and savory dish since the ingredients absorb all the flavors. For a meatless version of this dish, see Kan Shao Green Beans (page 270). The kan shao technique can also be used with eggplant or shrimp.

1 pound green or wax beans

½ cup ground pork or beef (4 ounces)

1 tablespoon dry sherry

1 teaspoon cornstarch

3 tablespoons fermented black beans, coarsely chopped

1 tablespoon minced peeled gingerroot

2 garlic cloves, minced

1 teaspoon crushed red pepper, to taste

3 tablespoons dark soy sauce

1 teaspoon sugar

3 tablespoons canola, corn, or peanut oil

1. Snap the ends and string the beans. Break them into 2-inch lengths. Rinse and set aside to drain in a colander.

2. Mix the meat with the sherry and cornstarch. Set aside.

3. Mix the black beans, gingerroot, garlic, and red pepper in a small dish. Set aside. Combine the soy sauce, sugar, and ½ cup water in another small bowl. Set aside.

4. Heat the oil in a wok or stir-fry pan over medium-high heat. Add the black bean mixture and stir a few times until aromatic. Stir up the meat mixture and pour it into the pan. Turn the heat to high and stir-fry until the meat turns color and separates, about 2 minutes.

5. Add the green beans and the soy sauce mixture. Stir a few times and then reduce the heat to medium. Cook, covered, for 5 minutes. Remove the lid and stir constantly over high heat for about 5 minutes, or until the liquid is almost gone. Serve hot.

Szechuan Stir-fried Eggplant with Pork

Serves 3 to 4, or 5 to 6 as part of a multicourse meal

*A*lthough this dish contains no fish, the eggplant is cooked in the same type of flavorings that are used in the highly savory ''fragrant fish sauce'' of Szechuan (Sichuan) Province. This dish contains very little meat, and you can make it without any meat at all, if you like. If your eggplant is garden fresh, leave the skin on for added texture, otherwise peel it entirely or peel it in strips. Omit the crushed pepper for a less spicy version.

禧

1 to 1¼ pounds eggplant, regular or Asian

1 teaspoon salt

3 tablespoons thinly sliced scallions plus additional for garnish, green and white parts

1 tablespoon minced peeled gingerroot

1 teaspoon minced garlic (about 1 clove)

1 to 3 teaspoons crushed red pepper, or to taste

1 tablespoon Szechuan hot bean sauce

1 tablespoon cider vinegar

1 teaspoon sugar

1 tablespoon dark soy sauce

⅓ cup ground lean pork (3 ounces)

1 tablespoon sherry

1 teaspoon cornstarch for the pork plus 2 teaspoons, dissolved in 1 tablespoon water for sauce

3 tablespoons canola, corn, or peanut oil

1 cup water

1. Wash the eggplant and trim off the stem. Leave the skin on if eggplant is very fresh and the skin tender. Otherwise peel or peel in strips. Quarter the eggplant lengthwise and cut each quarter into 1-inch long pieces. If the eggplant is large, cut it into eighths first; the pieces should be bite size. Place in a colander, sprinkle with salt, toss, and let stand for 20 minutes. Rinse, drain, and pat dry. Set aside.

2.   In a small dish, mix together the 3 tablespoons of scallions, ginger-root, garlic, and red pepper. Set aside. In another small dish, combine the hot bean sauce, vinegar, sugar, and soy sauce. Set aside. In a third bowl, stir together the pork, sherry, and 1 teaspoon cornstarch. Set aside.

3.   Pour the oil into a wok or stir-fry pan and place over high heat. Heat the oil to hot but not smoking. Test by dipping a piece of eggplant into the oil; it should sizzle. Stir the eggplant into the hot oil. The eggplant will initially absorb all the oil but will release it as it cooks. Do not add more oil. Cook, stirring and pressing the eggplant against the bottom of the pan with the back of a spatula, for about 6 minutes, or until it is soft and turns dark. Add the pork and stir-fry until the meat changes color and becomes crumbly. Add the scallion mixture and stir for 1 minute.

4.   Add the bean sauce mixture and water and stir to mix. Cover the pan, reduce the heat to medium, and simmer, stirring occasionally, for 2 to 3 minutes, or until tender. Remove the cover and thicken the sauce with the cornstarch slurry. Transfer to a shallow platter and sprinkle with thinly sliced scallions. Serve hot.

Meat-stuffed Cucumbers

**Serves 4 to 5, or 6 to 8 as part of a
multicourse meal**

豬肉

M y mother often prepared this dish for us when we were young, perhaps because the ingredients are easy to obtain and the finished dish can be kept warm while waiting for stragglers to come to the dinner table. It's a typical family-style recipe that's not served in restaurants. Any leftover ground meat should be formed into small meatballs and cooked alongside the cucumbers.

健康

4 medium cucumbers

¾ pound ground lean pork or beef

½ cup corn flakes or bread crumbs

2 teaspoons dry sherry

3 tablespoons plus 2 teaspoons dark soy sauce

3 tablespoons cornstarch

About ¼ cup all-purpose flour, for dredging

3 tablespoons canola, corn, or peanut oil

½ teaspoon salt, or to taste

1 teaspoon sugar

1. Peel the cucumbers, leaving alternating ½-inch-wide strips of skin behind for color. Trim off about ½ inch from each end and then cut the cucumber into 2-inch pieces. Carefully hollow out the inside by removing the seeds with a teaspoon. Discard the seeds and set the cucumber pieces aside.

2. Place the meat in a bowl. Add the corn flakes, sherry, the 3 tablespoons soy sauce, 2 tablespoons of the cornstarch, and 3 tablespoons water. Stir the mixture together well. Mix the remaining 1 tablespoon cornstarch with ¼ cup of water. Set aside.

3. Tightly fill each cucumber piece with the meat mixture. Spread the meat out at both ends to form a plug to prevent the meat from shrinking back into the cucumber as it cooks. Dip the ends in flour.

4. Pour the oil into a deep skillet and place over high heat. When the oil is hot, place the stuffed cucumbers, meat end down, in the pan and brown well. Turn to brown the other end. Place cucumbers on their side and add 1 cup water, the 2 teaspoons soy sauce, salt, and sugar. Cover and simmer on low heat for 20 to 30 minutes, or until the cucumbers are tender and trans-lucent. Turn occasionally for even cooking.

5.   Remove the cover and baste for 5 minutes. With a slotted spoon, transfer the cucumbers to a heated platter. Skim the fat off the sauce. Turn the heat up to medium and when the gravy boils stir in the cornstarch mixture. Stir until the gravy thickens, then pour it over the cucumbers. Serve hot.

Note   If you are not serving the cucumbers right away, cover the pan and keep hot in a low oven. There are no crisp vegetables that will overcook. The dish also heats up well in the microwave.

Lion's Head

Serves 6 to 8, or 10 as part of a multicourse meal

This famous dish from Yangchow (Yangzhou), near Nanking (Nanjing), is another of my mother's favorites. She used to say that a good Lion's Head should be so tender that it cannot be picked up with chopsticks; you have to use a spoon. Her comments from her book describe the dish well:

"New customers of our restaurant are always surprised about this dish and ask if it is really made from a lion's head. Of course it is not. Chinese people like to put words like dragon, phoenix, or lion into names of dishes, because in Imperial China, dragon and phoenix symbolized emperors and their dishes. So, to use these names indicates the high quality of the food. As for lion, it is the king of the jungle. To use its name means high quality and large size. In the menu, Lion's Head is actually large meatballs, the size of a baseball or tennis ball."

2 pounds ground pork (4 cups)

⅓ cup dark soy sauce plus 1½ tablespoons for the gravy

2 teaspoons dry sherry

2 teaspoons light brown sugar

½ teaspoon salt, or to taste

4 tablespoons cornstarch

2 pounds Chinese cabbage, preferably napa, washed and cut into 2-inch pieces

2 tablespoons canola, corn, or peanut oil

Pork

(continued)

1. Place the meat in a bowl. Add the ⅓ cup of soy sauce, the sherry, 1 teaspoon of the brown sugar, salt, 1 tablespoon of the cornstarch, and ½ cup cold water to the meat. Use your hands to mix together well. Let stand for at least 15 minutes.

2. In a deep plate, mix the remaining 3 tablespoons of cornstarch with 2 tablespoons of cold water into a thin paste. Divide the meat into 8 portions and form each into a ball with your hands.

3. Heat the oil in a stir-fry pan, preferably nonstick, over medium heat. Coat the meatballs with the cornstarch paste, tossing gently between your hands for even coating. They will be sticky and the cornstarch paste watery.

4. Brown the lightly coated meatballs in the hot oil for about 5 minutes, or until evenly browned. Do not crowd the pan; cook in batches, if necessary. Handle the meatballs gently as they will be soft. I find it easiest to use 2 spatulas to turn the meat, carefully loosening the bottom before turning. Transfer each browned piece gently with a slotted spoon to a flameproof casserole. Reserve the oil that is left in the pan for later use.

5. Combine the remaining 1½ tablespoons soy sauce and 1 teaspoon sugar with ½ cup water and add it to the pot with the meatballs. Cover and simmer over low heat for 1½ to 2 hours, or until the meatballs are cooked through.

6. Meanwhile stir the cabbage into the same pan used to brown the meatballs. If necessary add the cabbage in stages, waiting for the first to wilt and make room for the next batch. Cook over medium-high heat for about 5 minutes, or until all the cabbage has wilted.

7. Remove the cover from the casserole and lift the meatballs out with a slotted spoon and place on a dish. Skim the fat from the liquid. Spread the cabbage around the casserole and arrange the meatballs over the cabbage. Simmer, covered, for about 10 minutes to heat through. Serve hot from the casserole.

Note   This is a good dish for entertaining, especially if your meal includes a number of stir-fry dishes. Cook the meatballs the day before. Early on the day you will serve the dish, cook the cabbage with the meatballs and set aside until ready for its last 10 minutes of reheating.

Steamed Meat Cake

**Serves 3 to 4, or 5 to 6 as part of a
multicourse meal**

Steamed Meat Cake and rice are a real Chinese home favorite. I introduced this dish to our New York sales representative, Tom Scafati, one day as we had dinner in New York's Chinatown. In Chinese restaurants the meat cake is sometimes enriched with preserved duck eggs or dried and salted fish, and he was a little leery at first. But it was love at first bite!

禧

1 pound ground pork (2 cups)

½ cup canned water chestnuts, drained and minced

1 tablespoon fermented black beans, minced

1½ tablespoons thinly sliced scallions

2 teaspoons grated peeled gingerroot

1 teaspoon dry sherry

½ teaspoon light brown sugar

1 tablespoon cornstarch

1 egg

1. Use you hands to mix all the ingredients together in a mixing bowl. Press the meat evenly into a 9-inch pie pan or similar heatproof dish with a rim.

2. Place a steamer filled with water over high heat and bring it to a boil as described on page 36. Be sure your steamer is large enough to hold the pan or dish with room for the steam to circulate freely and for you to be able to get the pan out. Place it in the steamer, reduce the heat to medium, and maintain a steady boil. Cover the steamer and cook the meat cake for 10 to 15 minutes, or until the meat is cooked through and has liquid all around it. The time depends on how thick the meat cake is. Test for doneness by using a fork or knife to cut into the center of the cake to see if the meat is cooked. If it is still pink, steam a few minutes more and test again.

3. When the meat cake is done, turn off the heat and remove the plate from the steamer. Serve the meat cake hot, directly from the pan or dish.

Pork

207

Sweet and Sour Pork, Cantonese Style

Serves 2, or 4 as part of a
multicourse meal

*T*he traditional southern Chinese sweet and sour dish is made with much less batter than in this recipe, but this is the one Americans know best. For best results use lean pork that is free of gristle. The batter must be prepared exactly as described and the pork fried twice at a temperature no less than 375°F. to ensure crispness. A deep-fry basket makes it easy to remove the cooked pork from the oil.

The same ingredients and technique can be used with chicken, shrimp, or beef. Cooking times need to be adjusted accordingly.

健康

½ cup peeled and roll-cut carrots (page 46)

1 small green bell pepper, seeded, cored, and cut into 1-inch cubes (½ cup)

½ cup canned pineapple chunks, well drained

½ cup all-purpose flour

¼ cup cornstarch plus 3½ tablespoons dissolved in ⅓ cup water

½ teaspoon baking powder

1 tablespoon beaten egg plus enough water to make ½ cup

1 teaspoon canola, corn, or peanut oil

About ½ pound lean boneless pork chops, cut into 1-inch or smaller cubes (about 1 cup)

1 teaspoon dry sherry

¼ teaspoon salt

Dash black pepper

Canola, corn, or peanut oil, for frying

¾ cup sugar

⅓ cup ketchup

1 tablespoon light soy sauce

¼ teaspoon salt

⅔ cup water

½ cup cider vinegar

Pork

1. In a small saucepan of boiling water, parboil the carrots for 1 minute. Add the green pepper to the same water. As soon as it comes back to a boil, drain the vegetables and rinse in cold water to stop cooking. Add the pineapple to the vegetables and set aside.

2. Combine the flour, ¼ cup cornstarch, baking powder, egg mixture, and oil in a mixing bowl and beat with a wooden spoon until the mixture is a smooth paste. Set aside.

3. In another bowl, stir the pork, sherry, salt, and pepper together. Set aside.

4. In a wok or stir-fry pan, heat 2 inches of oil to a temperature of 375°F. to 400°F. Dip the marinated cubes of pork into the batter to coat completely. Carefully drop the pork into the hot oil, 1 piece at a time. Deep-fry until light golden brown. Remove with a wire skimmer, spread out on paper towels, and let cool. Reserve the oil in the pan. (You may deep-fry the pork to this point in advance and keep it in the refrigerator for a few days or in the freezer. The oil may be strained and kept for a day or two; otherwise use fresh oil for the second frying.)

5. Make the sweet and sour sauce only when ready to proceed with the second frying. Combine the sugar, ketchup, soy sauce, salt, and water in a 2-quart saucepan. Bring to a boil and add the vinegar. When the liquid comes back to a boil, stir in the cornstarch solution. Cook until the sauce thickens. Add the parboiled vegetables and the pineapple to the sauce, then add 1 tablespoon of hot oil from the deep-fry pan to give the sauce a shine.

6. While preparing the sauce, reheat the deep-fry oil to 400°F. for a second frying. Add all the pork to the oil and fry until the pieces are heated and crisped. (Frozen or refrigerated pork should be brought to room temperature before being cooked.) Remove with a wire skimmer and drain on paper towels. (If not ready to serve the dish immediately, you can keep the sauce warm on the stove and the pork warm in a 325°F. oven for 10 minutes, no longer. Put together just before serving.)

7. Put the pork in a deep plate and pour the sweet and sour sauce over. Serve immediately.

Sweet and Sour Pork, Northern Style

豬 肉

Serves 3 to 4, or 5 to 6 as part of a multicourse meal

*T*his traditional northern Chinese version of sweet and sour pork does not require the batter or double deep-frying of the Americanized Cantonese style. Here I've given a recipe for the familiar sweet and sour sauce made with ketchup and, as a variation, a dark sauce made with black Chinkiang vinegar.

福

1 pound lean pork loin

¼ teaspoon pepper

1 egg

1 tablespoon light soy sauce

3 tablespoons cornstarch

⅓ cup white or cider vinegar

⅓ cup sugar

⅓ cup water

2½ tablespoons ketchup

¼ teaspoon salt

1 cup canola, corn, or peanut oil, for frying

1 tablespoon and 2 teaspoons cornstarch dissolved in 3 tablespoons water

1 tablespoon canola, corn, or peanut oil (optional)

1 cup canned pineapple chunks, drained

1. Cut the pork into ¾-inch cubes and toss with the pepper. Stir the egg, soy sauce, and 3 tablespoons cornstarch together in a bowl. Add the pork and stir to coat well. Let stand for 10 minutes.

2. For the sweet and sour sauce, combine the vinegar, sugar, water, ketchup, and salt in a saucepan. Stir together and set on an unlit burner while cooking the pork.

3. Heat the cup of oil in a wok or stir-fry pan to 350°F. Gently drop half of the pork, 1 piece at a time, into the hot oil and fry until light brown and crisp, about 6 minutes. Stir gently with a wire skimmer so all sides brown and the pieces don't stick together. Remove the pork from the oil with the skimmer and spread out on paper towels. Keep warm in a low oven. Bring the oil back to 350°F. and fry the remaining pieces the same way.

4.   Turn on the burner under the sauce to medium. Bring the mixture to a boil and stir in the cornstarch slurry. Continue stirring until the sauce thickens and turns translucent. If desired, add the tablespoon of oil to give the sauce a glaze. Stir thoroughly. Add the pineapple and heat just until warm. Transfer the pork to a serving platter and pour on the hot sauce. Serve immediately.

Variation   Omit the vinegar, ketchup, and pineapple from the sweet and sour sauce and add ¼ cup plus 1 tablespoon Chinkiang vinegar. Prepare as in steps 2 and 4. Sprinkle the finished dish with 2 tablespoons toasted sesame seeds. To toast seeds, spread them on an ungreased baking pan and toast in a 350°F. oven for about 10 minutes, or in a dry skillet over low heat, stirring occasionally, until golden.

Sweet and Sour Spareribs, Shanghai Style

Serves 2, or 4 as part of a multicourse meal

*W*hen *my husband and I visited my mother's ninety-three-year-old sister in Szechuan (Sichuan) Province, she made these ribs for us. So we would feel welcome and at home, she instructed her family to prepare the Liao family's home-style dishes from Jiading, a suburb of Shanghai. These and other wonderful dishes were lovingly and swiftly readied in a tiny six- by six-foot outdoor kitchen with a two-burner bottled gas stove. No oven. The sink, with only cold water, was outside on the other side of the wall. I carefully watched the housekeeper, Er-jie (second sister), prepare the ribs and was able to re-create the dish at home — so well that my husband declared it just as tasty as what we ate in China.*

A very important ingredient in this recipe is the black rice vinegar called Chinkiang vinegar. It is named after the city in which it is brewed. That city, spelled Zhenjiang in pinyin, *is located in the Jiangsu Province, in which my mother's home town, called Jiading, is located. So you see this dish was very specially chosen for our visit. There really is no substitute for this rich, flavorful vinegar. Ask for it in Asian markets.*

1 large egg

1 tablespoon dark soy sauce plus 1 teaspoon for the sauce

2 tablespoons cornstarch plus 2 teaspoons cornstarch, dissolved in 3 tablespoons water

1 pound pork spareribs or baby back ribs, cut across the bone into 1-inch-wide strips (ask your butcher to do this)

1 cup canola, corn, or peanut oil

5 tablespoons Chinkiang vinegar

3 tablespoons sugar

1 teaspoon dry sherry

1 teaspoon sesame seed oil

1.   In a large mixing bowl, lightly beat the egg with 1 tablespoon soy sauce and the 2 tablespoons of cornstarch until it makes a thin paste. Cut between the bones of the ribs to separate. Add to the paste and stir to coat. Let stand for about 15 minutes.

2.   Pour the oil into a wok or stir-fry pan and place over medium-high heat. When the temperature reaches 300°F., carefully add the ribs, a batch at a time, and fry for about 6 minutes, or until they are browned and crisp. Stir gently to keep the ribs from sticking together. Remove with a wire skimmer and place on paper towels. Repeat with remaining ribs.

3.   In a small bowl mix together the vinegar, sugar, sherry, sesame seed oil, the remaining teaspoon of soy sauce, and 3 tablespoons water. Stir until sugar is dissolved. Pour into a clean wok, stir-fry pan, or deep skillet and heat over medium-high heat. When the sauce comes to a boil, add the fried ribs and stir a few times. Add the cornstarch slurry and stir until sauce has thickened and all the ribs are evenly coated. Transfer to a platter. Serve hot.

Spareribs in
Black Bean Sauce

**Serves 3 to 4, or 5 to 6 as part of a
multicourse meal**

M ost people think of spareribs as a long affair calling for a two-fisted eating technique, but the Chinese don't usually serve such large pieces of meat. They cut the meat into small portions that can be handled with chopsticks. Ask your butcher to cut across the bones into 1-inch strips. You can then cut them apart through the meat into separate little pieces at home.

3 tablespoons fermented black beans, coarsely chopped

1 tablespoon dry sherry

2 teaspoons sugar

2 tablespoons light soy sauce

2 teaspoons minced garlic

1 teaspoon crushed red pepper (optional)

1 tablespoon canola, corn, or peanut oil

1½ pounds pork spareribs, trimmed, cut into 1-inch lengths, and ribs separated

1½ teaspoons cornstarch, dissolved in 1 tablespoon water

1. Combine the black beans with the sherry, sugar, soy sauce, garlic, red pepper, and ¾ cup water in a small bowl and mix well. Set aside.

2. Heat the oil in a wok or stir-fry pan over high heat until hot but not smoking. Test by dipping a sparerib into the oil; it should sizzle. Add the spareribs to the hot oil and brown for 4 to 5 minutes. Stir in the black bean mixture, cover, and cook over medium-low heat for 20 to 25 minutes, stirring occasionally, until ribs are cooked. Test by taking out a thick piece of rib and cutting through the meat. If meat is very pink, continue cooking until it tests done.

3. Remove the cover and turn the heat up to medium-high. When the sauce boils, add the cornstarch slurry and stir until the sauce thickens. Serve immediately or set aside and reheat later.

Pork

Shanghai-style Pork Chops

Serves 4

*E*ating a whole pork chop with chopsticks is simple — provided you are adept with them and have no qualms about taking bites out of a piece of meat and then putting it down on your plate while you eat some rice. This dish is clearly not one to serve at banquets, where casual home-style eating habits are deemed inappropriate.

健康

3 tablespoons dark soy sauce

1 tablespoon light brown sugar

½ cup water plus 2 tablespoons

1 tablespoon canola, corn, or peanut oil

4 pork chops, on the bone or boneless, about ¾ inch thick

½ cup thinly sliced onion

1.　In a small bowl, mix together the soy sauce, sugar, and water. Set aside.

2.　Pour the oil into a stir-fry pan with a wide flat bottom or into a 10-inch nonstick skillet and place over medium-high heat. When the oil is hot enough for the meat to sizzle, add the pork chops. Brown on both sides, about 3 minutes per side. Transfer to a plate, leaving the oil and meat juices in the pan.

3.　Stir the onion into the same pan and cook until the edges are lightly browned, 2 to 3 minutes. Return the chops to the pan and pour in the soy sauce mixture. Cover and cook over medium-low heat for 5 minutes. Turn once halfway through cooking for even cooking and flavor.

4.　Remove the cover and baste for 30 seconds. Transfer to a serving platter. Serve hot.

Pork

White-cooked Pork with Garlic Dressing

Serves 4 to 5, or 6 to 8 as part of a multicourse meal

*T*he term *white-cooked refers to cooking in water or broth without any heavy seasoning so that the meat remains light in color. Since such dishes are served cold, they can be prepared a day or two ahead, making them convenient for parties. White-cooked Pork is usually served as an appetizer, but it is a refreshing change on a hot summer's night with a fresh salad of mixed greens.*

福

1¼ to 1½ pounds pork tenderloin or boneless pork loin roast

4 slices unpeeled gingerroot, 1 × ⅛ inch each

2 tablespoons dry sherry

2 scallions, white and green parts, cut into 3-inch pieces

2 garlic cloves, minced

3 tablespoons light soy sauce

1 teaspoon rice vinegar

2 teaspoons light brown sugar

1 teaspoon sesame seed oil

½ teaspoon hot chili oil, or to taste (optional)

2 tablespoons water or reserved cooking juices

Cilantro sprigs, for garnish

1.   Trim away the fat from the pork. Place the meat, gingerroot, sherry, and scallions in a 2½-quart saucepan. Cover with 6 cups of water, or enough to completely cover the meat. Bring to a boil over medium-high heat. Reduce the heat to low and simmer gently, uncovered, for 45 minutes to 1 hour, or until the temperature on an instant-read thermometer registers 150°F. to 160°F. or meat is just evenly pink at center.

2.   Drain the meat, reserving 2 tablespoons of the cooking liquid for the dressing, if desired, and discard the gingerroot and scallions. Cool the meat to room temperature and refrigerate for at least 2 hours or overnight so the meat firms up for easier slicing.

3.   When ready to serve, mix together the garlic, soy sauce, vinegar, sugar, sesame seed oil, hot chili oil, if using, and water or reserved cooking

Pork

216

juices. Slice the chilled meat ⅛ inch thick. Arrange the slices in an overlapping pattern on a platter. Garnish the center of the platter with cilantro sprigs. Just before serving, pour the dressing over the meat or serve it in a small bowl as a dip.

Shanghai Red-cooked Ham

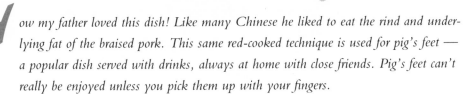

Serves 5 to 6, or 8 to 10 as part of a multicourse meal

How my father loved this dish! Like many Chinese he liked to eat the rind and under-lying fat of the braised pork. This same red-cooked technique is used for pig's feet — a popular dish served with drinks, always at home with close friends. Pig's feet can't really be enjoyed unless you pick them up with your fingers.

4 pounds fresh ham, pork butt, or shoulder
1 cup dark soy sauce
½ cup sugar
1 tablespoon dry sherry
2 slices unpeeled gingerroot, 1 × ⅛ inch each
4 whole star anise
1 cup water

1.   Bring a large pot of water to a boil and carefully lower the pork into the boiling water. Let soak for 2 to 3 minutes. Drain and rinse in cold water.

2.   Place the ham in a Dutch oven or large pot and add all the rest of the ingredients. Bring to a boil over medium-high heat, cover, and reduce the heat to low. Maintain a simmer for about 2 hours or more, until the meat is cooked and tender. Turn the ham over occasionally to encourage even cooking, flavor, and color and replenish water as necessary.

3.   Uncover and increase the heat to medium. Boil gently, basting, until the gravy is reduced to about 1 cup. This will take 15 to 20 minutes. Skim off the fat. Serve hot or cold.

Note   The leftover gravy, called "lu," can be saved and used to cook hard-boiled eggs or to flavor Half Moon Eggs in Soy Sauce (page 253).

Pork

Chinese Cabbage with Sweet Sausage

Serves 3 to 4, or 5 to 6 as part of a multicourse meal

I always keep Chinese sausages and napa cabbage on hand. The sausages, which are air dried, have a pleasantly sweet taste and are available in Asian markets. They keep in the refrigerator for a month or more and in the freezer for much longer. Since napa cabbage keeps a long time in the vegetable crisper, I always have the makings of this emergency dish at my fingertips.

禧

1½ pounds napa cabbage

3 Chinese sausages (about 5 ounces)

3 tablespoons canola, corn, or peanut oil

1 slice unpeeled gingerroot, 1 × ⅛ inch

½ cup Chinese Chicken Broth (page 64) or water

½ teaspoon salt

½ teaspoon sugar

2 teaspoons cornstarch, dissolved in 1 tablespoon water

1. Rinse the outside of the cabbage and remove any yellow or discolored leaves. Split the cabbage in half through the root and then cut each half into quarters. Each quarter should be 3½ to 4 inches wide. If the cabbage is very large, cut each quarter in half again. Trim away the thick root end from the cabbage heart, and then cut the quarters across into 2-inch sections. Set aside.

2. Slice the sausages on the diagonal ¼ inch thick. Set aside.

3. Heat the oil in a wok or stir-fry pan over high heat until hot but not smoking. Test by dipping a piece of sausage into the oil; it should sizzle. Add the sausage and gingerroot to the hot oil and stir a few times. Add the cabbage and stir for about 1 minute. Add the broth, cover the pan, and reduce the heat to medium-high. Simmer for 5 to 8 minutes, or until the cabbage is wilted and tender. Stir occasionally for even cooking.

4. Add the salt, sugar, and cornstarch slurry and stir until the liquid is thickened. Discard the gingerroot, if desired. Serve hot.

Pork

218

牛 肉 羊 肉 *Beef and Lamb*

Neither beef nor lamb is as popular in China as is pork. China, with a land mass larger than that of the United States, has only ten percent arable land. The rest is mountains or desert. With a fifth of the world's population residing in China, how to feed everyone has always been a pressing issue. Cattle and sheep need land to graze, but with so little flat land available for growing crops, the Chinese could not afford to use it for grazing animals. Pound for pound, soy beans provide more protein than beef. The land had to be used to grow food for people, not for animals.

If beef is not easily available, why then are there so many beef recipes? Most of the dishes that use beef originally called for pork and were adapted in America, where beef is king. Beef is rarely used, however, in white-cooked or soup dishes. This is because beef has a stronger and more pronounced flavor than pork. It tastes better in heavier, soy sauce–based sauces and gravies.

Because meat is easily available in this country and as a concession to Western tastes, larger and larger amounts of meat found their way into recipes. In general, the Chinese like to have more vegetables than meat, but here in America many people want the opposite. We learned in our restaurant business that some Westerners would be upset and feel they weren't getting their money's worth unless the dish had a good portion of meat in it. This attitude is changing as more and more nutritional studies show that a diet high in animal protein is not healthy. Although larger portions of meat are used here than in China, each serving is still only about four ounces of beef for each person. And because stir-frying is so flexible, you can further reduce the amount of beef in a recipe and increase the vegetables, if you wish. You will, of course, need to adjust the seasoning and cooking time accordingly.

The cut of beef I prefer for stir-frying is flank steak, although you can use other cuts such as blade, sirloin, or top round. (When I do use blade steak, I trim away the large gristle running through the center of the meat before slicing.) Flank steak is very easy to slice. I usually buy a whole flank steak and slice it all up, using only what I need and freezing the rest in 1- or 2-cup portions for future use. I don't recommend buying meat that is already sliced and packaged for stir-frying. It's often more expensive and usually improperly cut.

Lamb is not a popular meat in China as a whole, mainly because of its strong aroma and flavor. Northern China, however, has many lamb dishes, having been introduced to that meat in the thirteenth century by the invading Mongols and Tartars. Since many of these nomadic invaders were Moslem, their influence is still felt in some of the very fine Moslem restaurants in and around Beijing that feature lamb.

Beef and Scallions in Oyster Sauce

牛肉羊肉

**Serves 3 to 4, or 5 to 6 as part of a
multicourse meal**

C onsider this a master recipe for a beef stir-fry. In place of the scallions, you could use
asparagus or zucchini slices. Harder vegetables, such as broccoli and carrots, should be
parboiled for about a minute before being added.

健康

1 pound flank steak, sliced (page 42)

2 teaspoons cornstarch

1 tablespoon dry sherry

1 teaspoon sugar

2 tablespoons dark soy sauce

3 tablespoons oyster sauce

3 tablespoons canola, corn, or peanut oil

1 slice unpeeled gingerroot, 1 × ⅛ inch

1 garlic clove, crushed and peeled

About 10 scallions, white and green parts, cut into 2-inch lengths, bulb split
    (3 cups)

1 medium red bell pepper, seeded, cored, and sliced into ½-inch strips

1.   Place the beef in a bowl, stir in the cornstarch, sherry, sugar, soy
sauce, and oyster sauce, and mix well. Set aside.

2.   Pour the oil into a wok or stir-fry pan and set over high heat. Add
the gingerroot and garlic and push them around the pan until they sizzle and
the oil is hot. Be careful not to burn the garlic. Stir the meat up again and
pour it into the pan. Stir briskly for about 1 minute, or until the beef loses its
pink color.

3.   Add 2 tablespoons of water to the pan and stir in the scallions and
pepper. Stir over high heat for 2 minutes more, or until the beef is cooked
and the vegetables are tender-crisp. Discard the gingerroot and garlic, if desired. Serve hot.

Beef with Mixed Vegetables

**Serves 4 to 5, or 6 to 8 as part of a
multicourse meal**

*T*his is a good dish to make when your vegetable drawer holds small amounts of many different vegetables. You should have about six to eight cups in all. I've given specific proportions in this recipe, but you can vary them according to what you have on hand. Keep the vegetables in separate bowls to add them one at a time, starting with the vegetables that take longer to cook. Bean sprouts and such leafy vegetables as spinach or watercress don't work well together with chunky vegetables since the ingredients in a Chinese dish should be uniform in shape. I like the heightened flavor fermented black beans give to this dish, but if you have difficulty finding them, just do without.

福

1 pound flank steak, sliced (page 42)
4 tablespoons dark soy sauce
1 tablespoon cornstarch
1 tablespoon dry sherry
1 teaspoon sugar
3 tablespoons canola, corn, or peanut oil
2 cups broccoli florets
1 cup cauliflower florets
½ cup sliced carrots
½ cup water
1 cup red bell pepper chunks
1 cup sliced celery
1 (8-ounce) can sliced water chestnuts, drained (1 cup)
2 slices unpeeled gingerroot, 1 × ⅛ inch each
1 garlic clove, crushed and peeled
1 tablespoon fermented black beans, coarsely chopped (optional)
Salt

1. Place the meat in a bowl, stir in the soy sauce, cornstarch, sherry, and sugar, and mix well. Set aside.

2. Heat 1 tablespoon of the oil in a wok or stir-fry pan over high heat until hot but not smoking. Test by dipping a vegetable into the oil; it should sizzle. Add the broccoli, cauliflower, and carrots to the hot oil and stir-fry for 1 minute. Add ¼ cup of the water. Reduce the heat to medium, stir a few times, and cover the pan. Cook for 2 minutes. Add the pepper, celery, and water chestnuts and stir-fry for another 2 minutes, or until tender-crisp. Transfer the vegetables to a shallow platter.

3. Add the remaining 2 tablespoons of oil to the same pan. Add the gingerroot and garlic and stir around the pan until the oil is hot but not smoking; the gingerroot and garlic will begin to sizzle. Stir up the beef again and pour it into the pan. Stir constantly until the beef is almost cooked, about 2 minutes. Add the remaining ¼ cup water and the black beans, if using. Stir to mix and return the vegetables to the pan. Taste and add salt, if desired. Stir thoroughly. Serve hot.

Note If the sauce seems thinner than you'd like (some vegetables release more liquid than others), thicken with 1 teaspoon cornstarch dissolved in 1 tablespoon water.

See pages 42–43 for directions for slicing the beef.

Beef with Asparagus

Serves 3 to 4, or 5 to 6 as part of a multicourse meal

M y mother taught me to remove the small lower leaves that look like scales on the asparagus spear for a neater appearance and to get rid of any lingering sand or grit. The
very first time I saw an asparagus plant was at the Greenough farm in Massachusetts.
We used to have annual picnics there with the Greenough family and their guests. I
remember meeting a relative of theirs, Beverly Sills, who had not yet been discovered
by the general public, and the composer Dan Pinkham. My mother was particularly
thrilled with the fresh vegetables. We would go into the fields and pick our own vegetables for lunch.

1 pound flank steak, sliced (page 42)

2 teaspoons cornstarch

1 tablespoon dry sherry

2 tablespoons dark soy sauce

½ teaspoon sugar

1 pound asparagus

3 tablespoons canola, corn, or peanut oil

¼ cup water

1 slice unpeeled gingerroot, 1 × ⅛ inch

1 large onion, sliced ½ inch thick (1 cup)

1. Place the beef in a bowl, stir in the cornstarch, sherry, soy sauce,
and sugar, and mix well so the meat is well coated. Set aside.

2. Snap or cut off the tough ends of the asparagus and strip off the small
leaves on the spear up to 2 inches from the tip. Wash the asparagus and cut
on the diagonal into 2-inch pieces.

3. Heat 1 tablespoon of the oil in a wok or stir-fry pan over high heat
until hot but not smoking. Test by dipping a piece of asparagus in the oil; it
should sizzle. Add the asparagus and stir-fry for about 30 seconds. Add the
water. Stir briefly and cover. Cook, covered, for 1 to 2 minutes, just until the
vegetables are tender-crisp. Pour the asparagus onto a serving platter.

4. Put the remaining 2 tablespoons of oil into the same pan, add the gingerroot and stir around the pan until it begins to sizzle. Stir in the onion and cook for about 1 minute, stirring constantly. The onions should wilt but not brown. Stir up the beef again and turn it all into the pan. Stir constantly. When the beef is almost done, about 2 minutes, return the asparagus to the pan and stir thoroughly until reheated. Discard the gingerroot, if desired. Serve immediately.

Beef with Broccoli

Serves 3 to 4, or 5 to 6 as part of a multicourse meal

Chinese restaurants often serve this over a bed of freshly steamed rice as a one-dish meal for people who want a quick lunch or snack, or who are dining alone.

1 pound flank steak, sliced (page 42)

3 tablespoons dark soy sauce

1 tablespoon cornstarch

1 tablespoon dry sherry

1 teaspoon sugar

1 pound broccoli

3 tablespoons canola, corn, or peanut oil

¼ cup water

1 slice unpeeled gingerroot, 1 × ⅛ inch

1 garlic clove, crushed and peeled

½ teaspoon salt, or to taste

(continued)

Beef and

Lamb

1.   Place the beef in a bowl and add the soy sauce, cornstarch, sherry, and sugar. Stir until well mixed. Set aside.

2.   Peel the stalks of the broccoli. Cut off the flower head, leaving a 2-inch or shorter stem on the florets. Roll-cut the stems as described on page 46 and cut the broccoli into bite-size florets about 2 inches long. You should have about 4 cups.

3.   Heat 1 tablespoon of the oil in a wok or stir-fry pan over high heat until the oil is hot but not smoking. Test by dipping a piece of broccoli into the oil; it should sizzle. Add the broccoli and stir constantly for about 30 seconds. Stir in the ¼ cup water, reduce heat to medium, and cover the pan. Continue cooking, stirring occasionally for another minute or two until broccoli is tender-crisp. Remove from the pan and spread out on a plate. Do not pile into a bowl, as the heat generated by the broccoli will overcook the pieces on the bottom.

4.   With the heat still on high, pour the remaining 2 tablespoons of oil into the same pan. Add the gingerroot and garlic and stir around the pan a few seconds until they are fragrant and begin to sizzle. Stir up the beef again and add to the pan. Stir until the meat is almost done, about 2 minutes. Return the broccoli and mix thoroughly. Taste and add salt if necessary. Remove the gingerroot and garlic, if desired. Serve hot on a platter.

牛肉羊肉 Beef with Cauliflower and Tomatoes

Serves 3 to 4, or 5 to 6 as part of a multicourse meal

*Y*ou may never have thought of stir-frying tomatoes, but they work very well as long as they are firm and you do not overcook them. I prefer to use cherry tomatoes in this dish because they stay neat and look so lovely with the white cauliflower.

健康

1 pound flank steak, sliced (page 42)

2 tablespoons dark soy sauce

1 tablespoon cornstarch

1 tablespoon dry sherry

1 teaspoon sugar

¾ pound cauliflower

8 to 10 cherry tomatoes or 2 medium tomatoes

3 tablespoons canola, corn, or peanut oil

¼ cup water

1 slice unpeeled gingerroot, 1 × ⅛ inch

2 tablespoons fermented black beans, chopped

1.   Place the beef in a bowl. Add the soy sauce, cornstarch, sherry, and sugar and stir together. Set aside.

2.   Separate the florets from the stem of the cauliflower and cut them into bite-size pieces. Set aside. Cut the cherry tomatoes in half or cut regular tomatoes into eighths. Set aside.

3.   Heat 1 tablespoon of the oil in a wok or stir-fry pan over high heat until the oil is hot. Add the cauliflower and stir 1 minute. Pour in the water, reduce the heat to medium, and cook, covered, until the cauliflower is tender-crisp, 3 to 5 minutes. Stir occasionally for even cooking. Remove the cauliflower from the pan and spread out on a plate.

4.   Add the remaining 2 tablespoons of oil to the same pan. Place the pan over high heat and add the gingerroot. Stir the gingerroot around the pan until the oil is hot but not smoking and the gingerroot is sizzling. Stir up the beef mixture again and pour it into the pan. Stir until the meat changes color and is almost cooked, about 2 minutes.

5.   Add the black beans and stir to combine. Add the tomatoes, stir about 1 minute, and return the cauliflower to the pan. Mix thoroughly with a couple of big stirs. Transfer to a serving platter and discard the gingerroot, if desired. Serve immediately.

Beef with Green Beans

Serves 3 to 4, or 5 to 6 as part of a
multicourse meal

*y mother was very skilled at choosing the perfect combination of entrees for a meal.
She believed that at least one dish should have a sauce that would go with white rice.
With its rich, savory sauce, this dish is certainly one of them. Fermented black beans
make it especially flavorful.*

1 pound green beans

¾ pound flank steak, sliced (page 42)

2 tablespoons dark soy sauce

1 tablespoon cornstarch

1 tablespoon dry sherry

1 teaspoon sugar

3 tablespoons canola, corn, or peanut oil

¼ cup water

1 slice unpeeled gingerroot, 1 × ⅛ inch

3 tablespoons fermented black beans, coarsely chopped

1. Break off and discard the ends of the beans. Snap the beans in half
or thirds to make pieces about 2½ inches long. Rinse and set aside.

2. Place the beef in a bowl, add the soy sauce, cornstarch, sherry, and
sugar and mix well. Set aside.

3. Heat 1 tablespoon of the oil in a wok or stir-fry pan over high heat
until the oil is hot but not smoking. Test by dipping the tip of a spatula into
the beef mixture and then into the oil; it should sizzle. Add the green beans
and stir for about 1 minute. Add the water and reduce the heat to medium.
Cover the pan and cook the beans for 6 to 9 minutes, or until tender-crisp.
Pour the beans and any liquid onto a platter.

4. Add the remaining 2 tablespoons of oil to the same pan and raise
the heat to high. Add the gingerroot and black beans and stir them around
the pan until they sizzle and become fragrant. Stir the beef mixture up again
and pour it to the pan. Stir for about 2 minutes, or until the beef is no longer
pink.

5.   Return the beans with any liquid on the platter to the pan and stir for 30 seconds, or until thoroughly mixed and heated. Discard the gingerroot, if desired. Serve immediately.

Beef in Oyster Sauce

Serves 3 to 4, or 5 to 6 as part of a multicourse meal

Oyster sauce, a rich, savory condiment made with oyster extract, is widely used in southern Chinese cooking. It makes a wonderful gravy for even the simplest of ingredients, and does wonders for the beef and onions in this recipe. For a very special treat, use a Vidalia onion if available, in place of the yellow onion.

禄

1 pound beef flank steak, sliced (page 42)
1 tablespoon cornstarch
1 tablespoon dry sherry
1 tablespoon dark soy sauce
2 teaspoons sugar
3 tablespoons canola, corn, or peanut oil
1 large onion, peeled and quartered
2 slices unpeeled gingerroot, 1 × ⅛ inch each
2 garlic cloves, crushed and peeled
¼ cup water
4 tablespoons oyster sauce

1.   Place the beef in a bowl, stir in the cornstarch, sherry, soy sauce, and sugar, and mix well. Set aside.

2.   Heat the oil in a wok or stir-fry pan over high heat until hot but not smoking. Test by dipping the tip of a spatula in the beef mixture and then into the oil; it should sizzle. Add the onion, gingerroot, and garlic. Stir constantly for 1 minute. Do not brown.

3.   Stir up the beef mixture again and pour it into the pan. Stir briskly for about 2 minutes, or until the beef is almost done. Add the water and oyster sauce and stir over high heat for 1 minute or less, or until the beef is cooked and the ingredients are well mixed and heated through. Discard the gingerroot and garlic, if desired. Serve immediately.

Beef and

Lamb

Beef with Red Onions

**Serves 3 to 4, or 5 to 6 as part of a
multicourse meal**

My mother, my brother Stephen, and I had this dish many times as we went by train
from Quangzhou (Canton) to Shanghai. As we traveled north, away from the areas
of abundant produce, the train's cooks would turn more and more to root vegetables,
which keep well without refrigeration. You may substitute Spanish or Vidalia onions.

1 pound flank steak, sliced (page 42)

1 tablespoon cornstarch

1 tablespoon dry sherry

3 tablespoons dark soy sauce

1 teaspoon sugar

4 tablespoons canola, corn, or peanut oil

1 slice unpeeled gingerroot, 1 × ⅛ inch

2 medium red onions, peeled and cut into 1-inch chunks (about 2 cups)

1 small red bell pepper, seeded, cored, and cut into 1-inch chunks

¼ cup water or broth (optional)

1.   Place the beef in a bowl, stir in the cornstarch, sherry, soy sauce, and sugar, and mix well. Set aside.

2.   Pour 2 tablespoons of the oil in a wok or stir-fry pan and set over high heat. Add the gingerroot and stir around the pan until the oil is hot; the gingerroot will sizzle. Add the onions and stir for about 30 seconds. Add the pepper and cook, stirring constantly, for another 30 seconds, or until the vegetables are tender-crisp. Remove from the pan and spread out on a plate.

3.   Add the remaining 2 tablespoons of oil to the same pan. When it is hot, stir up the beef mixture again and add it. Stir constantly for about 2 minutes, adding ¼ cup water, if desired, for more gravy and to keep the meat from sticking to the pan. Stir until the meat is almost done. Return the vegetables to the pan and stir for about 30 seconds to mix. Serve hot.

*Beef and

Lamb*

Beef with
Mixed Sweet Peppers

**Serves 3 to 4, or 5 to 6 as part of a
multicourse meal**

I like the colorful contrast that green, red, and yellow bell peppers give to this dish, but
if you are unable to get red or yellow peppers, substitute all green ones.

禧

1 pound beef flank steak, sliced (page 42)

3 tablespoons dark soy sauce

1 tablespoon cornstarch

1 tablespoon dry sherry

1 teaspoon sugar

4 tablespoons canola, corn, or peanut oil

1 green pepper, seeded, cored, and cut into 1-inch chunks

1 red bell pepper, seeded, cored, and cut into 1-inch chunks

1 yellow bell pepper, seeded, cored, and cut into 1-inch chunks

1 slice unpeeled gingerroot, 1 × ⅛ inch

1 (8-ounce) can sliced bamboo shoots, drained (about 1 cup)

½ teaspoon salt, or to taste

1.   Place the beef in a bowl, stir in the soy sauce, cornstarch, dry sherry,
and sugar, and mix well. Set aside.

2.   Heat 2 tablespoons of the oil in a wok or stir-fry pan over high heat
until hot. Test by dipping a spatula into the beef mixture and then into the
oil; it should sizzle. Add the peppers and stir for 1 minute. Transfer to a platter.

3.   Heat the remaining oil in the same pan and add the gingerroot. Stir
a few times until it is fragrant and begins to sizzle. Stir up the beef mixture
again and pour into the pan. Stir constantly for about 2 minutes, or until beef
is almost done. Add the bamboo shoots and return the peppers to the pan.
Stir well for 30 seconds or more to reheat the vegetables. Taste and add salt,
if desired. Serve hot.

Beef with Snow Peas

H ere's an old favorite that everyone seems to love.

健康

1 pound beef flank steak, sliced (page 42)

2 tablespoons dark soy sauce

1 tablespoon dry sherry

1 tablespoon cornstarch

1 teaspoon sugar

3 tablespoons canola, corn, or peanut oil

2 slices unpeeled gingerroot, 1 × ⅛ inch each

¼ cup broth or water (optional)

¼ pound snow peas, ends snapped off and strings removed

1 (8-ounce) can sliced water chestnuts, drained (1 scant cup)

1. Place the beef in a bowl, stir in the soy sauce, sherry, cornstarch, and sugar, and mix well. Set aside.

2. Pour the oil into a wok or stir-fry pan and place over high heat. Add the gingerroot and stir around the pan until the oil is hot; the gingerroot will sizzle. Stir up the beef again and pour it into the hot oil. Stir constantly for about 2 minutes. If the meat sticks to the pan, add a few tablespoons of broth or water, a little at a time. Do not add more than ¼ cup.

3. Add the snow peas and water chestnuts and continue stirring for about 1 minute, or until the snow peas are tender-crisp. Transfer to a platter and remove and discard the gingerroot, if desired. Serve immediately.

Beef with Zucchini

A t the end of the summer, when all the gardeners you know are trying to give away
their surplus zucchini, this stir-fried dish is not only delicious but economical. Small
zucchini are better than large.

福

1 pound flank steak, sliced (page 42)

3 tablespoons dark soy sauce

1 tablespoon cornstarch

1 tablespoon dry sherry

1 teaspoon sugar

2 to 3 tablespoons water

3 tablespoons canola, corn, or peanut oil

1 slice unpeeled gingerroot, 1 × ⅛ inch

1 garlic clove, crushed and peeled

1 medium red onion, peeled and cut into wedges (about 2 cups)

3 small zucchini, sliced ¼ inch thick (about 3 cups)

½ teaspoon salt (optional)

1.   Place the beef in a bowl, stir in the soy sauce, cornstarch, sherry,
and sugar, and mix well. Set aside.

2.   Place the oil in a wok or stir-fry pan and place over high heat. Add
the gingerroot and garlic and stir around the pan with a spatula until they
begin to sizzle. Do not brown. Add the onion and stir constantly for 1 minute.
Stir the beef mixture up again and add to the pan. Cook another minute,
adding water, a tablespoon at a time, to keep the meat from sticking to pan.

3.   Add the zucchini and cook for about 2 minutes, stirring constantly.
Taste and add salt, if desired. Serve hot.

Curried Beef

Serves 3 to 4, or 5 to 6 as part of a multicourse meal

urry is not native to China, but the Chinese do like curried meat dishes. If I am serving a curry dish as a single entree, I make a vegetable side dish and serve plenty of hot white or brown rice with an array of condiments, such as chopped roasted peanuts, cilantro, and a generous bowl of Spicy Mango Chutney (page 330).

1 pound flank steak, sliced (page 42)

4 tablespoons cornstarch

2 tablespoons curry powder

2 teaspoons sugar

1 tablespoon chili powder

2 cups water

3 tablespoons canola, corn, or peanut oil

2 cups sliced onion

2 carrots, peeled and roll-cut (page 46)

1½ teaspoons salt, or to taste

1. Place the meat in a bowl, stir in 1 tablespoon of the cornstarch, and mix well. Set aside.

2. Stir together the curry powder, sugar, and chili powder with ½ cup of the water in a small bowl. Set aside. Mix the remaining 3 tablespoons of cornstarch with another ½ cup of the water. Set aside.

3. Pour the oil into a wok or stir-fry pan and place the pan over high heat. When the oil is hot but not smoking, add the onion and carrots; they should sizzle. Stir for about 2 minutes, add the meat, and stir constantly for about 2 minutes, or until the beef has turned color but is not completely cooked. It should be pink in the center.

4. Add the curry mixture, stir a few times, and add the remaining 1 cup of water. Bring the mixture to a boil, reduce the heat to very low, and simmer gently for 10 minutes. Add salt to taste. Mix the cornstarch solution again, pour it in, and stir until the sauce is thickened. Serve hot.

Spiced Soy Sauce Beef

*M*y mother used to prepare this dish for picnics because it is so good cold. In China, the meat is sliced very thin and arranged in an overlapping design on a cold platter for banquets. The meat is delicious alone or even between slices of bread spread with mayonnaise. It runs the gamut from picnic to banquet!

3 to 3½ pounds pot roast or boneless chuck
1 tablespoon dry sherry
⅓ cup dark soy sauce
2 tablespoons sugar
1 cup water
3 slices unpeeled gingerroot, 1 × ⅛ inch each
2 whole star anise

1.   Trim off the excess fat from the meat. Keep the meat in one piece. Combine the sherry, soy sauce, sugar, and water in a small bowl or measuring cup. Stir until sugar is dissolved.

2.   Place the meat, gingerroot, and star anise in a large heavy pot. Pour the soy sauce mixture over the meat and bring to a boil. Reduce the heat and simmer, covered, for 3 hours or more, until meat is tender but still firm. Turn the meat occasionally for even cooking and to prevent it from sticking to the pan. If the liquid dries out before the beef is tender, add ¼ to ½ cup of water, as needed.

3.   Remove the meat from the pot, reserving the cooking juices. Cool the meat at room temperature until thoroughly cool and firm. Cut the meat into thin slices no longer than 3½ inches; cut in half if longer. Sparingly drizzle the sauce over the meat and serve.

Spicy Beef with Carrots and Celery

Serves 3 to 4, or 5 to 6 as part of a multicourse meal

*T*he traditional method of preparing this Szechuan dish is to deep-fry the shredded beef in oil first. Shredding the meat with the grain gives it a chewy texture and frying makes it dry and crispy. I have adapted the recipe to use a stir-fry method, which is faster and lower in fat — and every bit as delicious.

1 pound flank steak, shredded (see page 42)

2 tablespoons dark soy sauce

1 teaspoon dry sherry

2 teaspoons grated peeled gingerroot

4 tablespoons canola, corn, or peanut oil

1½ cups shredded carrots (about 3 medium)

2 cups shredded celery (about 4 stalks)

1 to 3 teaspoons crushed red pepper, or to taste

½ teaspoon salt, or to taste

1 teaspoon cornstarch, dissolved in 1 tablespoon water

1. Place the beef in a bowl, stir in the soy sauce, sherry, and gingerroot, and mix well. Set aside.

2. Heat the oil in a wok or stir-fry pan over high heat until hot but not smoking. Test by dipping the end of a spatula into the beef mixture and then into the oil; it should sizzle. Stir the beef up again and add it all. Stir briskly for about 2 minutes, or until the shreds separate and are no longer pink. Remove the beef with a slotted spoon to a plate, leaving the liquid in the pan.

3. Return the pan to high heat, add the carrots, and cook for 30 seconds. Add the celery and red pepper and stir for 1 minute. Return the beef to the pan and stir a few times. Taste the gravy and add salt, if desired. Add the cornstarch mixture and stir until the gravy is thickened. Serve immediately.

禄

Note   If you like, substitute ½ to 1 fresh chili, chopped, for the crushed red pepper.

See pages 44–45 for directions for shredding the flank steak and vegetables.

Tangy Stir-fried Beef Salad

Serves 4 to 6

Although this salad is not traditional, it fits right in with our contemporary, health-conscious lifestyle. Serve the salad with chow mein noodles, pita bread, or French bread.

健康

1 pound flank steak, shredded (page 44)

3 tablespoons dark soy sauce

1 tablespoon dry sherry

1½ teaspoons grated peeled gingerroot

2 tablespoons sugar

1 tablespoon cornstarch

3 tablespoons canola, corn, or peanut oil

½ teaspoon crushed red pepper, or more to taste (optional)

4 cups shredded iceberg lettuce

2 cups grated carrots (about 2 medium)

¼ cup chopped chives or scallion, white and green parts

3 tablespoons chopped cilantro or parsley

½ cup rice vinegar

3 tablespoons sugar

2 teaspoons sesame seed oil

1 tablespoon balsamic or red wine vinegar

(continued)

1. Place the beef in a bowl, stir in the soy sauce, sherry, ½ teaspoon of the gingerroot, sugar, and cornstarch, and mix well. Set aside.

2. Heat the oil in a wok or stir-fry pan over high heat. When the oil is hot, add the beef mixture and stir briskly for about 1 minute. Add the red pepper, if using. If the cornstarch begins to stick to the pan, add 2 to 3 tablespoons water and continue stirring until the meat is cooked. Transfer the meat to a colander set over a bowl and allow the meat to drain and cool while preparing the vegetables and dressing. Lightly press meat against the colander to help drain excess moisture.

3. Toss the lettuce, carrots, chives, and cilantro together in a large salad bowl. Set aside.

4. Combine the rice vinegar, sugar, remaining 1 teaspoon of gingerroot, sesame seed oil, and vinegar together in a small bowl or lidded jar. Mix or shake well until the sugar is dissolved.

5. With a slotted spoon, add the beef mixture to the salad greens. Discard excess gravy. Pour on the dressing and toss to mix thoroughly. Serve immediately.

福

Note   See pages 44–45 for directions for shredding the flank steak and lettuce.

Chinese-style Beef Stew

Serves 6 to 8

*T*his stew with lots of root vegetables actually improves with age. After a day in the refrigerator, the flavors meld together and the overall taste is much better than when it was just made. Serve with white or brown rice, noodles, or steamed or crusty bread, the way my husband likes it.

Beef and Lamb

238

2 tablespoons canola, corn, or peanut oil

2 pounds stewing beef, such as chuck or top round, cut into 2-inch cubes

3 cups beef stock or 2 bouillon cubes dissolved in 3 cups hot water

3 tablespoons ketchup

1 tablespoon dry sherry

2 tablespoons dark soy sauce

2 slices unpeeled gingerroot, 1 × ⅛ inch each

2 whole star anise

2 tablespoons light brown sugar

1 garlic clove, crushed and peeled

½ teaspoon ground dried orange peel or a 2-inch square of dried or fresh orange
  peel with no white pith

12 to 14 small white boiling onions (about ½ pound), trimmed and peeled

3 carrots, peeled and roll-cut into 1½-inch lengths (about 2 cups)

2 sweet potatoes, 1 to 1¼ pounds, peeled and cubed into 1½-inch pieces

Salt to taste

3 tablespoons cornstarch, dissolved in ¼ cup water

1.   Pour the oil in a large heavy saucepan or Dutch oven and place over high heat. Pat the meat dry, and when the oil is hot, brown in a single layer. Don't put all the meat in at one time, or the temperature in the pan will drop and the meat will steam instead of sear. Brown all sides. Transfer the browned meat to a bowl as you add new pieces. Continue until all the meat is browned.

2.   Return the meat to the pan and stir in the scallions. Add the stock, ketchup, sherry, soy sauce, gingerroot, star anise, brown sugar, garlic, and orange peel. The meat should be just covered. If not, add more stock or water. Bring to a boil. Cover the pan, reduce the heat, and simmer for 1½ to 2 hours or until the meat is easily pierced with a fork. If you like the meat fork tender, cook for the longer time.

3.   Add the onions, carrots, and sweet potatoes and simmer covered for about 40 minutes or until the vegetables are tender. Remove and discard the orange peel, garlic, gingerroot, and star anise. Taste and add salt if necessary.

4.   Bring the stew back to a boil. Stir in the cornstarch slurry and stir gently until the liquid is lightly thickened. Serve hot.

Note   For easy removal, tie the gingerroot, star anise, garlic, and square of orange peel in a piece of cheesecloth.

Jellied Lamb Loaf

**Serves 6 as a main course or
10 as an appetizer**

*H*ere's another recipe from my mother's Joyce Chen Cook Book. *My mother liked to prepare this unusual dish as a cold appetizer for dinner parties. You can make it days ahead and unmold it the day of the party. Here's what my mother had to say about this dish: "In ancient China, Jellied Lamb with Fine Wine was among the most enjoyable things for poets, philosophers, and scholars. Even now it is still the favorite dish of many people. My father was fond of it. Lamb is supposed to be 'warm' so it is widely relished in winter. The refrigerator, however, has not yet become common in China, so we make jellied lamb only in the winter to have it set firm. We used pig rind for the jelly, added during the cooking. Here, plain gelatin is more convenient."*

禧

2 to 2½ pounds lamb shoulder chops, shanks, or other stew cuts, well trimmed
½ cup light soy sauce
2 tablespoons sugar
1 tablespoon dry sherry
1 medium carrot, washed and cut into 4 pieces
2½ cups water
2 tablespoons unflavored gelatin, softened in 1 cup cold water
½ teaspoon salt, or to taste
1 thinly sliced scallion, white and green parts, or parsley sprigs, for garnish

1.   Put the lamb, soy sauce, sugar, sherry, carrot, and water in a heavy pot or Dutch oven. Stir a few times and bring to a boil. Cover and simmer for 1½ to 2 hours or until the meat is very tender and easily pulled from the bone. Stir occasionally to prevent burning. Remove the pan from the heat and let cool with the cover off.

2.   When the mixture is cool enough to handle, drain the liquid into a measuring cup and skim off the fat. (Or refrigerate the juices until the fat solidifies.) You should have about 2 cups of meat juices. If there is not enough, add water to make 2 cups and return the liquid to the pan.

3.   Pick the meat from the bones and discard the carrot pieces, bones, gristle, cartilage, and large pieces of fat. Break the meat with your hands into small pieces, about ½ inch. Return the meat to the pan and bring to a boil.

4.   Remove from heat and add the softened gelatin and salt. Pour everything into a 9-inch loaf pan to cool. Refrigerate until firm.

5.   Serve cold, cut in slices or squares. Or unmold the loaf for a dramatic presentation by dipping the loaf pan for a second or two in hot water, running a knife around the edges and turning it upside down on an oblong or oval platter. Garnish with scallions or sprigs of parsley.

健康

Lamb with Scallions and Bamboo Shoots

Serves 3 to 4, or 5 to 6 as part of a
multicourse meal

A lthough lamb is not very popular in China, it is sometimes eaten during the winter months because it is believed to help keep the body warm.

福

1 pound boneless lamb loin, sliced (page 42)

2 tablespoons hoisin sauce

2 tablespoons dark soy sauce

1 tablespoon cornstarch

1 tablespoon dry sherry

1 teaspoon sugar

3 tablespoons canola, corn, or peanut oil

2 slices unpeeled gingerroot, 1 × ⅛ inch each

1 garlic clove, crushed

¼ cup water or broth

1 (8-ounce) can sliced bamboo shoots, drained (1 cup)

5 scallions, green and white parts, cut into 2-inch pieces, bulb split

1 teaspoon sesame seed oil

1.   Combine lamb with the hoisin sauce, soy sauce, cornstarch, sherry, and sugar in a bowl and mix well. Set aside.

2.   Pour the oil into a wok or stir-fry pan and place over medium-high heat. Add the gingerroot and garlic and stir around the pan until the oil is hot; they will begin to sizzle. Do not brown.

3.   Stir up the lamb mixture again and pour into the pan. Stir thoroughly for about 1 minute until the lamb begins to change color and separate.

4.   Stir in the water or broth, add the bamboo shoots, and cook for 1 to 2 minutes, stirring constantly, or until the lamb is almost cooked. Add the scallions and stir for 1 to 2 minutes, or until the scallions are wilted and the lamb is fully cooked. Drizzle on the sesame seed oil and give the ingredients a few quick tosses. Discard the gingerroot and garlic, if desired. Remove from the heat. Serve hot.

Bean Curd
and Eggs

In China, bean curd, or tofu, is widely used. It is very nutritious, low in fat, inexpensive, and easy to digest. In a country where meat is scarce and famine chronic, its value as a ready source of protein and calcium is immeasurable. The Western world is beginning to discover bean curd as a healthy substitute for meat with none of the fat and cholesterol.

Bean curd comes in many different textures, forms, and flavors. A good place to sample the extensive variety is at a restaurant that caters to vegetarians. Our Chinese nanny/housekeeper, or *amah* as she was called, is now retired and lives next to a Buddhist monastery on one of the Hong Kong harbor islands. When we visit her, she often takes us to the monastery for a meal. There, skilled vegetarian cooks (the nuns and monks themselves) make dishes look and taste like meat and seafood, all from vegetables and bean curd!

Although freshly made bean curd has a subtle sweet fragrance, generally it has no discernable flavor of its own. Many Westerners, unfamiliar with bean curd, find the bland flavor — and more often the soft texture — unpalatable. But the Chinese never eat bean curd plain; they enjoy it with the flavors it takes on from the sauces and ingredients with which it is cooked. I have seen many converts after they've tasted their first well-prepared bean curd dish!

Most stir-fry dishes use Chinese-style firm bean curd and not the soft Japanese or even softer silken bean curd. Japanese bean curd, however, can be used in some stir-fry dishes, such as Szechuan Spicy Bean Curd, that have no other vegetables. The texture will be very soft and custardlike. Japanese bean curd will *not* tolerate the heat of deep-frying.

Since chickens are popular and easily available, it stands to reason that eggs are also. We use both fresh and preserved eggs for entrees as well as to flavor other dishes. My mother would make a point of getting farm-fresh eggs whenever possible.

We all enjoy preserved duck eggs, available in Asian markets, as a side dish or as a flavoring for other dishes. The best known is the Shanghai specialty, the Hundred-Year-Old Eggs (sometimes hyperbolically called Thousand-Year-Old Eggs). Unshelled eggs are packed in soil, ash, and lime and then coated with rice husks. They are buried for one hundred days and come out looking very different from they way they did when they went in. The egg white becomes a transparent black-brown and the yolk is greenish and sometimes runny. Sounds awful, right? For those who love it, it is very tasty indeed. Shelled and quartered, these eggs are part of elaborate cold platters at banquet feasts. They are also drizzled with soy sauce and sesame seed oil and eaten with breakfast congee. My husband still cringes a bit when I crack open my Hundred-Year-Old Egg for breakfast.

Duck eggs are also preserved in brine. They are frequently added to steamed dishes such as Steamed Meat Cake or hard boiled and eaten at breakfast or as a snack with congee or steamed bread. My mother used to make her own salted eggs at home before they were readily available in stores. Although she also made many of her own pickles and preserves, those large crocks filled with eggs on the counter are what I remember best.

Mushrooms with Bean Curd

**Serves 3 to 4, or 5 to 6 as part of a
multicourse meal**

*T*he delicate texture of this easy dish pairs nicely with those that feature colorful, crisp vegetables. I always keep bean curd on hand in the refrigerator or freezer for quick dishes such as this.

健康

1 pound firm tofu (bean curd)

2 cups fresh mushrooms (about ¾ pound)

2 tablespoons canola, corn, or peanut oil

1 teaspoon salt

1 tablespoon soy sauce

1½ teaspoons cornstarch, dissolved in ½ cup water

1 teaspoon sesame seed oil

2 tablespoons thinly sliced scallions

1.   Drain the tofu, if necessary, and cut it into 1 × ½-inch pieces.

2.   Trim the ends of the mushrooms. Clean the mushrooms with a brush. Rinse quickly in cold water and slice ¼ inch thick. Set aside.

3.   Heat the oil in a wok or stir-fry pan over high heat until hot but not smoking. Test by adding a piece of mushroom to the oil; it should sizzle. Add all the mushrooms and stir for about 2 minutes, or until they turn a darker color. Add the tofu, salt, and soy sauce and cook, stirring constantly, for about 3 minutes. Add the cornstarch slurry and stir until the gravy thickens. Drizzle with sesame seed oil, sprinkle with scallions, and give a couple of big stirs. Serve immediately.

*Bean Curd
and Eggs*

Szechuan Spicy Bean Curd

Serves 3 to 4, or 5 to 6 as part of a
multicourse meal

*T*his classic Szechuan dish is called Ma Po Tofu *in Chinese, a rather unappetizing name. Translated literally, it means pockmarked grandmother's tofu, named after the woman who created it. The soft, Japanese-style tofu (bean curd) is preferred for this dish. It has a smooth, silken consistency when cooked. For a vegetarian dish, omit the ground meat.*

福

1 pound soft tofu (bean curd)
2 tablespoons hot bean paste
1 garlic clove, minced
1 teaspoon grated peeled gingerroot
2 teaspoons dry sherry
1 tablespoon soy sauce
$\frac{1}{2}$ teaspoon crushed red pepper, or to taste
1 teaspoon Szechuan peppercorns, toasted and ground
3 tablespoons canola, corn, or peanut oil
$\frac{1}{2}$ cup ground pork or beef (4 ounces)
1 cup Chinese Chicken Broth (page 64) or water
2 teaspoons cornstarch, dissolved in 2 teaspoons water
2 tablespoons thinly sliced scallions
1 teaspoon sesame seed oil.

1. Drain the tofu and cut it into 1-inch cubes. Set aside. Stir the hot bean paste, garlic, gingerroot, sherry, and soy sauce together in a small bowl. Set aside. Combine the red pepper and ground peppercorns together in another small dish. Set aside.

2. Heat the oil in a wok or stir-fry pan over medium-high heat until hot but not smoking. Stir fry the ground meat until it separates into small pieces. Add the hot bean sauce mixture and stir a few times. Add the broth or water and pepper mixture and stir a few times to mix. Add the tofu. Stir gently to combine and bring the mixture to a boil. Reduce the heat to low and simmer, uncovered, for about 5 to 6 minutes to reduce the liquid by about a quarter.

3.   Add the cornstarch slurry and stir until the sauce is thickened. Pour onto a serving platter and sprinkle with scallions and sesame seed oil. Serve hot.

Bean Curd with Crabmeat

Serves 3 to 4, or 5 to 6 as part of a multicourse meal

A light dish that allows the subtle flavor of crab to come through — a pleasant change from the usual bean curd dishes with dark sauces.

1 pound firm tofu (bean curd)

¾ cup fresh lump or 1 (6-ounce) can crabmeat, drained (about ¾ cup)

1 teaspoon dry sherry

3 tablespoons canola, corn, or vegetable oil

2 slices unpeeled gingerroot, 1 × ⅛ inch each

1 cup canned chicken broth

2 tablespoons cornstarch, dissolved in ¼ cup water

1 egg white, lightly beaten

½ teaspoon salt, or to taste

3 tablespoons thinly sliced scallions

1.   Drain the tofu and cut it into 1-inch cubes. Set aside. Mix the crabmeat with the sherry. Set aside.

2.   Pour the oil into a wok or stir-fry pan and place over medium-high heat. Add the gingerroot and stir around the pan until the oil is hot but not smoking; the gingerroot will begin to sizzle. Add the crabmeat and broth and stir gently. Add the tofu. Simmer over medium-low heat for about 4 minutes.

3.   Raise the heat to high and when the mixture comes to a boil, slowly stir in the cornstarch slurry and stir until thickened. When the mixture just begins to boil again, stir in the egg white. Remove the pan from the heat, taste, and add salt as needed. Discard the gingerroot, if desired. Transfer to a serving dish and sprinkle the scallions over the top. Serve hot.

Bean Curd

and Eggs

Bean Curd with Black Mushrooms and Bamboo Shoots

Serves 3 to 4, or 5 to 6 as part of a multicourse meal

A flavorful vegetarian dish that provides protein. The tender textures contrast well with crispy deep-fried or vegetable dishes.

1 pound firm tofu (bean curd)

1 cup dried black mushrooms (about 1 ounce)

2 tablespoons dark soy sauce

1 tablespoon oyster sauce

1 teaspoon sugar

3 tablespoons canola, corn, or peanut oil

1 (8-ounce) can sliced bamboo shoots, drained (1 cup)

2 scallions, white and green parts, thinly sliced

1. Drain the tofu and place on a cutting board. Slice horizontally in half. Slice each half crosswise into pieces about 1¾ inches long, ½ inch wide, 1 inch thick. Set aside.

2. Soak the mushrooms in hot water to cover for 15 minutes, or until soft. Drain, squeeze out excess water with your hands, and cut off the stems with scissors. Cut the caps in half or if they are 2 inches or larger, into quarters. Set aside.

3. Mix the soy sauce, oyster sauce, sugar, and 2 tablespoons of water in a small dish. Set aside.

4. Heat the oil in a wok or stir-fry pan over medium–high heat. When the oil is hot but not smoking, add the bamboo shoots and mushrooms; they should sizzle. Stir for about 1 minute to heat. Add the tofu and the soy sauce mixture and stir gently so as not to break up the tofu. Stir for about 3 minutes, or until the ingredients are well heated. Transfer to a serving dish and garnish with scallions. Serve hot.

Bean Curd, Family Style

Serves 3 to 4, or 5 to 6 as part of a multicourse meal

*N*utritious, quick, and easy, the soft bean curd contrasts nicely with the mixed vegetables. For variation, use bok choy in place of green cabbage, and fresh mushrooms for the dried black. For a spicy version, add 1 teaspoon crushed red pepper to the hoisin sauce mixture.

1 cup dried black mushrooms (about 8 pieces)
1 pound firm tofu (bean curd)
3 tablespoons hoisin sauce
2 tablespoons dark soy sauce
2 teaspoons cornstarch
3 tablespoons canola, corn, or peanut oil
2 garlic cloves, crushed and peeled
2 slices unpeeled gingerroot, 1 × ⅛ inch each
½ pound green cabbage, cut into 1½-inch chunks (about 3 cups)
1 medium red or green bell pepper, seeded, cored, and cut into 1½-inch chunks
1 (8-ounce) can sliced bamboo shoots, drained (1 cup)

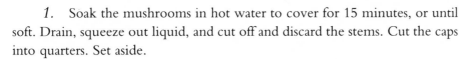

1. Soak the mushrooms in hot water to cover for 15 minutes, or until soft. Drain, squeeze out liquid, and cut off and discard the stems. Cut the caps into quarters. Set aside.

2. Drain the tofu and place on a cutting board. Slice the tofu horizontally into three even pieces. Keeping the pieces together, cut through from corner to corner into four triangles. There should be a total of 12 triangular pieces. Set aside.

3. Mix the hoisin sauce and soy sauce with 2 tablespoons water in a small dish and set aside. Dissolve the cornstarch in ¼ cup water and set aside.

4. Heat the oil in a wok or stir-fry pan over high heat. When the oil is hot, add the garlic and gingerroot and stir until fragrant. Add the cabbage and stir-fry for 3 minutes. Add the peppers, bamboo shoots, and mushrooms, and cook for 2 minutes. It is alright if the cabbage begins to brown in spots.

(continued)

Bean Curd

and Eggs

5.   Add the hoisin sauce mixture and tofu to the pan and cook 2 minutes (If using crushed red pepper, add it), until the tofu is heated through. Stir gently so the tofu does not break into pieces. Stir in the cornstarch mixture and stir another 30 seconds until the ingredients are thoroughly coated. Discard the gingerroot and garlic. Serve immediately.

Fried Bean Curd with Broccoli

Serves 3 to 4, or 5 to 6 as part of a multicourse meal

*S*erve this meatless dish as an entree alone or with white or brown rice for a well-balanced meal. Or use it as a vegetable dish in a multicourse dinner. For deep-frying the bean curd, I use a method I call shallow-frying that calls for only one cup of oil. You can substitute storebought deep-fried bean curd in this recipe.

1 pound firm tofu (bean curd)
1 cup canola, corn, or peanut oil
1 pound broccoli
2 tablespoons dark soy sauce
2 teaspoons dry sherry
2 tablespoons fermented black beans, coarsely chopped
1 teaspoon sugar
2 garlic cloves, peeled and thinly sliced
1 (8-ounce) can sliced bamboo shoots, drained (1 cup)
1 tablespoon cornstarch, dissolved in 2 tablespoons water

1.   Drain the tofu and place on a cutting board. Slice horizontally into three even pieces. Keeping the pieces together, cut through from corner to corner into four triangles. You should have a total of 12 triangles. Blot with paper towels. Set aside on paper towels for 15 minutes or more.

2.   Cut the broccoli into 1½-inch florets. Peel the stalk with a paring knife and roll-cut the stalk into 1½-inch pieces as described on page 46.

Bean Curd

and Eggs

3. Combine the soy sauce, sherry, black beans, sugar, and ½ cup water in a small bowl. Stir until the sugar dissolves. Set aside.

4. Heat the oil in a wok or stir-fry pan over medium-high heat to 350°F. The oil is ready when tofu sizzles when a point is placed in the oil. Slip half the tofu into the hot oil and fry until golden brown. Turn and fry the other side. When both sides are browned (this should take about 10 to 15 minutes), remove from the oil with chopsticks, tongs, or a slotted spatula and place on a plate lined with a double layer of paper towels. Repeat with remaining tofu. Set aside.

5. Reserve 2 tablespoons of the cooking oil and discard the rest. Place 1 tablespoon in the same pan used to cook the tofu or in a clean pan. Heat the oil over high heat until it is hot. Add the broccoli and stir for about 30 seconds. Add ¼ cup water, reduce heat to medium, cover and continue cooking, for another minute or two, or until tender-crisp. Remove and spread on a plate. Set aside.

6. Add the second tablespoon of reserved oil to the same pan and add the garlic. Stir around the pan until fragrant and sizzling, but do not let it burn. Add the bamboo shoots, soy sauce mixture, and fried tofu to the pan and stir-fry over medium-high to high heat for 1 to 2 minutes.

7. Return the broccoli to the pan and stir a few times. When the liquid boils add the cornstarch slurry. Stir until the sauce thickens. Serve hot.

Chilled
Bean Curd Salad

Serves 4 to 6 as a side dish

*T*his country-style dish is traditionally made with lightly mashed bean curd. If you find that unappetizing — as my husband does — cut the bean curd into very small cubes.

福

1 pound fresh soft tofu (bean curd), drained
5 teaspoons light soy sauce
1 teaspoon sesame seed oil
2 tablespoons thinly sliced scallions, green and white parts
1 tablespoon minced dried shrimp (optional)

1.   Blanch the tofu for 1 minute in enough boiling water to cover it. Drain and place in a bowl of ice water for 5 minutes to cool. When cool, drain the bean curd and pat dry with paper towels. Transfer to a shallow serving dish and coarsely crumble it with the back of a fork or cut it into ½-inch cubes.

2.   Add the soy sauce, sesame seed oil, and scallions. Toss a few times and garnish with minced dried shrimp, if desired. Serve cold.

Half Moon Eggs in Soy Sauce

豆腐蛋

**Serves 4 as part of a
multicourse meal**

My mother often made this for family meals when we needed an extra dish. The eggs are cooked just like sunny-side-up eggs, but before the whites set, the eggs are folded over. The yolks should be runny and the edges of the whites crisp. The eggs go well with rice.

禄

1½ tablespoons dark soy sauce
½ tablespoon light brown sugar
4 tablespoons canola, corn, or peanut oil
4 large eggs
1 tablespoon thinly sliced scallions or minced onion

1.   Mix the soy sauce, sugar, and 2 tablespoons of water together in a small bowl. Set aside.

2.   Pour 2 tablespoons of the oil into a nonstick 10-inch skillet and place over medium-high heat. When the oil is hot, break 2 eggs into the skillet, keeping the eggs from running into each other. When the edges of the whites are light brown and the yolks are still soft, fold the eggs over with a spatula so that it forms a half-moon shape. You may need to hold the edges down with the tip of a spatula until the whites fuse together. Transfer the eggs to a platter and fry the remaining 2 eggs in the same manner, adding another tablespoon of oil if necessary. Transfer these eggs to the platter.

3.   Add the scallions to the pan and stir around a few times. Return the fried eggs to the pan and pour the soy sauce mixture over. Shake the pan gently to heat and coat the eggs with sauce. Transfer the eggs and sauce to a serving dish. Serve immediately.

Variation   Flavor the fried eggs with leftover red-cooked sauce from such dishes as Soy Sauce Chicken (page 182), Shanghai Red-cooked Duck (page 187), or Shanghai Red-cooked Ham (page 217).

Bean Curd

and Eggs

Egg Foo Yung, Family Style

Serves 3 to 4, or 5 to 6 as part of a multicourse meal

E gg Foo Yung used to be very popular in Chinese restaurants. Even before I was a teenager, I helped in the family restaurant and packed many an Egg Foo Yung to go. In the restaurant, the eggs were deep-fried into small round pillows and then covered with a simple brown sauce. In my mother's family-style recipe, the eggs are pan-fried into a looser form, more akin to an omelet. It calls for less oil, and the eggs can be served with or without the brown sauce.

The ingredients for the Egg Foo Yung should all be shredded, as described on pages 44–45.

5 large eggs

1 teaspoon salt (if using canned crabmeat, reduce to ½ teaspoon)

1 teaspoon dry sherry

Dash black pepper

½ cup fresh or canned lump crabmeat or shredded cooked pork, chicken, ham, beef, or shrimp

½ cup shredded celery, no leaves

½ cup dried black mushrooms, softened in hot water for 15 minutes, squeezed dry, stems removed, and shredded

1 cup fresh bean sprouts or drained and shredded bamboo shoots

¼ cup thinly sliced onion

3 tablespoons canola, corn, or peanut oil

1. Gently beat the eggs with the salt, sherry, and pepper. Add the crabmeat, celery, black mushrooms, bean sprouts, and onion and mix well.

2. Heat the oil in a nonstick wok or stir-fry pan over medium-high heat until the oil is hot but not smoking. Test by dipping the end of a spatula into the egg mixture and then into the oil; it should sizzle. Add the egg mixture to the hot oil. Let the eggs sit without stirring until the bottom is slightly set but the top is still runny. With a spatula, turn sections of the eggs over. Con-

Bean Curd

and Eggs

tinue turning the eggs until the mixture is set on both sides. Remove to a serving platter. Serve immediately.

健康

Variation   Serve the Egg Foo Yung with a restaurant-style brown sauce. Make the sauce before cooking the eggs.

Mix together 1 cup Chinese Chicken Broth (page 64) plus ½ teaspoon salt or 1 cup of canned chicken broth, ½ teaspoon ketchup, 1½ teaspoons light soy sauce, and 2 tablespoons flour, mixed with 2 tablespoons cold water into a smooth paste, in a saucepan. Cook over medium heat, stirring constantly with a wire whisk. Bring to a boil and stir until the sauce is thickened. Simmer 2 minutes to eliminate the raw taste of the flour. Pour the sauce freely over the cooked eggs.

Egg Garnish

Makes two 10-inch pancakes

*W*hen I was a girl, I would make an egg pancake using this recipe and fold it up to fill *a sandwich, but mostly the recipe is used to make a versatile garnish for salads and soups. It resembles very thin noodles and it works wonderfully for many dishes, such as salads and soups, where you'd like a little color.*

If you use a nonstick skillet, which I prefer, you can use less oil. Too much oil will make it difficult to form a thin pancake since the eggs will slide as you tilt the pan.

2 eggs
½ teaspoon salt
½ teaspoon dry sherry
2 teaspoons canola, corn, or peanut oil

1.   Beat the eggs with the salt and sherry. Heat 1 teaspoon of the oil in a 10- to 11-inch skillet over medium heat and smear it evenly over the bottom of the pan with a paper towel. Pour in half the egg mixture and tip the pan back and forth to spread out the egg into a very thin pancake. Use a spatula to help push the egg to its thinnest. Cook until the edges turn light brown and begin to curl. This will take less than 1 minute.

(continued)

2.   With a spatula, transfer the egg pancake to a cutting board and cut it into 4 even strips. Pile the strips on top of one another, turn sideways, and cut across the strips to make fine shreds. Repeat with the remaining egg mixture and oil.

Mandarin Eggs

豆腐蛋

Serves 3 to 4, or 5 to 6 as part of a multicourse meal

*A*lthough this dish is traditionally made with egg yolks only, I have reworked my mother's original recipe to use whole eggs. The chicken broth thins the eggs so they remain soft and custardlike.

禄

4 large eggs

⅓ cup finely minced canned water chestnuts

1 tablespoon thinly sliced scallion, green and white parts

1½ cups Chinese Chicken Broth (page 64) plus ½ teaspoon salt or canned chicken broth

¼ teaspoon salt to taste

2 tablespoons cornstarch

½ teaspoon dry sherry

4 tablespoons canola, corn, or peanut oil

2 tablespoons minced Smithfield ham

1.   Beat together the eggs, water chestnuts, scallion, broth, salt, cornstarch, and sherry.

2.   Heat the oil in a nonstick stir-fry pan or skillet over high heat until hot but not smoking. Test by dipping the end of a spatula into the egg mixture and then into the oil; it should sizzle. Add the eggs to the hot oil and stir gently but constantly in the same direction until the eggs thicken to form a soft custard, about 4 to 5 minutes. Be sure not to miss the outside edges!

3.   Transfer to a serving platter and garnish with ham. Serve immediately.

Bean Curd

and Eggs

Mock Crab Omelet

Serves 2, or 3 to 4 as part of a
multicourse meal

During our first trip to China after President Nixon opened relations in 1972, we had this omelet at Number One Uncle and Aunt's house in Shanghai. (In China, we refer to our relatives by their relationship vis-à-vis our parents.) My mother was delighted with the dish and developed the recipe to feature on our public television documentary called "Joyce Chen's China."

The dish is designed to taste and look like crab. Freshwater crabs are popular in the winter when they are in season, especially the full-bodied female with eggs. Everyone hopes for those! The carrots resemble the bright orange crab roe; the potatoes, the white crabmeat; and the wood ears, the dark membrane that lines the top shell. And since the Chinese eat crab with a vinegar and ginger dip, the seasonings used are reminiscent of those flavors.

2 medium potatoes, peeled and cut in half (about 1 pound)

1 medium carrot, peeled and cut in thirds

2 tablespoons dried wood ears (about ¼ ounce)

1 teaspoon minced peeled gingerroot

1½ tablespoons cider vinegar

2 large eggs

1 teaspoon dry sherry

3 tablespoons canola, corn, or peanut oil

1 teaspoon salt

1 tablespoon thinly sliced scallions, green parts only

1.   Boil the potatoes and carrots together in a saucepan until tender. Plunge the vegetables into cold water to cool. When cool, mash them coarsely with the back of a fork. The texture should remain somewhat lumpy. Spread out on paper towels to absorb the excess moisture.

2.   Soak the wood ears in 2 cups of hot water for 15 minutes, or until soft. Drain, rinse, and squeeze out excess water. Coarsely chop.

3.   Mix the gingerroot with the vinegar. Set aside. In a separate bowl, beat the eggs with sherry. Set aside.

(continued)

4. Heat the oil and salt in a nonstick stir-fry pan or 10-inch skillet over high heat. When the oil is hot and fragrant, add the potatoes and carrots and stir gently. Avoid vigorous stirring as this will make the potatoes mushy. Cook for no more than 2 minutes. Stir in the wood ears and scallions, add the beaten eggs, and stir them into the vegetables gently but thoroughly until the mixture begins to become firm. Pour the vinegar and ginger mixture over the eggs and stir to mix thoroughly. The eggs should be soft, so be careful not to overcook them. Transfer the eggs to a platter. Serve immediately.

Chinese Omelet

with Crabmeat

Serves 3 to 4, or 5 to 6 as part of a
multicourse meal

 Chinese omelet is more like loose scrambled eggs than a formed omelet in the Western sense. If you don't like runny eggs, cook them a little longer.

1 (6-ounce) can crabmeat (about ¾ cup)

6 large eggs

1 teaspoon dry sherry

1 teaspoon salt

1 tablespoon thinly sliced scallions, white and green parts

4 tablespoons canola, corn, or peanut oil

1. Place the crabmeat with the liquid from the can in a mixing bowl. With your hands, separate the crabmeat into flakes and discard any pieces of cartilage. Set aside.

2. Beat the eggs with the sherry, salt and scallions until well mixed but not foamy. I use a pair of chopsticks or a fork so as not to overbeat. Add the crabmeat and mix together thoroughly.

3. Heat the oil in a wok or stir-fry pan, preferably nonstick, over high heat until hot but not smoking. Test by dipping the tip of the spatula into the egg mixture and then into the oil; it should sizzle. Add the eggs to the hot oil and with a spatula turn the eggs from the edges to the center, allowing the uncooked egg mixture to run onto the exposed pan surface. Continue until the eggs are lightly set but not dry. Remove from the heat. Serve immediately.

*V*egetables 蔬菜

egetables are perhaps the most important ingredient in Chinese cooking. They can be found in just about every dish. The Chinese are particularly fond of leafy greens such as spinach, water spinach, mustard greens, watercress, and leafy Chinese cabbages. As a child I never understood why other children hated spinach. We loved the way my mother prepared it. The first time I had spinach cooked Western-style at school — soft, mushy, and tasteless — I understood why my friends had such an abhorrence for spinach.

Any vegetable that is found in a supermarket can be used for Chinese cooking. Specialty Chinese vegetables are interesting and nice to have when available, but they are not necessary for good home cooking. Freshly picked vegetables are far superior to ones that have been out of the ground for days or even weeks; they are much preferred by the Chinese. My mother was thrilled when she could get fresh-picked vegetables and fruits; she loved to visit local farms. One of our favorites is probably the only farm left in Belmont, a suburb of Boston. The farmer, Angelo Sergi, picked his vegetables daily, and if he didn't have what my mother wanted in the stand, he let her go out into the fields and pick it herself.

It was at Sergi's farm that we would also pick wild greens. My mother's favorite is green amaranth (*Amaranthus retroflexus*), commonly known as pig weed. We called it fox tails because of its insignificant green flowers that grew in long spikes. (Do not confuse this with foxglove or *Digitalis,* a flowering garden plant that is poisonous.) My mother would stir-fry the freshly picked amaranth greens with garlic and a little oil.

Another wild green we would pick was shepherd's-purse (*Capsella Bursa-pastoris*), so called because the heart-shaped seedpods that line the flower spikes resemble the leather pouches shepherds used to carry. There was a particularly good growth of shepherd's purse in front of our local post office. My mother and I would sometimes go there to get some of the tender young greens. They would be blanched, chopped up, and added to our Peking Ravioli or wonton filling.

A selection of recipes from this chapter will make a satisfying vegetarian meal. Because vegetables are so prominent in many Chinese dishes, there are recipes in the meat chapters that can be made without the meat. I have sometimes made such suggestions.

Stir-fried Asparagus

Serves 4, or 5 to 6 as part of a multicourse meal

*A*lthough the asparagus is not indigenous to China, the Chinese have added it to their repertoire and use it in many dishes. This simple stir-fry relies on the sweet freshness of springtime asparagus for flavor rather than on heavy spices. It's a dish that pairs well with Western foods like broiled or grilled fish or chicken.

健康

1 pound asparagus

2 tablespoons canola, corn, or peanut oil

½ teaspoon salt, or to taste

2 garlic cloves, thinly sliced

½ cup water

1 red bell pepper, seeded, cored, and sliced into 2-inch-long julienne strips

1¼ teaspoons cornstarch, dissolved in 1 tablespoon water

1.   Cut or snap the tough ends from the asparagus. Remove the leaf scales from the bottom of the spears. Wash thoroughly under running water and drain. Roll-cut into 1½-inch lengths as described on page 46.

2.   Pour the oil into a wok or stir-fry pan and place over high heat. Add the salt and garlic and stir around the pan until the oil is hot; the garlic will begin to sizzle. Add the asparagus and stir for about 1 minute. Pour in the water and cook, covered, over medium-high heat for about 2 minutes, or until the asparagus are tender-crisp.

3.   Stir in the red pepper and stir for 30 seconds to 1 minute, or until the pepper loses its raw look. Stir up the cornstarch slurry and pour it into the pan, stirring until the liquid thickens. Remove from the heat, taste, and add salt as desired. Serve hot.

Broccoli in Oyster Sauce

**Serves 4 to 5, or 6 to 8 as part of a
multicourse meal**

*T*he rich flavors of the oyster sauce and dark soy sauce will not overpower the broccoli. For an interesting variation, try using Chinese broccoli, available in Asian markets.

福

1½ pounds broccoli

3 tablespoons oyster sauce

1 tablespoon dark soy sauce

1 teaspoon sugar

1 teaspoon cornstarch

2 tablespoons canola, corn, or peanut oil

1 garlic clove, crushed and peeled

¼ cup Chinese Chicken Broth (page 64) or water

1.   Cut 2-inch-long florets from the top of the broccoli. Peel the tough outer skin from the stalks and roll-cut into 2-inch lengths as described on page 46.

2.   Blend the oyster sauce, soy sauce, sugar, cornstarch, and 3 tablespoons water together in a small bowl. Set aside.

3.   Pour the oil into a wok or stir-fry pan and place over high heat. Add the garlic and stir around the pan until the oil is hot; the garlic will sizzle. Turn the broccoli into the pan, stirring until the pieces turn a darker green. Pour the broth into the pan, reduce the heat to medium, and cover. Steam the broccoli for about 4 to 6 minutes, or until tender-crisp.

4.   Stir in the oyster sauce mixture. Stir until the sauce has thickened and the broccoli is completely coated. Discard the garlic, if desired. Transfer to a platter. Serve immediately.

Stir-fried Cauliflower and Broccoli

Serves 3 to 4, or 5 to 6 as part of a
multicourse meal

*T*he contrasting colors of these two vegetables make a simple dish special. You could also use only one vegetable with, perhaps, a garnish of two tablespoons minced Smithfield ham for color and flavor.

禄

½ pound cauliflower

½ pound broccoli

2 tablespoons canola, corn, or peanut oil

1 garlic clove, crushed and peeled

½ cup Chinese Chicken Broth (page 64) or water

½ teaspoon salt

2 teaspoons cornstarch, dissolved in 2 tablespoons water

1.   Cut the cauliflower and broccoli into bite-size 2-inch-long florets. Peel the stem of the broccoli and roll-cut as described on page 46 to the same length as the florets.

2.   Pour the oil into a wok or stir-fry pan and place over high heat. Add the garlic and stir around the pan until the oil is hot but not smoking; the garlic will begin to sizzle. Add the cauliflower and stir for about 2 minutes. Add the broccoli and stir for 1 minute.

3.   Add the broth or water and cover the pan. Turn the heat to medium and simmer for 4 to 6 minutes, or until the vegetables are tender-crisp. Stir occasionally. If you like the vegetables more tender, cook them longer.

4.   Uncover the pan, sprinkle with salt, and stir to mix thoroughly. Turn the heat to high, add the cornstarch slurry, and stir until the gravy thickens. Discard the garlic clove, if desired. Serve hot.

Vegetables

Stir-fried Napa Cabbage

**Serves 4, or 5 to 6 as part of a
multicourse meal**

*H*ere is a simple family-style vegetable dish. You could use other kinds of Chinese cabbage, but I prefer napa cabbage, not only for its delicate flavor and texture but also because it keeps very well in the refrigerator and makes a perfect emergency ingredient.

壽

1 pound napa cabbage

2 tablespoons canola, corn, or peanut oil

2 slices unpeeled gingerroot, 1 × ⅛ inch each

1 chicken bouillon cube, dissolved in ½ cup hot water

1½ teaspoons cornstarch, dissolved in 2 tablespoons water

1. Remove and discard any tough, wilted, or discolored leaves from the cabbage. Cut the cabbage lengthwise into 2-inch-wide wedges. Cut out the core and cut the wedges crosswise into 3-inch lengths. Separate the leaves. Set aside.

2. Pour the oil into a wok or stir-fry pan and place over high heat. Add the gingerroot to the oil and stir around the pan until the oil is hot; the gingerroot will sizzle. Add the cabbage and stir for about 2 minutes.

3. Pour the chicken broth into the pan, stir a couple of times, and reduce the heat to medium. Cover and cook for another 2 minutes, stirring occasionally, or until the desired tenderness is achieved. If too much of the liquid evaporates add a few tablespoons of water. There must be liquid in the pan to bind with the cornstarch.

4. Uncover the pan, turn the heat to high, and add the cornstarch slurry. Stir until the liquid is thickened. Discard the gingerroot, if desired. Serve hot.

Variation   Add ¼ cup dried shrimp, rinsed and drained, to the cabbage when adding the chicken bouillon in step 3.

Vegetables

Ginger-glazed Carrots
and Parsnips

Serves 4 as a side dish

*T*he natural sweetness of these root vegetables is enhanced by the light ginger glaze. This dish is a particularly good accompaniment for roast pork or poultry.

健康

2 tablespoons canola, corn, or peanut oil

4 medium carrots, peeled and roll-cut into 1-inch pieces (page 46)

3 medium parsnips, peeled and roll-cut into 1-inch pieces (page 46)

¼ cup water

¼ teaspoon salt

4 teaspoons light brown sugar

1 teaspoon grated peeled gingerroot

Freshly ground black pepper

1 tablespoon chopped parsley

1. Heat the oil in a wok or stir-fry pan over high heat until hot but not smoking. Add the vegetables; they should sizzle. Stir for about 2 minutes. Add the water, reduce heat to medium, cover, and cook, stirring occasionally for even cooking, for 5 to 6 minutes, or until the vegetables are tender. A fork should go in easily with just a little resistance.

2. Uncover the pan and sprinkle on the salt, sugar, gingerroot, and a dash of pepper. Turn the heat to high and stir for about 1 to 2 minutes to reduce the liquid to a glaze. Transfer to a shallow platter and sprinkle with parsley. Serve immediately.

Shanghai Bok Choy
with Black Mushrooms

**Serves 2, or 3 to 4 as part of a
multicourse meal**

*Y*ou'll have to make a trip to a Chinese market to find Shanghai bok choy but these *tender little cabbages with their lovely jade color and delicate flavor are well worth the effort. In China, the hearts of Shanghai bok choy are considered a delicacy and are often served at banquets.*

福

8 dried black mushrooms
1 tablespoon soy sauce
Dash black pepper
1 teaspoon sugar
$\frac{1}{2}$ teaspoon dry sherry
$\frac{1}{2}$ teaspoon salt
$\frac{1}{2}$ pound Shanghai bok choy
2 tablespoons canola, corn, or peanut oil
1 slice unpeeled gingerroot, 1 × $\frac{1}{8}$ inch
1 (8-ounce) can sliced bamboo shoots, drained (1 cup) (optional)
2 teaspoons cornstarch, dissolved in 2 tablespoons water

1.   Soak the mushrooms in 1¼ cups hot water for 15 minutes to soften. Squeeze out the excess water with your hands. With scissors, trim off and discard the woody stems. Strain the soaking liquid, reserving 1 cup. Add the soy sauce, pepper, sugar, sherry, and salt to the mushroom liquid. Set the mushrooms and the liquid aside separately.

2.   Trim away and discard any yellow or discolored leaves from the bok choy. Clean thoroughly under running water. Pull the larger outer leaves from the head one by one and cut them in half or thirds lengthwise. When you reach the very tiny center leaves, cut the whole core in half or quarters to match the size of the leaves.

3.   Bring 6 cups of water to a boil and blanch the cabbage for 2 minutes. Drain and cool immediately in cold water to refresh and stop the cooking. Gently squeeze out the excess water and set the leaves aside.

4.   Pour the oil into a wok or stir-fry pan and place over medium-high heat. Add the gingerroot and stir around the pan until the oil is hot; the gingerroot will sizzle. Add the mushrooms, bamboo shoots, cabbage leaves, and the mushroom liquid. Stir until boiling. Add the cornstarch slurry. Stir until the sauce thickens. Taste and add salt, if necessary. Discard the gingerroot. Serve immediately.

Note   For a banquet-style presentation, place the cabbage leaves in a sunburst shape on a platter. Pile the mushrooms and bamboo shoots in the center. Serve hot.

Stir-fried Celery

C elery is a terrific stir-fry ingredient — crisp, low in fat, high in fiber, economical, and usually on hand in the refrigerator. Carrots add a bright color contrast to the light green celery stalks. You could also use a red bell pepper.

禧

1 pound celery
2 tablespoons canola, corn, or peanut oil
1 garlic clove, thinly sliced
½ teaspoon salt
3 carrots, peeled and cut on the diagonal ¼ inch thick
½ cup canned chicken broth
1 teaspoon cornstarch, dissolved in 1 tablespoon water

1.   Separate the celery stalks and wash thoroughly, paying special attention to grit in the grooves on the outside of the stalks. Trim off the leaves and a little from the root end of each stalk. String the tough outer stalks. Slice each stalk on the diagonal ½ inch thick. You should have a little more than 4 cups.

2.   Pour the oil into a wok or stir-fry pan and place over medium-high heat. Add the garlic and salt and stir around the pan until the oil is hot; the garlic will begin to sizzle. Add the carrots and cook for about 1 minute.

3.   Add the celery and broth, lower the heat to medium, and simmer, covered, for 3 to 5 minutes, or until the vegetables are tender-crisp. Stir occasionally for even cooking. Uncover and add the cornstarch slurry. Stir until the liquid thickens. Taste and add salt, if desired. Serve hot.

健康

Variation   Add ¼ cup dried shrimp, rinsed and drained, to the pan when adding the celery in step 3. Reduce the salt in step 2.

Stir-fried Green Beans

**Serves 3 to 4, or 5 to 6 as part of a
multicourse meal**

Home-style Chinese cooking is surprisingly simple, often using just a few ingredients. These green beans, for example, are cooked with a minimal amount of seasonings, relying instead on the natural flavor of the vegetable. This is an excellent side dish for Western foods.

1 pound green or wax beans
2 tablespoons canola, corn, or peanut oil
½ cup Chinese Chicken Broth (page 64) or water
1 teaspoon salt
1 teaspoon sugar

1.   Snap off the tips of the green beans and break each bean into 2 or 3 pieces about 1½ to 2 inches long.

2.   Heat the oil in a wok or stir-fry pan over high heat. When the oil is hot enough to sizzle when a bean is dipped in, add all the beans and stir for 2 minutes. Add the broth or water and salt. Stir and cover the pan. Reduce the heat to medium and cook for about 6 to 9 minutes, or until the beans are tender to your liking. Stir occasionally for even cooking.

3.   Add the sugar and cook, uncovered, for 1 minute, stirring frequently. Serve hot.

Note   If you like a garlicky taste, add 2 minced garlic cloves with the broth in step 2.

Vegetables

Kan Shao Green Beans

**Serves 4, or 5 to 6 as part of a
multicourse meal**

Y ou can also use Chinese long beans in this recipe. Break them into pieces about one
and a half inches long. The texture will be a little softer.

1 pound green beans
¼ cup fermented black beans, chopped
1 tablespoon minced peeled gingerroot
2 garlic cloves, minced
1 tablespoon crushed red pepper, or to taste
3 tablespoons canola, corn, or peanut oil
2 tablespoons light soy sauce
1 teaspoon sugar
½ cup water

1.   Snap off the ends of the beans and break them into pieces about 1½ to 2 inches long. Set aside.

2.   Combine the black beans, gingerroot, garlic, and red pepper in a small dish. Set aside.

3.   Heat the oil in a wok or stir-fry pan over medium-high heat until hot but not smoking. Add the black bean mixture, it will sizzle slightly when added. Stir until fragrant.

4.   Add the green beans, soy sauce, and sugar. Stir a few times and add the water. Stir to mix, cover, and cook over medium heat for 5 minutes. Uncover the pan, turn the heat to high, and cook for 5 minutes, or until the beans are tender and the liquid has evaporated. Stir frequently to ensure even cooking and to prevent burning as the liquid evaporates. Serve hot.

Red-mouthed Green Parrot

**Serves 2 to 3, or 4 to 5 as part of a
multicourse meal**

Chinese poets describe spinach with pink roots as a "red-mouthed green parrot." My mother often took us to a farm stand and asked if we could pick spinach ourselves; that way we could pull it up with the sweet pink roots still attached. We would leave about half an inch of the root attached, then scrape it clean with our fingernails or a small knife. Although the pink makes a prettier dish, you can use regular loose spinach. The small amount of sugar in the recipe brings back the natural sweetness of just-picked vegetables.

禧

1 pound spinach, preferably with pink roots attached
2 tablespoons canola, corn, or peanut oil
2 garlic cloves, crushed and peeled
½ teaspoon salt
1 teaspoon sugar

1. Fill the sink with cold water and put the spinach in the water. Separate the large leaves with their stalks. Leave the smaller leaves attached to the root. Scrape the pink root with your fingernails or a paring knife. Lift the spinach from the water and place in a colander. Discard the water and repeat the washing two more times. There should be no grit in the bottom of the sink after the last washing. Drain well and leave the spinach leaves whole.

2. Pour the oil into a wok or stir-fry pan and place over high heat. Add the garlic and salt and stir around the pan until the oil is hot; the garlic will begin to sizzle. Do not let the garlic burn or it will become bitter.

3. Add the spinach; the oil will sizzle. Stir until the spinach begins to wilt. Sprinkle on the sugar and continue stirring until well wilted, 1 to 2 minutes. (I find chopsticks best for stirring greens.) Spread flat on a shallow platter and serve immediately.

Vegetables

Stir-fried Watercress
with Fu Ru

**Serves 2 to 3, or 4 to 5 as part of a
multicourse meal**

*F*u ru is a kind of bean curd that is fermented in salt and wine until it develops a
strong salty flavor and pungent aroma. It is often called "Chinese cheese." It is sold
in jars in Chinese grocery stores.

禧

2 bunches fresh watercress, 12 to 14 ounces
3 small cakes fu ru, about 1 inch square and ½ inch thick
2 tablespoons canola, corn, or peanut oil
1 garlic clove, crushed and peeled
1 slice unpeeled gingerroot, 1 × ⅛ inch

1.   Wash and drain the watercress, discarding any discolored leaves. Cut
the sprigs in half.

2.   With a small spoon, cream the fu ru with 2 tablespoons water in a
small bowl. The mixture will be a little lumpy. Set aside.

3.   Pour the oil into a wok or stir-fry pan and place the pan over high
heat. Add the garlic and gingerroot and stir around the pan until the oil is hot;
the garlic and gingerroot will begin to sizzle. Add the watercress and stir until
wilted, about 1½ to 2 minutes. Chopsticks are helpful for stir-frying because
of the stringy nature of the watercress.

4.   Add the fu ru and stir thoroughly until well mixed, about 30 seconds.
Serve immediately.

Vegetables

272

Mushrooms, Bamboo Shoots, and Snow Peas

Serves 3 to 4 as part of a multicourse meal

*T*he Chinese like to use the number three in dishes. In Chinese this dish is known as *Three Delights*. Each ingredient has a distinct texture and appearance that make the dish delightful to eat and delightful to look at.

福

½ cup dried black mushrooms

2 tablespoons light soy sauce

1 teaspoon sugar

3 tablespoons canola, corn, or peanut oil

½ pound snow peas, ends snapped off and strings removed

½ teaspoon salt

1 (8-ounce) can sliced bamboo shoots, drained (1 cup)

1½ teaspoons cornstarch, dissolved in 1 tablespoon water

1.   Soak the mushrooms in 2 cups hot water for 15 minutes, or until soft. Drain and squeeze the liquid, reserving ½ cup. Strain and mix with the soy sauce and sugar. Set aside. Trim off the mushroom stems with scissors and cut the caps in half. Cut large caps into quarters so all the pieces will be of uniform size. Set aside.

2.   Heat 2 tablespoons of the oil in a wok or stir-fry pan over high heat until hot but not smoking. Test by dipping a snow pea in the oil; it should sizzle. Add the salt and then the snow peas. Stir constantly until the peas turn a darker green, about 1 minute. Transfer to a platter and spread out to stop cooking.

3.   Add the remaining 1 tablespoon of oil to the same pan. Stir in the bamboo shoots and mushrooms with the mushroom liquid mixture. Stir and cook for about 2 minutes. Add the cornstarch slurry. Stir until the sauce thickens. Return the snow peas to the pan and mix thoroughly. Serve immediately.

Vegetables

273

Stir-fried Chinese Water Spinach with Fu Ru

Serves 2 to 3, or 4 to 5 as part of a multicourse meal

*T*he Chinese call water spinach hollow hearted vegetable, since the long stem is hollow like a reed. The Chinese, especially southerners, love these greens for their tender, arrow-shaped leaves and crisp stems. In Chinatown you can ask for it by its Cantonese name, ung tsoi. Buy a lot — it will shrink to less than half its volume when cooked.

This dish is a real down-home, country recipe that is popular in Cantonese restaurants in Chinatown but usually known only to the Chinese. It is never printed on the menu in English, and it is not always available. If you want it, you'll have to ask for it. Just ask if they have ung tsoi with fu ru today. The waiter will surely be surprised!

1½ pounds Chinese water spinach
3 cakes fu ru, plain or chili flavored
2 tablespoons canola, corn, or peanut oil
2 garlic cloves, crushed and peeled
¼ cup water

1. Wash the water spinach thoroughly in lots of water and drain. Trim away and discard any rotting leaves. The ends tend to be tough, so cut or break off about 2 inches from the bottom of the stems. Cut or break the remaining spinach into 3-inch pieces. Water spinach is very crisp so it will break easily.

2. Remove the fu ru from the jar. Place in a small bowl and mash with the back of a spoon with 1 tablespoon of water to make a paste. It will not be completely smooth but will become so when it cooks.

3. Pour the oil into a wok or stir-fry pan and place over high heat. Add the garlic and stir until the oil is hot; the garlic will sizzle. Add the water spinach and stir until the leaves have wilted. Add the ¼ cup water and stir for about 2 minutes. Chopsticks are easier to use than a spatula here since the water spinach gets stringy as it cooks.

4. Add the fu ru paste and stir thoroughly until dissolved. Cook for 2 minutes or so, stirring. Transfer to a serving dish and serve hot.

Note Even the same brand of fu ru may vary in flavor intensity. If the fu ru tastes lighter than you'd like, add another cake to the dish or flavor with some salt.

Quick Asparagus Salad

Serves 3 to 4 as a side dish

*O*ften the simplest way to prepare a vegetable is the best. Use very fresh asparagus and cook them just until tender-crisp.

1 pound asparagus
3 tablespoons light soy sauce
1 teaspoon sesame seed oil or hot sesame oil

1. Cut or snap off the tough ends of the asparagus and cut off the small wedge-shaped leaves up to 2 inches from the tip. Wash well and roll-cut as described on page 46 or cut on the diagonal into 1½-inch lengths.

2. Bring 6 cups of water to a boil in a saucepan over high heat. Add the asparagus pieces. As soon as the water returns to a boil, drain and quickly cool in cold water to stop the cooking. Drain well. (The asparagus can be cooked a day ahead and refrigerated.)

3. Just before serving, place the asparagus in a serving bowl and toss with the soy sauce and sesame seed oil. Serve at room temperature.

Vegetables

275

Vegetarian's Delight

蔬菜

As with Beef with Mixed Vegetables (page 222), this recipe can be a flexible combination of vegetables. I don't recommend stir-frying as an excuse for cleaning out the refrigerator, but we often find ourselves with little bits and pieces of vegetables that are not enough to make anything on their own. Of course, you can prepare this any time you crave lots of colorful, crunchy vegetables as a side dish with other Chinese or Western entrees. In addition to the vegetables you may want to add some fried or dried bean curd or softened golden needles and wood ears. Adjust the amount of broth, cornstarch, and salt for larger quantities of ingredients.

I use chicken bouillon cubes dissolved in water when I don't have chicken broth on hand or need just a small amount. You can use homemade or canned broth instead. Adjust the salt accordingly.

健康

3 tablespoons canola, corn, or peanut oil
2 slices unpeeled gingerroot, 1 × ⅛ inch each
1 garlic clove, crushed and peeled
7 to 8 cups mixed vegetables, such as broccoli, cauliflower, zucchini, summer
    squash, beans, bell pepper, carrots, bamboo shoots, and water chestnuts
1 chicken bouillon cube, dissolved in ⅓ cup hot water
½ teaspoon salt, or to taste
3 teaspoons cornstarch, dissolved in 2 tablespoons water

1. Heat the oil in a wok or stir-fry pan over high heat. When the oil is hot, add the gingerroot and garlic; they should sizzle. Stir a few times and add the vegetables, the harder root vegetables first and the more tender ones last.

2. Add the dissolved bouillon and cover the pan. Cook over medium heat for 1 to 2 minutes, or until the vegetables are tender-crisp. Stir occasionally for even cooking.

3. Uncover the pan, season with salt to taste, and mix in the cornstarch slurry. Stir until the liquid thickens. Discard the gingerroot and garlic, if desired. Serve hot.

Bean Sprout Salad
with Egg Garnish

Serves 4 to 6

With the exception of cucumbers and radishes, raw vegetables do not appeal to the Chinese palate. Here the bean sprouts are parboiled to remove that unappetizing raw taste. Be sure to remove the bean sprouts just as the water begins to bubble and to refresh the sprouts immediately in plenty of cold water so they will remain crisp. Add some shredded cooked chicken or diced ham to the salad before garnishing with the egg for a light luncheon dish.

福

2 ounces snow peas, ends snapped and strings removed (1 cup)
1 pound bean sprouts
2 tablespoons light soy sauce
1 teaspoon sesame seed oil
1 recipe Egg Garnish (page 255)

1. Bring 10 cups of water to a boil in a large saucepan over high heat. Plunge the snow peas into the water for 10 seconds. Remove with a strainer and rinse immediately with cold water to stop the cooking. Return the water to a boil and add the bean sprouts. Just as the water begins to bubble again, drain the sprouts in a colander. Rinse immediately with cold water until all the warmth is gone. Allow the vegetables to drain thoroughly.

2. Shred the snow peas on the diagonal to about the same length as the bean sprouts and toss the vegetables together in a serving bowl. Mix the soy sauce and sesame seed oil together in a small dish. Just before serving, toss the dressing with the vegetables and scatter the garnish on top. Serve immediately.

Vegetables

Spicy Sweet and Sour Cabbage

Serves 6 to 8

*T*his dish is often served as part of a Chinese-style cold platter; it is a great choice any time your menu calls for cole slaw or sweet and sour red cabbage. The relish may be eaten warm, but my mother always chilled it overnight to improve the flavor and texture.

禄

2 pounds napa or Chinese celery cabbage

½ tablespoon crushed red pepper, or to taste

½ cup light brown sugar

⅓ cup cider vinegar

2 tablespoons light soy sauce

1 teaspoon salt

3 tablespoons canola, corn, or peanut oil

1. Remove and discard any tough or discolored outer leaves of the cabbage. Cut it into quarters lengthwise and cut out and discard the core. Cut each quarter across into 4-inch pieces. Shred lengthwise into ½-inch-wide strips. Toss to separate the leaves.

2. Combine the red pepper, sugar, vinegar, soy sauce, and salt in a mixing bowl. Set aside.

3. Pour the oil into a wok or stir-fry pan and place over medium-high heat. When the oil is hot but not smoking, add the cabbage; it should sizzle. Stir constantly until the leaves become limp and the stems loose their raw look, about 5 minutes. Remove the pan from the heat and stir in the pepper mixture.

4. Transfer the cabbage to a large platter and spread it out to prevent overcooking. Stir occasionally to distribute the flavoring evenly. When completely cooled, lightly drain from the liquid and serve. Or refrigerate in the liquid and drain before serving.

Note The cabbage tastes best if left to stand for at least 1 hour in the liquid. It may be kept in the refrigerator for several days.

Celery Salad

*T*his salad is atypically Chinese in that it uses raw vegetables. Instead of blanching the vegetables, you shred and soak them in salted ice water for greater crispness. The recipe itself is quick and easy, but the shredding may take some time. A mandoline shredder makes quick work of the carrots, but I find that the celery, because of the strings, doesn't come out as well and has to be shredded by hand.

禧

2 teaspoons salt
4 cups finely shredded celery (about 8 stalks) (page 45)
1 cup finely shredded carrot, about 1 medium
1 tablespoon finely shredded peeled gingerroot (optional)
3 tablespoons light soy sauce
1 teaspoon sesame seed oil

1. Dissolve the salt in 7 cups ice water. Soak the celery, carrot, and gingerroot for at least 30 minutes but no more than 1 hour. Drain, cover, and store the vegetables in the refrigerator until ready to use.

2. Just before serving, transfer the vegetables to a serving bowl, mix in the soy sauce, and drizzle with sesame seed oil. Toss a few times to mix. Serve immediately.

健康

Note Do not add the soy sauce too early as it will stain the vegetables and spoil the presentation.

Vegetables

Quick Cucumber Salad

Serves 4 to 6 as a side dish

A *simple-to-make salad that can be served as a side dish or an hors d'oeuvre. Children love it as a snack.*

福

1 pound seedless or regular cucumbers
3 tablespoons light soy sauce
1 teaspoon sesame seed oil

1.   Seedless cucumbers do not need to be peeled, but for a different presentation you can peel away strips of peel. Split the cucumber lengthwise and cut on the diagonal into slices ¼ inch thick. If using regular cucumbers, partially peel, split in half, and scoop out and discard the seeds. Cut as for seedless cucumber. Place in a serving bowl.

2.   Just before serving, toss with the soy sauce and sesame seed oil. Serve cold.

Cucumbers in Garlic and Chili Dressing

Serves 4 to 6 as a side dish

*I*f you like strong flavors, you'll love this chilled salad. For a less spicy taste, reduce the red pepper to half a teaspoon.

1 pound seedless or regular cucumbers

1 teaspoon salt

3 tablespoons Chinkiang black vinegar

1 tablespoon plus 2 teaspoons sugar

2 garlic cloves, peeled and minced

2 teaspoons grated peeled gingerroot

1 teaspoon crushed red pepper

1 teaspoon light soy sauce (optional)

1.   Wash the cucumber, split in half lengthwise, and cut on the diagonal into slices ¼ inch thick. If using regular cucumbers, partially peel, split in half lengthwise, and scoop out and discard the seeds. Cut as for seedless cucumber. Place the cucumbers in a bowl and toss with the salt. Let stand for 10 to 15 minutes.

2.   Mix the vinegar, sugar, garlic, gingerroot, red pepper, and soy sauce, if using, in a small bowl. Stir until the sugar is dissolved.

3.   Rinse the cucumbers in cold water, drain thoroughly, and pat dry with paper towels. Transfer to a bowl and toss with the dressing. Serve at room temperature or chilled.

Vegetables

Sliced Cucumbers with Spicy Peanut Dressing

Serves 4 to 6 as a side dish

I use the very crisp long, seedless cucumber for this dish. The cucumber doesn't have to be peeled since it's not waxed but wrapped in plastic to prevent moisture loss.

1 pound seedless or regular cucumbers
¼ cup smooth peanut butter
¼ cup water, Chinese Chicken Broth (page 64), or canned chicken broth
½ teaspoon salt, or to taste
¼ teaspoon Szechuan peppercorns, toasted and ground
1 tablespoon sesame seed oil
1 teaspoon crushed red pepper

1. Split the long cucumber in half lengthwise and cut on the diagonal into thin slices. If using regular cucumbers, peel alternating strips of the skin away, leaving some green for color, split in half lengthwise, and scoop out and discard the seeds. Cut on the diagonal into thin slices.

2. Mix the peanut butter with the broth or water, salt, Szechuan peppercorns, sesame seed oil, and red pepper into a smooth, thin paste.

3. Just before serving, mix the peanut dressing with the cucumber slices. Serve cold.

Minute Sweet and Sour
Cucumber Salad

Serves 4 to 6 as a side dish

*T*his amazingly simple salad is very good with barbecued or grilled meats. The cucumbers make you feel refreshed the minute you start to eat them.

1 pound seedless or regular cucumbers
½ teaspoon salt
2 tablespoons light brown sugar
2 tablespoons cider vinegar
½ teaspoon light soy sauce
½ teaspoon sesame seed oil

1. Split the cucumber in half lengthwise and cut on the diagonal into slices ¼ inch thick. If using regular cucumbers, partially peel, leaving alternating strips of green skin behind, split in half lengthwise, and scoop out and discard seeds. Cut as for seedless cucumber.

2. Place the cucumber slices in a bowl, sprinkle with salt, and toss. Let stand for 15 minutes to draw out liquid. Drain and transfer to a serving bowl. (You may wish to rinse the salt off the cucumbers in cold water and pat dry with paper towels, but it is not necessary.)

3. Mix the sugar, vinegar, and soy sauce in a small dish until the sugar is dissolved. When ready to serve, pour the dressing and sesame seed oil over the cucumbers and toss well. Serve chilled or at room temperature.

Steamed Eggplant Salad

**Serves 3 to 4, or 5 to 6 as part of a
multicourse meal**

As soon as eggplants began to ripen in my mother's garden, she would make this dish. The skin on her just-picked eggplants was so tender she didn't even peel them. As she was preparing the eggplant, my mother would remind us that it was one of her father's favorite dishes. This salad can be served hot, warm, or cold. The flavor is robust but not overwhelming.

健康

1 pound eggplant
3 tablespoons cider vinegar
3 tablespoons light brown sugar
2 teaspoons sesame seed oil
1 tablespoon light soy sauce
½ to 1 tablespoon minced or grated peeled gingerroot
1 teaspoon minced garlic

1. Cut off and discard the stem. Peel the eggplant unless it is garden-fresh or very young. Cut the eggplant into 6 or 8 wedges. Spread the wedges in a steaming basket in a saucepan over water as described on page 36. The perforated steaming dish is necessary to allow any bitter juices to drain off into the boiling water. Cover the pan, bring the water to a boil, and steam for 8 to 10 minutes, or until the eggplant is very soft and easily pierced by a fork. Do not let the water boil into the eggplant. Drain. (The eggplant may be steamed in advance and stored, covered, in the refrigerator until ready to dress.)

2. While the eggplant is steaming, combine the vinegar, sugar, sesame seed oil, soy sauce, gingerroot, and garlic in a small bowl or lidded jar and mix or shake thoroughly.

3. Place the eggplant in a serving dish, pour the dressing over, and mix gently. Serve hot, warm, or chilled.

Note The eggplant will be very soft and fall apart. Don't be alarmed. This salad is not particularly beautiful to look at, but it's sensational to eat!

Vegetables

Sweet and Sour Radish Salad

Serves 4 as a side dish

Whenever we bought radishes at our local farm stand, my mother checked them carefully. They had to be crisp and not too spicy. We would buy extra and snack on them — spread with peanut butter — while watching TV. Even when I was very young, my mother let me prepare this dish seeing how much I enjoyed smashing the radishes with the cleaver.

20 radishes (2 bunches)
½ teaspoon salt
2 tablespoons light brown sugar
2 tablespoons cider vinegar
½ teaspoon sesame seed oil

1. Trim away both ends of the radishes. Wash the radishes well and drain. If the ends are discolored, scrape away the discoloration.

2. Crush each radish with the broad side of a Chinese cleaver. Cut large ones in half before crushing them. Crush just enough to crack the radish so it will absorb the dressing better.

3. Place the radishes in a bowl and sprinkle with salt. Let stand for 15 minutes. Drain and transfer to a serving bowl.

4. Mix the sugar and vinegar together in a small bowl and pour over the radishes. Drizzle with sesame seed oil, and toss to blend. Serve.

Variation   Use hot sesame seed oil in place of the regular or add about ½ teaspoon of a hot sauce like Tabasco to the dressing.

Substitute a long seedless cucumber for the radishes. Cut it in half lengthwise and into thin slices. Salt and let sit for 15 minutes. Drain and dress as in step 4.

Wilted Spinach with Mustard Dressing

Serves 6 to 8 as a side dish

My mother remembered this cold dish from her childhood in Beijing (Peking) and developed this recipe to re-create it. She says that the Chinese like to use older spinach with long stalks for their crunchy texture. Sometimes near the end of spinach season, you can find such older spinach sold at farm stands.

2 pounds spinach
2 tablespoons dry mustard powder
½ teaspoon cider vinegar
1¼ teaspoons salt, or to taste

1. Separate the spinach and discard any yellowed or wilted leaves. Wash thoroughly in cold water, changing the water at least three times to be sure every bit of sand is rinsed away. Drain thoroughly.

2. Mix the mustard powder with 2 tablespoons cold water into a thick paste. Gradually add 2½ tablespoons more water, the vinegar, and ¼ teaspoon of the salt. Stir into a thin paste.

3. Bring 6 to 8 cups of water to a boil in a large saucepan. Add the spinach. As soon as the spinach wilts (before the water boils again), drain in a colander. Refresh immediately by plunging into a bath of cold water to cool the spinach and set the color. Drain and gently squeeze the water out with your hands.

4. Cut the spinach into small pieces and transfer to a serving bowl. Mix with the mustard dressing and remaining salt to taste. Serve cold.

Small Eats

mall eats are the kind of snacks the Chinese enjoy at almost any time of the day or night. Instead of candy and processed foods, we eat what is sometimes called street food because it is sold on street corners or in small fast-food restaurants. Most of the appetizers and small eats in this chapter may be served Western style, as finger foods with drinks or at the table as the first course of a Chinese-style meal.

Many recipes in other chapters could actually fit in here. Noodles and fried rice, for instance, are often served as a midnight snack. Some desserts in the book, such as Steamed Egg Cake (page 347) and Sweet Red Bean Soup (page 342), could be listed here since they are often served as part of dim sum. You can see how versatile Chinese food is.

Appetizers served at formal Chinese banquets are generally cold platters with a variety of meats, seafood, and vegetables thinly sliced and arranged in elaborate auspicious designs, such as a phoenix, a dragon, or a lucky Chinese character. Many of the ingredients used in Chinese cold platters are unusual foods that are appreciated for their special appearance and texture. Some are exotic, like Hundred-Year-Old Eggs, shredded jellyfish, and sliced abalone. These may be combined with more conventional ingredients such as Pickled Carrots and Daikon, Cucumbers in Garlic and Chili Dressing (page 281), Drunken Chicken, and Red-cooked Gizzards and Livers.

Less formal meals may also start with cold appetizers, but the foods are not arranged in fanciful designs. Choose one, two, or three cold dishes from this or other chapters to serve in small dishes at the beginning of a meal for an authentic Chinese dinner. I like to serve cold appetizers at a dinner because they can be made in advance.

I have found that most Americans do not seem to like cold appetizers as much as hot appetizers — egg rolls, spring rolls, spareribs. Hot appetizers are usually served as substantial dim sum (*dian xin* in Mandarin), which means "dot the heart." The hot platters popularly known as Pu Pu Platters are not traditionally Chinese. Dim sum is served at teatime, but it can be a brunch, a whole meal, or a snack. The Cantonese have made this a tradition, and in Hong Kong at noon the many tea shops that specialize in dim sum are packed with people. The dim sum are wheeled around on carts, usually by women, and the customer picks from the myriad of items offered. At the end of the meal, the maitre d' counts the number of empty dishes and tallies up the bill.

My mother liked to tell about a famous tea shop next to a lake in China; the dining room was built on piles out over the water. As one unscrupulous gentleman ate, he would throw the dishes into the water so that his bill would be smaller!

Wontons

福 These celebrated meat dumplings can be fried or boiled to be served as hors d'oeuvres, appetizers, snacks, in soups, or as a meal in themselves. If you serve them deep-fried as hors d'oeuvres, allow four wontons per person; if boiled as a snack or light meal, ten to twelve per person. If you're putting them in a soup to be served as an appetizer, allow four to six per person; in a soup that's served as a meal, ten to twelve per person.

Filling Wontons

Wonton skins are available in the produce department of most supermarkets. A one-pound package contains about sixty skins. Any unused portion of the package will freeze well as will leftover filling. Be sure to thaw the skins thoroughly before using or they will crack and break. Since wonton skins dry out quickly, place a damp kitchen towel or moistened plain white paper towels over the skins and the formed wontons as you work.

(If you can't find wonton skins, cut egg-roll skins into four even pieces.) The simplest and fastest way to do this is to take one egg roll skin and fold it in four to mark the skin; unfold and place over the stack of wrappers, like a template, and cut carefully through the stack along the folds of the skin.

When the Chinese make wontons, they use only about half a teaspoon of filling in each. If you like more filling, you can use up to one teaspoon. Don't overstuff or the wontons won't seal securely, and you will end up with

empty wonton skins and the filling at the bottom of your pot. One cup of filling (pages 293–294) will fill about a pound of wonton skins, depending on how much filling is used.

Uncooked wontons will keep for a few days in the refrigerator and longer in the freezer. To freeze, place them in the freezer on a cookie sheet. When they are frozen, hit the tray against the edge of the counter to dislodge them. Transfer to a plastic bag, seal, and place in the freezer. Frozen wontons will keep for a month or more. It is not necessary to thaw before using.

Folding Wontons

The technique for folding wontons that will be boiled is the family-style method my mother taught me. I like to use a restaurant-style fold for deep-fried wontons because they fry up puffed and important looking. You can, however, use either fold for either cooking method, just be sure to fold the wonton so that there is a little space between the filling and the sealed corners. This way the hot liquid can circulate around the wonton and cook the filling evenly. Line up the folded wontons neatly on a tray and cover with a damp cloth until ready to cook.

Family-style fold for boiled wontons

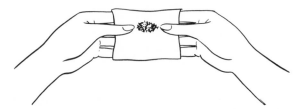

1. With a table or butter knife, place a rounded ½ teaspoonful of filling in the center of a wonton skin. Support the skin on the fingers of both hands with your thumbs on top.

2. Fold the back edge over the filling until the back edge meets the front edge.

3. Using the thumbs, press the skin down around the filling to help center it and hold it in place. Keep the index fingers under the back of the wonton.

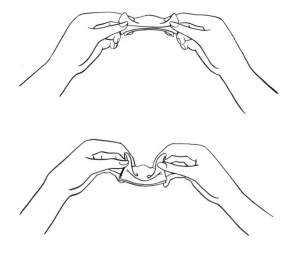

4. Now fold the back edge over again covering your thumbs.

5. Push the top corners up with your thumbs and hold them between your thumbs and your index fingers.

6. Using your finger, wet the top left corner with water or lightly beaten egg white. Bring the top right corner to the top left, and overlap the corners pressing them together to secure.

7. You now have a completed wonton that looks like a nurse's cap with the "wings" or flaps, standing up. Arrange the formed wontons on a baking tray dusted lightly with flour and cover them with a dry cloth. If the room is very dry, cover with a damp cloth. Proceed with instructions for Boiled Wontons.

Restaurant-style fold for deep-fried wontons

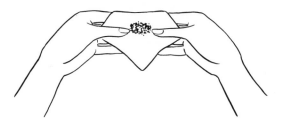

1. With a table or butter knife, place a rounded ½ teaspoonful of filling in the center of a wonton skin. Support the skin on the fingers of both hands with your thumbs on top and with one corner facing you.

2. Fold the back corner over the filling, until the back edge meets the front edge.

3. Using the thumbs, press the skin down around the filling to help center it and hold it in place. Keep the index fingers under the back of the wonton.

4. Fold the back edge halfway toward you, covering your thumbs.

5. Push the top corners up with your thumbs, holding the corners between your thumbs and index fingers.

Small Eats

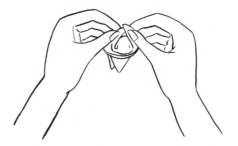

6.   Using your finger, wet the left corner with water or lightly beaten egg white. Bring the right corner to the left, and overlap the corners pressing them together to secure.

7.   Arrange the wontons on a baking tray lightly dusted with flour and cover them with a dry cloth. If the room is very dry, cover with a damp cloth. Proceed with instructions for Deep-fried Wontons.

Boiled Wontons

Bring 3 quarts of water to a boil in a 6-quart pot over medium heat. Add as many wontons as can swim freely about. Stir gently with a wooden spoon and cover the pot. Return to a boil and immediately add 1 cup cold water. With the pot covered, let the water return to a boil, then remove the pan from the heat. Let the wontons stand in the hot water with the cover on for 5 minutes. Scoop out the wontons with a wire skimmer and drain well. Serve with cider vinegar, Chinkiang vinegar, or a soy sauce dip (page 324). Be careful not to overcook the wontons or the skins will become too soft and lose their "bite."

Store leftover boiled wontons, covered, in the refrigerator. Reheat in a nonstick skillet with 1 tablespoon oil. Cook as you would home-fried potatoes — brown one side, turn, and brown the other side.

Deep-fried Wontons

Pour 2 inches of canola, corn, or peanut oil into a wok or stir-fry pan and heat to 350°F. When the oil is hot, drop in the wontons, a few at a time, stirring and turning for even browning, and fry until golden brown. Bring the oil back to temperature before frying a second batch. Remove with a wire skimmer and drain on paper towels. Transfer to a serving platter and serve as soon as possible so the wontons remain crispy. Serve hot with Chinese mustard and duck sauce or Sweet and Sour Sauce (page 327).

Store leftover deep-fried wontons in the refrigerator or freezer. Reheat on a baking sheet in a 450°F. oven for 15 minutes. It is not necessary to defrost frozen wontons before reheating.

Pork Wontons

Makes about 50 to 60 wontons

*P*ork wontons can be boiled or deep-fried. Serve the fried wontons hot with Chinese mustard and duck sauce or Spicy Mango Chutney (page 330). Serve drained boiled wontons with a soy sauce dip (page 324) or add them to soup as on page 66.

健康

½ pound ground lean pork (about 1 cup)

1 tablespoon soy sauce

1 tablespoon sesame seed oil or vegetable oil

2 tablespoons broth or water

¼ teaspoon salt

1 teaspoon finely minced scallion

1 teaspoon cornstarch

1 teaspoon dry sherry

1 pound wonton skins

Combine all the ingredients except the wonton skins in a bowl. Stir together until well mixed. Fill, fold, and cook the wontons as described on pages 288–292.

Turkey Wontons

Makes about 60 to 90 wontons

My childhood friend Anna Ku Lau makes a wonton filling with ground turkey. She mixes in frozen chopped spinach and puts a small piece of raw shrimp into every wonton before folding. I find it easier to chop the raw shrimp and mix it right into the ground meat. Be sure to squeeze out as much water from the spinach as you can so the filling does not get too wet. These wontons may be boiled or deep-fried.

福

½ pound ground turkey

1 tablespoon plus 1 teaspoon soy sauce, light or dark

1 tablespoon canola, corn, or peanut oil

¼ teaspoon salt

⅓ cup frozen chopped spinach, thawed and water squeezed out

1 tablespoon minced scallion

1 teaspoon cornstarch

1 teaspoon dry sherry

¼ cup small shrimp, chopped fine (about 2 ounces)

1 to 1½ pounds wonton skins

Combine all the ingredients except the wonton skins in a bowl and stir together until well mixed. Fill and deep fry or boil according to the directions on pages 288–292.

Peking Ravioli

Makes 32 ravioli

*T*he Chinese term for these dumplings when they are boiled is jiao zi; when they are pan-fried, they are called guo tie, or potstickers, because they stick to the pot when cooked. My mother coined the name Peking Ravioli, because when she started serving them in our restaurant in the 1950s, no one had seen anything like them before. Borrowing from our Italian neighbors in Boston let customers know that these were dough pockets with a filling. Interestingly, although the name potsticker is common now, just about all the Chinese restaurants in the Boston area still call them Peking Ravioli because of my mother's influence. In the Chinese tradition, when our family gathered together, we would all make the ravioli, and at the end of the meal we would announce how many each of us had eaten. This is one of my mother's most treasured recipes.

I am giving you my mother's recipe as she gave it to me, including directions for boiled and fried ravioli. Plan on six to eight pieces per person as a main meal and two to three as an appetizer.

2 cups all-purpose flour
⅔ cup lukewarm water
1 pound napa or Chinese celery cabbage
1½ teaspoons salt
¾ pound ground pork
1½ tablespoons dark soy sauce
1 tablespoon dry sherry
½ teaspoon sugar
1 or 2 tablespoons canola, corn, or peanut oil or bacon drippings (use 2
    tablespoons if the meat is very lean)
1 tablespoon sesame seed oil

1.   Mix the flour and water together in a large mixing bowl with a wooden spoon. Remove from the bowl and knead on a lightly floured work surface for 4 minutes, or until the dough becomes smooth and elastic. If the dough seems too dry, add a few drops of water and continue kneading. Cover the dough with a damp towel and allow to rest, or as the Chinese say "wake up," for 30 minutes or more.

(continued)

2. While the dough is resting, wash and drain the cabbage. Chop into coarse chunks, then mince very fine. Sprinkle 1 teaspoon salt over the cabbage while mincing. Place in a cloth bag or in a double layer of cheesecloth. Squeeze out enough liquid to make 1 cup. Discard the liquid. Put the remaining ingredients into a large bowl and add the cabbage. Mix well — by hand is the best way. Set aside.

3. Using the palms of your hands, roll the "waked up" dough into two even ropes 16 inches long. Cut each rope into sixteen 1-inch pieces and shape the pieces into small balls. Flatten them with the palm of your hand and dust with flour. With a rolling pin, roll each piece into a 3-inch circle. If the dough sticks to the work surface or the rolling pin, dust with more flour. Cover the circles with a dry cloth to keep them from drying out.

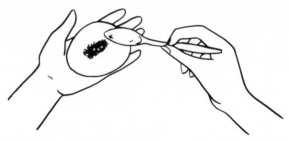

4. Place a heaping teaspoon of filling, in a log shape, in the center of a circle of dough.

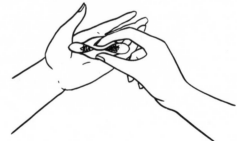

5. Fold the dough in half and pinch the edges together just at the center of the half circle until that point is sealed.

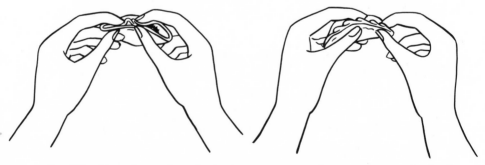

6. Working from the pinched center toward one corner, pinch the edges together between your thumb and forefinger, pleating the dough in 3 or 4 places as you go. Repeat on other side.

7.   The pleats will create an attractive arched half moon. Be sure to seal the dumpling tightly, pinching the whole edge one more time after it has been formed.

8.   Place the ravioli on a floured surface with the pleated edges on top and cover with a dry cloth (or a damp cloth if the air is very dry) to keep them from drying out. Cook immediately according to directions for Boiled or Fried Peking Ravioli or refrigerate for several days or freeze for several weeks. To freeze, arrange the ravioli on a floured cookie sheet, and place in the freezer. When they are frozen, bang the pan on the edge of the counter to loosen them, put them in a plastic bag, seal it, and return it to the freezer. Do not drop them into a freezer bag while they are soft or they will lose their shape and stick together. Frozen Peking Ravioli do not need to be thawed before cooking.

壽

Note   Some supermarkets now sell prepared Peking Ravioli, or Potsticker, skins made from the same egg-and-flour dough used for wontons and egg-roll skins. (Don't buy wonton wrappers or egg-roll skins, because they're too thin and won't hold up.) These are often made by Japanese companies and are marketed under the Japanese name of *gyoza*. (Peking Ravioli are popular for lunch in Japan.) Chinese brands are available in Chinese grocery stores. Ready-made skins are not as soft as homemade skins so you will need to use some water or egg white to secure the seal. They are also thinner so cooking time should be reduced slightly.

Boiled Peking Ravioli

The Chinese prefer to boil their Peking Ravioli and eat them as a whole meal usually with a dip made of vinegar, light soy sauce, and Hot Chili Oil (page 329). The host sets a cruet of each on the table, and the guests mix the dip themselves. My family and I actually prefer to eat the boiled ravioli with just cider vinegar or Chinkiang vinegar. Sometimes we tease people about that because when the Chinese say "eat vinegar," it means to be jealous.

The cooking water is sometimes served as a refreshing hot beverage after the meal. I personally find it tasteless, but many Chinese are partial to it.

Bring 5 quarts of water to a boil in a stockpot. Slip the dumplings into the boiling water, one at a time, being sure there is enough room to allow them to swim about freely. Stir a few times to prevent sticking, cover, and cook over medium-high heat until the water boils again. Watch the pot; the water can foam up and boil over easily. As soon as the water returns to a boil, add 1 cup cold water, cover, and continue cooking over medium heat. When the water boils again, add another 1 cup cold water, cover, and let the water return to a boil for the third time. Remove from heat and let stand, covered, for 2 to 3 minutes. This procedure ensures that the filling cooks through.

If using ready-made skins, reduce the standing time to about 1 minute.

Remove the dumplings with a wire skimmer or slotted spoon and drain briefly in a colander. Transfer to a plate or shallow platter and serve immediately with vinegar, oil, and soy sauce.

Store leftover boiled ravioli, covered, in the refrigerator. To reheat, pan-fry in a covered nonstick skillet over medium heat with about 1 tablespoon oil until heated through and lightly browned on one side.

Fried Peking Ravioli

In America, the more popular way to serve Peking Ravioli (potstickers) is not boiled, which the Chinese prefer, but pan-fried. By a clever combination of pan-frying, boiling, and steaming, the dough is browned while the meat filling is cooked through. Serve the fried dumplings with the same type of dips as for boiled dumplings.

Heat an 8- or 9-inch heavy nonstick skillet over medium-high heat until hot. Pour 1 tablespoon oil into the pan and spread it over the entire cooking surface. Starting at the outside of the pan, arrange the dumplings carefully in concentric circles, facing in the same direction and touching each other lightly. Put 2 dumplings in the center facing each other.

Add ½ cup cold water, cover, and cook over medium-high heat for 6 to 7 minutes, or until the water has evaporated. Lower the heat and cook, covered, for 2 minutes, or until the dumplings are golden brown on the bottom.

Loosen the dumplings from the bottom of the pan with a spatula without disturbing the arrangement. Select a serving plate that will fit over the skillet. Place it, upside down, on top of the skillet. Holding it in place, invert the pan and give a little shake so the loosened dumplings will fall out onto the plate. The brown bottom will now be on top. Serve immediately with vinegar, oil, and soy sauce.

Store leftover fried ravioli, covered, in the refrigerator. To reheat, pan-fry in a covered skillet over medium-heat with about 1 tablespoon oil but no water.

Joyce Chen's
Original Egg Rolls

Makes 28 egg rolls

My grade school holds an annual fund-raising event called *The Buckingham Circus.* When I was in the second grade, my mother donated her own Chinese egg rolls. She put the egg rolls on the food table, and then walked through the circus with me. When we returned to the table, the egg rolls were gone. She first thought they were not acceptable and had been put away, but one of the mothers told us that the egg rolls were an instant hit and sold out almost immediately. My mother was so happy that she went home and made more that very day. They became known as Mrs. Chen's egg rolls and were the start of my mother's reputation as a cook.

This is my mother's original recipe and here are some of her own notes:

"This is the exact filling used in the egg rolls which I made especially for the schools. This is not authentic. Chinese egg roll is called spring roll which symbolizes the coming of Spring. We serve them during the New Year holidays or as a snack in the afternoon. The spring roll is smaller-sized with thinner skin, and beef is never used for filling as the beef is not common in China.

"If you live in a city with a Chinatown or Asian market, then it is much easier to use machine-made egg-roll skins which are sold in Chinese noodle factories in five-pound packages. If they do not want to separate the package for you, then keep the unused portion in the freezer wrapped in separate smaller packages for future use in making egg rolls or wonton. Defrost the egg-roll skins thoroughly before use. The best way to fry is to wrap a few egg rolls, enough to fit in pan, and fry them while wrapping the others.

"Since there is quite a procedure to making egg rolls, I suggest making enough to please your family and your friends."

(continued)

½ *pound lean ground beef*

1 teaspoon dry sherry

1½ teaspoons cornstarch

¼ teaspoon black pepper

1 tablespoon light brown sugar

1 tablespoon thick or dark soy sauce (If using dark soy sauce, reduce salt by
    ½ *teaspoon)*

2 tablespoons canola, corn, or peanut oil

3½ teaspoons salt

3 slices unpeeled gingerroot, 1 x ⅛ inch each

2 large celery stalks, shredded (page 45)

1 medium onion, thinly sliced (about 1 cup)

1½ pounds cabbage, shredded (page 45), (about 8 cups packed)

2 tablespoons flour

1 pound bean sprouts, about 4 cups tightly packed

2 pounds egg-roll skins (about 28 sheets)

1 egg, beaten with 2 tablespoons cold water

Vegetable oil, for deep-frying

1. Mix the beef with the sherry, cornstarch, pepper, brown sugar, and soy sauce in a large bowl. Set aside.

2. Heat the oil in a wok or stir-fry pan over high heat. Add the salt and gingerroot. Add the celery and onions and cook for about 3 minutes. Add the beef mixture and stir constantly until it is cooked and separates into small pieces, about 2 minutes.

3. Transfer to a colander set over a large bowl and drain off the excess liquid. Set aside the liquid. Spread the meat on a large baking sheet to cool. Discard the gingerroot.

4. Return the reserved liquid to the wok and cook the cabbage in it over high heat until transparent and soft, about 6 minutes. If liquid is scant, add 2 tablespoons of oil to wok. Stir constantly. You may need to cook the cabbage in batches.

5. When all the cabbage is cooked, drain off any liquid, pressing the cabbage against the sides of the colander. Transfer the cabbage to a large bowl, sprinkle with the flour, and mix together thoroughly, using your hands. Keep the cabbage and beef mixtures in the refrigerator until ready to use. The filling should not be used while warm.

6. When ready to assemble the egg rolls, mix the cabbage and beef mixtures together. Mix in the bean sprouts by hand, lightly crushing them as you mix. You should have about 10 cups of filling.

7.   Pour 1 inch of oil into a wok and heat to 350°F. to 375°F. while wrapping the egg rolls.

8.   Place a generous ⅓ cup of filling in the center of an egg-roll skin.

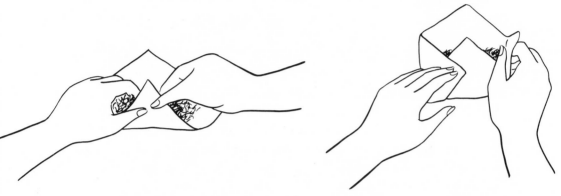

9.   Fold over 1 corner of the skin to cover the filling, then fold over the right and left sides to form an envelope.

10.   Brush the top with the egg mixture and finish rolling.

11.   Roll neatly and tightly, making sure that all the filling is sealed securely in the wrapper. If it isn't, the egg roll may burst open in the oil.

(continued)

Small Eats

12.   Immediately deep-fry the egg rolls, 3 to 5 at a time, until golden brown. Do not let the egg rolls sit before frying, or the filling will soak through the wrapper and they will not fry up crisp and puffy. Turn the egg rolls occasionally as they cook.

13.   Remove the egg rolls and stand them on end in a colander lined with paper towels. Place the colander over a pan to catch any excess oil. If you are going to serve at a later time, line up the egg rolls on a rack to cool thoroughly. Never pile the hot egg rolls; the wrappings will turn soft and lose their crispness.

Note   Fried egg rolls can be kept in the refrigerator for 4 to 5 days or frozen for about 1 month. Only the bean sprouts will lose their good texture. Reheat the rolls in a covered skillet over very low heat for 20 minutes — 40 minutes if frozen — turning once, halfway through heating. They can also be reheated in a 400°F. oven for 10 to 12 minutes (15 to 18 minutes if frozen). Place the egg rolls on a rack over a baking pan to drain off the excess oil and to help recrisp the surface.

Variation   Substitute ½ to ¾ pound ground turkey for the beef and increase the oil used in step 2 to 3 tablespoons. Add 3 tablespoons additional oil in step 4 when stir-frying the cabbage.

Pan-fried Scallion Cakes

Makes twelve 4-inch cakes or six 6-inch cakes

*T*hese pan-fried cakes made of unleavened dough are commonly sold by street vendors in northern China. The cakes take a bit of time to make but are definitely worth the effort. I make the smaller size for passing with drinks and the larger ones for more substantial servings. For a traditional vegetarian version, omit the bacon and increase the salt to taste.

健康

3 cups all-purpose flour

1 teaspoon salt, or to taste

1 cup hot water

2 cups thinly sliced scallions, green and white parts (about 15–18)

½ cup chopped bacon (optional)

6 teaspoons sesame seed oil, for brushing

Canola, corn, or peanut oil for frying

1.   To make the dough by hand, combine the flour and salt in a mixing bowl. Gradually mix in the water with a spoon until a rough dough is formed. Add more water by droplets if necessary to incorporate all the flour. Transfer the dough to a lightly floured work surface and knead until smooth. Cover with a damp cloth or damp paper towels. Let rest for 30 minutes.

2.   To make the dough in a food processor, put the flour and salt in the workbowl fitted with a metal blade and pulse about 5 seconds to mix. With the machine running, pour the hot water through the feed tube and process for 20 seconds, or until a ball forms. If the dough appears dry and does not form a ball, stop the machine and take a good look. Sometimes it simply needs a few seconds to fully absorb the liquid. If after examination the dough is dry, add a few droplets of water until a rough dough is formed. Transfer the dough to a lightly floured surface, knead by hand, and cover as in step 1.

3.   Roll the dough under the palms of your hands on a lightly floured surface into a rope about 12 inches long and 1¼ to 1½ inches in diameter. Cut the rope into twelve 1-inch pieces or six 2-inch pieces for larger cakes. Roll each piece into a ball. Place the balls under a damp cloth or paper towels to keep them from drying out.

(continued)

Small Eats

4.   Roll out each ball of dough into a circle about 5 or 7 inches in diameter, depending on the size the finished cake is to be, and about ¹⁄₁₆ inch thick. Brush sesame seed oil to within ½ inch of the edge, using about ½ teaspoon for the small cakes and 1 teaspoon for the large. Sprinkle the oiled part with 2 to 4 tablespoons scallions, 1 to 2 heaping teaspoons bacon, if using, and salt.

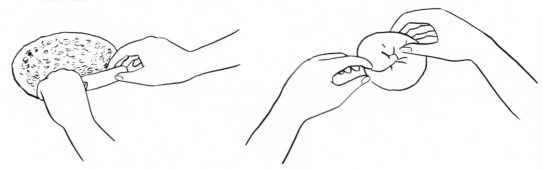

5.   Roll up the circle into a cigar shape, pinch the ends closed, and coil into a circle, tucking the ends under slightly. Press very gently with the palm of your hand to flatten.

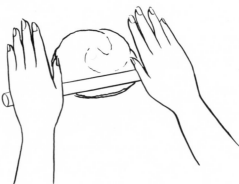

6.   With a rolling pin, gently roll into either a 4- or 6-inch circle. Be careful when rolling so that the trapped air bubbles do not burst. Some air bubbles may pop and break the surface. This is all right, but if there are too many holes, the scallions will fall out into the oil and burn. Place the cakes on a lightly floured board or baking sheet, cover with a towel, and continue until all are done. (If not frying immediately, stack the cakes, separated by lightly floured sheets of wax paper, and store them in a sealed plastic bag in the refrigerator.)

7.   When ready to cook, heat a 10- or 12-inch well-seasoned cast-iron or nonstick skillet over medium heat. When the pan is hot, add 3 tablespoons oil and wait a few seconds for it to heat. Add the cakes to the pan; they will sizzle. Add only as many cakes as will fit in a single layer without crowding. Cook about 3 minutes on each side, or until both sides are golden brown. Remove and place on paper towels. Add more oil to the pan, as necessary, and repeat until all the cakes are cooked.

8.   Cut 4-inch cakes into quarters, 6-inch cakes into eighths. Serve hot. Sprinkle with additional salt, if desired.

Note   If the cakes are not to be served right away, let them cool thoroughly, stack them, pack them in plastic bags, and refrigerate. When ready to serve, reheat on an ungreased cookie sheet in a 350°F. oven for about 15 minutes. Be careful not to overbake as the cakes will dry out and get tough. Do not reheat in a microwave oven; it is sure to make them tough.

Minute Scallion Pancakes

Makes two 10-inch pancakes

*W*hen we were children, my mother would often make this quick version of Pan-fried Scallion Cakes (page 303) as an after-school snack — or even for breakfast. The pancakes can be made smaller and cut into wedges, then rolled and pierced with a toothpick for an appetizer or hors d'oeuvre.

> 1 large egg
> ⅔ cup all-purpose flour
> ⅓ cup thinly sliced scallions, about 2 stalks, white and green parts
> 1 strip bacon, minced, or 1 heaping tablespoon dried shrimp, minced
> ¼ teaspoon salt, or to taste
> ½ cup Chinese Chicken Broth (page 64) or canned chicken broth
> 4 teaspoons canola, corn, or peanut oil

1.   Mix all of the ingredients, except the oil, together in a mixing bowl. You will have a thin paste.

2.   Heat a 10-inch well-seasoned cast-iron or heavy nonstick skillet over medium heat and pour in 2 teaspoons of the oil. Tip the pan back and forth to spread the oil evenly over the bottom and to heat it up. Pour half the batter into the skillet and spread it out to the sides of the pan with a spatula. Cook until the edges are lightly browned, then flip the pancake over to brown the other side. This should take less than 1 minute. Remove from the pan and repeat with the remaining oil and batter. Serve hot.

Chinese-style
Barbecued Spareribs

Serves 4 as main course, or 8 to 10 as an appetizer

*I*f you judge from our restaurant, everyone loves Chinese spareribs. You'll be happy to find out how easy they are to prepare at home. The cooks at the restaurant prepare the spareribs ahead of time up to the final browning step. After the first cooking, the ribs are refrigerated; they are browned only when ready to be served. You can do the browning on an outdoor grill if you like. Serve the ribs with Chinese duck sauce and Chinese mustard or with Spicy Mango Chutney (page 330). (See page 214 for an explanation of Chinese-style spareribs.)

壽

2 racks spareribs, Chinese style (about 2 pounds each)

3 tablespoons dark soy sauce

4 tablespoons hoisin sauce

1 tablespoon dry sherry

1 tablespoon light brown sugar

1 tablespoon honey

½ teaspoon five-spice powder

2 garlic cloves put through a garlic press (optional)

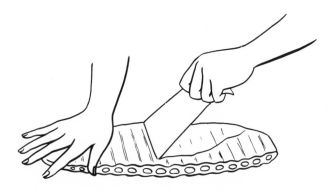

1. Trim the fat from the ribs and peel off the tough, paperlike membrane covering the inside of the ribs.

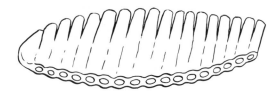

2.   Make 1½-inch-long cuts between the bones at the thicker part of the ribs. This allows the marinade to penetrate better and provides even cooking.

2.   Stir the remaining ingredients together in a small bowl. Rub the sauce all over the ribs and place them in a plastic bag or bowl. Marinate in the refrigerator for at least 1 hour or overnight.

3.   When ready to roast, preheat the oven to 350°F.

4.   Place the ribs on a rack over a roasting pan partially filled with water. Be sure that the ribs do not touch the water. Roast for 50 minutes, replenishing the hot water as necessary. Halfway through the cooking, brush the ribs with sauce, turn them over, and baste the other side.

5.   Turn the heat up to 450°F. and roast for 5 to 8 minutes on each side, or until browned and crisp. Remove from the oven and separate the ribs.

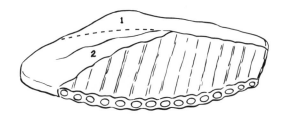

Note   Chinese-style spareribs have been trimmed of the soft, bony end called the chine bone (1) and have the brisket flap (2) removed. This makes for a more attractive uniform slab that will cook more evenly than regular spareribs. They are often available in markets and marked "Chinese style." Otherwise, buy regular spareribs and trim them. Save the brisket flap for other recipes that call for a small amount of sliced, shredded, or ground pork.

Variation   Substitute an orange-based marinade for the more familiar restaurant-style one. Combine 2 teaspoons sugar, 3 tablespoons dark soy sauce, 1 tablespoon dry sherry, 2 tablespoons ketchup, 2 tablespoons honey, 1 tablespoon hoisin sauce, ½ teaspoon five-spice powder, and 3 tablespoons frozen orange juice concentrate in a small bowl. Marinate the ribs as described in step 2 and continue with the recipe.

Pork Strips,
Chinese Restaurant Style

Serves 8 to 10 as an appetizer

*T*his Chinese-American version of Cantonese roasted pork (tsa tso) was one of the most popular appetizers on our restaurant menu. I used to put slices of this pork between pieces of French bread for lunch. Those were the days before we stopped serving French bread. I'm sure some of you remember that French bread was de rigueur at all Chinese restaurants in the 1950s. My parents learned the hard way when a disgruntled customer exclaimed as he left our restaurant when it first opened, "What kind of Chinese restaurant is this anyway? You don't even serve French bread!"

My mother's method of roasting pork over a pan of water does two things: it prevents the marinade from burning and it keeps the meat moist and juicy. I use tenderloin, a lean cut, instead of the more traditional strips of fatty pork.

2 pounds pork tenderloin or boneless center cut pork loin roast
1½ tablespoons dark soy sauce
2½ tablespoons hoisin sauce
1 tablespoon dry sherry
⅛ teaspoon five-spice powder
1 tablespoon honey

1. Trim any fat and gristle from the meat and place in a plastic bag or a dish. Set aside.

2. Stir the remaining ingredients together in a small bowl. Pour over the meat and rub in with your fingers. Seal the bag or cover the dish and place in the refrigerator to marinate for at least 1 hour or overnight. The longer the meat marinates, the tastier and more tender it will become.

3. When ready to roast, preheat the oven to 300°F.

4. Place the meat on a rack set over a baking pan partially filled with water. Do not let the meat touch the water. Roast for 1½ to 2 hours, or until the meat is cooked to your liking or a meat thermometer reads 160°F. when inserted in the meat. It will still be slightly pink at the center at 1½ hours. Baste the meat 2 or 3 times with the marinade and turn the meat over halfway through the cooking. Replenish the water as necessary. Transfer to a cutting board and let rest for 15 to 20 minutes. Slice thin. Serve hot or cold.

Note   For parties, cut the pork into bite-size cubes and serve with toothpicks. Leftover pork can be used in other recipes calling for small amounts of cooked meat such as fried rice and salads.

福

Fried Shrimp Balls

Serves 10 as an appetizer

My mother formed the shrimp paste into balls with two moistened spoons. I find it easier to refrigerate the shrimp paste for a couple of hours to firm it up, then roll the balls between my palms, oiled to keep the paste from sticking. You may need to re-oil your hands a couple of times before all the balls are formed.

Provide Szechuan Peppercorn and Salt Dip (page 332) and dip the shrimp balls lightly before eating.

1 pound shrimp, shelled and deveined
2 slices bacon
5 whole fresh (peeled) or canned water chestnuts
1 teaspoon dry sherry
½ teaspoon salt
3 tablespoons minced parsley
3 to 4 cups vegetable oil, for deep-frying
Parsley sprigs, for garnish
Lemon wedges, for garnish

1. Rinse the shrimp and drain well. Process the shrimp, bacon, and water chestnuts in a food processor fitted with a steel blade. Process until you have a smooth paste, about 15 seconds. Transfer to a bowl and stir in the sherry, salt, and parsley. Set aside.

2. Pour 1½ inches of oil into a wok or stir-fry pan and heat to 350°F. over medium heat. While the oil is heating, roll the shrimp paste into 1-inch balls. Oil a plate and your palms with cooking oil. Scoop up a heaping teaspoon of shrimp paste and roll it between your palms into a smooth ball. Place the ball on the oiled plate and continue until all the paste is used up.

3. Slip the shrimp balls into the oil, about 10 at a time. Do not crowd the pan. The balls need to swim freely in the oil to brown evenly. Cook until the balls rise to the surface and are light brown, about 3 to 4 minutes. Remove the shrimp balls with a wire skimmer or slotted spoon and spread on a tray lined with paper towels. Keep the shrimp balls in a warm oven. Do not pile them in a bowl. Transfer to a platter garnished with parsley sprigs and lemon wedges. Serve hot or warm.

Note   The shrimp balls may shrivel a bit if left too long after frying. They taste just as good, but they do look best when served right after frying. Leftover shrimp balls may be added to soups or noodle dishes.

Variation   Roll or dip half of the shrimp balls in sesame seeds before deep-frying.

Chinese Shrimp Chips

Makes about 130 pieces

Shrimp chips are made of shrimp, starch, and salt. They are sold dried and boxed and look like pink poker chips. When they are dropped into hot oil, they puff up to almost triple their size and become crispy like potato chips. The ones I like best are the Pigeon brand from Shanghai. Small, medium, and large sizes are available. The small ones puff to the size of a potato chip and are perfect to serve at parties. The big ones fry up to the size and shape of the sole of a shoe!

My husband sometimes complains that frying shrimp chips smells up the house. It's true; the odor of the shrimp and oil can be strong and clinging. To avoid that, especially when I am frying up a big batch for a dinner party, I set up the frying pan on the porch on a portable butane burner. I sometimes even wear a shower cap to protect my hair from the odor.

健康

5 cups vegetable or canola oil
1 (1½-pound) package small shrimp chips

1. Pour the oil into a wok or stir-fry pan at least 12 inches in diameter. The oil must be at least 1 inch deep. Add more oil if it is not. Place the pan over the burner and heat to about 325°F., or until a shrimp chip slipped into the oil sizzles and puffs.

2. Fry 8 to 10 chips at a time. Stir the chips as they begin to sizzle at the bottom of the pan. In a few seconds, they will puff up and rise to the surface. Stir and push them down a couple of times, using the back of a wire skimmer. Don't let them float in the hot oil too long, or they will scorch.

3. When the chips are light pink and do not puff any more, remove them immediately with the skimmer and put them into a clean brown paper bag to drain. Give the bag a few gentle shakes to help drain all the excess oil. Transfer the fried chips to a basket or bowl lined with paper towels. The chips are best eaten immediately, but they may be set aside for later use.

Note Humidity in the air will soften the fried chips and make them rubbery. If it is humid, cool the chips completely to avoid condensation and place in a plastic bag. Seal tight until ready to eat. The chips are best eaten the same day.

Cantonese-style Barbecued Chicken Wings

Serves 3 to 4 as main course, or 6 to 8 as an appetizer

*T*his sauce is the same as that for barbecued spareribs (page 306). It works just as well on chicken. The red coloring that many Americans are used to seeing in restaurant-style barbecued dishes is not traditional in Chinese home cooking, and I do not use the red dye here.

禄

2 to 2½ pounds chicken wings, about 12 to 16 pieces
3 tablespoons dark soy sauce
4 tablespoons hoisin sauce
1 tablespoon dry sherry
1 tablespoon light brown sugar
1 tablespoon honey
½ teaspoon five-spice powder
2 garlic cloves put through a garlic press (optional)

1. Rinse the chicken wings and pat dry. Cut off the wing tips with scissors, and cut the wings into 2 sections through the joint. Discard the wing tips or save them for making broth.

2. Stir the remaining ingredients together in a plastic bag. Add the chicken pieces, tightly seal the bag, and marinate in the refrigerator for 2 hours or overnight. Turn the bag occasionally so the chicken marinates evenly.

3. Preheat the oven to 400°F.

4. Remove the wings from the marinade and arrange in 1 layer in a roasting pan. Roast for 15 to 20 minutes, or until almost cooked. Turn the wings over and cook 10 minutes more until completely done. If you like, slide the wings under the broiler for the last 3 minutes for a darker finish. Serve hot or cold.

Variation Substitute the same weight of thighs, drumsticks, or whole legs. Increase the cooking time by 15 minutes.

Red-cooked Chicken Gizzards and Livers

Serves 6 to 8 as an appetizer

*I*n China, the gizzards are one of the most expensive parts of a chicken. This may seem strange, but the Chinese like the taste, texture, and flavor of the giblets and since each chicken has only one gizzard, liver, and heart, they become true delicacies. The gizzards in particular are eagerly received at Chinese banquets, where they are sliced and served as part of cold appetizer platters.

This recipe always reminds me of the time the Chinese navy came to Boston to claim an old American navy vessel that was being given to Taiwan. When my mother heard that these poor sailors were not allowed off the base, that they had only institutional Western food, and were homesick for Chinese home cooking, she made arrangements with the United States government to allow them off the base for a day of sight-seeing and a good Chinese meal. We took them to Lexington and Concord, Massachusetts — the birthplace of America — and then to our restaurant for a hearty meal.

My mother, a stickler for detail, found out that these sailors were originally from Fujian Province, an area noted for garlicky food. Among other things, she served Peking Ravioli (page 295) with a dip of fresh minced garlic. For the rest of the day, which we spent visiting a local museum, we didn't have to worry about losing anyone, we could just smell their trail!

When the ship was ready to sail back to Taiwan, my mother's parting gift was a load of frozen giblets. The sailors were thrilled with their valuable and delicious gift.

1½ pounds chicken gizzards and/or livers
½ cup dark soy sauce
¼ cup sugar
1 slice unpeeled gingerroot, 1 × ⅛ inch
1 whole star anise
2 teaspoons dry sherry
1 scallion
Cilantro sprigs, for garnish

1.   Rinse the gizzards and/or livers and remove any fat and membrane threads with your hands. Drain.

2.   Place in a heavy saucepan and add the soy sauce, sugar, gingerroot, star anise, sherry, scallion, and ¼ cup water. Cover and bring to a boil. Reduce the heat and simmer gently for 20 to 25 minutes, stirring occasionally, or until the giblets are cooked through. To test, take a gizzard out and slice it open; no blood should show.

3.   Turn the heat to high and bring the sauce to a boil. Stir the giblets for a few minutes until they develop a deep, dark color and the sauce becomes slightly syrupy. Cool the giblets in the cooking liquid.

4.   Remove the giblets from the sauce. Slice the gizzards lengthwise into thin slices and cut the liver into bite-size pieces. Serve at room temperature or chill and serve cold garnished with sprigs of cilantro.

健康

Oven-roasted Oyster Sauce Chicken Wings

Serves 3 to 4 as a main course, or 6 to 8 as an appetizer

*T*he Chinese frequently deep-fry chicken wings, but this oven-roasting method makes a dish that is substantially lower in fat. The wings are very good with Spicy Mango Chutney (page 330).

I often pack chicken wings in the picnic basket; they taste great cold. Just bring extra napkins!

健康

2 to 2½ pounds chicken wings, about 12 to 16 pieces
1 teaspoon grated peeled gingerroot
1 tablespoon dry sherry
3 tablespoons dark soy sauce
3 tablespoons oyster sauce
1 teaspoon sugar

1. Rinse the chicken wings and pat dry. Cut off the wing tips with scissors, and cut the wings into 2 sections through the joint. Discard the wing tips or save them to make chicken broth.

2. Combine the remaining ingredients in a plastic bag. Mix well. Add the chicken wings, seal the bag, and marinate in the refrigerator for 2 hours or overnight. Turn the bag occasionally.

3. Preheat the oven to 400°F.

4. Place the wings on an ungreased baking pan and roast for 15 to 20 minutes, or until the chicken is almost cooked. Turn the wings over and cook 10 more minutes until done. If you'd like a darker color, finish the wings under the broiler for the last 3 minutes of cooking. Serve hot, cold, or at room temperature.

Porcelain Tea Eggs

Makes 12 eggs

*T*ea eggs are popular street food in China and can be purchased from street vendors, even in such major cities as Hong Kong and Taipei. As the eggs simmer in the dark savory liquid, it seeps through cracks in the shells to form a lacy pattern similar to the crazed glaze of ancient Chinese porcelain teacups, hence the name. A long cooking is necessary for the eggs to absorb the rich flavors of the cooking liquid.

12 eggs
3 tablespoons black tea leaves
3 tablespoons dark soy sauce
2 tablespoons salt
3 whole star anise

1.   Place the eggs in a medium saucepan and cover with cold water. Bring the water to a boil and simmer the eggs for 15 minutes. Drain the eggs and place in bowl of cold water to cool.

2.   Drain the cooled eggs. Cup your hand over an egg and gently roll it on the countertop to form cracks over the entire surface of the shell. Do not peel. Repeat with the remaining eggs.

3.   Place the tea leaves, soy sauce, salt, and star anise in the same saucepan. Stir to dissolve the salt. Return the eggs to the saucepan and add just enough water to cover the eggs. Bring the water to a boil, reduce the heat, and simmer for 1 hour. (The eggs may be refrigerated in the shell in the cooking liquid for several days.) Drain the eggs and cool at room temperature. Just before serving, remove the shells and cut the eggs into quarters.

Bacon-wrapped
Water Chestnuts

Makes 24

*C*anned water chestnuts are fine in this dish, but do use fresh water chestnuts if they are available.

禄

24 whole water chestnuts, fresh or canned
2 tablespoons light brown sugar
8 strips bacon, cut into 3-inch-long pieces
24 round toothpicks, soaked in hot water for 1/2 hour

1.   Preheat the oven to 450°F.

2.   Drain the canned water chestnuts or rinse and peel the fresh water chestnuts and rinse again. Place the water chestnuts and the brown sugar in a bowl and toss together until the sugar coats the chestnuts. Set aside.

3.   Wrap a piece of the bacon around each chestnut and secure with a toothpick, piercing into the water chestnut just to the other side.

4.   Place in a single layer on an ungreased baking pan and bake for about 15 minutes, or until the bacon is golden brown. Serve hot.

壽

Note   Prepare the water chestnuts through step 3 and refrigerate until ready to bake.

Black Mushroom Caps
and Winter Bamboo Shoots

Makes 4 to 6 servings as an appetizer

A savory appetizer that can be put together quickly with ingredients always on hand, this goes nicely with drinks. It can be made ahead and refrigerated to serve cold or at room temperature.

2 cups dried black mushrooms

2 (8-ounce) cans whole bamboo shoots (about 2 cups)

3 tablespoons dark soy sauce

3 teaspoons sugar

1½ teaspoons grated peeled gingerroot

3 tablespoons canola, corn, or peanut oil

Parsley sprigs, for garnish

1. Soak the mushrooms in hot water to cover for 20 minutes. When they are soft, squeeze out the water and cut off the woody stems and discard. Scissors work best. Cut the caps into bite-size pieces.

2. Drain the bamboo shoots and cut into bite-size pieces. Mix the soy sauce, sugar, and gingerroot together in a small bowl and set aside.

3. Pour the oil into a wok or stir-fry pan and place over medium-high heat. When the oil is hot but not smoking, add the mushrooms and bamboo shoots; they should sizzle. Stir for about 2 minutes. Lower the heat and pour in the soy sauce mixture, stirring over the heat until most of the liquid is absorbed. Transfer to a serving plate and garnish with parsley. Serve hot, warm, or cold with toothpicks.

Pickled Carrots and Daikon

Serves 6 to 8 as a side dish

Chinese restaurants in Chinatown often serve pickles such as these to their Asian diners as a complimentary appetizer while they read the menu. I have always considered it a shame that they don't offer the same courtesy to everyone, but they seem to think that their other guests will not enjoy these more unusual dishes. If you see something on a neighboring table that you would like to try, but don't find on the menu, don't be shy — ask for it even if you have to point to another table to get the idea across.

健康

3 medium carrots (about ½ pound)
1 pound daikon (white icicle radish)
½ cup rice vinegar
½ cup sugar
¼ teaspoon salt

1. Wash and peel the carrots and radish. Cut both vegetables into matchsticks, about 2 inches long and ⅛ inch thick.

2. Plunge the carrots into a saucepan of boiling water. Remove from the heat immediately and let stand for 30 seconds. Add the daikon to the same water as the carrots and let stand for 1 minute. Drain the vegetables, rinse in cold water, and drain thoroughly in a colander, shaking off the excess water. Pack the vegetables tightly in a jar with a tight-fitting lid.

3. Combine the vinegar, sugar, and salt in a small bowl and stir until the sugar is dissolved. Pour the liquid over the vegetables and cover the jar tightly with the lid. If the liquid does not quite cover the vegetables (no more than ½ inch of vegetables should stick out), invert the jar occasionally to mix or add liquid as necessary. The pickling juices will increase somewhat in volume as moisture is drawn out of the vegetables. Refrigerate for at least 24 hours before eating.

Note The pickles will keep in the refrigerator for 2 to 3 weeks.

Oven-roasted Spiced Peanuts

Makes 4 cups

*T*hese roasted peanuts are sold in stores and by street vendors in China, but they are easy to make at home. Peanuts are a symbol of long life and they are always served during the lunar New Year to ensure good luck in the year to come.

壽

1½ teaspoons salt
¼ cup hot water
¼ teaspoon five-spice powder
1 pound blanched peanuts

1.   Preheat the oven to 300°F.

2.   Dissolve the salt in the hot water and stir in the five-spice powder.

3.   Place the peanuts in an ungreased roasting pan. Add the seasoned liquid and mix well. Spread out the peanuts in a single layer. Roast for about 1 hour, or until the peanuts are a very light brown. Stir every 15 minutes so the nuts brown evenly and absorb the spicy flavors.

4.   Let the nuts cool. Store in a lidded jar, a tightly sealed plastic bag, or a covered tin until ready to serve. The peanuts will keep, tightly covered, for about 3 weeks.

Note   Blanched peanuts are available at health food stores.

Table Dips

Condiments and table dips are frequently served to accompany different dishes. In a Chinese home, these dips are served with specific dishes; in restaurants they are placed on the table as a matter of course. Restaurant tables are often lined with cruets of soy sauce, vinegar, and chili oil so that diners may use them singly or mix them according to taste. Many Westerners do not realize that soy sauce is meant to be used as a dip, not to be poured over rice or food.

Westerners have become so familiar with certain favorites that they expect to find them on the table regardless of what they are eating. The sweet and pungent duck sauce and Chinese mustard so popular in the East Coast of America are automatically placed at every table where Westerners are seated. They are not usually served to Chinese customers in the Far East.

Chinese restaurants on the West Coast seem to serve a more diverse selection of dipping sauces. This may be due to the influence of a larger Asian population, but even so, most Westerners are not exposed to the wide variety of sweet, salty, or spicy table sauces that the Chinese serve with different foods. Besides the simple table dips that can be made at home, there are prepared sauces, like hoisin sauce, shrimp sauce, and oyster sauce, that can be used at the table or in the kitchen.

I have made suggestions following recipes that call for dipping sauces. Some meats are white-cooked, that is, cooked without any flavoring; for these, dips are very important to give the food flavor. Steamed or poached seafood is also served with dips.

Soy Sauce Dips

Soy Sauce Dips are served with white-cooked dishes, such as White-cooked Chicken (page 178) or White-cooked Pork with Garlic Dressing (page 216), when there is very little flavor in the meat itself. The dip provides the taste. The Chinese also like these dips with dumplings, like Peking Ravioli (page 295) or Boiled Wontons (page 292). In many Chinese restaurants soy sauce, vinegar, and hot oil are placed on the table and diners mix their own dips according to their preference. Some people like to add a small amount of cider vinegar or Chinkiang vinegar and light brown sugar to the dips as well.

Soy Sauce Dip with Sesame Oil

¼ cup light soy sauce
½ teaspoon sesame seed oil

Stir the soy sauce and oil together in a small bowl when ready to serve.

Soy Sauce with Garlic Dip

¼ cup light soy sauce
½ teaspoon sesame seed oil
2 garlic cloves, peeled and minced
1 teaspoon Chinkiang vinegar

Stir the soy sauce, oil, garlic, and vinegar together in a small bowl when ready to serve.

Soy Sauce with Ginger and Scallion Dip

¼ cup light soy sauce
½ teaspoon sesame seed oil
2 teaspoons grated peeled gingerroot
2 teaspoons thinly sliced scallions

Stir the soy sauce, oil, gingerroot, and scallions together in a small bowl when ready to serve.

Chinese Mustard

his mustard, another condiment that is very popular in Chinese-American restaurants, is frequently paired with sweet and pungent duck sauce and served with such appetizers as egg rolls and spareribs. It is very easy to make at home. As with other mustard, it gets sharper if made a day ahead.

健康

2 tablespoons mustard powder
⅛ teaspoon salt
4 tablespoons cold water
½ teaspoon cider vinegar

Mix the mustard powder and salt in 2 tablespoons of the cold water until it becomes a smooth paste. Add the remaining water and vinegar and mix thoroughly into a smooth thin paste. Cover and refrigerate for at least 1 hour or overnight before serving. The mustard will separate; stir well before serving.

Just mixed mustard sauce will taste bitter. It must rest at least an hour (overnight is better) to mellow and develop that strong, sharp, pungent taste. It is better to make it a day ahead and store it in the refrigerator for later use.

Unlike hot dog or Dijon-style mustards, Chinese mustard sauce will be thin and runny. If you like it thicker, add more mustard powder. Chinese mustard will keep a couple of weeks covered in the refrigerator; however, it is best to make small amounts each time so it will be fresh.

Table Dips

Hoisin Sauce Dip

oisin sauce may be used right from the bottle, but thinning it with a little soy sauce and garnishing it with sesame seed oil makes it easier to spread. They also add fragrance. Use this to spread on Mandarin Pancakes for Moo Shi Pork (page 118) or Peking Duck.

福

¼ cup hoisin sauce
2 tablespoons light soy sauce
½ teaspoon sesame seed oil

Mix the hoisin sauce with the soy sauce in a small bowl until smooth. Transfer to a small dish and drizzle with sesame seed oil. Leftover hoisin sauce can be stored in the refrigerator, tightly covered, almost indefinitely.

Sweet and Sour Sauce

Makes about 1³/₄ cups

Sweet and Sour Sauce can be used in place of duck sauce as a dip or condiment with fried finger foods of any sort. It should be served hot, warm, or at room temperature. If it has been refrigerated, reheat over low heat, stirring constantly, until warm.

禄

1 tablespoon canola, corn, or peanut oil

1 garlic clove, crushed and peeled

²/₃ cup sugar

¹/₄ cup ketchup

¹/₂ cup cider vinegar

2 tablespoons light soy sauce

¹/₃ cup water

2 tablespoons cornstarch, dissolved in ¹/₃ cup water

Heat the oil in a saucepan over medium heat. Brown the garlic and discard. Combine the sugar, ketchup, vinegar, soy sauce, and ¹/₃ cup water. Pour into the pan with the oil and stir constantly with a spoon or wire whisk until the mixture is smooth and comes to a boil. Add the cornstarch slurry and stir until the sauce thickens and takes on a sheen. Keep warm over very low heat, stirring occasionally to prevent scorching, until ready to serve, or serve at room temperature.

Hot Chili Sauce

*T*his easy-to-make, versatile sauce can be freshly made in small quantities for dipping or for garnishing noodles. It can also be used like chili oil (page 329) to spice up stir-fry dishes by adding a little at the end of the cooking. The Chinese say that hot food "opens one's appetite," and the aroma of freshly infused peppers is indeed very appetizing.

1 tablespoon crushed red pepper
¼ teaspoon chili powder
⅛ teaspoon ground black pepper
2 tablespoons canola, corn, or peanut oil

1. Mix the red pepper, chili powder, and black pepper together in a heatproof bowl. Heat the oil in a small saucepan over medium heat until a flake of red pepper foams immediately when dropped into the oil. If the pepper flake burns remove the oil from the heat and let it cool slightly. Test again. When the oil is ready, remove from the heat and pour over the dry spices. The oil should foam in the bowl and sizzle as it is poured. Avoid looking in the bowl or breathing in the steam to avoid irritation.

2. Stir the sauce and transfer to a small condiment dish to cool. Serve for individual dipping.

Hot Chili Oil

Makes about 1 cup

A clear orange-red oil, this is meant not for cooking but to use as a dip or garnish for salads or to add spiciness to stir-fry and noodle dishes. Hot oil can be purchased at Asian markets, but it is really very simple to make your own.

禧

2 tablespoons crushed red pepper
1 tablespoon Szechuan peppercorns
5 slices unpeeled gingerroot, 1 × 1/8 inch each
1 cup canola, corn, or peanut oil
3 tablespoons sesame seed oil

1.   Mix the red pepper, Szechuan peppercorns, and gingerroot together in a 1-quart heatproof bowl. Heat both oils in a small saucepan over medium heat to 250°F. to 275°F., or until a flake of red pepper immediately foams when dropped into the oil. Remove from the heat and immediately pour over the pepper mixture. The oil should foam and sizzle as it is poured. Do not put your face over the bowl or breathe in the steam.

2.   Cover the bowl and allow the oil to cool. Let stand overnight to thoroughly infuse. Strain through a fine sieve or cheesecloth. Discard the solids.

3.   Store in a tightly lidded jar away from heat and sunlight for 6 months. Refrigerate for longer periods.

健康

Note   Instead of using sesame seed oil, my mother sometimes infused sesame seeds along with the spices.

Spicy Mango Chutney

Makes about 9 cups chutney

*T*his recipe comes from Deli Bloembergen, a close family friend and former neighbor who was born in Indonesia and lived there until she was a teenager. As a child, she spent many hours watching the family cook who was Indonesian. The chutney goes especially well with Asian dishes, curries in particular. It's also delicious with such fried foods as egg rolls and fried wontons.

福

5 firm mangoes, about 3 inches in diameter

2 cups (packed) light brown sugar

1½ cups wine or cider vinegar

1 cup golden raisins

1 red bell pepper, seeded, cored, quartered, and cut crosswise into slivers

3 large onions, peeled and chopped (about 4 cups)

1 teaspoon ground cardamom

4 teaspoons chili powder

2 teaspoons ground cinnamon

4 teaspoons ground coriander

2 teaspoons garlic powder

4 teaspoons grated peeled gingerroot or 4 teaspoons ground ginger

2 teaspoons grated lemon peel or dried lemon peel

2 teaspoons salt

½ teaspoon Tabasco (optional)

1. Rinse and peel the mangoes. Hold the mango in one hand and with a small knife in the other, cut the flesh off from around the pit in big hunks. Cut the pieces into ½- to 1-inch chunks. Discard the pit. Do this over the pot you will cook in to catch the mango juices.

2. Place all the ingredients in a large heavy-bottomed nonreactive saucepan, such as stainless steel or enamel-coated steel, and bring the mixture to a boil. Turn the heat to low and simmer gently, uncovered, for 30 minutes, or until tender. Stir often as the chutney burns easily.

3. Pour the hot mixture into clean jars with tight-fitting lids. Cover the jars while the chutney is hot or allow it to cool slightly first. Store in the refrigerator for about 6 months. For longer storage, pour the hot mixture into hot sterilized canning jars and seal with sterilized two-part lids.

Table Dips

330

Note   To make half a recipe, use 3 mangoes and 1 cup of vinegar. Halve the rest of the ingredients and proceed as directed. If you double the recipe, you must cook it in two batches. For best results, do not make more than one batch at a time.

Variation   Substitute two 8-ounce boxes of dried apricots for the mangoes. Cut each apricot in half with scissors.

Ginger and Vinegar Seafood Dip

My mother always made this traditional seafood dip to go with steamed crabs. It is also served with other seafood, like fried shrimp or steamed fish, as well as savory dumplings, such as Peking Ravioli (page 295) and Boiled Wontons (page 292).

In China the most famous crabs are the Shanghai freshwater hairy crabs, so called because of the hairs that grow over the large claws. They are in season very briefly in late fall. Live crabs travel from Shanghai to Hong Kong tightly tied with bamboo string and packed in bamboo baskets. Garishly colored posters and neon signs herald their arrival throughout the city. The taste is exceptional — the best part is the body with lots of roe — with prices to match!

¼ cup cider vinegar
1 tablespoon minced or shredded peeled gingerroot
2 tablespoons light brown sugar, or to taste
2 teaspoons light soy sauce, or to taste (optional)

Mix together the vinegar, gingerroot, sugar, and soy sauce, if using, in a small bowl when ready to serve.

Variation   For a less seasoned dip, omit the sugar and soy sauce.

Table Dips

331

Szechuan Peppercorn
and Salt Dip

健康

A dry dip, this is most often served with deep-fried foods such as Fried Shrimp Balls (page 310), but can be used to flavor such diverse foods as fried chicken and salads. It makes an excellent salt substitute in stir-fry dishes. Serve at the table in a small dipping dish. Use it with a light touch; a little goes a long way. It can be stored, tightly covered, in the cupboard.

2 teaspoons Szechuan peppercorns
4 tablespoons salt

1. Put the peppercorns and salt in a dry heavy skillet and heat over medium. Shake the pan constantly until the peppercorns smoke lightly and you hear a light cracking sound and smell a fragrant aroma. Do not let the peppercorns burn. Shake the pan for another 30 seconds. Remove from heat and continuing shaking the pan for another 30 seconds.

2. Pour the salt and peppercorns into a mortar and grind with a pestle to a fine consistency. Or process in a small food processor until fine. Or place between sheets of heavy paper and roll with a rolling pin. Strain through a sieve, discarding the particles that do not fall through.

Desserts

*D*aily desserts are not part of Chinese cuisine, and you'll find that the dessert chapter in a Chinese cookbook is usually rather thin. Since few people had ice boxes or refrigerators, chilled desserts were not popular; dairy products — ice cream and the like — simply weren't available. And since no one had ovens, there was no tradition of baking. When dessert was served at home, it was simple fare, like fruit or easy-to-prepare sweet soups made from beans or pureed nuts. Elaborate sweets were reserved for festivals and special occasions and tended to be rich and heavy.

It's been said that the people of Shanghai have a sweet tooth, so it's no wonder that my mother, my cousins, and I (all from Shanghai) love sweets. Many of the recipes in this chapter are a result of that. I find that hot fruit desserts, light chiffon or angel food cake, custard, sherbet, or ginger– or green tea–flavored ice cream make an excellent ending to a Chinese meal.

Fruit Desserts

The Chinese enjoy fruits after a meal — a tradition that is carried on, in a way, at Chinese-American restaurants that serve orange quarters or pineapple chunks with fortune cookies. Many tropical fruits are popular in the Far East. Most are difficult to obtain fresh, but the canned variety is still refreshing and light. With all of the last-minute stir-fry preparation, it is nice to be able to sit down and relax with a cool bowl of fruit.

Canned Fruit

These canned fruit, available in Asian markets and sometimes in larger supermarkets, make a perfect ending to a Chinese meal.

Longans The Chinese name for this small, translucent, white round fruit is dragon's eye. Chill the can and serve the longans with their syrup.

Loquats A yellow fruit about the size of a small apricot. Chill the can and serve in small dessert bowls with the syrup.

Lychee Nuts Chill the can and serve the lychees alone or with a ginger syrup (page 336) garnished with fresh berries. A twenty-ounce can contains about twenty-four lychees.

Fresh Fruit

Almost any fresh fruit can be served at the end of a Chinese meal. The fruit should be perfectly ripe and as unblemished as possible. Ripe fruit that is less than perfect can be cut up and marinated in a fruit liqueur like Chambord, Grand Marnier, or ginger liqueur. Top-quality fruit is best served unadorned. I chill the fruit and place it on pretty dessert plates of a contrasting color, garnished with a sprig of mint or lined with a pretty leaf from our grapevine.

The following are some of my favorite fruits. You can add favorites of your own. Remember, you don't have to serve a lot as long as what you do serve is ripe and sweet. Let the bounty of mother nature be your guide.

Berries It doesn't sound very Chinese, but fresh berries are such a satisfying way to end a meal and since their season is so short, I take advantage of every opportunity to serve them. Since we grow blueberries, raspberries, and blackberries in our garden, a favorite dessert of ours is a bowl of just-picked berries with a dollop of sweetened whipped cream. Local strawberries are always welcome, too.

Mangoes My father loved ripe mangoes more than any other fruit. When I was a child, we would buy mangoes by the case and keep them in the basement to ripen slowly. Each day my father would inspect them, gently pressing the flesh and smelling for that sweet, almost heady fragrance that told him they were ready. Not all the mangoes in the box ripened at the same time, so when there was only one fruit ready, my father would bring it upstairs and we would all lean over the dining table as he almost ceremoniously peeled the skin to expose that deep yellow flesh. He then divided the fruit among us — except for my brother Stephen, who was allergic to mangoes. As a special treat, one of us would be allowed to scrape the remaining mango off the skin.

Mangoes are most flavorful and affordable during the months of June and July. They are hardly ever ripe enough to eat when purchased, so you have to get your mangoes about a week before you plan to serve them. Let them ripen at room temperature. A mango is ripe and ready to eat when the skin is rosy red and the flesh is tender and gives to a gentle squeeze. The stem end should smell sweetly fragrant.

Ripe mangoes are very juicy and difficult to eat gracefully. It would be cruel and unusual punishment to serve a whole mango to a guest. See page 337 for directions on cutting and serving mangoes.

Melons Nothing is so refreshing at the end of a meal as a slice or wedge of chilled ripe melon.

Cantaloupe melons. This sometimes ordinary fruit can be out of this world when properly ripened. I serve a small wedge already sliced away from its rind. If you have both cantaloupe and honeydew, a dish of melon cubes makes a very attractive dessert.

Honeydew melons. Asians love the honeydew melon. When it's ripe and sweet with a lot of juice, there's nothing that can compare to it. In Japan there is a melon much like our honeydew. You see the melons beautifully packaged in wooden presentation boxes with a part of the stem still attached. These melons can cost up to $100 each!

Watermelon. The Chinese are partial to watermelon. For many years cold drinks were not easily available in China, and the summer beverage came from a slice of watermelon. In China, my mother and her friends would take a whole watermelon on a picnic. The watermelon was placed in a net and lowered into a cool well. On more formal occasions, serve a small wedge or triangle of watermelon to each person or cut the watermelon into small pieces and serve them in dessert dishes. I like to serve seedless watermelon for easier eating and yellow watermelon for a change when it's available.

Oranges Oranges are believed to be lucky and are given as tokens of good fortune during the lunar New Year. Mandarin oranges appear in the market around February — just in time for the lunar New Year. Many kinds of easy-to-peel oranges are called tangerines or mandarins.

One of my favorite varieties is the Honey tangerine, also known as the Murcott. It is a little tighter skinned than some of the others, but the flesh is as sweet as its name implies. Other kinds of mandarins are the tiny clementines and bright orange mineolas. Serve a whole mandarin to each guest. I also use canned mandarin oranges in several of my desserts.

Peaches and Nectarines The peach is a symbol of long life; it is always held by the god of longevity. Cut them into cubes (toss peaches with lemon juice to prevent discoloring) and serve in little dessert bowls, garnished perhaps with a strawberry or a dash of Grand Marnier or Chambord liqueur.

Persimmons Persimmons were another of my father's passions. They grow abundantly in northern China; in the winter months they are lined up on the rooftops to sweeten and dry. Persimmons have a short season, from

October to January. Except for the Fuji persimmon, the ripe fruit is soft and the thin tomatolike skin a bit shriveled. Underripe persimmons are very astringent and impossible to eat. Fuji persimmons are hard and crisp. I was afraid to buy them because I always thought they were not yet ripe. Then one day one was served to me. To my surprise and delight, it was sweet and crisp, just like an apple. To serve soft persimmons, place a fruit, with stem side down, on a plate. Cut an X at the tip so the persimmon may be peeled easily. Each person peels the skin halfway down, then eats the soft flesh with a small dessert spoon.

Lychees with Sweet Ginger Sauce

Serves 4

The lychee is not a nut but a juicy soft, white fruit. It's not easy to obtain fresh lychees even during their short season in the summer, but the canned ones, although not quite as tasty as the fresh, are perfectly acceptable and refreshing. They are available in Asian markets and some larger supermarkets.

健康

1 (20-ounce) can lychees in syrup
1 tablespoon coarsely chopped peeled gingerroot
2 tablespoons light brown sugar
Sprigs of fresh mint, for garnish (optional)

1.   Drain the lychees, reserving the syrup. You should have about 1 cup of syrup. Set aside. Place the lychees in a bowl. Set aside.

2.   Combine the gingerroot, sugar, ¼ cup of water, and the lychee syrup in a small saucepan. Bring to a boil, reduce the heat to low, and simmer for 5 minutes. Remove from the heat and allow it to cool for 15 minutes. Strain and discard the gingerroot.

3.   Let the liquid cool to room temperature and add it to the drained lychee nuts. Cover and refrigerate for 1 hour or overnight. Serve the lychees in small dessert bowls with the ginger sauce. Decorate with a sprig of fresh mint, if desired.

Porcupine Mangoes

Serves 2

*I*n Asia mangoes are enjoyed by nearly everyone. Ripe mangoes are indescribably delicious but messy to eat. Here's a neat way to serve mangoes even at dinner parties.
The first time I saw this done, I thought the mangoes looked a bit like the back of a
porcupine, with the bright yellow cubes of fruit sticking up.

1 ripe mango
2 mint sprigs, for garnish

1.   With a sharp knife, slice the flesh off either side of the pit. Cut as
close to the pit as you can. The pit is flat at the widest part of the mango.

2.   Holding a piece that was just sliced off, make evenly spaced diagonal
cuts in a diamond design through the flesh but not into the skin. Do the same
for the other piece.

3.   Holding a mango piece in your hands, push the center up so that
the skin flips up and the mango pieces separate and stand out. Serve with a
sprig of mint. Or slice off the cubes and serve them in a dessert bowl with a
fork or toothpicks.

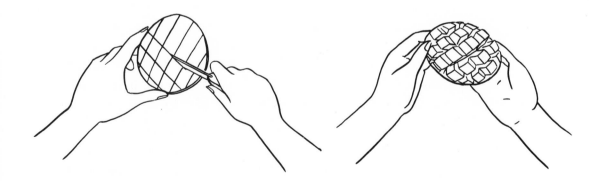

Note   There is always some flesh left on the mango pit. I consider it
the cook's reward.

Desserts

Poached Pears in
Spiced Ginger Sauce

Serves 6

*T*his light fruit dessert was inspired by Western poached fruit recipes. You might drizzle a teaspoon or two of ginger liqueur or brandy over each serving of pears or garnish
with toasted sliced almonds, shaved chocolate, slivers of crystallized ginger, or a sprig
of fresh mint. Serve with Almond Ginger Cookies (page 348).

禄

1 lemon
6 firm pears, Bosc, Anjou, or Bartlett
½ cup plus 2 tablespoons sugar
3 tablespoons candied ginger, minced (about 1 ounce)
6 whole cloves
1 cinnamon stick (about 2 inches)
3 cups water

1.   Cut 1 heaping tablespoon of julienne strips from the lemon peel.
Avoid taking any of the bitter white pith. Set aside. Cut the lemon in half.
Halve the pears, core with a melon baller, and peel. Squeeze the juice of the
lemon over the pears. Set aside.

2.   Combine the sugar, ginger, cloves, cinnamon, lemon peel, and 3
cups of water in a saucepan large enough to hold the pears. Bring to a boil,
stir to dissolve the sugar. Add the pears and reduce the heat to a simmer.
Cook, covered for 15 to 25 minutes, or until the pears are tender. Insert a
toothpick or cake tester into a pear; if it goes in easily, the pears are ready. Be
careful not to overcook or they will become too soft and mushy.

3.   Uncover the pan and cool in the cooking liquid. Transfer the pears
to a bowl, strain the liquid, and return to the pears. Serve warm or cold with
the cooking liquid in individual dessert dishes.

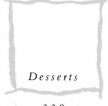

Desserts

Almond Tea

Serves 4

My mother recalls how vendors in Peking (Beijing) used to sell almond tea from door to door in the morning, afternoon, and evening. It was made by hand grinding soaked raw rice and almonds together. My mother took out the elbow grease by using pure almond paste and fresh rice flour. Using pureed nuts to make thick sweet soups is quite common in China. Almonds, walnuts, peanuts, and black and white sesame seeds are all popular.

Asian markets often carry powdered instant sweet soups that just need to have water added. Some from Japan come in thick pouches that can be heated in boiling water. All of these are easy, but none taste as good as soups made from scratch.

壽

⅓ cup rice flour

2 tablespoons almond paste

4 cups cold water

⅓ cup sugar

1 teaspoon almond extract

Light brown sugar, for garnish (optional)

1.   Combine the rice flour, almond paste, and ½ cup of the water in a blender. Blend on high until you have a very smooth thin paste. Add the remaining water, 1 cup at a time, and continue blending until smooth.

2.   Transfer the liquid to a heavy-bottomed saucepan and heat over medium heat, stirring constantly, until it boils. You must keep stirring to keep the liquid from burning on the bottom or becoming lumpy. When it comes to a boil, add the sugar and almond extract and stir to dissolve thoroughly. Remove from the heat and serve hot in cups, mugs, or bowls. Sprinkle with ½ to 1 teaspoon brown sugar, if desired. If not serving immediately, press a piece of plastic film directly on the surface of the tea to prevent a skin from forming. Remove plastic wrap when reheating.

Note   I sometimes use sweet rice flour, also called glutinous rice flour or powder, for a thicker consistency. I prefer a brand called Mochiko (the Japanese name for sweet rice flour) made by Koda Farms in California and sold under their Blue Star label. If you like the tea thinner, simply add more water and adjust the sugar to taste.

Desserts

The Emperor's Nectar

Serves 6 to 8

*T*he name for this soup dessert, with its tiny glutinous rice balls and orange segments, was coined by our friend Barry Lockard as we were sitting at the table one winter evening enjoying this dessert. He insisted that I include it in my book. It's a good dessert to follow a spicy meal of Szechuan food.

健康

1 (13-ounce) jar or 1½ cups sweet rice wine, both liquid and rice
½ cup sugar
½ cup glutinous rice flour
1 (11-ounce) can mandarin orange segments in syrup

1. Combine the rice wine, 6 cups of water, and the sugar in a 3-quart or larger saucepan.

2. Mix the rice powder with 3 to 3½ tablespoons water to make a dry dough. Working with ¼ teaspoon at a time, roll the dough between your palms into tiny pearl-shaped balls. You should have about 50 balls. Line the rice balls on a plate and set aside.

3. Bring the rice wine mixture to a boil over medium heat. Drop in the rice balls a few at a time until all the balls are in the hot liquid and stir. When the balls float to the surface, they are cooked. The mixture will remain very liquid. Add the mandarin oranges with their syrup. Taste and add more sugar, if desired. Serve hot in bowls.

福

Note This dessert is best served fresh, but it does reheat very well. Store it in the refrigerator; the rice balls will soften, but that does not affect the taste. Reheat gently in a saucepan over medium heat, stirring so the rice balls don't burn.

Orange and Pearl Tapioca Sweet Soup

Serves 6

*I*n China, this slightly thick soup is often served at formal banquets. When my cousin May Chen first came to America from Shanghai, I made it for her as a midnight snack. It really hit the spot and reminded her of home.

禄

¼ *pound large pearl tapioca (about ¾ cup)*
½ *cup sugar, or to taste*
1 teaspoon almond extract
1 (11-ounce) can mandarin oranges in syrup

1. Soak the tapioca in 2 cups of cold water for at least 2 hours or overnight.

2. Pour the soaked tapioca with the soaking water into a saucepan and add another 3 cups of water. Bring to a boil over medium heat. Cover and simmer over very low heat for 30 minutes. Stir occasionally to avoid burning.

3. Remove the saucepan from the heat and let stand, covered, for 20 minutes. The tapioca pearls will become completely transparent.

4. Add the sugar, almond extract, and mandarin oranges with their syrup. Stir until the sugar is dissolved. Bring to a boil over medium heat, stirring occasionally. Stir gently to avoid breaking the orange segments. Serve hot in Chinese rice bowls or dessert bowls.

Note   The tapioca thickens as it cools. If the soup gets too thick (it should have the consistency of heavy syrup), thin it with water and add more sugar to taste.

Desserts

Sweet Red Bean Soup

Serves 6 to 8

甜點

*R*ed bean soups are especially popular in the southern part of China. For special occasions, this soup is sometimes enriched with lily root segments and lotus seeds. In summer it is often made thicker and sweeter and served cold over shaved ice (a favorite with the Japanese) or thinned with water and light cream into an iced drink.

Red azuki beans may be purchased in Asian markets or health food stores.

禧

1 cup azuki beans (8 ounces)
2-inch square dried tangerine peel (optional)
1 cup granulated or (firmly packed) light brown sugar, or to taste

1. Rinse the beans and discard any black or damaged ones. Cover the beans with cold water and soak overnight or for at least 4 hours. Drain.

2. Place the beans and tangerine peel, if using, in a large saucepan with 8 cups of water. Bring to a boil, reduce the heat, and simmer, partly covered, stirring occasionally, until tender, about 1½ to 2 hours.

3. When the beans are tender and beginning to break apart, add the sugar. Stir to dissolve and remove from the heat. Serve hot or at room temperature in hot weather.

健康

Note The soup can be made in advance, and refrigerated, covered. Reheat just before serving. Place in saucepan over medium heat and be sure to stir frequently as the beans fall to the bottom of the saucepan.

Variation A thicker version of this soup can be made by adding 5 tablespoons of glutinous rice with the beans in step 2. You may want to add more than 1 cup of sugar in step 3. The soup thickens as it cools. When reheating, add more water and sugar to taste, if desired.

Almond Float

Serves 6

My mother adapted this dessert from a classic Chinese recipe and it quickly became a favorite at our first restaurant on Concord Avenue in Cambridge. She substituted gelatin for the agar agar called for in the original recipe. She used almond extract instead of grinding almonds by hand and added mandarin oranges.

I've made Almond Float into a festive dessert for the Fourth of July by combining the white almond jelly with red strawberries and blueberries for a patriotic red, white, and blue dessert. If you do that, be sure to make a double portion of the syrup so everything will float.

1 tablespoon unflavored gelatin
⅓ cup cold water
¾ cup boiling water
⅔ cup sugar
1 cup milk
1½ teaspoons almond extract
2 (11-ounce) cans mandarin orange segments in syrup, chilled

1. Sprinkle the gelatin into a 10-inch square baking dish. Add the cold water and let stand until the gelatin softens, about 3 minutes. Add the boiling water and ⅓ cup of the sugar and stir until the sugar and gelatin have dissolved. Pour in the milk and 1 teaspoon of the almond extract. Cover the dish with plastic wrap and chill in the refrigerator for at least 3 hours or overnight. It will be softly firm.

2. To make the syrup, mix the remaining ⅓ cup of sugar, 2 cups of water, and the remaining ½ teaspoon of almond extract together in a small bowl and stir until the sugar is dissolved. Chill the syrup in the refrigerator.

3. To serve, cut the almond gelatin into ½-inch squares. With a rubber spatula, carefully scrape the cubes out of the dish and place in a serving bowl. Add the 2 cans of mandarin orange segments with their syrup to the bowl. Pour on the chilled almond syrup. Stir gently to mix. Serve in small dessert bowls with enough liquid so that the almond gelatin floats.

Variation Add raspberries, blueberries, or quartered strawberries along with the mandarin oranges.

Desserts

Eight Treasure Pudding

Serves 6 to 8

E ight Treasure Pudding is not difficult to make, but it is usually reserved for special occasions and banquets. The Chinese like to refer to dishes so as to express wealth, prosperity, longevity, happiness, and so on. The candied fruit that crowns the pudding represents the treasures, precious gems like rubies, jade, and onyx.

2 cups glutinous rice

3 tablespoons vegetable shortening

¼ cup assorted dried fruit, such as Maraschino cherries, cut in half; dark or golden raisins; candied citron; candied kumquats, cut into thin shreds; candied ginger, cut into thin shreds; Chinese black or red dates, pits removed and cut into slivers

⅔ cup plus 2 tablespoons sugar, divided

1 cup canned sweetened red bean paste

2 tablespoons cornstarch, dissolved in 3 tablespoons water

½ teaspoon almond extract

1. Soak the rice in at least 4 cups of cold water for 2 hours; it will almost double in volume. Drain in a strainer and put in a 1½-quart heatproof bowl. Add 1¾ cups of water and steam over boiling water for 30 minutes. (For this recipe, the steamer is the best way to cook the rice because it prevents any burning or hard crust from forming.) Allow the rice to cool enough to be handled. It should remain warm.

2. Coat a heatproof 1½-quart bowl generously with 1 tablespoon of the shortening. Arrange the dried fruit in a design on the bottom and up the sides of the bowl. The design will be on the top of the pudding when it is unmolded. Set aside.

3. When the rice is cool enough to handle, transfer to a large mixing bowl and mix in the remaining 2 tablespoons of shortening and ⅓ cup of the sugar. Mix with your hands to keep the rice grains from breaking.

4. Press half the rice around the sides and bottom of the prepared bowl, being careful not to disturb the fruit design. The rice should be thicker at the bottom than around the sides.

5.   Spoon the bean paste into the center of the bowl on top of the rice. Press lightly with a rubber spatula to flatten. Add the remaining rice around and on top of the bean paste. Press gently as you work to eliminate any air pockets. Smooth the surface with a rubber spatula.

6.   Heat water in a steamer large enough to hold the bowl with enough room above it for the steam to circulate freely. Seal the top of the bowl with plastic wrap, cover the pan with a lid, and steam for 1 hour over simmering water. (Covering the bowl with plastic prevents any condensation from dripping onto the rice. The old Chinese way to do this was to wrap the steamer lid with a cloth. Be sure to remove the plastic carefully so that the accumulated water doesn't fall into the rice.) The pudding can stay in the steamer with the water at a simmer until ready to unmold and serve. The extra steaming will not affect its quality.

7.   To make the sauce, combine 1½ cups of water and the remaining sugar in a small saucepan. Bring to a boil and stir until the sugar dissolves. Slowly pour in the cornstarch slurry and stir until the sauce thickens and becomes translucent. Stir in the almond extract and keep warm.

8.   Remove the pudding from the steamer and carefully remove the plastic wrap. Run the tip of a knife around the edge of the pudding to loosen. Be careful not to disturb the fruit design. Place a rimmed platter — it needs some depth to capture the sauce that will be poured over the pudding — over the bowl and invert so the pudding unmolds onto the platter. Pour the sauce over. Serve immediately.

Note   The pudding is meant to be served hot. You can prepare it ahead of time and steam it while having dinner, or prepare it and seal it with aluminum foil or plastic wrap and refrigerate or freeze until ready to steam. Freezing and reheating does not alter the taste or texture of this dessert. The sauce, however, should be freshly made. The cooked pudding can also be reheated by steaming.

Almond Rice Pudding

Serves 6 to 8

*A*lthough rice pudding made with dairy products is not Chinese, I like a well-made rice pudding — and, of course, I always have rice on hand. This recipe is adapted from The Periyali Cookbook. *The Periyali Restaurant in New York City has the best rice pudding I've ever tasted. Instead of cooking the rice on the stove, where it has to be monitored and stirred almost constantly for about an hour, I cook it in a steamer. The rice cooks evenly, won't burn, and doesn't need to be stirred while cooking.*

4 cups low-fat milk

2 pieces lemon peel, about ¾ × 4 inches each

¾ cup long-grain rice

¾ cup sugar

1 egg yolk

½ cup heavy cream

1 teaspoon almond extract

Toasted sliced almonds, for garnish

Ground cinnamon, for garnish

1.   Combine the milk, lemon peel, and rice in a 1½-quart heatproof bowl. Bring water to a boil in a steamer and steam the rice for 40 to 50 minutes, or until the grains are tender. The mixture will remain very soupy.

2.   Transfer the rice and the liquid into a 3-quart or larger saucepan. Separate the rice grains with a wooden spoon or fork. Heat over medium heat just until the liquid comes to a boil. Stir frequently to prevent sticking.

3.   In a small bowl, mix the sugar into the egg yolk with a fork until the mixture is crumbly. Stir in a few spoonfuls of the hot liquid from the rice to warm the egg. Remove the rice from the heat and quickly stir in the egg mixture, stirring constantly to prevent the yolk from cooking.

4.   Return the pan to the stove and continue cooking over low heat for a few minutes. Stir constantly to prevent burning and a skin from forming on the surface. Add the cream and continue stirring until the mixture is steaming. Remove from the heat and stir in the almond extract. Stir for 1 minute, then pour the pudding into a serving bowl. If not serving immediately, press plastic wrap on top of the pudding to prevent a skin from forming. Serve warm or chilled with a generous sprinkling of toasted almond slivers and cinnamon.

Desserts

Steamed Egg Cake

Serves 6

When the Chinese make cakes or bread, they steam them. It may seem unusual, but the results are quite delicious — and healthy, too, when you consider that this recipe calls for no butter, oil, or shortening. The steamed cake can be eaten hot, warm, or cold. It's at its best piping hot, right from the steamer. For a festive touch, my mother sometimes dusted the top of the cake lightly with colored sugar crystals.

福

3 eggs, separated
½ teaspoon pure vanilla extract
1 cup all-purpose flour
¼ teaspoon baking powder
1¼ cups sugar

1. Line the bottom of an 8-inch round cake pan with wax paper or aluminum foil. Bring water to a boil in the bottom of a steamer. The water should not be high enough to touch the bottom of the cake pan.

2. While the water is coming to a boil, beat the egg yolks with the vanilla and ⅓ cup of water just until blended. Sift the flour with the baking powder. Add the sugar and sift again. Stir the flour mixture into the egg yolks.

3. Beat the egg whites until stiff but not dry. Fold the whites into the batter and pour the batter into the prepared pan. Rap the pan sharply on the counter several times to remove any large air bubbles.

4. Place the pan in the steamer and steam over medium-high heat for 20 to 25 minutes, or until a toothpick inserted into the cake comes out clean. Remove the cake from the steamer.

5. Invert the cake pan onto a plate, pull off and discard the paper, and turn the cake right side up. It is best served hot or warm.

Desserts

Almond Ginger Cookies

Makes about 4 dozen 2¹⁄₂-inch cookies

These cookies were inspired by a recipe given to me by Valarie Hart Ross, our Oregon sales representative. The cookies are rich in almond flavor and have the cracked surface of traditional Chinese almond cookies.

Chinese almond cookies are commonly garnished with whole blanched almonds but I use natural almonds. I'm lucky to have a steady supply since my brother-in-law Cliff Ohmart, who is an entomologist, collects them in the almond groves of California. He goes into the groves to check the trees and almonds to determine the optimum time for farmers to spray. He always has more than he needs.

禄

2¹⁄₂ cups unbleached all-purpose flour
1 teaspoon baking powder
3 teaspoons ground ginger
¹⁄₂ teaspoon salt
³⁄₄ cup vegetable shortening
1 cup (firmly packed) light brown sugar
¹⁄₄ cup honey
1 large egg
¹⁄₂ cup almond paste (4 ounces)
About 48 whole almonds

1.   Preheat the oven to 350°F.

2.   Sift the flour, baking powder, ginger, and salt together into a mixing bowl. Set aside.

3.   Blend the vegetable shortening with the brown sugar, honey, and egg in a food processor fitted with a steel blade until smooth. Cut the almond paste into small pieces, add to the mixture, and process until it is smooth and the almond paste well incorporated. Add the flour mixture a third at a time, turning the processor on and off at 5-second intervals, until a firm dough is formed.

4.   Roll about 1 rounded tablespoon of dough between the palms of your hands into a ball. Continue with all the dough. Place on an ungreased cookie sheet 2 inches apart. Press an almond into the center of each.

5. Bake for 10 to 12 minutes, or until the cookies are lightly browned. Cool for about 1 minute on the sheet, then transfer to a rack. Cool thoroughly. Store in a tightly sealed container.

Ginger Pound Cake

Makes two 9 × 5-inch cakes

Ginger is often used at the end of Chinese meals as a digestive. This ginger-flavored cake is a perfect ending to a Chinese meal and goes exceptionally well with Chinese tea.

3 cups unbleached all-purpose flour
1 tablespoon baking powder
½ teaspoon salt
¾ cup light cream
2 teaspoons pure vanilla extract
2¼ cups sugar
1½ cups (3 sticks) butter, at room temperature
6 eggs, at room temperature
1 cup candied ginger (8 ounces)
¼ cup poppy seeds (optional)

1. Preheat the oven to 350°F. Butter two 9 × 5-inch loaf pans and line the bottoms with parchment or wax paper. Butter the paper and dust the pans lightly with flour, tapping out the excess.

2. Sift 2½ cups of the flour with the baking powder and salt. Set aside. Stir the cream and vanilla together. Set aside.

3. With a stand mixer or a handheld beater, cream the sugar and butter together until light and fluffy. Beat in the eggs, one at a time, beating well after each one. With a spoon or the beater on slow speed, add the flour mixture alternately with the cream and stir until smooth. Increase the beater speed to high and beat just until smooth.

(continued)

4.   Toss the candied ginger with a few tablespoons of the remaining ½ cup of flour and cut into small diced pieces. Fold the ginger, remaining flour, and poppy seeds, if used, into the batter until well mixed. Divide the batter evenly between the 2 loaf pans and tap them on the counter to remove any air pockets.

5.   Bake for about 1 hour, or until the loaves are golden brown and the cakes pull away from the sides of the pan. A cake tester inserted in the center should come out clean. Set the pans on racks and cool for about 30 minutes. Unmold, remove the paper, and turn the loaves right side up to cool completely.

Note   This keeps in the refrigerator up to 2 weeks or in the freezer for 2 months.

Index

Index

353

Index

Index